FOCUS ON FACTS
2004
THE WORLD AND EUROPE
A
HIDDEN AGENDA
BEHIND A HALL OF MIRRORS

BY

ALEXANDER NILES

CONTENTS

	INTRODUCTION.	4
Ch. 1	A STORY OF UNTOLD WEALTH.	8
Ch. 2	A HISTORY OF GLOBAL GOVERNMENT	52
Ch. 3	INTERNATIONAL ZIONISM - ITS CONNECTION TO FREEMASONRY AND COMMUNISM.	72
Ch. 4	WORLD ORDER - THE HIDDEN AGENDA OF GLOBAL FINANCIERS.	83
Ch. 5	THE ILLUMINATI AND FREEMASONRY.	96
Ch. 6	MARXIST POLICIES - A HALL OF MIRRORS.	149
Ch. 7	THE INTERNATIONAL POLICY OF MARXISM.	171
Ch. 8	THE EUROPEAN UNION - A STAGING POST TO GLOBALISM.	221
Ch. 9	THE SYSTEMATIC DISTRUCTION OF BRITAIN AND THE COMMONWEALTH.	251
Ch. 10	AMERICA-THE BASTION OF CAPITALISM?	267
Ch. 11	COLLECTING OUR THOUGHTS.	354
Ch. 12	AUSTRALIA - ABOARD THE GLOBAL ONE WAY TRAIN.	385
Ch. 13	THE UNITED NATIONS.	396
Ch. 14	THE COUNCIL ON FOREIGN RELATIONS.	413
Ch. 15	THE BILDERBERG GROUP.	438
Ch. 16	THE TRILATERAL COMMISSION.	462
	SUMMARY.	485
	BIBLIOGRAPHY.	528

Published by P.E.Publishing Ltd.

Berkshire, England.

First Published in book form in Great Britain 2004.
© 2004 Alexander Niles.

Non-Fiction.

Printed by Booksdurge.com.

Layout and Design by P.E. Publishing Ltd.

Web Sites: www.focusonfacts.co.uk
www.focusonfacts.com

E Mail: pepltd@avnet.co.uk

FOCUS ON FACTS
THE WORLD AND EUROPE
a
HIDDEN AGENDA

Behind a Hall of Mirrors
By
Alexander Niles

P.E. Publishing Ltd.
Non Fiction.
All Rights Reserved.
ISBN 0-9525920-8-8

INTRODUCTION

It is strange indeed how fate directed me to research this book. My intention was to expose the hidden group behind the politicians who were outwardly controlling the events within the European Union. It was only when a friend of mine, a journalist employed by the international press, advised me to investigate the owners of the international press that I started to unearth details of a far larger plan. What I found was damaging to World Democracy. It included the European Union just as a small part. The plan was incredible in its thoroughness and secret in its execution.

EUROPE AS PART OF A GAME PLAN

The future of Europe and its direction is of great importance to over three hundred and ninety million people affected by the decisions our politicians are making in Europe. This compels me to write 'Hidden Agenda'. However, knowing what I have researched to be true, I cannot isolate Europe from the whole. I believe if we can change direction in Europe we can deal a mighty blow to the forces behind the well documented plan for World Government: The plan that most of our powerful press barons support and have hidden from our view for this entire century.

The plot that I will exhibit is very detailed and has been in place and eroding our national power for two hundred years.

I will show you precisely how Europe falls into the plan and how our politicians and media have been sucked into the scheme.

The book explains how everything that happens in the world today is directed, not by our governments, but by a small group of very powerful financiers who create wars and inflation, organise the collapse of the Soviet Block, control world Jewry and Arab oil wealth, and own the vast majority of the world's commodities such as Uranium, Gold, Silver, Diamonds, Copper, Bauxite and so on.

They also control world finance from the United Nations World Bank and onwards down to national debt. They even control our personal debt to a great extent. In this way they believe they have the world and its people at their feet.

All this is hidden from us by a hall of mirrors, held in place by a media, press and television, that has long since been owned and controlled by their men. All this century we have only been told what they want us to know and I will show how this works in our day to day life. The policies to entrap the world come directly from Karl Marx's international policy, where deception (the mirror) is used to distract our attention from their real objective.

I will show how these super rich finance capitalists have used Marxist policies to capture the world for their own power lust and when their plan is finally complete the world will be governed by Marxism which will control it by dictatorship, and you will see how Europe fits these plans.

It is essential for us to know the truth so we can combat their global plans. Everything I will show you will be supported by previous writings and backed by evidence from these books and substantiated by undiluted facts from history. Some of our best known politicians have been key players in this drama during and after the Second World War. Three Presidents of the United States of America gave

Russia large areas of the world that was not theirs to give, Roosevelt, Truman and Eisenhower. I will disclose the reasons, described in a welter of written non-fiction. I will expose one of Britons prime ministers as a Marxist sympathiser.

During the late sixties and early seventies the Right Honourable Edward Heath campaigned for, and took us into, the European Union. At this time the official white paper **(1)** on Britain's Entry into Europe stated quite categorically: 'There is no question of any erosion of essential national sovereignty'. It was not true.

Edward Heath also stated: 'There are some in this country who fear that in going into Europe, we shall in some way sacrifice independence and sovereignty.... these fears, I need hardly say are completely unjustified...'. A statement made in a television programme running up to the referendum. **(1)**

Yet well before he made this statement the Lord Chancellor wrote him a letter, emphasising that in his view 'the surrenders of sovereignty involved are serious...' and '...ought to be brought out in the open now...' (Full letter printed in the same paper dated 14th. December 1960). **(2)** Even before that he had a meeting with Jean Monnet (the founding father of the European Union) who told him quite clearly that the plan for Europe was Federal, but on no account was he to tell the electorate this as they would vote against federalisation. **(3).** This is just one example of the Hidden agenda all through the world and the European Union, orchestrated by global government supporters.

In suppressing this information and misinforming us about the Federal intention of the European plan the Right Honourable Edward Heath, in my opinion, committed an act of high treason against our Sovereign State and its people and probably influenced the outcome of the referendum held under the Right Honourable Harold Wilson.

All over Europe politicians of all parties have submitted to the ogre of the European Union in the face of consistent opposition from the people of the nations. It is not that the people oppose a European free trade zone, they don't; what they can't agree with is a one way street to monetary union followed by federal single government, and loss of control over our forces; the 'Hidden Agenda'.

Pro-Europeans in England will never discuss this issue as if the 'F' word is a taboo. Yet the very politicians who would hand over sovereignty to Europe are the very politicians who built up Britain's national debt in a spiral of competition with their respective opposition till our nation's debt, owned by the international bankers, was so large that politicians could not see a way out of their self-imposed national debt. Then Europe offered to nullify those debts if we joined a federal Europe. This policy seemed to the politicians the only way out without telling the nations about their spendthrift policies. This is the big carrot to draw us into the trap of single currency, the one way street with no return.

To spring this trap and dress it up as a necessary policy for Europe, the co-operation of most of our national press was essential. They ignore the worries of the people and maximise the 'Essential for a fair Europe' ideal, which has never ever had any meat on its crumbling bones.

The whole European Union is a deception designed to disorientate the nations and their people from sovereignty in readiness for the next stage, World Government. (another mirror).

The single currency is designed as a one way street to make sure we don't escape. It has been described by europhiles as essential to good trading. (This is another mirrored deceit.)

I will show how the financiers use their power to censor the press so they only print stories they pass. This even extends to titles outside their control.

It is essential that we give this deceitful plan publicity, so that the people can decide which way they want to go when we reach the referendum. The nation must be clear in its mind what is at stake and how to react. Time is short and we must use it to the best effect. I ask you to read this book and, if you support what I am saying, help me to get the message to the people of the World. We are unlikely to have much help from the press.

In the last chapter I will discuss some measures to help create a successful campaign for a free Sovereign World. This matter is far too important to us all for it to go through on the nod from our politicians. We must take the initiative.

In writing this book I have a formidable problem to overcome. I have to attack international Zionist financiers as they are behind the movement for World control. Since the war, this group, who have been severely criticised by some brave members of the Jewish race for the practice of usury, the same usury that forced them out of Babylon, have used the dreadful holocaust in Germany to silence criticism of their actions throughout the world. The book will show why this is so.

If we are under threat from a secret group with a hidden agenda, it is our right and duty to expose the details. If that should cross the line of Semitism it makes it no less necessary to attack the source of the threat to Europe, world democracy and freedom. I will show exactly how International Zionism controls our lives and suggest how it can be stopped. This is not a threat to the Jewish race; on the contrary I hope they will join us in an attempt to halt this plan of a few greedy men. My attack is directed towards the people who threaten our democracy and that does not include the vast majority of the Jewish faith. I will expose the excesses of a few who wish to dominate the world by hidden agenda. By simple argument I hope to neutralise their hold on the media with a reasoned response that will open up a free debate.

At this point you must expect an interesting table of events engulfing our world. I feel it is important for you to clear your mind of all the influences developed in your life by the media, which is, at best, slanted and, at worst, a pack of lies. There are of course exceptions.

What you are about to read will turn everything you have ever learned from the media on its head. I only hope I have presented my research in such a way that you will appreciate the full impact of what I relate. Your reaction is vital to the course of the world.

Time is short and we can no longer afford to say, 'What can we do?' This is an attitude that will hand the world to this group, intent on a world dictatorship.

In writing this book I have lit the fire. It is up to you to feed the flames and keep it burning till we win our future freedom.

We have seen Bush, the American President and Blair, the British Prime Minister give a pressing reason to go to war. Every shred of evidence shows that neither government had any substantiated evidence that positively showed there were weapons of mass destruction after 1991.. Yet these two men stuck together and claimed these weapons did exist. Now even America's own expert in Iraq David Kay has resigned and stated categorically that in his opinion, since the first Iraq war, there never has been such weapons. This means that at its best these two leaders gave us quarter truths fabricated with information that was totally spun. The reason is these two men are controlled by the power of the Anglo American establishment who in turn own American and British national debts. This group wished to control Iraq's vast oil reserves rather than to let Saddam Hussein sell it to China and France at discounted prices, a deal already agreed. In doing so they risked a World War and although this did not happen they have succeeded in increasing the World terrorism threat by at least ten fold.

Our politicians ignore the peoples wishes, as we have seen, in favour of this unelected body and its demands, when ever called upon to do so.

American and British soldiers have died needlessly because of this and many innocent Iraq's died under blitz and terror bombing. What this book will prove is how this powerful force came into existence and where it stands today until people power stops it. I also predict the future unless we stand up to our real enemies within.

A message to readers in the United Kingdom.

I would like to thank everyone who helped technically to create this book and the hundreds of writers that I quote who have compromised their profession to tell you the truth. We must win this battle if we are to survive. Every person that knows the truth is a victory towards that end. So I would ask you to help me to get 'The World and Europe' distributed by telling your friends all about it and enrolling them onto our supporters list on the website. We need to work fast as it is uncertain when the single currency issue will be upon us. This will be our main chance to voice our opinion, don't waste it.

CHAPTER ONE

A STORY OF UNTOLD WEALTH

(This chapter is essential to understanding the book, its direction and motivation).

In 1763 in the city of Frankfurt on Main in the district of Hesse, (Germany) Meyer Amschel Rothschild founded a banking dynasty that today finances many nations throughout the world and, at the same time, through their sphere of influence, control the main resources of the world such as oil, uranium, gold, diamonds and a large list of commodities.

So from what beginnings did this remarkable man launch his influence on the world and how did it grow into such a decisive force?

He was born on the 2nd. February 1744 in a rough tenement at the back of the Judengasse.

The street was a ghetto that housed the Jewish merchants and traders of the city. They were locked in their quarters at night to prevent them from mixing with the rest of the town. This early prejudice, along with the treatment given to Jews, formed a pattern in behaviour that today registers itself in the attitude towards business transacted by the banks with their customers **(direction)**.

In those days, in a city of around thirty-three thousand people, of which three thousand were Jewish, the main business was as merchants or the natural combination of money lender, later known as merchant bankers.

Frankfurt was in a fortunate trading position, right in the middle of five major trading routes and a fine supply facility on the river Main which was linked to the Rhine.

The Jewish population, which arrived at the time of the Roman occupation, were mostly merchants or craftsmen and most of the male population were literate, a remarkable achievement in those times of general illiteracy. The persecution was constant, with laws to control their movements which limited their ability to trade and made their life a misery. They were generally called Jew, 'the accursed race' and at times even massacred. They could not own land, only property on the land and they were taxed excessively.

In this atmosphere Meyer Amschel Rothschild grew up and quite remarkably prospered in business. Germany was in those days a loose network of some one hundred principalities, each one governed by an absolute sovereign. Most areas, like Frankfurt, minted its own currency and would only accept others in solid silver to the same weight. Therefore travellers had to change currency before they could trade in the area. This is where the bankers made their living. If they were shrewd they could increase their exchange commission; Rothschild was one of the brightest.

The Judengasse was, to most observers, a nightmare of a street, with its tall thin buildings blocking out most of the daylight and a cobbled street, so narrow that a cart could not turn within it. The open sewers flowed down the street over spilling where blockages occurred, giving a constant reek of sewage.

Meyer Amschel Rothschild was the fourth child of eight, of which five survived the squalor and filth of the times and their situation. He was brought up with a strict

Jewish education, being well versed in the Torah and Talmud. Learning was the strength of the Jewish child and set him above and apart from his gentile contemporaries, that is with the exception of languages.

Despite the depravation surrounding the inhabitants of the Judengasse, the community thrived and curiously, these socially deprived people prospered, especially Rothschild through his industry.

His languages were Juden-Deutsch, Hebrew and from his learning of the Talmud, Aramaic. The Talmud imparts knowledge to the reader in law, memory concentration, systematic thought and total logic. These teachings add dimensions that put the recipient in a superior position to all gentiles he might trade with in his lifetime; perhaps one of the main reasons Jews are so successful.

His great disadvantage was the inward looking Ghetto culture which ignored the outside world and failed to teach him simple German; a disadvantage he suffered when writing important correspondence in his business life.

At the early age of ten he started work in the family money changing business. At the age of eleven he was sent to the Jewish Seminary of Fürth. In October of the same year his father died of small-pox and in June 1756 his mother also passed away.

He returned home to a small inheritance and launched what was to be the start of the most remarkable business success the world has known.

His first job was to learn banking outside the Judengasse, so he took up an apprenticeship in Hanover with Wolf Oppenheim, a friend and colleague of his father, who had left the Judengasse to develop a five branch bank of importance. Here he was to learn the secrets of successful finance and above all the etiquette of being a court Jew, a way of escaping the humiliations that his religion imposed on him from outside the Jewish quarters. Samuel Oppenheim had become court factor to no less a noble than the Austrian Emperor and financed his wars with Louis XIV and the Turks.

The court Jew was an important part of German aristocratic life as the various princes of territories were in constant need of funds for wars and troops to fight and protect their territories.

Across Europe the culture of the Jewish race provided a constant contact loan system, second to none, that captured the lucrative market of money lending to the rich, for their political extravagances.

Rothschild stayed in Hanover from 1757 to mid 1763, learning the art of banking and especially providing war loans which would eventually be the cause of his meteoric business success.

He gained knowledge of foreign trade, bills of exchange and as a sideline he learned the art of collecting rare coins. This was to be a great asset in obtaining his first big contract. In the meantime he met a nobleman, General von Estorff, an ardent collector, who gave him commissions to obtain rare coins for his collection.

1763 saw his return to Frankfurt, his home.

His inheritance gave him one quarter of his parents home. He joined his brother Calmann in partnership in his exchange shop and started a coin section for the collectors as well as jewels and antiques. He knew that selling coins would not make him wealthy but it would draw in people that mattered. His target, was the Crown

Prince Wilhelm, the son and heir to the Landgraf of Hesse, the state ruler. Not only was he rich and powerful but his cousin was King George III of England and he was married to the daughter of the Danish King. He was ruler of a small territory called Hanau. This was to be the time when coins paid off for Prince Wilhelm was a coin collector. The Prince was a modernist, frequenting Masonic lodges and secret societies. This was to be Rothschild's first introduction to the secret debating societies of the European centre of

middle-class intellectuals. **(Direction).** The Prince's first purchase of medals and coins took place in June sixty-five at the Frankfurt fair. By 1769 he asked for and obtained the honorary title of court factor; from this moment on he was not to look back.

His next task was to find a wife and he courted and married Guttle Schnapper, also from the Judengasse, when he reached the required age of twenty-five, on the twenty-ninth of August 1770. She brought with her a dowry of two- thousand-four-hundred Gulden, a small fortune.

As his main line, he developed his coin and medal business, buying and selling whole collections as well as single coins. He made contact with all the important people in the area, travelling round the local towns to build his trade.

He ran a catalogue mail order business to promote his business, covering all Germany. He even sold coins to the King of Bavaria. By August 1771 he had his first child, a daughter Schönche, followed by three sons and two daughters.

By eighty-two his brother and partner died leaving him the sole owner of the business. But, as yet, his break in the banking world had not occurred. However his luck was about to change. The hard work he had put into softening Prince Wilhelm, the crown Prince of Hesse, gave him his long awaited opportunity. Wilhelm struck a deal with George III to supply soldiers for his wars. This was a very profitable business, netting the Prince several million Gulden in seventy-six alone. He was paid in bills of exchange and required banks to bid to cash them so he could then invest his fortune. Rothschild was one of several banks given credit to discount the bills and so he got his foot in the door and he kept it there. Even now, the crown Prince seemed reticent towards Rothschild's persistent endeavours to handle his financial affairs. However in his attempts to obtain the Prince's business he made a very important friend of Buderus, an employee of the Prince who was destined to become head of his treasury.

In the meantime Rothschild met Prince Karl Anselm and became his banker. Anselm was the ruler of Thurn and Taxis and they happened to run the most highly praised postal service covering central Europe. Rothschild was to learn that an efficient postal service gave him an edge over his competitors when it came to up-to-date information.

By 1783 Rothschild managed to get a gate pass to leave the ghetto at night at a time when his business success as a banker was beginning to take an upward turn. His long friendship with Buderus was showing signs of delivering business to his house.

1784 saw a marked improvement in his status when he bought a house in the Judengasse to house his family only. By this time he had six surviving children and his wife was to give birth to four more.

The new house, that doubled also as the centre for his new banking business was to help towards the expansion of his business interest.

In 1785, the father of Prince Wilhelm, the Landgraf of Kassel and Hesse, died, leaving his son his entire fortune and properties; a considerable fortune.

The Prince became Wilhelm IX., said to be the richest man in Germany. His father before him had made his fortune by selling soldiers to noblemen wishing to go to war.

Buderus, the new Landgraf's agent visited Frankfurt occasionally and Rothschild managed his personal increasing assets.

Rothschild, sensing victory, kept up the pressure on Wilhelm IX., selling him coins at near cost price but still Wilhelm gave the majority of his business to the gentile bankers of Frankfurt who had served his father.

Gradually the Landgraf began to trust Rothschild and gave him a small credit rating which he increased slowly. But however hard he tried, business was slow. Rothschild, having seen the advantages of a good courier service, decided to launch his own to handle his generally increasing business. This gave him an advantage over his competitors. Fast news was first news and first news made money. Now his sons were old enough to help him in the business and they surpassed their father's greatest hope. But he needed the big break. He continued to pressure for a larger slice of the Landgraf's business and was encouraged by Buderus.

Rothschild was a dedicated worker, starting early in the morning and working through to late each night. All his other sides were flourishing. He went into the wholesale business, holding large stocks of English cotton, wool and flour. At this time, his night pass out of the Judengasse, granted to him by the council after pressure from the Landgraf, was a great asset and gave him an edge over his fellow traders.

In October ninety-two French troops of the revolution appeared outside Frankfurt. The Landgraf, fearing for the safety of his considerable fortune, retreated to Kassel with his army. Frankfurt surrendered and was immediately fined for harbouring French aristocrats, enemies of the Republic.

A strange thing happened in Frankfurt. In most of the surrounding territory the Jewish residents welcomed the French liberators as they had recognised Jewish rights in Paris. But strangely the Frankfurt Jews accused the invading troops of aggression.

When, after two weeks, the French victors were forced out of Frankfurt by Prussian troops, the Jews all rejoiced. Finally the Landgraf decided to join the Prussian led coalition to fight the French intrusion.

The war of coalition against France drew Frankfurt deeper into the vortex of action. The armies of the coalition had their headquarters in Frankfurt with the armies in the surrounding area. Rothschild negotiated supply of food, clothing, horses and equipment as well as acting as the paymaster for the troop's wages. **(Direction).**

It was a mammoth task, involving millions of Gulden. A task perhaps only Rothschild could have undertaken with his network of useful contacts. He became a war agent. **(Direction).** This was his first big break and by ninety-six he was assessed for tax at the rate of fifteen-thousand Gulden, the maximum.

Rothschild, to control his business, hired a German speaking gentile called Geisenheimer to look after his stock taking control after a sad incident of internal theft by an employee. Geisenheimer was also a freemason of the L'Aurore, a French lodge. This is a pointer that Rothschild's orthodox views were changing as Geisenheimer, through his Masonic lodge was trying to reform the Jewish religion and Rothschild was probably drawn to his ideas. This very lodge became illuminated through Weishaupt's influence, and is more than likely to be where

Rothschild first heard of this form of masonry. (see chapter two). **(This is an important 'Direction' in the history of the Rothschilds).**

Suddenly Napoleon's troops were outside Frankfurt's walled city and the Judengasse was evacuated to a town nearby. The fire caused by the cannons wiped out half the Judengasse, leaving Rothschild's building untouched. Rothschild's business moved out of the Judengasse although his family remained inside its walls.

Rothschild's eldest son, Amshel, married the daughter of another court agent. His eldest daughter Schönche married Moses Wormes. To show his wealth, he gave a thirty-thousand Gulden present to the couple for their wedding gift he also made Amschel a junior partner in the firm. Following on from this he also made Nathan and Solomon junior partners of a company with assets of four-hundred and fifty-thousand Gulden. A sizeable amount in those days.

Buderus, Rothschild's friend, was promoted to the Landgraf's paymaster general, a position of immense power, giving Rothschild's business its first big chance to get a sizeable part of the banking business.

By ninety-eight Rothschild's business was nearly at full strength with four out of his five sons already working in the bank. His son Nathan was showing signs of being the brightest star and in a strange way Geisenheimer, the mason, had a remarkable influence on the direction of the family.

At this time, Nathan, after a confrontation with a salesman, decided to go to England and carry out the buying direct, cutting out the middleman. This move, emphasised at this point, that the merchant business was booming and that banking was still the second best.

This move was to eventually establish the English branch of Rothschild's banking house and the beginning of a new era of development.

Geisenheimer, as he spoke English, was released from his duties to accompany Nathan.

At the turn of the century Rothschild's dream was maturing. He successfully negotiated state loans and sold bonds at a profit and the bank's movement into financing states had begun. Another important step forward. **(Direction).**

With his axiom of maximising turnover by minimising profit, he was sweeping his competitors from the floor. This policy, with the constant help of Buderus, enabled him to defeat the Landgraf's loyal banks and take over as his main banker. He gained the main share of the Landgraf's business by 1807.

At this time the Rothschild business had reached a high point. On the one side, his merchant business was trading in colonial goods, coins, antiques, textiles and his latest addition, wine. On the other side banking was developing into government loans and financing wars and army requirements. **(This is a major Direction to note).**

In Vienna, on the 29th. of January 1800, the Habsburg Emperor, Franz II, appointed Rothschild and his son Amschel as imperial court agents, a privilege that had many assets, including authority to carry arms. This was in recognition of the assistance Rothschild had given to the Emperor against the aggression from France.

A most important exemption was the tax levied in the Holy Roman Empire which was waived for the two Rothschilds. But the Roman Empire was crumbling and everywhere, local officials ignored the Roman rights, so this appointment was somewhat watered down.

In 1802 Solomon Rothschild joined the local Masonic Lodge of L'Aurore which was one of the French discipline German lodges that had adopted Illumination (see chapter two). **(4).** The same year Meyer Rothschild became the Landgraf's chief court agent.

Meanwhile Nathan, who had settled well in England, set up his operation in Manchester at the heart of the textile industry. The Industrial Revolution was beginning to have effect and demand for military cloth was constantly growing, thanks to the Napoleonic War. It did not take him long to treble his twenty-thousand pound stake and he soon became Manchester's most important customer. He sent most of his purchases back to his father in Germany. It is interesting to note that the textiles for war supplies were paying handsomely. **(Direction).**

Back in Frankfurt Rothschild was about to change direction, by converting an exchange shop and warehouse into a bank. The reason was he wanted to be ready to handle large government loans with assistance from his friend Buderus and the money of the Landgraf.

Rothschild's persistence had at last brought him his main goal, access as lending agent to the Landgraf's considerable wealth, estimated at over forty-five million pounds.

At first he was very cautious, discounting his lending as a bookie would today, worried by heavy bets. It gave him, for the first time, ability to lend large amounts to government for wars or even national development. He moved the Landgraf's investments into bonds, buying at a low price and selling at maturity, making sizeable profits for the Landgraf and himself. The Rothschilds were becoming rich beyond belief.

Two loans to the Danish court **(Direction)** showed his efficiency was paying dividends. His old rival Bethmann's bank was losing out to his resourcefulness. Back in Frankfurt Rothschild was becoming involved in the education of Jews and founded a school that would not only teach the Torah but expand the knowledge to Voltaire, **(direction)** and other influences. Among the subjects were languages and social philosophy. Needless to say the Jewish population were worried by this departure from strict Jewish teaching; so were the Gentiles of Frankfurt as they saw it as a way to gain further concessions for the Jewish population. **(Direction).**

War between Prussia and France, which had simmered on and off for many years, broke out again.

The treaty of Lunéville extended France's influence to the Rhine. It also brought Wilhelm the title of Elector in 1803.

Wilhelm, the Elector of Hesse, played both sides to see where the best deal lay. He leased twenty-thousand soldiers to Prussia while negotiating with Napoleon for the city of Frankfurt to be given into his charge. After heated exchanges, nothing came of his endeavour. Napoleon was incensed by Wilhelm's refusal to support his efforts in Germany and sent his army to Kassel to remove him and his wealth once and for all.

Wilhelm terrified for his wealth, packed the best part of his collection of antiques, silver, coins and medals, most of which Rothschild had sold to him, into his chests. In other chests he packed all the records of his wealth and investments.

His aim was to ship his crates to Bremen on route to England but he was so mean that he refused to pay an extra fifty Thaler requested by the boatman and had to hide over one hundred crates in secret passages in his castles and palace.

Napoleon's troops reached Kassel on the 31st. October 1806.

Wilhelm escaped to his brother at Gottdorf, but his hiding places were well known and it did not take long to find huge hoards of gold and silver along with his coin collection. Worse, the search turned up most of the crates containing his record of accounts. However the French Governor General, like many others, was overcome with temptation and declared less than half of his findings. A sum of eleven million Thaler was declared to Napoleon. He was bribed to return the remaining cases to the Elector on receipt of two-hundred and sixty-thousand francs in cash. These crates contained the bonds and cash vouchers and other assets as well as his accounts.

Rothschild agreed to hide four crates containing privy council documents but myths since have popularised the rumour that Wilhelm hid his entire wealth as well as his wines. This was rumour only, encouraged by some members of the family.

About this time Rothschild, in a secret agreement, made Buderus a silent partner in his bank on payment of twenty- thousand Gulden. Buderus became a business adviser. This was an inspired move by Rothschild.

The Elector was not disposed to trust one man but in exile he became more and more dependent on Rothschild's good service; another turn of fortune for the fast developing assets of his dynasty. The Elector now depended entirely on Buderus and Rothschild in turn was given many new profitable duties especially in England and gradually he was handling most of the Elector's investments and had overall financial control.

By 1807 Rothschild was worth two million Gulden. In the same year he opened a temporary office in Hamburg to help Calmann, one of his sons, to handle the Elector's business in exile.

In the meantime Frankfurt once and for all time lost its connection with the Holy Roman Empire, and was enrolled in the Confederation of the Rhine under French control. The new rulers removed all restriction of movement from the Jewish population.

Rothschild, unwilling to miss an opportunity, tried hard to get on the right side of Karl Von Dalberg, the Prince-Bishop of Mainz, Napoleon's man in Frankfurt, who sided with Napoleon when he saw the development of events. Dalberg turned out to be a bitter disappointment to the Jewish population. Rather than remove remaining restrictions from the Jewish population, as Napoleon had done elsewhere, he re-imposed old restrictions and made the Jews, who had moved out of the Judengasse after the fire, move back into their ghetto and suffer its restrictions once more.

Another turn in Rothschild's fortune took place a year earlier when Napoleon announced the Edict of Berlin, closing all ports to British goods. Trade with England was made illegal. Traders found with goods would have them confiscated and persistent offenders jailed.

This was like a red rag to a bull. The traders, especially Rothschild, with his son in a position to arrange direct delivery, prospered as never before, as the prices started to rise. The family spread out over Europe to form a wholesale distribution chain with ships for transport laid on by the English government in an attempt to break the blockade; they seemed impervious to the law, where opportunity for profit was concerned. Once more while others might falter the Rothschilds risked all and reached for their pot of gold.

In Frankfurt at this time Rothschilds' association with the Elector became a problem when Napoleon's police chief, Savagnier, put the whole Rothschild family under house arrest while he searched the house and the books for dealings with the Elector. To Rothschild's delight nothing serious was found; possibly a bribe was paid, but this was not clear. From there on he would be more careful. The way Rothschild handled himself impressed the Elector, who offered a place for one of his sons on his staff. With gratitude Rothschild declined as he needed all his sons to develop his banking business since his illness. This might have been a bluff but he sensed the need to give more power to his sons.

Nathan, who handled the Elector's finances in England was asked to do the biggest deal yet for the Elector by investing a total of five-hundred and fifty-thousand pounds, to be bought in Rothschild's name to hinder sequestration. This gave Nathan an inflated credit standing in the city which he used to good effect. The deal itself brought a large profit to the bank.

Nathan was made an English citizen in 1804 and opened a bank counting house in Saint Swithin's Lane, very close to the Bank of England.

By 1810 Rothschild, in recognition of his sons' hard work, gave them the right of signature and extra shares in the business profit. However he retained voting power. Provision was also made to cover his other two sons.

Nathan, as a English citizen, was excluded but a separate secret agreement was struck by his father. Rothschild sensed he was coming to the end and in true form was guaranteeing the continuance of his dynasty. From this point he began to relax and let his able sons take up the reins.

He turned his energy to getting equal rights treatment for the Jews of Frankfurt. He negotiated a deal (Bribe) with Dalberg and brought the price down from a million Gulden to four-hundred and forty-thousand Gulden.

On the 7th. of February 1811 Dalberg proclaimed the equality of all residents but a rider was added, 'Provided the city lost no revenue.' Therefore the Jewish community must find the equivalent of all the extra taxes imposed on the Jewish community. On the twenty-eighth of December Dalberg finally signed a new agreement for equal rights with the rider removed; a victory for Rothschild and the power of money.

A plot of land in the Judengasse, bought by the three eldest sons was now used to build a new bank to cope with their increased fortunes; it was, at last, a modern, purpose-built office.

Solomon and Amschel lived outside the Ghetto in the city but Meyer Amschel Rothschild, their father, who could afford to live anywhere, would not move out of the Judengasse. It had, after all, housed his life's work and his fortune, and formed a world power in banking. Again we see how fortune shone on Rothschild's decisions. Dalberg wanted to visit Paris to attend the baptism of Napoleon's son and needed eighty-thousand Gulden to make the journey in style. Other bankers refused his request but Rothschild lent him the money and in return received a passport for his son Jacob (James) who wished to go to Paris and start a new branch. Dalberg also introduced him to the French Treasury. With this introduction they launched the next branch of their bank.

By now they were concentrating mostly on banking and the merchant side was being run down. As luck was on his side, shortly after his run down of trade, the French troops confiscated all English goods and burned them in public. Rothschild's fine was smaller than most of the bankers at under twenty-thousand francs against one trader's of over a million francs.

Nathan, in England, was buying bills that Wellington was cashing at high discount to keep his army fed. With the profit from the bills he bought gold to the value of eight-hundred-thousand pounds. When the English government heard of his purchase they bought it from him at a handsome profit and came to an agreement to keep Wellington, now desperate for cash, supplied with money during his campaign in Portugal. He undertook, through his network of contacts (Sphere of influence) to move gold and keep the money flowing. **(Direction)**. At this point we have to ask ourselves, "why, with all its superior sea power England could not do the job itself?"

The gold was shipped to Paris where Jacob, (James) through his hastily arranged contacts, changed them to bills payable at Portuguese banks.

Although Rothschild charged for this as a service, he saved the Treasury a great deal of money. Some say as much as two-hundred million pounds of transfers were made in this way, right under Napoleon's nose, while he believed it was a sign of the collapse of England.

The profit to the Rothschilds must have been large and showed how once again they were prepared to go further than the other bankers to make a killing.

Life was coming to an end for Meyer Amschel Rothschild. His final act was to call his sons to his bedside; but only Amschel and Calmann were present in the time left. On his death bed he counselled his sons to stick together so they could become the richest men in Germany. His business fortune was left in five equal shares to his five sons. Amschel was to be in charge of the Frankfurt bank A M Rothschild. Nathan controlled the English branch of N M Rothschild. Jacob, known later as James was in charge of the Paris branch of J M Rothschild. Solomon was in charge of the Vienna branch of S M Rothschild. Last but by no means least there was Calmann, later known as Carl, who was in charge of C M Rothschild.

The banks were all controlled under the same account to make sure they continued to co-operate with each other and prosper.

Meyer Amschel Rothschild's private wealth was dispersed to his daughters and his wife. A small amount was left to a Christian foundation, not strangely Jewish. He died on the 19th. of September 1812. The King was dead, long live the Kings. His sons heeded his words and stuck together, increasing their fortunes many times. They were to become the richest bankers in Europe and create a multi-national banking consortium. The nineteenth century writer, Heine, described James (Jacob) as the "Profit of a new religion, the religion of money. "How wondrous that once again it is the Jews that invent this new religion." **(5).**

But wealth on this scale was a new phenomenon and **direction** will show us how this wealth moulded the world into its present shape from the modest beginnings of a man, hemmed in by his religion and circumstance, yet had the vision to develop such a powerful bank. This is not a story about Jews or Gentiles but about circumstances that develop empires like Rothschild and his sons in a **'direction'** and how a goal was set. This goal has been carefully planed and precisely executed. A plan that takes into account the way the world treated the founder, Meyer Amschel Rothschild. A plan with terrible consequences for the freedom and democracy of the world. I believe **'Direction'** of action proves my analysis. You must judge this when you have read the full story.

CHAPTER ONE, PART TWO.

ROTHSCHILD x FIVE = POWER

The collapse of Napoleon's army in Russia had a devastating effect on Europe. A shift at the centre of power was about to take place. Caution was needed as the bank had customers on both sides of the war. Everywhere in Germany the people felt a new freedom from the French oppressors. Gradually the opportunists who had sided with Napoleon broke loose. Prussia fell in behind Russia. 1813 saw Napoleon again win two battles in Saxony but he did not drive the enemy out of their position. Finance for the alliance was offered and accepted from England. Both Prussia and Russia increased their armies. Even Metternich, after his famous meeting with Napoleon in 1813, changed his nation's policy and backed the Prusso-Russian alliance **(6)**. The Elector of Hesse, Wilhelm, asked the Emperor of Austria to re-instate him as soon as possible. Never at a loss to protect his property, he reminded the Emperor of his undertaking;' to guarantee him against any loss'. He contributed to war funds and sent troops to help the coming offensive.

Buderus was asked to obtain the money and the House of Rothschild supplied the one-hundred-thousand thaler. This was planned, with the financial assistance of Rothschild, and heralded the turning point in the Napoleonic war'**s,** the day of Leipzig on the 18th. October 1813, the day the whole of Germany was liberated up to the Rhine.

The Confederation of the Rhine collapsed; Dalberg voluntarily resigned and the King of Westphalia fled in panic. By the 11th. of November the Elector of Hesse returned from Prague and the general atmosphere favoured the House of Rothschild.

The next move shows us how the founder had taught his sons to read politics.
(Direction).

It was Nathan who saw the opportunity that would both boost his power and prestige, let alone his wealth, and at the same time make himself indispensable to the coalition against Napoleon.

The opportunity arose when the Prince Regent of England wished to re-pay one-hundred-thousand pounds to the Elector and Nathan was ordered to re-invest the money in consols. This brought him in direct touch with the private royal finances. At this time great demands were being made on England for the Napoleonic Wars and Rothschild was called in by Herries and given the task of transferring the money to Europe and the Coalition. The money was to supply Wellington with finance to make his big push into France. Nathan had to work in secret to protect his brother James behind enemy lines. As Wellington wanted French money Nathan had to go to Holland to obtain such a large quantity. He then dispatched the money to Wellington's headquarters. He kept up a flow of money to Wellington and not only did he make a fortune from his efforts he also gained prestige with the English King and government, indeed later, he claimed it was the best deal he had ever done.
(Direction).

The future was to bring Nathan business with Austria. Metternich was the man of the moment and with his influence and the hard lobbying of Amschel Rothschild, first Nathan handled the officers' pay; but as the wars ended abruptly it spoiled further advancement at that moment. On the 31st. of March the Coalition entered Paris and Napoleon abdicated.

The Rothschilds still pressed to be allowed to have 'the honour' of handling the financial affairs of the Austrian government; still the Austrian officials resisted. Rothschilds already had part of the lending accounts of Prussia and by paying money in advance of due payment they tried to impress the Austrian officials with their strength and ability. This failed. At one time all five brothers were employed in an attempt to win Austria's business. Rothschild bid for the transfer of moneys from occupied countries, in this case Belgium, to the three coalition countries Prussia Austria and Russia, but Austria, still unaware of the strength of Rothschild or loyal to another bank, gave the business to Bethmann, Rothschild's Frankfurt rival.

The great advantage of having branches in different countries enabled the Rothschilds to issue bills to save transport of moneys. There were few banks with their standing and they cornered the market at a time when money transport was both costly and dangerous. Nathan, the genius, was the key inspiration for this idea. It was Nathan's drive that helped England, Prussia, Austria and Russia to beat Napoleon. He now set his sights on the Bourbons who had returned to Paris with his financial backing. As was typical of the Rothschilds they allowed others to get credit and glory from the moment while they accumulated profit in silence; the way they best liked it. **(Direction)**.

Louis XVIII returned to his throne but it was short lived as Napoleon was on his way back from Elba, and with the help of the Illuminati **(7)** took over the government and once again the Bourbon King fled.

At this time the congress of Vienna was discussing Europe's future. Napoleon hoped they would follow his policy but they didn't. They decided to rush through changes, one of which was a German Confederation encompassing thirty-nine communities or principalities giving each independence under a common government. To the Rothschilds advantage Frankfurt was chosen as the power base.

Once again the four powers, would engage Napoleon's power. This time Rothschild, through Nathan and Solomon, secured the transfer of money to the Prussian Government and when the two-hundred-thousand pounds sent, was found to be inadequate, Solomon on the spot increased the loan by one-hundred and fifty thousand pounds without consulting his brothers but at a high charge which the English Government promptly agreed to cover. For this initiative he would get his reward. Nathan approached Herries, their contact inside the English government, to get an annoyance removed by the Austrian government. The Baron von Hügel, the Austrian representative in Frankfurt, conveyed the English request to Metternich and Stadion, the new finance minister, and, not only did they stop demands for the Rothschilds to take up military service but also opposition to their handling the English transfers were removed. Once again the house of Rothschild was to prosper from war.

Napoleon's fortune did not last long. By the 18th. of June eighteen-fifteen he was decisively beaten at the Battle of Waterloo. This time he was banished to Saint Helena. Rothschild's great asset during all these years of conflict was his arrangements by which he could be informed quickly of important world developments. This above all else gave the Rothschilds advantage over their rivals; he actually gave Herries and the English Government the news of the battle of Waterloo one day before the government's own messenger. This impressed the English government and the people. **(Direction)**. The Rothschilds used this recognition to their advantage. However Austria still showed signs of mistrust towards the Rothschilds.

Herries, once again, took the Austrians to task over their prejudice against the bank of Rothschild and Baron von Limburger gave a written undertaking on behalf of the English Government to make good any loss that might occur in transfer. This and the news that Metternich and Stadion were receiving news daily about the good services of the Rothschild brothers finally won the bank Austria's business. A long and hard fought battle had been won. **(Direction)**.

Meanwhile back in Frankfurt Buderus von Carlshousen was elevated to Privy Councillor and President of the Chamber as Wilhelm's envoy to the Federal Diet. His close connections with the Rothschilds insured the Rothschilds that their special position with the Elector, which had taken second place to the war business, in Rothschilds schedule, with millions changing hands, was restored.

Once again the Rothschilds were diverted from local matters when the Coalition inflicted war indemnity on France of seven-hundred-million Francs. Rothschilds saw great profit in distributing this war bounty to the Coalition countries. They faced formidable competition from the four Austrian banks and even Barings, an English banking house. Rothschild and his associate Gontard won the transfer contract for Austrian payments at one and a quarter percent commission. Shortly after this Rothschild and Gontard were commissioned to move part of the French indemnity money.

James, in Paris, broke the neutrality of Barbier, Austria's financial representative and Rothschilds gained about half the business for the French indemnity money which was again to make them a fortune.

The manner in which they handled this business brought them recognition from Austria's Emperor Francis. Amschel and Solomon were ennobled on the 25th. of September 1816 and on the 21st. of October of the same year Carl and James. A coat of arms was granted to the Rothschild family in 1817. They could now put von in front of their names. Today this means little but then power was in the hands of the ennobled.

Shortly afterwards Nathan and James sought further power as honorary consuls for Austria, a diplomatic post in England and France and after much debate and many manoeuvres, were granted the posts. This again shows how they followed up everything further and longer than their opposition. These positions opened many closed doors. **(Direction)**.

The Rothschilds now had standing power and a considerable fortune made astutely by good contacts, who were generously treated, Buderus as a shareholder in the Rothschild Bank as an example, and by hard work and ultimately by collaboration between the five brothers with the genius of Nathan to lead them towards the power of the moment.

By sticking to the principle the Elector of Hesse taught their father, to deal with the top, where bad debt was less likely; and from this advice they prospered.

By their speedy information service that brought them news before their rivals.

By financing countries at war, where money was needed to supply troops, armaments and food for the battles; with certainty of financial strength. This all formed a pattern of development. **(Direction)**.

Yet Nathan the motor, wished to increase the power of his already unbeatable banking house with its steadily increasing sphere of influence.

Nathan did a deal with Prince Hardenberg to straighten out the Prussian finances in exchange for help in favour of the Frankfurt Jewish community, still suffering from prejudice. The Prince took up the cause and asked Amschel in turn to put pressure on his brothers to agree to the loan to his government. Both Nathan and Amschel saw this loan as a good opportunity to earn money. Nathan concluded the deal with Rother, the Prince's representative, who in his report to Berlin stated "It is widely stated, and is, indeed, almost a fact, that he (Nathan) entirely regulates the rate of exchange in the city. (London)."

The loan brought added fortune to the Rothschilds but set a precedent for their bank as the first big state loan, encouraging them to develop this line of business. **(Direction)**.

1821 saw the death of the Elector Wilhelm; his eldest son succeeded him and inherited his power and wealth.

This son had led a playboy life of extravagance on borrowed money from the Rothschilds, but on accession he paid off his debt.

Rothschild no longer needed the Elector. Power politics were his future and, being up with the leaders of the pack, his concentration.

A congress in Aachen of the victorious powers was set up to establish a policy concerning relations with France and other duties of a victor. The Rothschilds lost no time in getting Gentz, Prince Metternich's secretary, to call their tune. They even managed to persuade Gentz to take up the matter of the Frankfurt Jews.

Gentz was to become a great asset and was duly rewarded. He showed them the details of the men who mattered in Europe, met Metternich for the first time, and filled their books with contacts, so essential to bankers on the move.

Meanwhile, in England, Nathan handled a twelve million pound deal with the Treasury at almost no profit so he could chase off the competition. His position was secure as he was known as the banker of England.

James, in Paris, was increasing his business, through war indemnity.

Back in Frankfurt things were not so good. Buderus had a stroke. This man, through his steadfast petitioning on their behalf to the Elector had made it possible for the Rothschilds to expand and prosper. Then he helped them to use the money to develop their business. Although they no longer needed this help, without it, the Rothschild bank would never have reached its heights. Like the Elector, they owed Buderus a great gratitude; unlike the Elector, Rothschild recognised this in bank shares.

The bank negotiated the transfer of money from Naples to Austria, from France to Austria and from Milan to Austria. At these times the secrecy of transfer was paramount, so, for confidential information, the Rothschild courier service was extended to bypass the other services which were both slow and prone to letter reading. They even offered this service to governments and began a profitable service, some of which gave them some important information.

On the 3rd. of march 1820 Nathan was appointed Austrian Consul in London. Shortly afterwards, Rothschild and Parish shared the fifty-five million Gulden loan for Prince Metternich.

The first part of the loan was twenty-million Gulden over a long period, netting the banks eighteen million Gulden on completion. This caused uproar and the bankers were accused of usury and the government of incompetence. Today these circumstances are common-place with all government loans.

The bonds were issued as lottery bonds and on opening there was high demand from the public. The bonds began climbing from one-hundred, one-twenty, one-fifty and higher. This prompted Stadion to issue the remaining thirty-five million Gulden only four months later. Rothschild and Parish paid over 35,000,000 Gulden over twelve months and repayment was 76,821,515 Gulden; plus a commission of 1,400,000 Gulden. This proved the most lucrative loan yet and heralded the emphasis on state loans as their future priority. **(Direction)**.

Solomon Rothschild now set up shop in Vienna, living in a hotel, as Jews were not allowed to buy houses.

Business was opening up everywhere. Rothschild became the natural first choice bank.

Naples was in a state of war, and Austria, that controlled the territory, had to act to dampen down the revolt. Rothschild was brought in to finance the war but was to arrange loans at the expense of Naples. He saw how Austria depended on his good offices so he placed money at their disposal to secure the Naples' business exclusively for his bank.

Carl Rothschild was sent to Naples, stopping off at Vienna, to speak with Stallion. From there he went to Laibach. On the 24th. of March 1821 the forward troops entered Naples without resistance. Carl left for Florence on the 31st. of March. From there he proceeded to Naples to view the situation and make his offer. Naples soon became another country to borrow money to finance its obligations. **This is a system used by every debt ridden country today, giving the bankers control of all debt ridden nations.**

The Rothschilds gave the outward appearance of conservatism but they always had it in mind that liberal elements could take power, so they carefully fostered liberal friends like Duke Louis Philippe of Orléans. On the 11th. of August James von Rothschild was made consul-general in Paris for the Austrian government.

Meanwhile back in Naples, Austria was demanding payment of reparations and advised the Neapolitan authorities to get in touch with Carl Rothschild in Naples who was authorised to collect moneys due. The first payment of 500,00 Gulden was due on the 31st. of august and 700,00 Gulden a month for three months, and a final payment of 1,400,000 Gulden in January 1822. The bonds covering the loans increased from 60 to 76.5 percent. Not a bad profit. Another loan was concluded with Naples authority for nearly 17,000,000 ducats at the end of November 1821 at a remarkably high underwritten price of 67.3 percent.

Effectively what this did was to ensure that the total cost of the Austrian army was borne by Naples at a crippling cost to its people. Rothschild, in the meantime, made a killing.

The Rothschilds had now achieved a position of real power. Everyone needed them on their side so restrictions of Jews were relaxed from practical necessity. Rothschild could either hinder or promote deals. Their friendship with Gentz, Metternich's secretary grew stronger and although it cost Solomon dearly, his contacts were invaluable.

Meanwhile Naples was getting further in debt, with a new finance minister, Medici, trying hard to change course. But even his considerable skills could not do the impossible. Two more loans were given. Each time the bonds rose through the Rothschild's skill. However Naples' debt had risen from 28,000,000 to 104,000,000 ducats, an impossible debt for such a small Nation. **(Direction)**

Carl, who had moved to Naples on a temporary basis, decided to build the fifth branch there, completing a new centre for the Rothschild Empire.

On the 29th. September 1822 all the brothers and descendants of both sexes were accorded the title of Baron by the Austrian Emperor and the original design for their coat of arms was accepted. The motto "Concordia Integritas Industria" showed the harmony of the five brothers.

This produced the desired effect socially and further increased their power and influence. The desire to enlarge their empire was phenomenal.

A civil war in Spain had been in progress since 1820 and the King was a virtual prisoner of the member of the Cortes. Metternich decided to attend the Congress of Sovereigns with Gentz and the Emperor on the 20th. October 1822 at Verona. This time they took Solomon Rothschild with them to arrange finance for any rescue operation that was decided in Congress.

Solomon, on arrival in Verona, learnt of wide spread rumours that his bank had negotiated a loan with the Spanish government which was in power, and due to the revolution, the very government that was holding the King. Although discussions may well have taken place, no loan was agreed. Solomon had to squash the damaging leak if he was to hold credibility with Metternich.

In a letter to Metternich he denied having anything to do with the revolutionary Government, which was true. Nathan had, however, discussed the matter but no loan had been granted.

This taught the Rothschilds a lesson, if you lend to both sides, use agents for at least one. **(Direction)**.

Solomon's explanation was accepted and Gentz introduced Solomon to the Tsar's representatives with whom he negotiated a loan for 6 million pounds and received an honour from Russia (the order of Vladimir). James also was honoured.

Solomon now opened a courier service between Verona, Paris and Vienna, linking their newly conquered territory. This link made and saved them much money in the uncertain months ahead, using advanced knowledge to best effect. After much delay the Congress decided to send aid to the Spanish King.

Nathan asked to be made Consul General in London in recognition of his previous work for Austria. The Emperor, with recommendation from Metternich, granted the elevation without argument.

A new problem arose; the four brothers following the power flow in Europe were swayed by conservative leanings, while Nathan, in England, a liberal land, and the richest nation in the world, had to, at least show support for liberal ideas or he would lose out on business. As business was all important, politics must be adopted to suit the government of the day. **(Direction)**.

In 1823, James, through his friendship with Count de Villèle, offered a loan to assist the financial weakness at the Treasury. James knew the campaign against Spain would necessitate a loan so he just sat back and waited. Once more Metternich got the news of James' efforts to halt the war between France and Spain. But events saved the Rothschilds as the force crossed the border and penetrated deep into Spain without opposition.

The Rothschilds deposited a letter of credit with the Madrid Bank through their sphere of influence to pay for the army's occupation. On the 23rd. of May the Duke of Augoulême entered Madrid and set up a Regency without opposition. However the King was carried off to Cadiz.

Villèle, to pay for the Spanish exercise, floated a loan for twenty-two million francs. In competition with other bankers, Rothschild bid 89.55% winning the loan from his nearest rival of 87.75%. Soon after they placed the bonds on sale, they rose to 91.25%. Again the Rothschilds beat the opposition (who dares wins). The end came soon to the Spanish war. The King was released after payments were made through Rothschild and, James, in recognition of his part, received the Cross of the Legion of Honour, and of course increased wealth from profitable trading.

Again a shared loan came shortly afterwards, to support the King, a shared loan of 125,000,000 pesetas was suggested, at 60 percent, with a guaranteed mortgage from Spain's colonial revenue and a formal guarantee from France. France refused to sign the guarantee. The offer was withdrawn.

The power of the Rothschilds was now so great that they did not need to use other banks in the larger deals.

At last Gentz delivered his promise to the Jews of Frankfurt. Count Buol was withdrawn from office and Baron von Münch Bellinghousen took over and quickly repealed the anti Jewish laws of Frankfurt by August 1822. The Jews were counted as Israelite citizens and the Ghetto was freed and the inhabitants were at liberty to move inside the city. At last the consistent pressure, applied on Metternich through Gentz, paid off for the Rothschilds.

In April 1823, Austria borrowed a further 30,000,000 Gulden. Four firms provided the loan including Rothschild; receiving 36,000,000 million 5 percent bonds, payable at 82 Gulden per cent. 1829 saw new business in Brazil. Shortly afterwards, in league with Barings Bank they jointly underwrote a loan for Austria. 150,000,000 three percent bonds plus a savings bond but this was rejected by the Upper House and caused much indignation against the government and the House of Rothschild.

Carl, in the meantime, began fostering goodwill in Naples with the local dignitaries as he was resolved to stay in Naples and see an end to Austria's involvement. So he was set on founding the Naples branch of the House of Rothschild, the fifth power house.

One of the most extraordinary endeavours undertaken by the Rothschilds was to suggest to the King of Naples that for his personal protection he should recruit an Irish army, which would alleviate the troubles in Ireland, supply the King with a loyal army and by doing so, develop good business. It illustrates how this banker went outside the remits of banking to make a deal. **(Direction).** On this occasion the deal fell through when the King of Naples died.

1824 saw a new profitable Spanish loan that came to nothing. James married his niece Betty, the nineteen year old daughter of Solomon; a pattern of marriage developed by the Rothschilds to keep the business safely in family circles.

Not every loan was successful. An indemnity of one-hundred and fifty-million Francs had to be paid by Haiti who could not meet the demand. The loan, syndicated, Rothschild being involved, was finally indemnified by the French government but still made a loss.

Not only did the Rothschilds lend money to governments but made a habit of lending money to people in power and of standing. The reason was that it put them under a social business obligation. (Direction).

At the beginning of 1826, John Parish, the banker and Rothschild's partner in some deals, collapsed. **(8).** In a letter to Metternich he described the brothers Rothschild as "Heartless persons, only interested in their money bags, who, standing under the special protection of Metternich, have behaved in a most ungrateful manner to him". **(9).** In a letter to Solomon he accused him of squeezing him out, although he had introduced him to important French and Austrian business. This was not true but the essence of what he said was accurate in that the Rothschild partners were ruthless. **(Direction).**

The family also knew how to use literary talent to praise their house and control the aggressive press through contacts. (Sphere of influence).

Gentz was one of those literary pens who often wrote glowing reports of the family in between agreeable dinner parties and 'financial transactions' as recorded in Gentz's own diary. An example of his work can be seen in the 'Conversational Encyclopaedia' published by Brockhous 1826. **(10).**

Now the business had five centres, control was its largest problem, due to the poor communication system available in those days. So each brother had a wide parameter of decision. Carl was the most isolated, not being on one of the main European routes. He had to go to Paris or London to confer regularly. So the House of Rothschild continued to finance governments.

Solomon in the meantime set about the task of organising the estates of Marie-Louise, Napoleon's ex-wife. Metternich had approached him for his advice and

Rothschild responded and set about sorting out a very complicated deal to realise her assets.

So impressed was she with Solomon's dedication to her problems, she retained him as her adviser and trustee for her estates. Once again this association brought in many new opportunities that were not missed by the House of Rothschild.

The Rothschilds' greatest attribute was to be able to predict the political future accurately. This was helped by their courier service, bringing early news. **(Direction).**

The Rothschild Empire was central Europe. Russia was a dangerous area for a Jewish banker but it was in their mind for future development, but not yet. They employed Wellington as a political adviser.

Rothschilds, through their endeavours, built a reputation such that all parties rushed to their door to tap their resources for their domains.

Prussia applied for a loan, this time 5,000,000 at four percent through Solomon. This was the first of several loans to Austria, Prussia and France.

In 1830 a bombshell hit France. By 323 votes to 125 the electors voted the government out of office. This set the King's followers in turmoil.

The King dissolved the hostile chamber before it met and ordered a new election under different rules. France was in an uproar of indignation. Paris revolted and by the 24th. of July the royal troops were forced back on Saint Cloud where the King sat waiting for events to pass. On the 31st. of July Charles X and his entire entourage fled in panic.

This was the moment for Louis Philippe, the Duke of Orleans, the liberal, to make a timely entrance. James Rothschild immediately changed allegiance to Philippe, thus forsaking a conservative administration for a Liberal one. (Direction).

Metternich's plan for a peaceful world took a knock. Once again he first got the news indirectly from the Rothschilds news service. However, through events out of their control the house of Rothschild was to momentarily experience a fall in their wealth. Liberalism took heart from the events in Paris, and cities in Germany started to rise.

The Rothschilds changed ship and denounced wars at any cost to save their House.

The new King used James as a messenger of good will to Metternich.

The Rothschilds set to work eagerly to keep the powers in Europe informed of developments so they could nip any sign of revolution in the bud. Things were going too fast for safety. James was even given an audience with the new King, Philippe, to discuss events, showing how important to European affairs the Rothschilds had become.

Revolution was in the air in Germany, Italy, Spain and Belgium affecting Holland. As a result Belgium and Holland separated and the house of Orange fell. News from Vienna showed severe repression was planned against all signs of revolution. Metternich also planned action against France to restore the old order.

The Rothschilds, in fear of further war and its effect on the money market, did their best to calm Metternich and his call for war.

The Rothschilds lost no time in using all their contacts to pressurise the powers. Negotiations took place between Metternich and Philippe, through Solomon and James, each in direct touch with their side, by-passing the ambassadors and using the trusted Rothschild courier system. So, war was not always the catalyst for their profit and their feverishly active efforts to convince the power centres of Europe were to save their investments and the very existence of their bank. Once more a fine gesture but one with self interest in mind. **(Direction)**.

We have now studied the first eighty years in the history of the House of Rothschild, from the founder to the five sons. From this we get a definite pattern that indicates the all important '**Direction**'.

Back in his early days Meyer Amschel Rothschild learned that the big money was to be made from financing the power hungry princes at war.

To enable him to achieve this aim he targeted Wilhelm, the Elector of Hesse, to obtain his business and use his wealth to promote his aim. Soon war became his company's fortune, not only through finance, but through war supplies. Nathan's transfer to England promoted this increase in his fortune.

His sons eventually opened four more branches in England, France, Austria, and Italy. the brothers opened a fast courier service to link their branches.

Their success came from dealing with the top men in Europe and tapping into their decisions.

Money was their only motivation. Power became their engine. Monopoly of banking their aim; control of nations through their debt, their target. Nothing was sacred that came in their way, politics, ethics and friendships would all be used or sacrificed for their god, Money.

We see from this early history of the House of Rothschild that war and government loans became the bulk of their business. No other bank was so successful in such a corrupting business.

We also know from history that the progress of the Rothschilds, from this point on, depended largely on the financing of wars. Nearly every war that took place right up to the Second World War was partly financed by the Rothschilds either directly or through agents. In some indeed, like the American Civil War between North and South, they had an agent in both camps, lending money. When they wished to hide their involvement they used agents or other banks within their sphere of influence.

This happened again in the second world war when money was lent to the Third Reich through the Warburg controlled Mendelsohn bank of Amsterdam and later the J. Henry Schroeder bank, of Frankfurt, London and New York. **(11)**. I need hardly point out these were Jewish controlled banks, putting a new complexion on the second world war. This shows clearly the Three hundred bankers in action, setting Europe up for a war to favour their aims of world domination.

The Russian Bolshevik revolution was perhaps their greatest diversion in their lending pattern; however we heard that they wanted to trade in Russia, and this was their first chance. But it was more. Rothschild and others had funded first Weishaupt and then Karl Marx to design Rothschild a way to world control. This was the moment to test it, and it worked. **(Direction)**.

They continued to finance Russia after the Revolution and together with members of the three-hundred bankers they supplied Russia's financial needs right up to the so called collapse of Communism. Their prize of course has been the rich mineral and oil reserves, largely untapped.

In financing Russia after the Revolution they financed first Lenin Then Stalin. This means that they financially helped the largest holocaust in the history of the world where twenty-two and a half million people died at the hands of Stalin. Because of this, I claim, they have no moral right to censor the world when it wishes to criticise International Zionist actions, that will effect the democracy and well being of all peoples in the world. **(12)**.

On this basis I canvass support to expose the Hidden Agenda of the International Finance Capitalists, and their threat to the world, far greater than any war, as it is unseen.

> "The movement among the Jews is not new. From the days of Sparticus-Weishaupt to those of Karl Marx, and down to Trotsky (Russia), Bela Kun (Hungary), Rosa Luxemberg (Germany), and Emma Goldman (United States), this world-wide conspiracy for the overthrow of civilisation and for the reconstruction of society on the basis of arrested development, of envious malevolence, and impossible equality, has been steadily growing".
>
> **Winston Churchill. In the Illustrated Sunday Herald, February 8th. 1920.**

CHAPTER ONE, PART THREE.

ROTHSCHILDS AND THEIR SPHERE OF INFLUENCE 1992

We turn now to their influence in the recent past. Changes have occurred in the lists, and titles have changed, but the list is as accurate as possible covering the sphere of influence at the end of 1992 to the end of 1994. Some material comes from previous years company records, where latest filed lists have not been entered in company house.

THE HOUSE OF ROTHSCHILD

There are fifty-one living members of the house of Rothschild. The present overall head of the family, by male primogeniture is the British Baron Rothschild (Born 1936); the heir is Nathaniel Philip Victor James (Born 1971). Seventeen are males over the age of twenty-one and are thereby eligible to become Freemasons and their names are in bold type. Of the remaining five males, three are presently (18-8-94) due to reach their twenty-first birthday by the year two-thousand and their names are in italics. The year of birth for each individual is in parentheses.

The Rothschilds are descended from Meyer Amschel Rothschild (1744-1812), the founder of the dynasty, through three of his five sons: Solomon Mayer (1774-1855); Nathan Mayer (1777-1836) and James Mayer (1774-1855); descent from each respectively is indicated by an appropriate letter (S), (N), (J). Amschel Mayer (1773-1855) died childless and Carl Mayer (1788-1855) has no living descendants with the Rothschild name. (Note. Meyer Amschel Rothschild changed his first name to Mayer in 1782, it is thought, to sound more German).

The English Rothschilds are the descendants of Nathan Mayer through his son Lionel Nathan (1808-1879). The French Rothschilds belong to two lines; the elder, all female, being descended from Nathan Mayer through his son Nathaniel (1812-1870) and the younger, descendants of James Mayer. Bettina Jemima (Born 1924) is the last of the Austrians.

ROTHSCHILDS LIVING FAMILY

	NAME	BORN
AUSTRIAN	Bettina Jemima (S)	1924
ENGLISH		
	Miriam Louisa (N)	1908
	Elizabeth Charlotte (N)	1909
	Kathreen Annie Pannonica (N)	1913
	Sarah (N)	1934
	Nathaniel Charles Jacob Baron (N)	1936
	Hannah Mary (N)	1962
	Beth Matilda (N)	1964
	Emily Magda (N)	1967
	Nathaniel Philip Victor James (N)	1971
	Victoria Katherine (N)	1953
	Amschel Mayer James (N)	1955
	Kate Emma (N)	1982
	Alice Miranda (N)	1983
	James Amschel Victor (N)	1985
	Edmund Leopold (N)	1916
	Katherine Juliette (N)	1949
	Nicholas David (N)	1951
	David Lionel (N)	1955
	Charlotte Henrietta (N)	1955
	Naomi Louisa Nina (N)	1920
	Leopold David (N)	1927
	Renée Louise Marie (N)	1927
	Sir Evelyn Robert Adrian (N)	1931
	Jessica (N)	1974
	Anthony James (N)	1977
	David Mayer (N)	1978
FRENCH		
	Nichole (N)	1924
	Monique (N)	1925
	Philippine Mathilde Camille (N)	1935
	Guy Edouard Alphonse Paul Baron (J)	1909
	David René James (J)	1942
	Lavinia Anne Alix (J)	1975
	Stephanie Anne Marie Helene (J)	1977
	Alexandre Guy Francesco (J)	1980
	Edouard Etienne Alphonse (J)	1957
	Jacqueline Rebecca Louise (J)	1911
	Bethsabee Louise Emile Beatrix	1914
	Diane Cecile Alice Juliette (J)	1907
	Beatrice Juliette Ruth (J)	1939

Eric Alain Robert David (J)	1940
Robert James (J)	1947
Cecile Leonie Eugenie Gudule Lucie (J)	1913
Elie Robert Baron (J)	1917
Michel Nathaniel Robert Eugene (J)	1946
Raphael Benjamin Jacob (J)	1976
Ester Eva (J)	1979
Nelly Rachel Cecile (J)	1947
Elizabeth Clarice Ester Gustava (J)	1952
Edmond Adolphe Maurice Jules Jaques (J)	1926
Benjamin Edmund Maurice (J)	1963

ROTHSCHILD BANKS AND THEIR LISTED INTERESTS

REGISTERED OFFICE	N. M. Rothschild and Sons Ltd. New Court, St. Swithin's Lane, London EC4P 4DU.
DIRECTORS	* Indicates Directors of Rothschilds Continuation Ltd.
CHAIRMAN	Sir Evelyn De Rothschild*.
DEPUTY CHAIRMAN	David de Rothschild*.
VICE CHAIRMAN	Sir Michael Richardson.
MANAGING DIRECTORS	Antony Alt; John Bishop; Russel Edey; Bernard Myers*.
EXECUTIVE DIRECTORS	M Aish; Charles Alexander; Antony Allen; Richard Bailey; Caroline Banszky; D. Bendel; Peter Bird; C. Cornforth; Graham Curds; Penelope Curtis; R. Davey; P. Ffolkes Davis; Antony Fry; Alan Graham; Jeremy Gray; Benoît Guerin Timothy Hancock; Nigel Higgins; Peter Johns; Charles Keay; Martyn; W. Lamarque; Oliver Letwin; Simon Linnett; R. Lonsdale; C. Mercey; H. De la Moriniere; Robert Perry; Michael Phair; Charles Price; Jonathan Scherer; A. Stuart; Philip Swatman; Paul Tuckwell; M. Westerman; James Yates; Nicholas Wrigley.

NON_EXECUTIVE DIRECTORS.	Edmund de Rothschild* (Retiring at AGM 1994;) Eric de Rothschild*; Leopold de Rothschild: The Hon. Amschel Rothschild; Lord Armstrong if Ilminster; David Blackett; Peter Byrom; The Right Hon. Sir Frank Cooper; Sir John Fairclough; Christopher French; Ruben Goldberg; John Green-Armytage; Robert Guy; Graham Hearne; Georges Karlweis; The Right Hon. Norman Lamont; Grant Manheim.

SUBSIDIARIES
1 LIFE ASSURANCE.

J Rothschild Assurance Holdings Plc.

SJPC owns 51.02% of ordinary shares and 66.7% of redeemable convertible preference shares. JRAH holds a 10% interest in Scottish Amicable International.

J Rothschild Assurance
J Rothschild International Assurance

JRIA was formed at the end of 1992 to offer life assurance and investment products throughout the European Union as well as in expatriate markets throughout the world. Operating from the International Financial Services centre in Dublin. It has established relationships with Midland Bank overseas, Svenska Handelsbanken, Bank of Bermuda and Hambros Bank (Jersey). Chief executive: David Benyon, former Managing Director of Midland Bank Financial Services.

2 INVESTMENT MANAGEMENT.
J Rothschild Investment Management Ltd.
J Rothschild Capitol Management Ltd.
Main activity: Management of RIT capitol Partners Plc
IFM holdings Ltd.
SJPC owns 80% of the share capital, and the American International Group owns the remaining 20%.
Global Asset Management (Incorporated in Bermuda)
SJPC owns 29.7% of the share capital.

3 INVESTMENT BANKING.

J Rothschild, Wolfensohn and Co.
Joint venture between SJPC and James D Wolfensohn Inc. SJPC owns 50% of the
share capital. Advises clients on merger, acquisitions and divestitures, strategic alliances, joint ventures and financial strategy throughout Western and Eastern Europe.

4 INVESTMENT HOLDING AND INVESTMENT DEALING.

J Rothschild Holdings Plc.
J Rothschild Securities Ltd.

St James's Place Capital Plc.

Registered office   27 St James' Place, London SW1A 1NR.
Board of Directors:

The Lord Rothschild	Joint Chairman of SJPC and Non-Executive Director RIT Capitol Partners Plc. In 1971 became Chairman of Rothschild Investment Trust Ltd predecessor company to SJPC. **He is a member of the Bilderberg Group.**
Sir Mark Weinberg	Joint chairman of SJPC and since 1993 a non-executive director of RIT Capitol Partners Plc. Chairman of J Rothschild Assurance Holdings Plc. and has been deputy chairman of the Securities and Investment Board.
The Viscount Weir	Vice-Chairman and Non-Executive Director of SJPC. Member of its Audit Committee and its Remuneration and Conflicts Committee. predecessor. J Rothschild Holdings. He joined the Board of RIT and Northern, a predecessor company, at the time of its formation in 1982 on the merger of RIT with Great Northern Investment Trust, of which he was Chairman. He is Chairman of Weir Group Canadian Pacific. He was formally a **Director of the Bank of England** and British Steel Corporation.
The Hon Clive Gibson	Joined J Rothschild Holdings in 1985 and was appointed an

	executive Director of that Company in 1986. He is also a non-executive Director of RIT Capital Partners Plc.
Maurice Hatch DFC	A non-executive Director of SJPC and a member of its audit committee and its remuneration and Conflicts Committee, he was formerly senior partner of Saffery Champness, Chartered Accountants. Director of Saga Group Ltd and was until recently a member of the Board of the Securities and Futures Authority Ltd.
Anthony Loehnis CGM	non-executive Director of SJPC and a member of its audit committee & its Remuneration and Conflicts Committee. He is a Director of J Rothschild Assurance Holdings Plc, J Rothschild International Holdings Plc and Bank of Tokyo International Ltd. He was formerly a Director of S G Warburg and an executive Director of the Bank of England.
The Lord Rees-Mogg	A non-executive Director of SJPC and a member of its Remuneration and Conflicts Committee. He was **Editor of the Times for fourteen years, and until recently chairman of the Broadcasting Standards Council.** He is chairman of Pickering and Chatto (Publishers) Ltd and of International Business Communication Holdings Ltd. Director of the General Electric Company and Private Bank and Trust Company Ltd.
Andrew Stafford-Deitsch	
	Joined J Rothschild Holdings in 1983 and was appointed an executive Director of that

company in 1985. Chief Executive Officer of J Rothschild. Wolfensohn and Co. and also a non-executive Director of Capitol Partners Plc.

Nathaniel de Rothschild

A non-executive Director of SJPC. Currently President of Nathaniel de Rothschild Holdings Ltd. 1982-1984 co-chairman of the New York based investment banking firm Rothschild Inc. and from 1973 he was with the Banque Rothschild in Paris, where he was the Vice Chairman of the Management board at the time Of its Nationalisation in 1982. Management board at the time

PRINCIPAL SHAREHOLDERS.

Investment management clients of Mercury Asset Management Group.	37,318,557	13.65%
The Lord Rothschild.	35,284,187	12.89%
Clay Finley Inc.	16,800,000	6.14%
Amp Asset Management Plc and connected interests.	13,643,536	4.98%
Accounts managed by Scudder Stevens and Clark Inc.	10.000.000	3.65%

Political Contributions.   (to year ending 31.3.94)

Conservative Party	£25,000
Centre for policy studies	£1,000

James C Smith; The Hon Jeremy Soames; Sir Derek Thomas; Lord Tombs of Brailes (Retiring at AGM 1994); Charles Tracy; Henderson Tuten; Alan Wheatley; George Wong.

COMMENTARY ON DIRECTORS.

Lord Armstrong of Ilminster was head of the **Home Civil Service** from 1981 to 1987 following eight years as secretary to the Cabinet. He was appointed to the board of NMR in October 1988. He is Chairman of the Bristol and West Building Society and of Biotechnology Investments Ltd. and a non-executive director of BAT

Industries, **Carlton Television**, Inchcape, RTZ, and the Shell Transport and Trading Company.

Sir John Fairclough was given the **Freedom of the City of London** in 1989 and is likely therefore to be a Freemason. He joined the board of NMR in 1990. He was with IBM 1957-1986 when he was appointed **Chief Scientific Advisor to the Cabinet**. He is chairman of Rothschild Ventures Ltd., related collaterally to NMR as a subsidiary of Rothschilds Continuation Ltd., and is also Chairman of the Engineering Council. He is a non-executive Director of Lucas Industries and Oxford Instruments.

Sir Michael Richardson is a **Freemason** and friend of Baroness Thatcher who was recruited to NMR in 1981 by Sir Evelyn de Rothschild. He won for NMR, against stiff opposition, the contract to handle the six-billion sell-off of British Gas. This was followed by similar contracts for the privatisation of BP in 1987 and the Electricity Generating Companies in 1989.

Dr James C. Smith was made a **Freeman and Liveryman** of The City of London in 1984, therefore the probability of his being a Freemason is very high. He is Chairman of Eastern Electricity, a Director of National Grid Holding Plc. and a non- executive director of ERA Technology Ltd. He is a past President of the Institute of Electrical Engineers and a member of the CBI Education and Training Affairs Committee. He joined the board of NMR in May 1991 and is due to become Chairman of the Audit Committee at the 1994 AGM.

Sir Derek Thomas joined **the Foreign Office** in 1970 and became British Ambassador to Italy in 1987. During his career in the Foreign Office, **he was involved in negotiations leading up to the UK membership of the EC**. He joined the Boards of NMR, Rothschild Europe BV and of Rothschild Italia SpA in 1990. He is a Director of Christow Consultants Ltd., a member of the Export Guarantees Advisory Committee and **Chairman of Committee on the City's Liberalisation of Trade in Service.**

The Lord Tombs of Brailes, who retires from the board at the AGM 1994 has been a Freeman of the City of London since 1980 and a **Liveryman since 1981**. Almost certainly a Freemason.

ACTIVITIES.

NMR is the World's leading financial advisor on privatisation and has recently been appointed to advise the Dutch government on the privatisation of its post and telephone utility, KPN; the Italian government on the planned sale of oil and gas company ENI; and the Peruvian government on the privatisation of Electroperu. It has also advised the Polish, Chech, and the Hungarian Telecoms, the first privatisation of its kind in Eastern Europe. In the UK it advises Railtrack on the restructuring of British Rail and the government on the privatisation of British Coal. NMR has also been the chief financial advisor to the People's Republic of China.

DIRECTOR COMPANY LISTS.   Notes.

The chart shows the links between, principally, the Rothschild network; Oppenheimer dominated mineral/mining companies with close South African associations, Rothmans' International known to have close South African links through the Rupert family, and the various elements of the British Media.

Not listed is the control of the Argus Printing and Publishing Company, in South Africa, by Charter Consolidated, a company linked into Minorco along with its subsidiary, Johnson Mathey.

Much is circumstantial, much has to be inferred; no less legitimately than in any other field of analysis and not all connections are based on current directorships. However, recent past office, or a significant association with a company are read as establishing a positive and durable influence and involvement.

Analysis demonstrates that the Rothschild network is vast; without exhausting the scope and restricting mainly British companies, the list, for the purposes of this analysis, is shown below. This is condensed to a single column in the chart, although individuals may well be linked to one or more individual companies in practice.

Sources, such as Dunn and Bradstreet, the Directory of Directors, Who's Who, and annual company reports, must be regarded as accurate as a continuing pattern of change due to retirement, affiliation, acquisition, amalgamation and so on, allows.

ROTHSCHILD NETWORK.
(Numbers to be used against Company lists)

Lord Alexander of Weedon	010 033 179
Lord Armstrong	149 179 212 249 326
	399 571 588 671 721
E.L. Baillieu	042 149 179 650 701
J.W. L Baillieu (3rd Viscount)	015 170 650
R.L. Baillieu	043 100 171
R. E. Bell	160 161 162
Stanley Berwin	149 434
Sir Derek Berkin	002 053 057 058 17 210
	431 541 650 651
David Blackett	149 153 174
A. H. Bloom	151 653
Tony Bromovsky	175
Lord Camoys	002 034 036 054 149
Sir Roderick Carnegie	042 076 172 173 179
	253 268 650 673 700
N. Comninus	149 154
Sir Frank Cooper	149 546 695 724
J. D. Crackwell	149 163
J. E. Craig	011 149 164
Sir Peter Derha	170 588 650 673
Baron Derwent	122 149 723
Sir John Fairclough	149
Sir Alister Frame	020 179 216 238 482

Name	Numbers
	560 651 747
Sir Campbell Fraser	150 211 249 361
C. P. Gibson	149 151
J. M. Green-Armytage	099 149 234
Lord (Sidney) Greene	179 753
G. J. Hearne	149 221 452 486 575
Sir Martin Jacomb	001 002 033 034 052 053 054 055179 210 303 360 542 657
J. W. P Johnston	149 165 166
James Joll	149 300 382 65
Richard Katz	177
Baron Philipe Lambert	096 151
Oliver Letwin	149 721
Sir Sidney Lipworth	035 149 249 300 365 653
Martin Littman	089 179 303 369 491
Patrick L. MacDougall	011 146 149 263
Sir Clous Moser	149 324 365 374 405 678
Harold Mourgue	149 389 553 565 591 603
George F. Naylor	179 216
Sir David Nicholson	056 065 069 171 216 252 569
Sir David Orr	007 179 212 254 571 680
Daniel Pekarsky	178 651
Robert Pirie	149 155 178 673
Lord Rees-Mogg	074 114 115 149 152 365 373 375 377 403 405 563 731
Jacob Rees-Mogg (Son)	149
Sir Michael de R. Richardson	069 097 108 149 155 168 169 696 697.
S. W. Roditi	149 152 163
Baron David de Rothschild	176
Edmund de Rothschild	156
Baron Elie de Rothschild	157
Sir Evelyn de Rothschild	037 149 184 249 253 405
Lord (J. N.) Rothschild	145 149 151 155 157 158
Leopold de Rothschild	038 149 154 159 304 331
Hans zv. Schloss	149
Sir Philip Shelbourne	003 100 108 149 253 565 727
Sir Philip Sherbourne	062 100 108 149 565 673
Lord Sieff	149 365 366 471 652 682
Lord Soames (dec)	149
Hon J. B. Soames	149 655
A Stafford-Dietsch	095 096 149 151
Lord Swathling	028 062 102 149 167 252 360 394 658
Amy Yip York Tak	076 081 153

Nils Taube	116 149 152 163 166 167 373 604
Sir Donald Tebbit	179 653 654 723
Sir Derek Thomas	177 723
Lord Tombs	149 223 237 251
Sir Antony Tuke	002 053 179 307 472 671
Rt. Hon. Peter Walker	149 210 168 488 501
Hans zv. Schloss	149
Sir Mark Weinberg	149 309 365 653
Viscount Weir	024 149 151
John H. Weston-Smith	149 309 434
James D. Wolfensohn	145 680

Companies Within The Sphere of Influence.
Group 1   Banks.

1   Bank of England
2   Barclays include. BZW and overseas.
3   Midland
4   Lloyds
5   Royal Bank of Scotland
6   Orion Bank
7   Bank of Ireland
8   Royal Trust Bank
9   Grindlays
10 National Westminster
11 Standard Chartered
12 J P Morgan
13 Yorkshire Bank
14 Nordic Bank
15 Bank National de Pari
16 Bank of Montreal
17 Bank of Nova Scotia
18 Chase Manhatton
19 Chemical Bank
20 Toronto Dominion Bank
21 Royal Bank of Canada
22 National Bank of New Zealand
23 B.B.M.E.
24 Hong Kong and Shangh Banking Corporation.
25 Bankers Trust Co N.Y.
26 Citicorp
27 Canadian Imperial Bank
28 Ottoman Bank
29 Bank of Scotland
30 (Spare)
31 T.S.B.
32 First National Investment Corpn.
33 (Spare)
34 (Spare)
35 (Spare)
36 American Express Amex
37 La Banque Privee S.A.
38 Banco B.I.C.E. (Chile)
39 Bank Nazional del Lavaro
40 Banque de L'Indochine et de Suez.
41 Banque de Paris et de Pays
42 A.N.Z. Banking Group
43 Banque Belge

Group 2   Merchant Banks, Finance, Trusts.

49 Charterhouse Japhael
50 Morgan Grenfell
51 James Capel
52 Kleinwort Benson

53	Merchant's Trust	54	Merchantile Credit
55	Touche Remnant	56	Union Discount Co
57	C.R.A. (Australia)	58	(Spare)
59	Hogg Robinson	60	Stratton Investment Trust
61	S.G.Warburg	62	(Spare)
63	Beresford	64	Hill Samual
65	Lazard (UK and abroad	66	Merril Lynch
67	(Spare)	68	Barings
69	Invesco	70	Singer Friedlander
71	Union Group	72	Selincourt
73	Hambros	74	M and G
75	Morgan Stanley	76	Morgan Guaranty Trust
77	City and Foreign	78	Consolidated Venture
79	Globe	80	Schroder
81	First Pacific spec Assets	82	Temple Bar Investment Trust
83	Candover Investments	84	Charterhouse Group
85	Lloyds developement Cap.	86	Scottish Inv. Trust
87	American Trust	88	Kleinwort Grievson
89	Amerada Hess Corp (US)	90	Meyer International
91	Edpar Investments	92	City of London Trust
93	Lloyd Bowater	94	Leopold Joseph Holdings
95	Amersham Intl. inv. Trust	96	Anglo Group Plc
97	English and Intl. Trust	98	Alantic and General Trust
99	English and Scottish Inv	100	Ansbacher
101	Guiness Peat	102	Philip Hill Inv. Trust
103	Leverhulme Trust	104	Mercury Securities
105	Agriculture Mort. Grp.	106	Save and Prosper
107	Foreign and Colonial Inv.	108	Drayton Group/Corp/ Far Eastern Trust
109	Electra	110	M.A.I.
111	Brown Shipley	112	Boustead
113	London and Strathclyde	114	Ston Eston Inv.
115	Sinclair Stevenson	116	Electric and General Inv. Trust
117	International Commercial Bank	118	Blue Arrow
119	Goldman Sachs	120	Sheraton Securities
121	P.K. Banken/English trust	122	Tanks Consolidated Inv
123	Solomon		

Invesco sphere of influence includes M.I.M./Brittania/(78)(97)(108).

Group 3 Rothschild sphere of influence

145	J. Rothschild, Wolfenson and Co.	146	Amex Bank (formally Rothschild intercont)
147	Rothschild Frankfurt	148	Rothschild Concordia (Swiss)
149	J. & N. M. Rothschild	150	Charterhouse J Rothschild

151 R.I.T. & Northern
153 N. M. Rothschild (Hong Kong)
155 Rothschild N. America Inc.
157 Rothschild Bank AG (Swiss)
159 Five Arrows
161 Groundside Ltd
163 Bishopsgate Progressive Management Trust
165 Atlantic and General Trust

167 Precious Metal Trust
169 N M Rothschild Intl. N.V
171 Dawney Day
173 Comalco
175 Kilda Investments
177 Rothschild Italia
179 R.T.Z.

152 St James Palace Capital
154 Old Court International Capitol
156 Rio Algom
158 Rothschild Cont Holdings AG (Swiss)
160 Gladecore Investments
162 Sheldon Investments
164 Greyfriars Inv. Co.

166 Global Asset Mgnt. (Inc. Bermuda)
168 Smith New Court
170 Rothschild (Australia)
172 C.R.A.
174 Rothschild (Singapore)
176 Rothschild et Ci Banque
178 Rothschild Canada

Minerals and Mining.

180 Amgold
182 Anglo-American (South America)
184 De Beers
188 Foseco
190 Minerals and Resources Corp. (Bermuda).

181 Charter Con. Now Minorco.
183 Minorco (include. Charter Consolidated
185 Premier Consolidated
189 Guiness-Mahon
191 Spare

Group 5 Fuel and Power.

209 Cluff Oil
211 British Petroleum (Inc. Overseas companies)
213 Scottish Power
215 (Spare)
217 Powergen
219 Burmah/Castrol
223 S.S.E.B.
225 North Sea Assets
227 Aberdeen Petroleum
229 Phillips Imp. Petroleum
231 North Sea & General Plc
233 Exxon/Standard Oil
235 Gulf Oil (Canada)
237 Energy Council
239 Premier Consolidated Oilfields

210 British Gas
212 Shell (All companies)
214 (Spare)
216 Lasmo
218 Dome Petroleum
222 Sovereign Oil & Gas
224 Clyde Petroleum
226 Pict Petroleum
228 C.E.G.B.
230 Texaco
232 (Spare)
234 Kelt Energy
236 Ultramar
238 Davy Corporation
240 N.I.K.E. Canada Power Corp.

Group 6 Multinationals and Links; Identified major players.

249 B.A.T.
251 Weir Group
253 I.B.M.
255 Chrysler Corp.

250 I.C.I.
252 Rothmans
254 Unilever
256 London Docklands Development Corp.

257 Hollinger Group
259 Seagrams
261 Lex Group
265 Christies
267 Burroughs Corp.
269 Ford Motor Company
271 De Benedetti

258 Du Pont
260 Olympia & York
264 Sotherby's
266 Monsanto
268 General Motors
270 Alcan
272 Olivetti

Group 7 Insurance/Assurance.

300 Lloyds/Lloyds-Abbey Life
302 Hartford Insurance Group
304 Sun Alliance/Life
306 Pearl Assurance
308 Allianz. Insurance
310 Legal & General Insurance
312 Leeds Perm. Bldg. Socy.
314 Nationwide Anglia

301 Alliance and Leicester
303 Commercial Union
305 Equitable Life
307 Royal Insurance
309 Abbey National
311 Halifax
313 Standard Life Assurance
315 National and Provident Bldg. Socy.

316 Medical & General
318 Scottish Widows
320 Woolwich Equitable Bldg. Socy.
322 General Accident

317 M.G.M. Assurance
319 Prudential
321 Household Mortgage Corp.
323 Maritime Life Ass. Coy of Canada

324 Equity & Law
326 Bristol & West Bldg. Socy
328 Friends Prov. Ass. Socy
330 Transatlantic Holdings
332 (Spare)
334 Swiss Reinsurance Co.

325 Australia Mutual Prov.
327 Phoenix Assurance
329 Guardian Royal Excg.
331 London Insurance Plc.
333 Royal Exchange Ins.
335 Jardine Matheson

Group 8 The Communication Media.

360 Telegraph Newspaper
362 Spectator
364 Brasseys
366 The Independent
368 W.H. Smith
370 Daily Mail

361 Scottish Television
363 United Newspapers
365 The Arts
367 Reuters
369 Granada Group
371 Daily Express (See Utd. Newspapers)

372 Yorkshire Television
374 Reed International
376 Rank Organisation
378 Goldcrest Films & Tel. Hldgs
380 New York Times
382 Pearson Group
384 Hunterprint
386 Capitol Radio
388 B-Sky-B
390 Provisional Press
392 Northcliffe Newspapers
394 London Weekend Tele.
396 London Weekend Tele.
398 Trident Television
400 Independent Tele. News
402 Century Hutchinson
404 Ladbrooke

373 Pickering and Chatto
375 News International Corp. The Times
377 Sidgwick & Jackson
379 Guardian Newspaper
381 Pearl & Dean
383 M.C.C.
385 Tyne-Tees Television
387 TV-AM
389 Thames Television
391 Local Radio
393 Channel 4 Television
395 (Spare)
397 Grampian Television
399 Carlton Comm/Tele.
401 ITV Publications
403 B.B.C.
405 The Economist.

Group 9   Property and Construction.

430 Slough Estates
432 Wiggins-Teape
434 British Land
436 Tarmac
438 Land Securities
440 Mountleigh
442 R.M.C.
446 Wates City of London
448 (Taylor Woodrow)
450 Costain
452 B.P.B. Industries
454 Temple Cloud Properties

431 Wimpey
433 Balfour Beatty
435 Blue Circle
437 Stanhope Estates
439 Rugby Industries
441 Allied London Properties
445 Taylor Woodrow
447 Redland
449 Alfred McAlpine
451 M.E.P.C.
453 Y.J. Lovell
455 Hong Kong Group

Group 10   Food, Drink, Health and Retailing.

470 Smith-Klein-Beecham
472 Savoy Hotel
474 Whitbread
476 United Biscuits
478 Dairy Crest
480 (Spare)
482 Glaxo
484 Cadbury-Schweppes
486 Reckitt and Coleman
488 Tate and Lyle
490 Tesco
492 G.U.S.

471 Marks and Spencer
473 J. Sainsbury
475 R.J.R. Nabisco
477 Booker McConnell
479 British Sugar
481 Sears
483 Hepworth
485 Storehouse
487 (Spares)
489 Guinness
491 Burton Group
493 Boots

494 (Spare)
496 Unigate
498 Colgate-Palmolive
500 (Spare)
502 Vaux Group
504 H.J.Heinz

495 Forte
497 R.H.M.
499 Grand Metropolitan
501 Dalgety
503 Allied Lyons

Group 11 Major Companies/ other Multinationals.

540 B.I.C.C.
542 Hudson Bay Company
544 Cookson
546 Morgan-Crucible
548 B.A.A.
550 Yorkshire Chemicals
552 Racal
554 La Porte Industries
556 P&0
558 G.K.N.
560 Plessey
562 Hawker-Siddeley
564 British Aerospace
566 Pilkington
568 S.T.C.
570 Trafalgar House
572 Vickers

574 Chloride
576 (Spare)
578 American Cyanamid Co
580 Ferranti
582 Powell-Dyffryn
584 B.P.C.C.
586 I.M.I.
588 Lucas Industries
590 Allied Steel & Wire Hlds
592 Wire Ropes Ltd.
594 British Alcan
596 General Electric (USA)
598 Rockwell
600 Chillington Corp.
603 John Swire Group
605 Dylon International
607 Haliburton Group
609 R.H. Macy (USA)
611 Hoover

541 Smiths Industries
543 B.E.T.
545 British Airways
547 Coats-Viyella
549 Cable and Wireless
551 British Telecom
553 Thorn-E.M.I.
555 Canadian Pacific
557 De la Rue
559 B.O.C.
561 Wellcombe
563 G.E.C.
565 Rolls-Royce
567 Ciba-Geigy
569 B.T.R.
571 Inchcape
573 Johnson-Mathey (See ChartCon/Minorco)

575 Courtaulds
577 N.V. Phillips
579 Gestetner
581 Scapa
583 Waterford/ Wedgewood
585 Hanson
587 Strong and Fisher
589 Whessoe
591 (Spare)
593 (Spare)
595 T.I. Group
597 Laird Group
599 Anglo Eastern Plantation
601 James Beatie
604 Inmos
606 Avon Cosmetics
608 Ocean Transport and Trading
610 Woolworths

Group 12 Royal/National Links.

650 Australia
652 Israel
654 Zimbabwe
656 Eire/Northern Ireland
651 Canada
653 Africa/South Africa
655 Royal Family
657 Europe/E.E.C.

Group 13 Organisations/Foundations/Pressure Groups.

670 United (Atlantic) World College
671 Trilateral Commission
672 Institute of Economic Affairs
673 Harvard University
674 North Atlantic Assembly
675 Fabian Society
676 World Health Assembly
677 Centre for Policy Studies
678 London School of Economics
679 Kissinger Associates
680 Bilderberg Group
681 Rockefeller Trust/Foundation/Fellowship
682 Policy Studies Institute
683 Council on Foreign Relations
684 Ditchley Foundation
685 British North Atlantic/North American Committee
686 Royal Institute of International Affairs
687 Aspen Institute
688 Bow Group
689 Rhodes Scholar/Trust
690 Yale University
691 Georgetown Centre for Strategic Studies
692 International Institute for Strategic Studies
693 Massachussets Institute of Technology
694 Ford Foundation
695 Leverhulme Trust
696 Rank Foundation
697   Wellcome Foundation
698   698 Business Roundtable
699 Guggenheim Foundation
700 Brookings Institute
701 Freemasonry
702 **Atlantic Trust for International Affairs, Paris.**
703 **The Centre for Strategic and International Studies Washington.**
704 Churchill Memorial Trust
705 Carnegie Institute
706 World Wide Fund

Group 14 Government Office/Regulatory Bodies/Quangos.

720 Ministry of Health
721 Cabinet Office
722 Department of Trade and Industry
723 Foreign and Commonwealth Office
724 Civil Service
725 Advisory Council on Applied Research and Development
726 Bank for Economic Reconstruction and Development
727 City Take-overs and Mergers Commission
728 Securities and Investment Board
729 Monopolies and Mergers Commission
730 The Newspaper Panel
731 **Broadcasting Standards Council**
732 **Agriculture Priorities Board for Resources, Agriculture and Food**
733 **Agriculture and Food Research Council**
734 Milk Marketing Board
735 **Ministry of Agriculture**
736 Science and Engineering Research Council
737 Industrial Development Advisory Board
738 National Economic Development Advisory Council
740 Commonwealth Development Corporation
741 Medical Research Council
742 Northern Ireland Office
743 United Nations
744 NATO
745 Foreign Intelligence Advisory Board
746 Council of Lloyds
747 United Kingdom Atomic Energy Authority
748 National Farmers' Federation (Australia)
749 Independent Broadcasting Authority (Was ITA).
750 Acid Rain (Envoy, Canada)
751 Confederation of British Industry
752 Horserace Betting Levy Board
753 Trades Unions

Company Directorships.
(Numbers to be used against the Company lists).

Robin W. Adam	021 211 216 322 451 651
Sir Campbell Adamson	065 309 403 436
Rudolff I. J. Agnew	011 187 585
Lord Airlie	005 060 322 655
Sir Lindsey Alexander	004 211 300 562
Lord Alexander of Weedon	010 033 179 671
Sir Geoffrey Allen	254 575 576

Sir Derek Alun-Jones	187 307 374 558 580
Michael Angus	103 254 553
Anne Armstrong (US Diplomat)	268 607 673 683 684 745
Lord Armstrong	149 179 212 249 326 399 571 588 671 721
Dr. John Ashworth	369 721
Dr. David Atterton	001 002 188 376 471 586 670 725
Sir John Atwill	451 650 670
C.C. Baillieu	729 746
E.L. Baillieu	042 149 179 650 701
J.W.L. Baillieu (3rd Viscount)	015 170 650
R.L. Baillieu	043 100 171
Robin Baillieu	011 112 113 300
C.F. Baird	016 233 250 673 683 685
Mrs Mary Baker	002 319 389
Prof. Sir James Ball	002 216 253 310 685
Sir John Baring	001 060 068 211 307
Francis Baron	368 372
Sir Peter Baxendall	212 304 562 651
Robert A Beck	230 319
R. E. Bell	160 161 162
W. E. Bell	212 221 450
D. V. Bendall	039 040 050 606 744
Sir Christopher Benson	256 304 365 451
Stanley Berwin	149 434
Sir Timothy Bevan	002 035 543
Roger Bexon	065 211 233 540 554 651
Sir Derek Birkin	002 053 057 058 179 210 431 541 650 651
Colin Black	052 078 082 109 224 318
Conrad Black	**257 360 671 680**
Viscount Blackenham	065 382 451
David Blackett	149 153 174
A. H. Bloom	151 653
Werner Michael Blumenthal	019 267 681 698
R. H. Bonham-Carter	001 041 061 080 104 673 739
Charles W. Brady	069 189 673
Christopher Brand	394 402 471 472 485
M. D. Bridgland	042 250 650 698
Tony Bromovsky	175
Peter Bronfman	257 652
Tore Browdalah	253 254 262
P. C. D. Burnall	182 582
M. W. Burrel	065 372 382 388
Willard C. Butcher	018 230 698 739
Sir Michael Butler	073 365 657 673 697 723 743

Sir Adrian Cadbury	001 253 484
Earl of Cairns	061 249
Philip Caldwell	018 269 671 673 698
Lord Camoys	002 034 036 054 149
Sir Roderick Carnegie	**042 076 172 173 179 253 268 650 673 700**
Lord Carrington	**257 365 679 680**
Dougal A. Carroll	007 252 656
Lord Catto	024 050 306 325 375 563 650
Sir Peter Cazalet	211 233 556 557 558
Godfrey J. Chandler	078 085 368
Sir Robert Clark	001 031 064 212 249 449 470 586
W.M.. Clark	009 042 334
John Clater	014 063 064 107 189 305
John Martin Clay	001 073 379
Alan W. Clements	189 232 250 549 570
Sir Colin Corness	001 061 314 368 447 448 575 673
D. W. Colson	235 360
N. Comninus	149 154
P. J. D. Cooke	360 390
Sir Frank Cooper	149 546 695 724
M. J. Cooper	219 239
R. M. Cox-Johnson	120 121 239 256
J. D. Crackwell	149 163
J. E. Craig	011 149 164
John Cordingley	073 212 216 231
Sir Derek Crichton-Brown	252 370 650 671
Dr Chester Crocker	183
Earl of Cromer (Dec)	001 012 019 068 075 076 212 253 370 674
D. J. Cunningham	003 679
The Hon. Ed. D. G. Davies	078 082
David John Davies	018 064 335 451 455 592 673
Dr. Margeret Davies	007 485
Peter Davis	369 374 473
Hon W.G. Davis	240 259 269 651 701 750
Sir Graham Day	017 217 218 484 553 564 597
Carlo de Benedetti	076 271 272 699 702 703
D. de Bruyne	212 250 393
The Rt. Hon. Edmund Dell	**101 212 250 393**
Sir Peter Derham	170 588 650 673
Baron Derwent	122 149 723
Robert Dickinson	002 008 385
Kenneth H. M. Dixon	217 372
Marquess of Douro	189 252 304 330 391
George Duncan	004 092 093 321 366 543 554 589 590 678
Sir Kenneth Durham	018 050 254 564 610 673 685 695 732

A. E. Earle	651 678 684
Mrs Diana Eccles	385 473
Sir Donald Eckersley	325 650 748
Sir Michael Edwardes	181 183
David Elstein	389 652
P. J. Elton	064 187 270
H. Garfield Emerson	651
James Evans	367 390
J. R. Evans	021 270 651 676 681 689
Sir John Fairclough	149
Malcolm Field	368 451
Sir Leslie Fletcher	011 080 376 442
Sir Archibald Forster	003 233 653
Sir Alistair Frame	020 179 216 238 482 560 651 747
Sir Michael Franklin	002 500 657 721 722
Sir Campbell Fraser	150 211 249 361
Stephen Friedman	119 671
Viscount Garmoyle	061
Louis V. Gerstner	475 671
A.B. Giamatti	683 690 694
C. P. Gibson	149 151
P. J. Gillam	011 211 678
R. V. Giordano	228 367 499 559 673
Tim Gold Blyth	389 543
Sir Nicholas Goodison	028 031 322 365
Lord Gormley	**752 753**
J. M. Green-Armytage	099 149 234
D. B. Green	399
M. P. Green	399
Lord (Sidney) Greene	**179 753**
R. H. Grierson (Formally Griessmann)	006 061 238 255 365 475 563 657 671
Angus M. M. Grossart	005 078 086 087 225 226 378 651
John H. Gutfreund	123 671
Peter Gyllenhammer	018 262 367 382 687
J. H. Hale	016 270 382 651 685
Ronald Halstead	035 219 238 373 470 490 578 579 677
R. N. Hambro	073 180 360 653
J. D. Hamilton	031 444 446
Paul Hamlyn	374 375 387
David W Hardy	078 105 256 317 567
Earl of Harrowby	006 010 582 671 686 702
G. J. Hearne	149 221 452 486 575
H. J. Heinz (b. 1908)	504 684 690 705 706
Sir Denys Henderson	002 250 304 403

Sir Nicholas Henderson	073 074 107 264 403 436 655 723
R. A. Henderson	052 053 220 305 484 571
J. W. Herbert	181 572
R. A. E. Herbert	010 056 094 105 324 471
Prof. Rosalyn Higgins	678 686 690 743
Rt. Hon. Terence Higgins	261 671 686 690
Sir Christopher Hogg	064 367 575 694
Sir Trevor Holdsworth	553 558 685 686 704
Sir John Harvey-Jones	229 250 374 499
Sir Simon Hornby	368 382
A. R. Hughes	360 598
Lord Hunt of Tanworth	015 253 254 319 684 721 724
Ian Irvine	367 374 386 387 388
Sir Martin Jacomb	001 002 033 034 052 053 054 055 179 210 303 360 542 657
Sir Alex Jarratt	002 003 250 319 374 541 657 721
Earl Jellicoe	061 238 264 488 546 689
J. W. P Johnston	149 165 166
James Joll	149 300 382 652
Norman Jones	004 022 300 650
David Justham	250 396 586
Richard Katz	177
Henry Keswick	024 252 263 304 671
J. C. L. Keswick	222
S. J. Keynes	049 121 239 304 749
Nick Kinnesburg	223 313 547
Dr. Henry Kissinger	**018 257 609 671 679 680 681 683**
A. S. B. Knight	257 360 365 367 375 680
Sir Arthur Knight	575 671 678 686
Thomas A Lebrecque	018 671
Peter Laister	383 553 571 559
Henry Lambert	002 105 304 545
Baron Philipe Lambert	096 151
K. P. Legg	022 023 026 027
Peter Leslie	001 675
L. E. C. Letts	050 209 599
Oliver Letwin	149 721
Lord Lever	069 365 379
Leon Levy	061 109
D. C. Lewis	369 575
Sir Sidney Lipworth	035 149 249 300 365 653
Mark Littman	089 179 303 369 491 671
R. E. B. Lloyd	064 310 572 684 737 738 751
Sir Richard Lloyd	031 064 310 572 591 593 684
Wm. R. Loomis	065 183

John Hugo Loudon (b. 1905)	006 018 212 269 694 702 706
Patrick L. MacDougall	011 146 149 263
John Macomber	018 475 566
Sir Ian MacGregor	065 384 440 494
Prof. Roderick MacFarquar	403 671 673 674 675 681 686 694 695 723
Donald F. McHenry	032 683 694 700 705
Sir Kit Mahon	001 003 062 365
T. J. Manners	065 217 238 581
F. N. Mamsanger (b. 1911)	611 684 701
Prof. Laurence Martin	385 681 690 691 693
James Maxin	261 262 553
John W Mayo	061 252
E. S. Marguiles	063
Sir Patrick Meaney	003 250 376 451
John Mellon	374 673
H. S. Mellor	219 501
R. P. B. Michaelson	061
Quentin Morris	078 369 573 583 678
Sir Ian Morrow	073 110 381 587 597
Sir Jeremy Morse	004 250 310 674
Sir Clous Moser	149 324 365 374 405 678
Sir Denis Mountain	017 376 441 650 651 653
Harold Mourgue	149 389 553 565 591 603
David C. Nash	250 484 499
George F. Naylor	179 216
Sir David Nicholson	056 065 069 171 216 252 569
Sir Robin Nicholson	035 211 432 721
M D Nightingale	049 599 600 675
Sir Edwin Nixon	010 095 253 307
Miss O'Cathain	003 481 490 494
J. Ogilvie-Thompson	002 180 183 184 186
A. E. Oppenheimer	181
N. F. Oppenheimer	183 184
Sir David Orr	007 179 212 254 571 680
Sir Michael Palliser	002 062 212 249 477 659 671 692 721 723
Sir Derek Palmar	009 064 108 363 372 677
Ian Park	035 367 391 392
C. H. Parker	181 573
Sir Lional Peach	109 111 253 314 481
D. A. E. R. Peake	015 052
Daniel Pekarsky	178 651
N. Peltz	440 489
Brian Peppiat	061 109
D. L. C. Peretz	608

Robert Phillis	396 399 400 401
Sir A. Pilkington	015 211 561
Robert Pirie	149 155 178 673
Sir Leo Pliatzky	236 396 545 724
Sir Eric Pountain	003 436 586 601
L. T. Preston	012 211 596
Charles H Price	230 380 545 585
D. W. J. Price	061
Lord Prior	002 473 476 563
Jay Pritzker	063 123
W. B. Purves	003 023 024
Sir John Quinton	002 676 720
F. D. Radler	257 360
John Raisman	004 212 365 482 572
Lord Rawlinson of Ewell	024 360 568 695
Lee R. Raymond	233 671
Lord Redesdale	018
Paul Reichmann	260 437
Gavin Relly	180 183 186
Lord Rees-Mogg	**074 114 115 149 152 365 373 375 377 403 405 563 731**
Jacob Rees-Mogg	149
Christopher Reeves	050 066 308 540
Lord Remnant	029 056 236 650
H. J. Reuton	051 599
Sir Peter Reynolds	307 314 379 493 497
Sir Michael de R Richardson	**069 097 108 149 155 168 169 696 701**
Viscount Ridley	002 008 385 655
Lord Rippon	069 383 671
Cedric E. Richie	017 183 651
Sir Ralph Robins	011 080 565
N. J. Robson	008 028 031
S. W. Roditi	149 152 163
Sir Frank Rogers	360 390
Lord Roll of Ipsden	001 030 061 671 674 680
Baron David de Rothschild	176
Edmund de Rothschild	156 671
Baron Elie de Rothschild	157
Sir Evelyn de Rothschild	037 149 184 249 253 360 405
Lord (J. N.) Rothschild	145 149 151 155 157 158
Leopold de Rothschild	038 149 154 159 304 331
P. M. Samuel (Heir to Viscount Bearsted)	064 212 605 656
Hans zv. Schloss	149
Sir David Scholey	006 056 061
C. F. Sedcole	254 374 488 675

Lord Sharpe of Grimsdyke	228 266 399 437 549 678
N. M. Shaw	027 055 230 444 488 541 651
A. J. Shepperd	061 561
Sir Alfred Shepperd	061 561
Sir Patrick Sheehy	211 249
Sir Philip Shelbourne	003 100 108 149 253 503 565 727
Lord Sieff	149 365 366 471 652 682
Wilmott Sitwell	061 368
David Sneddon	367 390 391
Dr Brian Smith	063 238 250 480 549 550
Prof. Roland Smith	305 483 564
Lord Soames (dec)	149
Hon. J. B. Soames	149 655
Antony M. Solomons	069 070
Colin Southgate	217 319 553 559 588
Sir James Spooner	002 059 473 546 547 602
A. Stafford-Dietsh	095 096 149 151
Nigel Stapleton	254 374
Antony W. Stenham	025 252 254 365 376 386 432
Lord Stevens	064 069 077 078 108 363
H. A. Stevenson	061
H. D. Stevenson	256 382 385 480
Murray Stewart	063 106 213
Michael C. Stoddart	061 078 109 584
Sir Richard Storey	367 390
A.G. Stoughton-Harris	307 314 379
G. Strowger	440 499
Lord Swaythling	028 062 102 149 167 252 360 394 568
Nils Taube	116 149 152 163 166 167 373 604
Alfred Taubman	264 609
Sir Donald Tebbit	179 653 654 723
Norman R. Tebbit	**118 362 481 543 551**
A. J. Tennant	015 329 333 489
Sir Derek Thomas	177 723
Ward Thomas	372 385 397 398
Lord Thompson of Monteith	005 250 320 657 684 723
Bill Thomson	212 547
Sir Christopher Tidbury	002 054 306 475 502
Laurence Tisch	609
Lord Tombs	149 223 237 251
Sir Ian Trethowan	002 375 389 403 553 684
Sir Christopher Tugendhat	010 229 303 559 684 686
Sir Antony Tuke	002 053 179 307 472 671
J. W. Utz	252 650
Cyrus Vance	**671 673 681 684 690**
Bruce Vaughan	501 650
David Veit	065 382

R. Vine	002 032
Paul Volcker	**018 250 671 673**
R. K. A. Wakeling	181 573
Sir Peter Walters	002 211 435 553
Rt. Hon. Peter Walker	**149 210 168 488 501**
N. W. Way	070 399
Michael David Weill	233 382 671
Sir Mark Weinberg	149 309 365 653
Viscount Weir	024 149 151 251
David Welham	212 499
Sir Eric Weiss	188 670
John H. Weston-Smith	149 309 434
James G. West	078 083 084 437
James White	261 447 470 588
John Wilkinson	385 403 653
P. S. Wilmott-Sitwell	061 073 368
James D. Wolfensohn	145 680
Lord Wolfson	**492 652**
E. J. Worledge	249 432
P. J. Wrangham	003 023 024 051 117
Walter Wristow	026 367 596 683
Amy Yip York Tak	076 081 153
Baroness Young	010 471 723
R. Neil Young	028 088 227

Remember this list was prepared from a cut off date of 1992.

From these lists you will recognise many names that have been active in supporting the European Union, these are the main gainers from global government as they support collectivism. This list is to show the power and influence the Bank has over our lives and its inter-linking influence with other groups, eleven years ago, an influence that is still maintained although changes have taken place over the years till today.

CHAPTER TWO
PART ONE
HISTORY OF GLOBAL GOVERNMENT

If I said that the lust for a world government is traceable back to the Old Testament and that several attempts, some linked, have already been made to achieve this; the critics would say it was virtually impossible as over such a long period of time, no order, however strong, could survive. I would remind them how religion has survived all man's attempt to discredit it which proves it is a strong force. So is Satanism, and it is through this powerful medium of evil that we see today a plan hatched in Babylon, is still the inspiration of today's attempt to capture the world for its exclusive evil. Dr R.P. Oliver wrote; "Since subtle conspirators must be very shrewd men, not likely to be deceived by auto suggestion, hypnosis or drugs we should have to conclude that they are in contact with a force of pure evil. That conclusion will give pause to the irreligious and sceptical". **(13)**.

In the Books of Isaiah, Ezekiel and Revelations we see the full picture of how Lucifer had a mighty place in heaven and as his name implies, 'Son of the Morning' had position and attributes of knowledge and wisdom. He decided this was not enough and wanted ultimate power. For this disloyalty he was banished from heaven to earth and began to do evil in the world against God. **(14)**. Then came God's revenge on Lucifer **(1 5)**. Henceforth he became Satan.

In the New Testament Satan is called 'God of this world' **(16)**, and that he disguises himself as an angel of light. **(17)** and in **(18)**. **(Deception and a source of the name Illuminati)**.

If you are a believer, God put Adam on earth as his representative, but he fell for the evil, in the form of the apple recommended to him by the snake **(Satan in disguise; deception)**. As a result God realised man would follow Satan's ways. **(19)**. God therefore decided to flood the earth and save only two of each species (Noah's Ark). For a time this worked and all beings lived in fear of God.

We now get an early case of 'power corrupts absolutely'. Nimrod saved his people from the wild beasts of the forest, which had multiplied from Noah's rescue operation. He became a hero of his people. Up to this point he had done only good for his people, but power corrupts and Satan helped him to banish God from his people's minds. Hislop, in his great work states; "All tradition from the earliest times bears testimony to the apostasy of Nimrod, and his success in leading men away from the patriarchal faith, and delivering their minds from the awe of God and fear of the judgements of heaven that must have rested upon them while yet the memory of flood was present, and according to all the principles of depraved human nature, this too, no doubt, was one grand element in his fame; for men will readily rally around anyone who can give the least appearance of plausibility to any doctrine that will teach them that they can be assured of happiness. **(20)** (see

Weishaupt's policy page 6o). Though their hearts and natures are unchanged, and although they live without god in the world." **(22).**

Nimrod introduced immoral standards (See Weishaupt's policy page 6o) to please his people. So the people built themselves a walled city to keep the wild animals from their streets and they built a tower to heaven.

Nimrod knew his people needed a God to believe in. He had destroyed God in his people's minds and quickly needed a replacement.

They turned their attention to the snake (Satan's Deception) because it was promised that this snake would give them the knowledge of good and evil. It was named the 'Enlightener' or 'Illuminator' (See Weishaupt policies page 6o) of mankind. They also worshiped the sun and the giver of light. So was established the symbol of the sun with the serpent coiled around its surface. **(23).**

Nimrod's desires grew; he conquered all lands between Babylon and Lybia (most of the known world) and so his Satan based religion spread round most of the world. But God had his revenge on Nimrod when Shem, Noah's son, led an Egyptian revolt against Nimrod and cut up his body and sent a part to each of his kingdoms as an example to the people who would stray away from the True God. Thus, according to Hislop, the pagan religion, born of Satan, was forced underground. **(24).** Symbols were used henceforth to hide their true worship of the sun serpent and bind the followers to the Sovereigns of Babylon. Some are the very symbol used today in Freemasonry.

Nimrod was succeeded by his wife Semiramis, who held her people in a spell of licentious Satanism. She cleverly mixed truth with Satanism to hold her people's attention and to capture the undecided. Her rule achieved great success even against the twelve tribes of Israel.

So taken in were the Israelites that Elijah told God he was the only follower left to worship the true God and he lived in constant danger. But God told him there were seven-thousand followers still in silent faith.

Corinthians **(25)** says Satan is transformed into an angel of light and righteousness, using **'deception'** to further his cause. At this time it was widely believed that Satan ruled the earth and it was not until Jesus Christ appeared that people began to realise that Satan, with all his 'hall of mirrors' and elaborate deceptions, was an impostor. Even then Jesus was put to the test by Satan **(26)** during his fast when Satan offered him 'all' if he would worship Satan. Then came Jesus' famous rebuttal; "Get thee behind me, Satan: For it is written you shall worship the Lord your God and him only shall you serve. **(27).**

After this ordeal Christ succeeded Satan as ruler of the world, except in the eyes of some. Those people have carried through Satan's will over the centuries **till this day.**

The history of Christianity has been built on such strong ground that with all Satan's efforts over the centuries, he has not been able to topple the true faiths from their sure foundation, but it did not stop him trying, and he is still at work with his devious ways corrupting the world and his latest attempt is Globalism.

Satan's master plan is to take the high ground of politics without getting into an armed conflict. As you read through the pages of this book you will see how this dreadful scheme now controls a large part of the world; it does so through willing Satanists, political opportunists, financial gainers and a host of people caught up in the web of this master plan through its sphere of influence.

Cleverly, Satan introduced his ace in the shape of Simon Magus, the first exponent of the many untrue religions to plague the earth. His aim was to corrupt the Christian teaching with a mixture of true religion and his paganism as the cream on the top of the pie. In many references in the bible we have witness of pagan attempts to use true religion for Satan's purpose**.** **(28).** Simon Magus and his disciples tried to lead true Christians into his path to Satan. **(29).** To the debased minds of human nature the Luciferian's way seemed enlightened **(Illumination, direction)** but through all the ways of pagan Satan, the truth of real Christianity shines through as a light that is inextinguishable. Simon Magus used his name to confuse his paganism with Simon the Apostle and convert his followers to Satan's path.

What is so conclusive is the thread of the policy of deception that weaves its path through history to the Illuminati of Weishaupt, through to Marxism, right through to the European Union and its eventual goal Global Government. All through the centuries they have used the same thread of deception that Lucifer practised in his early days.

Simon Magus, as Satan's disciple, went to Rome and overcame the minds of many citizens with his pagan half truths. He even took on the name of Simon Peter, whereas Peter, the true disciple of Jesus was never in Rome. So this impostor 'put on Peter's clothes' and led his followers into the way of Satan. His fame spread far and wide and a temple to his ideology was built in the centre of falsehood, Mesopotamia, taking up the cloth of Nimrod, the founder of the Pagan religion of Babylon.

Out of the multitude of pagan religions, we see clear evidence in many contemporary works that the Catholic religion was born. **(30).** But true Christians believe the new religion was another deception by Peter Magus, also well covered in Hislop's 'The Two Babylons'. **(31).**

To prove the case of the deception of the founder of Roman Catholicism we have to go no further than Werner Keller's description of Simon Peter's death and burial. Apparently Simon Peter (Simon Magus) was secretly taken to a pagan burial spot called Vatican Hill**. (32).** If anyone doubted this argument, if the true Peter was the one, he would never have been buried on the Vatican Hill, a pagan cemetery. He was a Jew and a life long campaigner against paganism, so he would never have been buried in a pagan cemetery. I am at pains to add that the followers of the Roman Catholic church today firmly believe in Christ.

In the fourth century AD. Emperor Constantine adopted Peter Magus's paganised religion as the official religion of the expanding Roman Empire and through its great expansion was formed, what was to become known as The Roman Catholic Church. As time passed it became an accepted church of Christ. From history we know of the murders, moral decline and abuse of power practised by the heads of this church which must open our minds when we understand the early history of its deception. Hurlbut put it clearly; "The church gradually usurped power over the state and the result was not Christianity, but a more or less corrupt hierarchy controlling the nations of Europe, making the church mainly a political machine" **(33).** This was truly named the dark ages and was an early attempt at world domination.

The Reformation period in Europe promised a new beginning. A questioning of the church's abuse. But instead of forming a single strong church it fostered many selfish churches of convenience, man's corrupt ideas to hide his satanic desires behind the wall of a false mirror. Nevertheless the Roman Catholic Church today is the most formidable opponent of Communism whatever its past history.

CHAPTER TWO, PART TWO.
ILLUMINATI
A PLOT BORN IN GERMANY IN 1776 THAT THREATENS TO DESTROY WESTERN DEMOCRACY
(Under other names, such as the Bilderberg Committee.)

The world had seen another Great Empire, the Roman Empire expand its influence into the known world and through moral decline and the greed of man, collapse.

This was the second formidable attempt to rule the world, the effects of which were still to be found in Europe and Germany in particular in the eighteenth century.

Germany had reasonable freedom for the expansion of thought and from the Universities a whole host of new philosophers were expanding their ideas to audiences within the newly formed Masonic Lodges, where all matters including subversion could be discussed without the fear of prosecution, within reason.

We will discuss how these came about in chapter five; suffice it to say that the secret debating lodges formed by a combination of Jewish desire to crush other religions, in league with satanic evilness to rule the earth, combined to give every encouragement to those who wished to change the order of Christian and political stability.

In the year 1776 three major events took place; two of which we read about in all our history books. The third, and most important of all, has been concealed by most Encyclopaedia's and history books. In this year Adam Smith wrote his famous book 'Wealth of Nations' **(34)** which formed the basis of capitalism in readiness for the industrial revolution.

The American Declaration of Independence was written in this year. Both have good coverage in our history books.

The one event which strangely has had little publicity was the formation of the Illuminati within the Lodge of Theodore (Proofs of Conspiracy page 58) on May the first of this year by Adam Weishaupt, a Professor of Canon law at Ingolstadt University, (Proofs of Conspiracy Page 58) whose work was to become the basis for Communism throughout the world. It has had a profound effect on everyone's lives. It is quite amazing to me to find how this has been carefully and deliberately left out of history. It explains the foundation for everything that happens in world politics today and shows the devious underhand deceptions enacted upon the peoples of the world.

Luckily some researchers have made painstaking efforts to expose the history of this Satanic movement and it is to them we must be grateful.

Weishaupt, of Jewish parentage, (Refer to Rakovski interview page 108) who converted to Roman Catholicism, was brought up a Jesuit till he broke with the Order. He formed his own organisation within the Masonic movement dedicated to a Satanic philosophy with a plan to crush Christianity and create a 'World Order' by disrupting nations and their governments.

Although this movement was short-lived in Germany, as it was ordered to close by the Elector of Bavaria, its policy has been perpetuated, through Masonic Lodges, to this day. We learn from 'Towards World Government' by Deirdre Manifold **(35)** that Weishaupt was employed by the Rothschild family (Also reference in Rakovski interview page 108.) to 'Give form and precision to their plan for World Government' and to back this evidence up, many years later James P Warburg stated to a sub-committee on Foreign Relations on February the 17th. 1950 that, 'We shall have world government, whether or not we like it------ by conquest or by consent'. **(Direction)**.

So Weishaupt built his organisation within the Masonic lodge of Theodoré in Munich. He exercised a haughty arrogance and his self praised superior knowledge led him to believe he alone should rule the world. Financed by his Banking backer, he set about his revolutionary plans. The secret ceremonies of his order were designed to take the innocent and turn them gradually into his revolutionaries, without telling them his secret of Illumination. His desire was to crush their religion and rubbish their nations.

So well did he design his deceitful path to Illumination that bored Princes and Noblemen flocked to his cause like lemmings to their own destruction. This can be likened to today where normal business men and politicians follow the drive for federalisation and single currency in Europe, the for-runner to global government, without knowing who drives the people of the world into federalisation and on to oblivion.

Unless we wake up and take heed of past history to realise the true threat to our being we will be swallowed up by this pagan monster and from there on be in slavery to his every desire. Few would oppose an evolution that took us into Europe as a sovereign state. Most thinking people oppose a single currency, not for itself but as a one way mechanism that forces Sovereign states into a Federal Europe without an escape clause in the true Weishaupt style, within a **hidden agenda. (Illumination)**.

From the introduction of the Americanist Classics reproduction of Professor John Robison's book 'Proofs of a Conspiracy' **(36),** one of the books that tells us the true history of Masonry and the Illuminati, we get a vivid picture of the deception involved in the order, even amongst its own initiates.

Professor Robison was heralded in his day as a remarkable Scientist and Philosopher. He was a member of the esteemed Royal Society and professor of natural Philosophy at Edinburgh University. Invited by Weishaupt to join the Illuminati, he went to Europe to investigate the new Masonic order and wrote his account of what he found; 'Proofs of Conspiracy'. At the same time a French schoolmaster, Abbe Barruel wrote a four volume book called 'Memoirs Illustrating the History of Jacobinism' in 1799. **(37).** Both books accurately support each other's text, giving us a true picture; so important to understanding the source of Communism today.

Robison tells us that the order of Illumination, practised at the lodge Theodoré and established by Weishaupt had immediate effect and overwhelming success in drawing in the young intellectuals destined to be the future journalists, lawyers, politicians, professors and teachers as well as the sons of nobles. The method of teaching made each a spy of all. (Seen in Marxist Russia).

The practice of Illumination spread quickly through Germany and Europe but particularly in France as Weishaupt's lodge was linked to The Grand Orient; a group of two-hundred and sixty-six lodges in France ruled by the infamous Duke of Orleans.

So how was a policy, so anti-democratic and anti-Christian, able to draw such appeal? Again Robison tells us of the inner truths of Illumination that only a few top members of the lodges fully knew, the hidden policy. That policy, entailed a detailed plan to overthrow civil governments and abolish religion, replacing it with a dictatorship of his order of Illumination throughout the world. Weishaupt we learn, was so puffed up with his own importance, that he saw his plan as the future of the world and his Illuminated followers as a higher intelligence who were the only ones fit to control politics and destiny, yet these trainee disciples of his Satanic dreams, knew nothing of his plan, but revelled in the simplicity of the false utopia. **'Illumination' painted a picture of liberty and equality to make man universally happy and free of care.**

At this moment I must pause to reflect; Haven't I seen this utopia in the American constitution and on reflection I see on their own dollar note the broken pyramid with the top illuminated and the eye of Lucifer starring out and the words in Latin that translate into **"New World Order"** and I ask myself, how far has Illumination penetrated the civilised world today despite its disappearance from view.

The truth is that Weishaupt came to promote his deception upon the young and hungry intellectuals of the world who were eagerly searching for new ways to happiness and he cleverly disguised his plans to suit their dreams. This is what made his false utopia so addictive to these young minds. He erected a hall of mirrors, reflecting their desires but hidden behind these mirrors were his devious satanic plan born in Babylon and fostered in his warped, but clever mind. It was a plan to dominate the world. I have to make a parallel here to the armies of ordinary people today, who without knowing it, are pushing the world towards Weishaupt's goal because their work orders them to do certain jobs, which seem quite innocent, but press another button towards the global corruption of our world.

The politicians who have physically lied to our nations about the true agenda of the European Union to hide what they know will not be accepted. They are the directors of companies who follow the bankers regardless of personal conviction. Indeed the civil servants who hold the secrets of the European Union and will not disclose them to the people.

Where you find hidden Agendas inside organisations that wish to rule our lives we should either open those agendas to public debate or if it is impossible withdraw from their deception till the debate is honestly opened. This applies equally to the United Nations, the Trilateral Commission and the Bilderberg committee which we will deal with in chapter sixteen.

Now we must look at the evidence of association that makes the Global Power theory into a proven conspiracy. We have already seen the evidence in Deirdre Manifold's book **(38)** that the Rothschilds, in the latter part of the eighteenth century, employed Weishaupt (This is also mentioned on page 98 of the next report in the Rakovski interview) to produce a clear path to world government. She goes on to state; "Weishaupt recruited some two thousand paid followers, promising them success in this life even if they would not live to see world government. These included some of the most intelligent men in the field of letters, education, the sciences, finance and industry." **(38)**.

At the Elector of Munich's inquiry, where members of the Illuminati were questioned about the Lodge of Illuminati within the Lodge Theodoré, "It was repeatedly stated to the elector, that members of the lodge Theodoré had unguardedly spoken of this order as one that in time would rule the world." This was a future promise of Illumination to initiates, without disclosing the path to its achievement. **(39). (Deception)**.

In the book by Professor Robison **(40)** he states, "The first and immediate aim is to get the possession of riches, power, and influence, without industry; and, to accomplish this, they want to abolish Christianity; and then desolate manners and universal profligacy will procure them the adherence of all the wicked, and enable them to overturn all the civil governments of Europe; after which they will think of farther conquests, and extend their operations to the other quarters of the globe, till they have reduced mankind to the state of one indistinguishable chaotic mass."

He goes on to say, "Their founder, I dare say, never entertained such hopes, nor troubled himself with the fate of distant lands. But it comes in his way when he puts on the mask of humanity and benevolence: it must embrace all mankind, only because it must be stronger than patriotism and loyalty, which stand in its way". **(The reason that national sovereignty must be removed within the European Union to further their cause).**

These are but a few quotes of many that point to world domination by the Illuminati. Like most despotic plans, their inner thought became exposed by shear chance; a messenger, carrying the plans of Illuminati was killed by an electric storm. These plans, of the French Revolution, found their way back to the Bavarian Government. They immediately banned the society of Illumination in 1783. The members went underground and rose again as literary reading societies, under the name of the German Union, with the same hidden agenda.

This is proved in Weishaupt's earlier statement in a letter to Cato; "I have considered everything, and so prepared it, that if the order this day should go to ruin, I shall in a year re-establish it more brilliant than ever." As Shakespeare said, "What is there in a name".

A footnote to Illumination comes in the form of a instruction to a prospective regent (A high grade of Illuminati). **"If a writer publishes anything that attracts notice, and is in itself just, but does not accord with our plan, we must endeavour to win him over or decry him".** This could have been straight from Marx and shows direction practised by our controlled media all over the world today.

So the Illuminati moved into literary reading houses dominating print with their propaganda. In Germany they had success. A report remarked "All the German schools and the benevolent society are at last under our control" and "Lately, we have got possession of the Bartholomew Institution for young clergymen........through this we shall be able to supply Bavaria with priests". (Classic Marxist infiltration) If it started this long ago, today it must have penetrated all their targeted agenda.

They also concentrated their efforts in corrupting the French Masonic lodges of the Grand Orient with Illumination.

The French were ready for revolution, and in particular the Duke of Orleans, who was power hungry. They made ready pupils. France cried out for change, and the Illuminati seized their first big opportunity to put their theories into practice.

In 1786 the lodge of Philalethes in Paris, run by Mirabeau, the Duke de Lauxun and Abbe Perigoro asked the German lodge of Illumination to send further instructions. This was their opportunity to try out their World Revolution to gain global power that the Rothschilds had instructed Weishaupt to develop. The hidden agenda of this scheme was designed to kill religion, lower moral standards and break up domestic life style by destroying marriage vows and removing children from the influence of their parents during their education. This was the exact pattern of development in France after the revolution.

Mirabeau drew the evil Duke of Orleans into his lodge and he was filled with the power and corruption of the order. He was completely absorbed by Weishaupt's evil Illumination, that in his oath of allegiance he vowed, that the interests and the object of the order shall be rated by him above all other relations, and that he will serve it with honour, his fortune, and his blood. He did just that. The leaders of the French Revolution fed him lies and bled him of his fortune to fund their revolution. This cheating way they learned from Weishaupt himself. The crown, that they dangled like a carrot, the Duke's great desire, led him to his destruction. He never rose to this height, he was guillotined in 1793. But before this he used his wealth to try and bribe the loyal soldiers to join the Republican cause with first women then money, amounting to over fifty-thousand pounds in total. So blinded with Illumination was he that he knew nothing of his users plans. But he was powerful, as Grand Master of the Order of the Grand Orient; which made him the head of two-hundred and sixty-six lodges. He converted them all to Illumination. Illumination and its army of converts within these lodges of the Grand Orient caused the French Revolution and by their corruption within the Royal camp weakened the resistance to their power.

Working from within, there is no doubt that the atrocities of the Revolution were orchestrated by the Masonic movement. They whipped the crowd into a frenzy. The peace surrender was prepared by the Masons. To this and other points Mr Lefranc bore witness. **(41).** From this point on, after the terrible atrocities, murdering the aristocracy at will in a vile manner, France became a Republic. It is wrong to suppose Illumination was the only trigger for revolution, of which there were many, but Illumination, through Masonic allegiance led, and the others followed, as I stated before, like lemmings over the cliff.

All the decisions were passed down to each lodge through its political committee and revolution was therefore equalised throughout France. By Masonic plans of Illumination and through this process the link between the lodges and the Jacobin club was Illumination. Credit must be given to Weishaupt's plan as in a short space of time it instructed some two-hundred and sixty-six lodges to his ways and prepared them for revolution.

Robison states; "Hence it has arisen that the French aimed, at the very beginning, at overturning the whole world". **(42).** After the revolution had captured the whole of France we see secret Masonic revolutionary societies at work before even the opening of the National Assembly.

It fell to the Jacobin Club to lead the Illuminated brethren. So was heard, all over France, and spreading round Europe through the Masonic connection, all the old clichés of Illumination: World Citizens, Liberty and Equality, The Rights of Man, Morality, the defamation of kings and priests and the preaching of Atheism.

One of the most grotesque laws of the assembly was to form an assassination group to execute their enemies, executions passed by word of mouth without trial. A move of complete despotic anarchism.

Two important manifests appear in Robison's, 'Proofs of a Conspiracy' **(43)**. One from the Grand National lodge signed by the Duke of Orleans which implores all lodges of Europe to prepare for revolution. The other manifest implores all the lodges to establish secret schools of education to enlighten the children in their doctrine. To support writers in favour of the revolution while marginalising patriotic writers opposing revolution. **(Direction)**.

The planners of Illumination saw two goals in view, destroying Religion and Morality, as pre-requisite to the next stage. This alone should warn the people of its end desires but Illumination relies on ignorance to protect its cause.

So, although the source of Illumination had been prescribed in Germany, they went on to control France and would do so on and off through the troubled years of Napoleon, where, on occasions, he also controlled Germany and Europe. So at the first attempt the Illuminati had immediate success and the French had a satanic orgy of killing.

We must at this moment remember that the Rothschilds employed Weishaupt to design a plan for the conquest of the world. This support through Masonry was done in secrecy, which was essential for the Rothschilds as openly he was financing Mitternich's efforts to halt France's expansionist policy and in England's effort to support Metternich and his alliance. A man who finances both sides of a war must be unprincipled and only concerned with maximising his profit, or making a fortune while planning a hidden agenda. I believe the Rothschilds were following the second option. **(Direction)**.

The unshakeable truth remains that the French Revolution of 1789 was the first big gain for world revolution brought about by the Masonic lodges of the Grand Orient, planned by Weishaupt and put into action by people mesmerised by its Satanic deception. A pattern you will see that follows through history. Two moves above all helped this Satanic gain. Firstly Weishaupt planted trained subversives within government. **(Direction)**.

Secondly he was at pains to control the press. These two **'Directions'** will crop up regularly throughout this book.

As a final note to this part of the chapter Sir Walter Scott, in his second volume of, 'Life of Napoleon Bonaparte' **(44)** points to the fact that events leading up to the French Revolution were all created by the Money Barons--The Illuminati's financiers.

Let us at this point reflect on the seven aims of the Illuminati;

1 Abolition of all governments. (National). (The EU is doing this through Federalisation).
2 Abolition of private property. (Through inheritance tax).
3 Abolition of inheritance. (Through inheritance tax).
4 Abolition of patriotism. (By federalisation).
5 Abolition of all religions. (Through infiltration and drawing religions into politics).
6 Abolition of the family. (Through moral decline and marriage).
7 The creation of a New World Order. (World government by dictatorship).

Who will bring this about? The top council of the Illuminati or as time elapses whoever they call themselves. (The United Nations). Remember Weishaupt saying that if they were closed down that within a year they would rise again under the guise of the moment. Today it is the Council on Foreign Relations and the United Nations. (See Chapter 16).

The lodge of the Illuminati are broken down into three classes;

1   Novices, Minervals and lesser Illuminati.
2   Freemasons (Ordinary) and Scottish Knights.
3   The Mystery or hidden class. This contains two grades of 'Priest' and 'Regent' and 'Magus' or 'King'. (Weishaupt or successor). Only group three, the Guardians, know the full secret of Illumination. The others are fed 'feel good' news only.

The second group only learns the essential details to promote the lodge and recruit the first group. Only a few members of the second group will get promotion to the third group when the elite are sure of their commitment. So most of them work for revolution and dictatorship outside religion without knowing it. You will see shortly how Karl Marx adopted Illumination and changed its name to Communism.

The Illuminati hide behind organisations such as in America, 'The Council for Foreign Relations' which has its counter parts in most European countries, including England, all of which promote Global Government actively behind the scenes.

So you might well ask, how did an embryo idea spread so fast?

Easily. They attract the higher minds, professors, and teachers to the lower grades of Illuminati and surround education with their disciples. (Carroll Quigley is a good example). Now Universities turn out students well versed in global economy taught to them by their Illuminated teachers. A modern example is President Clinton, a strong advocate of Globalism, taught by none other than Carroll Quigley, a professor of Princeton University. President Clinton is a Rhodes Scholar (Which you will see is Illuminati in training for high office). The horror story opens up to expose where it stands today. We will look behind the mirrors that conceal the hidden agenda.

As in other secret groups the top men were named after famous characters from the past. Weishaupt himself was named Sparticus as is his successor today.

CHAPTER TWO, PART THREE.
ILLUMINATI IN THE 20th. CENTURY

At this stage it is important that you should have sight of how Illumination progressed and my example comes from a significant speech by Arnold Toynbee from his address to the Institution of Scientific Study of International Relations, June 1931: a product of the League of Nations, the for-runner to the United Nations, it was a teaching ground for International Affairs for the Illuminated delegates from some twelve countries whose delegates, mostly civil servants and members of, in England as an example, the Royal Institute of International Affairs, London School of Economics, (A breeding ground for Illuminism) and the Woodrow Wilson Chair of International Politics at Aberystwyth.

Toynbee was an Oxford graduate of classical studies and afterwards became a classical tutor of history at Oxford. 1915 he began working for British Intelligence, 1919 he was a delegate to the Paris Peace Conference. He helped to formulate the Versailles Treaty, which is now seen as a major contributor to the Second World War.

At the Versailles Conference the League of Nations was formed, whose ultimate intention, without consultation, was to create a 'World Government' without democratic representation. **Everything that I will discuss has this as its end objective, the European Union being no exception.**

To prove this point let me quote you a few examples from Toynbee's address which will leave you in no doubt where he stood. He was an official from government office, that indicates at least where a sizeable number of civil servants and politicians stood, as he was by no means alone.

He starts with a rather obvious statement, not at first showing his hand, talking about tendencies he said; "The formula that I would suggest for our consideration is this: in the 'Post War' period the principle tendency in International Affairs has been the tendency of all human affairs to become international". **(45).** I say this is natural because all civil servants try to expand the territory they work in to create larger units to man manage. He goes on to say: "Really the present economic unification of the world was implicit in the first circumnavigation of the globe, more than four centuries ago, by Western navigators". This is absolute rubbish. Those explorers were after the riches of their discoveries in those days which lines up completely with today's exploiters, the International Finance Capitalists, who want a world order so they can control the resources and riches of the world's nations for their own incessant greed.

He says: "The cure (For Anarchy) may come through a voluntary, Pacific, rational and constructive effort, such as we are making in our day----**an effort to deprive the local states of their sovereignty** for the benefit of society as a whole, without at the same time depriving them of their existence". **(Deception). Exactly what the European Union is all about. The hidden agenda that proves Edward Heath avoided the truth when speaking to the nation.**

He goes on to say the alternative is all out war till the strongest nation wins. This is rich, as the bankers, his masters, have funded both sides on every war in the last two hundred years.

Left alone from interference from behind politics from the power bankers, the world would find peace and compromise as the economic reality. Funding of wars creates more problems than it solves, especially when that funding is for selfish personal gain. But that has mostly been its aim as bankers in prior knowledge of events make big profits as the Rothschilds demonstrated.

He moves nearer his inner thought when he says; "It is true that, in the Russian atmosphere, the Marxian Social Philosophy appears to be undergoing a metamorphosis. It appears to be turning with amazing rapidity into a substitute for orthodox Christianity with Marx for Moses and Lenin for the Messiah and the collected works of Marxism for the scriptures of this new Russian church Militant". This is a comparison so beset with bias that it explodes the mind. To liken Christianity and Moses to Marxism and Lenin shows his past training by the Illuminati that developed into Marxism. It also shows a clear example of the attempt to remove religion and promote Satanism through Communism, Marxism and Illumination.

Referring to federation he said; "What Prussia is today, France, Great Britain and Italy, yes and even the United States, are likely to become tomorrow. For the sake of peace and prosperity of the world, I devoutly hope that my prophecy will become true". What he is trying to say is that states like Prussia federalised, why can't others do the same for peace. Simply there is no precedent in the world today that shows mature nations federalising successfully. It did not stop World War Two in that part of the world so it was a very bad example to give in the hindsight of history. Federalisation is fraught with dangers and insurmountable complications and is doomed to failure. **It is the European line he takes, straight from the book of the Illuminati, to prepare Europe and fix it on a one way street to total World Order. (Dictatorship).**

He continues talking about the force of resistance in the free thinking world; "We shall admit that we are engaged on a deliberate and sustained and concentrated effort to impose limitations upon the sovereignty and independence of the fifty or sixty local sovereign independent states which at present partition the habitable surface of the earth and divide the political allegiances of mankind". This is I repeat, a sure sign that, at each of those steps forward, the principle of local sovereignty is really being encroached upon and its sphere of action reduced (Just study what the EU has done to our life and its constant interference in internal matters) and its power of evil restricted. (The bankers power is Satanic and evil, not the power of the sovereign state).

"It is just because we are really attacking the principle of local sovereignty that we keep on protesting our loyalty to it so loudly. The harder we press our attack upon the idol, the more pains we take to keep its priests and devotees in a fool's paradise". I am one that escaped their hypnosis. This quite clearly shows the Hidden Agenda of the European Union at its embryo stage. It also shows how completely Toynbee was brainwashed by Illumination. **It also quite clearly shows that the Europe plan was rigidly Federal from the start and that sovereignty was the main obstacle to overcome to achieve their aim.** So it stands to reason that if we can stop Federalism we stop their move to the second but last stage to World Domination.

You will also note the skills of Marxist deception to achieve their aim. The word 'We' appears often in his speech. It refers to the cloned collective of Illuminati cum-Marxist, one worlders' and their leaders, the Guardians. All this vividly shows Illumination had spread world-wide by the thirties and had successfully penetrated the halls of power as Weishaupt predicted it would, putting their implants behind and surrounding the seat of government. We see more about this in chapter ten.

I now turn to the Ghost Theme of this book. In 1905 a form of an address was handed to a Russian, Professor Nilus, which became known as 'The Protocols of the meetings of the Learned Elders of Zion'. It was translated into English by Victor Marsden in 1920, **(46)** after the Russian Revolution, and from this moment a controversy built up around its authenticity and the International Zionist movement quickly moved to have it classed as a forgery. It was banned in Russia, Switzerland and South Africa. In Russia, a death penalty was imposed for possessing a copy, I don't want to go into the arguments for or against its authenticity except to pose the question, what is it a forgery of? This has never been answered by its accusers and leaves their argument slightly meaningless.

Its contents, of which you will read, a part at the end of each chapter, accurately predicts the events of the world until today. When you realise it was published in 1905 in Russian, therefore it was at least that old, it is in any estimation, a remarkable document; or plan, by very powerful people that is gradually being fulfilled as a **hidden agenda.**

Most unbiased view believes it to be the latter and it is for that reason I ghost it into the book to show how accurately it predicts events this century, but with a cynical likeness to the Illumination of Weishaupt/Marx and their plan for World Government, financed by the bankers.

The key to understanding the ethnic origin of the bankers involved comes from Walter Rathenau, a Jew himself and a banker of the Kaiser who wrote in an article in Weiner Frei Presse, December 24th. 1912. "Three hundred men, each of whom knows all the others, govern the fate of the European continent and they elect their successors from their entourage". That's part of the picture.

Confirmation came when Jean Izoulet, a member of the Jewish alliance, 'Israelite Universëlle' stated in his Paris 'La Capitale des Religion' in 1931 **(47)**: "The meaning of history of the last century is that today three-hundred Jewish financiers, all masters of lodges, (Masonic), rule the world". Yes I repeat RULE THE WORLD. Weishaupt's Illumination come true! Not quite yet. However this disclosure gives us the proof of the Masonic connection with International Zionism. The truth is this document most likely came from the high command in a Masonic lodge, probably predominately filled with bankers at all levels. This explains the Jewish form of wording (e.g. Goyim, meaning all others but Jews).

Another important leader to my line of thinking is an article in the 'Jewish World' of the 15th. March 1923; "Fundamentally Judaism is anti-Christian". (Again a thought out of Illumination).

Despite all this, to prove its rightful position in history as a very important document, I only wish to show how accurate it was in content, whatever its history was in practice. After each Protocol I will make my comments in relation to its content and the chapter it is linked to in the book.

PROTOCOL ONE

Taken from the Protocols of the Learned Elders of Zion

THE BASIC DOCTRINE

Putting aside fine phrases we shall speak of the significance of each thought: by comparison and deduction we shall throw light upon surrounding facts.

What I am about to set forth, then, is our system from the two points of view, that of ourselves and that of the goyim. (Non Jew).

It must be noted that men with bad instincts outnumber good men, and therefore the best results in governing them are attained by violence and terrorisation, and not by academic discussions. Every man aims at power, everyone would like to become a dictator if only he could, and rare indeed are the men who would not be willing to sacrifice the welfare of all for the sake of securing their own welfare.

What has restrained the beasts of prey who are called men? What has served as their guidance hitherto?

At the dawn of society they were subjected to brutal and blind force; afterwards, to law which is the same force, only disguised. I draw the conclusion that by the law of nature right lies in force.

Political freedom is an idea but not a fact, and one must know how to use it as a bait whenever it appears necessary to attract the masses of the people to one's party for the purpose of crushing another who is in authority. This task is rendered easier if the opponent has himself been infected with the idea of freedom, so-called **Liberalism,** and for the sake of the idea, is willing to yield some of his power. It is precisely here that the triumph of our theory appears; the slackened reins of government are immediately, by the law of life, caught up and gathered together by a new hand, because the blind might of the nation cannot for one single day exist without guidance, and the new authority merely fits into the place of the old already weakened by Liberalism.

In our day the power which has replaced that of the rulers who were Liberal is the power of gold. Time was when faith ruled. Freedom is an impossible ideal to achieve because no one knows how to use it with moderation.

It is enough to hand over a people to self-government for a certain length of time for that people to be turned into a disorganised mob. Thereafter there arises internecine strife, which soon devolves into class warfare, in the midst of which states burn down and their importance is reduced to that of a heap of ashes.

Whether a state exhausts itself in its own convulsions, whether its internal discord brings it under the power of external foes, in any case it can be accounted irretrievably lost: it is in our power. The despotism of capital, which is entirely in our hands, reaches out to it a straw that the state, willy-nilly, must take hold of: if not, it goes to the bottom.

Should anyone of a Liberal mind say that such reflections as the above are immoral I would put the following questions: If every state has two foes and if in regard to the external foe it is allowed and not considered immoral to use every manner and art of conflict, as for example to keep the enemy in ignorance of plans of attack and defence, to attack him by night or in superior numbers, then in what way can the same means in regard to a worse foe, the destroyer of the structure of society and commonweal, be called immoral and not permissible?

It is possible for any sound logical mind to hope with any success to guide crowds by the aid of reasonable counsels and arguments, when any objection or contradiction, senseless though it may be, can be made, and when such objection may find more favour with people, whose powers of reasoning are superficial? Men in masses and the men of masses, being guided solely by petty passions, paltry beliefs, customs, traditions and sentimental theorism, fall a prey to party dissension, which hinders any kind of agreement even on the basis of a perfectly reasonable argument. Every resolution of a crowd depends upon a chance or packed majority, which, in its ignorance of political secrets, puts forth some ridiculous resolution that lays in the administration a seed of anarchy.

The political has nothing in common with the moral. The ruler who is governed by moral is not a skilled politician, and is therefore unstable on his throne. He who wishes to rule must have recourse both to cunning and to make believe. Great national qualities, like frankness and honesty, are vices in politics, for they bring down rulers from their thrones more effectively and more certainly than the most powerful enemy. Such qualities must be the attributes of the kingdoms of the goyim, but we must in no wise be guided by them.

Our right lies in force. The word 'Right' is an abstract thought and proved by nothing. The word means no more than:- 'Give me what I want in order that thereby I may have proof that I am stronger than you.

Where does right begin? Where does it end?

In any state where central authority is weak, and where laws and rulers have lost their personality amid the flood of rights ever multiplying out of Liberalism, I find a new right, to attack by the right of the strong, and to scatter to the winds all existing forces of order and regulation, to reconstruct all institutions and to become the sovereign lord of those who have left to us the rights of their power by laying them down voluntarily in their Liberalism.

Our power in the present tottering condition of all forms of power will be more invincible than others, because it will remain invisible until the moment when it has gained such strength that no cunning can any longer undermine it.

Out of the temporary evil we are now compelled to commit will emerge the good of an unshakeable rule, which will restore the regular course of the machinery of the national life, brought to nought by Liberalism. The result justifies the means. Let us, however, in our plans, direct our attention not so much to what is good and moral as to what is necessary and useful.

Before us is a strategic plan from which we cannot deviate without running the risk of seeing the labour of many centuries brought to naught.

In order to elaborate satisfactory forms of action it is necessary to have regard to the rascality, the slackness, the instability of the mob, its lack of capacity to understand and respect the conditions of its own life, or its own welfare.

It must be understood that the might of the mob is blind, senseless and unreasoning force, ever at the mercy of a suggestion from any side. The blind cannot lead without bringing them into the abyss; consequently members of the mob, upstarts from the people even though they may have a genius for wisdom, yet have no understanding of the political, cannot come forward as leaders of the mob without bringing the whole nation to ruin.

Only one trained from childhood for independent rule can understand the meaning of the words that can be constructed from the political alphabet.

A people left to itself, that is, to upstarts from its midst, brings itself to ruin by party dissension's excited by the pursuit of power and honours and disorders arising there-from.

Is it possible for the masses of the people calmly and without petty jealousies to form judgements, to deal with the affairs of the country, which cannot be mixed up with personal interests?

Can they defend themselves from an external foe? It is unthinkable, for a plan broken up into as many parts as there are heads in the mob loses all homogeneity, and thereby becomes unintelligible and impossible to execute.

It is only with a despotic ruler that plans can be elaborated extensively and clearly in such a way as to distribute the whole property among the several parts of the machinery of the state: from this the conclusion is inevitable that a satisfactory form of government for any country is one that is concentrated in the hands of one responsible person. Without an absolute despotism there can be no existence for civilisation which is carried on not by the masses but by their guide, whosoever that person may be. The mob is a savage and displays its savagery at every opportunity. The moment the mob seizes freedom in its hands it quickly turns to anarchy, which in itself is the highest degree of savagery. Behold the alcoholised animals, bemused with drink, which freedom permits them to consume to excess. It is not for us and ours to walk that road. The peoples of the goyim are bemused with alcoholic liquors; their youth has grown stupid on classicism and from early immorality, into which it has been inducted by our special agents, by tutors, lackeys, governess in the houses of the wealthy, by clerks and others, by our women in their places of dissipation frequented by the goyim. Among the latter I also include the so-called "Society Ladies", voluntary followers of the others in corruption and luxury.

Our countersign is, force and make-believe. Only force conquers in political affairs, especially if it is concealed in the talents essential to statesmen. Violence must be the principle, and cunning and make-believe the rule of governments which do not want to lay down their crowns at the feet of agents of some new power. This evil is the one and only means to attain the end, the good. Therefore we must not stop at bribery, deceit and treachery when they shall serve towards the attainment of our end. In politics one must know how to seize the property of others without hesitation if by it we secure submission and sovereignty.

Our state marches along the path of peaceful conquest, has the right to replace the horrors of war by less noticeable and more satisfactory sentences of death, necessary to maintain the terror which tends to produce blind submission. Just but merciless severity is the greatest factor of strength in the state: not only for the sake of gain but also in the name of duty, for the sake of victory, we must keep to the programme of violence and make-believe. The doctrine of squaring accounts is precisely as strong as the means of which it makes use. Therefore it is not so much by the means themselves as by the doctrine of severity that we shall triumph and bring all governments into subjection to our super-government. It is enough for them to know that we are merciless for all disobedience to cease.

Far back in ancient times we were the first to cry among the masses of the people the words "Liberty, Equality, Fraternity", words many times repeated since those days by stupid poll-parrots who from all sides round flew down upon these baits and with them carried away the well-being of the world, true freedom of the individual, formerly so well guarded against the pressure of the mob. The would-be wise men of the goyim, the intellectuals, could not fathom these abstract words; did not note the contradiction of their meanings and interrelation; did not see that in nature there is no equality, cannot be freedom: that nature herself has established inequality of minds, of characters, and capacities, just as immutably as she has established subordination to her laws: never stopped to think that the mob is a blind thing, that upstarts elected from among it to bear rule are, in regard to the political, the same blind men as the mob itself, that the adept, though he be a fool, can yet rule, whereas the non-adept, even if he were a genius, understands nothing in the political, to all these things the goyim paid no regard; yet all the time dynastic rule rested upon these tenets: for the father passed on to the son a knowledge of the course of political affairs in such a wise that none should know it but members of the dynasty and none could betray it to the governed. As time went on the meaning of the dynastic transference of the true position of affairs in the political were lost, and this aided the success of the cause.

In all corners of the earth the words "Liberty, Equality, Fraternity" brought out our ranks, thanks to our blind agents, whole legions who bore our banners with enthusiasm. And all the time these words were canker-worms at work boring into the well-being of the goyim, putting an end everywhere to peace, quiet, solidarity and destroying all the foundations of the goya states. As you will see later, this helped us to triumph: it enabled us to grasp, among other things, the master card, the destruction of privileges, or in other words of the very existence of the aristocracy of the goyim, that class which was the only defence peoples and countries had against us. On the ruins of the natural and genealogical aristocracy of the goyim we have set up the aristocracy of our educated class headed by the aristocracy of money. **(The Illuminati, the Rothschilds and the bankers).** The qualifications for this aristocracy

we have established is wealth, which is dependent upon us, and in knowledge, for which our learned elders provide the motive force.

Our triumph has been rendered easier by the fact that in our relations with the men whom we wanted we have always worked upon the most sensitive chords of the human mind, upon the cash account, upon the cupidity, upon the insatiability for material needs of man; and each one of these human weaknesses, taken alone, is sufficient to paralyse initiative, for it hands over the will of men to the disposition of him who has bought their activities.

The abstraction of freedom has enabled us to persuade the mob in all countries that their government is nothing but the steward of the people who are the owners of the country, and that the steward may be replaced like a worn out glove.

It is this possibility of replacing the representative of the people which has placed them at our disposal, and, as it were, given us the power of appointment.

COMMENT

In referring to men with 'Bad Instincts' as the non-Illuminated, they justify 'violence' and 'terrorisation' rather than discussion. We see this in action, first in the French Revolution, then the more sophisticated re-match during the Russian Bolshevik Revolution and after. (Weishaupt's plan carried forward by Marx and his disciples like Lenin.

The Protocol states, 'Political freedom is an idea but not a fact'. With this I agree but this has been brought about by the power of Illumination which has encircled our domestic process to use it as a toy in a power game. It states, Liberalism, handed to them on a plate, power, because as Liberalism waters down power, so Illumination takes up the reigns of power to lead people to their twisted fate.

The Protocol states Gold is the fountain of all power and all Gold is in their hands. (The bankers). On religion they say the time was when faith ruled the world. It still does but seems to be under constant attack from all quarters, press, television, morality and pressure of life. It is therefore remarkable it still exists. Through their agents, the Illuminati have rebutted religious education, lowered the moral standards repeatedly for over sixty years and forced pornography into our homes.

Their comment about 'Frankness' and 'Honesty' being vices in politics is alas true but again only perhaps so because of the hidden agenda behind politics ruled by the Illuminated group of three-hundred bankers. 'Right' becomes the next attack and they state quite clearly that Liberalism multiplies rights out of all proportion to need and good government. They see this clearly, they should. They planted the Liberal thinking into government through education, universities, and foundations. (America in particular). They took it right into the power houses of government, through politics and the civil service. A deep and lasting penetration. That the Illuminated ones have achieved slowly, but conscientiously, since 1789, the year of the French Revolution, such a complete infiltration, is a frightening reality, but as it is so hidden from our gaze it remains somewhat illusive to expose, giving them the benefit of the doubt. We must face the fact that this is for real.

President Clinton is an example of a person driven by the beliefs of his University tutor Carroll Quigley and his Rhodes Scholarship, both disciplines completely possessed by Illumination. Liberalism is one of Illuminations main weapons to soften the underbelly of government in readiness for revolution. They go on to say, and this is very important; Our power in the present tottering conditions of all forms of power will be more invincible than any other, because it will remain invisible until the moment when it has gained such strength that no cunning can any longer undermine it". This means their agenda will remain hidden from view till no force can crush them. **(Deception).** This is their soft underbelly, exposure is their greatest dread, while they manipulate our lives towards their goal, behind the scenes, through all available channels. So political parties, the civil service, the teaching profession, the professional world of lawyers and solicitors, media including our press have all been infiltrated and stand poised to act when Illumination sounds the gong. That will be the moment when we cannot escape their clutches.

'Before us is a strategic plan from which we cannot deviate without running the risk of seeing the labour of many centuries brought to nought'. Interesting. This infers that it is a plan that came from way back when. It probably did because philosophers like Weishaupt and Marx were well read and King Solomon was probably the instigator of their diabolical plan. So the Protocols seem to say the plan is laid down and must be completed intact, so if the Protocols are a true plan we can expect the future to mirror the Protocols, as they have this century, unless we have the courage to say, now we know their plot, up till now we have done their bidding in ignorance, but no more, in the light of knowledge. This seems to me an eminently sensible way forward.

'Only one trained from childhood for independent rule can understand the meanings of the words that can be constructed from the political alphabet'. Proof that they are training their army of students from an early age to become the advocates and working bees in the large hive of the world. **(Marxist policy).**

'It is only with a despotic ruler **(Dictator)** that plans can be elaborated---'. Meaning, quite clearly, there aim is to rule by dictatorship.

'Behind the alcoholised animals, bemused with drink which freedom permits them to consume to excess'. To this you can add drugs and again it is a part truth, but the bankers promote these products through Liberalism, their invention as well, and they gain great profit from money laundering, as well as de-stabilising democracy, the main target of their **Hidden Agenda.**

They tell us that 'Force' and 'Make believe' are their countersign and the progress of their work is living proof of this as they have been behind all the wars and have built a whole host of mirrors to hide the truth of their actions. They have infiltrated society to manipulate its movement without the fear of recognition. The main evil in the world is their work crafted by their hidden hand.

'In politics one must know how to seize the property of others without hesitation if by it we secure submission and sovereignty'. This is almost describing the European Union, setting a trap, through single currency, to snare countries into a one way street of no return and relinquish our control of our financial future and our sovereignty. **(Pure Marx).**

They claim to be the first to call for 'Liberty, Equality, and Fraternity', a collection of meaningless words, as Shakespeare might of said, 'Signifying nothing', in the hands of the Illuminati. But it conjures up in the innocent minds of the normal person a sanctuary of correctness. They use the mirror image to hide the truth and therefore the sentiments are worthless. Freedom (Liberty) will probably never exist. Equality has long proved by Karl Marx to be a myth. Communism was the greatest example of elitism in our time. **(Mirror deception).** But these words have helped the Illuminati crush the aristocracy and replace it with their own aristocracy of wealth seen in the three-hundred bankers corrupting the world. So in the first Protocol we have come full circle, back to the bankers that hired Weishaupt then Marx to design a policy to conquer the world. Today this plan is getting dangerously near completion which only exposure and concerted action by the people can now halt.

From this first Protocol you will begin to see the pattern and threads that runs through Weishaupt's Illumination and Karl Marx's Communist plan. It is no coincidence that the two philosophers combined with the powerful three-hundred bankers, and using the somewhat dated ideas of King Solomon, are linked to this plan. Neither is it coincidence that the plan is plainly Anti Christian as was its source, Solomon, who was planning to conquer Christianity and establish his form of Judaism in its place. Today that form has taken on the mantle of Illumination and next to Christianity is the second most powerful force in the world today. For **true Christianity** to hold its place it needs our support as never before.

> "In the desires of a terrible and formidable sect, you have only reached the first stages of the plans it has formed for that general Revolution which is to overthrow all thrones, all altars, annihilate all property, efface all law, and end by dissolving all society".
>
> **The Abbe Barruel (1797) writing on the Anti-Christian Conspiracy.**

CHAPTER THREE

INTERNATIONAL ZIONISM IT'S CONNECTION TO FREEMASONRY AND COMMUNISM.

"Unless Bolshevism is nipped in the bud immediately, it is bound to spread in one form or another over Europe and the whole world, as it is organised and worked by Jews who have no nationality, and whose one object is to destroy, for their own ends, the existing order of things". **(48).**

A revealing document that would have been suppressed today as Anti-Semitism. It was left out of reprints of this White Paper at that time, showing the power of the International Zionist lobby even in 1919.

To support this statement there are many examples of similar evidence but this next one gives us the same message some nineteen years later in an article by Hilaire Belloc; a Jewish writer, "As for anyone who does not know that the present

Bolshevik movement in Russia is Jewish, I can only say that he must be a man who is taken in by the suppression of our deplorable press".

These two articles, one official, give us a very clear picture that Bolshevism and Revolution in Russia were International Zionist led, (and as we will find out in chapter five, financed). We will also find that Weishaupt was Jewish, the founder of the Illuminati and the instigator of the French Revolution, and from this comes Communism, a policy of the Illuminati that Carl Marx, also Jewish, was paid to develop. From this policy the International bankers financed the drive to take over Russia; a vast untapped continent of rich resources and political illiteracy. That is the key to the bankers' original desire which gave them a rich testing ground for their dictatorial development of political anarchy to prepare the way for their final goal, world control.

To find out why International Zionism was so dominant within the Masonic movement we have to go back in history to Freemasonry in the 16th. century. The rise of Protestant power in the 16th. century disturbed the mystical body of Christ, according to Thomas Walsh in his authoritative work 'Philip II', which in chapter XVI describes Freemasonry.

He describes a secret organisation that is spreading the gospel of Naturalism, a policy diametrically opposed to Christian teaching. He claims that if the leaders of the 'False' Jews (The Khazar Tribe) did not start this secret society, they surely played a large part in its anti-Christian activities to influence weak Christians to join their society. He goes on to show how Freemasonry uses Jewish symbolism's. A prospective mason walks to the East, towards Jerusalem, to rebuild the temple destroyed in the fulfilment of the prophecy of Christ.

"The Grand Orient and Scottish Rite lodges, sources of so many modern revolutions, are more militant, more open and apparently more virulent than some of the others which they are leading into a single world organisation by gradual steps". **(49).**

Bernard Lazare, a Jewish writer confirms the presence of Jews at the birth of Freemasonry. "It is certain, that there were Jews at the cradle of Freemasonry- Cabalistic Jews, as is proved by some of the rites that have been preserved. During the years that preceded the French Revolution they very probably entered in great numbers into the councils of the society and founded secret societies themselves. There were Jews around Weishaupt; and Martinez De Pasqualis, a Jew of Portuguese origin, who organised numerous groups of Illuminati in France, (Grand Orient) recruiting many novices to whom he taught the doctrine of reintegration. The lodges, founded by Martinez, were Mystical, whilst the other orders of Freemasonry were rather Rationalist. This permits one to say that the secret societies represented the two sides of the Jewish mind; practical Rationalisation and Pantheism". **(50).** Both modes of Jewish thinking are opposed to ordered submission to God through Jesus Christ.

So in the life of Phillip II 1527-1598 there grew a Masonic movement not unlike it is today but only just beginning to grow; an enlargement that has created the largest secret society in the world. Throughout its growth the Jewish influence developed along naturalistic lines but unlike its Jewish mentors it remained a secret society even hiding its Jewish character and its naturalism from its initiates and pretending to be a highly correct and Christian organisation; even today its members do not know its intention to destroy Christianity and in particular the Roman Catholic Church and replace it with their form of naturalism which is close to atheism.

Once again I quote from a respected author; "The Jews have swarmed into it (Freemasonry) from the earliest times and controlled the higher grades and councils of the ancient and accepted Scottish Rite since the beginning of the 19th. century". **(51).**

Monsignor Dillon, in "Freemasonry Unmasked", regards the society as the secret power behind Communism and sees the absorption of Weishaupt's "Illuminati" into Freemasonry, and the complete take-over of the Grand Orient by this Atheistic Rite, as the next stage in Masonic development. The editor of this publication makes a studied comment about history since the French Revolution. First the 'Declaration of the Rights of Man' was passed almost without alteration, taken straight from the lodges of Freemasonry. This document, in a hidden manner, renounces the Christian Doctrine for naturalism and therefore technically made France the leader in Freemasonry's drive towards atheism. It is only the people who have bravely fought to retain Christian belief up till today that delays their plan.

The next move strengthened the influence of the Jewish settlers. The Constituent Assembly 1789-1791, the Deputies of which were almost exclusively Jewish (Father Lémann, 'L' Entree Des Israélites Dans La Sociéte Francaise' Page 356.) voted decisively for Jewish emancipation. As this assembly were mostly Freemasons from the revolution it was a forgone conclusion as to the result. Mirabeau, a leader of the Masons of high degree and also a leader of the revolution was a friend and devotee of Weishaupt and had close links with the Jewish group in Berlin. It was a Mr A Duport who finally swung the debate in favour of Jewish emancipation. It was one of many favours the Masons would perform for the Jewish community.

Thus the Christians of France suffered a double blow, the official acceptance of naturalism by the state and the acceptance of those, through the masonic lodges, who imposed this naturalism upon them. It was a crushing blow to the French people. Amongst the Freemasons who made this happen were L'Abbé Gregoire and Tallyrand, Bishop of Auten.

Monsignor Dillon's preface states **(52)**; "Modern history since 1791 is, to a large extent, the account of the domination of state after state by the anti-supernatural supernaturalism of Freemasonry, behind which has been steadily emerging the still more strongly organised anti-supernatural supernaturalism of the Jewish nation.

That is why the post-revolutionary epoch has witnessed, in country after country, persistent attacks upon the programme of 'Christ the King'. It goes on to say, and this is so obvious today; "After every successful Masonic revolution, since the first in 1789, the world soon began to hear of the countries entering upon the path of 'Progress' by the introduction of 'Enlightenment' **(Illuminati = Direction)** reforms, such as the separation of the church and state (or the putting of all religions on the same level) the legalisation of divorce, the secularisation of schools, the suppression and banishment of religions orders and congregations, the glorification of Freemasonry, the nationalisation of property and the un-restrained licence of the press".

In 1922 the Grand Lodge of France proclaimed that its main task was to form a United States of Europe, (To lead to a world federation) so it is easy to see how today, we, the Nations of Europe, are being blindly lead into a Masonic trap planned within the Masonic movement which would eventually give freemasonry, tremendous dominating power over our Sovereign Nations. At that time the moral law taught through Christian teaching would no longer be permissible and moral and sociological decline would accelerate.

Europe is where we can say "No" to a single currency leading to federalisation, and where we can save our Sovereign Nation.

So what about English Freemasonry? It has been said that it was not tainted by the influx of Jewish entrants and therefore was not led down the same path. But in Sir Alfred Robbin's book 'English Speaking Freemasonry' **(53)**, he gives us evidence to the contrary. He writes, "The foundations on which Freemasonry so long has stood are a reverential belief in the eternal, with an inter realisation of his revealed will and word. It recognises that both belief and revelation exist in many forms...in England many lodges are composed of...Jews (Zionists)".

So the Masonic movement, with close links between lodges all over the world, has set itself up as the opposition of Anti-Christ to Christ and this applies to American and British Masonry despite protest and denial by their governing bodies.

It has been further stated that because English Masonry includes 'The Great Architect of the Universe' it must be Christian. This is not so, because it does not accept 'The Mystical Body of Christ' and is therefore anti-supernatural and anti-Christian, as it puts all forms of religion on the same level as Christ, like Buddha and Mohammed.

The reason Masonry uses the 'The Great Architect of the Universe' is to hide their true aims behind religion **(Deception)** and fool their initiates into believing they are true Christians.

It is easy at this stage to see how Voltaire's works of organised Atheism, directed against all religion, but particularly the Roman Catholic Church took hold through the Masonic lodges of Europe. His influence had great bearing on Weishaupt's policy of the Illuminati and he was well read amongst the European

Jewish community who set their sights on destroying the Roman Catholic influence all over Europe.

Voltaire was born, Francis Arouet, but like Marx, chose to change his name, to Voltaire. He was born to a middle class family of Catholic faith and like Weishaupt attended a strict Jesuit Seminary and grew to hate his educators, spending the rest of his life, like Weishaupt, organising the intellectual hatred for whom he considered his jailers.

He was destined to be a lawyer and had the ability to reach to the top of this profession, but like many of his time he became distracted by the "isms" of the time which occupied many a hopeful student. Vice became his pleasure and Atheism his vehicle to attack the very roots of Roman Catholicism. His words fell as sweet music on the ears of the corrupt society of Paris as the church was the only body to attack their abandoned morality. He went too far in attacking the government in 1727 and ended up as a guest of the Bastille.

In exile in England, he perfected his debauchery and Atheism, and joined the Masonic Movement, becoming addicted to its secrecy and saw its power within the French society he wished to destroy; a society, as he saw it, controlled by the Roman Catholic Church on the one hand and the sanctimonious pomposity of authority that imprisoned him on the other.

So on returning to Paris he took up his task of attacking government and religion with the passion of a man possessed. His writings matured while in England and found their home in corrupt society. It too was under attack from the Church.

He was exalted when told of the suppression of the Jesuits. He set about designing his plan to crush the Church and replace it with his Atheistic idea of brotherhood without marriage, family, God, property or law; a vile plan for a debauched society, without order, brought about by an evil mind. He was the epitome of immorality. Quite probably, although we cannot be certain, his vile creed and inhuman vigour in pushing his thoughts upon the privileged of Paris played a decisive role in the French Revolution. He certainly set the minds of his followers on a path towards the atrocities that were witnessed during this infamous revolution, where every decency was abandoned by the mob that brutally butchered the King and his court, the government and the church.

Condorcet, in his 'Life of Voltaire' says; "He did not see all that which he accomplished, but he did all that we see. Enlightened observations prove to those who know how to reflect, that the first author of the Great Revolution was without doubt Voltaire".

From his secret society of the brotherhood (Freemasonry) his thoughts were taken up and developed by Weishaupt and the highly planned operation to create the French Revolution was sent to the Grand Orient Lodges by Weishaupt as you will see in chapter five. Now perhaps it is a good time to examine the birth of the Masonic movement.

Monsignor Segur, Bishop of Grenoble, studied early Freemasonry and he believed that Faustus Socinus, the nephew of Laelius Socinus, the founder of the Unitarians, later known as Socinians, was the originator of early Freemasonry.

Faustus, while in Lyons, heard of the death of his uncle in Zurich and went to collect his papers and belongings. In the papers he found Uncle Laelius had been involved in a conference of Heretics at Vicenza in 1547 at which a plan for the destruction of Christianity was evolved: A policy Reviving Arianism, a doctrine attacking the Trinity and the Incarnation. The plan was exposed to the Republic of

Venice and two of its leaders were executed. Those left, including Ochinus went underground. In the 'Veil Removed' Abbé le Franc, a victim later of the French Revolution, claims that the success of Faustus Socinus in spreading his uncle's theories was enormous. His aim, like Voltaire, was to destroy the Church and replace it with his temple for all followers of Anti-Christian creeds.

To fool its novices, like Weishaupt's Illuminati, it was promoted as Christian but lacking all Christian attributes of faith, hope, or love.

He aimed to attract Unitarianism and the members of the confederation formed to attract Christianity at Vicenza, attracting the rich, the learned and the powerful, of the world. (Where have we heard this before?).

He praised all the anti-Christ associations, Trinitarians and Anti-Trinitarians alike, Lutherans and Calvinists. He knitted them into a single garment of hatred aimed at the Roman Catholic Church to add force to their cause, its destruction.

His idea was that they were all brothers and his disciples were called 'United Brethren', 'Polish Brothers', 'Moravian Brothers', 'Brother Masons', and at last 'Freemasons'.

Dillon tells us that the Abbé Lerudan, as early as 1747, wrote that, "The real secret of Freemasonry consisted, even then, in disbelief in the divinity of Christ, and in a determination to replace that doctrine, which is the very foundation of Christianity, by naturalism or rationalism".

Socinus, having established his sect in Poland sent his disciples to Germany, Holland and England to preach his creed.

In 'Le Voile Levé, the Abbé Lefranc believes Oliver Cromwell was a Socinian and it was he who brought Freemasonry to England. Cromwell's sympathy did not extend to the Church as his policies show.

Monsignor Secur tells us that Cromwell gave the title Freemasons to the secret society and also invented the allegory of the temple of Solomon, so much used in Masonry right up till today. This temple, destroyed by Christ, was to be restored by Freemasonry after Christ and the Christian order, was obliterated by conspiracy and revolution. He goes on to connect modern Freemasonry with the Jews and the Templars as well as Socinus. Dillon agrees, that the Jews, before the Reformation, formed secret societies for their own protection and towards the destruction of Christianity, which persecuted them. The rebuilding of the temple of Solomon was the dream of their lives. It is therefore not impossible, that they admitted into their secret societies the Templars ripe for revenge. Dillon also agrees with Abbé Lefranc that Cromwell was connected to the Socinus Brotherhood and therefore Freemasonry.

In the footnote to Dillon's lectures a very bold statement is found; "One of the works that anti-Christ will do, it is said, is to re-unite the Jews, and to proclaim himself as their long looked-for Messiah. As it is now generally believed, he is to come from Masonry and be of it; this is not impossible, for in it, he will find the Jews, the most inveterate haters of Christianity, the deepest plotters, and the fittest to establish his reign".

Lefranc thinks that Socinus blended the brotherhood with the ancient guild of working Masons which had existed as an honourable society for the protection of craftsmen for many centuries before his time. The irony of which can be seen when you realise the main customers for their skills were the churches throughout England and Europe. But as with all these secret societies the actual aim was withheld from the craftsmen and they lived in hope of an increase of demand for their skills.

The first known link between Freemasonry and the Anti-Christian movement is dated 1535 and was called the Charter of Cologne, which if genuine, is the earliest known reference to Freemasons displaying Anti-Christian rituals within their lodges. The main move in this trend came much later in the 18th. century when the Socinus Brotherhood led to the Illuminati of Weishaupt (See chapter five).

To bring back the Pretender, the Jacobites formed a Scottish, English and Irish constitution. The English constitution included the Mother Lodge of York and the London Lodge, which later split in 1717 to form the Grand Lodge of London. It was from this time that the Jacobites took their rites to France to help the cause for the Stuarts. It was then that Lord Derwentwater opened the Mother Lodge of Paris. From here Masonry spread to Ireland 1729, to Holland in 1730, and to Germany 1736. This was the period of Voltaire's corruption of Masonry and as with the French Lodges, the exponents of Masonry were generally of low morals and allowed Voltaire's views to capture the agenda of their newly founded lodges.

Masonry became a power in Europe in the 18th. century, strengthened by the bond between the separate lodges, financed by the wealth of some members (Bankers) and the unscrupulousness of the brotherhood of Masons. It was just one step from Illumination.

With Voltaire's influence, Freemasonry rapidly spread through the upper classes of France and Germany and the European states. In France and Europe it had an English, Scottish and local obedience (ritual), all of which had separate officials, all joining in singular brotherhood. The Duke of Orleans, Grand Master of the Scottish Masonic body in France, joined with others and formed the Grand Orient of France. The lodges for women named 'Lodges of Adoption' were formed and led by the Duchess of Bourbon, sister of the Duke of Orleans, bringing an untapped source of influence to the hitherto male dominated order. Society rapidly joined the Masons and were promoted in the Army, Navy, in Law, the public services and in the top end of education and the press, ready for the internal corruption of society and destabilisation of France.

Two events secured the end result of the French Revolution. Firstly Illumination took hold of Saint Martin in France. Adam Weishaupt, the founder of the Illuminati being behind this move which developed rapidly thanks to the preparation of Freemasonry by Voltaire, covering the core of Weishaupt's policy. Secondly was the introduction of female lodges which played a large part in corrupting the royal court and demoralising society in Paris.

A Portuguese Zionist, named Martinez Pasqualis, was to introduce Illumination to the lodges of Lyon, this spread throughout the high society of France immorality, anarchy and atheism, corrupting the pillars that supported the structures of France. All planning was centred within the newly formed collection of Masonic lodges called the Grand Orient and with the core plan of Adam Weishaupt they added their debauched plans for murder and destruction that reached new heights of human atrocity.

Dillon states that Voltaire's will to; "Do God and man injury" was as great as Weishaupt's, and it must be given some credence. But Voltaire was a destroyer. Weishaupt realised that if you destroy a pillar of a temple, unless you replace it with another, the temple will collapse. So Weishaupt had his answer, Communism.

In researching his life I have become convinced that if Weishaupt had not existed, Communism, if born, would not have survived infancy and indeed I may well not have been writing this book. But he did and his dynamic plan for what became to be known as Marxism, after its author, was more correctly Weishaupt's plan to destroy his main enemy the Roman Catholic Church and replace it with his conceited idea of superior rule under Marxist dictatorship. I would go further and say that if he had had no part in Masonic intrigue, the use of the Masonic orders for organising and spreading Communism would have receded and died. But alas his evil intent is in a commanding position today through secrecy and deception, **and financing by the bankers.**

To understand the reasoning for Weishaupt's union with Freemasonry you should read chapter six of 'Freemasonry Unmasked' by Monsignor Dillon. **(54).** In short it held his plans in secret while spreading his rite to continents all over the world. Without Masonry's service his plans would not today be a threat to world democracy. Weishaupt remained head of the Illuminati till his death, spreading his doctrine over the world to America under the evil Satanist General Pike; to Italy and Massini, his future successor, and Switzerland, Spain and England. He also Illuminated Palmerston who used his position to promote Masonry and the Illuminati to the detriment of England. All this was accomplished through Masonry. So how did he attach his evil intent to this secret society?

After Weishaupt had spent five years studying for his 'New World Order' his first introduction to his new parish (The world) took place when Saint Martin decided to test Illuminism in France and a meeting of all deputy Masons took place at Lyons under the title 'Convent of the Gauls'. Weishaupt thought of this as a stepping stone to a world convent where his aims could be truly wed to Freemasonry. This convent acted as a testing ground for his wish to join with Freemasonry to spread his evil aims.

The Illuminism of Saint Martin was an easy convert and began a terrible evil that was to spread throughout the Masonic world. His plan was to set his Illumination of Masonry as a hidden degree above the generally practised degrees of Masonry, into the grey area of this secret society. It was to be a secret society within a secret society where only chosen masons and others could be enrolled by invitation only.

Following the success at Lyons the World Convent of Wilhelmsbad of 1781 was organised to bring about the marriage between Weishaupt's Illuminati and the World Council of Freemasonry. Deputies from all the countries where Masonry had reached, attended this convention; the British Empire, the newly formed United States of America, all countries of Europe; but the largest attendance came from Weishaupt's strongholds of Germany and France.

Between Baron Knigg, Weishaupt's man, and Dittfort, also under his influence, the Illuminati controlled most of the council of deputies. It was at this convention that he set in motion the plans for the French Revolution. At the end of the convention Weishaupt had made his targeted link with world-wide Freemasonry that delivered him his tool to secretly, through Masonry, start and execute his plot to crush the Roman Catholic Church and replace governments throughout the world with his form of Marxist Communism; to hold the majority under dictatorship while his chosen group of Freemasons, International Finance Capitalists, International Zionists and followers, enjoyed the fruits of his revolution. That this plan is in an advanced state today, through secrecy and contempt for democracy, may be a surprise for you. But I can assure you that it is true.

Why the warning of the revolution was unheeded by the courts of Europe remains to this day a matter for speculation. The death of the courier, carrying plans for the Revolution who was killed by lightening at Ravensburg led to the secret papers falling into the hands of the Bavarian Elector who published them and sent copies to all the interested States in Europe including France, the subject for the abuse. The most likely answer to why his warning remained unheeded was because each state probably saw gain in ignoring the threat. But France's rejection was almost certainly the result of the Illuminati's agents who had penetrated the government and the courts, who had taken over the decision from the weakened power. This was after all the main reason why the Illuminati were so successful with the French Revolution in 1789.

So the leaders of the Illuminati, a few of whom I name, Mirabeau, Fouché, Talleyrand, Lafayette, Robespierre, Murat, Cambaceres and Danton, led the French revolution from the Masonic Lodges of the Grand Orient. They won of course, as France had been disarmed in advance. Weishaupt knew this only too well. To end this proof of association let us look again at the words of Monsignor Secur; "See to what a point the reign of Jesus Christ was menaced at the hour the Revolution broke out. It was not France alone that it agitated, but the entire Europe. What do I say? The world was in the power of Masonry. All the lodges of the world came in 1781 to Wilhelmsbad represented by delegates from Europe, Asia, Africa, and America; from the most distant coasts discovered by navigators they came, zealous apostles of Masonry... they all returned imbued with the Illumination of Weishaupt, that is Atheism, and animated with the poison of incredulity with which the orators of the convent had inspired them. Europe and the Masonic world were then in arms against Catholicity. Therefore, when the signal was given, the shock was terrible, terrible especially in France, in Italy, in Spain, in the Catholic nations which they wished to separate from the Pope, and cast into schism, until the time came when they could completely de-Christianise them".

To support this we have a passage from John Robison's 'Proof of a Conspiracy' **(55).** Bear in mind while you read this that he was a Mason, but was so horrified when he found out the true policy of the Illuminati that he wrote his book which is today one of two books that give us a full picture of the Illuminati and Masonry at that time.

"I have been able to trace these attempts, made, through a course of fifty years, under the specious pretext of enlightening the world by the torch of philosophy, and of dispelling the clouds of civil and religious superstition which kept the nations of Europe in darkness and slavery. I have observed these doctrines gradually diffusing and mixing with all the different systems of Free Masonry; till, at last, **an association has been formed for the express purpose of rooting out all the religious establishments, and overturning all the existing governments of Europe.** I have seen this association exerting itself zealously and systematically, till it has become almost irresistible; and I have seen that the most active leaders in the French Revolution were members of this association, and conducted their first movements according to its principles, and by means of its instructions and assistance, formally requested and obtained: and, lastly, I have seen that this association still exists, still works in secret, and that not only several appearances among ourselves show that its emissaries are endeavouring to propagate their detestable doctrines among us, but that the association has lodges in Britain corresponding with the mother lodge at Munich ever since 1784.

"If all this was a matter of mere curiosity, and susceptible of no good use, it would have been better to have kept it to myself, than to disturb my neighbours with the knowledge of a state of things which they cannot amend. But it shall appear that the minds of my countrymen are misled in the very same manner as were those of our continental neighbours...If I can show that the reasoning's which make a very strong impression on some persons in this country are the same that actually produced the dangerous association in Germany; and that they had this unhappy influence solely because they were thought to be sincere, and the expressions of the sentiments of the speakers. If I can show that this was all a fraud, and that the leaders of this association disbelieved every word that they uttered, and every doctrine that they thought; and that their real intention was to abolish all religion, overturn every government and make the world a general plunder and wreck...I cannot but think that such information will make my countrymen hesitate a little, and receive with caution, and even distrust, addresses and instructions which flatter our self conceit".

I think you will agree these are two very different sources, one from religion and one within Masonry, which come together and give use substantial proof of the plans of the Illuminati together with the earlier evidence that proves the connection between International Zionism (The bankers and International Zionist members of the European lodges) and masonry, which, through the Illuminati, became involved in Communism. We continue this search for the truth in chapter five.

PROTOCOL ELEVEN

The State Council has been, as it were, the emphatic expression of the authority of the ruler; it will be, as the 'show' part of the Legislative Corps, what may be called the editorial committee of the laws and decrees of the ruler.

This then, is the programme of the new constitution. We shall make law, Right and Justice ONE In the guise of proposals to the Legislative Corps, TWO. By decrees of the President under the guise of general regulations, of orders of the Senate and of resolutions of the State Council in the guise of ministerial orders. THREE. And in case a suitable occasion should arise-in the form of a Revolution in the State.

Having established approximately the 'modus agendi' we will occupy ourselves with details of those combinations by which we have still to complete the revolution in the course of the machinery of State in the direction already indicated. **By these combinations I mean the freedom of the press, the right of association, freedom of conscience, the voting principle, and many another that must disappear for ever from the memory of man**, or undergo a radical alteration the day after the promulgation of the new constitution. It is only at that moment that we shall be able at once to announce all our orders, for, afterwards, every noticeable alteration will be dangerous, for the following reasons: if this alteration be brought in with harsh severity and in a sense of severity and limitations, it may lead to a feeling of despair caused by fear of new alterations in the same direction: if, on the other hand, it be brought in, in a sense of further indulgences it will be said that we have recognised our wrongdoing and this will destroy the prestige of the infallibility of our authority, or else it will be said that we have become alarmed and are compelled to show lenience for which we shall get no thanks because it will be supposed to be compulsory...Both the one and the other are injurious to the prestige of the new constitution. We desire that from the first moment of its promulgation, while the people of the world are still stunned by the accomplished fact of the Revolution, still in a condition of terror and uncertainty, they should recognise once for all that we are so strong, so in expugnable, so superabundantly filled with power, that in no case shall we take any account of them, and so far from paying any attention to their opinions or wishes, we are ready and able to crush with irresistible power all expression or manifestation thereof at every moment and in every place, that we have seized at once everything we wanted and shall in no case divide our power with them...Then in fear and trembling they will close their eyes to everything, and be content to wait what will be the end of it all.

The goyim are a flock of sheep, and we are their wolves. And you know what happens when the wolves get hold of the flock?

There is another reason also why they will close their eyes: for we shall keep promising them to give back all the liberties we have taken away as soon as we have quelled the enemies of peace and tamed all parties...

It is not worth while discussing how long they will be kept waiting for the return of their liberties...

For what purpose then have we invented this whole policy and insinuated it into the minds of the goy without giving them any chance to examine its underlying meaning? For what indeed, if not in order to obtain in a roundabout way what is for our scattered tribe unattainable by the direct road? It is this which has served as the basis of our organisation of **secret Masonry which is not known to, and whose aims are not even so much as suspected by, these goy cattle attracted by us into the 'show' army of Masonic Lodges in order to throw dust in the eyes of their fellows.**

God has granted to us, his chosen people, the gift of the dispersion, and in this which appears in all eyes to be our weakness, has come forth all our strength, which has now brought us to the threshold of sovereignty over all the world.

There now remains not much more for us to construct upon the foundation we have laid.

COMMENT

In this protocol we see the real colours of the secret society. Abolition of the freedom of the press. This is almost complete world wide. The Media and the publishing houses are nearly all in their hands. The right of association; **abolished**. Freedom of conscience; **abolished.** Freedom of the vote; **abolished.** These freedoms must disappear for ever 'they' say.

To show their dictatorial power they state that on no account will 'they' take any notice of our opinions. 'They will hold the power and not share it. Dictatorship without mercy.

Masonry, seems, according to 'them' as much as a decoy (deception) as a channel to revolution. It states quite clearly that 'their' secrets are not known, even by their fellow Masons.

The Jewish people were dispersed by God all over the world as punishment for their behaviour. They were outcasts because of their practice of usury. It was meant to weaken their endeavours. But usury, to the Khazar Tribe, is their strength. But only as long as we, their so called Goyim sheep, allow it to happen. Now we see this plan is against our very basic rights, we must stop it. It is only a small but ruthless group, linked to a small but wealthy group of International Zionists, that are intent on corrupting the world for their own greed. You are now beginning to see the likeness between 'their' statements in the protocols and Weishaupt and Carl Marx and their policies, with the background of the International Finance Capitalists guiding their path, in absolute command.

CHAPTER FOUR

WORLD ORDER, THE HIDDEN AGENDA OF GLOBAL FINANCIERS

PART ONE
THEIR PATH THROUGH FINANCIAL CONTROL

Because we are too busy existing in today's rat race, and because our so-called free press hides the truth from us, we believe the International Finance Capitalists are an upstanding group of financiers who try and solve international financial problems for the good of the world in general, and to help the poorer countries manage their economies more efficiently. But of course we would be wrong. They act to increase their own wealth. International finance capitalism is the greed trail of usurers and is a tightly knit group of the richest men in the world **who think nothing of creating wars or international financial crises for their own gain, of which the Second World War and the Wall Street collapse of 1929 are typical examples. They are totally ruthless.**

The 1929 financial collapse created waves all over the world but none so severe as in Germany. This was part of the reason that they created the collapse, to weaken Europe, because at the other end they calculated they would come out of it **in control of Germany by their financial loans to Hitler's regime, so they could use Germany as a buffer to Stalin and Russia, the monster they created in Communism that they had partly lost to Stalin by his power grab.** They weren't sure they could control Stalin till later when he came under their control through finance. Germany was their insurance policy in case things went wrong. They would use this monster in a terrible world war. They, the bankers, wanted war as it would drive the world nearer to Communism, despite of the obvious policies of Hitler their trump card to world control. Hitler was their man to fulfil their agenda. This statement that I have just made reverses everything we have been told by our media. However, all of my statement is supported by facts. Facts that although in print have been marginalised by the distributors of published works because those distributors are owned or controlled by the very financiers who control world lending and the Media. Nothing happens naturally where they are concerned, so let us study them carefully in the next two chapters.

MONEY MAKERS - USURERS

The following quotation introduces the subject admirably; "This brings us to the currency of America. Since the war of secession, 1865, the entire country has, financially speaking, been an Empire of ignorant subjects, and the owners of the large banks in New York have been the economic Monarchs. The codification of this situation took place in 1913, when the Federal Reserve system was created by law. It provided for a system of twelve central banks upon which the central government would be dependent for its finance. These banks are privately owned, and, issue money against government bonds, which are sold through these banks. Thus the American war effort in the Second World War earned approximately $7,500,000,000. in interest for the owners of this system. The only currency known in America is this private issue of these central banks. This currency is spoken of as 'Secured by Government Bonds'. These bonds however are payable only in this currency. The whole system is simply a device for private control of the economic life of the country. The volume of currency may be increased or decreased at the will of Finance-Capitalism, and in a country without a state, this is a technique of domination...Finance Capitalism belongs to a past age, the age of money. Even in America, it has passed into second place, and has become a mere technique of the absolute domination of the cultural disorder. More important as a technique is the control of men's minds, and an understanding of America and its potentialities for Europe necessitates a knowledge of its propaganda system". **(56)**.

But first let us look at how England led the field in handing over its sovereign right to create its own money to a group of bankers who have since had taxes created to fund the interest debt charge for money created from nothing. We have to go back to 1694 to find the cradle of the lending era which has enslaved the people of England ever since. **Debt gives the lender control so National and personal debt enslaves countries and people, to the will of the lender. Debt has become the norm to most people by mortgage loans, and Nations by national debt.**

In 1694 William III asked a William Patterson to lend him £1,200,000 to go to war. Patterson and his fellow bankers set up the Bank of England to make the loan and the King agreed they could create a further similar amount for themselves, prompting Patterson to remark "The bank hath benefit of interest on all moneys it creates out of nothing". This was the start of the United Kingdom's debt. Today we see the result in forecasts of the 'Gilt Edged Securities' in our financial columns which represent the bonds given by government as security; it is all created paperwork that represents the worst usury ever imposed on Nations. But governments could, and should side-step this charge by being their own creators of money, but instead they have always heeded the original warning of the bankers that governments were too weak and too subject to contemporary pressures to be trusted to handle financial creation objectively. This is neither true nor relevant as an adequate safeguard can be built into any system to guard against politicians who wish to abuse our money system. What is fully plain is that we allow this system to continue that holds us in bondage to the Will of the International Finance Capitalists today.

The International Banker has made it his business to be close to government and interested in promoting government debt. Their business is, as we saw in chapter one, devoted mainly to the use of government bonds as collateral and as a added value (You saw Rothschild making extra profit over and above interest charges on bond sales over the launch price). This made them devoted to deflation as it increased bond values. All this was carried out within a secret structure that the International Finance Capitalists (Merchant Bankers) devised themselves to maximise the influence on political decisions. Today with the combination of their influence and Multi-National Companies, they can and do walk over national interests and ignore local politics accordingly. So how did they create money? Quite simply, they printed it; but why were they allowed to get away with it is another matter.

The system is this, and it applies all over the world: The government wants to increase money supply by say £1,000,000,000. or in any currency. The bankers agree and government bonds (Gilts) are printed to that value. The bank prints, at the cost of printing only, £1,000,000,000. of currency (Note at **printing cost only**). Then it lends it to the government at between 8-10% interest per annum till they reduce the money supply or redeem their bonds; this has got to be the worst form of usury ever.

From the small beginnings of William's loan the public sector debt of the UK rose to £204,174,000,000. Or put it another way, over two hundred and four billion pounds in 1991-1992 costing taxpayers £16,691,000,000 debt charges and an economic briefing forecasting £26,000,000,000 by 1995-1996. This means twelve pounds a week for every tax payer. What this means to our main services is devastating – Health, Education, and Defence are all under-supplied with money to feed the greedy bankers rather than creating our own money supply in an ordered manner and spending the saved debt charges on our services and reducing taxes. The present system cannot continue; some brave politician must challenge this folly and stop the very source of the International Finance Capitalists great wealth because they have another agenda to wreck our freedom and create a world dictatorship. What I am saying, is that if all countries took financial control of their money creation, under controlled guidelines, no nation need be in debt to outside forces except perhaps in extreme cases of famine and disaster.

Examples do exist of countries using their own money creation but most have been crushed by the International Finance Capitalists, as any weakness is bad for business, showing they will crush alternative competition..

Guernsey is one example that re-built its sea defences without public debt. In 1912 Australia set up a government owned Commonwealth Bank which financed Australia's part in the First World War, lending $700,000,000, then after the war they financed the Trans-Australia Railroad. But in 1923 Sir Denies Miller died and the bank became a privatised clone and followed the lines of the finance capitalists.

The Reserve Bank of Australia also financed the Second World War under the watchful eye of H C Combs, but as strong personalities die, the Finance Capitalists seem to bear in on the vacuum left by their loss. They were taken over by the Finance Capitalists.

The most powerful resistance was shown by Canada's premier MacKenzie King who used the Bank of Canada to finance their part in the World War 11 at near to zero rate of interest with budget deficits over twenty-five percent of gross national product. Once again the International Finance Capitalists targeted this crack in their armour and closed it.

In the words of C H Douglas "Just as the banks created money out of nothing, so they bought the war debts for nothing, and our income tax, surtax and death duties are what we pay them for having created and appropriate for their own use, the national debt... Taxation is legalised robbery". The bankers are truly pirates of finance.

So, where does it put us? It puts us in debt, even if personally we do not owe a penny. That's where it puts us. Is it necessary? **No, if we as a country controlled our own money supply we would be out of debt and outside the political interference from the International Finance Capitalists (Merchant bankers), who gain from our debt.**

The Bank of England was nationalised in 1949 by a Labour government but the Merchant Bankers, lending the money, were not, and consequently the creation of money remained in private hands. So once again the bankers side-stepped legislation and a, far from successful, attempt to nationalise our money supply remained in place, leading some to believe that the government was in control of money creation.

So why do politicians allow this to happen? Just look at the lucrative jobs they get when they retire from politics. You need look no further than the Rothschilds' sphere of influence to see the names that once adorned our media as politicians to see the bankers buy silence and offer these jobs as sops to them for not tackling the main problem the world faces today which is usury from fake interest on paper debt created from nothing. Interest for next to nothing for the bankers. But even worse we are, as nations, held in subservience through this falsely created debt. The Economic Research Council's report in 1981 states; "...It is apparent that no new money (Credit) can be created except through the banking system, which issues it as interest-bearing debt owed to them by the nations. The result of this has been the piling up of an enormous burden of debt on which succeeding generations of our people will have to pay huge sums each year in the form of interest and sinking funds". This official message could not be put more clearly. Now let us take note of another tentacle of the octopus. Let us just remind ourselves of the financiers links with our perceived enemy in this quotation; **"Marxism, you say, is the bitterest opponent of Capitalism, which is sacred to us. For the simple reason that they are opposite poles of the earth and permit us to be its axis. These two opposites, Bolshevism and ourselves, find ourselves identified in the International. And these two opposites, the doctrines of the two poles of society, meet in their unity of purpose, the renewal of the world from above by control of wealth, and from below by revolution". (57).** <u>So, the bankers are the modern Trojan Horse harbouring the enemy within. The capitalists that fund Communism, that wishes to destroy us.</u>

Now let us pass to the USA and study how they have coped with the debt problem and where they stand today. In 1790 Meyer Amschel Rothschild made a bold but considered statement, **"Permit me to issue and control the money of a nation and I care not who makes its laws".** With this arrogant statement he started on the road to control, with help from his colleagues in banking. The emergent power that they have today over America and through their control of Wall Street, the world financial markets, is proof of their success. Remember those words well. The next year 1791, he established, with his colleagues the United States Bank that, renamed today, gives his banking influence power equal to Rockefellers and Morgan today.

It was a time of fast expansion as the thirteen colonies changed into States. Those that were well organised and cash rich had the upper hand. The Rothschilds were certainly that. The new United States encouraged the use of coinage by minting gold and silver into coins at no charge and the State banks, who pretended to be in public ownership, were in reality owned by Rothschild and others who emigrated to America to seize the banking initiative. These banks, by government acceptance, were incorporated and allowed to issue paper money against gold stocked to its issue value. But as any system of trust, the bankers lent without gold to support their loans and some failed when called upon to cover their loans. The big problem was that there was not enough coined money to cover the rapid expansion.

I must express clearly that the First Bank of the United States was named to fool the people that it was an organ of government and as such was to be fully trusted. **(Deception).** As indeed the name 'The Bank of England' was used for the same end, **(Deception).** Of course both were privately owned by the Rothschilds and colleagues and were placed to fulfil the very words of Meyer Amschel Rothschild we have just read. Today the first bank has been renamed the Federal Reserve Bank. Perhaps one in a thousand Americans know it is a private concern, that shows how well the deception worked.

Dr Quigley, in 'Tragedy and Hope' **(58)** shows how the large banking Dynasties led by Rothschild in Europe and later Rockefellers and Morgan in America have joined with an elite band of Merchant Bankers to control world markets. They knew from experience that countries need credit for emergencies and by fulfilling their needs Quigley states that the Democratic leaders became subservient to the bankers demands, allowing the bankers to control political appointments and even deciding political issues **(Hidden power).** Quigley, a believer in the power of the bankers continues; "In time they brought into the financial network the provincial banking centers, organised as commercial banks and saving banks, as well as insurance companies, to form all these into a single financial system on an international scale, which manipulated the quantity and flow of money so that they were able to influence, if not control, governments on one side and industries on the other. The men who do this...aspired to establish dynasties of international bankers and were at least as successful at this as were many of the dynastic political rulers". **(58).**

Quigley goes on to name names and says; "The greatest of these dynasties, of course, were the descendants of Meyer Amschel Rothschild (1743-1812) of Frankfurt, whose male descendants, for at least two generations, generally married first cousins or even nieces. Rothschild's five sons, established at branches in Vienna, London, Naples, and Paris, as well as Frankfurt, co-operated together in ways which other International Banking dynasties copied but rarely excelled...

"The names of some of these banking families are familiar to all of us and should be more so. They include Baring, Lazard Erlanger, Warburg, Shroder, Seligman, The Speyers, Mirabaud, Mallet, Fould and above all Rothschild and Morgan". **(59).**

At this point of learning, it is useful to look back, before the bankers' eclipse of American Democracy, to 1750, the point before the great American Abraham Lincoln, won the civil war between the North and South and established the modern idea of a United States.

When Benjamin Franklin travelled to England to represent the Colonies, he was asked to explain how the Colonies were increasingly prosperous while England, the motherland, was in relative poverty? He replied; "That's simple; in the colonies we issue our own money. It is called colonial scrip. (Money). We issue it in proper proportion to make the products pass easily from the producers to the consumers. In this manner, creating ourselves our own paper money, we control its purchasing power, and we have no interest to pay to no one".

This was the speech that undid the good passage of the future of the United States. The bankers, led by Rothschild, moved to have a law passed by the English Parliament, prohibiting the Colonies from issuing their own money. One year later a frustrated Franklin admitted; "The Colonies would gladly have borne the little tax on tea and other matters had it not been for the poverty caused by the bad influence of the English bankers on the parliament; which has caused in the Colonies hatred of England, and, the revolutionary war".

So, when America won its independence it made a supreme effort to protect itself against what they conceived as their enemy, not England but the bankers who had hijacked them.

The American constitution, signed at Philadelphia in 1787 in article 1, section 8, paragraph 5 states; "Congress shall have power...to coin money and to regulate the value thereof". Thus from the start they set up a defence against the bankers but the bankers were not about to give up. They sent their agent to the foot of power to infiltrate government; his name, Alexander Hamilton. He, with skill and ammunition, advocated a Federal Bank to be owned by private bankers, his masters. He argued for the creation of debt money, tempting politicians with its short term advantage, of achieving the impossible immediately; stating that national debt in reason would be a national advantage. But his trump card was debt money (Loan money) only, issued by private banks, would be acceptable by other nations. This was a banker's lie that they used to lock governments into their debt system.

He began to get support for the bankers, but Thomas Jefferson, the Secretary of State was strongly opposed, but President Washington was seduced by Hamilton's argument and in 1791, a Federal Bank, The Bank of the United States was formed with private bankers owning this deception aimed at the people of America. A deception that still exists today.

But the bank was short lived, only eleven years, thanks to Thomas Jefferson and Andrew Jackson. Still the bankers fought on.

Nathan Rothschild, from England, issued his threat; "Either the application for renewal of the charter is granted, or the United States will find itself in a most dangerous war". Jackson replied; "You are a den of thieves-vipers. I intend to rout you out, and by the eternal God, I will rout you out".

Rothschild issued orders to the British Government; "Teach these impudent Americans a lesson, bring them back to Colonial status". So started the war of 1812 against America.

Under Rothschild's orders thousands of good Americans were killed but what did Nathan care as long as they came to heal. They did in 1816 when the banks charter was renewed.

The next challenge came from Abraham Lincoln who printed, under the original provisions of the constitution 450 million dollars, a debt free issue, known in history as the greenbacks. But still the bankers fought on. Finally in December 1913 the congress voted in the Federal Reserve Act.

Charles A Lindbergh Senior said; "This act establishes the most gigantic trust on earth. When the President signs this bill, the invisible government of the monetary power will be legalised...**the worst legislative crime of the ages, is perpetrated by this banking and currency bill**".

In the words of Louis Even, from this moment on he recalls; **"There is always enough money to make war, but not always enough for working people to make a living wage"**. Yet these Finance Capitalists have falsely set themselves up as the friend and ally of the working class through their false creed. **(Communism-Illuminati, call it what they will, equals 'Deception').**

Ask yourself one simple question, why is money created out of nothing in the hands of the bankers who are profiteers when the nation, which always needs money to run the services such as health, social services and its responsibilities like providing housing has to go cap in hand to bankers to borrow money at usurious rates when it is the currency of the nation in the first place? The answer is simple. The bankers were prepared to do anything to protect their sole right to create money for their own banking interests, for profit at high interest, and that meant that they would kill Presidents or go to war to protect their rights.

On June 1963 John F Kennedy made an attempt to strip the Federal Reserve Bank of its power to create money, at a cost to the US government, under Executive Order No. 11110 he gave his government the power to create and issue money without the consent of the Federal Reserve Bank. This meant Kennedy's order gave the Treasury the power to print silver certificates against silver bullion held at the treasury. By this method Kennedy circulated $4,300,000,000 in notes. The hope and effects of this bill were enormous and heralded a new debt free start for America. By passing this act, Kennedy was well on his way to putting the Federal Reserve Bank out of business. The reason was that The federal reserve notes were backed by nothing while Kennedy's notes were fully backed by silver deposits.

This Executive Order 11110, could, and should, have prevented the National Debt from spiralling to its present level of over six trillion dollars. But unfortunately John F Kennedy was assassinated, perhaps as a future warning to those who would meddle with the bankers domain, who knows? It had its effect; six months later all attempts to change to national creation of money were dropped and the bankers won another war.

You have just read of two events that took place in the sixties. The death of John F Kennedy, which we all remember as if it was yesterday, covered by the whole media. Yet the other, that has had far reaching and disastrous consequences for the people of America has had no publicity, and passed relatively unknown through the body politique. I refer of course to Executive Order 11110; to regain the right for the American people to print their own money. Why can such a far reaching order be unknown by most Americans? Now is the time to study the media to find the answer.

"Permit me to issue and control the money of a nation and I care not who makes its laws".

Meyer Amschel Rothschild. 1790.

THE MEDIA

The words Free Press, applied to our media are a **deception.** No press is free from influence. But unfortunately our press has gone further than just being under the influence of its proprietors, it has fallen into the hands of the International Finance Capitalists who use their association with the power brokers of the Illuminati to censor our press to suite their own agenda; towards a 'New World Order'. But don't take my word for it. Remember Kennedy's effort to bring back money creation to the US government? Ask around if anyone can remember it. Do a bit of your own research in Encyclopaedias. It can be found, but only in what is termed marginalised publications. They are not available through main stream book shops and get no media publicity. They therefore end up with small readership and have a marginalised impact.

As a means of proof that media is owned by the financial elite I have a remarkable statement made by an editor of no less than the 'New York Times', John Swinton. At a banquet given in his honour on his retirement he gave this explosive response to the toast; 'An Independent Press'. This reply tells the full story. **It was meant to be for internal ears only**, but it escaped, thanks to democratic sources.

"What folly is this, toasting an independent press. Everyone present here tonight knows there is no such thing as an independent press. You know it and I know it. There is not one of you who dare to write his honest opinions, and if he did, you know beforehand it will never appear in print. I am paid two hundred and fifty dollars a week to keep my honest opinions out of the papers I am connected with. Others are paid similar salaries for similar work. The business of the journalist is to destroy the truth, to lie outright, to pervert, to vilify, to fawn at the foot of Mammon, and so sell himself, his country and his race for his daily bread. You know this and I know it, and what folly it is to be toasting an Independent Press! We are the tools and vassals of the rich men behind the scenes. We are jumping jacks - They pull the strings and we dance. Our talents, our possibilities and our lives are the property of these men. We are intellectual prostitutes".

That gives us a very good idea where the press stands but is it universal or is it partial? You only have to look back to the sphere of influence of the Rothschilds to see a clearer picture and they are just one merchant bank involved in the Illuminati's drive to World Government; there are over three hundred involved.

They do not control all the media, but because the press depend on advertising especially from multi-nationals to pay the costs for printing their papers, they are in a catch twenty-two situation, as the bankers control the multi-nationals and can apply pressure to stop a paper, if they so wish.

Increasingly the bankers control the media as they have made a point of buying up the important national newspapers all this century. First was Robert Maxwell, who until his death was buying up press and communication media here and in America, funded by the bankers and fully supporting the Illuminati and its path to dictatorship.

Then came Rupert Murdoch, a media mogul from Australia, who boasts that he changes minds. He did in Australia, winning his chosen candidate an election, and when necessary, changing his mind to another candidate, if they did not follow his line.

In the last election he claimed his support for Blair, in the Sun, won Blair the election. It may have gone a long way to doing so but the Tories disarray was the main cause, and, 'who created that out of nothing?' the press of course. We have seen after the election the Labour camp has exactly the same problems; members with something to hide, but the press was selective and assassinated the Conservative party alone. So Blair rode his shining white horse to victory on a tide of selected stories. This is the way the press is used by the International Finance Capitalists and in perfect accord with the doctrine of the Illuminati that control their thinking.

Murdoch's News International is now a problem to all national interests as he now owns a large and specialised section of the world media and seems to have endless finance to keep buying. In England he owns the Times, The Sunday Times, The News of the World, The Sun, and a large selection of lesser titles, Harper Collins is in his group, one of the largest publishers, and television B Sky B. He dominates the media in Australia and is an increasing worry to those who see the danger in his domination in America. He has moved into Europe and is now buying up media in the Middle and Far East, the countries of the Pacific Rim. So where does he get his finance from? You will see his company listed in the Rothschild sphere of influence, one of several sources, all involved in the Bankers drive to World Government.

The power he can yield is immense, he can black news that he considers against the bankers interests. He can promote politicians through ignoring others. His organisation is full of potential dangers to democracy and shows signs of its ability to use it as in our last election.

You may argue that the Sun was hostile to The European Union. I say, that when the time comes it will swing behind Europe and in doing so will seem to be the more genuine **(Deception)**. It is my opinion that a large section of the press today is a deceit.

A classical example of the media's selective handling of news came in 1972 when Professor Sutton gave his testimony to a sub-committee of the Republican convention. Up to this time the media had been at pains to show Russia as a fearful giant in the cold war years leading the world in arms and technical superiority and endangering the balance of power. They led us to believe that the technology, they did not have, they stole, through a superior spy force and that the West was in continual danger from their superior armoury.

What Professor Sutton had to say should have sent shock waves around the world. It was the sort of news that sells print; news editors pray for, and newspapers make a reputation by printing first. But when it was released to the major wire services nothing went to print. Congressman John Schmitz sent it to Associated Press and United Press International, the result was similar only two minor covers printed a small article in each case. James Gibb Stuart, in his book "Hidden Menace to World Peace" **(60)**, who knows all about the media, had this to say; "Those who are new to the subject may find it difficult to accept, at this early stage, that there could be such a thing as a complete media boycott on certain types of news and views--What the author has described as inconvenient knowledge. In the hurly-burly which is normally associated with news gathering and print deadlines, it may seem incredible that anyone should find the time to check and monitor a whole range of sensitive items; that they should bother; and that it could on occasions result in a virtual news blackout on matters of national importance".

On the Sutton testimony he had this to say; "Western peoples have long been encouraged to believe that one of the great virtues of their 'Open' societies is that they have absolute freedom of communication; that a free press exists to provide the public with 'All the news that's fit to print'. It is in fact a lynch-pin of the democratic system, the assurance that through a multiplicity of news outlets we will get a balanced picture of what is happening in the world around us, and thus be in a position to make logical judgements when it comes to choosing political policies and electing governments.....In this case (Sutton's testimony) what were the consequences of domestic public opinion being denied an opportunity to study Professor Sutton's grave allegations that it was mainly American technology which had made a nuclear superpower out of the Soviet Union? For a start, it was still the year 1972, and American soldiers were still being killed in Vietnam, possibly by weaponry which had been helped into existence by courtesy of their own State Department".

On the subject of the media's role in this suppression of vital news, James Gibb Stuart had this to say; "That precious privilege of free speech is still available but to what extent could it ultimately be jeopardised by a censorship which is now so subtle as to be invisible to the non-discerning. A disturbing aspect about the 'Spiking' of the Sutton testimony was that it covered the whole spectrum of publications, whether they be right, left or centre. You might wonder who could create and enforce that degree of unanimity. And having done it once, were they liable to do it again and again and again?"

The book that gives full details of Professor Sutton's evidence, so carefully researched and all verifiable, is 'National Suicide' **(61),** and is well worth reading. But it was a marginalised book so its important message was not aired satisfactorily.

The year 1976 is a landmark in the history of press censorship. It ended the career of one of Britain's top investigative journalists, Gordon Tether, a financial Times reporter, who probed deeply into the Bilderberg Conferences of top level bankers, civil servants, politicians and military personnel. He posed the question that if they were acting within democratic bounds secrecy was unnecessary. But it continues to be secret today and is a secret planning group behind world government, financed by the bankers. But more about that in chapter sixteen.

In chapter seven we will go further into the methods used by the media and controlled by the bankers. I will show how the media subtly angles its news to influence and control our minds and I will cite some important examples of mind influence or auto suggestion carried on by even the BBC.

In closing this chapter we have started to realise the media is not our 'Knight in shining armour' that the system would have us believe. I have shown you how the media chooses the news it wishes to show you and withholds other news that gives a more balanced picture. You have also seen that they sack journalists who speak out of line. There are many examples.

The media is fast becoming the property of the bankers and comes under their control financially as well as politically. It moves, year by year, into fewer hands, closing the gap where news, contrary to their wish can escape.

At this point it is appropriate to remember the words in the Protocols that say if various press articles appear between papers that disagree they will still control both sources, as it is good to show the press as free agents **(Deception).**

The important matter to bear in mind is that as these bankers control the press; it is not free, and they can at any time clamp down on media divergence, to suit their path to dictatorship. This gradual creeping control of our media Television, Radio,

Press and publications has happened over a century and its subtle introduction is not easy to detect unless you know their devious ways. I hope I have fired your interest enough to watch and observe because we hold the key to democracy by openness and numbers. Our job, yours and mine, is to seek out and expose any secrecy.

> "Not a single announcement will reach the public without our control. Even now this is already being attained by us inasmuch as all the news items are received by a few agencies, in whose offices they are focused from all parts of the world...We shall have a sure triumph over our opponents since they will not have at their disposition organs of the press in which they can give full and final expression of their views..."
>
> **From Protocol Twelve. On the Media.**

PROTOCOL SIX

We shall soon begin to establish huge monopolies, reservoirs of colossal riches, upon which even large fortunes of the goyim will depend to such an extent that they will go to the bottom together with the credit of the States on the day after the political smash....

You gentlemen here present who are economists, just imagine the significance of this combination!....

In every possible way we must develop the significance of our Super-Government by representing it as the protector and benefactor of all those who voluntarily submit to us.

The aristocracy of the goyim as a political force, is dead--we need not take it into account; but as landed proprietors they can still be harmful to us since as such they are self-sufficient. It is essential therefore for us at whatever cost to deprive them of their land. This object will be best attained by increasing the burdens upon landed property--in loading lands with debts. These measures will check land-holding and keep it in a state of humble and unconditional submission.

The aristocrats of the goyim, being hereditarily incapable of contenting themselves with little, will rapidly burn up and fizzle out.

At the same time we must intensively patronise trade and industry, but, first and foremost, speculation, whose part is to provide a counterpoise to industry: the absence of speculative industry will multiply capital in private hands and will serve to restore agriculture by freeing the land from indebtedness to the land banks. We want industry to drain off from the land both labour and capital and by means of speculation transfer into our hands all the money of the world, and thereby throw all the goyim into the ranks of the proletariat. Then the goyim will bow down before us, if for no other reason but to get the right to exist.

To completely ruin the industry of the goyim we shall bring to the assistance of speculation the luxury which we have developed among the goyim, that greedy demand for luxury which is swallowing up everything. **We shall raise the rate of wages which, however, will not bring any advantage to the workers, for, at the same time, we shall produce a rise in prices of the first necessaries of life alleging that it arises from the decline of agriculture and cattle-breeding; we shall further undermine sources of production, artfully and deeply by accustoming the workers to anarchy and to drunkenness, and side by side therewith taking all measures to extirpate from the face of the earth all the educated forces of the goyim.**

In order that the true meaning of things may not strike the goyim before the proper time we shall mask it under an alleged ardent desire to serve the working classes and the great principles of political economy about which our economic theories are carrying on an energetic propaganda.

PROTOCOL EIGHT

We must arm ourselves with all the weapons which our opponents might employ against us.

We must search out the very finest shades of expression and knotty points in the lexicon of legal justification for those cases where we shall have to pronounce judgements that might appear abnormally audacious and unjust, for it is important that these resolutions should be set forth in expressions that shall seem to be the most exalted moral principles cast into legal form. Our directorate must surround itself with all these forces of civilisation among which it will have to work.

It will surround itself with publicists, practical jurists, administrators, diplomats and finally, with persons prepared by a special super-educational training in our special schools. These persons will have cognisance of all the secrets of the social structure, they will know all the languages that can be made up by political alphabets and words; they will be made acquainted with the whole underside of human nature, with all its sensitive chords on which they will have to play. These chords are the cast of mind of the goyim, their tendencies, shortcomings, vices and qualities, the particularities of classes and conditions. Needless to say that the talented assistants of authority, of whom I speak, will not be taken from among the goyim, who are accustomed to perform their administrative work without giving themselves the trouble to think what its aim is, and never consider what it is needed for. The administrators of the goyim sign papers without reading them, and they serve either for mercenary reasons or for ambition.

We shall surround our government with a whole world of economists. That is the reason why economic sciences form the principle subject of the teaching given to the Jews. Around us again will be a whole constellation of bankers, industrialists, capitalists and--the main thing--millionaires, because in substance everything will be settled by the question of figures.

For a time, until there will no longer be any risk in entrusting responsible posts in our States to our brother Jews, we shall put them in the hands of persons whose past and reputation are such that between them and the people lies an abyss, persons who, if they disobey our instructions, must face criminal charges or disappear - this in order to make them defend our interests to their last gasp.

COMMENT

In Protocol six they state that they will monopolise the world finance to such an extent that on the day of 'Political Smash' we will go down together with all States (That refers to all States carrying a debt burden).

They claim the Aristocracy is dead as indeed it nearly is, but they fear continual power from landowners. So their solution is land tax and death duties, both of which have crippled landowners. So why are they scared of landowners? Because they can be self sufficient.

They admit to encouraging speculative industry as money ends up in their hands. Whereas if industry is stable, money goes back to restore agriculture. They want industry to drain both labour and capital from the land and into their hands so they get absolute control. So what they are saying is that they have planned the demise of agriculture. (Is the BSE crises part of their plan?). It is obvious to us all, that they are succeeding in ruining Britain's agriculture and particularly our beef trade; once it was one of our large exports; now nothing. I will be covering the subject in chapter seven.

Then we see their reasoning. They will increase wages but at the same time food will rise, wiping out the gain, and they will use the decline of agriculture and beef as the reason. They will encourage drunkenness, and lower educational standards to the top achievers. We have seen this programme unwrapping itself in the last twenty years and yet another prediction comes true. Then they state they will hide their aims from us by propaganda. **(Deception and diversion).**

Protocol eight is a description of their house keeping.

CHAPTER FIVE
PART ONE.
THE ILLUMINATI AND FREEMASONRY.

Now we must study the Illuminati under a magnifying glass. To do so I will repeat some points from chapter two. This chapter is very important in understanding the Illuminati and where they stand today. It also shows how Karl (Levi) Marx joined the Illuminati and developed Marxism as a practical programme towards world order. (Government).

Adam Weishaupt was born on February 6th. 1748. Although his parents were Jewish, (Refer to Rakovsky's interview Page 108) his father converted to Catholicism and he was brought up in a Jesuit seminary. The Jesuit order was very strict and although he attained his intellectual superiority from his education, it left him with a distinct hatred of Jesuits and a desire to get even with his Jesuit educators, and he absorbed the writings of the French philosophers who were both anti-Christian and subversive.

He spent five years absorbing Satanism and subversion while planning his grand policy to overthrow the established society in the world and replace it with what he called 'Novus Ordo Seclorum', (New World Order). It is no coincidence that today this Latin statement appears on the back of a dollar note with the Satanic eye of Lucifer staring out. I will deal with that later.

At this time Germany, and particularly the scholars were searching for new ideas to change what they perceived as an elitist society, totally corrupted by power and wealth with monarchy and the church as its twin pillars of corruption.

Germany was the classroom of philosophy because it had a freedom of expression banned by the church in most of the other countries. This is undoubtedly why philosophy led revolution stemmed from middle class Germany and, two philosophers above all succeeded; Adam Weishaupt and Karl (Levi) Marx. They were both of Jewish descent, both Atheists, and both arrogantly sure of the superiority of their own minds.

We are in the age of Rationalism, an age where every philosopher searched for the right way forward through the biblical and historical myths of the time. Waiting for them in timeless leisure was their inspiration, Satan. He had failed miserably in the Dark Ages to influence man in his ways but knew man would succumb if he planted the right fruits in his path. What Satan did not realise was that there were one or two people around who were just as evil.

In front of our two despots could clearly be seen the Church that had been destroyed by human depravity. They assumed this human corruption was a sign that the teachings of the bible were wrong. What they had observed was Satan's hand at work who had corrupted man and man's stewardship of the Church; with the complications of their mind they could not see this simple truth. Hurst's **(62)** shows; "Rationalists openly attack all established beliefs with a deep seated conviction that all religions were false". What they did not discriminate between was the True Christianity and Pagan look-a-likes. They came to the conclusion that there was no God and that "The only god of man was man himself". **(63).**

I could go on quoting endless examples; suffice it to say that the point was well covered. Therefore by the second half of the eighteenth century all students of philosophy were weaned on a false premise, that Christianity was a lie and realism was an open book, without words, to be filled with their thoughts.

So after five years meditation Weishaupt, now a professor of Canon Law at Ingolstadt University in Bavaria, started the secret society of the Illuminati. His aim was to capture the minds of the intelligentsia that gathered in the Masonic lodges and coffee houses of Europe and use his secret formula, designed to be compatible with Masonic Enlightenment to entrap them as his tools to capture the world by infiltrating power behind government. That he knew that this was where real power lay, was to his credit.

Weishaupt's plan was so attractive to the young intellectuals and indeed more mature professors that quickly he gathered his first disciples, some two thousand, to go to all Masonic lodges that would adopt his rites and spread his message of male emancipation as his own God at peace with himself and the world. He named himself Sparticus.

Because, some eight years later, the Bavarian Elector had the Illuminati banned, the foolish think it was no longer a problem or a threat to the world. This was and is today, a serious misjudgement of resourcefulness of the Illuminati, to be able to change like a chameleon, to deceive all that behold them with their simple message of Illumination behind which, to this day, hides a Satanic plan to dominate the World, by dictatorship. Two books that prove the Simon Magus followers (Satan) have joined the Illuminati at the top level were written by the Reverend Arriaga PnD, a Mexican Priest. **(64).**

The name Illuminati comes from the bible **(65)** meaning 'the bearers of light', a deception. From this Weishaupt interpreted it as 'Brilliance' which exactly explains the heart of his plan to use the top brains of the world to fulfil his plan of world domination. As a University professor it is not surprising that he chose the bankers of Frankfurt as his means to finance his end. His motto 'Novus Ordo Seclorum' (New World Order) is also found in every American pocket today, printed on the dollar note and is the final ambition of the United Nations. On the dollar note it is no coincidence that it appears in pride of place with Lucifer's eye looking out from the split top of the pyramid surrounded by light, the Illumination. It shows clearly where America stands; totally controlled by the modern Illuminati which now comes under many names, some of which I will deal with later.

It is, thanks to a man named Lanze, that the plans of Illuminati are known today. He was a courier, working for the Illuminati, who was unlucky enough to be struck by lightening in Regensburg while riding to Paris from Frankfurt with documents sent by the Illuminati to the Grand Master of the Grand Orient Masonic Order led by the Duke of Orleans. These papers exposed the plan for a revolution and the Bavarian Elector immediately sent copies of the documents to all governments affected, including Paris, which the French government chose to ignore. He also prescribed the Illuminati.

A short four years later the consequences of this folly by the French authority became too clear when the Illuminati, well established in two-hundred and sixty-six lodges of the Grand Orient led the French Revolution and won. It is interesting to note that Sir Walter Scott said in his book on Napoleon Bonaparte; "Quite clearly that the events leading up to the French Revolution were all created by the money Barons in the Illuminati".

The book that gives us the fullest picture possible of the inside workings of the Illuminati is 'Proofs of Conspiracy' **(66)** by John Robison AM., a professor at Edinburgh University, a Mason himself, invited by Weishaupt to join the Illuminati and one of the few outsiders who saw the whole plan. His book is of the greatest importance in understanding the Illuminati; how they linked with Freemasonry all over the world and how, today, what happened two-hundred years ago threatens our very survival. Only the power of true religion or the evil power of Satan could outlive its founder's life. It is easy to blow this thought away by saying the Illuminati died in 1785 when Bavaria banned it. But we have already heard Weishaupt's response to that possibility. He would rise again bigger and better than ever. This was no idle threat; he did; as the French Revolution of 1789 and Bolshevik revolution of 1917 bear testimony. So because we cannot see his name in neon lights today, it does not mean he is not amongst us. Let us take a quick look again at the composition of the Illuminati. Group one is the Minervals, the apprentice Illuminati, keen to learn the secrets of Illumination. They were the ones, who, without knowing the dreadful purpose of the secret society, would promote it round the world and capture the intelligent thinkers from Universities and Colleges.

The second level was for existing Freemasons and Scottish Knights, mostly members of the lodges they Illuminated. The third level consisted of two grades of Priest and Regent, and the final upper level of Magus and King. Magus being recognition of Satan's' disciple, Simon Magus, and the Guardians of the Illuminati.

It was only from Priest level that they knew the true aim of Illumination; to abolish religion and create a 'World Order' through dictatorship. The first group were fed the good news, that they wished, to make of the human race, without any distinction of nation, condition, or profession, one good and happy family".

As usual under Masonry, they all swear an oath to remain silent and adopt a singular loyalty to the cause **(67)**. The threat of death is used to hold initiates to silence **(68)**. Only when he reached the inner circle would he learn the seven point plan to world domination (See page 62, chapter 2).

On page 64. of 'Proofs of Conspiracy' **(69)** Professor Robison discloses Weishaupt's plan to take Christians into his order and gradually wean them off religion by promises and trickery. Weishaupt in a letter to Cato (One of his disciples) said "The most admirable thing of all is that great Protestants and Reform Theologians who belong to our order really believe they see in it the true and genuine mind of Christian Religion. Oh man, what can not you be brought to believe". **(70)**.

His whole plan is built on deceit and today many innocent people do his bidding without even knowing of his society because his control of education has been around so long it has perverted our whole system of learning. (See chapter nine).

Masonry gave the Illuminati a safe haven to disappear into when the going got hot. This was demonstrated in Germany in 1785 when it was banned only to re-appear as Reading Unions throughout Germany.

Weishaupt was a con-man par excellence; a man who used deceit and a hall of mirrors to mesmerise his graduates. Through deceit, he hid the real agenda, an agenda no person in their right mind would accept. It was Protestant Princes who introduced Weishaupt to the Masonic order, which was his passport to rapid expansion throughout the world. In him they saw their chance to destroy the Catholic Church.

In 1782 at the Masonic Congress at Wilhelmsbad the knot was tied between the Masonic order and the Illuminati, linking over three million Masons to Weishaupt and his Satanic plan for world domination.

A Mason who attended the meeting was later to refuse to tell what was planned at the meeting as his oath would not allow him to speak; however the Comte de Vireu, when asked about the meeting said; "I will not confide them to you. I can only tell you that this is very much more serious than you think. The conspiracy that has been woven is so well thought out that it will be, so to speak, impossible for the Monarchy and the Church to escape from it". **(71).** After this meeting the Comte spoke of Masonry as evil.

In the next few years the Jewish population began to be accepted and one of the first movements to welcome them was Masonry, who lifted the ban. At this time the Illuminati headquarters moved to Frankfurt to attract the finance needed by Weishaupt for his rapidly growing organisation. It was at this point the Jewish bankers of Frankfurt were seduced by the message of the Illuminati and joined the lodge that promoted the Illuminati. Rothschild was the main spokesman for the group of Jewish bankers and became involved with Weishaupt to the extent of financing him to produce a plan for a world government. (See Rakovsky interview page108, 'The World and Europe'. Also Deidre Manifold, 'Towards World Government' page 3.). **(82).**

At this moment Weishaupt's plans for the French Revolution were exposed when his courier was killed by lightening on his way to Paris and the Duke of Orleans.

This led to the apparent demise of the Illuminati in Germany; so it hid behind Masonry while Weishaupt retired to the estate of the Duke of Saxe-Gotha, his friend and benefactor.

From there he put the final touches to his plan for a revolution in France and encouraged people to think that the Illuminati was dead, which is almost chapter and verse from his statement in Robison's book **(72)** which says; "The great strength of our order lies in its concealment; never let it appear in any place in its own name, but always covered by another name, and another occupation". This is 'Deception'. It is interesting to note at this point that the lie of disbanding the Illuminati has been adhered to by historians ever since. It is this amazing power over intellectuals that still exists today and has been handed down through academics ever since.

Well we know his initiates won the French Revolution in 1789, their first major success, now let us see who the Illuminati, under any other name, targeted next.

For this we must first turn to America. The Illuminati arrived too late to effect the outcome of the American Revolution, but not too late to establish themselves behind government and, therefore to expand their hold from the early period when administration was new, inexperienced and willing to explore new ideas. Before the states or colonies were brought together as a federation of states with a written constitution the Illuminati had fifteen lodges under its control. The Colombian Lodge in New York was established in 1785 and prominent politicians such as De Witt Clinton, Horace Greeley and later Clinton Roosevelt were members. Virginia saw another Lodge a year later with non other than Thomas Jefferson as a member. It was Jefferson who came to Weishaupt's defence when he was exposed in Germany and branded a revolutionary.

It is interesting to note that while the Illuminati were trying to establish a foothold in America, academics were warning America of its danger; David Pappen, President of Harvard University and Timothy Dwight, President of Yale.

The Illuminati's activities had also come to the attention of George Washington by 1796, and in his farewell address he warned the nation to take care not to get too involved with the 'Foreign world'.

In a plea to his people he said; "---the jealousy of a free people ought to be constantly awake, since history and experience prove that foreign influence is one of the most baneful foes to Republican government---".

Unfortunately the Federation of America did not heed its founder's words too well; Weishaupt's corruptive Illuminati under many different names grew rapidly and prospered.

In 1796 John Adams, a mason himself but outside Illumination, opposed Thomas Jefferson for the Presidency. It was too soon for the Illuminati to win but they were always busy infiltrating the seats of learning, establishing their men in behind the seats of power and multiplying their supporters. They always used other names to channel their deceitful propaganda through to pervert the minds of the people.

As the Illuminati virtually disappeared; to follow their path you only have to look for other groups with new names that preach the same creed for destroying religion and Sovereignty while promoting a New World Order and there they are.

Although very little seemed to happen till the second quarter of the nineteenth century, the Illuminati were busy at work in the lapse, building their organisation and infiltrating especially the Universities, even though warning from within these establishments had been clearly given.

By 1829 they laid on a lecture tour by Fanny Wright, a English woman and member of the Illuminati. She toured America preaching equal rights, equal opportunity, Emancipation, atheism, Communism (In the early guise) and free love; a hotchpotch of Illumination and destabilisation. This started the first move to link the Atheists and Nihilists and Subversives into a organisation under Communism. Clinton Roosevelt became its supremo and immediately identified his cause with the working class; a complete mirror to hide his agenda behind. In his book, **(73)** Clinton Roosevelt cannot hide the power of the Illuminati which influences his every word and controls his last thoughts.

In 1830 Adam Weishaupt died and in his death he tried to deceive the world that he repented his sins by re-joining the Catholic Church. It was his final act in a life of **deception.**

In 1834, Giuseppe Mazzini, a Guardian and an evil revolutionary from Italy took over as the Director of World Revolution within the loose collection of Illuminati groups around the world.

At the same time Mordecai Marx Levy, joined a branch of the Illuminati named 'The League of the Just'. Mr Levy, of Jewish parentage, later changed his name to Karl Marx. As an unemployed Philosopher he was hired by the bankers of Frankfurt to write the Communist Manifesto, for their New World Order. What he actually came up with was a re-write of Weishaupt's plan. It was, to the interested bystander, a document with nothing new to offer, using ideas from Hegel and other philosophers and combining them in a document that spelt out the Illuminati's seven points of policy. **For twenty years or more it didn't even use the name of its author as the recognised source.**

Meanwhile Mazzini had appointed a new Supremo for America, one General Albert Pike. Pike was borne on 29th. of December 1809 and his education ended at Harvard. He was an evil genius, speaking sixteen languages, mostly ancient, of superior intelligence and an openly acknowledged worshipper of Lucifer. He joined the army and became Brigadier General while serving in the Civil War on the side of the Confederacy. He brought together an army of savages from the Red Indian tribes and set upon a course of despotic barbarity to such a degree that England nearly intervened to halt his lust for carnage.

Pike was the Sovereign Grand Commander of the ancient and accepted Scottish rite of Freemasonry. At this time Mazzini approached him with his simple plan.

Mazzini realised that to attract other Masonic lodges with their own Masonic rites, he must not interfere in their established practices that had been built up during the past history of the Masonic movement. His idea was to create a secret super rite above the three main rites which would remain unknown. To enter these higher rites would be by invitation only and it would be named the Higher Degree. From this Mazzini aimed to control all Freemasonry. **(74)**. He adopted Weishaupt's name, Sparticus).

Pike re-organised 'The Illuminated' part of Masonry under the name, The New and Reformed Palladian Rite; establishing three supreme councils, one in Charleston NC, his own state, the second in Berlin, Germany; and the third in Rome, Italy.

Historians have confirmed this marriage of Illumination to Freemasonry. Dr. Bataille confirms, "This super rite, which is Masonic Luciferian Spiritism, must not be confused with the machinery of High Masonry. Palladianism is the cult of Satan (Lucifer) in the inner shrines of a rite superimposed on all the rites. It is a cult, a religion". **(75)**.

As final proof of Pike's commitment to Lucifer (Satan), in his instructions issued on July 14th. 1889 to the now twenty three supreme councils of the world (grown from three) he states, "That which we say to the crowd is, 'We worship God, but it is the God one adores without superstitions'. To you Sovereign Grand Instructors General, we say this, that you may repeat it to the brethren of the 32nd., 31st., and 30th. degrees. The Masonic religion should be, by all of us initiates of high degrees, maintained in the purity of the Luciferian doctrine". **(76)**.

The problem, for the world to recognise the evil events of this secret society, is because of its hidden agenda. Hidden behind an old and established, albeit quaintly secret, order of Masonry. By adding the higher degrees onto Masonry, the Illuminati hide behind an already hidden society. Today it is the action of the 33rd. degree and above we must fear. The Protocols of the Elders of Zion was signed by the representatives of Zion of the 33rd. degree. The proof just shown should make us all fearful for our future wherever we are in the world. Secrecy means that there is something to hide. Masonry would have us believe it is harmless fun for their members. This frightening proof shows a very different side to the story.

In England today the Masonic movement claims it is not a secret society but a society with secrets. I must ask why then do Masons in general believe there are only three degrees in their lodge? They seem to know nothing of the 4th. to the 33rd. degree which has a separate headquarters as proof of its secrecy. The 4th. to the 33rd. degree have their headquarters at 10, Saint James, London. In this building the supreme council resides. This behaves and acts as a society within a society and it is totally secret. Members are obtained by invitation only and high ranking Civil Servants, wealthy business men, bankers and top members of our military services are included in their list of members. To Masons in the know this building is known as the 'The Grand East'. Within the building a room is named The Chamber of Death'.

The Supreme Council, the head of British Masonry, bears an uncanny resemblance in name to Pike's 23 Supreme councils of the world. Was this one of the 23 councils he referred to in his address? If so the link with British Masonry is complete and far from being harmless business men, seeking relaxation they could well, behind their closed doors, be planning our total fall from democracy. Can we afford to give them the benefit of the doubt? I think not.

The British Museum has a letter from Pike to Mazzini outlining their plan to conquer the world. It includes three World Wars. That makes one to go. The third is when the Nihilists and Atheists take part in the conflict and the world will fight to destroy these revolutionaries and when they succeed they will be ungoverned and ready to be Illuminated, having destroyed both Atheism and Christianity.

"The only statement I care to make about the Protocols is that they fit in with what is going on. They are sixteen years old and they have fitted the world situation up to this time. They fit it now.

Henry Ford, in the New York World, February 17th, 1921.

CHAPTER FIVE, PART TWO.
ILLUMINATION + EDUCATION = CONTROL

It is difficult for anyone to understand how an operation such as the Illuminati could have had such a devastating effect on the world with only a few thousand followers. The secret to their success is firstly that everything they do is secret; a hidden agenda. Hidden even from their own followers. Secondly, and the key to their success, was Weishaupt's recognition of the necessity to control both Education and the Media. The reason that their control of Education is not generally recognised today is because they control the Media and the literary world and if anyone steps outside their permitted boundaries they are immediately marginalised. To put it bluntly they censor the output of all the media to protect their secrets. This means everything they do can be, and is hidden, except some courageous journalists and writers, who have ignored their power to bring you the truth, and have published. The problem is that they cannot get normal distribution and normal press coverage; both essential to selling the quantities that are required to inform the people.

So Weishaupt set about his plan to control thinking at Universities in Europe, America and England. We have already seen how he approached Professor Robison, a man of world renown, but failed to inspire him with his plan. Robison published his book before the media was bought out by the bankers. It remains the heart of the case against Weishaupt's policy.

Lady Queenborough clearly shows the importance of the educated mind, "A mind that is positive cannot be controlled. For the purpose of the occult's dominion, minds must therefore be rendered passive and negative in order that control may be achieved. Minds consciously working to a definite end are a power, and power can oppose power for good or evil. The scheme for world dominion might be doomed by recognition of this principle alone, but, as it is unfortunately unrecognised, it remains unchallenged". (Agenda hidden by censorship). **(77)**.

It was the cream of University thinking that Weishaupt, in Germany and Albert Pike, in America, targeted. Carroll Quigley, author of 'Tragedy and Hope', openly admits he was a member of the Elite Illuminated Intelligentsia and as an insider saw how the conspiracy grew and took over the education system in America. He also shows how it crept into the English education system first at the top level, for example John Ruskin at Oxford University. In his book (Quigley) 'Tragedy and Hope', he states; "Until 1870 there was no professorship of fine art at Oxford, but in that year, thanks to a Slade bequest, John Ruskin was named to such a chair. He hit Oxford like an earthquake, not so much because he talked of fine arts, but because he also talked about the Empire and England's downtrodden masses, and above all because he talked about all three of these things as moral issues". **(78)**.

Whether or not Ruskin had been Illuminated he was saying exactly what Weishaupt would have said if he had been alive in 1870. He built up a Utopia for the privileged undergraduates of Oxford to aim their sights at, and sent them out into the world to accomplish his vision of a world ruled by the elite and privileged students under his spell. (Pure Illumination).

"He told them (his students) that they were the possessors of a magnificent tradition of education, beauty, rule of law, freedom, decency, and self-discipline; but this tradition could not be saved, and did not deserve to be saved, unless it could be extended to the lower classes of England itself and to the non-English masses through the world". **(79)**.

He goes on to say that if knowledge was not extended to the working classes and the majority in the world, the upper class English man would be submerged by the majorities and lost for ever.

This challenge to Ruskin's Illuminated students found its takers all from privileged families. One such student was non other than Cecil Rhodes, who kept a copy of Ruskin's lecture in his wallet for the rest of his life, reading it for inspiration (Illumination, just like a drug). Most of us know a little about Cecil Rhodes but not enough. The BBC programme on 'The Life of Cecil Rhodes', controlled by the bankers, was far from accurate and left out all connection with the Illuminati. This is not surprising as it has been written out of history. Rhodes' energy was boundless. For his business he raided South Africa, taking over the gold and diamond deposits, monopolising the diamond and gold mines, naming his company De Beers Consolidated Mines for diamonds and Consolidated Goldfields, for gold. We find behind this successful man finance from Lord Rothschild and his colleague Albert Beit. Rhodes became Prime Minister of Cape Colony 1890-1896 and controlled politicians in South Africa and back home in England, enabling him to push forward his highly controversial plans for South Africa.

In his mind, programmed by Ruskin, and encouraged by Rothschild, was his desire to make a Grand Federal body to control and govern the English speaking people and to eventually incorporate the whole world into his federation. To this end he spent his considerable fortune in accordance with plans laid in his mind by Ruskin. It is from this you learn the danger of influenced teaching when the influence is evil. To guarantee the future after his death he set up two important safeguards that his life's work would continue. He formed a Rhodes scholarship to develop Ruskin's influence and insure that his work continued towards a 'New World Government'. (Illumination under another name. (Direction). Between Ruskin and the Rhodes Scholarship at Oxford, the world today has been infiltrated by Illuminated scholars, the power of whom cannot be underestimated.

The second safeguard to the continuance of Rhodes' work started on February 5th. 1891 when Rhodes' group of Ruskin trained graduates joined a group from Cambridge University led by William Stead, and from it was formed a Secret Society along Weishaupt's lines containing a outer circle named 'The Association of Helpers'. Among Ruskin's disciples we find such names as Arnold Toynbee, Alfred (Lord) Milner, Arthur Glazebrook, George (Later Sir George) Parkin, Philip Littleton Gell and Henry (Later Sir Henry) Birchenough. The Cambridge group contained Reginald Baliol Brett (Lord Esher), Sir John B Seely, Albert (Lord Grey) and Edmund Garrett. All these graduates devoted their lives to Ruskin's dream.

Quigley goes on to show how these graduates and others became the movers and shakers of Imperialism. They formed a secret society of which Rhodes was leader (for a short time till he died). Stead, Brett (Lord Esher) and Milner (Lord) formed the executive, while Lord Rothschild, Arthur (Lord) Balfour, Lord Grey and others were listed as potential members of a circle of Initiates. The other group already mentioned 'The Association of Helpers', later became known as 'the Round Table Organisation'. This was founded by Lord Milner, as a tribute to Rhodes, in 1910 and until 1913 he was busy forming groups in British Dependencies and America. The Round Table was largely supported by Sir Abe Bailey's funds and Rhodes bequests. By this time this group was having a large and increasing influence on England's foreign policy. In 1919 they founded the 'Royal Institute of International Affairs' (Chatham House), supported financially by Sir Abe Bailey and the Astor Family. (Owners of, 'The Times').

Following on from this, in 1925 the Institute of Pacific Affairs was launched and covered twelve countries in the Pacific linking up with the Round Table and the Institute of International Affairs. Meanwhile a parallel group was set up in 1884, again inspired by Ruskin's ideas to bring education to the poor and began as the Settlement House, with Toynbee, Milner, Gell, Grey, Seely and Michael Glazebrook. They lived in the slums of the East End to educate the working class. Toynbee died a year before it opened but Toynbee Hall was named in his honour. From this they developed the modern Adult Education system and the Extension of University Education. This was on the surface a wonderful move but they infiltrated it with their Illuminated teachers.

Milner, as Governor General of South Africa employed a group of young men from Oxford University and Toynbee Hall to assist his administration known as the Milner Kindergarten. It was these recruits who spread out to organise the Round Table.

This whole group was Illuminated through Ruskin but I have to say the probability is that they knew little if anything about Weishaupt or the Illuminati. It had now been passed on by other names but, behind the honourable motives that they displayed publicly, hid the evil intentions of Weishaupt, Mazzini and Pike, unknown to Rhodes and Ruskin's band of Disciples.

Today, if you confronted any member of the Round Table with these facts of history, they would quite honestly say, "Its absolute nonsense. We are a group of privileged business men brought together to do charity". Most Masons would say the same. Yet lurking behind their main body, a few leaders direct their agenda with evil intent to drive the world to global dictatorship.

Most developed states have a council dedicated to driving their country towards global government. In England, the Royal Institute of International Affairs is the centre of Illuminati and they are funded by International bankers. In America, its equivalent, the Council On Foreign Relations, almost totally governs America's foreign policy with influence stretching into the United Nations, The Bilderberg Committee and the Trilateral Commission. All with a strong banker influence.

The Institute for Pacific Affairs controls most of Asia and most European nations have equivalent councils.

This brings us near to a full picture of the power house that has built up from the Illuminati of Weishaupt and penetrated our bastions of power to influence and pervert its direction, succeeding because it has been done secretly through education. The media, meant to be our protector against such plans, is owned by the International bankers behind Weishaupt's plan so they will not expose the plotters but are used to divert our attention away from their progress. So they continue to proceed towards their greedy goal. There is one thing certain, the power and influence gathered together by Ruskin and built on by Rhodes and Milner is immense and has in its wake brainwashed several generations of students towards their goal; students who have never heard of Weishaupt.

I will deal more thoroughly with several of the components later in the book.

This brings us right up to today in this section of the major plan for world government, but this is only one tentacle of the octopus of Illumination. Next we study Communism.

CHAPTER FIVE, PART THREE.

MARX. A TOTAL FAILURE? COMMUNISM A WORLD OF MIRRORS.

When we think of Karl Marx our mind automatically turns to Communism. Strangely this is not because Karl Marx was a genius but solely because the Illuminati used Marx and built his image in the minds of the people as the Father of Communism to hide their attempt to dress up their revolution under any other name. Remember Weishaupt's remark about hiding behind names.

Karl Marx was in his entire life a complete domestic failure. A failure in his work brought about by his obsessive jealousy of his associates and their success and because of his highly debatable conclusions which were never completely thought through and because he always came across evidence to disprove them. He produced policies that went nowhere. He championed the working class but in the main they rejected him and his violent changes out of instinct, and apart from a few disciples he never fired the imagination of enough people to make his policies relevant. If the Illuminati and their backer, the Rothschilds, had not wished it to continue it would be dead and buried today.

In his personal life he was no more successful. Most of his life, he lived off the goodwill of his friends, especially his friend Engel, who sent him money throughout their friendship. His wife had six children, all of whom lived in abject poverty and because of the lack of food and poor living conditions, three died of starvation and two more committed suicide. On his death in 1883 only six people attended his funeral.

In his life, we know that he wrote the Communist Manifesto in 1848 but this was by request from above. It was Baron Lionel Rothschild who paid Marx to establish a policy to take over the world. (New World Order). It was the Communist Manifesto that he wrote for Rothschild, and his name did not appear on the document for over twenty years. He just followed his paymasters' request and based his policy document on the seven pillars of the Illuminati.(page 60) We have already learned that Marx was a member of 'The League of the Just' an illuminated secret society.

In Rakovsky's exposure of the power behind the Bolshevik Revolution he named the ruling elite at that time; the Bank Kuhn Loeb and Company, the Schiff's, the Warburg's and the group of Eastern bankers Baruch, Lippmann and Rothschild.

They led the Finance International. In 1864 Marx founded the first International Working Mans Association (re-named Socialist International). It broke up through feuding caused by Marx and was re-named and moved to New York and merged with the Socialist Party in 1868. The second Socialist International (Funded by Rothschild) was founded in Paris on July 14th. 1889. It was controlled by Labour Unions because the working class had little interest since the collapse of the First International. So behind Communism even at this early stage was an enormously powerful group of Bankers intent on subversive activity that might lead to war. (Their aim). It had a four fold effect for them. It brought them great financial gain from war, interest from financing the aftermath, enormous gains through the arms trade that they controlled, and the secret agenda which was to weaken Nations in readiness for their Weishaupt style take-over. Their aim; government with ultimate control of all resources.

So now we begin to see Communism as a mirror hiding from view the real intent of revolution. A convenient mirror to attract all the venom of Western Capitalism and act as an item of hate and potential war for the western world to concentrate its defence upon, which again had beneficial effects for the bankers. It boosted the arms industry, making the super rich richer still, and occupying the West in a fruitless spiral of defence expense.

So Communism turns out to be a false reflection of what the Media, in the bankers sphere of influence, has claimed to be the evil of our time. I suggest you reflect on this as the conclusion is that our media has consistently lied to us all this Century. It is in fact the International Finance Capitalists who are the world's true enemy, hiding behind the hall of mirrors, having created and financed every war this Century, and created endless money crises all over the world for their financial gain, leaving the people of the world in relative poverty.

In 1905 the Bolsheviks led a uprising planned by the Intelligentsia of the Illuminati, funded by the international bankers, including Warburg and Rothschild.

Lenin led the uprising. Leon Trotsky was a young man at the time, but as if from nowhere he became the leading figure at Petrograd, eclipsing Lenin. The reason was his association with the bankers. He had married Sedova, whose family was associated with the Warburg's, and Jacob Schiff, the funders of the uprising. But it failed to shake the Tsar's guards, and Lenin escaped to France.

However this did not stop them planning. The Tsar was being undermined by Rasputin in league with the Tsarina so his profile was becoming exposed. Nine years later a shot was fired killing the Arch Duke Ferdinand and the blame was placed on Trotsky and his financiers. It started World War One, predicted in the 'Protocols of the Elders of Zion'.

In 1917 Lenin, Trotsky and the Bolsheviks came back this time to capture Russia from the Imperial Guard and brutally murder the Tsar and his family. But Russia was a massive territory and it did not all fall to the mirror, Communism. It took seven years to stabilise the country by which time the people would have gladly helped another revolution to rid themselves of their suppressers. But no one came forward to their aid in their time of need. However Lenin died and Stalin snatched power, leaving the bankers in a state of animated limbo. He was not their man at this point. So then began their big flirtation to win him over but in the meantime Stalin suppressed his people, purged the Bolsheviks and embarked upon the worst Holocaust the world has ever seen where **twenty two and a half million peasants, mostly from country areas, died directly through his policies.** As the bankers continued to finance Russia they also financed this holocaust, which incidentally included Jewish peasants, in this dreadful figure.

Included in the Bolsheviks that Stalin imprisoned was one Christian G Rakovsky, former Soviet Ambassador in Paris; friend of Trotsky and the International with inside knowledge of the power behind Communism. It is his words that we will analyse when we study his replies to Stalin's questions. He is interrogated by Gavriil (Gabriel) G Kus'min on the 26th. January 1938, a NKVD operator. As French was Rakovsky's language an interpreter was present; a doctor of medicine named Landowsky, who carefully kept a secret copy of his translations. The script appears in full in 'Red Symphony'; we will study just parts that are all relevant to support what you have already read. The interrogation takes place in 1938, just before the Second World War and therefore holds some surprises that will turn your whole conception of Communism, Hitler and the Jewish events completely on its head.

The appearance of the Rakovsky interview in Red Symphony was a very important revelation that today we must use to prove the existence of a group of International Bankers and Intellectuals who are arrogant enough to think they should rule the world without democratic approval. We have already seen the arrogance of Paul Warburg, organiser and board member of the Federal Reserve Bank, when he said, "We shall have world government whether or not we like it. The only question is whether world government will be achieved by conquest or consent".

What this document gives us is proof from within Russia and indeed the NKVD, the forerunner to the KGB, that Communism was created by the Bankers, financed by the same group of bankers, and Russia was throughout its existence as a Communist State, used by those same bankers to manipulate the world into a position for final take-over under their dictatorship.

Therefore the importance of these papers, covering an examination of Rakovsky's knowledge of the world events in relation to the bankers, Russia's Revolution and Stalin, cannot be over emphasised. You must remember while reading this interview that Rakovsky **(80)** was an intellectual Trotskyist under the threat of death from Stalin, who feared pure Communists.

I abbreviate the speakers as follows; Gabriel is 'G', Rakovsky is 'R', and My comments 'C', in brackets.

I can only cover the part of the interview that is totally relevant to this book, but the whole interview can be found in 'Red Symphony' and is well worth reading.

Remember; Rakovsky is in jail, waiting sentence under Stalin's purge of Trotskyites, and unless he can be helpful to Stalin's cause, he will face the death penalty.

RAKOVSKY

G   Therefore as ordinary spies, for money?

R   **For money? Nobody received a single mark from Germany. Hitler has not enough money to buy, for example, the Commissar for Foreign Affairs of the USSR, who has at his disposal, freely, a budget which is greater than the total wealth of Morgan and Vanderbilt, and who does not have to account for his use of the money.**

C   (Russia, still in revolution, has countless money at its disposal. Is this not strange or does is show the bankers endless purse?)

G   With a small difference, Rakovsky; at present there is Socialism in the USSR, not the Tsar.

R   You believe that?

G   What?

R   In the existence of Socialism in the USSR?

G   Is the Soviet Union not Socialist?

R   **For me only in name.** It is just here that we find the true reason for opposition. Agree with me, and by the force of pure logic you must agree, that theoretically, rationally, we have the same right to say--no, as Stalin can say--yes. And if for the triumph of Communism, defeatism can be justified, then he who considers that Communism has been destroyed by the Bonapartism of Stalin and that he betrayed it, has the same right as Lenin to become a defeatist.

R   I have already agreed that there exists formal Communism. All that you enumerate are merely forms.

G   Yes? For what purpose? From mere obstinacy?

R   Of course not. This is necessity. It is impossible to eliminate the materialistic evolution of history. The most that can be done is to hold it up. And at what price? At the cost of its theoretical acceptance, in order to destroy it in practice. The force which draws humanity towards Communism is so unconquerable that that same force, but distorted, opposed to itself, can only achieve a slowing down of development; more accurately--to slow down the progress of permanent revolution.

G   An Example?

R   The most obvious--with Hitler. He needed Socialism for victory over Socialism; it is this his very anti-Socialist Socialism which is National Socialism. Stalin needs Communism in order to defeat Communism. The parallel is obvious. But, notwithstanding Hitler's anti-Socialism and Stalin's anti-Communism, both, to their regret and against their will, transcendentally create Socialism and Communism, which we, the Communist-Marxists, must inevitably inherit.

R   We agreed that at the present moment the opposition cannot be interested in defeatism and the fall of Stalin, insofar as we do not have the physical possibility of taking his place. This is what we both agree. At present this is an incontrovertible fact. However, there is in existence a possible aggressor. There he is, that great Nihilist, Hitler, who is aiming with his terrible weapon of the Wehrmacht, at the whole horizon. Whether we want it or not, but will he use it against the USSR? Let us agree that for us this is the decisive unknown factor. Do you consider that the problem has been correctly stated?

G   It has been well put. But I can say that for me there is no unknown factor. I consider the attack of Hitler on the USSR to be inevitable.

R   Why?

G   Very simple; because he who controls it is inclined towards attack. Hitler is only the condottiere of International Capitalism.

R   I agree that there is a danger, but from that to the assumption on this ground of the inevitability of his attack on the USSR--there is a whole abyss.

G   The attack on the USSR is determined by the very essence of Fascism. In addition he is impelled towards it by all those Capitalist States which have allowed him to re-arm and to take all the necessary economic and strategical bases. This is quite obvious.

R   You forget something very important. The re-armament of Hitler and the assistance he received at the present time from the Versailles Nations **(Direction)**-- were received by him during a special period, when we could still have become the heirs of Stalin in the case of his defeat, when the opposition still existed....Do you consider this fact to be a matter of chance or only a coincidence in time?

G   I do not see any connection between the permission of the Versailles powers of German re-armament and the existence of the opposition...The trajectory of Hitlerism is in itself clear and logical. The attack on the USSR was part of his programme already a long time ago. The destruction of Communism and expansion in the East--these are dogmas from the book "Mein Kampf", that Talmud of National Socialism....but that your defeatists wanted to take advantage of this threat to the USSR -- that is, of course, in accordance with your train of thought.

R   Yes, at first glance this appears to be natural and logical, too logical and natural for the truth.

G   To prevent this happening, so that Hitler would not attack us, we would have to entrust ourselves to an alliance with France...but that would be a naiveté. It would mean that we believe that Capitalism would be willing to make sacrifices for the sake of saving Communism.

R   If we shall continue the discussion only on the foundation of those conceptions which apply for use at mass meetings, then you are quite right. But if you are sincere in saying this then, forgive me, I am disappointed; I had thought that the politics of the famous Stalinist police stand on a higher level.

G   The Hitlerist attack on the USSR is in addition, a dialectical necessity; it is the same as the inevitable struggle of the classes on the international plane. At the side of Hitler, inevitably, there will stand the whole global Capitalism.

R   And so, believe me, that in the light of your scholastic dialectics, I have formed a very negative opinion about the political culture of Stalinism. I listen to your words as Einstein could listen to a school boy talking about physics in four dimensions. **I see that you are only acquainted with elementary Marxism, i.e. with the demagogic, popular one.**

C   (From this we gather Marxism has two policies; one open Communism, the second a secret agenda only for the eyes of the elite).

G   If your explanation will not be too long and involved, I should be grateful to you for some explanation of this "relativity" or "quantum" of Marxism.

R   Here there is no irony; I am speaking with the best intentions...In this same elementary Marxism, which is taught even in your Stalinist University, you can find the statement which contradicts the whole of your thesis about the inevitability of the Hitlerist attack on the USSR. You are also taught that the cornerstone of Marxism is the assertion that, supposedly, contradictions are the incurable and fatal illness of Capitalism... Is that not so?

G   Yes, of course.

R   But if things are in fact such that we accuse Capitalism of being imbued with continuous Capitalistic contradictions in the sphere of economics, then why should it necessarily suffer from them also in politics? The political and economic is of no importance in itself; this is a condition or measurement of the social essence, but contradictions arise in the social sphere, and are reflected simultaneously in the economic or political ones, or in both at the same time. It would be absurd to assume fallibility in economics, and, simultaneously, infallibility in politics--which is something essential in order that an attack on the USSR should become inevitable--according to your postulate-- absolutely essential.

G   This means that you rely in everything on the contradictions, fatality and inevitability of the errors which must be committed by the bourgeoisie, which will hinder Hitler from attacking the USSR. I am a Marxist, Rakovsky, but here, between ourselves, in order not to provide the pretext for anger to a single activist, I say to you that with all my faith in Marx I would not believe that the USSR exists thanks to the mistakes of its enemies...and I think that Stalin shares the same view.

R   But I do think so... Do not look at me like that, as I am not joking and am not mad.

G   Permit me at least to doubt it, until you will have proved your assertions.

R   Do you now see that I had reasons for qualifying your Marxist culture as being doubtful? Your arguments and reactions are the same as any rank and file activist.

G   And they are wrong?

R   Yes, they are correct for a small administrator, for a bureaucrat and for the mass. They suit the average fighter...They must believe this and repeat everything as it has been written. Listen to me by way of the completely confidential. **With Marxism you get the same results as with the ancient esoteric religions. Their adherents had to know only that which was most elementary and crude, insofar as by this, one provoked their faith, i.e. that which is absolutely essential, both in religion and in the work of revolution.**

C   (Confirming secrecy of direction. Only releasing details of policy to the public that are essential. Hiding from public gaze anything that uncovers their secret direction).

G   Do you not now want to open up to me the mystical Marxism, something like yet another Freemasonry?

R   No. No esoterics. On the contrary, I shall explain it with the maximum clarity. Marxism, before being philosophical, economic and a political system, is a conspiracy for the revolution. And, as for us, the revolution is the only absolute reality, it follows that philosophy, economics and politics are true only insofar as they lead to revolution. The fundamental truth, lets call it subjective, does not exist in economics, politics or even morals; in the light of scientific abstraction it is either truth or error, but for us, who are subject to revolutionary dialectic, it is only truth. And insofar as to us, who are subject to a revolutionary dialectic, it is only truth, and therefore the sole truth, then it must be such for all that is revolutionary, and such it was to Marx. In accordance we must act. Remember the phrase of Lenin, in reply to someone who demonstrated by way of argument that, supposedly, his intention contradicted reality: "I feel it to be real" was his answer. Do you not think that Lenin spoke nonsense? No, for him every reality, every truth was relative in the face of the sole and absolute one: the revolution. Marx was a genius. If his works had amounted to only the deep criticism of Capitalism, then even that would have been an unsurpassed scientific work; but in those places where his writing reaches the level of mastery, there comes the effect of an apparently ironical work. **"Communism" he says "must win because Capital will give it that victory, though its enemy".**

C   (This is an extraordinary statement, said with frightening confidence. Because 'They', the bankers and their associates, control the money supply of the world and are **capitalists**, and at the same time fund Communism).

R.   Such is the magisterial thesis of Marx....Can there be a greater irony? And then, in order that he should be believed, it was enough for him to depersonalise Capitalism and Communism, having transformed the human individual into a consciously thinking individual, which he did with extraordinary talent of a juggler. Such was his sly method, in order to demonstrate to the Capitalists that they are a reality of Capitalism and that Communism can triumph as the result of inborn idiocy; since without the presence of immortal idiocy in 'Homo Economico' there could not appear in him continuous contradictions as proclaimed by Marx. **To be able to achieve the transformation of 'Homo Sapiens' into 'Homo Stultum' is to possess magical force, capable of bringing man down to the first stage of the zoological ladder, i.e. to the level of the animal.**

C   (From free men of the world to man chained in servitude. This is the bankers plan for the masses. The secret of Communism/Illuminati.).

R.   Only if there is 'Homo Stultum' in the epoch of the apogee of Capitalism could Marx formulate his axiomatic position: contradictions plus time equal Communism. Believe me, when we who are initiated into this, contemplate the representation of Marx, for example the one which is placed above the main entrance to the Lubianka, then we cannot prevent the inner explosion of laughter by which Marx had infected us; we see how he laughs into his beard at all humanity.

R   You can be sure that if Marx believed that Communism will achieve victory only thanks to the contradictions in Capitalism, then he would not have once, ever, mentioned the contradictions on the thousands of pages of his scientific revolutionary work. Such was the categorical imperative of the realistic nature of Marx: not the scientific, but the revolutionary one. The revolutionary and conspirator will never disclose to his opponent the secret of his triumph... He would never give the information; he would give him dis-information which you use in counter-conspiracy. Is that not so?

R   **Have you not felt this intuitively? Have you not noticed how in Marx words contradict deeds?** He declares the necessity and inevitability of Capitalist contradictions, proving the existence of surplus value and accumulation, i.e. he proves that which really exists. He nimbly invents the proposition that to a greater concentration of the means of production corresponds a greater mass of the proletariat, a greater force for the building of Communism, is that not so? Now go on: at the same time as this assertion he founds the International. Yet the International is, in the work of the daily struggle of the classes, a "reformist" i.e. an organisation whose purpose is the limitation of the surplus value and, where possible, its elimination. For this reason, objectively, the International is a counter-revolutionary organisation and anti-Communist, in accordance with Marx's theory.

C (Marx clearly had two policies. One for open display and to satisfy the masses, Communism as practised in Russia. But behind this was a terrible policy of suppression, by dictatorship and censorship and the iron rule of law. This was the second policy of Marx designed for the elite bankers and others to keep the masses servile. This is what they want to adapt to help their plan for world rule by dictatorship.).

G Now we get that Marx is a counter-revolutionary and a anti-Communist.

R Well, now you see how one can make use of the original Marxist culture. (Make it mean anything to suit the occasion). It is only possible to describe the International as being counter-revolutionary and anti-Communist, with logical and scientific exactness, if one does not see in the facts anything more than the directly visible result, and in the texts only the letter. One comes to such absurd conclusions, while they seem to be obvious, when one forgets that words and facts in Marxism are subject to strict rules of the higher science: the rules of conspiracy and revolution.

C (This means you can't trust Communism. For what they say, is not what you get. It is a policy based on continual evolution and deception.).

R Don't you suspect that the much mentioned contradictions of Capitalism, and in particular the financial ones, are also organised by someone?...By way of basis for these deductions I shall remind you that in its economic struggle the proletarian International coincides with the Financial International, since both produce inflation, and wherever there is coincidence there, one should assume, is also agreement. Those are his own words.

G I suspect here such an enormous absurdity, or the intention of spinning a new paradox, that I do not want to imagine this. It looks as if you want to hint at the existence of something like a Capitalistic second Communist International, of course an enemy one.

R Exactly so. When I spoke of the Financial International, I thought of it as of a Comintern, but having limited the existence of the "Comintern", I would not say that they are enemies.

C (Proof of the meeting point between Capitalism of the bankers and Communism of the International. This was the reason the bankers took up this policy and have since used it as their vehicle to world government.).

R Bear in mind the "five-pointed star", like the Soviet one, which shines all over Europe, the star composed of the five Rothschild brothers with their banks, who possess colossal accumulations of wealth, the greatest ever known...and so this fact, so colossal that it misled the imagination of the people of that epoch, passes unnoticed with Marx.....One had killed Kings, Generals, Bishops, Policemen, Priests and other representatives of the hated privileged classes; one robbed and burnt palaces, churches and even centres of science, but though the revolutions were economic-social, the lives of the bankers were respected, and as a result the magnificent buildings of the banks remained untouched...According to my information, before I had been arrested, this continues even now...

C (This confirms that the bankers were involved in financing the Spanish Revolution. The mob burned and wrecked Palaces, Churches, and even centres of Science, but left untouched the bank buildings and the bankers.).

G Where?

R In Spain....Don't you know it? As you ask me, so tell me now: Do you not find this very strange? Think, the police...I do not know, have you paid attention to the strange similarity which exists between the Financial International and the Proletarian International. I would say that one is the other side of the other, and the back side is the proletarian one as being more modern than the financial.

G Where do you see similarity in things so opposed?

R Objectively they are identical. As I had proved, the Comintern, paralleled, doubled by the reformist movement and the whole of Syndicalism, calls forth the anarchy of production, inflation, poverty and hopelessness in the masses. Finances, chiefly the Financial International, doubled, consciously or unconsciously by private finances, create the same contradictions, but in still greater numbers...Now we can already guess the reasons why Marx concealed the financial contradictions, which could not have remained hidden from his penetrating gaze, if finances had not had an ally, the influence of which objectively revolutionary, was already then extraordinarily important.

G An unconscious coincidence, but not an alliance which pre-supposes intelligence, will and agreement....

R Let us leave this point of view if you like. Now let us better go over to the subjective analysis of finances and even more: let us see what sort of people personally are at work there. The international essence of money is well known. (This is at the heart of the drive for Globalism). From this fact emerges that the organisation which owns them and accumulates them is a cosmopolitan organisation. Finances in their apogee-- as an aim in themselves, the Financial International--deny and do not recognise anything national, they do not recognise the state; and therefore it is anarchical and would be absolutely anarchical if it--the denier of any national state--were not itself, by necessity, a state in its own basic essence. The state as such is only power. And money is exclusively power.

The Communistic super-state, which we are creating already during a whole century, and the scheme of which is the International of Marx. Analyse it and you will see its essence. The scheme of the International and its prototype of the USSR--that is also pure power. The basic similarity between the two creations is absolute. It is something fantastic, inevitable, since the personalities of the authors of both were identical. The financier is just as international as the Communist. Both, with the help of differing pretexts and differing means, struggle with the national bourgeois state and deny it. Marxism in order to change it into a Communist state; from this comes that the Marxist must be an Internationalist; the financial denies the bourgeois national state and his denial ends in itself; in fact he does not manifest himself as an internationalist, but as a cosmopolitan anarchist... That is his appearance at the given stage, but let us see what he really is and what he wants to be. As you see, in rejection there is clear similarity individually between Communist-Internationalists and financial-cosmopolitans; as a natural result there is the same similarity between the Communist International and the Financial International...

G   This is a chance similarity subjectively and objective in contradictions, but one easily eroded and having little significance and that which is modest radical and existing in reality.

R   Allow me not to reply just now, so as not to interrupt the logical sequence... I only want to decipher the basic axiom: money is power. Money is today the centre of global gravity. I hope you agree with me?

G   Continue, Rakovsky, I beg you.

R   The understanding of how the Financial International has gradually, right up to our epoch, become the master of money, this magical talisman, which has become for people that which God and the nation had become formerly, is something which exceeds in scientific interest even the art of revolutionary strategy, since this is also an art and also a revolution.

C   (This confirms that finance (The bankers) rules the world. But only to them has money become a 'God' and 'Internationalism' their aspiration, most of us have to stick to reality.).

R   I shall explain it to you. Historiographers and the masses, blinded by the shouts and the pomp of the French Revolution, the people, intoxicated by the fact that it had succeeded in taking all the power from the King and the privileged classes, did not notice how a small group of mysterious, careful and insignificant people had taken possession of the real royal power, the magical power, almost divine, which it obtained almost without knowing it. **The masses did not notice that the power had been seized by others and that soon they had subjected them to slavery more cruel than the King, since the latter, in view of his religious and moral prejudices, was incapable of taking advantage of such power.**

C   (While the French Revolution raged, the Illuminati - Masonic group took over the power of France.).

R   So it came about that the supreme Royal power was taken over by persons, whose moral, and intellectual and cosmopolitan qualities did allow them to use it. It is clear that these were people who had never been Christians, but cosmopolitans.

G   What is that for a mythical power which they had obtained?

R   They had acquired for themselves the real privilege of coin money...Do not smile, otherwise I shall have to believe that you do not know what moneys are...I ask you to put yourself in my place. My position in relation to you is that of the assistant to the doctor, who would have to explain bacteriology to a resurrected medical man of the epoch before Pasteur. But I can explain your lack of knowledge to myself and can forgive it. Our language makes use of words which provoke incorrect thoughts about things and actions, thanks to the power of the inertia of thoughts, and which do not correspond to real and exact conceptions. I say: Money. It is clear that in your imagination there immediately appeared pictures of real money of metal and paper. But that is not so. Money is now not that; real circulating coin is a true anachronism. If it still exists and circulates, then it is only thanks to atavism, only because it is convenient to maintain the illusion, a purely imaginary fiction for the present day.

G   This is a brilliant paradox, risky and even poetical...

R   If you like it, this is perhaps brilliant, but it is not a paradox. I know--and that is why you smiled--that States still coin money on pieces of metal or paper with Royal busts or national crests; well, so what? A great part of the money circulating, money for big affairs, as representative of all national wealth, money, yes money--it was being issued by those few people about whom I had hinted. Titles, figures, cheques, promissory notes, endorsements, discount, quotations, figures without end flooded the States like a waterfall. What are in comparison with these the metallic and paper moneys?...Something devoid of influence, some kind of minimum in the face of the growing flood of the all-flooding financial money. They, being the most subtle psychologists, were able to gain even more without trouble, thanks to a lack of understanding. **In addition to the immensely varied different forms of financial moneys, they created credit-money with a view to making its volume close to infinite. And to give it the speed of sound...it is an abstraction, a being of thought, a figure, number; credit faith...**

Do you understand already?...Fraud; false moneys, given a legal standing....using other terminology, so that you should understand me. **Banks, the stock exchanges and the whole world financial system--is a gigantic machine for the purpose of bringing about unnatural scandals, according to Aristotle's expression; to force money to produce moneys--that is something that if it is a crime in economics, then in relations to finances it is a crime against the criminal code, since it is usury.**

C **(Credit money, created by the International Finance Capitalists has enslaved the nations of the world in deep debt with falsified money, only given a legal standing because the bankers own national debts.** It is pure usury. It enables the bankers to create financial crises whenever they wish for their own gain, i.e. the Wall Street collapse 1929.).

R I do not know by what arguments all this is justified: by the proposition that they receive legal interest...Even accepting that, and even that admission is more than is necessary, **we see that usury still exists, since even if the interest received is legal, then it invents and falsifies the non-existent capital.** Banks have always by way of deposits or moneys in productive movement a certain quantity of money which is five or perhaps even a hundred times greater than there are physically coined moneys of metal or paper. I shall say nothing of those cases when the credit-moneys, i.e. false, fabricated ones, are greater than the quantity of moneys paid out as capital. Bearing in mind that lawful interest is fixed not on real capital but on non-existing capital, the interest is illegal by so many times as the fictional capital is greater than the real one.

Bear in mind that this system, which I am describing in detail, is one of the most innocent among those used for the fabrication of false money. **Imagine to yourself, if you can, a small number of people, having unlimited power through the possession of real wealth, and you will see that they are the absolute dictators of the stock-exchange; and as a result of this also the dictators of production and distribution and also of work and consumption. If you have enough imagination then multiply this by the global factor and you will see its anarchical, moral and social influence, i.e. a revolutionary one...Do you now understand?**

R The Capitalistic system of production is determined by finance. The fact that Engels states the opposite and even tries to prove this, is the most obvious proof that finances rule bourgeois production. So it is and so it was even before Marx and Engels, that finances were the most powerful instrument of revolution and the Comintern was nothing but a toy in their hands. (The bankers). But neither Marx or Engels will disclose or explain this. On the contrary, making use of their talent as scientists, they had to camouflage truth for a second time in the interests of the revolution. And that both of them did.

G   This story is not new. All this somewhat reminds me of what Trotzky had written some ten years ago.

R   Tell me...

G   When he says that the comintern is a conservative organisation in comparison with the stock-exchange in New York, he points at the big bankers as being the inventors of the revolution.

R   Yes, he said this in a small book in which he foretold the fall of England... Yes, he said this and added: "Who pushes England along the path of revolution?"... and replied: "Not Moscow, but New York".

C   (This is true, and is at the heart of understanding of what is happening today).

G   But remember also his assertion that if the financiers of New York had forged the revolution, then it was done unconsciously.

R   The explanation which I had already given in order to help to understand why Engels and Marx camouflaged the truth, is equally applicable also to Leo Trotzky.

G   I value in Trotzky only that he, in a sort of literary form, interpreted an opinion of a fact, which as such was too well known, with which one had already reckoned previously. Trotzky himself states quite correctly that these bankers "carry out irresistibly and unconsciously their revolutionary mission".

C   (Trotzky says the bankers carry out their drive to revolution unconsciously. I don't think so. They know exactly the perimeter of their game play, after all they created the illusion, Communism, through the Illuminati to hide their real agenda, world domination.).

R   And they carry out their mission despite the fact that Trotzky has declared it? What a strange thing! Why do they not improve their actions?

G   The financiers are unconscious revolutionaries since they are such only objectively, as the result of their intellectual incapacity of seeing the final consequences.

R   You believe this sincerely? You think that among these real geniuses there are some who are unconscious? You consider to be idiots people to whom today the whole world is subjected? This would really be a very stupid contradiction!

G   What do you pretend to?

R   I simply assert that they are revolutionaries objectively and subjectively, quite consciously.

G   The bankers! You must be mad?

R   I, no...But you? Think a little. These people are just like you and me. The circumstance that they control moneys in unlimited amounts, insofar as they themselves create them, does not give us the opportunity of determining the limits of all their ambitions... **if there is something which provides a man with full satisfaction then it is the satisfaction of his ambition. And most of all the satisfaction of his will to power. Why should not these people, the bankers, have the impulse towards power, towards full power? Just as it happens to you and to me.**

G   But if, according to you--and I think the same--they already have global political power, then what other power do they want to possess?

R   I have already told you: Full power. Such power as Stalin has in the USSR, but world-wide.

G   Such power as Stalin's, but with the opposite aim.

R   Power, if in reality it is absolute, can be only one. The idea of the absolute excludes multiplicity. For that reason the power sought by the Comintern and "Comintern", which are things of the same order, being absolute, must also in politics be unique and identical: Absolute power has a purpose in itself, otherwise it is not absolute. And until the present day there has not yet been invented another machine of total power except the Communist state. Capitalistic bourgeois power, even on its highest rung of the ladder, the power of Caesar, is limited power since if, in theory, it was the personification of the deity in the Pharaohs and Caesar's in ancient times, then nevertheless, thanks to the economic character of life in those primitive states and owing to the technical under-development of the state apparatus, there was always room for individual freedom. Do you understand that those who already partially rule over nations and worldly governments have pretensions to absolute domination? **Understood that that is the only thing which they have not reached...**

C   (Ultimate power.).

G   This is interesting; at least as an example of insanity.

R   Certainly, insanity in a lesser degree than in the case of Lenin, who dreamt of power over the whole world in his attic in Switzerland or the insanity of Stalin, dreaming of the same thing during his exile in a Siberian hut. **I think that dreams of such ambitions are much more natural for the moneyed people, living in the skyscrapers of New York.**

C   (Direction. This clearly states the bankers driving force)..

G   Let us conclude: Who are they?

R   You are so naive that you think that if I knew who "They" are, I would be here as a prisoner?

G   Why?

R   For a very simple reason, since he who is acquainted with them would not be put into a position in which he would be obliged to report on them... This is an elementary rule of every intelligent conspiracy, which you must well understand.

G   But you said that they are the bankers?

R   Not I; remember that I always spoke of the Finance International and when mentioning persons I said "They" and nothing more. **If you want that I should inform you openly then I shall only give you facts, but not names, since I do not know them. I think I shall not be wrong if I tell you that not one of "them" is a person who occupies a political position or a position in the World Bank.** As I understood after the murder of Rathenau in Rapallo, they give political or financial positions only to intermediaries. Obviously to persons who are trustworthy and loyal, which can be guaranteed a thousand ways; thus one can assert that bankers and politicians-- **are only men of straw... even though they occupy very high places and are made to appear to be the authors of the plans which are carried out.**

G   Although all this can be understood and is also logical, but is not your declaration of not knowing only an evasion? As it seems to me, and according to the information I have, you occupied a sufficiently high place in the conspiracy to have known much more. You do not even know a single one of them personally?

R   Yes, but of course you do not believe me. I have come to that moment where I had explained that I am talking about a person and persons with a personality...how should one say?...a mystical one, like Ghandi or something like that, but without any external display. Mystics of pure power, who have become free from all vulgar trifles. I do not know if you understand me? Well, as to their place of residence and names, I do not know them...Imagine Stalin just now, in reality ruling the USSR, but not surrounded by stone walls, not having any personnel around him, and having the same guarantees for his life as any other citizen. By which means could he guard against attempts on his life? He is first of all a conspirator, however great his power: he is anonymous.

    G   What you are saying is logical, but I do not believe you.

    R   But still believe me; I know nothing; if I knew then how happy I would be! I would not be here, defending my life. I well understand your doubts and that, in view of your police education, you feel the need for some knowledge about persons. To honour you and also because this is essential for the aim which we both have set ourselves, I shall do all I can in order to inform you. **You know that according to the unwritten history known only to us, the founder of the First Communist International is indicated of course secretly, as being Weishaupt. You remember his name? He was the head of the Masonry which is known by the name of the Illuminati; this name he borrowed from the second anti-Christian conspiracy of that era--gnosticism. This important revolutionary, Semite and former Jesuit, foreseeing the triumph of the French Revolution decided, or perhaps he was ordered (some mention as his chief the important philosopher Mendelssohn) to found a secret organisation which was to provoke and push the French Revolution to go further than its political objectives, with the aim of transforming it into a social revolution for the establishment of Communism.**

    C   (This is startling news. Weishaupt is the author of the first Communist International. This confirms his link with Communism and Masonry. Now we see the formal start of Communism after the French Revolution. So Communism and the Illuminati are the same thing.).

In those heroic times it was colossally dangerous to mention Communism as an aim; from this derive the various precautions and secrets, which had to surround the Illuminati. More than a hundred years were required before a man could confess to being a Communist without danger of going to prison or being executed. This is more or less known. **What is not known is the relations between Weishaupt and his followers with the first of the Rothschilds. The secret of the acquisition of wealth of the best known bankers could have been explained by the fact that they were the treasurers of this first Comintern. There is evidence that when the five brothers spread out to the five provinces of the financial empire of Europe, they had some secret help for the accumulation of these enormous sums; it is possible that they were those first Communists from the Bavarian catacombs who were already spread all over Europe. But others say, and I think with better reason, that the Rothschilds were not the treasurers, but the chiefs of that first secret Communism. This opinion is based on that well-known fact that Marx and the highest chiefs of the first International--already the open one--and among them Herzen and Heine, were controlled by Baron Lionel Rothschild, whose revolutionary portrait was done by Disraeli (in Coningsby) the English Premier, who was his creature, and has been left to us. He described him in the character of Sidonia, a man, who, according to the story, was a multi-millionaire, knew and controlled spies, Carbonari, Freemasons, secret Jews, gypsies, revolutionaries etc. etc.**

    C   (Rakovsky discloses the link between the Rothschild bankers, their amazing rise, the Illuminati and Communism. He believes Baron Lionel Rothschild to be the chief of Communism. Now everything begins to fall into place thanks to Rakovsky.).

R   All this seems fantastic. But it has been proved that Sidonia is an idealised portrait of the son of Nathan Rothschild, which can also be deduced from that campaign which he raised against Tsar Nicholas in favour of Herzen. He won this campaign.

If all that we can guess in the light of these facts is true, then, I think, we could even determine who invented this terrible machine of accumulation and anarchy, which is the Financial International. It is an act of genius: to create with the help of Capitalism accumulation of the highest degree, to push the proletariat towards strikes, to sow hopelessness, and at the same time to create an organisation which must unite the proletarians with the purpose of driving them into revolution. This is to write the most majestic chapter of history. **Even more: remember the phrase of the mother of the five Rothschild brothers: "If my sons want it, then there will be no war". This means that they were the arbiters, the masters of peace and war**, but not emperors. Are you capable of visualising the fact of such a cosmic importance? is not war already a revolutionary function? War--The Commune. **Since that time every war was a giant step towards Communism.** As if some mysterious force satisfied the passionate wish of Lenin, which he has expressed to Gorky. Remember: 1905-1914. Do admit at least that two of the three levers of power which lead to Communism are not controlled and cannot be controlled by the proletariat. Wars were not brought about and were not controlled by either the Third International or the USSR, which did not yet exist at that time. Equally they cannot be provoked and still less controlled by those small groups of Bolsheviks who plod along in the emigration, although they want war. This is quite obvious. The International and the USSR have even fewer possibilities for such immense accumulations of capital and the creation of national or international anarchy in Capitalistic production. **Such an anarchy which is capable of forcing people to burn huge quantities of foodstuffs, rather than give them to starving people, and is capable of that which Rathenau described in one of his phrases i.e.: "To bring about that half the world will fabricate dung, and the other half will use it".**

C   (A crime against the starving but a step towards Communism, so the bankers have used this ploy.).

R   And after all, can the proletariat believe that it is the cause of this inflation, growing in geometric progression, this devaluation, the constant acquisition of surplus values and the accumulation of financial capital, but not usury capital, and that as the result of the fact that it cannot prevent the constant lowering of its purchasing power, **there takes place the proletarization of the middle classes, who are the true opponents of revolution.**

C   (The true enemy of the Communist Revolution is the thinking middle-class).

R   The proletariat does not control the lever of economics or the lever of war. But it is itself the third lever, the only visible and demonstrable lever, which carries out the final blow at the power of the Capitalistic State and takes It over. Yes, they seize it, if "They" yield it to them....

G   I again repeat to you that all this, which you have set out in such a literate form, has a name which we have already repeated to excess in this endless conversation: the natural contradictions of Capitalism and if, as you claim, there is yet someone else's will and activity apart from the proletariat, then I want you to indicate to me concretely a personal case.

R You require only one? Well, then listen to a small story: "They" isolated the Tsar diplomatically for the Russo-Japanese War, and the United States financed Japan; speaking precisely this was done by Jacob Schiff, the head of the bank of Kuhn, Loeb and Company, which is the successor of the House of Rothschild, whence Schiff originated. He had such power that he achieved that States which had colonial possessions in Asia supported the creation of the Japanese Empire, which was inclined towards xenophobia; and Europe already feels the effects of this xenophobia. **From the prisoner-of-war camps there came to Petrograd the best fighters, trained as revolutionary agents; they were sent there from America with the permission of Japan, obtained through the persons who had financed it. The Russo-Japanese War, thanks to the organised defeat of the Tsar's army, called forth the revolution of 1905, which, though it was premature, but was very nearly successful; even if it did not win, it still created the required political conditions for the victory of 1917.**

C (So we learn, America took part in training the subversives that entered Russia to overthrow the Tsar and his government in 1905, financed by Wall Street bankers.).

R I shall say even more. Have you read the biography of Trotzky? Recall its first revolutionary period. He is still quite a young man; after his flight from Siberia he lived some time among the émigrés in London, Paris, and Switzerland; Lenin, Plekhanov, Martov and other chiefs look on him only as a promising newcomer. But he already dares during the first split to behave independently, trying to become the arbiter of the reunion. In 1905 he is twenty-five years olds and he returns to Russia alone, without a party and without his own organisation. Read the reports of the revolution of 1905 which have not been "pruned" by Stalin; for example that of Lunatcharsky, who was not a Trotzkyite. Trotzky is the chief figure during the revolution in Petrograd. This is how it really was. Only he emerges from it with increased popularity and influence. Neither Lenin, nor Martov, nor Plekhanov acquire popularity. They only kept it and even lose a little. How and why there rises the unknown Trotzky, gaining power by one move greater than that which the oldest and most influential revolutionaries had? Very simple; he marries. **Together with him there arrives in Russia his wife--Sedova. Do you know who she is? She is associated with Zhivotovsky, linked with the bankers Warburg, partners and relatives of Jacob Schiff, i.e. of that financial group which, as I had said, had also financed the revolution of 1905. Here is the reason why Trotzky, in one move, moves to the top of the revolutionary list. And here, too, you have the key to his real personality. Let us jump to 1914. Behind the back of the people who made the attempt on the Archduke there stands Trotzky, and that attempt provoked the European war.**

C (Trotzky marries the daughter of Zhivotovsky, associated with the Warburg's and related to Jacob Schiff, the financier of the revolution. The picture gets clearer. We also learn that Trotzky was behind the plot to assassinate the Archduke Ferdinand that started the First World War.).

R Do you really believe that the murder and the war--are simple coincidences?.... as had been said at one of the Zionist congresses by Lord Melchett. Analyse in the light of "Non-coincidence" the development of the military actions in Russia. "Defeatism" is an exemplary word. The help of the Allies for the Tsar was regulated and controlled with such skill that it gave the allied ambassadors the right to make an argument of this and to get from Nicholas, thanks to his stupidity, suicidal advances, one after the other. The mass of the Russian cannon fodder was immense, but not inexhaustible. A series of organised defeats led to the revolution. When the threat came from all sides, then a cure was found in the form of the establishment of a democratic republic--an "Ambassadorial Republic" as Lenin called it, i.e. this meant the elimination of any threat to the revolutionaries. **But that is not yet all. Kerensky was to provoke the future advance at the cost of a very great deal of blood. He brings it about so that the democratic revolution should spread beyond its bounds. And even still more: Kerensky was to surrender the State fully to Communism, and he does it. Trotzky has the chance in an "unnoticed manner" to occupy the whole state apparatus. What a strange blindness! The Bolsheviks took that which "they" gave them.**

C (This argues with our history books. Kerensky hands Russia to the Bolsheviks (Communists) and Rakovsky says, 'They', the bankers, gave it to them. Once again the Capitalist/Communist International takes the day and our media does not inform us. That seems strange doesn't it?).

G You dare to say that Kerensky was a collaborator of Lenin?

R Of Lenin--no. Of Trotzky--yes; it is more correct to say, a collaborator of "them".

G An absurdity!

R You cannot understand... precisely you? It surprises me. If you were to be a spy and, while hiding your identity, you were to attain the position of commander of the enemy fortress, then would you not open the gates to the attacking forces in whose service you actually were? You would not have to become a prisoner who had experienced defeat? Would you not have been in danger of death during the attack on the fortress if one of the attackers, not knowing that your uniform is only a mask, would have taken you for the enemy? Believe me: despite the statues and mausoleum--Communism is indebted to Kerensky much more than Lenin.

G You want to say that Kerensky was a conscious and voluntary defeatist?

R **Yes to me that is quite clear. Understand that I personally took part in all this. I shall tell you even more: Do you know who financed the October revolution? "They" financed it, in particular through those same bankers who had financed Japan in 1905, i.e. Jacob Schiff, and the brothers Warburg; that means through the great banking constellation, through one of the five banks who are members of the Federal Reserve, Through the bank of Kuhn, Loeb and Company; here there took part also other American and European bankers, such as Guggenheim, Hanauer, Breitung, Aschberg, the "Nya Banken" of Stockholm. I was there "by chance", there in Stockholm, and participated in the transmission of funds. Until Trotzky arrived I was the only person who was an intermediary from the revolutionary side. But at last Trotzky came; I must underline that the allies had expelled him from France for being a defeatist. And the same allies released him so that he could be a defeatist in allied Russia... "Another chance". Who arranged it? The same people who had succeeded that Lenin passed through Germany. Yes, "They" were able - and sent him on to Russia, to get the defeatist Trotzky out of a Canadian camp to England giving him the chance to pass freely through all the allied controls; others of "Them" - a certain Rathenau, accomplishes the journey of Lenin through enemy Germany.**

C (This is where Rakovsky opens up and discloses names. These are the bankers who financed the Bolshevik Revolution and Russia right up till today. From this you see, 'They', the bankers, meddling to fulfil their programme, financing and moving the revolutionaries around to suit their target in this case the Tsar of Russia.).

R   If you will undertake the study of the history of the revolution and civil war without prejudices, and will use all your enquiring capabilities, which you know how to apply to things much less important and less obvious, then when you study information's in their totality, and also study separate details right up to anecdotal happenings, you will meet with a whole series of "Amazing chances".

G   All right, let us accept the hypothesis that not everything was simply a matter of luck. What deductions do you make here for practical results?

R   Let me finish this little story, and then we shall both arrive at conclusions. From the time of his arrival in Petrograd, Trotzky was openly received by Lenin. As you know sufficiently well, during the interval between the two revolutions there has been deep differences between them. All is forgotten and Trotzky emerges as the master of his trade in the matter of the triumph of the revolution, whether Stalin wants this or not. Why? This secret is known to the wife of Lenin - Krupskaya. She knows who Trotzky is in fact; it is she who persuaded Lenin to receive Trotzky. If he had not received him then Lenin would have remained blocked up in Switzerland; this alone had been for him a serious reason, and in addition he knew that Trotzky provided money and helped to get a colossal international assistance; a proof of this was the sealed train. Furthermore it was the result of Trotsky's work, and not of the iron determination of Lenin that there was the unification round the insignificant party of the Bolsheviks of the whole Left-wing revolutionary camp, the social-revolutionaries and the anarchists. It was not for nothing that the real party of the "non-party" Trotzky was the ancient "Bund" of the Jewish proletariat, from which emerged all the Moscow revolutionary branches, and to whom it gave 90% of its leaders; not the official and well-known Bund, but the secret Bund, which had been infiltrated into all the Socialist parties, the leaders of which were almost all under its control.

C   (Trotzky was the go-between for the bankers and the Bolsheviks. He organised the sealed train with the arms and finance for the revolution. We also see how Trotzky controlled the infiltrated Jewish organisers of the Bund into the Socialist Party under the direct command of the bankers.).

G   And Kerensky too?

R   Kerensky too..., and also some other leaders who were not Socialist, the leaders of the bourgeois political fractions.

G   How is that?

R   You forget about the role of Freemasonry in the first phase of the democratic bourgeois revolution?

G   Were they controlled by the Bund?

R   Naturally, as the nearest step, but in fact subject to "Them."

G   Despite the rising tide of Marxism which also threatened their lives and privileges?

R   Despite all that: obviously they did not see that danger. Bear in mind that every Mason saw and hoped to see in his imagination more that there was in reality, because he imagined that which was profitable for him. As a proof of the political power of their association they saw that Masons were in governments and at the pinnacle of the States of the bourgeois nations, while their numbers were growing all the time. Bear in mind that at that time the rulers of all the Allied nations were Freemasons, with very few exceptions.

This was to them an argument of great force. They fully believed that the revolution would stop at the bourgeois republic of the French type.

C   (Note that the leaders of most nations were also Masons.).

G   In accordance with the picture which was given of the Russia of 1917 one had to be a very naive person to believe all this...

R   They were and are such. Masons had learned nothing from that first lesson which, for them, had been the Great Revolution, in which they played a colossal revolutionary role; it consumed the majority of Masons, beginning with the Grand Master of the Orleans Lodge, more correctly the Freemason Louis XVI, in order then to continue to destroy the Girondistes, the Hebertistes, the Jacobins etc. ....., and if some survived it was due to the month of Brumaire.

G   Do you want to say that the Freemasons have to die at the hands of the revolution which has been brought about with their co-operation?

R   Exactly so. You have formulated a truth which is veiled by a great secret. I am a Mason, you already knew about that. Is that not so? Well, I shall tell you this great secret, which they promise to disclose to a Mason in one of the higher degrees, but which is not disclosed to him either in the 25th, nor the 33rd, nor the 93rd, nor any other high level of any ritual. It is clear that I know of this not as a Freemason, but as one who belongs to "Them"...

G   And what is it?

R   Every Masonic organization tries to attain and to create all the required prerequisites for the triumph of the Communist revolution; this is the obvious aim of Freemasonry; it is clear that all this is done under various pretexts; but they always conceal themselves behind their well-known treble slogan. (Liberty, Equality, Fraternity - Trans.) You understand? But since the Communist Revolution has in mind the liquidation, as a class, of the whole bourgeoisie, the physical destruction of all bourgeois suicide of Freemasonry as an organization, and the physical political rulers, it follows that the real secret of masonry - is the suicide of every more important Mason.

C   (Most Masons know nothing of the aims of their top men. Masonry, at the top, is directed towards a Communist Revolution and the destruction of democracies, but also the suicide of the Masons themselves. Except of course the Illuminated ones.).

You can, of course, understand that such an end, which is being prepared for every Mason, fully deserves the secrecy, decorativeness and the inclusion of yet another whole series of secrets, with a view to concealing the real one. If one day you were to be present at some future revolution then do not miss the opportunity of observing the gestures of surprise and the expression of stupidity on the face of some Freemason at the moment when he realises that he must die at the hands of the revolutionaries.   How he screams and wants that one should value his services to the revolution! It is a sight at which one can die ... but of laughter.

G   And you still deny the inborn stupidity of the bourgeoisie?

R   I deny it in the bourgeoisie as a class, but not in certain sectors. The existence of madhouses does not prove universal madness. Freemasonry is also a madhouse, but at liberty. But I continue further: the revolution has been victorious; the seizure of power has been achieved. There arises the first problem: peace, and with it the first differences within the party, in which there participate the forces of the coalition, which takes advantage of power. I shall not explain to you that which is well known about the struggle which developed in Moscow between the adherents and opponents of the peace of Brest-Litovsk. I shall only point out to you that which had already become evident then and was later called the Trotskyist opposition, i.e. these are the people, a part of whom have already been liquidated and the other part is to be liquidated; they were all against the signing of the peace treaty. That peace was a mistake and an unconscious betrayal by Lenin of the International Revolution. Imagine to yourself the Bolsheviks in Versailles at the Peace Conference, and then in the League of Nations, finding themselves inside Germany with the Red Army, which had been armed and increased by the Allies. The Soviet State should have participated with arms in the German revolution... Quite another map of Europe would then have emerged. But Lenin, intoxicated with power, with the help of Stalin, who had also tasted the fruits of power, supported by the national Russian wing of the party, having at their disposal the material resources, enforced their will. Then was born "Socialism in one country," i.e. National-Communism, which has to-day reached its apogee under Stalin. It is obvious that there was a struggle, but only in such a form and extent that the Communist State should not be destroyed; this condition was binding on the opposition during the whole time of its further struggle right up to the present day. This was the reason for our first failure and all those which followed. But the fight was severe, cruel, although concealed in order not to compromise our participation in power. Trotzky organised, with the help of his friends, the attempt on Lenin's life by Kaplan. On his orders Blumkin killed the Ambassador Mirbach. The coup d'etat which was prepared by Spiridonova with her social-revolutionaries had been co-ordinated with Trotzky. **His man for all these affairs, who was immune from all suspicions, was that Rosebud, a Lithuanian Jew, who used the name of O'Reilly, and was known as the best spy of the British Intelligence.**

C   (This puts a new light on one of Britain's most successful spies. It appears, according to Rakovsky he was one of, 'Them'.).

R   In fact he was a man from "Them." The reason why this famous Rosenblum was chosen, who was known only as a British spy, was that in case of failure the responsibility for assassinations and conspiracies would fall not on Trotzky, and not on us, but on England. So it happened. Thanks to the Civil War we rejected conspiratorial and terrorist methods as we were given the chance of having in our hands the real forces of the State, insofar as Trotzky became the organiser and chief of the Soviet Army; before that the army had continuously retreated before the Whites and the Territory of the USSR was reduced to the size of the former Moscow Principality. But here, as if by magic, it begins to win. What do you think, why? As the result of magic or chance? I shall tell you: when Trotzky took over the top command of the Red Army then he had by this in his hands the forces necessary to seize power. A series of victories was to increase his prestige and forces: it was already possible to defeat the Whites. **Do you think that official history was true which ascribes to the unarmed and ill-disciplined Red Army the fact that with its help there was achieved a series of victories?**

G   But to whom then?

R   To the extent of ninety per cent they were indebted to "Them." You must not forget that the Whites were, in their way, democratic. The Mensheviks were with them and the remnants of all the old Liberal parties. Inside these forces "They" always had in their service many people, consciously and unconsciously. When Trotzky began to command then these people were ordered systematically to betray the Whites and at the same time they were promised participation in a more or less short time, in the Soviet Government. Maisky was one of those people, one of the few in the case of which this promise was carried out, but he was able to achieve this only after Stalin had become convinced of his loyalty. This sabotage, linked with a progressive diminution of the help of the Allies to the White generals, who apart from all that were luckless idiots, forced them to experience defeat after defeat. Finally Wilson introduced in his famous 14 Points, the existence of which was enough in order to bring to an end once and for all the attempts of the Whites to fight against the USSR. The Civil War strengthens the position of Trotzky as the heir of Lenin. So it was, without any doubt. **The old revolutionary could now die, having acquired fame. If he remained alive after the bullet of Kaplan, he did not emerge alive after the secret process of the forcible ending of his life, to which he was subjected.**

G   Trotzky shortened his life? This is a big favourable point for our trial! Was it not Levin who was Lenin's doctor?

R   Trotzky?....It is probable that he participated, but it is quite certain that he knew about it. But as far as the technical realisation is concerned,....that is unimportant; who knows this? "They" have a sufficient number of channels in order to penetrate to wherever they want.

C   (Here, Rakovsky says the bankers can accomplish any task they want.).

G   In any event the murder of Lenin is a matter of the greatest importance and it would be worth while to transfer it for examination to the next trial ...What do you think, Rakovsky, if you were by chance to be the author of this affair? It is clear that if you fail to achieve success in this conversation...The technical execution suits you well as a doctor...

R   I do not recommend this to you. Leave this matter alone; it is sufficiently dangerous for Stalin himself. You will be able to spread your propaganda as you wish; but "They" have their propaganda which is more powerful and the question as to "qui podest" - who gains, will force one to see in Stalin the murderer of Lenin, and that argument will be stronger than any confessions extracted from Levin, me or anyone else.

G   What do you want to say by this?

R   That it is the classical and infallible rule in the determination of who the murderer is, to check who gained..., and as far as the assassination of Lenin is concerned, in this case the beneficiary was his chief - Stalin. Think about this and I very much ask you not to make these remarks, as they distract me and do not make it possible for me to finish.

R   Our failures, which get worse every year, prevent the immediate carrying out of that which "they" have prepared in the post-war period for the further leap of the revolution forward. The Treaty of Versailles, quite inexplicable for the politicians and economists of all nations, insofar as nobody could guess in projection, was the most decisive precondition for revolution.

C   (The Versailles Treaty was a decisive act towards revolution. This means the politicians were doing the bankers' bidding.).

G   This is a very curious theory. How do you explain it?

R   The Versailles reparations and economic limitations were not determined by the advantages of individual nations. Their arithmetical absurdity was so obvious that even the most outstanding economists of the victorious countries soon exposed this. France alone demanded as reparation a great deal more than the cost of all her national possessions, more than one would have to pay if the whole of France had been converted into a Sahara; even worse was the decision to impose on Germany payment obligations which were many times greater than it could pay, even if it had sold itself fully and given over the whole of its national production. In the end the true result was that in practice Germany was forced to carry out a fantastic dumping so that it could pay something on account of reparation. And of what did the dumping consist? An insufficiency of consumer goods, hunger in Germany and in corresponding measure unemployment in the importing countries. And since they could not import there was also unemployment in Germany. Hunger and unemployment on both sides; all these were the first results of Versailles...Was this treaty revolutionary or not? Even more was done: one undertook an equal control on the international plane. Do you know what that undertaking represents in the revolutionary plane? It means to impose an anarchical absurdity to force every national economy to produce in sufficient volume all that it needs, while assuming that to attain that one does not have to take account of climate, natural riches and also the technical education of directors and workers. The means for compensation for inborn inequalities of soil, climate, availability of minerals, oil, etc., etc. in various national economies, were always the circumstance that poor countries had to work more. This means that they had to exploit more deeply the capacities of the working force in order to lessen the difference which arises from the poverty of the soil; and to this are added a number of other inequalities which had to be compensated for by similar measures; let us take the example of industrial equipment. I shall not expand the problem further, but the control of the working day carried through by the League of Nations on the basis of an abstract principle of the equality of the working day, was a reality in the context of an unchanged International Capitalist system of production and exchange and established economic inequality, since here we had to deal with an indifference to the aim of work, which is a sufficient production. The immediate result of this was an insufficiency of production, compensated for by imports from countries with a sufficient natural economy and an industrial self-sufficiency; insofar as Europe had gold, that import was paid for by gold. Then came the apparent boom in America which exchanged its immense production for gold and gold certificates, of which there was plenty. **On the model of any anarchy of production there appeared at that period an unheard of financial anarchy. "They" took advantage of it on the pretext of helping it with the aid of another and still greater anarchy: the inflation of the official money (cash) and the a hundred times greater inflation of their own money, credit money, i.e. false money. Remember how systematically there came devaluation in many countries; the destruction of the value of money in Germany, the American crisis and its phenomenal consequences...a record unemployment; more than thirty million unemployed in Europe and USA alone. Well, did not the Versailles Peace Treaty and its League of Nations serve as a revolutionary pre-condition?**

C   (The Versailles Treaty indirectly brought about inflation in money, causing devaluation and destruction of money in Germany and America, causing mass unemployment all over the world. All planned and executed by the bankers to create a Second World War.).

G   This could have happened even if not intended. Could you not prove to me why the revolution and Communism retreat before logical deductions; and more than that: they oppose Fascism which has conquered in Spain and Germany...What can you tell me?

R   I shall tell you that only in the case of the non-recognition of "them" and their aims you would be right....but you must not forget about their existence and aims, and also the fact that in the USSR power is in the hands of Stalin.

G   I do not see the connection here...

R   Because you do not want to: you have more than sufficient deductive talents and capabilities of reasoning. I repeat again: for us Stalin is not a Communist, but a Bonapartist.

G   So what?

R   We do not wish that the great preconditions which we had created at Versailles for the triumph of the Communist Revolution in the world, which, as you see, have become a gigantic reality, would serve the purpose of bringing victory to Stalin's Bonapartism...Is that sufficiently clear to you? Everything would have been different if in this case Trotzky had been the dictator of the USSR; that would have meant that "They" would have been the chiefs of International Communism.

G   **But surely Fascism is totally anti-Communist, as in relation to the Trotzkyist and the Stalinist Communism...and if the power which you ascribe to "Them" is so great, how is it that they were unable to avoid this?**

R   Because it was precisely "they" who gave Hitler the possibility of triumphing.

G   You exceed all the boundaries of absurdity.

R   **The absurd and the miraculous become mixed as the result of a lack of culture. Listen to me. I have already admitted the defeat of the opposition. "They" saw in the end that Stalin cannot be overthrown by a coup d'état, and their historical experience suggested to them the decision of a repetition with Stalin of that which has been done with the Tsar. There was here one difficulty, which seemed to us insuperable. In the whole of Europe there was not a single aggressor-state. Not one of them was geographically well placed and had any army sufficient for an attack on Russia. If there was no such country then "They" had to create it. Only Germany had the corresponding population and positions suitable for an attack on the USSR, and it was capable of defeating Stalin; you can understand that the Weimar Republic had not been invented as an aggressor either politically or economically; on the contrary, it was suited to an invasion. On the horizon of a hungry Germany there sparked the meteor of Hitler. A pair of penetrating eyes fixed their attention on it. The world was the witness to his lightning rise. I shall not say that all of it was the work of our hands, no. His rise, uninterruptedly increasing in extent, took place as the result of the Revolutionary-Communist Economy of Versailles. Versailles had had in mind not the creation of preconditions for the triumph of Hitler, but for the proletarization of Germany, for unemployment and hunger, as the result of which there should have triumphed the Communist Revolution. But insofar as, thanks to the existence of Stalin at the head of the USSR and the International, the latter did not succeed and as a result of an unwillingness to give up Germany to Bonapartism, these preconditions were somewhat abated in the Davis and Young Plans, in expectation that meanwhile the opposition would come to power in Russia...; but that, too, did not happen; but the existence of revolutionary preconditions had to produce its results. The economic predetermination of Germany would have forced the proletariat into revolutionary actions. Through the fault of Stalin the Social-International Revolution had to be held up and the German proletariat sought inclusion in the National-Socialist revolution.**

C   (Now comes the most remarkable part. The bankers saw Stalin as a problem to their plan. So they created an opponent to balance the power in Europe.

The chosen country was Germany, which had been bankrupted by the Versailles Treaty.).

R   This was dialectical, but given all the preconditions and according to common sense the National Socialist revolution could never have triumphed there. That was not yet all. It was necessary that the Trotzkyists and Socialists should divide the masses with an already awakened and whole class consciousness-- in accordance with instructions. With this business we concerned ourselves. But then more was needed: **In 1929, when the National-Socialist Party began to experience a crisis of growth and it had insufficient financial resources, "They" sent their ambassador there. I even know his name: It was one of the Warburg's. In direct negotiations with Hitler they agreed as to the financing of the National Socialist Party, and the latter received in a couple of years millions of dollars, sent to it from Wall Street, and millions of Marks from German financiers through Schacht; the upkeep of the S.A. and S.S. and also the financing of the elections which took place, which gave Hitler power, are done on the Dollars and Marks sent by "Them".**

C   (From this historic interview we clearly find that the bankers of New York financed Hitler. Yes, Hitler. Yet we have been forced to abstain from comment on all Jewish matters since World War 11. No section of our community should have such a blanket censorship on responsible comment. This is by far the most important reason why we know little of these events and is a totally unhealthy situation. We have seen how the International Bankers control our media and censor our news. Our search for the truth is of utmost importance for a free and democratic world).

G   Those who, according to you, want to achieve full Communism, arm Hitler, who swears that he will uproot the first Communist nation. This, if one is to believe you, is something very logical for the financiers.

R   You again forget the Stalinist Bonapartism.   Remember that against Napoleon, the strangler of the French Revolution, who stole its strength, there stood the objective revolutionaries--Louis XVIII, Wellington, Metternich and right up to the Tsar-Autocrat...This is 22 carat, according to the strict Stalinist doctrine. You must know by heart his theses about colonies with regard to imperialistic countries. Yes, according to him the Kings of Afghanistan and Egypt are objectively Communists owing to their struggle against his Britannic Majesty; why cannot Hitler be objectively Communist since he is fighting against the autocratic "Tsar Koba I"? (Stalin). After all there is Hitler, with his growing military power, and he already extends the boundaries of the Third Reich, and in future will do more... to such an extent as to have enough strength and possibilities to attack and fully destroy Stalin...Do you not observe the general sympathy of the Versailles wolves, who limit themselves only to a weak growl? Is this yet another chance, accident? Hitler will invade the USSR and as in 1917, when defeat suffered by the Tsar then gave us the opportunity of overthrowing him, so the defeat of Stalin will help us to remove him...Again the hour of the world revolution will strike.   Since the democratic States, at present put to sleep, will help to bring about the general change at that moment, when Trotzky will take power into his hands, as during the civil war. Hitler will attack from the West, his generals will rise and liquidate him...Now tell me, was not Hitler objectively a Communist? Yes or no?

G   I do not believe in fairy tales or miracles...

R   Well if you do not want to believe that "They" are able to achieve that which they had already achieved, then prepare to observe an invasion of the USSR and the liquidation of Stalin within a year. You think this is a miracle or an accident, well then prepare to see and experience that...But are you really able to refuse to believe that of which I have spoken, though this is still only an hypothesis? You will begin to act in this direction only at that moment when you will begin to see the proofs in the light of my talk.

G   All right, let us talk in the form of a supposition, what will you say?

R   You yourself have drawn attention to the coincidence of opinions, which took place between us. We are not at the moment interested in the attack on the USSR, since the fall of Stalin would pre-suppose the destruction of Communism, the existence of which interests us despite the circumstance that it is formal, as that gives us the certainty that we shall succeed in taking it over and then converting it into real Communism. I think that I have given you the position at the moment quite accurately.

G   Splendid, the solution...

R   First of all we must make sure that there would be no potential possibility of an attack by Hitler.

G   If, as you confirm, it were "They" who made him Führer, then they have power over him and he must obey them.

R   Owing to the fact that I was in a hurry I did not express myself quite correctly and you did not understand me well. If it is true that "They" financed Hitler, then that does not mean that they disclosed to him their existence and their aims. The ambassador Warburg presented himself under a false name and Hitler did not even guess his race; he also lied regarding whose representative he was. (True Illuminati). He told him that he had been sent by the financial circles of Wall Street who were interested in financing the National-Socialist movement with the aim of creating a threat to France, whose governments pursue a financial policy which provokes a crisis in the USA.

G   And Hitler believed it?

R   We do not know. That was not so important, whether he did or did not believe our explanations; our aim was to provoke a war ... and Hitler was war. Do you now understand?

G   I understand. Consequently I do not see any other way of stopping him as the creation of a coalition of the USSR with the democratic nations, which would be capable of frightening Hitler. I think he will not be able to attack simultaneously all the countries of the world. The most would be - each in turn.

R   Does not a simpler solution come to your mind - I would say - a counter-revolutionary one?

G   To avoid war against the USSR?

R   Shorten the phrase by half ... and repeat with me "avoid war"... is that not an absolutely counter-revolutionary thing? Every sincere Communist imitating his idol Lenin and the greatest revolutionary strategists must always wish for war. **Nothing is so effective in bringing nearer the victory of revolution as war**.

C   (War is the promoter of revolution. That is clear.). This is a Marxist-Leninist dogma, which you must preach. Now further: Stalin's National-Communism, this type of Bonapartism, is capable of blinding the intellect of the most pure-blooded Communists, right up to the point at which it prevents their seeing that the transformation into which Stalin has fallen, i.e., that he subjects the revolution to the State, and not the State to the revolution, it would be correct.

G   Your hate of Stalin blinds you and you contradict yourself. Have we not agreed that an attack on the USSR would not be welcome?

R   But why should war be necessarily against the Soviet Union?

G   But on what other country could Hitler make war? It is sufficiently clear that he would direct his attack on the USSR; of this he speaks in his speeches. What further proofs do you need?

R   If you, the people from the Kremlin, consider it to be quite definite and not debatable, then why did you provoke the Civil War in Spain? Do not tell me that it was done for purely revolutionary reasons. Stalin is incapable of carrying out in practice a single Marxist theory. If there were revolutionary considerations here, then it would not be right to sacrifice in Spain so many excellent international revolutionary forces. This is the country which is furthest from the USSR, and the most elementary strategical education would not have allowed the loss of these forces...How would Stalin be able in case of conflict to supply and render military help to a Spanish Soviet Republic? But this was correct. There we have an important strategic point, a crossing of opposing influences of the Capitalist States...It might have been possible to provoke a war between them. I admit that theoretically this may have been right, but in practice--no. You already see how the war between the democratic Capitalist and Fascist States did not begin. And now I shall tell you: If Stalin thought that he himself was capable of creating an excuse sufficient in order to provoke a war, in which the Capitalist States would have had to fight among themselves, then why does he not at least admit, if only theoretically, that others, too, can achieve the same thing, which did not seem possible to him?

G   If one is to agree with your assumptions then one can admit this hypothesis.

R   That means that there is yet a second point of argument between us: the first -- that there must be no war against the USSR; the second -- that it would be well to provoke it between the Bourgeois States.

G   Yes, I agree. Is that your personal opinion, or "Theirs"?

R   I express it as my opinion. I have no power and no contact with "Them", but I can confirm that in these two points it coincides with the view of the Kremlin.

G   That is the most important thing and for that reason it is important to establish this beforehand. By the way, I would also like to know on what you base yourself in your confidence that "They" approve this.

R   If I had the time in order to explain their full scheme, then you would already know about the reasons for their approval. At the present moment I shall condense them to three:

G   Just Which?

R   One is that which I have already mentioned. Hitler, this uneducated and elementary man, has restored, thanks to his natural intuition, and even against the technical opinion of Schacht, an economic system of a very dangerous kind. **Being illiterate in all economic theories and being guided only by necessity he removed, as we had done it in the USSR, the private and international capital. That means that he took over for himself the privilege of manufacturing money, and not only physical moneys, but also financial ones; he took over the untouched machinery of falsification and put it to work for the benefit of the State.** He exceeded us, as we, having abolished it in Russia, replaced it merely by this crude apparatus called State Capitalism; this was a very expensive triumph in view of the necessities of pre-Revolutionary demagogy...Here I give you two real facts for comparison. I shall even say that Hitler had been lucky; he had almost no gold and for that reason he was not tempted to create a gold reserve. Insofar as he only possessed a full monetary guarantee of technical equipment and colossal working capacity of the Germans, his "Gold Reserve" was technical capacity and work...something so completely counter-revolutionary that, as you already see, he has by means of magic, as it were, radically eliminated unemployment among more than seven million technicians and workers.

G   Thanks to increased re-armament.

R   What does your re-armament give? If Hitler reached this despite all the bourgeois economists who surround him, then he was quite capable, in the absence of the danger of war, of applying his system also to peaceful production...Are you capable of imagining what would have become of this system if it had infected a number of other States and brought about the creation of a period of autarky...For example the Commonwealth. If you can, then imagine its counter-revolutionary functions...The danger is not yet inevitable, as we have had luck in that Hitler restored his system not according to some previous theory but empirically, and he did not make any formulations of a scientific kind. (Rakovsky's view which is ignoring Hitler's reading of Gottfried Feder advised in "Mein Kampf"). This means that insofar as he did not think in the light of a deductive process based on intelligence, he has no scientific terms or a formulated doctrine; yet there is a hidden danger as at any moment there can appear, as the consequence of deduction, a formula. This is very serious. Much more so that all the external and cruel factors in National-Socialism. We do not attack it in our propaganda as it could happen that through theoretical polemics we would ourselves provoke a formulation and systematisation of this so decisive economic doctrine. There is only one solution-- War.

G   And the second motive?

R   If the Termidor triumphed in the Soviet Revolution then this happened as a result of the existence of the former Russian nationalism. Without such, a nationalism Bonapartism would have been impossible. And if that happened in Russia, where nationalism was only embryonic in the person of the Tsar, then what obstacles must Marxism meet, in the fully developed nationalism of Western Europe? Marx was wrong in respect to the advantages for success of the revolution. Marxism won not in the most industrialised country, but in Russia, where the proletariat was small. Apart from other reasons our victory here is explained by the fact that in Russia there was no real nationalism, and in other countries it was in full apogee. You see how it is re-borne under this extraordinary power of Fascism, and how infectious it is. **You can understand that apart from that it can benefit Stalin, the need for the destruction of nationalism is alone worth a war in Europe.**

C   (Here is the proof that the European Union, in following federalism, is part of the Bankers plan through Communism to remove Nationalism).

G   In sum, you have set out, Rakovsky, one economic and one political reason. Which is the third?

R   That is easy to guess. We have yet another reason, a religious one. **Communism cannot be the victor if it will not have suppressed the still living Christianity. History speaks very clearly about this: the permanent revolution required seventeen centuries in order to achieve its first partial victory--by means of the creation of the first split in Christendom. In reality Christianity is our only real enemy, since all the political and economic phenomena in the bourgeois States are only its consequences.**

C   (This makes another policy of the Bankers and Communism official. **Religion is its main enemy.**).

R   Christianity, controlling the individual is capable of annulling the revolutionary projection of the neutral Soviet or atheistic State by choking it and, as we see it in Russia, things have reached the point of creation of that spiritual Nihilism which is dominant in the ruling masses, which have, nevertheless, remained Christian; this obstacle has not yet been removed during twenty years of Marxism.   Let us admit in relation to Stalin that towards religion he was not Bonapartistic. We would not have done more than he and would have acted in the same way.   And if Stalin had dared, like Napoleon, to cross the Rubikon of Christianity, then his nationalism and counter-revolutionary power would have been increased a thousand-fold. In addition, if this had happened then so radical a difference would have made quite impossible any collaboration in anything between us and him, even if this were to be only temporary and objective...like the one you can see becoming apparent to us.

G   And so I personally consider that you have given a definition of three fundamental points, on the basis of which a plan can be made. That is what I am in agreement about with you for the present. But I confirm to you my mental reservations, i.e. my suspicion in relation to all that which you have said concerning people, organisations and facts. Now continue to follow the general lines of your plan.

R   Yes, now this moment has arrived. But only a preliminary qualification: I shall speak on my own responsibility. I am responsible for the interpretation of those preceding points in the sense in which "They" understand them, but I admit that "They" understand them, but I admit that "They" may consider another plan to be more effective for the attainment of the three aims, and one quite unlike that which I shall now set out. Bear that in mind.

G   Very well, we shall bear it in mind. Please speak.

R   We shall simplify. Insofar as the object is missing for which the German military might have been created--to give us power in the USSR -- the aim now is to bring about an advance on the fronts and to direct the Hitlerist advance not towards the East, but the West.

G   Exactly. Have you thought of a practical plan of realisation?

R   I had had more than enough time for that at the Lubianka. I considered. So look: if there were difficulties in finding mutually shared points between us and all else took its normal course, then the problems comes down to again trying to establish that in which there is similarity between Hitler and Stalin.

G   Yes, but admit all this is problematical.

R   But not insoluble, as you think. In reality problems are insoluble only when they include dialectically subjective contradictions; and even in that case we always consider possible and essential a synthesis, overcoming the "morally-impossible" of Christian meta-physicians.

G   Again begin to theorise.

R   As a result of my intellectual discipline--this is essential for me. People of big culture prefer to approach the concrete through a generalisation, and not the other way round. With Hitler and with Stalin one can find common ground, as, being very different people. They have the same roots; if Hitler is sentimental to a pathological degree, but Stalin is normal, yet both of them are egoists: neither one of them is an idealist, and for that reason both of them are Bonapartists, i.e. classical Imperialists. And if just that is the position, then it is already not difficult to find common ground between them. Why not, if it proved possible between one Tsarina and one Prussian King...

G   Rakovsky, you are incorrigible...

R   You do not guess? If Poland was the point of union between Catherine and Frederick--the Tsarina of Russia and the King of Germany at that time, then why cannot Poland serve as a reason for the finding of common ground between Hitler and Stalin? In Poland the persons of Hitler and Stalin can coincide, and also the historical Tsarist-Bolshevik and Nazi lines. Our line, "Their" line--also, as Poland is a Christian State and, what makes the matter even more complex a Catholic one.

G   And what follows from the fact of such treble coincidence?

R   If there is common ground then there is possibility of agreement.

G   Between Hitler and Stalin?... Absurd! Impossible.

R   In politics there are neither absurdities, nor the impossible.

G   Let us imagine, as an hypothesis: Hitler and Stalin advance on Poland.

R   Permit me to interrupt you; an attack can be called forth only by the following alternative: War or Peace. You must admit it.

G   Well, and so what?

R   Do you consider that England and France with their worse armies and aviation, in comparison with Hitler's, can attack the united Hitler and Stalin?

G   Yes, that seems to me very difficult...unless America...

R   Let us leave the United States aside for the moment, will you agree with me that as the result of the attack of Hitler and Stalin on Poland there can be no European war?

G   You argue logically; it would seem impossible.

R   In that case an attack or war would be useless. It would not call forth the mutual destruction of the bourgeois States: the Hitlerist threat to the USSR would continue in being after the diversion of Poland since theoretically both Germany and the USSR would have been strengthened to the same extent. In practice Hitler to a greater extent, since the USSR does not need more land and raw materials for its strengthening, but Hitler does need them.

G   This is a correct view...but I can see no other solution.

R   No, there is a solution.

G   Which?

R   That the democracies should attack and not attack the aggressor.

G   What are you saying, what hallucination! Simultaneously to attack and not attack...That is something absolutely impossible.

R   You think so? Calm down...Are there not two aggressors? Did we not agree that there will be no advance just because there are two? Well...What prevents the attack on one of them?

G   What do you want to say by that?

R   Simply that the democracies will declare war only on one aggressor, and that will be Hitler.

G   Yes, your arguments seem to be logical in the case if the conflict will be limited to four countries; but there are not four, but more, and neutrality is not a simple matter in a war on the given scale.

R   Undoubtedly, but the possible participation of many countries does not change the power relationships. Weigh this in your mind and you will see how the balance will continue, even if others or even all European States come in. In addition, and this is very important, not one of those States, which will enter the war at the side of England and France will be able to deprive them of leadership; as a result the reasons which will prevent their attack on the USSR will retain their significance.

G   You forget about the United States.

R   In a moment you will see that I have not forgotten. I shall limit myself to the investigation of their function in the preliminary programme, which occupies us at present, and I shall say that America will not be able to force France and England to attack Hitler and Stalin simultaneously. In order to attain that, the United States would have to enter the war from the very first day. But that is impossible. **In the first place because America did not enter a war formerly and never will do so if it is not attacked. Its rulers can arrange that they will be attacked, if that will suit them.**

C   (That is exactly what happened at Pearl Harbour.). Of that I can assure you. In those cases when provocation was not successful and the enemy did not react to it, aggression was invented. In their first international war, the war against Spain, of the defeat of which they were sure, they invented an aggression, or, more correctly, "They" invented it. In 1914 provocation was successful. True, one can dispute technically if there was one, but the rule without exception is that he who makes a sudden attack without warning, does it with the help of a provocation. Now it is like this: this splendid American technique which, welcome at any moment, is subject to one condition: that aggression should take place at a suitable moment, i.e. the moment required by the United States who are being attacked; that means then, when they will have the arms. Does that condition exist now? It is clear that it does not. In America there are at present a little less than one hundred thousand men under arms and a middling aviation: it has only an imposing fleet. But you can understand that, having it, it can not persuade its allies to decide on an attack on the USSR, since England and France have preponderance only at sea. I have also proved to you that, from that side there can be no change in the comparative strengths of the forces.

G   Having agreed with this, I ask you again to explain once more the technical realisation.

R   As you have seen, given the coincidence of the interests of Stalin and Hitler with regard to an attack on Poland, all comes down to the formalisation of this full similarity of aims and to make a pact about a double attack.

G   And you think this is easy?

R   Frankly, no. Here we need a diplomacy which is more experienced than that of Stalin. There ought to have been available the one which Stalin had decapitated, or the one which now decays in the Lubianka. In former times Litvinov would have been capable, with some difficulties, although his race would have been a great obstacle for negotiations with Hitler; but now this is a finished man and he is destroyed by a terrible panic; he is experiencing an animal fear of Molotov, even more than Stalin. His whole talent is directed towards making sure that they should not think that he is a Trotskyist. If he were to hear of the necessity of arranging closer relations with Hitler, then that would be enough for him to manufacture for himself the proof of his Trotskyism. I do not see a man who is capable of this job; in any event he would have to be a true-blooded Russian. I could offer my services for guidance. At the present moment I would suggest to the one who begins the talks, that they should be strictly confidential, but with great open sincerity. Given a whole wall of various prejudices only truthfulness can deceive Hitler.

G   I again do not understand your paradoxical expressions.

R   Forgive me, but this only appears to be so; I am forced by the synthesis to do so. I wanted to say, that with Hitler, one must play a clean game, concerning the concrete and most immediate questions. It is necessary to show him that the game is not played in order to provoke him into war on two fronts. For example, it is possible to promise him, and to prove at the most suitable moment, that our mobilisation will be limited to a small number of forces, required for the invasion of Poland, and that these forces will not be great. According to our real plan, we shall have to place our main forces to meet the possible Anglo-French attack. Stalin will have to be generous with the preliminary supplies which Hitler will demand, chiefly oil. That is what has come to my mind for the moment. Thousands of further questions will arise, of a similar character, which will have to be solved so that Hitler, seeing in practice that we only want to occupy our part of Poland, would be quite certain of that. And insofar as in practice it should be just like that, he will be deceived by the truth.

G   But in what, in this case, is there a deception?

R   I shall give you a few minutes of time so that you yourself can discover just in what there is a deception of Hitler. But first I want to stress, and you should take note, that the plan which I have indicated here, is logical and normal and I think that one can achieve that the Capitalistic States will destroy each other, if one brings about a clash of their two wings: the Fascist and the Bourgeois. I repeat that the plan is logical and normal. As you have already been able to see, there is no intervention here of mysterious or unusual factors. In short, in order that one should be able to realise the plan, "Their" intervention is not required. Now I should like to guess your thoughts; are you not now thinking that it would be stupid to waste time on proving the un-provable existence and power held by "Them." Is that not so?

G   You are right.

R   Be frank with me. Do you really not observe their intervention? I informed you, wanting to help you, that their intervention exists and is decisive, and for that reason the logic and naturalness of the plan are only appearances...Is it really true that you do not see "Them"?

G   Speaking sincerely, no.

R   The logic and naturalness of my plan is only an appearance. It would be natural and logical that Hitler and Stalin would inflict defeat on each other. For the democracies that would be a simple and easy thing, if they would have to put forward such an aim; for them it would be enough that Hitler should be permitted, make note "permitted" to attack Stalin. Do not tell me that Germany could be defeated. If the Russian distances, and the dreadful fear of Stalin, and his henchmen of the Hitlerite axe, and the revenge of their victims will not be enough in order to attain the military exhaustion of Germany, then there will be no obstacles to the democracies, seeing that Stalin is losing strength, beginning to help him wisely and methodically, continuing to give that help until the complete exhaustion of both armies. In reality that would be easy, natural and logical, if those motives and aims which are put forward by the democracies and which most of their followers believe to be the true ones, and not what they are in reality - pretexts. **There is only one aim, one single aim; the triumph of Communism; it is not Moscow which will impose its will on the democracies, but New York, not the "Comintern," but the "Capintern" on Wall Street. Who other than he could have been able to impose on Europe such an obvious and absolute contradiction? What force can lead it towards complete suicide? Only one force is able to do this: money. Money is power and the sole power.**

C   (The triumph of Communism is being directed by the bankers of New York, through the ultimate power, Money.).

G   I shall be frank with you, Rakovsky. I admit in you an exceptional gift of talent. You possess brilliant dialectic, persuasive and subtle: when this is not enough for you, then your imagination has command of means in order to extend your colourful canvas, while you invent brilliant and clear perspectives; but all this, although it provokes my enthusiasm, is not enough for me. I shall go over to putting questions to you, assuming that I believe all that you have said.

R   And I shall give you replies, but with one single condition, that you should not add anything to what I shall say, nor deduct.

G   I promise. You assert that "They" hinder or will hinder a German-Soviet war, which is logical from the point of view of the Capitalists. Have I explained it correctly?

R   Yes, precisely so.

G   But the reality of the present moment is such, that Germany has been permitted to re-arm and expand. This is a fact, I already know that, in accordance with your explanation this was called forth by the Trotskyist plan, which fell through thanks to the "cleanings-out" now taking place; thus the aim has been lost. In the face of a new situation you only advise that Hitler and Stalin should sign a pact and divide Poland. I ask you: how can we obtain a guarantee that, having the pact, or not having it, carrying out, or not carrying out the partition, Hitler will not attack the USSR?

R   This cannot be guaranteed.

G   Then why go on talking?

R   Do not hurry. The magnificent threat to the USSR is real and exists. This is not an hypotheses and not a verbal threat. It is a fact, and a fact which obliges. "They" already have superiority over Stalin; a superiority which cannot be denied. Stalin is offered only one alternative, the right to choose, but not full freedom. The attack of Hitler will come in any case of its own accord; "They" need not do anything to make it happen but only leave him the chance of acting. This is the basic and determining reality, which has been forgotten by you owing to your excessively Kremlin-like way of thinking... Egocentrism, Sir, egocentrism.

G   The right to choose?

R   I shall define it exactly once more, but shortly: either there will be an attach on Stalin, or there will come the realisation of the plan I have indicated, according to which the European Capitalistic States will destroy each other. I drew attention to this alternative, but as you see it was only a theoretical one. It Stalin wants to survive then he will be forced to realise the plan which as been proposed by me and ratified by "Them."

G   But if he refuses?

R   That will be impossible for him. The expansion and rearmament of Germany will continue. When Stalin will be faced by this gigantic threat...then what will he do? This will be dictated to him by his own instinct of self-preservation

G   It seems that events must develop only according to the orders indicated by "Them."

R   And it is so. Of course, in the USSR to-day things still stand like this; but sooner or later it will happen like that all the same. It is not difficult to foretell and to suggest for carrying out something, if it is profitable for the person who must realise the matter; in the given case Stalin, who is hardly thinking of suicide. It is much more difficult to give a prognosis and to force to act, as needed, someone for whom that is not profitable, but who must act nevertheless; in the given case, the democracies. I have kept the explanation for this moment to give a concrete picture of the true position. Reject the wrong thought that you are the arbiters in the given situation, since "They" are the arbiters.

G   "They" both in the first and the second case...Therefore we must deal with shadows?

R   But are facts shadows? The international situation will be extraordinary, but not shadowy; it is real and very real. This is not a miracle; here is predetermined the future policy...Do you think this is the work of shadows?

G   But let us see; let us assume that your plan is accepted...But we must have something tangible, personal, in order to be able to carry out negotiations.

R   For example?

G   Some persons with powers of attorney and representation.

R   But for what? Just for the pleasure of becoming acquainted with him? For the pleasure of a talk? Bear in mind that the assumed person, in case of his appearance, will not present you with credentials with seals and crests, and will not wear a diplomatic uniform, at least a man from "Them"; if he were to say something or promise, then it will have no juridical force or meaning as a pact.. Understand that "They" are not a State; "They" are that which the International was before 1917, that which it still is; nothing and at the same time everything. Imagine to yourself, it is possible that the USSR would have negotiations with Freemasonry, with an espionage organization, with the Macedonian Komitadgi or the Croatian Ustashi. Would not some juridical agreement be written?...Such pacts as the pact of Lenin with the German General Staff, as the pact of Trotzky with "Them" - are realized without written documents and without signatures. The only guarantee of their execution, is rooted in the circumstance, that the carrying out of that which has been agreed, is profitable for the parties to the pact, this guarantee is the sole reality in the pact, however great may be its importance.

G   From what would you begin in the present case?

R   Simple; I should begin already from to-morrow to sound out Berlin ...

G   In order to agree about the attack on Poland?

R   I would not begin with that... I would display my willingness to yield, and would hint about certain disappointments among the democracies, I would soft-pedal in Spain ... This would be an act of encouragement; then I would drop a hint about Poland. As you see---nothing compromising, but enough so that a part of the OKW (German High Command-Trans.), the Bismarckists, as they are called, would have some arguments to put before Hitler.

G   And nothing more?

R   For the beginning, nothing more; this is already a big diplomatic task.

G   Speaking frankly, having in mind the aims which have been dominant in the Kremlin until now, I do not think that anyone would at present dare to advise such a radical change in international policy. I propose to you, Rakovsky, to transform yourself in imagination into that person at the Kremlin who will have to take the decision... on the basis only of your disclosures, arguments, your hypotheses and persuasion, as I see it, it would be impossible to convince anyone. I personally, after having listened to you and at the same time, I shall not deny it, having experienced a strong influence from your explanations, of your personality, have not for a single moment experienced the temptation to consider the German-Soviet pact to be something realisable.

R   International events will force with irresistible strength...

G   But that would be a loss of valuable time. Consider something concrete, something which I could put forward as a proof of your veracity and credibility...In the contrary case I should not dare to transmit your information about our conversation; I should edit it with all accuracy, but it would reach the Kremlin archives and stay there.

R   Would it not be enough to bring about, that it is taken into consideration if someone, even in a most official manner, were to have a talk with some very important person?

G   It seems to me that this would be something real.

R   But with whom?

G   This is only my personal opinion, Rakovsky. You had mentioned concrete persons, big financiers; if I remember correctly, you had spoken about a certain Schiff, for example; then you mentioned another who had been the go-between with Hitler for the purpose of financing him. There are also politicians or persons with a big position, who belong to "Them" or, if you like, serve "Them". Someone like that could be of use to us in order to start something practical...Do you know someone?

R   I do not think it is necessary...Think: about what will you be negotiating? Probably about the plan which I have set out, is that not so? For what? At the present moment "They" need not do anything in this context; "Their" mission is "not to do." And for that reason you would not be able to agree about any positive action and could not demand it... Remember, consider well.

G   Even if that is so, yet in view of our personal opinion there must be reality, even if a useless one,...a man, a personality who would confirm the credibility of the power, which you ascribe to "Them."

R   I shall satisfy you, although I am sure of the uselessness of this. I have already told you that I do not know who is a part of "Them," but have assurances from a person who must have known them."

G   From whom?

R   **From Trotzky. From Trotzky I know only that one of "Them" was Walter Rathenau, who was well known from Rapallo. You see the last of "Them" who occupied a political and social position, since it was he who broke the economic blockade of the USSR. Despite the fact that he was one of the biggest millionaires; of course, such also was Lionel Rothschild.**

C   (At last he names one of 'them', a banker, Walter Rathenau.).

R   I can with confidence mention only these names. Naturally I can name still more people, the work and personality of whom I determine as being fully "Theirs," but I cannot confirm what these people command or whom they obey.

G   Mention some of them.

R   **As an institution - the Bank of Kuhn, Loeb & Co., of Wall Street; to this bank belong the families of Schiff, Warburg, Loeb and Kuhn; I say families in order to point out several names, since they are all connected among themselves by marriages; then Baruch, Frankfurter, Altschul, Cohen, Benjamin, Strauss, Steinhardt, Blom, Rosenman, Lippmann, Lehman, Dreifus, Lamont, Rothschild, Lord, Mandel, Morgenthau, Ezekiel, Lasky.**

C   (There comes a flood of names. All bankers, mostly Masons.).

R   **In the end I shall take the risk. Do you know if Davis is at present in Moscow? Yes, the Ambassador of the United States.**

G   I think he is; he should have returned.

R   Only an exceptional situation gives me the right, as I see it, against the rules, to make use of an official intermediary.
G   Therefore we can think that the American Government is behind all this...
R   Behind - no under all this..
G   Roosevelt?
C   (This is the most disturbing part yet. We see the American Ambassador is a Mason and linked to 'Them', the bankers. Behind him we also learn the Roosevelt's are controlled by 'Them', the bankers. This shows how deep world affairs have been penetrated by 'Them', the bankers.).
R   What do I know? I can only come to conclusions. You are all the time obsessed with the mania of political espionage. I could manufacture, in order to please you, a whole history; I have more than sufficient imagination, dates and true facts in order to give it veracity in appearance, which would be close to looking obvious. But are not the generally known facts more obvious? And you can supplement them with your own imagination, if you wish. Look yourself. **Remember the morning of the 24th. October 1929. The time will come when this day will be for the history of the revolution more important than October, 1917. On the day of the 24th. October there took place the crash of the New York Stock Exchange, the beginning of the so-called "depression," a real revolution. The four years of the Government of Hoover - are years of revolutionary progress: 12 and 15 millions on strike. In February, 1933 there takes place the last stroke of the crisis with the closing of the banks. It is difficult to do more than capital did in order to break the "classical American," who was still on his industrial bases and in the economic respect enslaved by Wall Street.**
C   (The Wall Street crash of October 1929 was controlled and engineered by the bankers to further their plan for revolution.).
R   It is well known that any impoverishment in economics, be it in relation to societies or animals, gives a flourishing of parasitism, and capital is a large parasite. But this American revolution pursued not only the one aim of increasing the power of money for those who had the right to use it; it pretended to even more. Although the power of money is political power, but before that it had only been used indirectly, but now the power of money was to be transformed into direct power. **The man through whom they made use of such power was Franklin Roosevelt. Have you understood? Take note of the following: In that year 1929, the first year of the American revolution, in February Trotzky leaves Russia; The crash takes place in October...The financing of Hitler is agreed in July, 1929. You think that all this was by chance? The four years of the rule of Hoover were used for the preparation of the seizure of power in the United States and the USSR; There by means of a financial revolution, and here with the help of war and the defeat which was to follow. Could some good novel with great imagination be more obvious to you? You can understand, that the execution of the plan, on such a scale, requires a special man, who can direct the executive power in the United States, who has been predetermined to be the organising and deciding force. That man was Franklin and Eleanor Roosevelt. And permit me to say that this two-sexed being is not simply irony. He had to avoid any possible Delilah.**
G   Is Roosevelt one of "Them"?

R   I do not know if he is one of "Them," or is only subject to "Them." What more do you want? I think that he was conscious of his mission, but cannot assert whether he obeyed under duress of blackmail, or he was one of those who rule; it is true that he carried out his mission, realized all the actions which had been assigned to him accurately. Do not ask me more, as I do not know any more.

C   (This shows clearly the catalogue of events the bankers prepared, and that Roosevelt was their puppet, by consent or by control).

G   In case it should be decided to approach Davis, in which form would you do it?

R   First of all you must select a person of such a type as "the baron"; he could be useful... Is he still alive?

G   I do not know.

R   All right, the choice of persons is left to you. Your delegate must present himself as being confidential, or not modest, but best of all as a secret oppositionist. The conversation must be cleverly conducted concerning that contradictory position into which the USSR has been put by the so-called European democracies, by their union against National-Socialism. This is the conclusion of an alliance with the British and French Imperialism, the contemporary real Imperialism, for the destruction of the potential Imperialism. The aim of the verbal expressions must be to conjoin the false Soviet position with an equally false one of American democracy...It also sees itself forced to support Colonial Imperialism for the defence of democracy within England and France. As you see, the question can be put onto a very strong logical foundation. **After that it is already very easy to formulate an hypothesis about actions. The first: that neither the USSR, nor the United States are interested in European Imperialism and thus the dispute is brought down to the question of personal hegemony; that ideologically and economically Russia and America want the destruction of European Colonial Imperialism, be it direct or oblique. The United States want it even more. If Europe were to lose all its power in a new war, then England, not having its own forces, with the disappearance of Europe as a force, as power, would from the first day lean, with all its weight and with the whole of its Empire, speaking the English language, on the United States, which would be inevitable both in the political and economic sense...**

C   (This shows how, 'They', directed affairs so Britain would be totally dependent on America to finance their war; and how, 'They', planned Europe's downfall to please the USSR and America to the detriment of Britain.).

R   Analyse what you have heard in the light of the Left conspiracy, as one might say, without shocking any American bourgeois. Having got to the point, one could have an interval for a few days. Then, having noted the reaction, it will be necessary to move further. Now Hitler comes forward. Here one can point to any aggression: he is fully an aggressor and of this there can be no doubt. And then one can go over to asking a question: What common action should be undertaken by the United States and the Soviet Union in view of the war between the Imperialists, who want it? The answer could be - neutrality. One must argue again: yes, neutrality, but it does not depend on the wish of one side, but also of the aggressor. There can be a guarantee of neutrality, only when the aggressor cannot attack, or it does not suit him. For this purpose, the infallible answer is the attack of the aggressor on another Imperialist State. From this it is very easy to go over to the expression of the necessity and morality, with a view to guaranteeing safety, for provoking a clash between the Imperialists, if that clash were not to take place of its own accord. And if that were to be accepted in theory, and it will be accepted, then one can regulate the question of actions in practice, which would be only a matter of technique. **Here is a scheme: (1) A pact with Hitler for the division between us of Czechoslovakia and Poland (better the latter). (2) Hitler will accept. If he is capable of backing a bluff for the conquest, i.e. the seizure of something in alliance with the USSR, then for him there will be full guarantee in that the democracies will yield. He will be unable to believe their verbal threats, as he knows that those, who try to intimidate by war threats, are at the same time partisans of disarmament and that their disarmament is real. (3) The democracies will attack Hitler and not Stalin; they will tell the people that although both are guilty of aggression and partition, but strategical and logical reasons force them to defeat them one by one: first Hitler and then Stalin.**

C   (Here 'They' show how Hitler will be guided to attack Europe, rather than the USSR, and the democracies will go to war against Hitler to create the Second World War. All planned by, 'Them', the bankers. It is worth noting this discussion took place in 1938 before the outbreak of war.).

G   But will they not deceive us with truth?

R   But how? Does not Stalin dispose of freedom of action in order to help Hitler in sufficient measure? Do we not put in his hands the possibility of continuing the war between the Capitalists until the last man and the last pound? With what can they attack him? The exhausted States of the West will already have enough on their hand with internal Communist revolution, which in the other case may triumph.

G   But if Hitler achieves a quick victory and if he, like Napoleon mobilises the whole of Europe against the USSR?

R   This is quite improbable! You forget about the existence of the United States. You reject the power factor, a greater one. Is it not natural that America, imitating Stalin, would on its part help the democratic States? If one were to co-ordinate "against the hands of the clock" the help to both groups of fighters, then there will be assured, without failure, a permanent extension of the war.

G   And Japan?

R   Is not China enough for them? Let Stalin guarantee them his non-intervention. The Japanese are very fond of suicide, but after all not to such an extent as to be capable of simultaneously attacking China and the USSR. Any more objections?

G   No, if it were to depend on me, then I would try... But do you believe that the delegate...?

R   **Yes, I believe. I was not given the chance of speaking with him, but note one detail: the appointment of Davis became known in November, 1936; we must assume that Roosevelt thought of sending him much sooner, and with that in mind, began preliminary steps; we all know that the consideration of the matter, and the official explanations of the appointment, take more than two months. Apparently his appointment was agreed in August...And what happened in August? In August Zinoviev and Kamenev were shot. I am willing to swear that his appointment was made for the purpose of a new involvement of "Them" in the politics of Stalin. Yes, I certainly think so. With what an inner excitement must he have travelled, seeing how one after another there fell the chiefs of the opposition in the "purges" which follow one on another. Do you know if he was present at the trial of Radeck?**

C   (Here we see the first move of 'Them' to get closer to Stalin. Later we will see Roosevelt continue this pursuit, for the bankers?).

G   Yes.

R   You will see him. Have a talk with him. He expects it already for many months.

G   This night we must finish; but before we part I want to know something more. Let us assume that all this is true, and all will be carried out with full success. "They" will put forward definite conditions. Guess what they might be?

R   This is not difficult to assume. The first condition will be the ending of the executions of the Communists, that means the Trotzkyists, as you call them. Then, of course, they will demand the establishment of several zones of influence, as I had mentioned. The boundaries which will have to divide the formal Communism from the real one. That is the most important condition. There will be mutual concessions for mutual help for a time, while the plan lasts, being carried out. You will see for example the paradoxical phenomenon that a whole crowd of people, enemies of Stalin will help him: note they will not necessarily be proletarians, nor will they be professional spies. There will appear influential persons at all levels of society, even very high ones, who will help the Stalinist formal Communism when it becomes if not real, then at least objective Communism. Have you understood me?

G   A little; you wrap up such things in such impenetrable casuistry.

R   If it is necessary to end, then I can only express myself in this way. Let us see if I shall not be able yet to help to understand. It is known that Marxism was called Hegelian. So this question was vulgarised. Hegelian idealism is a widespread adjustment to an uninformed understanding in the West of the natural mysticism of Baruch Spinosa. "They" are Spinosists: perhaps the matter is the other way round, i.e. that spinosism is "Them," insofar as he is only a version adequate to the epoch of "Their" own philosophy, which is a much earlier one, standing on a much higher level. After all, a Hegelian, and for that reason also, the follower of Spinosa, was devoted to his faith, but only temporarily, tactically. The matter does not stand as is claimed by Marxism, that as the result of the elimination of contradictions there arises the synthesis. It is as the result of the opposing mutual fusion, from the thesis and anti-thesis that there arises, as a synthesis, the reality, truth, as a final harmony between the subjective and objective. Do you not see that already? In Moscow there is Communism; in New York Capitalism. It is all the same as a thesis and anti-thesis. Analyse both. Moscow is subjective Communism, but Capitalism-objective-State Capitalism. New York: Capitalism subjective, but Communism objective. A personal syntheses, truth: the Financial International, the Capitalist-Communist one. "They."

C   (This explains the joining of the totally opposite power forms. A truly remarkable coming together for evil. A evil that will corrupt the world unless we can stop them).

The interview lasted six hours. Gabriel sat alone in the interview room for some time just coming to terms with his new knowledge. Rakovsky was not condemned to death. Hitler attacked Poland rather than his arch enemy Communism, of Russia. Stalin was now aware of the power of, 'Them'. It would influence the rest of his term in office. The interview speaks for itself and is the most important evidence to come out of Russia this century, detailing the plot of Communism to encompass the world.

Now we turn to the Protocol for this chapter. This, has in its content, demonstration of World Revolution, and the purpose and direction of Masonry.

"There is now definite evidence that Bolshevism is an international movement controlled by Jews; communications are passing between the leaders in America, France, Russia and England, with a view to concerted action".

Directorate of Intelligence, Home Office, Scotland Yard, London, in a monthly report to Foreign Embassies, 16th. July, 1919.

PROTOCOL FIFTEEN

When we at last definitely come into our kingdom, by the aids of coups d'état prepared everywhere for one and the same day, after the worthlessness of all existing forms of government has been definitely acknowledged (and not a little time will pass before that comes about, perhaps even a whole century) we shall make it our task to see that against us, such things as plots shall no longer exist. With this purpose we shall slay without mercy all who take arms (in hand) to oppose our coming into our kingdom. Every kind of new institution of anything like a secret society will also be punished with death; those of them that are now in existence, are known to us, serve us and have served us, we shall disband and send into exile to continents far removed from Europe. In this way we shall proceed with those goy Masons who know too much; such of these as we may for some reason spare, will be kept in constant fear of exile. We shall promulgate a law making all former members of secret societies liable to exile from Europe as the centre of rule.

Resolutions of our government will be final, without appeal. In the goy societies, in which we have planted and deeply rooted discord and Protestantism, the only possible way of restoring order, is to employ merciless measures that prove the direct force of authority: no regard must be paid to the victims who fall, they suffer for the well-being of the future. The attainment of that well-being, even at the expense of sacrifices, is the duty of any kind of government, that acknowledges as the justification for its existence, not only its privileges but its obligations. The principal guarantee of stability of rule, is to confirm the aureole of power, and this aureole is attained only by such a majestic inflexibility of might, as shall carry on its face, the emblems of inviolability from mystical causes from the choice of God. Such was until recent times, the Russian autocracy, the one and only serious foe we had in the world, without counting the Papacy. Bear in mind the example when Italy, drenched with blood, never touched a hair of the head of Sulla who had poured forth that blood. Sulla enjoyed an apotheosis for his might in the eyes of the people, though they had been torn in pieces by him, but his intrepid return to Italy ringed him round with inviolability. The people do not lay a finger on him, who hypnotises them by his daring and strength of mind.

Meantime, however, until we come into our kingdom, we shall act in the contrary way: we shall create and multiply free Masonic lodges in all the countries of the world, absorb into them all who may become or who are prominent in public activity, for in these lodges we shall find our principal intelligence office and means of influence. All these lodges we shall bring under one central administration, known to us alone and to all others absolutely unknown, which will be composed of our learned elders. The lodges will have their representatives, who will serve to screen the above-mentioned administration of Masonry, and from whom will issue the watchword and programme. In these lodges we shall tie together the known which binds together all revolutionary and Liberal elements. They will be composed of all strata of society. The most secret political plots will be known to us, and will fall under our guiding hands, on the very day of their conception. Among the members of these lodges, will be almost all the agents of international and national police, since their service is for us irreplaceable, in the respect that the police are in a position, not only to use their own particular measures with the insubordinate, but also to screen our activities and provide pretexts for discontents, et cetera.

The class of people who must willingly enter into secret societies are those who live by their wits, careerists, and in general people, mostly light minded, with whom we shall have no difficulty in dealing and in using to wind up the mechanism of the machine devised by us. If this world grows agitated, the meaning of that will be that we have had to stir it up, in order to break up its too great solidarity. But if their should arise in its midst a plot, then at the head of that plot will be no other than one of our most trusted servants. It is natural that we and no other should lead Masonic activities, for we know whither we are leading, we know the final goal of every form of activity whereas the goyim have knowledge of nothing, not even of the immediate effect of action; they put before themselves, usually, the momentary reckoning of the satisfaction of their self-opinion, in the accomplishment of their thought without even remarking that the very conception never belonged to their initiative but to our instigation of their thought...

The goyim enter the lodges out of curiosity or in the hope of getting a nibble from the public pie, and some of them in order to obtain a hearing before the public for their impracticable and groundless fantasies: they thirst for the emotion of success and applause, of which we are remarkably generous. And the reason why we give them this success is to make use of the high conceit of themselves to which it gives birth, for that insensibly disposes them to assimilate our suggestions without being on their guard against them in the fullness of their confidence that it is their own infallibility which is giving utterance to their own thoughts and that it is impossible for them to borrow those others...You cannot imagine to what extent the wisest of goyim can be brought to a state of unconscious naiveté through this high conceit of themselves, and at the same time how easy it is to take the heart out of them by the slightest ill-success, though it be nothing more than silencing the applause they enjoyed, and reducing them to slavish submission for the sake of winning a renewal of success... By so much as our disregard of success, if only they can carry through their plans, by so much the goyim are willing to sacrifice any plans only to have success. This psychology of theirs materially facilitates for us the task of setting them in the required direction. These tigers in appearance have the souls of sheep and the wind blows freely through their heads. We have set them on the hobbyhorse of an idea about the absorption of individuality by the symbolic unit of collectivism...They have never yet, and they never will have the sense to reflect that this hobbyhorse is a manifest violation of the most important law of nature, which has established from the very creation of the world, one unit unlike another and precisely for the purpose of instituting individuality...

If we have been able to bring them to such a pitch of stupid blindness, is it not proof, and amazingly clear proof, of the degree to which the mind of the goyim is undeveloped in comparison with our mind? This it is, mainly, which guarantees our success.

And how far-seeing were our learned elders in ancient times, when they said that to attain a serious end, it behoves us not to stop at any man or to count the victims sacrificed for the sake of that end...We have not counted the victims of the seed of the goy cattle, though we have sacrificed many of our own, but for that we have now already given them such a position on the earth as they could not even have dreamed of. The comparatively small numbers of the victims from the number of ours have preserved our nationality from destruction.

Death is the inevitable end for all. It is better to bring that end nearer to those who hinder our affairs than to ourselves, to the founders of this affair. We execute Masons in such wise, that none save the brotherhood can ever have a suspicion of it, not even the victims themselves of our death sentence; they all die when required as if from a normal kind of illness...Knowing this, even the brotherhood in its turn, dare not protest. By such methods we have plucked out of the midst of Masonry the very root of protest against our disposition. While preaching Liberalism to the goyim, we at the same time keep our own people and our agents in a state of unquestioning submission.

Under our influence, the execution of the laws of the goyim has been reduced to a minimum. The prestige of the law has been exploded by the Liberal interpretations introduced into this sphere. In the most important and fundamental affairs and questions, judges decide as we dictate to them; see matters in the light wherewith we enfold them, for the administration of the goyim, of course, through persons who are our tools, though we do not appear to have anything in common with them - by newspaper opinion or by other means...Even Senators and the higher administration accept our counsels. The purely brute mind of the goyim is incapable of analysis and observation, and still more, of foreseeing wither a certain manner of setting a question may tend.

In this difference in capacity for thought, between the goyim and ourselves, may be clearly discerned the seal of our position as the Chosen People and of our higher quality of humanness, in contradistinction to the brute mind of the goyim. Their eyes are open, but see nothing before them, and do not invent. (unless, perhaps, material things). From this it is plain that nature herself has destined us to guide and rule the world.

When comes the time of our overt rule, the time to manifest its blessings, we shall remake all legislatures, all our laws will be brief, plain, stable, without any kind of interpretations, so that anyone will be in a position to know them perfectly. The main feature, which they will hold in common, is submission to orders, and this principle will be carried to a grandiose height. Every abuse will then disappear, since all, down to the lowest unit, will be held responsible before the higher authority of the representative of power. Abuses of power, subordinate to this last instance, will be so mercilessly punished that none will be found anxious to try experiments with their own powers. We shall pursue jealously, every action of the administration on which depends the smooth running of the machinery of the state, for slackness in this, produces slackness everywhere: not a single case of illegality or abuse of power will be left without exemplary punishment.

Concealment of guilt, connivance between those in the service of the administration - all this kind of evil will disappear after the very first examples of severe punishment. The auréole of our power demands suitable, that is, cruel punishment for the slightest infringement, for the sake of gain, of its supreme prestige. The sufferer, though his punishment may exceed his fault, will count as a soldier falling on the administrative field of battle, in the interest of authority, principle and law, which does not permit that any of those who hold the reins of the public coach should turn aside from the public highway to their own private paths. For example: our judges will know that, whenever they feel disposed to plume themselves on foolish clemency, they are violating the law of justice, which is instituted for the exemplary edification of men, by penalties for lapse and not for display of the spiritual qualities of the judge...Such qualities it is proper to show in private life, but not in a public square which is the educational basis of human life. Our legal staff will not serve beyond the age of 55, firstly because old men hold more obstinately to prejudiced opinions and are less capable of submitting to new directions, and secondly because after this measure we will enjoy greater elasticity in changing the staff, which will thus the more easily bend under our pressure: he, who wishes to keep his place, will have to give blind obedience to deserve it. In general, our judges will be elected by us only from among those who thoroughly understand that the part they have to play is to punish and apply laws and not dream about the manifestations of Liberalism at the expense of the educational scheme of the state, as the goyim in these days imagine it to be. This method of shuffling the staff will serve also to explode any collective solidarity of those in the same service and will bind all to the interests of the government, upon which their fate will depend. The young generation of judges will be trained in certain views regarding the inadmissibility of any abuses that might disturb the established order of our subjects among themselves.

In these days, the judges of the goyim create indulgences to every kind of crimes, not having a just understanding of their office, because the rulers of the present age, in appointing judges to office, take no care to inculcate in them a sense of duty and consciousness of the matter which is demanded of them. As a brute beast lets out its young in search of prey, so do the goyim give their subjects places of profit without thinking to make clear to them for what purpose such a place was created. This is the reason why their governments are being ruined by their own forces through acts of their own administration.

Let us borrow from the example of the results of these actions, yet another lesson for our government.

We shall root government on which depends the training of subordinates for our state structure. Such posts will fall exclusively to those who have been trained by us for administrative rule. To the possible objection that the retirement of old servants will cost the treasury heavily, I reply, firstly, they will be provided with some private service in place of what they lose, and, secondly, I have to remark that all the money in the world will be concentrated in our hands, consequently it is not our government that has to fear expense.

Our absolutism will in all things be logically consecutive, and, therefore, our supreme will, in each one of its decrees, will be respected and unquestionably fulfilled: it will ignore all murmurs, all discontents of every kind and will destroy to the root, every kind of manifestation of them in act by punishment of an exemplary character.

We shall abolish the right of cassation, which will be transferred exclusively to our disposal - to the cognisance of our ruler, for we must not allow the conception among the people of a thought that there could be such a thing as a decision that is not right by judges set up by us. If, however, anything like this should occur, we shall ourselves cassette the decision, but inflict therewith such exemplary punishment on the judge for lack of understanding of his duty and the purposes of his appointment as will prevent a repetition of such cases...I repeat that it must be borne in mind, that we shall know every step of our administration, which only needs to be closely watched for the people to be content with us, for it has the right to demand from a good government a good official.

Our government will have the appearance of a patriarchal paternal guardianship on the part of the ruler. Our own nation and our subjects will discern in his person a father caring for their every need, their every act, their every interrelation as subjects one with another, as well as their relations to the ruler. They will then be so thoroughly imbued with the thought that it is impossible for them to dispense with this ward ship and guidance, if they wish to live in peace and quiet, that they will acknowledge the autocracy of our ruler with a devotion bordering on Apotheosis, especially when they are convinced that those whom we set up to not put their own in place of his authority but only blindly execute his dictates. They will be rejoiced that we have regulated everything in their lives as is done by wise parents, who desire to retain their children in the cause of duty and submission. For the people of the world, in regards to the secrets of the state, are ever through the ages only children under age, precisely as are also their governments.

As you see, I found our despotism on right and duty: the right to compel the execution of duty is the direct obligation of a government which watches over its subjects like a father. It has the right of the strong, that it may use it for the benefit of directing humanity towards the order, which is defined by nature, namely, submission. Everything in the world is in a state of submission; if not to man, then to circumstances or to its own inner character, in all cases to what is stronger. And so shall we be this something stronger for the sake of good.

We are obliged without hesitation to sacrifice individuals, who commit a breach of established order, for in exemplary punishment of evil lies, a great educational problem.

When the King of Israel sets upon his sacred head the crown offered him by Europe, he will become patriarch of the world. The indispensable victims offered by him, in consequence of their suitability, will never reach the numbers of victims offered in the course of centuries by the mania of magnificence, the emulation between the goy governments. Our King will be in constant communion with the peoples, making to them, from the tribune, speeches which fame will in that same hour distribute over all the world.

COMMENT

One of the dictatorship's first tasks seems to be to make secret societies illegal. This should tell us something as they have used them to gain power, and they know the advantage they have had over the world by using Masonry as their vehicle.

They will impose total submission to their laws, with the threat of death for dissenters. Death, they say, will deter others from following; otherwise law by dictatorship, not evolution.

They themselves will lead the Masonic movement and control its members, multiplying their lodges, and using Masons as their officials, while recruiting the army and police to their ranks to control the masses. They claim they will kill Masons when they are no longer of use to them. This might make these secret societies think for once.

This Protocol gives us a very vivid picture of life under the bankers' dictatorship and we can already see some of the preparations taking place in readiness for their take-over; the European Union being a striking example. Just reflect on the stupid rulings coming out of the European courts, and you can see what we are in for, in the future, unless we act to halt their progress.

"Unless Bolshevism is nipped in the bud immediately it is bound to spread in one form or another all over Europe and the whole world, as it is organised and worked by Jews who have no nationality and whose object is to destroy for their own ends the existing order of things".
British Government White Paper, Russia No. 1, 1919.

CHAPTER SIX
MARXIST POLICIES
A HALL OF MIRRORS

"A nation can survive its fools, and even the ambitious, but it cannot survive treason from within. An enemy at the gate is less formidable, for he is known and he carries his banners openly. But the traitor moves among those within the gate freely, his sly whispers rustling through all the alleys, heard in the very halls of government itself. For the traitor appears no traitor, he speaks in accents familiar to his victims, and he wears their face and their garments and he appeals to the baseness that lies dead in the heart of all men. He rots the soul of the nation; he works secretly; an unknown in the night, to undermine the pillars of the city; he infects the body politic so that it can no longer resist. A murderer is less to be feared". (81).
Marcus Tullius Cicero 105-43 BC.

If that had been written today, you could not have chosen better words to describe Marxism in practice. If you understand this simple explanation of a traitor you are beginning to appreciate Communism/Marxism/Illuminati.

You may well say, "How did it ever get further than the coffee bar debating rooms of Germany?" After all we have seen Karl Marx portrayed as a failure both as a Philosopher and as a father. The working class, the target and the beneficiary of his revolution, broadly rejected his revolutionary theories but the middle class intellectuals saw a new horizon in his message, a message largely incomplete as he could never balance his arguments and in the end fudged his policies, so much so that other philosophers began to drive holes in his theories. Time also showed falsehood in the main thrust of his policy, that Capitalism would enslave the working man and he would revolt. Marx wanted this to happen but as time went by, his policy theory was proved wrong. Capitalism improved the lot of the working man as seen today with all our automation, he is a winner in a buoyant world economy. It is when International Finance Capitalism linked with Marxism interferes with true Capitalism that the working man suffers. Our hidden enemy within our walls today, is the International Finance Capitalist and his army of henchmen, who have adopted Marxism for their own end (World Government) and move freely within our very government, controlling its every move, and he does it by the power of his loan debts as you have seen.

If Karl Marx had been left to promote his own policy with his handful of followers, shortly after his death his policies would have died with him, overtaken by the mountain of work produced by German Philosophers of his period. But his policy was picked up by Weishaupt's Illuminati, through the League of the Just, and he was invited to prepare the Communist Manifesto for a banking concern, one Baron Lionel Rothschild, who would pay him. So, he set about his work and in 1848 it was published, but for twenty years it did not even mention his name as the author.

That is because it was a work undertaken by the Illuminati for their patron Rothschild, **(82)** and it was he who wanted a plan for World Revolution towards a world government.

Weishaupt's Illuminati, already under many different names and guises, promoted Marxism through his organisation and linked Masonic lodges efficiently and quickly. So Marxism became a world revolution.

We must now examine how Marxism works and how it enters like a cancer into government and corrupts from within. What you see is Weishaupt's original policy developed and re-named. Weishaupt always said he would rise under borrowed names; this is the proof.

CHAPTER SIX, PART ONE

THE MEANING OF WAR WITHIN MARXISM:
NOW YOU SEE IT, NOW YOU DON'T.

We think of war as an armed conflict. Marxism believes revolution is a continual war, but with a difference. It can be an armed struggle. However it can also be one of many psychological corruptions Marxism uses to weaken a nation on target for the eventual revolution. Very few Western defence experts can take this on board, because it is so hidden from our view.

Communism/Marxism/Illuminati are in a continual war using different tools of their devised war play; deception, disinformation, corruption of education, decline of morality, fuelling discontent (i.e. unions), and the infiltration of key positions of influence, to name but a few. Until you can grasp this diverse policy of Marxism you will find difficulty in understanding how it can be so successful with its hidden agenda, using the enemy within.

Let us go back to 1989 to see a simple, but ingenious enactment of this policy which had me and most others fooled by its suddenness. I refer to the so called collapse of Communism in the Soviet Union and satellite states. It was as if a thunderbolt hit Communism and all had seen the light.

Instead it was a meticulously planned manoeuvre by the Finance Capitalists behind their puppet, Communist Russia, for their next big move towards World Government. The International Finance Capitalists want Europe federalised and they want the Communist block included so one quarter of the world would be ready for World Government. This could not happen if the Soviet Union remained a Communist block as Europe's people would reject it. So Communism was suspended to move forward. A remarkably confident move by the planners of this evil World Government, knowing that in the end all would be locked into Marxism without power to resist.

Marxism is the dialectical balance between the armed and the ideological struggle, and diversion is a major tool used outside the armed struggle to move the International Finance Capitalists revolution forward to the next stage while seemingly, in this case, to surrender. What it effectively does, is to put the free world off guard as many agents of the capitalists comment that Communism is finished and the Western world believes this diversionary propaganda, but these thought provoking capitalist agents are the enemy within, as Cicero aptly exposed. (at the start of this chapter).

Marxism, following on from the Illuminati, knew the first three stages of peaceful revolution were; 1. Gain control of the media. 2. Infiltrate and influence education. 3. Penetrate key appointments of government. As this book progresses you will see in practice how these three objectives work. Its origin goes back to the methods used in preparation for the French Revolution. What I must stress is that without the funding, first from the Rothschilds **(83)** and then from their banking associates, this practice, which has included the gradual purchase of the mainstream media throughout the world, would never have been able to achieve its aims. That a vast amount of money that has been available to keep Communism (Illuminati) afloat and moving rapidly forward, is the secret that Finance Capitalism wishes to maintain. In the open world the Finance Capitalists cannot afford to be seen cavorting with Communism; but the proof that they are is irrefutable and contained in all the pages of this book.

In education we have a different circumstance which has made a class of educated elitists adopt extreme Liberal thinking, playing right into the hands of the Illuminati plan from which Communism developed its policies. It is, alas, a self-destruct mechanism, as Weishaupt would confirm. They play their part and then they will be eliminated along with all liberal thinking that has brought the free world towards Communism. This, Weishaupt promised in his communications with his followers. Liberalism, not Socialism, was to be destroyed when they had brought the world to revolution and Illuminated the mechanisms of power. In chapter seven we will see the mechanisms used to accomplish this end, mostly put in place by Liberal reformers.

In proceeding chapters we will see the practice and full effect of the third policy, placing their own men in positions of influence. You will see a broad presence of infiltration from communists, Internationalists and opportunists. I stress once again this is not solely a Zionist plot but it is predominantly controlled by International Zionist influences.

At this moment we will learn about other policies Communism uses from its armoury for attack within a peaceful revolution. As I can find no better description of their aims I quote from 'On Target'. **(84).** First diversion; "Pundits delight in quoting the Chinese Sun Tzu, whose battlefield philosophy might be summarised as; "Why risk bloody confrontation with an opponent when he can first be reduced by rotting his brain and his belly? Destabilise him; take his eye off the ball. In a nutshell, 'Divert him'. Chambers twentieth century dictionary of 1901 defines diversion as the; "Act of diverting or turning aside; that which diverts...something done to turn the attention of an enemy from the principle form of attack". It is perhaps significant for Western strategists that later editions have been condensed and diffused to read, "...something done to turn, the attention...of an opponent".

"For Western Christendom the tragedy is that ignorance at the highest levels has lead to the acceptance that diversion, popularly and incorrectly termed - "Deception" - is applicable only to armed conflict, when in fact it exists in the form of a social, psychological - "Ideological" - attack at the very heart of our society during, what we are allowed conveniently to define as, "Peacetime".

Diversion, is, till now, invisible to most observers, in the central force of Marxism; the force that propels it towards revolution. I will now stick my neck out and make a bold statement. Diversion was used to hide the true thrust of the

Bolshevik/Marxist threat to Western peace. The whole programme of the Cold War was used to divert our attention from Marxist/Illuminati infiltration of our key positions of democracy, education, civil service, captains of industry, political advisers, even party politics and Marxism was only able to achieve this because of the power and influence of their financiers, the International Finance Capitalists. It is without question that their task would have been impossible without the enemy (To democracy) within.

Since the collapse of Communism in Russia another diversion has taken place. In general we believe the threat of Marxism has receded. We all feel safer. We think of the collapse as a near miracle. But we are wrong. It is simply a diversion to place the Communist block firmly in Europe ready for membership of the European Union and its next stage, still denied by politicians, Federalisation. You and I can stop it. We must stop it, unless we all desire to live under a Communist dictatorship led by the bankers; the same bankers that have created nearly all the wars in the last two hundred years. So where you now perceive no enemy; replace Communism with International Finance Capitalism and focus on them as our enemy. They always have been our hidden enemy.

Diversion is used in many fields today as On Target States; "In a lighter environment one might suggest that diversion can be 'Fun'. It is simply an indirect way of achieving one's aim. Nothing can be taken at face value in identifying diversion; everything potentially has a hidden, ulterior or secondary motive. At a personal level it is an every day and very human strategy. Diversion is a challenge to the imaginative and agile mind, as in the same way masking - 'Maskirouka' - as an essential element of diversion, suggests that nothing is what it seems.

"An example of these inter-related concepts was the case of the Soviet Intercontinental ballistic missiles (ICBM's) displayed on a military parade. They were merely mock-ups--not what they seemed. Thus the West was diverted with the implementation of expensive and unnecessary counter-measures! **(85).** The social, psychological, ideological--application of diversion is infinitely more subtle, and insidious; it is therefore much harder to identify and accept".

So what we learn from this is that Diversion can be applied to any form of activity to push forward the policy of Marxism to its eventual aim of unending revolution, not for only military use. Therefore we see this in Marxist infiltration into Western governments, the Media, Religion, Education, Resources and Agriculture, Moral Standing, and Law; to name but a few of the more important and sensitive areas. In chapter seven we will deal with these areas of Marxist infiltration and diversion, showing how, by use of a few people infiltrated into these areas they can manipulate policies to benefit their aims. When you have finished reading the next two chapters you will begin to understand why Britain has fallen from a world leader to a third world power. A policy planned in Russia and financed by Wall Street to benefit the revolution and do no harm whatsoever to the bankers behind the diversional policies who amass fortunes as they have prior knowledge of the events taking place.

All this diversion and decline would have been unworkable had the press been free to report honestly what was going on. It must be of utmost concern to us all that every attempt made by brave journalists, like Antony Sutton and Gordon Tether, failed; as their efforts were silenced or marginalised.

The press has treated matters of concern as a 'Conspiracy Theory' and derided it as such when they have had ample proof to show it was no theory but fact. I will show you in the next chapter how the media controls our minds and even programmes it to think their way, through auto suggestion. Just for the moment reflect on several matters that are relevant to Marxism and/or the Finance Capitalists. No journalist writes in favour of smoking. The press in general have gone out of their way to emphasise the dangers of Nuclear power and radiation, and no journalist dares to challenge the Holocaust. All these subjects have had one sided debate with few exceptions. But all matters can only be assessed intelligently if the debate is open and free, in this way we can all make intelligent decisions.

What you must realise is that Marxism, a policy financed by the International Finance Capitalists, is our real enemy not Russia or its people. Marxism, a clone of the Illuminati spread through the world within the secret societies of the Masonic movement, it is the power hidden behind a hall of mirrors that will eventually destroy us unless we can identify it and its agents and destroy them.

To identify them, we must first accept the continual war of Marxism and that it is International just as the bankers involved have no ties to a nation. Therefore the demise of one part of Communism (Russia) is irrelevant. The fact that organs of Marxism still exist, like the IRA is proof that Marxism is still active throughout the world.

Communism, since the French Revolution till today, has been financed by the bankers involved in International Finance Capitalism, names like Armand Hammer and Robert Maxwell, financed and traded with the Soviet Union, governments like Britain and America, controlled by the bankers, have been transferring technology and trading with Russia while Western armed forces, including our own, fought against the so called spread of Communism, Communism that already had a hold over their own actions. It was for exposing this hypocrisy that C. Gordon Tether retired early from the Financial Times **(86)**.

To add to the complications of Communism/Marxism we have to also understand Zionism. Zionism is so strong today that no journalist will even attempt to hint at the truth for fear of their livelihood. The Zionist movement was formed by Rabbi Moses Hess, the red Rabbi, he was also credited with giving coherence to the revolutionary ideals of Karl Marx. In 1982, Rabbi Dow Marmur, identified Marxist influence within the early settlements in Palestine, stating Zionism had become a largely secular, Marxist, movement. **(87). Khazar, non-Semitic Jews**, with no base in biblical terms in Palestine **have been the predominant revolutionaries in all Marxist insurrections in the West, and they predominate on both sides in South Africa.** Yet we have been told by our media that Russia ill treated the Jews, another diversion, another mirror. Russia was, and still is predominately controlled by The Bund management, taking their orders from the International Finance Capitalists who are again predominately from the Khazar tribe.

The Soviet Union not only armed the Zionist forces in Palestine in 1948 but supported their continued colonisation with emigrant support from Russia, so the media's insistence that Russia ill treated the Jewish population was not only false but another diversion; a mirror. Isn't it strange that in the history of the United Nations that no action has been taken over the suppression of the Palestinians during the settlement of Israel, while Saddam Hussein, doing the same thing in Iraq, has been bombed into submission? The answer lies in the agenda of the people controlling the UN, the International Finance Capitalists, who owned the oil rights, who as I have already said, are predominately International Zionists. Realise this and a whole history of conflicts become clear and you will begin to understand how the world is controlled by hidden forces.

The thoroughness of Soviet penetration and control of Western society and its institutions is only known by a small number of observers but its extent is response to detailed Soviet research and organisation since 1917. In a period of forty years state education (Not Private) is in a state of systematic deterioration. The Christian church, infiltrated by radical Liberals has failed to take the moral ground and entered into political interference, with minority pressure groups, thus influencing their direction. This change of direction has been planned and executed by a few Communist infiltrators, who have used their place within the World Council of Churches to attack the very heart of religion and plan its downfall. Likewise servicemen, politicians, intellectuals, academics and even ordinary citizens have been conditioned by media manipulation, and here is the evidence in a document found in Germany by the allied forces in 1919 which outlines the path for Communist revolution using diversionary tactics. You only have to follow each aim through the last seventy-five years to realise their policies have nearly succeeded.

1. Corrupt the young. Get them away from religion. Get them interested in sex.
2. Make them superficial. Destroy their ruggedness.
3. Get peoples minds off their governments by focusing their attention on athletics, sexy books, and plays (Soaps) and other trivialities.
4. Divide the people into hostile groups by constantly harping on controversial matters of no importance.
5. Destroy the peoples faith in their natural leaders by holding the latter up to contempt, ridicule and disgrace.
6. Always preach true democracy, but seize power as fast and as ruthlessly as possible.
7. By encouraging government extravagance, destroy its credit. Produce fear of inflation with rising prices and general discontent. (Part of banking strategy).
8. Incite unnecessary strikes in vital industries. Encourage civil disorders and foster a lenient and soft attitude on the part of the government towards such disorders.
9. By specious argument, cause the breakdown of the 'Old Moral', virtues, honesty, sobriety, self-restraint, faith in the pledged word, ruggedness.

Re-read these nine aims of world Communism printed in 1919. Now consider if they have achieved these aims or partly achieved them. These Marxist intentions were never denied, and at the third Communist International in 1919 were formally voiced from the platform. Later in 1923 Mikhail Borodin confirmed the thrust of Communism in an interview with Madame Chiang Kai-sheik. **(88)**.

To end my evidence of Marxist policy of diversion I quote from an up to date version given by Soviet defector Tomas D. Schuman, who detailed the subversion process to demoralise a population over a twenty year period. **(89)**. The target and policies can be summarised as follows;

Religion; politicise, commercialise, entertain, remove religious observance from schools.
Education; inculcate permissiveness and relativity.
Media; monopolise, manipulate, discredit, focus on false or divisive issues such as homosexuality, rather than defend sexual morality.
Culture; create false heroes and role models.
Law and Order; introduce a legislative rather than a moral code.
Social Relations; promote rights rather than obligations.
Security; attack intelligence agencies, the police and armed forces.
Internal politics; Generate disunity through party antagonism.

Foreign Relations; repeated capitulation to Soviet strategies and disharmony between Western powers.
Family and Society; break up and induce disloyalty.
Health; promote sporting entertainment rather than individual participation, unrealistic ideals of socialised Medicare and junk food.
Race; promote hatred and division through environmental rather than genetic arguments, and promotion of racial issues and enforced legislation.
Population; control through urbanisation, and eliminate patriotism and independence based on land ownership.
Labour; pit trades unions against society.

This abridged version gives us ample evidence of the Marxist aim to revolutionise our free society and in reading these aims you may think they are well on the way to accomplishing their aims. So you can see there has been a concerted campaign all this century to lower our Western standards in readiness for the revolution and to add to this Karl Marx himself stated that to prepare the world for revolution the family and its religion must be destroyed and privately owned property confiscated.

So we can see Marxism has a core of diversion up and running and is the reason why we cannot recognise our enemy but he **is within** and unless we wake up to his presence he will destroy us. Remember **Diversion** diverts our attention from their main aim, so at all times we must keep our eyes on the ball.

CHAPTER SIX, PART TWO.

SO WHAT DID MARX DISCOVER?

To start with, Marx centred his policy on the need of man. All his policies centred on man and supplying his needs, education, art, intellectual stimulus, down to shelter, clothing and food. His policy stated a man is a product of his own struggle in work and leisure and not a creation of any God. Therefore since society as a whole has been made by man for man it should be freely available to everyone. He claimed in primitive time a form of Communism existed where everyone shared the food and fruits of their labour but this came to an abrupt end when property was bought or given for service and became private. From this beginning gradually people split into two groups, the rich and the poor. The rich moved forward and became powerful by providing the needs of society by using the land to produce the food. They also owned the tools and factories of manufacture and then abused the poor by employing them at poverty rates to produce products that they sold for added value, capitalism.

He developed his policy at the beginning of the industrial revolution so he was only able to guess at the effects of Capitalism as it was too new but never the less he attempted to pre-empt the effects and told the working class that the capitalists would wear them down and keep them at poverty level, but this was an inaccurate guess because with the start of automation gradually wages improved and the lot of the working man improved, so the main pillar of Communism was proved to be false. This is probably why Communism never really caught on in the industrial world at the worker's level. However it found its takers in the intelligentsia and middle class, Liberal thinking, bourgeoisie. The very group he never identified and which makes a lie of his theories.

Marx based his thought on his observation that history progressed in stages; **(1).** The relationship between those that owned the factories of production and those that owned nothing. **(2).** The tools and the means of production. In the old world the freemen or owners controlled slaves, who managed the hand mills. Now in Marx's time the upper class was the capitalist and landowner and the workers tended the steam mills, but as time went by another class came into its own, the middle class of office workers and managers who upset the Marx theory and confounds its findings based on inaccurate guesses. Marx claimed the upper class that controlled production also controlled society, politics and government and influenced its intellectual direction. He claimed all the sciences were directly affected by this relationship. He also claimed the world reflected the relationships between the masters and slaves, according to the period, no one concept remaining after the change in the relationships. He also claimed that at each stage a relationship could only develop to a certain point and then no further development could take place. At this point a new class of people take over society and bring new development to the relationship. Marx claimed capitalism had reached this point and it was ready for change despite the fact it had advanced science, brought about the industrial revolution, created democracies and improved the lot of the working man.

His claim was, but he never proved it, capitalism would collapse through recession and depression. (But these recessions were and are still created by financiers). Marx also claimed the worker (Proletariat) made goods that he did not control and the added value was taken from him to enrich the capitalist.

So Marx saw the worker as a rising class who would rise up and revolt and take power. Marx claimed the coming of Communism was inevitable as it was the next natural move after capitalism. But he warned any take-over by revolution must be exactly planned and launched at the right moment. He claimed, under Communism, man could return to the original happiness. Where have we heard this before? Weishaupt's Illuminati of course, Communism being its clone.

As to how the revolution would take place Marx differed on this during his life. First he claimed revolution would have to be violent and would take fifteen to twenty years to complete. Later in his life Marx had changed his mind after living in England he thought Communism might come to power within the democratic system.

Russia adopted the first course with a violent revolution. Eurocommunism took the other root through the ballot box. However it does not water down Communism. We talk of mechanisms of power only, not content. Marx however, with Engels agreement, suggested different countries would use different paths to Communism.

CHAPTER SIX, PART THREE

EUROCOMMUNISM

In three countries of Europe Communism has achieved an unexpected success and seems to be progressing within the established democratic structure. This is happening in Italy, France and Spain, each country having its own local reason but as a group they had a overriding motive for their success, they followed a road to Communism by supporting and fighting for a democratic path to power. Today a respectable percentage of the electorate vote Communist allowing their representatives sometimes to share power in a proportional system of power sharing. Some observers have stated that the collapse of oppressive Communism in Russia caused this change but in truth it started well before 1989 and is satisfactorily explained by the path its leaders chose to take towards revolution.

Since 1917 the path Marxism took in Russia has been widely accepted as a model for revolution, however without violent intention Eurocommunism has in many ways built themselves a firmer foundation to launch revolution when the time is right.

The first danger we must conceive is that Eurocommunism has vowed to remain loyal to Marxism, but where it differs from other Communist states controlled through Moscow, who believe at some stage revolution will be the end of democracy, Eurocommunism believes that they can obtain the same result through peaceful and gradual transformation through the ballot box, not through sudden revolution. So according to its architects from France, Italy and Spain Eurocommunism is a party of tolerance, social justice, and individual liberty, supporting peaceful and democratic change.

So let us look at the origin of this so called Eurocommunism **(90)** in each of the three countries to see if in fact they are a breath of fresh air, all be it Communist air, or are they another diversion, hiding the truth.

EUROCOMMUNISM IN ITALY

The Italian Communist party (PCI) was founded in 1921 at a time when Italy was near to civil war. It was when Fascism was strong in Italy and one year later Benito Mussolini seized power and banned all other parties. So almost straight away they went underground. Italy was very important for Communism for it was the base for the Roman Catholic Church, the church Marx and Weishaupt declared their main target for destruction.

The intellectual father of the Italian Communist party was Antonio Gramsci, imprisoned by Mussolini. In his works written on Communism he declared Italy was a Catholic state and Communism must work within the political and religious structure and in time replace the authority and leadership of the church with Marxism, and to do this he said the church must be put into the political arena, then Communism could defeat it.

So Communism put on new clothes to present a democratic, caring role while planning to use Catholics to wreck the bourgeois state. In this way Communism would win over society and then they would attack and win the state. Religion would automatically commit suicide within this plan.

They joined the national liberation group in World War two to fight Fascism. Their reward after the war was to join with the others to form a democratic government opposed to Fascism. By 1946 in the elections nearly one fifth of the voters backed the Communists. But they suffered through Russia's policies of expansion which made people think twice about Communism.

Palmiro Togliatti, the post war leader took his party from around five thousand members in 1943 to two million three hundred thousand by 1951, a remarkable achievement; it now became a formidable force.

Togliatti supported Tito against Stalin in his dispute over Communism within Yugoslavia, saying they should have the right to take their own course within Communism. He continued to attack Stalin's stance as a dictator. He claimed, by taking part in political life through the ballot box his party could help to perfect Italian democracy. Under this path, created by its first two leaders, Italy paved the way to Eurocommunism as seen today.

That it is equally dangerous to World democracy is unquestionable. To Europe it is the balance that will tip Europe's scales when the former iron curtain countries come into the European Union and the frightening fact is Europe could well be swamped by Communism as failure in Eastern Europe could drive its voters back to Communism it knows, as a refuge rather than a statement.

There is no doubt that the news media and the liberals have propelled Communism forward in Italy. Liberalism is the enemy of democracy through its meddling attitude that lets Communism succeed. Communism therefore, needs Liberalism.

EUROCOMMUNISM IN FRANCE

The French Communist party was formed in 1920, just after the Russian Revolution. Its start was prompted by an army of supporters of revolution which had grown within Freemasonry and the Grand Orient, who were behind the French revolution in 1789. It is from that time that they had a major hold over government. So it had a very different start to that of Italy and fell in behind Lenin and later Stalin with an iron hand of discipline. It joined the Comintern and started to play its role during the thirties and the rise of Hitler.

Maurice Thorez, its leader, formed a popular front to oppose Fascism by joining the Communists, Socialists and Liberals into one defence. By 1936 a coalition of centre left, led by the Socialists, won an election with Communists asked to participate for the first time in government. But argument and disillusion wrecked the coalition which only lasted two years.

In 1936 the Communists won 14.76 per-cent of the vote, by 1946, after their work within the resistance, they polled 28.2 percent, a remarkable progress. Thorez made it quite clear the path to Communism was different in every country.

The French were however to go right-wing after the war and the party in general suffered when America stepped in to help.

In 1961 Thorez declared the single party system of Stalin was a mistake and his view was accepted at the 17th. and 18th. congress of the PCF. Their greatest victory came when they supported Mitterrand in 1965 for President and the coalition received 44.8 percent of the vote, but political discord ruined their chances in the assembly two years later, once more.

In 1969 the PCF moved to break up a strike of students and workers by separating them. This move showed them in a democratic light, and they continued to push this line when they supported Czechoslovakia and condemned the Soviet invasion. Their most important agreement, the union of the left took three and a half years to complete but brought about a union that has stood the pressures of the time. George Marchais, the leader of Communism in France during this period wrote a book entitled 'The Democratic Challenge', published in August 1973. In it he dedicates French Communism to a democratic system including freedom for the press. But in hind sight I feel he knew that the press was already in the hands of the bankers and therefore on their side.

In line with its thinking the PCF announced it disagreed with the 'Dictatorship of the Proletariat', this sealed their departure from the Soviet line and proved their independence. At last they had finally rejected Soviet style Communism.

However Communism is a movement that depends on deception and diversion, to this policy Eurocommunism is no exception.

EUROCOMMUNISM IN SPAIN

Spain is different to its two partners in so much as it is a relatively small party due to the fact that it has only recently been legalised, after the death of Franco, the ultra right dictator. At its conception it freed itself from Lenin and Stalinism. But it did this in relative secrecy at its foundation in 1921. The popular front, as in France won an election victory by a resounding 267 to 132. However the generals, led by Franco, refused to accept the democratic decision and entered the Spanish civil war. The right received support from Hitler and Mussolini and won the war.

Communists and their sympathisers from all over Europe formed the International Brigade to fight the Spanish republic but were defeated in 1939.

It was then that Franco became Spain's absolute leader. Franco then purged Spain, killing two hundred thousand of his opposition. This played a large part in disrupting the Communist party. Those that survived went underground. Franco continued his one man dictatorship and although not a Fascist, sent a troop to fight along side Germany against Stalin. This prompted the United Nations later to refuse Spain entry to their leftist club: in exile the PCE established itself in Paris. With advice from Stalin the Communist Party finished the civil war and infiltrated the trades union movement and by doing so regained a foothold in Spain.

Carrillo was a pure Marxist Leninist and it was not till 1968 and Russia's invasion of Czechoslovakia that he changed his mind. From this moment on he gradually became the policy-maker for Eurocommunism.

In 1974 he joined a broad left movement in Spain consisting of moderates and Liberals opposed to Franco. It was formed to give Spain democracy after Franco's death in 1975.

The first hint of power came when King Carlos appointed Adolfo Gonzalez as head of government who immediately released Communists imprisoned under Franco.

Carillo, encouraged, returned to Spain and declared his allegiance to Eurocommunism. In 1977 the PCE was legalised. He then swore Spain's

Communists to allegiance with democracy. In short he saw a road through democracy to gain Europe a more advanced Socialism.

There is one similarity that you see running through these short histories, each country involved, Italy, France and Spain had a problem with early Fascism dating back to its infancy. There is another thread of direction about these three countries, they all had systems of Proportional representation which favours coalitions, this, I am sure, was the deciding factor that led Communism to go down a road of democracy, but at any time in the future they can change tack. The danger that I have already stated is that Communism will swamp the future federalised state of Europe when we can kiss goodbye to our democracy as a small voice in a large impersonal state created by Communists for Communists. This will become apparent later on in this book. To enlarge your knowledge of European Communism I recommend 'Eurocommunism' By Stephen Goode to get a full picture of its history. **(90).**

Now lets get back into reality by reading official communications from our Embassy in Moscow to our government. These documents come from a collection of reports on 'Bolshevism in Russia' around 1919 at the height of the Bolshevik Revolution. **(90a).** The weight of evidence in these documents cannot be over estimated and brings Communism in power sharply into focus as these extracts will show.

CHAPTER SIX, PART FOUR
OFFICIAL GOVERNMENT PAPERS

Sir M. Findlay to Mr. Balfour. September 17th. 1918. Extract page 6.

"The foregoing report will indicate the extremely critical nature of the present situation. The danger is now so great that I feel it my duty to call the attention of the British and all other governments to the fact that if an end is not put to Bolshevism in Russia at once the civilisation of the whole world will be threatened. This is not an exaggeration, but a sober matter of fact; and the most unusual action of German and Austrian consuls-general, before referred to, in joining in protest of neutral legations appears to indicate that the danger is also being realised in German and Austrian quarters. I consider that the immediate suppression of Bolshevism is the greatest issue now before the world, not even excluding the war which is still raging, and unless, as above stated, Bolshevism is nipped in the bud immediately, it is bound to spread in one form or another over Europe and the whole world, as it is organised and worked by Jews who have no nationality, and whose one object is to destroy for their own ends the existing order of things. The only manner in which this danger could be averted would be collective action on the part of all powers".

Comment. A damning report that seems to have been ignored.

Mr. Lindley to Mr. Balfour, November 27th. 1818. Page 21.

"Principal reason why Bolsheviks have lasted so long is their unlimited supply of paper money, and I venture to recommend particular attention be paid to this side of the problem. This paper money enables them not only to pay their way in Russia but to build up credits abroad, which are to be used to produce chaos in every civilised country. It is the first time in history that an anarchist society has unlimited resources".

Comment. This move is almost certainly after advice and supply from the Finance Capitalists.

Mr. Alston to Earl Curzon, January 23rd. 1919. Page 28.

"The Bolsheviks can no longer be described as a political party holding extreme Communistic views. They form relatively small privileged class which is able to terrorise the rest of the population because it has a monopoly both of arms and of food supplies. This class consists chiefly of workmen and soldiers, and includes a large non-Russian element, such as Letts and Esthonians and Jews; the latter are specially numerous in higher posts. Members of this class are allowed complete licence, and commit crime against other sections of society...."

Mr. Alston to Earl Curzon, February 12th. 1919. Page 37.

"Bolsheviks ruthlessly 'nationalised' all property during first four or five months, including British firms like Contutshtim, Syssert, and Co, and they made constant demands on all moneyed merchant classes for huge contributions, with penalty of arrest and confiscation of all belongings unless paid promptly. Businesses of all kinds, banks, and houses were either placed under control of labour elements or nationalised, and to such a low level were industry and manufacture reduced that they practically came to a standstill. Systematic searches of houses and private individuals took place daily, and gold and silver ornaments, and even spare clothes, were taken without compensation. And merchants who attempted to resist or evade constant decrees from the local Soviet were immediately arrested. Robberies and murders were frequent, law and order were at very low ebb, and almost complete anarchy reigned. Local consular corps was formed in March 1918, consisting of consuls and representatives of some dozen different nationalities to act as an intermediary between Bolshevik Soviet and subjects of foreign powers, owing to the molestation of foreign subjects."

Workers International. Organ of the Petrograd Committee of the Russian Social-Democratic Labour party. August 7th. 1918. Page 83.

"The imaginary dictatorship of the proletariat has definitely turned into the dictatorship of the Bolshevik party, which attracted all sorts of adventurers and suspicious characters and is supported only by the naked force of hired bayonets in the country's. Their sham Socialism resulted in the complete destruction of Russian Industry, in the country's enslavement to foreign capital, in the destruction of all class organisations of the proletariat, in the suppression of all democratic liberty and of all organs of democratic state life, thus preparing the ground for a bourgeois counter-revolution of the worst and the most brutal kind".

Comment. (Hard words indeed from a party that should favour their revolution. Once again the mention of foreign capital backing the revolution).

Bolshevik Plans for World Revolution. Page 41.

"Bolshevism in Russia offers to our civilisation no less a menace than did the Prussians, and until it is as ruthlessly destroyed we may expect trouble, strikes, revolution everywhere. The German Military party is undoubtedly working hand in hand with Russian Bolsheviks with the idea of spreading Bolshevism ultimately to England, by which time they hope to have got over it themselves, and to be able to take advantage of our troubles. For Bolshevik propaganda unlimited funds are available. No other country can give their secret service such a free hand, and the result is that agents are to be found where least expected".

Appreciation of the Economic Situation, Compiled from Statistics in the Possession of His Majesty's Government. 1919. Page 70.

"It may be well asserted that, with production ever on the decrease (In some industries it has fallen to 5 percent of normal) and consumption on a starvation basis (e.g. the population of Petrograd, owing mainly to emigration consequent on unemployment and decease, has dwindled from two and a quarter millions to about six hundred and fifty thousand to seven hundred thousand), the economic system in Russia under Bolshevik influence has had the disastrous results of completely paralysing the trade and industry of the country.

A conclusive proof of Bolshevik economic bankruptcy is afforded by their latest budget statement of 1919, which runs as follows, in round figures:

Budget Statement 1919.

Expenditure	28 milliard roubles.
Revenue Deficit to be covered by fresh issues of paper.	
Taxes	2 milliard roubles
Contribution from the bourgeois classes.	10 milliard roubles
Currency (Fresh issue)	16 milliard roubles.
TOTAL	28 milliard roubles.

A deficit of 16 milliard roubles made up by printing new issue without an economic foundation to back it.

Transport. Page 75.

(a) General.--Without sufficient transport the existing Bolshevik regime is doomed. And they appear to have early realised the importance of obtaining control of the railways, although to this day they have a hard fight to maintain their domination, as is instanced by the hostile reception given to Radek when he attempted to address the Vologda Executive of the Railwaymen's Union.

(b) Rail Transport.--The railway personnel have shown a greater resistance to Bolshevism than any other branch of labour in Russia. This applies in the main to the operating executive--the repair and workshops being contaminated at an early date. The Railwaymen's Union 'Veksel' in the early days of Bolshevism vigorously combated extremist policy, but the Bolsheviks, by careful propaganda, gradually replaced the executive with men favourable to their views.

Comment. (Here you see the destruction of a vital service and the corruption of its union).

Speech by Zinoviev: reported in the Northern Commune, September 19th. 1918. no. 100.

"To overcome our enemies we must have our own Socialist Militarism. We must win over to our side, 90 millions out of the 100 millions of population of Russia under the Soviets. As for the rest, we have nothing to say to them; they must be annihilated".

Comment. (That foretells of the mass murder to come under the dictatorship of Stalin) **from a report of a meeting of the Conference of the Extraordinary Commission. Izvestia, October. 19th. 1918.**

Comrade Bokif gave details of the work of the Petrograd District Commission since the evacuation of the All Russian Extraordinary Commission to Moscow. The total number of arrested persons was 6220. 800 were shot.

Northern Commune (Quoted from 'Russian Life' Helsingfors, March 11th. 1919.

By order of the Military Revolutionary Committee of Petrograd several officers were shot for spreading untrue rumours that the Soviet authority had lost the confidence of the people.

All relatives of the officers of the 86th. Infantry Regiment (Which deserted to the Whites) were shot.

Treatment of the Bourgeoisie.

Orel---Today the Orel bourgeoisie commenced compulsory work to which it was made liable. Parties of the Bourgeoisie, thus made to work, are cleaning the streets and squares from rubbish and dirt. Isvestia, October 19th. 1918.

Mr. Lockhart to Sir G. Clerk. November 10th. 1918.

"Dear Sir George,
The following points may interest Mr Balfour:
1. The Bolsheviks have established a rule of force and oppression unequalled in the history of any autocracy.
2. Themselves the fiercest upholders of the right of free speech, they have suppressed, since coming into power, every newspaper which does not approve their policy. In this respect the Socialist press has suffered most of all. Even the papers of the Internationalist Mensheviks like 'Martov' have been suppressed and closed down, and the unfortunate editors thrown into prison or forced to flee for their lives.

The right of holding public meetings has been abolished. The vote has been taken away from everyone except the workmen in the factories and the poorer servants, and even amongst the workmen those who dare to vote against the Bolsheviks are marked down by the Bolshevik secret police as, counter-revolutionaries, and are fortunate if their worst fate is to be thrown into prison, of which in Russia today it may be truly said, 'many go in but few come out'.

Repression of democracy.-- "After the July Congress and the Anti-Bolshevik demonstration of the left Social Revolutionaries, non-Bolshevik Socialists were deprived of all political rights, hundreds of socialist workmen were thrown into prison and large numbers were shot. In addition 3000 workmen were thrown out of employment in the railway repairing shops in Moscow simply on the ground of their social Revolutionary sympathies".

Metal Trades. "The metal trade was practically at a standstill, due to the shortage of fuel and raw materials, probably not more than 40 percent of the plant on all branches being in operation. Labour was thoroughly disorganised, owing to political and economic disturbances and shortage of food products which forced the work-people to leave their occupations for long periods in search of food. The stocks of what little fuel, copper, lead, &c, that remained were being gradually exhausted, and no hope of recovery could be expected in the near future. Physically the metal trades entail a heavy strain on the workers, whose stamina was thoroughly exhausted by shortage of food".

Recent Legislation "All lands, buildings, machinery, &c, were now nationalised, without any compensation being paid to the former owners. The result has been an utter deadlock, all private enterprise being killed. Money is being hidden to an enormous extent, the absence of which is being made good as quickly as ever possible by the Soviet's printing presses; private printing establishments being taken over for this purpose. It is estimated that the quantity of paper currency in circulation is now over 30,000,000,000 roubles, roughly 100 times the present gold reserve. A great quantity of false money is also being printed and being brought into circulation, especially the 20 and 40 rouble notes. All private trading is being taken over by the government and the stocks are being confiscated".

"Gold articles over a certain weight are confiscated, with the result that some have disappeared, being hidden by the owners. The system of education has been entirely altered. All religious instruction has been abolished, and in its place a form of state Socialistic instruction substituted. The peasantry now refuse to send their children to the state schools and they remain without education. Clothing, such as winter overcoats, belonging to private people are being confiscated for the benefit of the red army. No man is supposed to possess more than one suit of clothes, two changes of linen, or two pairs of boots; anything above this is requisitioned for so-called state purposes. All furniture is nationalised".

"As regards food distribution, it is admitted even by the Bolsheviks that in no department of government is there such a corruption as among the numberless officials who control the food administration. The organisation of the food

distribution is, of course, mainly governed by the fact that there is scarcely any food to be distributed".

Mr. Alston to Mr. Balfour. January 3rd. 1919. August 7th.-- "I called at temporary prison and saw Greenep, Wishaw, and Jerram. They are all well treated by their guards who are real Russians, unlike most of their leaders, who are either fanatics or Jewish adventurers like Trotsky and Radek".

Bourgeoisie. "The position of the bourgeoisie defies all description. All who employ labour down to a servant girl, or an errand boy, or anyone whose wants are provided for ahead, that is, all that do not live from hand to mouth, are considered under Bolshevism as bourgeoisie. All newspapers except the Bolshevik ones have been closed, and their plant and property confiscated. New decrees by the dozen are printed daily in the press, no other notification being given. Non-observance of any decree means confiscation of all property. All government securities have been annulled and all others confiscated. Safe deposits have been opened, and all gold and silver articles confiscated. All plants and factories have been nationalised, as also the cinemas and theatres. This nationalisation or municipalisation means to the unhappy owner confiscation, since no payment is ever made. Payments by the banks from current or deposit accounts have been stopped. It is forbidden to sell furniture or to move it from one house to another without permission. Persons living in houses containing more rooms than they have members of their families have poor families billeted in the other rooms, the furniture in these rooms remaining for the use of the families billeted there. Hundreds of houses have been requisitioned for official or semi-official use, and thousands of unhappy residents have been turned out on the streets at an hour's notice with permission to take with them only the clothes they stood in, together with one change of linen. Houses are controlled by a poverty committee, composed of the poorest residents of the house. These committees have the right to take and distribute amongst themselves from the occupiers of the flats all furniture they consider in excess. They also act as Bolshevik agents, giving information as to movements. A special tax was levied on all house property amounting practically to full value of the same. Failure to pay in fourteen days resulted in municipalisation of property. All owners and managers of works offices, and shops, as well as members of the leisured classes, have been called up for compulsory labour, first for the burial of cholera and typhus victims, and later for cleaning the streets &c. All goods lying at the custom house warehouses have been seized and first mortgaged to the government bank for 100,000,000 roubles. Any fortunate owner of these goods, which were not finally confiscated, had the possibility of obtaining them on payment of the mortgage. All furniture and furs stored away have been confiscated. All hotels, restaurants, provision shops, and most other shops, are now closed after having had their stocks and inventories confiscated. Just before we left, a new tax was brought out, the extraordinary revolutionary tax. In the government newspapers there were printed daily lists of people, street by street, district by district, with the amount they must pay into the government bank within fourteen days on pain of confiscation of all property. The amounts, I noticed, ranged from 2000 roubles to 15,000,000. It is impossible to imagine how these sums can be paid".

Sir C. Eliot to Mr. Balfour. February 24th. 1919.

"An appeal to all democratic parties to unite against Bolsheviks has been published by the Omsk Government. Reasons given are as follows:-

1. Dictatorship of one class was claimed by Bolsheviks, and people of other classes were placed outside the law and starved.

2. Bolsheviks have deprived educated classes of their votes, as they do not admit universal suffrage.
3. Bureaucracy has been set up in place of municipal and village government, which has been abolished.
4. Political organisations have replaced law courts".

Sir C. Eliot to the Earl Curzon. March 5th. 1919.

"Commissaries consisted of un-intellectual labourers from 20-30 years old, who condemned people to death, without making any accusation against them, frequently personally taking part in the murder of their victims".
The Press.-- "Only two daily papers are issued in Moscow, i.e., the 'Isvestia of Soviet' and 'Pravda', these papers are edited by leading Bolsheviks, and of course contain only opinions and statements likely to further the cause of Bolshevism, and nothing is allowed to be published in any way antagonistic to or critical of Bolshevism".

Mr. Alston to Earl Curzon. February 5th. 1919.

"From the examination of several labourer and peasant witnesses I have evidence to the effect that the very smallest percentage of this district was pro-Bolshevik, majority of labourers sympathising with the summoning of the Constituent Assembly. Witnesses further stated that Bolshevik leaders did not represent Russian working classes, most of them being Jews".

The Reverend B. S. Lombard, to Earl Curzon. March 23rd. 1919.

"I have been for ten years in Russia, and have been in Petrograd through the whole of the Revolution.
"I spent six weeks in the Fortress of Peter and Paul, acted as Chaplain to His Majesty's Submarines in the Baltic for four years, and was in contact with the 9th. (Russian) Army in Romania during the Autumn of 1917 whilst visiting British Missions and hospitals, and had ample opportunity for studying Bolshevik methods. It (bolshevism) originated in German propaganda, and was, and is being, carried out by International Jews".

At this point I do not want to influence your thoughts. I just wish to ask you one question, Would you wish to live under such a regime? If not we must do our utmost to stop 'The One World Order'.

PROTOCOL TEN.

TODAY I begin with a repetition of what I said before, and I beg you to bear in mind that government and peoples are content in the political with outside appearances. And how, indeed, are the goyim to perceive the underlying meaning of things when their representatives give the best of their energies to enjoying themselves? For our policy it is of the greatest importance to notice this detail; it will be of assistance to us when we come to consider the division of authority; freedom of speech, of the press, of religion (Faith); of the law of association, of equality before the law; of the inviolability of property, of the dwelling; of taxation (the idea of concealed taxes), of the reflex force of the laws. All these questions are such as ought not to be touched upon directly and openly before the people. In cases where it is indispensable to touch upon them they must not be categorically named; it (the law) must merely be declared without detailed exposition that the principles of contemporary law are acknowledged by us. The reason for keeping silence in this respect is that by not naming a principle we leave ourselves freedom of action, to drop this or that out of it (the law) without attracting notice; if they were all categorically named they (the law) would all appear to have been already given.

The mob cherishes a special affection and respect for the geniuses of political power and accepts all their deeds of violence with admiring response: "rascally, well yes, it is rascally, but it's clever...a trick, if you like, but how craftily played, how magnificently done, what impudent audacity!"...

We count upon attracting all nations to the task of erecting the new fundamental structure, (like the European Union), the project for which has been drawn up by us. This is why, first and foremost, it is indispensable for us to arm ourselves and to store up in ourselves that absolutely reckless audacity and irresistible might of spirit which in the person: of our active workers will break down all hindrances in our way.

When we have accomplished our coup d'état we shall say then to the various peoples: "Everything has gone terribly badly, all have been worn out with sufferings. We are destroying the causes of our own torment-- nationalities, frontiers, differences of coinage. You are at liberty, of course, to pronounce sentence upon us, but can it possibly be a just one if it is confirmed by you before you make any trial of what we are offering you". ....Then will the mob exalt us and bear us up in their hands in an unanimous triumph of hopes and expectations. Voting, which we have made the instrument which will set us on the throne of the world by teaching even the very smallest units of members of the human race to vote by means of meetings and agreements by groups, will then have served its purposes and will play its part then for the last time by an unanimity of desire to make close acquaintance with us before condemning us.

To secure this we must have everybody vote without distinction of classes and qualifications, in order to establish an absolute majority, which cannot be got from the educated propertied classes. In this way, by inculcating in all a sense of self-importance, we shall destroy among the goyim the importance of the family and its educational value and remove the possibility of individual minds splitting off, for the mob, handled by us, will not let them come to the front nor even give him (the goyim) a hearing; it (the goyim) is accustomed to listen to us only who pay it (the goyim) for obedience and attention. In this way we shall create a blind, mighty force which will never be in a position to move in any direction without the guidance of our agents set at its head by us as leaders of the mob. The people will submit to this regime because it (the goyim) will know that upon these leaders will depend its earnings, gratifications and the receipt of all kinds of benefits.

A scheme of government should come ready-made from one brain because it will never be clinched firmly if it is allowed to be split into fractional parts in the minds of many. It is permissible, therefore, for us to know of the scheme of action but not discuss it lest we disturb its artfulness, the interdependence of its component parts, the practical force of the secret meaning of each clause. To discuss and make alterations in a labour of this kind by means of numerous votes is to impress upon it the stamp of all the reasoning and misunderstanding which has failed to penetrate the depth and extent of its plotting's. We want our schemes to be enforceable and suitably concocted. Therefore we ought not to fling the work of genius of our guide to the fangs of the mob or even to a selected company.

These schemes will not turn existing institutions upside down just yet. They will only effect changes in their economy and consequently in the whole combined movement of their progress, which will thus be directed along the paths laid down in our schemes.

Under various names there exists in all countries approximately one and the same thing. Representation, Ministry, Senate, State Council, Legislative and Executive Corps. I need not explain to you the mechanism of the relation of these institutions to one another, because you are aware of all that; only take note of the fact that each of the above-named institutions corresponds to some important function of state, and I would beg to remark that the word 'important', I apply not to the institution but to the function, consequently it is not the institutions which are important but their functions. These institutions have divided up among themselves all the functions of government--administrative, legislative, executive, wherefore they have come to operate as do the organs in the human body. If we injure one part in the machinery of State, the State falls sick, like a human body, and...will die.

When we introduced into the state organism the poison of Liberalism its whole political complexion underwent a change. States have been seized with moral illness--blood poisoning. All that remains is to wait the end of their death agony.

Liberalism produced Constitutional States, which took the place of what was the only safeguard of the goyim, namely Despotism; and a constitution, as you well know, is nothing else but a school of discord, misunderstanding, quarrels, disagreements, fruitless party agitation's, party whims--in a word, a school of everything that serves to destroy the personality of State activity. The tribune of the 'talkeries' has, no less effectively than the press, condemned the rulers to inactivity and impotence, and thereby rendered them useless and superfluous, for which reason indeed they have been in many countries deposed. **Then it was that the era of republics became a possibility that could be realized; and then it was that we replaced the ruler by a caricature of a government by a president, taken from the mob, from the midst of our puppet creatures, our slaves.** This was the foundation of the mine which we have laid under the goy people, I should rather say, under the goy peoples.

In the near future we shall establish the responsibility of presidents.

By that time we shall be in a position to disregard forms in carrying through matters of which our impersonal puppet will be responsible. What do we care if the ranks of those striving for power should be thinned, if their should arise a deadlock

from the scarcity of finding presidents, a deadlock that will finally disorganise the country?...

In order that our scheme may produce this result we shall arrange the elections in favour of such presidents as have in their past some dark, undiscovered stain, some 'Panama' or other--then they will become trustworthy agents for the accomplishment of our plans, being afraid, on the one hand, of revelation, and eager, on the other, for what everyone who has attained power desires, namely, the retention of the privileges, advantages and honour connected with the office of president. The chamber of deputies will protect and elect presidents, but we shall take from it the right to propose new, or make changes in, existing laws, for this right will be given by us to the responsible president, a puppet in our hands. Naturally, the authority of the president will then become a target for every possible form of attack, but we shall provide him with the means of self-defence in the right of an appeal to the people, for the decision of the people over the heads of their representatives that is to say, an appeal to that same blind slave of ours-- the majority of the mob. Independently of this we shall invest the president with the right to declare a state of war. We shall justify this last right on the ground that the president shall justify this last right on the ground that the president as chief of the whole army of the country must be able to command it, should it be needed to defend the new republican constitution, since the right to defend it will belong to him as the responsible representative of this constitution.

It is easy to understand that these conditions the key of the shrine will lie in our hands, and no one outside ourselves will any longer direct the force of legislation.

Besides this we shall, with the introduction of the new **Republican Constitution**, take from the chamber the right of interpellation on government measures, on the pretext of preserving political secrecy, and, further, we shall by the new constitution reduce the number of representatives to a minimum thereby proportionately reducing political passions and the passion for politics. If, however, they should, which is hardly to be expected, burst into flames, even in this minimum we shall nullify them by a stirring appeal and a reference to the majority of the whole people....Upon the president will depend the appointment of presidents and vice-presidents of the chamber and the senate, instead of constant sessions of Parliaments we shall reduce their sittings to a few months. Moreover, the president, as chief of the executive power, will have the right to summon and dissolve Parliament, and, in the latter case, to prolong the time for the appointment of a new parliamentary assembly. But in order that the consequences of all these acts which in substance are illegal, should not, prematurely for our plans, fall upon the responsibility established by us of the president, we shall instigate ministers and other officials of the higher administration about the president to evade his dispositions by taking measures of their own, for doing which they will be made the scapegoats in his place.... This part we especially recommend to be given to be played by the Senate, the Council of State, or the Council of Ministers, but not to an individual official.

The president will, at our discretion, interpret the sense of such of the existing laws as admit of various interpretations; he will further annul them when we indicate to him the necessity to do so. Besides this, he will have the right to propose temporary laws, and even new departures in the government constitutional working, the pretext both for the one and the other being the requirements for the supreme welfare of the State. By such measures we shall obtain the power of destroying little by little, step by step, all that at the outset when we enter on our rights, we are

compelled to introduce into the constitutions of the States to prepare for the transition to the imperceptible abolition of every kind of constitution, and then the time is come to turn every form of government into our despotism.

The recognition of our despot may also come before the destruction of the constitution; the moment for this recognition will come when the peoples, utterly wearied by the irregularities and incompetence--a matter which we shall arrange for-- of their rulers, will clamour: "Away with them and give us one king over the earth who will unite us and annihilate the causes of discords--

frontiers, nationalities, religions, state debts--who will give us peace and quiet which we cannot find under our rulers and representatives".

But you yourselves perfectly well know that **to produce the possibility of the expression of such wishes by all the nations it is indispensable to stir up the people's relations with their governments in all countries so as utterly to exhaust humanity with dissension, hatred, struggle, envy and even to use torture, starvation, the inoculation of decease and want, so that the goyim see no other course open to them than to take refuge in our complete sovereignty in money and in all else.**

But if we give the nations of the world a breathing space the moment we long for is hardly likely ever to arrive.

COMMENT

In this protocol you see the intricate planning that has taken place to prepare this plan. You begin to see that every detail has been taken care of and every eventuality discussed.

It is becoming very clear that 'Diversion' the main policy of the Illuminati under Weishaupt, and Marxism under Karl Marx, is to be used to effect, and that Marxism is a strong thread through the Protocols. When you read this you can't help comparing our leaders today to see if they fit into the description given in this protocol. It seems to be a very accurate description of the President of the United States and his army of radical advisers.

We see them entering our democratic system and corrupting it from within, using Liberalism to degenerate our nations. We see that, like the Illuminati and Marxism, they want to Federalise nations to eliminate borders, remove nationality to cancel our sovereignty, disband religion, the greatest power that holds us together, flood us with state debts which has already been accomplished, and when they have completed this they will have us ready for revolution. Just think of each of these triggers and ask yourself, how far to achieving their aims have they travelled by now and how long have we got to upset their plans? The answer to that is, not long.

The admission comes at the end; that if they give us a breathing space their day of power may never come. We must strive to make this come about.

CHAPTER SEVEN
THE INTERNATIONAL POLICY OF MARXISM

The world-wide policy of Marxism is what most concerns us. As you have seen in the last chapter Marxism is in a state of continual war. But war in their definition not ours. War is to them diversion, infiltration and disruption. It includes a policy of gradual change that appears to be evolution rather than infiltration. It targets key points that it considers important to bring about a revolution. In this way they can effect change in a country, ready for revolution, with a comparatively few specialised infiltrators, highly trained for their job.

We are now going to study six of the eight areas of government chosen by Marxism, and put them under the microscope to find out how they are used to bring about change towards its eventual goal, World Government. This infiltration has been accomplished over a long period, at least a century, and without the connections of the International Finance Capitalists could not have achieved its deep penetration that enables it to influence and change direction of the bodies within our society. At this stage let us remember Weishaupt's policy to get inside power and corrupt it from within in readiness for revolution. Marxism is Illuminati under another guise and **deception,** and **diversion** its trademarks.

CHAPTER SEVEN, PART ONE.
HIDDEN INFILTRATION OF WESTERN GOVERNMENTS

When we talk about infiltration we are discussing a policy of **deception** because the infiltrators are pretending to be, in the case of politics, Labour, Conservative or Liberals, or in America, Democrats or Republicans. They have been tutored from a young age to accomplish a task and all energy is given to achieving that task. Each candidate is given a cover story that corresponds with the task he must perform and only his directional fanaticism is a clue to his true identity which is easily confused with enthusiasm for their work. So most planted agent Provocateurs get away with their cover stories for a considerable time, and many get away with them completely. Behind each agent is a team that decides each move. A sizeable number of infiltrators have been positioned by the International Zionist movement with its powerful influence in Britain and America.

The other avenue of influence is in key positions of the Civil Service. Again, International Zionism eases many into position but a second and most worrying Group, Mossad, the official State Security of Israel, plays a considerable roll on an international basis. Worrying because, as a so called ally, it has special relations with MI5 and MI6 in this country and the CIA in America, allowing it access to classified material. (Remember Zionism was founded by Rabbi Moses Hess as well as Communism.)..Just make a check on how may recent spies caught in the west were International Zionists.

Today in Britain and America it is difficult to find a position of influence that is not occupied by a International Zionist in public and industrial life, (see the Rothschild sphere of influence), so it is not surprising they can influence the direction of policies to suit their agenda. Again Marxism, without this support, is a non-starter. Marxism today owes its hidden success to its co-revolutionaries, influence which in turn uses Marxism to obtain its goal. Over the years we have seen many spies who have worked for Marxism against Britain's interests, none more notorious than the Cambridge gang, Burgess, McLean, Philby, and Blunt all of whom left University and took up key roles in government and the Secret Service. This group was eventually exposed, but their controller, none other than Lord Victor Rothschild, continued to influence politics and became head of Edward Heath's 'Think Tank' in the seventies despite the fact that MI5 knew him as the spy ring controller. This is an example of their men being in place, in key positions, at the right time, to influence policies. One of Victor Rothschild's successes for Marxism was to influence Heath's government in passing over biological and scientific secrets to Russian scientists, but there is another secret that till today has remained hidden.

Victor Rothschild also controlled a group of Marxists in Oxford University. This cell at Oxford was organised by the head of Biology, also a Marxist, and had, as its political propaganda student, non other than a student called Harold Wilson. **(91)**. He used to hold meetings in his rooms and lecture students on Marxism. To support this I have a biology student who was present at several meetings with first hand knowledge of the events. You now begin to see how easily infiltration takes place when you have a few influential people in high places. They can also procrastinate when necessary to delay action against someone who is under suspicion. There is no greater example of this than the two government spies in America, Harry Dexter White and Alger Hiss, both of whom remained in their jobs long after they were first suspected of espionage. But more about them later.

Once Harold Wilson gained power he surrounded himself with a group of East European Jews, who financed his office and propaganda, in return they were honoured in our honours list. None of this is of great importance but the combination of Wilson's Marxist background mixed with his minders who controlled his actions with finance for his office in return for what can only be described as a helpful policy towards the Soviet Union and satellite countries, relaxing export regulations and passing over scientific and biological secrets developed in this country; this is worrying. During his whole period of office Wilson relaxed Britain's regulations to favour co-operation with Russia at a time when the cold war was, in the media anyway, at its peak. The deception over this policy is only just surfacing, but as this book progresses you will see how Marxism, International Zionism and Freemasonry have combined to envelope the very heart of government in both Britain and even to a greater extent America, where no government can legislate without the approval of this minority power group. It is ultimately the power of money combined with Zionist penetration of government that is easing Marxist policies upon the world while our media stands silent. If I can seek out and find the truth, so can they, (the Media), but in the hands of the bankers, they are powerless to print the truth..

It does not take much imagination to realise that with a Prime Minister in place, the infiltration of strategic offices can take place with the guidance and protection of power and Wilson's period of office certainly saw the ascendancy of bankers' power, that has moved into sensitive positions that have been responsible for the decline of our religion, the media, education, morality, agriculture and law and order and the family unit. In these key areas, a country can be de-stabilised and made ready for revolution. Check Weishaupt's seven areas of attack. (Page60).

PROTOCOL TWO
ECONOMIC WARS

It is indispensable for our purposes that wars, as far as possible, should not result in territorial gains: war will thus be brought onto the economic ground, where the nations will not fail to perceive in the assistance we give the strength of our predominance, and this state of things will put both sides at the mercy of our international Agenturs (agents), which possesses millions of eyes ever on the watch and unhampered by any limitations whatsoever. Our international rights will then wipe out national rights, in the proper sense of right, (this is what Federalisation is all about), and will rule the nations precisely as the civil law of states rules the relations of their subjects among themselves.

The administrators, whom we shall choose from among the public with strict regard to their capacities for servile obedience, will not be persons trained in the arts of government and will therefore easily become pawns in our game in the hands of men of learning and genius, who will be their advisers, specialists bred and reared from early childhood to rule t he affairs of the whole world. As is well known to you, these specialists of ours have been drawing the information they need to fit them for rule from our political plans, from the lessons of history, from observations made of the events of every moment as it passes. The Goyim are not guided by practical use of unprejudiced historical observation, but by theoretical routine without any critical regard for consequent results. We need not, therefore, take regard for consequent results. We need not, therefore, take any account of them--let them amuse themselves until the hour strikes, or live in hopes of new forms of enterprising pastimes, or on the memories of all they have enjoyed. For them, let that play the principal part which we have persuaded them to accept as the dictates of science. (theory). It is with this object in view that we are constantly, by means of our press, arousing a blind confidence in these theories. The intellectuals of the Goyim will puff themselves up with their knowledge and without any logical verification will put into effect all the information available from science, which our agentur specialists have cunningly pieced together for the purpose of educating their minds in the direction we want.

Do not suppose for a moment that these statements are empty words: think carefully of the successes we arranged for Darwinism, Marxism, Nietzcheism. To us Jews, at any rate, it should be plain to see what a disintegrating effect these directives have had upon the minds of the Goyim.

It is indispensable for us to take account of the thoughts, characters, tendencies of the nations in order to avoid making slips in the political and in the direction of administrative affairs. The triumph of our system, and of the machinery of which it is composed, which may vary according to the temperament of the peoples we encounter, will not be assured unless its practical application is based upon a résumé of the lessons of the past in the light of the present.

In the hands of the States of today there is a great force that creates the movement of thought in the people, and that is the press. The part played by the press is to keep pointing out requirements supposed to be indispensable, to give voice to the complaints of the people, to express and to create discontent. It is in the press that the triumph of freedom of speech finds its incarnation. But the Goyim States have not known how to make use of this force; and it has fallen into our hands. **Through the press we have gained the power to influence while remaining ourselves in the shade; thanks to the press we have got the gold in our hands, notwithstanding that we have had to gather it out of oceans of blood and tears. But it has paid us, though we have sacrificed many of our people. Each victim on our side is worth in the sight of God a thousand Goyim.**

COMMENT

Here we see reference to their international rights which will wipe out our national rights. We have seen this already demonstrated by the European Court of Justice with its political, deliberations that override our laws and make mockery of our justice system.

We see again that they (the bankers) use the press to brainwash the people as most of the National press is under their control. This we will see clearly in the next part to this chapter.

CHAPTER SEVEN, PART TWO.

THE MEDIA

Throughout our lives most people rely upon our media, Television, Radio and our National Newspapers, to tell us the truth about National and International affairs. That reliance includes the forming of our opinions on political matters from broadly what we read, as we do not have the scope or the time to set up our own investigations. We have always believed that our media gave us a more or less true picture of world events, even if, with national events, they play the party card, therefore we rely upon their integrity. It can be said that no politician controls as much power as the media unless they (the bankers) in turn control the media as they did in the Soviet Union.

So imagine a small group of motivated, multi-millionaires buying up the mass media in America and using it for their own ends to control the world politically. Imagine that ninety-nine percent of the world's news stems from three news collecting agencies that distribute the news world-wide, such as ABC, CBS, and NBC all of which are owned by the bankers. You can then see quite clearly that if those super rich financiers want to subtly angle the news to follow their political agenda, the whole world receives false news on which to base its views.

Now let's go back to Weishaupt, and the two aims of his Illuminati which are essentially in place before he follows his seven point plan. Firstly the infiltration and conversion of the teaching profession from the top down. Secondly the take over of the media. Who did he prepare this policy for? Not Communism, as the Illuminati turned out to be, when renamed, but the International Finance Capitalists led by the Rothschilds at that time, who could afford to buy up the media, allowing the policy to be in place at the turn of the century and now in Britain it is nearly ninety percent complete. I will study one company that is worrying democrats throughout the world, The News Corporation, run by Rupert Murdoch.

Subtle alterations to news can be as simple as giving high coverage to news from one source, while ignoring another, and even subtle changes of voice or choice of headline can alter our opinion. A very good example of this was demonstrated at the run up to the last election when all the sleaze stories were about the Tories. Then after the election, when Labour was elected, a flood of sleaze came out about Labour members when it no longer mattered. No one in the press can convince me these stories weren't known before the election, or at least some of them.

The Media Review lists eleven companies that dominate, as major players, in the global media monopoly. **(92).**

TIME WARNER INC. In 1993 it took over as the largest media company. (Now Aol and EMI to be included).

BERTELSMANN AG. No 2 in the media scene. Based in West Germany. In America owns Doubleday Books and RCA music. Bantam and Dell in the USA. Transworld in the UK. BCA Book Club and France's 'Lesoirs'.

NEWS CORPORATION Ltd. Rupert Murdoch's empire bought 20th. Century Fox. Television network is fighting ABC CBS and NBC to be up amongst the giants in media and news distribution. Owns most of Australia's media and television and in England he owns the Quality 'Times' and 'Sunday Times', 'the Sun', mass media, 'News of the World', and 'B Sky B', amongst others. In Europe and on the Pacific Rim he is buying into the media. Soon he will be the largest media company in the World.

MAXWELL COMMUNICATION CORPORATION. Maxwell's media conglomerate, with assets in America, England and Eastern Europe was giving Murdoch a run for his money until his demise after the missing pensions funds.

HATCHETTE SA. Not well known under this name in America, but it is the world's largest publisher of Encyclopaedias and magazines. 74 publications in ten countries, and moving into television.

WALT DISNEY CORPORATION. Much more than Mickey Mouse. It's a media monopoly and International business force.

TURNER BROADCASTING CORPORATION. 75 countries world-wide use their Cable Television News Network. They also control MGM and RKO film libraries. Especially for home videos.

GENERAL ELECTRIC. Owns NBC America's No 1 network controls. Major financial services such as GE., Capital and Kidder, Peabody Inc.

SONY CORPORATION OF JAPAN. Recently acquired CBS records and moving into Hollywood. A major player in the electronics industry.

TELE COMMUNICATIONS - UNITED ARTISTS. The largest and most aggressive cable operator, moving into cable programming. Already the worlds largest movie screen operator. Owns Blockbusters.

VIACOM INC. Establishing pay cable networks in Europe, the Pacific Rim and America. A rising player.

So what monster controls them and makes sure they tow the line? One word.
MONEY.
So where does this control come from?

First we must ask a question. What does Arnauld De Borchgrave, a cousin of the Rothschild's Belgium branch and friend of Dr. Henry Kissinger, former editor in chief of the ultra right Conservative 'Washington Times' and Max Frankel, top man at the 'New York Times', and a Liberal tabloid have in common? The answer is that they both belong to the Rockefeller funded 'Council for Foreign Relations'.

Rockefeller's influence on the media is immense according to Peter Borsnan, who says that the Rockefeller Family's Chase Manhatten Bank, and other institutions under Rockefeller, are among the largest in network stock (owners of network shares) in all these major media networks.

In CBS he controls 14%. Stock analysts say that, with only 5%, influence, and even outright control, can be exercised.

Right through the media you will find what you would conceive as opposing political views converging at the Council for Foreign Relations (CFR). A list of press participants is reprinted in 'On Target'. **(93).**

The CFR is run on pure Illuminati principles. Its purpose is to eventually control the minds of the people of the world through the media.

This is the proof that there is something very wrong within the so called free press.

The most worrying aspect of the Multinational (and bankers) control of the media must be the effect that is the reverse of enforced state control like the former Soviet Union, in the bankers scheme the Multinationals render National interests powerless. This interference is now exactly what we are seeing in the way news is handled; for example, about the Monarchy; the demise of our agriculture industry, morality, and the family; in all these issues the wish of the bankers takes precedence over sovereignty and good practice and family security.

The Monarchy has been particularly harshly treated in England and Australia by Murdoch's papers. Our agriculture has been decimated by the European Union and the press. The cause of this is more than likely to be the multinationals in the animal food business, and the chemical giants, who could well be using our agricultural demise to gain full control of world agriculture through their supply business, a policy again going back to Weishaupt's Illuminati. **Collectivism.**

The European Union wasted no time in banning English meat. Only, this was a concerted plan to make England dependent on imports and crush our farming industry. The EU had similarly, successfully, previously destroyed our Nuclear and Fishing Industries. At this point if you turn to the end of this chapter and read the highlighted part of the Twelfth Protocol you will see that their (the bankers) comment on the Media fits this context like a glove. Is this coincidence? Luck? Or planned?

The press is being used in its capacity as our informer to divert our thoughts and to misinform us about world matters and programme us to think kindly of their (the BBC's) agenda. The BBC at the time of writing this book uses Auto Suggestion to programme our minds towards global government. The practice was perfected by the KGB and has been used by our own BBC on several occasions. The first I recall was in the eighties when a BBC programme suggested that demonstrators should attack Mrs. Thatcher with missiles, and they did.

On this occasion the Auto Suggestion is visual. A balloon floats across our screen through tranquil settings at regular intervals, between programmes. You might say what's so ominous about that? Nothing, I reply, except that the balloon is decorated as a global world and the hidden message it holds is, global is tranquil, global is safe. The flash created in our subconscious ends up giving us the message which our mind accepts from our subconscious, we become programmed. Only when you know its aims can you counteract its effect. Now you can.

Thomas R. Dye wrote in 'Who's Running America' The Carter Years'. **(94).** "Television is the major source of information for the vast majority of Americans, and the people who control this flow of information are among the most powerful in the nation. Indeed, today the leadership of the mass media has successfully established itself as equal in power to the nation's corporate and governmental leadership".

The key to understanding why Communism is accepted by big business is that they both believe in collectivism. In both cases the Capitalist, and the Communist concept of power revolves around centralised administration which, to work, needs a totalitarian dictatorship. This is the key to understanding super Capitalism's flirtation with and use of Communism, to reach its final aim, political power that delivers absolute power. But be warned that if you think this sounds acceptable, remember it can only work through a dictatorship, and Communism has been discredited where ever it exists.

Nesta H. Webster had this to say in "Surrender of an Empire" **(95).** "Big business is by no means antipathetic to Communism. The larger big business grows the more it approximates to collectivism. It is the upper road of the few instead of the lower road of the masses to collectivism".

This proves that the bankers took this stance in and before 1931. There we see an early concept of the multinational company, accepting Communism as the way forward.

The H Du B report in 1989 made this interesting statement; "Communism is the instrument with which the financial world can topple national governments and then erect a world government with world police and world money. **(96).**

There is no greater proof of the media's censorship of news than when Antony C. Sutton exposed, with painstaking accuracy to the Republican Convention, details of Capitalist support and financial help to build Russia's industry at a time when America was outwardly deeply involved in the Cold War and even engaged in war in Vietnam. The full details are contained in Antony C. Sutton's book "National Suicide-Military Aid to the Soviet Union. **(97).** In his evidence to the Republican Congress he opened a debate that any free press Baron would give his last dollar to expose, he only had to check Sutton's impeccable research. But not one mainstream publication took up his torch or printed one column inch. It only appeared in about two low circulation publications. This proves conclusively that even fifty so called 'Conservative publications censored out anything that exposed the hidden agenda of the bankers who were by then ruling America's politics.

Walter Ratenau wrote about the group of three-hundred men who ruled the continent **(98)** and (Nester Webster's "The Surrender of an Empire". **(99).** From the foundation of revolution in 1919 **(100),** and the Fabian, Toynbee's speech in 1931 **(101),** which we have already discussed, we can see that careful preparations had already been made for World Government (The New World Order). Institutions had sprung up which debated this very process such as the Synarchist Movement, The Analeptic Institute, The Council for Foreign Relations (CFR), The Bilderberg Group and the Trilateral Commission (TC), supported by the tax free foundations and the Carnegie Institute for Peace.

Behind these institutions we find that the funds come from the bankers such as Rockefeller, whose involvement in the Council for Foreign Relations, the Trilateral Commission and The Bilderberg Group, which he funds combined with his high, but hidden involvement with the press, must pose the questions; "What is his motive? What is his agenda? Where is democracy?". Then study the list of attendees at the Council for Foreign Relations. You see the faces of the mass media occupying its seats (Over fifty press members), yet nothing is allowed to be reported especially from the Bilderberg Group. It is then that you realise that this is not the top planning centre for World Government, but it is not far removed. When you have taken this on board, ask yourself, surely the press are meant to report news and abuse, surely not make it and hide it? Again proof has shown that the press is controlled, and has fed us false news on important matters of politics for most of this century.

An example of selective news was given to the American People when in 1987 Mikhail Gorbachev stated; "We are moving towards a new world of Communism", adding; "We shall never turn off that road". NBC News, owned by the General Electric Company, broadcast only the first part to the American public. **(102)**.

So the agenda is softening the concept of Communism. In another field of entertainment Soviet defector Tomas Schuman exposed Communist entertainer Yves Montand as a groomed Soviet infiltrator who like many others in the literary field had passed through the Novosti Press Agency **(103)**.

Tariq Ali, a Trotskyist and a member of the revolutionary left, seen at many a demonstration in London against our democracy now writes even for the Sunday Times, spreading his creed of revolution amongst the young, especially teachers and television journalists while our government quietly, since 1959 handed over to the Soviet Union technology on agriculture, oceanography, fisheries, specialised secondary education, medicine as well as some classified material in Biology and other fields. One of the men behind this move to give Russia Technology was none other than Victor Rothschild.

Yet every attempt to get the above matters fairly treated by our press has met with rejection and silence while elements dangerous to national security, such as Tariq Ali, gain regular time on Television and radio and are paid to write articles for our press. Proof again of a hidden agenda in our Media. **(Deception)**.

This whole deception is covered in length by Colonel B.S. Turner in "Control of the Communications Media and Conditioning of the Public Mind". **(104)..**

Having read this chapter so far, does not the high-lighted part of this Protocol sum up this part in a paragraph?

Colonel Barry Turner, in his Sudbury paper on the Media, had this to say about the link in America with the Council for Foreign Relations. **(105)**.

"The Spotlight newspaper listed fifty leading United States media figures, all members of the Council for Foreign Relations, several also of the Trilateral Commission, who control the bulk of the national media. **(106)**. A wealth of information is also available from standard references, such as "Dun and Bradstreet", "Who's Who" and from company annual reports. In undertaking any analysis, account must be taken of recorded past associations, not necessarily at board level, that may be deemed to have established positive links. Conrad Black's Canadian Hollinger Group controls over 200 newspapers and Magazines in the

United States, Canada, Israel and the United Kingdom. In the United Kingdom It owns Telegraph Newspapers and the Spectator. Board memberships cover both the Bilderberg Group and the Trilateral Commission, and include Lord Carrington, Dr. Henry Kissinger, Paul Reichmann (The Reichmann brothers, linked to former cabinet minister Lord Young of Graffham, owners of global property developers Olympia and York, and responsible for the London's Dockland Development), Peter Bronfman (Seagram's Whiskey with a twenty percent holding in Du Pont Chemicals; brother Edgar, President of the World Jewish Congress), Sir James Goldsmith (Dec) Sir Martin Jacomb (Bank of England, Barclays and N.M. Rothschild's R.T.Z.), Sir Evelyn de Rothschild (De Beers Consolidated Mines, Chairman of N.M. Rothschild, merchant bankers to Hollingers and Telegraph Newspapers, and advisers or underwriters on numerous government and private floatations), Rupert Hambro (Anglo-American Corporation of South Africa), Lord Swaythling (Family name Montagu, Bank of England, N.M. Rothschild and Rothschild's Precious Metals Trust, London Weekend Television, and current Executive Chairman of Rothmans International with powerful links to South Africa through the Rupert family), Henry Keswick (Rothmans International) and Lord King (British Airways). That Chairman Conrad Black should be a Trilateralist, a Bilderberger and a member of the Institute for Strategic Studies cannot have been appropriate to the independence of former Editor-in-Chief Andrew Knight; yet he too, is a Bilderberger as is British Socialist elder statesman the Rt. Hon. Denis Healey.

"However circumstantial, there can be no smoke without fire in the influence and affiliations axiomatic to the matrix of company networks. Due regard must also be given to the continuous flux and cross-fertilisation of appointments. United Newspapers (Daily Express), own six national and seventy provincial newspapers, and ninety business magazines and newsletters. Chairman Lord Stevens's Invesco M.I.M. has been linked through its Drayton English and International Trust to Rothschild's Sir Michael Richardson (A senior freemason), and to the enterprises of the late Robert Maxwell (Evening Standard, 6th. December 1991; Daily Telegraph, 3rd. January 1992.). In turn, Maxwell's Pergamon Holdings held a twenty percent interest in Invesco that was sold to bankers Goldman Sachs. Goldman Sachs, who were closely connected with Maxwell, engaged former cabinet minister Leon Brittan, whose brother, Samual, writes for the Financial Times. United director Sir Derek Palmar is also Chairman of Yorkshire Television. Associated Newspapers (Daily Mail), own two national and sixteen provincial newspapers. Mail Director and Trilateralist, Australian Sir Robert Crichton-Browne, was succeeded as executive Chairman of Rothmans International by Lord Swathling in 1988. From here there is a knock-on connection with Anthony W. Stenham of the Banker's Trust Company of New York, the Rank Organisation and Capitol Radio, and with Sir David Nicholson of Invesco M.I.M. and Rothschild's Dawnay Day. The Australian, Rothschild and masonic links further encompass Major the Hon Robert Latham Baillieu (Dawnay Day), Lord James William Baillieu (Rothschild Australia), and the Hon Edward Latham Baillieu (N.M. Rothschild, R.T.Z. and the United Grand Lodge of England). (Please note that this paper was written in 1992 and changes will have taken place since.).

It shows clearly the strong hold of Zionist control, a totally inappropriate control, that is exercised over our media. Zionist presence is less than one percent of the British population yet it dominates our press; this is neither healthy nor desirable.

If you read this last section, with reference to the table of the sphere of influence of the Rothschilds at the end of the first chapter, you will see even more of the picture.

Colonel Barry Turner has this to say about the presence of the Zionist influence in every facet of our media. **(104).**

The Zionist Factor In The Control And Operation Of Our Media.

"Pervasive Jewish influence, cultural motivation and political strategy devolve inescapably from the Zionist-Marxist-Leninist-International Capitalist power triangle, and what is patently an integrated Israeli-American influence. The detail is factual; it is neither racial nor prejudiced; indeed, it is essential to restore a balance against the orchestrated power of Zionism and manipulation within the Jewish Diaspora. It is a fact that the Jewish population of the United Kingdom, at about 300,000, amounts to no more than 0.5 percent, rather more in the United States, yet on both sides of the Atlantic Jews occupy a totally disproportionate position in government and the key areas of national life.

"Essential to understanding these influences was the column written by the Sephardic Bishop Montefiore in the Church Times in January 1992 to distinguish between those Jews with genuine biblical links to Palestine, and the vast majority in the Diaspora; those adoptive, Khazar "Jews" of central Europe and the former Soviet Union, like Shamir and Maxwell, whose claims are entirely spurious (Church Times, 24th. January 1992; "The Myth of the Jews"). One is entitled to assume that control over the media in this manipulative power-play is such that Montefiore's definition, which was of explosive significance, was ignored by the Jewish Chronicle and the British media alike. Only the Daily Telegraph appeared to report Bishop Montefiore, three months later, when he distinguished between cultural anti-Semitism and political hostility to the Israeli State. (Daily Telegraph, 14th. April 1992 "Bishop warns on attitudes to Jews".).

"In 1913 Wickham Steed, in a simple assessment of Jewish influence under the Austrian Hapsburgs, was able to write, "The Jews control practically the whole press. They control also the financial and economic corporations". Today such a statement would be roundly condemned on principle as anti-Semitic. **(107).** In 1943, when it was still possible to comment rationally and objectively, seasoned journalist Douglas Reed who, like many commentators, had started in the 20s with no preconceptions, challenged a European newspaper proprietor on the Jewish strategy of progressive exclusion with the words: "You know very well that you haven't a single non-Jew on your staff of your newspaper, and you'll do the same for England..." **(108).** In the Preface to Reed's later "Controversy of Zion", was written; (109). "Reed found himself banished from the bookstands, all publishers' doors closed to him, and those books already written liable to be withdrawn from library shelves and 'lost', never to be replaced".

"The media reflect, virtually uncritically, the chronic identity crisis between the United States and The United Nations in the Middle East (Independent, 19th. August 1992, "U.N. was by-passed over 'no-fly' zone". Daily Telegraph, 27th. August 1992, "Tornadoes off to spy on Iraqi army"). Findley's "They Dare To Speak Out" **(110)** was expressly about suppression of other than a positive pro-Israeli position in the United States, and in the introduction to his work Findley related the fundamental problem of finding a publisher for his manuscript with the independence and courage to take it on. In the United Kingdom, Adams and Mayhew wrote that: "Over the past half century, and particularly since 1967, a deliberate and generally successful attempt has been made to cover up the truth about Palestine,...". They recorded not only explicit threats to employment and publication, but calculated personal attacks and systematic suppression at the highest levels, the crippling of a publishing chain and even the imperilment of the National Manchester Guardian newspaper; in each of the last two instances through an orchestrated campaign for withdrawal of subscriptions and advertising. (Adams, Michael and Christopher Mayhew. "Publish it not...The Middle East Cover-Up" Mayhew, Longman Group Ltd. '1975 pp 11, 52-55, 58-60, 63, 64, 66-105, 115, 122.).

"In 1991 Andrew J. Hurley described graphically how a tiny minority of Jews in the United States, perhaps two percent of the entire population, dominate United States foreign policy (As they do the security services). Through nation-wide influence in the media and financial networks, and through pressure groups such as the Anti-Defamation League (A.D.L.), they effectively block legislation and unseat elected representatives. It is revealing that Hurley's exposure received no publicity in the United Kingdom from media accustomed to the fulsome promotion of Jewish-Zionist-Holocaust oriented material. (Andrew J. Hurley. "Israel and the New World Order". Fithian Press, Santa Barbara, 1991.). The same power as that wielded over governments and public opinion in the case of South Africa is unmistakable in the case of Israel, where successive administrations evolving from terrorist groups of the 1930's and 1940's have flouted United Nations' resolutions 181, 242 and 338 in turn and concurrently maintained a campaign of genocide against the indigenous Palestinians. Israeli governments have remained virtually immune from meaningful diplomatic or political confrontation, and have at no time suffered more than a passing censure from the media in an unbroken sequence of biased reporting.

"Control of a substantial amount of British and foreign press, publishing, radio and television coverage, is overtly in the hands of individuals of Jewish origin whose dual, if not primary loyalty is frequently and expressly to the State of Israel. This pattern, with its source in the International Capitalist network linked to international Jewish organisations, is repeated in the English speaking Commonwealth of Australia and Canada. Leading names from no more than a random sample from the domestic media and entertainment industry include: Maxwell (DEC), Bernstein, Zelman Cowan (Former Chairman of the Press Council), Blom-Cooper (Chairman of the Press Council 1990), vice-Chairman Lord Barnett, Elstein, Grade, Isaacs, The Saatchi's, Michael Green (Related to Lord Wolfson and associated with Lord Young through marriage), Sieff, Weidenfeld, David Winter (Head of B.B.C. Religious Broadcasting), Winner, Sir Paul Fox, Michael and Jonathan Freedland, Linda Agran, Jenny Abramsky, Alan Yentob, Beeban Kid Ron, the late Stuart Young (Chairman of the B.B.C. and brother of Lord Young, former secretary of State for Trade and Industry, linked to Paul Reichmann of Hollinger and the Olympic and York property empire, Jewish Chronicle, 13th. November 1987.), Churchill biographer Martin Gilbert, Bernard Levin, Mordechai Richler, Adam Raphael, Steve Berkoff, Bob Dylan, Paul Symon, Bob Geldhof, Neil Sedaka, Ester Rantzen, Baroness Birk, creator of the avant-garde magazine "Nova", Eve Pollard, Wendy Henry, Melanie Phillips (Married to B.B.C. legal correspondent, Joshua Rozenberg), Felicity Green, Linda Kelcey, Maggie Goodman, Janet Daley, Barbara Amiel, Maureen Lipman, Clare Rayner and Rabbi Julia Neuberger.

In the United States it suffices to record that Neal Gabler wrote of Hollywood as a Jewish creation **(111)**, and David McClintick covered the dominant Jewish involvement in entertainment and finance in his "Indecent Exposure---A True Story of Hollywood and Wall Street". **(112).**

What is so worrying is not that Jewish influence should be so integrated into our media but that it should dominate it when the Jewish population is at the most 0.5 percent of the population. If no ulterior motive was being cynically applied to our media it would still be unacceptable. Now that we see it, it must become a matter of **National Importance** to change the situation to a balanced presence so that no small minority can wield so much disruptive power again. And disruptive it is, as you will see later in this chapter when we discuss morality.

Has any attempt been made to curb the attack from within our media on the pillars of our society, Religion, Morality, Education, The Monarchy, Sovereignty and Law and Order, or has indeed any part of the media itself taken a stand and set an example? On this Colonel Barry Turner has this to say:

The Calculated Assault On Western Society By The Media Power Base Of Finance Capitalism Through The Mass Communications And Entertainment Industries.

"Apart from Toynbee's revelations "The Trend Of International Affairs Since The War"; paper presented to the Fourth annual Conference for the Scientific Study of International Relations, Copenhagen, 1931, by Professor Arnold Toynbee. From 1925, Toynbee was Research Professor of International History at the London School of Economics and Political Science, and Director of Studies at the Royal Institute of International Affairs (R.I.I.A.); Director of Foreign Research at the R.I.I.A. from 1939-1943, and research Director of the Foreign office 1943-1946), evidence of an international conspiracy has come from numerous informed sources **(113) (114.) (115.)** and, significantly since the perceived collapse of the Communist bogey, such a possibility has predictably been the subject of numerous pre-emptive press articles scorning the "Conspiracy Theory". In 1988, Lord Anan wrote of the BBC's abrogation of its fundamental duty to the State; a loyal obligation axiomatic to any of those remaining media companies not consolidated in supra-national conglomerates. The contraventions he cited were not merely of balance or impartiality, but of palpable disloyalty. (Sunday Telegraph, 13th. November 1988; "The BBC: Its duty to the State". Anon stressed that the State is "The legal expression of the nation; repository of sovereignty; sole source of legal cohesion; source of the authority of the armed forces; agent of the law". Yet, allowing for increased vulnerability to exposure due to advances in communications technology, there is evidence of an orchestrated attack on the British Monarchy, on its constitutional role and on the integrity of the United Kingdom. That a BBC transmission should open with: "Twenty per cent of the Radio 4 Generation think

Royalty should be abolished..." was inductive and unsubstantiated. Why not "Eighty per cent of Radio 4 Generation think Royalty should be retained"? The television puppet series "Spitting Image" has been deliberately insulting and debasing (Daily Telegraph, 6th. December 1988; "The yahoo culture of Spitting Image"; Provincial press letter 7th. April 1989.). Billed as "The Big Debate", the double page TV Times feature "Do we really need the Royal Family?" was arguably contrived to condition or provoke passive or uncommitted public opinion, and one must ask "What debate; and at who's instigation?" (TV Times, 20-26th. October 1990.). Tabloid newspapers, largely those controlled by Murdoch and the late Robert Maxwell, neither British by birth or commitment like the International Finance Capitalist agencies behind them, have long mounted unprincipled and systematic attacks on the British Monarchy through innuendo, malicious cartoons, inductive composition and the skilful selection of photographs (The following selection typifies the nature of the attack), Sun 19th. October 1987, "33 days-that is how long since we saw the drifting Royals in public together"; "20th. May 1991, "Charles Di's rift over Camilla-Charles makes it so obvious he prefers to be with Camilla"; 21 May 1991, "Charles refused to let caring Di nurse him back to health-divorce is no royal option"; Daily Mirror 20th. October 1987, "Diana and Charles-That Marriage: What is the Truth?"; 22nd. October 1987, "Together again (but oh so briefly). Murdoch's nominally establishment orientated Sunday Times and the television networks, Sunday Times 6th. November 1988, "A marriage of opposites-He no longer understands her-nor even, it seems, much likes her"; 21st. January 1990, "For better, for worse? Our changing romance with the Royals"; 4th. February 1990, "Moving towards Monarchy PLC"; 30th. June 1991, "Can't pay, won't pay; Financial Times, the 12th. January 1990, "Time to hang up the Royal hat"; 30th. June 1990, "Queen should face her subjects at the polls"; "World in Action", Independent Television, 24th. June 1991. No less culpable than the Sunday Times, abetted by Murdoch's Sky Television resources, has been the Daily Mail in staging evocative public opinion polls that inevitably destabilise traditional loyalties (Daily Mail 15th. February 1991, "What you REALLY think of the Royals"; Sunday Times 17th. February 1991, "Some Royals are slackers says war poll".

"From no quarter of the British Media has there been any loyal counter-offensive, or from government circles, or from privy councillors committed by an oath of loyalty. That some 20 journalists should be involved in attacks on the British Monarchy; that James Whitaker should appear both for the Daily Mirror and the TV Times; that Andrew Morton should write both for the Sun and the Sunday Times; demands an answer to the policy imposed on, and imposed by, editors, and follows a parallel pattern in the destabilisation of other elements of the nation; within the Church, attrition through pressure groups against morality and social conventions, and the polarised struggle for power to the point of destruction in education.

"Visibility for left-wing oriented freedom of organisation and expression, presumably on the pretext of national security, has led to the induction of public acquiescence through a correspondingly high and uncritical media profile. Thus the freedom of action of the extreme left-wing to attack social conventions and morality, compared with the constraints induced against an organisation such as the Economic League, was demonstrated by the Campaign For Press And Broadcasting Freedom, which shares an address at 9 Poland Street, in London, with other left-wing pressure groups. The Campaign's "Media Manifesto" enjoys the support of the Marxist writer, Eric Hobsbawm and anti-nuclear campaigner Bruce Kent. Characteristically, its objectives include special treatment for black, disability, lesbian, gay, media education and women's issues, while it is opposed, in its opinionated concepts, to censorship, racism, sexism and anti-union bias. Therefore one must consider the attack on Law and Order through the police, as representative of the enforcement of conventional disciplines.

"Obdurate, internecine structural and functional problems in the ranks of the police there may be, of which the "canteen mentality" is one manifestation. But one must also ask, for example, if falsification in the Channel 4 "semi-documentary" "May The Force Be With You", the "reconstruction" of events dealing with the Police reported on BBC News in July 1987, or misrepresentations in the BBC 2 programme "Out Of Court", constituted deliberate subversion or the determined pursuit of genuine ideals? (Daily Telegraph 23rd. July 1986, "Two litres of blood in T.V. police film"; Daily Telegraph letter 21st. July 1987, "unnecessary reconstruction"; Daily Telegraph 13th. June 1986 "BBC accused of deliberate attack on justice system"). The Independent Newspaper suggestively reported the enquiry into violence during the newspaper demonstrations at Wapping, and complaints against the Police action by 2 pickets, trades union leaders and the media", with the headline "One law for the boys in blue?" (Independent 21st. December 1989.). In September 1991 the proliferation of such distortions precipitated a letter of protest to the Independent Newspaper from a senior Manchester police officer, yet only six months later an Independent Magazine cartoon depicted a police siege with the words: "He's a gun-toting maniac-do we shoot him or recruit him?" (Independent, 17th. July 1991; "Police deserve better"; Independent Magazine, 11th. January 1992.). The Rupert Murdoch owned Sunday Times reported proposals to protect the Police from snipers during riots with the overtly and unnecessarily emotive headline "Police plan a 'shoot to kill' policy in riots" (Times 8th. April 1990). This was followed by a report in Murdoch's Times newspaper that "Police keep racist image as public unease increases", as the result of a MORI poll conducted on behalf of the News Of The World; another Murdoch newspaper (Times 10th. April 1989). As with the headline "Power in need of arrest" to a Bernard Levin article, also in the Times 21st. April 1989), such presentations generate a negative image and repeatedly place the Police on the defensive; a pattern of journalism that eventually provokes a lengthy letter of protest to the Sunday Times from a Metropolitan Police officer (Sunday Times 24th. May 1992; "Don't the police take enough punishment?". Careful monitoring reveals little evidence of a comparable and sustained campaign by the media against those media, political, social and educational agencies and individuals that have militated for three decades, and continue to militate, against Law and Order. Nor is there significant evidence of material supportive of the police, as opposed to persistent scrutiny, exposure and triumphantly critical headlines. Worse, in a sustained campaign the so-called establishment press devoted whole pages to the purported innocence of the "Guildford Four", the "Birmingham Six", and Judith Ward, convicted of the M62 coach bombing; but such is the sickening distortion of priorities that when a soldier lost both legs in Northern Ireland, it was reported by the Daily Telegraph in a mere column inch. (Daily Telegraph, 14th. May 1992)".

When we look back to these events our minds were dominated by our conception of our press as **'Free'** so we thought of the reporting as accurate; but careful manipulation of news can be done gradually without our knowledge of tampering and the Communist way has been well practised in changing thought to its benefit. Remember at this point Zionism is linked to Communism by its founder Moses Hess.

The media has, like an octopus, many tentacles. To illustrate the full story of all its **directions**, it is possible, now we know its interconnections to Finance Capitalism, to study one of the power houses of the media that has been conspicuous for its rapid growth and political manipulations yet remained UN-censored. I refer of course to Rupert Murdoch's News International Group.

The most comprehensive report on the group and its Australian owner appeared in 'Spotlight', an American journal that tried to warn America of the dangers ahead if they allow their country to be dominated by the International Finance Capitalists. Bear in mind these articles were written in 1984 and has progressed further since the article's were written by Dan McMahon.

Précis of Spotlight article on Murdoch.

The article **(116)** on June 30th. 1984 starts by stating that Rupert Murdoch had, by that time, conquered Australia and Britain and had made serious inroads into European media and was now targeting the United States, having taken over the 'New York Post', 'Boston Herald', the 'San Antonio Express', the Chicago 'Sun Times', the 'New York' magazine and the 'Village Voice'. The article states that media analysts were already showing concern at his bid for Warner Communications, the world's largest Multi Media entertainment conglomerate.

With the power of this giant he could have film product to dominate European Satellite and cable television. So it poses main questions. Who is Rupert Murdoch? Who supports his ambitious programme and what is his aim? It also needs answers to two more; why would he, a self-declared Conservative Capitalist, keep a bust of Lenin in his office? What effect could Murdoch's hold on the American Media have on the industry of the United States and the public it serves?

Murdoch was the son of Keith Murdoch, a employee of a British newspaper in Australia, living between their house near Melbourne and his fathers country ranch. He was educated at Geelong Private School and finished his studies at Oxford University.

His father obtained a position and standing by a marriage to the daughter of a wealthy Jewish family, which propelled him from reporter to chairman of his newspaper from where he bought a title, Sir Keith Murdoch, and two further newspapers in Adelaide and a South Australian Radio Station in a mining town.

His mother brought him up in the Jewish faith but he has, for some reason, hidden his Jewish upbringing. But nevertheless he has shown a pro-Israel bias, which, with his background formed his editorial position taken by his papers.

His hatred of the Irish, stems from young Irish émigrés in Australia who taunted him, and goes as far as accusing them of disloyalty to the British Empire because of their refusal to fight in South Africa and Germany. He also classes as his enemies, Germans, Palestinians, the Arabs, free enterprisers of all races and most of all Anti-Zionists, his supreme traitors. This, in my view, places him firmly in the Communist camp.

His father asked Lord Beaverbrook to train young Rupert and he was introduced to the rich and powerful bankers such as Edgar Bronfman, the Canadian liqueur giant (and Zionist funder in North America) and Harry Oppenheimer, (The Chairman of Anglo American and De Beers Diamond and Gold cartel). Oppenheimer also owns all the English language newspapers in South Africa. On his father's death he inherited two tired newspapers in which he started to push the Marxist ideas which he had adopted while at Oxford. (Like Cecil Rhodes). With his title of 'Red Rupert' he began to include pro-Marxist editorials in his papers but it did not bring the money rolling in. (Now this tells us the full story; Zionist, Marxist, Capitalist. Ideally suited to International Finance Capitalists.).

Suddenly he bought a Sunday newspaper for $400,000 in Perth and then a string of titles. It was obvious that finance was behind him. Oppenheimer was his secret bank roll provider; the future agenda, global.

He bought out Sir Frank Packer and was nearing media monopoly with Lady Simon-Fairfax, a left wing publisher and head of the Women's International Zionist movement. In the seventies he bought further titles in England and then moved on to America.

In England he had contributed to the lowering of standards by placing nude women on Page three of the Sun and pandering to base instincts of man which has become his way to sell copy, but it did not stop him buying 'The Times' and 'Sunday Times' with all the prestige that is attached to these titles and in America's New York 'Village Voice' and 'Sun Times'.

When Murdoch takes over at a newspaper, it takes on sensationalism and develops a propagandistic message to the public; showing a strong bias to Israel and against Arabs, as seen clearly in the New York Post. Spotlight goes on to say in February 6th. 1984, "Rupert Murdoch, who commands a media monopoly of worldwide proportions, has joined an elite band of millionaire Marxists exemplified by Armand Hammer, Michel Fribourg, The Rothschilds, Edgar Bronfman, Harry Oppenheimer and Rupert Anton". **(116). (Comment; So Marxism and Capitalism are linked officially to the International Bankers).**

Murdoch, explaining this strange alliance in his more outspoken days at University had this to say, "There is no ideological difference between Communism and Capitalism, except that the latter should be more controlled and centralised. The two are complementary". He also said; "But the real enemy of society is rampant free enterprise. It leads to decentralisation and an uncontrollable economy. It dilutes power into the hands of the irresponsible". (Where have we heard that before? The Protocols.).

These speeches attracted the attention of the "Gang of Four" Financiers, as he was calling 'their tune'. Without their backing, Murdoch would probably still print local newsprint in Australia.

Bronfman, with his eye on the liquor trade in Australia, and Oppenheimer worried about Diamond potential, offered Murdoch finance and also affirmed their belief in Marxism. Murdoch used the offer when he returned to Australia and began the climb to a global media mogul.

Oppenheimer and Bronfman decided to groom Murdoch to take over the British press as successor to Beaverbrook.

"Spotlight" goes on to say, "Secret meetings were held between Murdoch and representatives of the billionaire duo. Murdoch would have access to whatever amount of financing was needed to monopolise the Australian media. He was to co-ordinate his policies with those of Bronfman and Oppenheimer, and use the power of his papers to ensure "The appointment of suitable politicians". If the formula were successful, it would be repeated in England and the United States". **(There is the proof of the use of press power to influence government).** As a part of the deal, Bronfman gained wide coverage on 'Pro Booze' stories within the Murdoch publications. Oppenheimer was not left out, Murdoch played, (The no diamonds in Australia game) and shut up politicians who disagreed.

Murdoch started taking over Television in Australia and even a trucking company and an airline. He had saturated Australia with his dominance and now controlled politics. England was next, and, as stated, power over politicians his target. He added 'The Times' and 'The Sunday Times' to his collection, promising to leave the editorial responsibility alone. But he didn't, and Harold Evans, its editor, resigned. A new editor toed Murdoch's line and followed his agenda.

Soon with real power in sight, he moved on to storm America's media, making one purchase after another. What ever he bought descended into the sleaze bracket to boost circulation, pandering to the lower instincts of man, the very thing we rely on our press not to do. Fabrication and slanting of stories become the hallmark of his publications, according to concerned parents of America, who monitored his stories, and said, "His papers level everything down to the lowest common denominator of obscenity and mediocrity. It is vile and vulgar and lying. Murdoch has no respect for decency. He appeals to the basest instincts".

The spokeswoman for the Liberal Press, Katherine Graham, owner of the Washington Post, took Murdoch under her wing and used him to try to topple a Press Magnate who did not dance to their tune. It failed. But Murdoch's 'Star' took off and established his credentials. He became the latest prodigy of the New York elite, but particularly the banking set, who speculated about his next move.

In 1976 the speculation was over; Murdoch bought the New York 'Post' from Dolly Shiff for $430 million and 'Village Voice' and 'New West' for $15 million from Clay Felker. The latter was a messy take-over, but, as usual, Murdoch got his way. America saw Murdoch's methods for the first time and it was not a pretty sight. The News sheets of America regularly discuss Murdoch's rise, but never mentioned the Bankers behind him; this is a press taboo.

So what does Rupert Murdoch really want? 'Opinion Control' is the goal, globally, through media monopoly. He succeeded in Australia when with his media power and help from his enforcers provided by Bronfman and Oppenheimer, referred to as the 'Zionist Mafia' by the 'Toorak Times' of Melbourne. The Mafia entered the Australian Labour Party, founded by Irish workers who were kicked out and replaced by leftist lawyers led by Murdoch's University friend Robert Hawke. The 'Zionist Mafia' sponsored Robert Hawke to be its leader and another lawyer Goff Whitlam, to become Labour Party leader. Old policies were dropped and Murdoch's brand of International Zionist/Marxist policies adopted.

In 1972 Murdoch told Whitlam that he was going to make him the next Prime Minister, but he would in return have to pursue Murdoch's agenda:-
1. Follow a 100% pro Israeli policy.
2. Borrow vast sums of money from the International Monetary fund and the International Banks.
3. Re-enforce laws guaranteeing Murdoch's media monopoly, and secure for
Oppenheimer a long list of mining leases in every state of Australia.

Following Whitlam's agreement, Murdoch, showing his future contempt for democracy, used his press and Television monopoly to push Whitlam into office.

But Whitlam, thinking that he now held power, reneged on his three point promise; whereupon Murdoch turned on Whitlam. Failing in his ploy to concoct scandals, he used the union boss Hawke, and the Governor General, to have Whitlam removed from office.

In 1983 Hawke was elected Prime Minister and he subordinated all Australia's interests to the 'Gang of Four' (Murdoch's backers). We must thank Spotlight for this knowledge and for having the courage to print it.

If this is to be Murdoch's pattern for dominating nations, whose media he has purchased with Banker money, the world must realise that democracy is in danger. This proves beyond doubt the International Bankers' intentions. We can, and must, stop them. Murdoch claimed after the 1997 election, that through his paper, 'the Sun', he had influenced voters to make Blair our new Prime Minister. If this is true, we must watch developments carefully. I, for one, do not trust Murdoch's stand against the European Union as it does not fit in with his International Agenda. Is it just another trick of diversion? I think we have now seen enough to realise that the media is being used by a minority group of Bankers intent on imposing its will on an ill-informed world because our media is in their hands. This is not only undemocratic but highly dangerous and must be addressed.

PROTOCOL TWELVE
CONTROL OF THE PRESS.

The word "freedom" which can be interpreted in various ways, is defined by us as follows:

Freedom is the right to do that which the law allows. This interpretation of the word will, at the proper time, be of service to us, because all freedom will thus be in our hands, since the laws will either abolish or create only that which is desirable for us according to the aforesaid programme.

We shall deal with the press in the following way: What is the part played by the press of to-day? It serves to excite and inflame those passions which are needed for our purpose or else it serves selfish ends of parties. It is often vapid, unjust, mendacious, and the majority of the public have not the slightest idea what ends the press really serves. We shall saddle and bridle it with a tight rein: we shall do the same also with all productions of the printing press, for where would be the sense in silencing the attacks of the press if we remain targets for pamphlets and books? The produce of publicity, which nowadays is a source of heavy expense owing to the necessity of censorship, will be turned by us into a very lucrative source of income to our state: we shall lay on it a special stamp tax and require deposits of caution-money before permitting the establishment of any organ of the press or of printing offices: these will then have to guarantee our government against any kind of attack on the part of the press. For any attempt to attack us, if such still be possible, we shall inflict fines without mercy. Such measures as stamp tax, deposit of caution-money and fines secured by these deposits, will bring in a huge income to the government. It is true that party organs might not spare money for the sake of publicity, but these we shall shut up at the second attack upon us. No one shall with impunity lay a finger on the aureole of the infallibility of our government. The pretext for stopping any publication will be the alleged plea that it is agitating the public mind without occasion or justification. **I beg you to note that among those making attacks upon us will also be organs established by us, but they will attack exclusively points that we have pre-determined to alter.**

Not a single announcement will reach the public without our control. Even now this is already being attained by us inasmuch as all news items are received by a few agencies, in whose offices they are focused from all parts of the world. These agencies will then be already entirely ours and will give publicity only to what we dictate to them.

If we have already contrived to possess ourselves of the minds of the goy communities to such an extent that they all come near looking upon the events of the world through the coloured glasses of those spectacles we are setting astride their noses; if already there is not a single state where there exist for us any barriers to admittance into what goy stupidity calls state secrets: what will our position be then, when we shall be acknowledged supreme lords of the world in the person of our king of all the world....

Let us turn again to the **future of the printing press.** Every one desirous of being a publisher, librarian, or printer, will be obliged to provide himself with the diploma instituted therefore, which, in case of any fault, will be immediately impounded. With such measures the instrument of thought will become an educative means in the hands of our government, which will no longer allow the mass of the nation to be led astray in by-ways and fantasies about the blessings of progress. Is there any one of us who does not know that these phantom blessings are the direct roads to foolish imaginings which give birth to anarchical relations of men among themselves and towards authority, because progress, or rather the idea of progress, has introduced the conception of every kind of emancipation, but has failed to establish its limits... All the so-called liberals are anarchists, if not in fact, at any rate in thought. Every one of them is hunting after phantoms of freedom, and falling exclusively into licence, that is, into the anarchy of protest for the sake of protest....We turn to the periodical press. We shall impose on it, as on all printed matter, stamp taxes per sheet and deposits of caution-money, and books of less than 30 sheets will pay double. We shall reckon them as pamphlets in order, on the one hand, to reduce the number of magazines, which are the worst form of printed poison, and, on the other, in order that this measure may force writers into such lengthy productions that they will be little read, especially as they will be costly. At the same time what we shall publish ourselves to influence mental development in the direction laid down for our profit will be cheap and will be read voraciously. The tax will bring vapid literary ambitions within bounds and the liability to penalties will make literary men dependent upon us. And if there should be any found who are desirous of writing against us, they will not find any person eager to print their productions. Before accepting any production for publication in print the publisher or printer will have to apply to the authorities for permission to do so. Thus we shall know beforehand of all the tricks being prepared against us and shall nullify them by outstripping them with explanations on the subject treated of.

Literature and journalism are two of the most important educative forces, and therefore our government will become proprietor of the majority of the journals. This will neutralise the injurious influence of the privately owned press and will put us in possession of a tremendous influence upon the public mind.... If we give permits for ten journals, we shall ourselves found thirty, and so on in the same proportion. This, however, must in nowise be suspected by the public. **(Hidden Agenda)** For this reason all journals published by us will be in appearance, of the most opposite tendencies and opinions, thereby creating confidence in us, and bringing over to us our quite unsuspicious opponents, who will thus fall into our trap and be rendered harmless.

In the front rank will stand organs of an official character. They will always stand guard over our interests, and therefore their influence will be comparatively insignificant.

In the second rank will be the semi-official organs, whose part it will be to attract the tepid and indifferent.

In the third rank we shall set up our own opposition, which, to all appearance, in at least one of its organs, will present what looks like the very antipothesis to us. Our real opponents at heart will accept this simulated opposition as their own and will show us their cards. **(Diversion)**.

All our newspapers will be of all possible complexions-aristocratic, republican, revolutionary, even anarchical--for so long, of course, as the constitution exists....Like the Indian Idol Vishnu, they will have a hundred hands, and every one of them will have a finger on one sector of public opinion as required. When a pulse quickens these hands will lead opinion in the direction of our aims, for an excited patient loses all power of judgement and easily yields to suggestion. Those fools who will think they are repeating the opinion of a newspaper of their own camp will be repeating our opinion or any opinion that seems desirable for us. In the vain belief that they are following the organ of their party they will in fact follow the flag which we hang out for them.

In order to direct our newspaper Militia in this sense we must take especial and minute care in organising this matter.

Under the title of central department of the press we shall institute literary gatherings at which our agents will without attracting attention issue the orders and watchwords of the day. By discussing and controverting, but always superficially, without touching the essence of the matter, our organs will carry on a sham fight fusillade with the official newspapers solely for the purpose of giving occasion for us to express ourselves more fully than could well be done from the outset in official announcements, whenever, of course, that is to our advantage. These attacks upon us will also serve another purpose, namely, that our subjects will be convinced of the existence of full freedom of speech and so give our agents an occasion to affirm that all organs which oppose us are empty babblers, since they are incapable of finding any substantial objections to our orders. Methods of organisation like these, imperceptible to the public eye but absolutely sure, are the best calculated to succeed in bringing the attention and the confidence of the public to the side of our government. Thanks to such methods we shall be in a position as from time to time, may be required, to excite or tranquillise the public mind on political questions, to persuade or to confuse, printing now truth, now lies, facts or their contradictions, according as they may be well or ill received, always very cautiously feeling our ground before stepping upon it.... **We shall have a sure triumph over our opponents since they will not have at their disposition organs of the press in which they can give full and final expression of their views,** owing to the aforesaid methods of dealing with the press. We shall not even need to refute them except very superficially.

Trial shots like these, fired by us in the third rank of our press, in case of need, will be energetically refuted by us in our semi-official organs

Even nowadays, take only the French press, there are forms which reveal masonic solidarity in action in acting on the watchword: all organs of the press are bound together by professional secrecy; like the augurs of old, not one of their number will give away the secret of his sources of information unless it is resolved to announce them. Not one journalist will venture to betray this secret for not one of them is ever admitted to practice literature unless his whole past has some disgraceful sore or other....these sores would be immediately revealed. So long as they remain the subject of a few the prestige of the journalist attracts the majority of the country-the mob follow after him with enthusiasm.

Our calculations are especially extended to the provinces. It is indispensable for us to inflame there those hopes and impulses with which we could at any moment fall upon the capital, and we shall represent to the capitals that these expressions are the independent hopes and impulses of the provinces. Naturally the source of them will be always one and the same-ours. We require that, until such time as we are in the plenitude of power, the capitals should find themselves stifled by the provincial opinion of the nation, i.e., of a majority arranged by our agentur. It is essential for our purpose that at the psychological moment the capitals should not be in a position to discuss an accomplished fact for the simple reason, if for no other, that it has been accepted by the public opinion of a majority in the provinces.

When we are in the period of the new regime prior to the transition to that of the assumption of our full sovereignty we must not admit any reservations by the press of any form of public dishonesty; it is necessary that the new regime should be thought to have so perfectly contented everybody that even criminality has disappeared... Cases of the manifestation of criminality should remain known only to their victims and to chance witnesses-no more.

COMMENT

This Protocol is really self explanatory. It exposes a plan to control the Media to such a degree that no self expression of freedom can be exercised. It has amazing detail as well, for example, where it says that among those making attacks on us will be organs established by us. They are going to pretend democracy exists when in fact they control the media. They go on to say, "Not a single announcement will reach the public without our control". Frightening. Even at this early stage, 1905, they had the News collecting agencies, of which there are three, in their control. That is at the beginning of this century. That is a sobering thought. How they are going to control thought through what is in print is another thing that gives me room for fear. Their control seems absolute. I know that when I come to publish this focus on facts, I am going to have a very difficult job in getting it first published and then distributed. So this process is already in their hands. But I have one or two tricks up my sleeve. In typical Marxist style they will use diversion to make us think there is opposition to their ways. It will be **a mirror of deception,** a fake democracy. **DIRECTION.**

CHAPTER SEVEN, PART THREE.

MORALITY

The level of morality within our society is a measurement of society's ability to exist or to disintegrate into a ungovernable state of lawless depravity. In history we have seen great empires in Babylon and in Rome crumble when moral depravity took over. Religion and morality, above all else, are the two main pillars of society and we should be very clear that if we allow either to degenerate, our treasured freedoms that still exist, will disappear for ever.

We have seen clear evidence from Weishaupt's Illuminati, followed by Karl Marx's Communism and from International Zionism, controlled by the International Finance Capitalists, that part of their peaceful revolution is to disarm religion as the main enemy and one of the tools they use is moral decline. They know full well what has worked before, and that alone is a good enough reason to use it again as an instrument for revolution. This is the reason why they need control of the media in all its forms; television, radio, the arts, theatre, cinema, the press and the literary world. If they control the media they can control our thinking, and our minds.

Gradually, during this century and in particular in the second half, our media, in all its forms, has passed into the hands of Zionist influence, directly through management, or indirectly through financial control. The result has been a well planned decline of morality that has as its end result not only the break up of the family but also the lawlessness seen increasingly at International football matches like the World Cup. This has nothing to do with patriotism but is a orchestrated demonstration to break up our National Sovereignty. The organisers of this thuggery, controlling its onslaught by mobile phones, are in the pay of the Marxist plan to destabilise our society and kill our sovereignty. (Inside information from a special branch officer).

Today our censorship of unsuitable material for use on television, radio and our cinema has declined to such an extent that it is non-existent. The job of censorship is virtually in the hands of the trade, who are motivated by sales; by lowering the moral standards they gain an increase in sales, or viewers, which, in turn bring in bigger rewards or advertising revenue.

Having proved their intent to use morality as a weapon in the Marxist struggle to destabilise our sovereignty and democracy, censorship cannot and must not be left to the capitalists within the media. Be quite clear. **This is their Hidden Agenda.** Let us now study how the plan to reduce our morality by the media-led-war is succeeding so far.

I turn again to Colonel Barry Turner's painstaking report on the media, to illustrate the evidence in support of this thesis that the media is driving our morality down a path to a dangerous level of lawlessness and depravity.

You only have to study the magazine racks in the book shops to see a whole host of teenage magazines, all of which compete with each other to reduce moral standards, to increase sales and, when questioned about the subject, give us a whole host of liberal thinking slogans to excuse themselves for openly enticing under-age children to start sex lives before their age allows. They then have the cheek to blame family life, instead of their deliberate attempt to pervert our children. Colonel Turner had this to say:-

A CATALOGUE OF DEPRAVITY IN THE MEDIA ASSAULT ON WESTERN SOCIETY.

Through the so-called "permissive sixties" to the 70s the sexual relationship was being cheapened and trivialised by influences at work in television, films, the theatre, mass communications media and advertising. In BBC transmissions invective proliferated **(117) (118)**. On the other hand, in 1975 the thirty-three year old writer and television producer Barry Cox vented his bile on censorship, and dismissed self-censorship that "obtains in the more modern media, such as films, broadcasting and the press" as "obsequious". He defended freedom of expression in a gallery display of phallic graffiti from lavatory walls, and considered hostility to the book 'Last Exit to Brooklyn' (released as a film early in 1990), with its homosexuality, as "a rather narrow view of social and sexual morality". **(119.).** The Obscene Publications Act of 1959 made constraints on published material less severe, and the Theatre Act of 1968 abolished the power of the Lord Chamberlain to censor stage plays. Books hitherto banned as obscene were to become compulsory examination reading in schools. **(120.).** The Royal Court Theatre, (where usherettes were later to sell condoms) **(121)**, staged 'Spring Awakening', in which a fourteen year old girl died of an abortion, two schoolboys kissed in an 'ecstasy of homosexual love', and the inmates of a juvenile prison indulged in a masturbation contest. **(122).** The nude, sexual theme continued, with obscenities, in stage productions such as: 'O! Calcutta', 'Che', 'Hair', and the plays of the homosexual Joe Orton. **(123) (124).** Booker referred to the years after 1966 as the heyday of erotic books, magazines and drug scandals. For the younger generation the Beetles heralded the advent of pop music. Along with other groups and with generous media exposure they set the pace of destabilisation by publicity flouting conventional morals and constraints on drug abuse. **(125) (126) (127).** The young have also been tempted into debt and the grasp of usury capitalism through the promotion of plastic credit cards. Easy cash credit is freely advertised in tabloid newspapers, as are erotic telephone contacts promoted through the images of sensuously posed girls. **(128).** Pornographic publications, that leave little to the imagination, flourish. **(129).** Teen age pop magazines, such as 'New Music Express', have promoted drug abuse and featured obscenities, blasphemy, and explicit sexual and homosexual material. The disclaimer by the editor of New Music Express **(130)**, could easily be refuted by reference to the pages of which he must have been well aware. **(131).** Neither does there appear to be any justification for the publicity accorded to the Jewish 'sex therapist' Dr. Ruth Westerheimer by BBC Television on the Wogan chat-show, or by a half page profile in the Daily Telegraph. **(132).** The down market tabloid press controlled by Maxwell (Dec) and Murdoch have concurrently become little better on occasions than Technicolor sex manuals, in which the nude and semi-nude couples are never depicted wearing wedding rings as they embrace. This same subliminal orthodoxy has been more subtly evident in the so-called establishment press with references, no less destined to condition the readership, to 'partner' rather than 'spouse', by routine acceptance of co-habitation and by inductive lines such as "...one-parent families are a fact of life", ...Why photos of penises and articles on orgasms are essential, and with 'Single motherhood losing its stigma...'.

In the United States the patter of Disc Jockey Howard Stern includes explicit sexual conversations, race and religion, and he offered match-making services to gays, lesbians, prostitutes and dwarfs. **(133).** In the United Kingdom, satellite television gives access to pornographic films from Europe. **(134).** Television comedies feature unmarried co-habitation, and the channel 4 programme 'Socially Unacceptable: Unmarried Mothers', dealt with changing attitudes to single parenthood, while the channel 4 serial 'Brookside' included a violent rape episode. **(135).** The programme 'Trouble with Sex' discussed the therapeutic aspects of sexual relations. **(136).** In December 1988, a channel 4 television programme, 'In The Club', about contraception, involved light hearted discussion of sexual experiences, and was referred to by Daily Telegraph journalist, Lesley Garner, as: "The first of a refreshing and surprisingly entertaining series". The Radio Times introduced the comedy series 'Blue Moon Detective Agency' with details of the heavily pregnant female partner 'Walking down the aisle' to marry, and the TV Times exploited the concept of unmarried co-habitation with a two page spread on pregnant star Melanie Griffith and her marriage plans. **(137).** In the works of BBC playwright Dennis Potter were included the heaving bottoms and obscenities of 'The Singing Detective', the obscenities of 'Jesus Son of Man' and the explicit sex scenes of 'Blackeyes'. **(138).**

Channel 4 productions seem particularly determined on the promotion of perversion through purportedly serious discussion, and through entertainment. The film 'Seventeen Rooms-Or What Lesbians Do in Bed' was cancelled, although a spokesman justified the film as "essentially comedy", but the French film 'Themrock' was transmitted, and included incest, orgies, perversion, violence, and cannibalism. **(139).** 'In The Pink: Breaking the Silence', in October 1987, discussed how lesbian mothers lived with their children. 'Out On Tuesday', a series for gays and lesbians, was considered by a Daily Telegraph reviewer as 'promotion', but was dismissed with the observation that they could 'Get on with it'. **(140).** On the 7th. March 1989, 'Out on Tuesday' dealt with changing attitudes to homosexuality in Germany between 1910 and 1945, and the following week the programme covered the attitude of adoption agencies to homosexual couples. The Daily Telegraph condemned the corrupting influence of 'Prick Up Your Ears', a salaciously homosexual film on the life of playwright Joe Orton, written by Alan Bennet and directed by Stephen Frears, also shown in March 1989. On the other hand, Telegraph Newspapers, along with the Times, regularly feature fulsome reviews of homosexual entertainment, accompanied quite unnecessarily by photographs of the embracing participants. In July 'The Survivor's Guide' concerned a counselling session on sexuality and sexual experiences, and included a homosexual couple. 'Chuck Solomon-Coming of Age', in December 1989, featured the life of a homosexual actor and director, Aids and the gay community of San Francisco. On the stage homosexuality appears commonplace, for example the play 'Gay Sweatshop Compromised Immunity' was based on the friendship between an Aids stricken homosexual and a young male nurse. **(141).** In 1990 the Royal Court Theatre starred Ian McKellen in a play based on homosexuality in Nazi Germany, which was sympathetically reviewed by John Gross in the Sunday Telegraph. **(142).** The Sunday Times observed on the masturbation, buggery, homosexual relations, explicit sex, violence, prostitution, and sadism in television productions such as 'The Last Of England', 'My Beautiful Launderette' (The author of which was sympathetically interviewed by Joan Bakewell on BBC 2), 'Sammy And Rosie Get Laid', 'Eat the Red' and 'Empire State'. **(143)**.

In November 1989 the Cambridge University Dramatic Society staged 'The Romans in Britain', which featured full frontal nudity, simulated homosexual rape, violence and obscene language. (144). The BBC serial on London life, 'Eastenders', featured a homosexual and a prostitute. The three part serial 'Oranges Are Not The Only Fruit', included a lesbian love scene between adolescents, and was defended by BBC Controller Alan Yentob, Director Beeban Kidron, the Head of BBC Television Drama, Mark Shivas and Producer Phillippa Giles. **(145)**. First reported in 1988, the BBC announced proposals for a homosexual film 'Two of Us', later scheduled for 14-16 year olds in the 1990 spring season of school transmissions. The film involves caressing, although kissing scenes were cut. The guide notes explained that homosexuality was part of normal development, but the Professional Association of Schoolteachers condemned the film as 'Promoting' homosexuality.

Since Colonel Turner wrote this in 1992 we have seen gay rights activists, led by adherents to Marxist philosophy campaign to reduce the age of consent of the homosexual act to sixteen. That means once more our legal system will reduce their level at least two years to fourteen and may well ignore complaints altogether. But this moves the act into the boundaries of Paedophilia.

The television has used homosexual and lesbian relationships on soaps and a BBC play called "Close Relations" showed nearly every type of minority perversion within one series which over-played family disintegration ten fold. The play was obviously shown to lower moral standards. The European Union has also ruled that pornography beamed in from Europe must be allowed in without blocking. If you go back to 1950 everything that has been mentioned would have been censored. When you make this comparison you see quite clearly the planned disintegration of moral standards. On this Barry Turner has this to say:

Manipulative Influence Of Progressive Centralisation And International Capitalist Control

Concern over the power of the media to determine what the public see and hear in the United Kingdom gave little cause for alarm through two Royal Commissions in 1947-49 and 1961-62, beyond limited newspaper amalgamation, and dual newspaper and television interests. **(146)**. In the United States neither Dye **(147)**, nor David Habastram **(148)**, made any bones about the concentration of power, or the individuals in whose hands that power was vested. Anthony Sampson undertook his customary detailed, but sanitised survey of the British media with no more than a passing mention of the concentration of power. **(149)**. Then in June 1988, the Financial Times reported: "The battle for television's soul-How satellites will shape TV in Britain". **(150)**. In May 1989 a House of Commons debate found members "United in opposition to media empires" **(151)**. Only three months later, the Independent newspaper reported that porn was "Set to be beamed at Britain" **(152)**, "The Alien Porn-Loopholes are letting the sleaze merchants mock Britain's law". The concentration of power that has progressively taken place, and that continues apace at a level of investment and financial support far beyond that accorded to productive domestic industries that create genuine wealth, demonstrates clearly the impotence of political shadow boxing about networks that are, in the words of Dye: "...probably now beyond the check of any institution in our society". **(153).** The palpable absurdity, the illusion of political will, and dishonesty towards the electorate, were encapsulated in the platitude of the then Home Secretary, the Right Hon. Douglas Hurd, that: "Broadcasting will not be ruled by tycoons". **(154).** Why only broadcasting?

Colonel Barry Turner goes on to show how, through government and media help, every encouragement and protection is given to the perversion mongers, while the groups that try to stop the decline of morality and family like Mary Whitehouse, and Lynette Burrows of the Family Education Trust, are scorned or marginalised by our media and government alike. This complicity by our elected servants is disgraceful.

Before we move on it would be appropriate to see a small part of Lynette Burrows purposeful book 'The Fight For The Family'. **(155).**

"The general public is being seriously misled in the matter of "Children's Rights". For most people, the idea of rights for children centre on their welfare: the need to protect them from harm and to provide them with the basic necessities of life. It would never occur to them that this necessary and benign intention is being misused by those who want to change the family from what they see as a bourgeois, paternalistic, oppressive institution to a new, radical activity unit where parents are merely caretakers of children, on sufferance from the State". (This is part of Weishaupt's policy to destroy the family unit. **(Direction).**

Now study this statement from the Children's Rights Office made in June 1995. "Traditionally, there has tended to be a presumption that parents' rights prevail until children can demonstrate a capacity for exercising their rights, but the obligation in article 5 (of the UN convention) to "act" in a manner consistent with the evolving capacities of the 'child' suggests that the presumption should be reversed: parents should exercise their rights to over-ride the actions of a child only where the child is not competent to understand fully the consequences of his actions, or where failure to intervene would place the child at risk or would cause harm to, or interfere with, the rights of others". Lynette Burrows says, "It is being suggested instead that others, outside the family, should supersede the right of parents to rear their children as they think fit, and that they, and not the parents, should decide when a child is "Competent". As the United Nations is the source of Law churned out by the European Union this attitude must shock us all when we realise the European Union can override our Law and therefore can take our children from us for no stated reason. The thought that the state can bring up a child better than a parent is ultimate arrogance. This disguises the planned break up of the family called for by Marxism and the Illuminati of Weishaupt. This plan enables them to be brainwashed by the state agenda. That's enough to say that you should read this book.

To safeguard ourselves against any further moral decline we should set up an Independent censor which will positively raise standards not lower them. We need a censor with moral bite.

The Encouragement Of Social And Moral Destabilisation In The Assault On Western Society

The consequences of this systematic massaging of public opinion coupled with infiltration and subversion of the professional establishment-invariably justified by the "chicken-and-egg" logic-was evident when the National Union of Teachers' Mr. Frank Howard declared that issues of sexuality should be taught in schools, with the uncorroborated opinion forming statement that '1 in 10 of the population is gay'. (156). And in the first months of 1992 BBC Television massaged this depravity with an early evening programme that involved teenagers in discussions about their sexual orientation. At peak afternoon viewing time, the same channel featured Jewish 'agony aunt' Claire Rayner in discussion on marital problems with a group that included a homosexual; an unquestionably subliminal transmission. Already, in 1971, educationalist Elizabeth Manners had foreseen violence and sexual scenes on television being drawn into the Law and Order debate, and cited the cost of vandalism and hooliganism from Southend to Manchester, both in schools and in the Universities. (157).

In 1986 the Reader's Digest magazine carried an article 'When Television Threatens Young Minds', concerning a twenty year record of the relationship of television violence and obscene language to real-life behaviour. (158). In the same year, campaigner Mrs Mary Whitehouse announced the results of a survey in which the incidence of obscenity was tabulated. (159). In 1987, the Sunday Times recorded the impact on the young of violence in video films available in the United States, the United Kingdom and Australia. (160). That year, the obituary for former BBC Director General, Sir Hugh Greene, stated that he presided over a period "Which fed the enormous flood of moral and social evil which afflicts us twenty five years later", and that he "scorned" Mary Whitehouse. (161).

In 1988, Mary Whitehouse spoke about the apparent determination of the BBC to question the validity of public and parliamentary anxiety. (162). Proposals to establish a Broadcasting Standards Council involved the prohibition of violence, explicit sexual acts and nudity only before 9 pm, but the newspaper article 'Television Bad Taste' revealed the arguments about the powers of the Council. (163).

Even in the run up to legislation under the obscene Publications Bill, Michael Grade, then BBC Director of Programmes, attacked the bill on the grounds that it would have "a devastating effect on creativity in every form in the country". A committee formed to fight the bill included film producer Michael Winner, liberal author John Mortimer Q.C., Paul Fox of Yorkshire Television, and Jeremy Isaacs, then Chief Executive of Channel 4 Television. (164). At the time of the Broadcasting Bill, Sir Richard Attenborough, Chairman of Channel 4 television, and Michael Grade, by then his Chief executive, both strongly opposed any government control over membership of the new Independent Television Commission. (165). Of these six individuals, it is of interest that four were Jewish and a fifth, Attenborough, has strong Jewish affiliations. One must wonder, therefore, at the perpetuation of this cult of obscenity by the BBC, and apparent determination to continue to destabilise, rather than to lead a return to acceptable standards; the defence of 'performers' Ben Elton and Alexei Sayle, and the defence of the Head of Comedy, James Moir by the Controller of BBC, Jonathan Powell. **(166).** Precisely what are the ideologies, motives and objectives of such individuals?

PROTOCOL FOURTEEN
ASSAULT ON RELIGION

When we come into our kingdom, it will be undesirable for us that there should exist any other religion than ours, of the one God with whom our destiny is bound up, by our position as the Chosen People and through whom our same destiny is united with the destinies of the world. We must therefore sweep away all other forms of belief. If this gives birth to the atheists whom we see to-day it will not, being only a transitional stage, interfere with our views, but will serve as a warning for those generations which will hearken to our preaching of the religion of Moses, that, by its stable and thoroughly elaborated system, has brought all the peoples of the world into subjection to us. Therein we shall emphasise its mystical right, on which as we shall say, all its educative power is based...

Then at every possible opportunity we shall publish articles in which we shall make comparisons between our beneficent rule and those of the past ages. The blessings of tranquillity, though it be a tranquillity forcibly brought about by centuries of agitation, will throw into higher relief the benefits to which we shall point. The errors of the goyim governments will be depicted by us in the most vivid hues. We shall implant such an abhorrence of them that the peoples will prefer tranquillity in a state of serfdom to those rights of vaunted freedom which have tortured humanity and exhausted the very sources of human existence, sources which have been exploited by a mob of rascally adventurers who know not what they do...**Unless changes of forms of government to which we instigated the goyim when we were undermining their state structures will have so wearied the peoples by that time that they will prefer to suffer anything under us rather than run the risk of enduring again all the agitations and miseries they have gone through.**

At the same time we shall not omit to emphasise the historical mistakes of the goy governments which have tormented humanity for so many centuries by their lack of understanding of everything that constitutes the true good of humanity in their chase after fantastic schemes of social blessings, never noticing that these schemes kept on producing a worse and never a better state of the universal relations which are the basis of human life...

The whole force of our principles and methods will lie in the fact that we shall present them and expound them as a splendid contrast to the dead and decomposed order of things in social life.

Our philosophers will discuss all the shortcomings of the various beliefs of the goyim. But no one will ever bring under discussion our faith from its true point of view since this will be fully learned by none save ours, who will never dare to betray its secrets.

In countries known as progressive and enlightened, we have created a senseless, filthy, abominable literature. For some time after our entrance to power we shall continue to encourage its existence in order to provide a telling relief by contrast to the speeches, party programme, which will be distributed from exalted quarters of ours...Our wise men, trained to become leaders of the goyim, will compose speeches, projects, memoirs, articles, which will be used by us to influence the minds of the goyim, directing them towards such understanding and forms of knowledge as have been determined by us.

COMMENT

From this Protocol we learn that they will use pornography to subdue the mass and keep their minds off politics. I think that this is already in practice in many Western nations. This business should be vigorously pursued till it becomes too costly for the filth peddlers to continue in business. It is the liberal reformers who have allowed this business to flourish. They must no longer control the agenda.

Because the enemy within our walls use a **Hidden Agenda** to attack our society it is difficult to positively identify any single action. But when you get a catalogue of immorality as Colonel Turner exposes in his excellent paper it becomes more identifiable and its source, as we have found with every tentacle of this octopus, leads us back to the centre, the International Finance Capitalists. Morality is a much larger subject that encompasses drugs, road rage and many other avenues but this would be a book in itself and I think you may now have a good understanding how they use part of their hidden agenda to destabilise our democracy.

CHAPTER SEVEN, PART FOUR.

RELIGION

We have already seen that both Weishaupt and Karl Marx considered religion as their main enemy. The Finance Capitalists, who are Zionist Atheists also see religion as a major obstacle to their progress. So you can see reference to all three groups linked through Freemasonry, actively engaged in efforts to destabilise the Christian world while promoting an atheistic form of Zionism.

Zionism, when criticised, reacts by hurling abuse at anyone who dares to question them on any level. The world, so horrified by the media, continually reminding them of the Holocaust, allows the Zionists to crush legitimate discussion that, in a true democracy, would allow a full debate to find the truth. But the world gets its information from the media and we now know who pulls the strings of that media, forming a world-wide censorship on all debating that might expose the bankers Hidden Agenda.

Their aim is mind control. The Christian religion is one of only a few open sources that can still influence the world against the bankers Satanic intentions. The Roman Catholic church has led the way in the fight against Communism. However the Communist infiltration of the World Council of Churches is almost complete and has had a disastrous effect on the direction, morale, and focus of this loose collection of Christian Churches throughout the world. (See 'Gospel According to Marx' By Joseph Harriss. (pp. 201-205, 'The World and Europe').

It is on this matter that I am concentrating my mind. While it goes without saying that many other matters have succeeded in bringing religion's presence to a crisis point within our communities, such as morality, already covered, industrialisation, diverting our attention from politics and religion to sport, while they (the Bankers) vandalise our religion and undermine our political base. A simple proof of this switch in our attention appeared on a 'B Sky B' poster where Murdoch used a script that likened football to religion, thus denigrating religion down to the level of football and all its fanatical problems. This was not a coincidence but a well planned ploy. This, isolated, seems petty, but in concert with all the other examples that occur represents a gradual brainwashing of the public.

My job is to show that infiltration has taken place that has paralysed our church procedure in favour of, at best, liberal, loose thinking and at worst, down right subversion, by infiltrated agents of Communism who have no place in our church as their final aim is to destroy it. The attack on Christianity is nothing new. It is its method that is different.

The laws of the Christian community, laid down by Moses in the Ten Commandments, stand as the pillars of Christianity. An attack on these is an attack on Christianity itself. To this the Pharisees added their own laws, diluting the true laws of Moses. The English common law is based on the Ten Commandments. Christian morality has developed through precedent and fairness, till today each case that goes before a court uses past cases to help the decision towards a just settlement. Not perfect, but considered one of the best in the world, until that is, along came the European Court Of Justice, influenced from behind a hidden screen by the bankers, the power brokers of the world. Through these courts our fishing industry has been shattered, our beef industry brought to its knees and Marxist IRA terrorists, set on the destabilisation of Britain, released and even compensated.

This alone is enough to warn us about the intent of the European Union and its Marxist Ideals. So history does repeat itself from the Pharisees to Europe.

The two pillars of Jewish law came from the Torah which was the Jewish interpretation of the laws of Moses and the Talmud which was the laws of the Pharisees interpreted and put into writing from its original oral form in the third and fourth century AD, now called simply the Jerusalem Talmud. This was superseded by the Babylon Talmud with a much developed discussion and far less factual statement, leaving it open to much interpretation. This version is the accepted Talmud, and was based on the thought of the minority of Jews responsible for the crucifixion of Christ. It is violently anti Christian, in some places, to obsession. Some of its moral statements are out of line with Christian morality and particularly the ten commandments of Moses. It is from this Talmud that Zionist Atheists, communists, Illuminati get their drive to destroy the Christian Religion, without the knowledge or approval of the vast majority of Jews.

Christ, **(167),** stated clearly that you cannot serve God and money. But a group of Khazar Jews were unimpressed. They spread over Eastern and central Europe and flowed into Germany to form the "Synagogue of Satan, who say they are Jews but are not". (Described in the book of Revelations) the Khazar Jews, known as the 13th. Tribe, **(168)** became the usurers of Europe, taking over the Financial World from the established bankers and controlling politics through their policy of National Finance. This applied particularly for wars, i.e. the Rothschilds, and influenced international banking that developed in the 18th. and 19th. century. So we see how the link was made through the International Bankers, using Atheism to destabilise the world through Communism, Religion being the Bankers greatest enemy. International Zionism has made sure that the Jewish race is blamed for its (International Zionism's) policies and actions when exposed; in true Weishaupt style.

However the true Jewish race is as innocent as the Christian Race. Because of International Zionist control of our Media, the Jewish race in general cannot be held responsible for the bankers intent. Those International Zionists involved must be separated and accused alone. The Jewish race is not under attack from this history but some of their most powerful sponsors are at the heart of this world conspiracy.

I take as proof of the attack on our Churches an article that appeared in Readers Digest February 1993 **(169)**, which clearly shows how the KGB infiltrated agents into the World Council of Churches. Before we go into this, it is worth noting that two books by Professor Ernest le Fever **(170)**, left no shadow of doubt that the World Council of Churches" has been deeply penetrated and that it had been under domination since the Delhi Conference of 1961.

Since then we have seen Church organs sponsor Communist Terrorist Organisations like ANC, without a reported outcry from true Christianity so opposed to Communism in any form.

THE GOSPEL ACCORDING TO MARX
BY JOSEPH HARRISS

Why have the interests of the World Council of Churches strayed so far from Christianity? Top-secret KGB files reveal one reason.

Before the opening service of worship at the last general assembly of the World Council of Churches (WCC) in Canberra, Australia, delegates passed through the smoke of burning leaves. This was a pagan cleansing rite. The congregation then listened to recorded insect noises and watched a male dancer impersonate a kangaroo.

The next day, as two painted, loin-clothed Aborigines cavorted, South Korean theologian Chung Hyun Kyung invoked the spirits of the dead and exhorted the audience of more than 4,000 to read the Bible "from the perspective of birds, water, air, trees" and to "think like a mountain".

Quite a display, but was it Christian? Some delegates protested against the animism, Spiritism and new age beliefs that were presented. "Pagan culture has infiltrated the WCC", says Vijay Menon, an Anglican delegate of Indian origin. "I left that behind to become a Christian".

Today the WCC, which includes 322 Churches in more than 100 countries, is a caricature of the ecumenical movement founded in 1948 by mostly European and American religious leaders. In its desire to accommodate radical anti-Western and third World pressure groups, the council has drifted from its original goal of Christian unity into the choppy waters of "secular ecumenism" ministering to society through political activism.

Now, Reader's Digest reveals a major reason why: for decades this vast organisation has been a target for manipulation by decidedly un-Christian forces.

Pastor Wolfhart Schlichting, head of the Lutheran society for missionary work in Germany, still remembers his shock over WCC Bible study materials he found during a 1989 visit to the Philippines. "Young people there were not really studying the Bible", he says. "These 'missionary' materials were preaching revolution".

The WCC's primary concern is now politics. "The council has jettisoned traditional Christian missionary activity and substituted political action designed to establish a new kind of world order", says Rachel Tingle, director of London's Christian Studies Centre.

Radical talk. To justify its political action, the WCC has encouraged "contextual theology for South Africa - all interpreting the Bible selectively to support radicalism. "Just as it was right for Jereboam to seek to oust Solomon", says one WCC publication, "it is right for all to throw off people from positions of authority".

Add increasing influence by feminist, ecological and other pressure groups, and you have a WCC out of touch with people in Western pews. When a study group at the Canberra assembly wanted to consult the Bible on a point, a WCC staff member protested, "Oh no. It's Christian imperialism to suggest that the bible has more to say than other books".

How WCC programmes have become politicised can be seen most clearly in the programme to combat Racism (PCR). "Around the world, Christians recognise the need for improving race relations", says the Reverend Billy Melvin, executive director of America's National Association of Evangelicals, "but the WCC concentrates on the 'white institutional racism' of the 'international capitalist economic system'."

Since 1970, the PCR has distributed more than £6.5 million to more than 130 organisations in some 30 countries-about half to revolutionary Marxist movements in Africa. It does not check to see that funds are actually used for humanitarian purposes. One grant of £55,000 went to the Patriotic Front in Rhodesia (Now Zimbabwe), which had murdered 1,712 black and 207 white civilians, along with nine missionaries and their children.

In South Africa, the WCC has long supported the African National Congress, with more than £850,000 in grants. Though the ANC leadership has disavowed such tactics, its members have used terrorist methods, including "necklacing", in which a petrol-soaked tyre is hung around the victim's neck and set ablaze.

In Namibia, more than £1.1 million in church money went to the SWAPO revolutionary group, even though it had imprisoned and tortured thousands of its own followers in concentration camps.

PCR grants, which last year totalled £247,120, are so controversial that they are not made from the regular WCC operating budget, but from the Special Fund contributors or the addresses of grant recipients.

Home Front. In Europe, British groups are the largest recipients of PCR grants. One beneficiary here is the Independent Immigration Support Programme, which links up with a number of campaigns to "elicit changes in the immigration appeals system".

Meanwhile, the WCC was strangely reticent on racism and oppression in Marxist countries. When the Ceusescu regime in Romania persecuted religious denominations and planned to bulldoze villages inhabited by ethnic minorities, the WCC refused to speak out forcefully. Says Bishop László Tökés, who sparked Romania's 1989 revolt that toppled the Communists, "The WCC was not interested in the Church's fight for freedom".

When religious dissenters in the former Soviet Union begged for support in the 1970s, the council said little. "The WCC failed to defend our Christian brothers in Eastern Europe and the USSR", says Father Gleb Yakunin, a courageous Russian Orthodox priest who spent years in Soviet prisons, labour camps and exile for his faith. "If the WCC had spoken out, the persecutors would have reduced their zeal".

Why was the WCC largely silent about the crushing of religious freedom in the Communist block? Why for the last 25 years has it strayed from its charter in order to support revolutionary and activist groups, oppose Western European defence policy, and denounce capitalism? Secret files from the KGB, the former Soviet Union's intelligence agency provide at least part of the answer.

Father Yakunin, now a deputy of the Russian Supreme Soviet's Commission on Freedom of Religion, has examined top secret monthly reports from the KGB Administration for Ideological Subversion. In an exclusive interview with Reader's Digest, he stated, "The KGB had a plan to penetrate and manipulate the WCC. Orthodox priests who were WCC delegates were often KGB agents acting on Communist Party orders".

Red Exports. How effective were they? "In my view", Yakunin said, "The WCC's radical-left activities helped the Soviet bloc spread Communist ideology in Africa, North and South America and the far East".

Witness one entry in the KGB reports: August 1969-"Agents 'Altar', 'Svyatoslav', 'Adamant', 'Magister', 'Roshchin', and 'Zemnogorsky' went to England to take part in the work of the WCC Central Committee.
"Agents managed to avert hostile activities and to place agent 'Kuznetsov' in a high WCC post".

A close study of KGB documents, co-ordinated with examination of records of the Russian Orthodox Church and other public reports, makes possible the identification of Kuznetsov. His name is Alexei Sergeyevich Buevsky, a lay member of the church's Moscow Patriarchate's Foreign Relations Department---and to this day a WCC Central Committee member. J.A. Emerson, a Dutch scholar and journalist, has called Buevsky "One of the most outspoken defenders of Soviet policy in numerous WCC meetings. He has helped to draft important WCC documents on International affairs".

Buevsky's presence on the committee gave his KGB contacts an unprecedented opportunity to influence the direction taken by the WCC. At that August 1969 Central Committee meeting in Canterbury, the WCC proclaimed that member churches should "become agents for the radical reconstruction of society".

Another later excerpt from KGB files bears witness to their success: July 1989 "According to a plan approved by the KGB leadership, efficient secret and organisational measures have been undertaken to ensure state security during events sponsored by the World Council of Churches in Moscow. As a result the WCC Executive and Central Committees adopted public statements (eight), messages (three), which corresponded to the political course of socialist countries". The memos go on and on, with 'Kuznetsov' popping up frequently.

In 1982 the WCC's Central Committee called for total nuclear disarmament. The statement came at a time when tensions were running high over Nato's decision to deploy Pershing missiles in Western Europe to counter Soviet SS-20's placed in Eastern Europe. In one passage the WCC asserted that "much would be gained in terms of European stability if Nato were to be less dependent on nuclear weapons". Yet the role the USSR might play in this "stability" was not mentioned.

Buevsky, along with other agents, probably ensured that WCC Central Committee members from Eastern Europe toed the Kremlin line. Regarding the election of Emilio Castro to the post of WCC general secretary in 1985, a KGB memo confirms that its agents supported Castro as "a candidate acceptable to us".

A liberation theologian from Uruguay, Castro was vocal in his appreciation of Marxism. At a 1989 reception in the Kremlin, he addressed the guests as "comrades" and remarked that Karl Marx "was dreaming out of the same biblical tradition from which we come...in that common dream, we hope that between us we will have many steps to take in common".

As the WCC marks its forty-fifth anniversary this year, the member Churches around the world are beginning to question its activities. The Orthodox Churches, with some 150 million faithful, have condemned "dangerous trends in the WCC". This sentiment is echoed by the Archbishop of Canterbury, George Carey. "The WCC's heart is in the right place, but it needs to be reformed", he says. "Fast".

It is doubtful, however, that its new General Secretary, 55-year-old German Theologian Konrad Raiser, is the man who can renew it. For ten years he served as deputy to West Indian Methodist Philip Potter, the former general secretary who was openly anti-Western and anti-capitalist. Raiser confirmed his commitment to PCR funding in his first press conference.

What can ordinary church-goers do to nudge the WCC towards reform? "First, they should raise questions with their church hierarchies about the WCC's activities", advises Father Richard John Neuhaus, president of the Institute on Religion in Public Life, in America. "They can also join a concerned renewal--reform group in their denomination. Finally, and I say this most reluctantly, they can cut back their contributions by the percentage their church gives to the WCC. This situation can be turned around by determined lay people".

Having flirted with the Delilah of paganism and danced with the Salome of Communist ideology, can the WCC return to the faith of its fathers? The Archdeacon of York, George Austin, having watched some areas of WCC theology

"Decline into gross heresy", thinks it is too late. "Perhaps the spirit", he states "is saying to the Churches that the WCC has served its purpose and now must die".

Sometimes we get to look behind the mirrors in front of our eyes and see the true story developing. This article gives us one of those rear glimpses, enough to see that Communism controls the World Council of Churches, and from there it can force change on the churches to accept reforms that will eventually be its destruction. The published aim of Marxism--Illuminati.

We have it in our power as people to join together in protest and reverse the decline. We could, as a last resort, withhold funding for the WCC in protest. Our society cannot overcome our enemies by sitting it out in hope it will go away. Action is needed now, before it is too late.

PROTOCOL FOUR

MATERIALISM REPLACES RELIGION

Every republic passes through several stages. The first of these is comprised in the early days of mad raging by the blind mob, tossed hither and thither, right and left: the second is demagogy from which is born anarchy, and that leads inevitably to despotism-not any longer legal and overt, and therefore responsible, despotism, but unseen and secretly hidden, yet nevertheless sensibly felt despotism in the hands of some secret organisation or other, whose acts are the more unscrupulous in as much as it works behind a screen, behind the backs of all sorts of agents, to change whom not only does not injuriously affect but actually aids the secret force by saving it, thanks to continual changes, from the necessity of expending its resources on rewarding long services.

Who and what is in a position to overthrow an invisible force? And this is precisely what our force is. Gentile Masonry blindly serves as a screen for us and our objects, but the plan of action of our force, even its very abiding place, remains for the whole people an unknown mystery.

But even freedom might be harmless and have its place in the State economy without injury to the well-being of the peoples if it rested upon the foundation of faith in God, upon the brotherhood of humanity, unconnected with the conception, for they have established subordination. With such a faith as this people, might be governed by a wardship of parishes, and would walk contentedly and humbly under the guiding hand of its spiritual Pastor submitting to the dispositions of God upon earth. **This is the reason why it is indispensable for us to undermine all faith, to tear out of the minds of the goyim the very principle of Godhead and spirit, and to put in its place arithmetical calculations and material needs.**

In order to give the goyim no time to think and take note, their minds must be diverted towards industry and trade. Thus, all the nations will be swallowed up in pursuit of gain and in the race for it will not take note of their common foe. But again, in order that freedom may once for all disintegrate and ruin the communities of the goyim, we must put industry on a speculative basis: as a result, what is withdrawn from the land by industry will slip through their hands and pass into speculation, that is, to our classes.

The intensified struggle for superiority and shocks delivered to economic life will create, nay, have already created, disenchanted, cold and heartless communities. Such communities will foster a strong aversion towards the higher political and towards religion. Their only guide is gain, that is Gold, which they will erect into a veritable cult, for the sake of those material delights which it can give. Then will the hour strike when, not for the sake of attaining the good, not even to win wealth, but solely out of hatred towards the privileged, the lower classes of the goyim will follow our lead against our rivals for power, the intellectuals of the goyim.

COMMENT

Here we see, predicted in the Protocols, what is actually happening in the World Council of Churches some ninety years later. You can see the mind of Weishaupt behind this planning. An evil mind of a Satanist who will use every diversion and every perversion to attain his secret hidden agenda. Hidden behind the walls of the Masonic movement. Is not the proof of happening enough to make us realise that the Protocols are more than just a lucky guess or the forgery the Zionists would have us believe? Is it not clear that they are the best warning to us of what is to come? Should we not take heed of the contents and begin to fight back by using some of their weapons to attack them?

CHAPTER SEVEN, PART FIVE.
EDUCATION

Within a state's responsibilities, education is the most important task it performs. It can make the difference between a focused, alert and progressive state and a state falling fast below the measured statistics of world performance.

Education is the future and, handled correctly, can give a cutting edge in a competitive world. It is not surprising that Weishaupt, as a professor, knew the importance of education and how to use it for his own evil intent. We have seen how he targeted education in France, America and Britain, to enslave the world in his dream for peaceful revolution. He sent out 2000 highly trained and motivated academics to revolutionise education, taking over the high ground at Universities in America and England. A good example of this was Ruskin who made such an impact on his students at Oxford University.

We saw how one man, Ruskin, influenced so many like minded students to take up his vision of a better world like Cecil Rhodes, who, through his endeavours, and helped by a team of students, spread Ruskin's teachings through the Empire, from which the Round Table movement developed through their influence. None of them probably knew the true source of their teaching, Weishaupt's Illuminati, they just saw the ideas as portrayed to them as a ideal way forward.

Weishaupt's policy went on to encompass thousands of teachers by influence of their peers at training colleges. All this would have failed, if, at the same time, Weishaupt, through the power of the bankers, had not taken over the Media and Publishing houses of the world. Their first target was the academic publishers who controlled information to the students. When they had completed this task, all history was subtly changed to reflect the aims of the revolution. The proof of this is the exclusion of all reference to Weishaupt and the Illuminati, even down to Encyclopaedias. Without accurate knowledge the people became reliant on the information available, most of which is now slanted towards a Marxist revolution. The teachers' union (National Union of Teachers), one of the most militant, is well infiltrated by Marxists, and it follows through down the line of teaching. It is in this situation, teaching, so well infiltrated, (by Marxist and followers of Weishaupt's Illuminati), stands today. It is no wonder therefore, that teaching is at a point of crisis; failing to deliver quality teaching, through a whole series of liberal interferences with the basic hard core requirement of education, the three "R's" You may therefore find it strange that none of this is my major concern. What is far more sinister and destabilising is the use of sex education to alienate children from family, and the church from its most important function, its responsibility to its parish within education. This is undoubtedly Weishaupt's policy to destabilise nations through lowering moral standards and breaking up the family unit. To do this they must discredit the church. What is surprising is that the initiation for this policy comes via many liberalised organisations from the United Nations. **(Direction).** The United Nations policy in turn comes from the Humanist Manifestos numbers. 1 and 2, of 1933 and 1973. A policy, in their words, for a secular society on a planetary scale. A policy where Jesus Christ has no part. These manifestos were signed by 300 leaders of thought and action, including John Dewey, educationalist, Sol Gordon Professor sex education, Julian Huxley of UNESCO, Betty Friedan feminist, and Alan Guttmacker population controller. It is also interesting to learn that they aspire to a world law and a world order. Could it be that the Humanist Movement is an Illuminati clone? We now see clearly the United Nations as a power tool of Destruction. **Our destruction.** The following is a talk given by Elizabeth Sugrue **(171),** a dedicated mother, determined to find out what was going wrong in her children's school in Southern Ireland. It is an eye opener that must leave us all deeply concerned.

THE HIDDEN AGENDA

Before I start, I would just like to mention that the teacher's Handbook for Primary Schools states that: "Each human being is created in God's image. He has a life to lead and a soul to be saved. Education is, therefore, concerned not only with life but with the purpose of life..." That handbook first appeared in 1971 and you can see that by 1984 things had been changing rapidly.

My interest in enquiring into Education in Ireland stemmed from reading two newspaper articles. The first article, entitled "Making Capital out of Aids" in the Times (London) in November 1986 dealt with some of the approaches to sex education by the family planners and it also dealt with the sources being promoted by the former British Health Education Council. R. Butt claimed that the family planners and sex educators were doing their best to bring to the attention of young people every kind of sexual activity without what they call "moralising", i.e. without offering any judgement as to the moral worth of these activities. At that time in Britain there was grave concern about:
1. The increasing numbers of young people with sexually transmitted diseases.
2. The rising illegitimacy rate.

3. The open promotion of homosexuality in some school text books for children under the age of seven.
4. The falling educational standards.
5. The rising in-discipline in schools.

The second article I read at that time was concerned with the findings of our own former controversial (Republic of Ireland) Health Education Bureau's "Survey of the Parents' Preference in Relation to Sex Education in Schools". One question asked respondents to indicate in which class they would like family planning to be taught to children aged 4 to 12 years approximately, who were attending Primary Schools. As our children were pupils at Primary schools, I decided to find out if there was a connection between the British Health Education Council and our Health Education Bureau and to establish why this Bureau showed an interest in including family planning in its proposed Health Education---Sex Education Programmes, bearing in mind the fact that it was illegal for children aged 4 to 12 to purchase contraceptives or to engage in sexual intercourse. At that time I innocently thought that the Irish Family Planning Association had been set up by a group of people who saw a gap in the market to supply contraceptives to adults to space the births of their children and in fact some of my acquaintances were its clients. I thought that "Health Education" meant educating people about keeping fit and eating the proper foods. I was totally unaware of the existence of the documents called "The Humanist Manifestos 1 and 2", which were published in 1933 and 1973. In its principles, which the Manifestos state are designed for a Secular Society on a planetary scale, we learn of the call to establish a "Religion" (But Jesus Christ is not to have any part in it). Instead, things are to be shaped for the needs of this age where people should have a right to suicide, divorce, abortion, euthanasia, and sexual freedom. Ethics is to be autonomous and situational. Anyone familiar with our controversial "Lifeskills---Personal development---Health Education Programmes" will see the similarity regarding ethics.

The world, we are told, must evolve a world-wide system of Television and Radio for information and education.

The signatories of these Manifestos look to the development of a system of **World Law and World Order** based upon transnational federal government. Moral education for children and adults is seen as an important way of developing awareness and sexual maturity. The sexual maturity which the Manifesto spelt out would be contrary to what most Christian parents would want for their children. In fact the Manifestos state that the many varieties of sexual exploration should not in themselves be considered "evil". Should there be any Humanists present could I say that I believe that you are entitled to have your own schools, but most Christians would not wish you to try to secularise their schools.

I am going to show how the Godless philosophy as expressed in the Humanist Manifestos is being promoted world-wide by the Federation of National Planning Associations, namely "International Planned Parenthood Federation", otherwise referred to as IPPF. This Federation also works through the United Nations and its agencies including the World Health Organisation, UNESCO, UNICEF, UNFPA, etc.

IPPF's programmes, called "Family Life Education" are designed to promote alternative lifestyles to marriage with children, including lesbianism, homosexuality, masturbation, sterilisation and abortion, and pre-marital adolescent sexual activity. Its publications regard adolescents from the age of ten. Its sex Education---Family Life Education programmes create a need for its services and then its members campaign for law reform in order for their children to gain access to such services. Should the Irish Government decide to decriminalise homosexual activity, that lobby will demand "equal rights" in the area of sexual education. IPPF's National Family Planning affiliates also promote Aids Education, Child Abuse Education and Stress Management courses for teachers etc. Its Family Life Education Programmes are promoted under different titles such as "Personal Development", "Lifeskills", "Health Education", "Social and Health Education" etc.

IPPF describes itself as an international non-governmental organisation which encourages the formation of national family planning associations to pioneer family planning services and to bring about a favourable climate of public opinion in which governments can be persuaded to accept responsibility for their provision of family planning programmes. It is a fact that as governments respond, IPPF's affiliates provide a nucleus of staff around which IPPF's programmes and services can build. This staff trains personnel (including government staff), and in this way IPPF's activities are integrated with government programmes. Its Management Handbook for family planning associations lists three stages of the development of family planning: first there is hostility, then limited toleration, and finally full recognition by governments. When it reaches the third stage the stated objective of a FPA as stated in the Management Handbook is: "To play a formative role in the development of social ethics, to select a specific role for the association in social development and the development of the individual". Bearing in mind IPPF's policies in the area of sexual morality, it is an important point for parents to note, because not many of them realise that National Family Planning Associations have had such interest in the development of the individual, IPPF issued a paper, "A Strategy for Legal Change" which was in fact a "four stage plan of action" for legal change in the area of family planning. This paper identified the direct and indirect laws which present obstacles or which may affect attitudes to family planning and "birth spacing in general". The direct laws are those relating to: "Contraception, abortion, voluntary sterilisation, services to adolescents, authorisation for paramedicals to provide contraceptives".

The indirect laws are those relating to: "The status of women, the family (marriage, divorce, inheritance, custody, adoption), employment and education, taxation and child allowances..."

IPPF's members carry out vigorous law-reform activities, and you can see what is going on in Ireland. Thirty years ago IPPF decided to target the captive audience in the classroom because of the resistance amongst adults to its programmes. Getting to the children at an early age would be more effective. One of IPPF's stated aims is to get sex education into all schools, colleges and Universities and then to have it made a compulsory subject. At school level getting Teachers' Unions and Parents' Councils to co-operate with national family planning associations, and having FPA members in key positions within departments of Education and Health assists in the implementation and integration of IPPF's programmes. Having a pupil's council at secondary level is seen as an asset, because the pupils will have a forum at which they can demand access to the services which the Sex Education--- etc. Programmes will have created. Scouts, Girl Guides, and Youth Clubs are also part of IPPF's agenda.

IPPF enjoys consultative status with all the UN important agencies including, as mentioned earlier, The World Health Organisation, UNESCO, UNFPA, UNICEF etc. It has stated that it uses its influence within these international bodies because the United Nations gains the commitment of governments through international

Charters and Declarations and because the UN also makes funds available for development programmes.

In the seventies IPPF and the World Confederation of Organisations of Teaching Profession (WCOTP) joined forces to discuss the need for Family Life Education in the curriculum. Any parents or teachers present who have studied the controversial Lifeskills---Personal Development---etc. programmes operating in our schools will see the similarity with IPPF's Family Life Education. Family Life Education programmes' stated objective include helping children in the process of clarifying or formulating their values and attitudes and also to assist in the development of effective communication and decision making skills, in matters relating directly or indirectly to family life and personal relationships. **I don't know how many parents, who have children at school, understand that these programmes target their values, attitudes and beliefs and aim to cut off your input and the teacher's input and the Church's influence.**

While parents are trying to pass on their Christian Values, particularly in the area of sexual morality, this global giant is working away. Its publications state that a conflict arises between the state and the family when its Programmes become part of the curriculum. It targets Parents for "Parenting Courses" (as a way of bringing the parents' values into line with the new values which the children may take on in the group setting in the classroom). In Ireland the programmes are not usually referred to as Family Life Education, or as Moral Education as mentioned in the Humanist Manifestos, they are called several names such as Pastoral Care---Lifeskills---Personal Development---Learning for life---Preparation for Life---Education for Life---Social and Personal Education---Health Education or Education for Living, and they are delivered from standard subjects such as Civics or Religious Education. **In fact Religious Education is seen as a key target in order to weaken the content of proper Christian Doctrine. This is done by having the children sitting in groups, discussing their attitudes and feelings, thus stopping them getting the proper Christian Doctrine.** In the 70's, while the Irish Family Planning Association was campaigning for Law Reform in the area of contraceptives our government set up a centre which was to operate as an expert in "Health Education" and it was called the "Health Education Bureau (HEB). Very early on it stated that it did not have the necessary resources and expertise for Health Education Programmes and it duly tapped into England to the **British Health Education Council.** It also brought experts from Scotland into Ireland to help get Health Education Programmes into our schools. The British Health Education Council had, according to the Daily Telegraph, been tied into the birth control movement since its inception in 1966. To give you an idea of how IPPF's affiliate members operate, **in Britain the key man at the top of the British Family Planning Association also held a top post at the Health Education Council, and both organisations set up an organisation called 'Family Planning Information Services' funded by the Health Education Council,** and I believe manned by the UK FPA. More recently this top man was guest of honour at the National Secular Society's dinner in 1987 where he spoke of work in law reform relating to free contraceptives, divorce, homosexuality and abortion.

In Ireland in the seventies, our Health Education Bureau stated that it would need the co-operation of our Health Boards and the teachers in order to deliver its programmes to the classrooms. Our Health Authorities, I think there were about thirty plus in the sixties, had been restructured into eight Health Boards and this made HEB's job much easier. The Health Boards had been given the power to get involved in "Health Education".

As some of you may know, parents were denied access to the HEB's Teacher Training Manual, they could have got a look at it in the HEB's offices but could not take it away, and as you know, you would have had to take it home to study it or to have it studied by psychologists and psychiatrists and get their critiques.

When I started to check out the situation in 1987 I rang the HEB and asked if I could have a list of the resources which they offered on sex education for Primary Schools. The first question I was asked was, are you a teacher? When I answered no, I was told sorry, they are only given out to teachers. I eventually got hold of the information using other channels.

Health Education Programmes were concerned not with knowledge and understanding but with decision making, with attitudes, values and feelings, and social skills, and they require a substantial shift towards less formal teachings to group work, role play, values clarification and of course, the decision making techniques. They are identical to IFFP's Family Life Education Programmes.

The Health Education Bureau's Teacher Training Manual (HEBTTM) stated that the main aim of Health Education was to equip young people with the skill to make responsible Health Decisions, elsewhere the Bureau stated that it was to teach about Sexual Decision Making. The HEB was slow to state what the word "Responsible" really meant, and of course they denied that they had any Sex Education Programmes. What the Bureau was doing was teaching our children a new way of making decisions using what the Bureau called the "Affective Component", in the area of sexual morality.

The main obstacles to implementing a comprehensive and effective "health promoting curriculum" are identified as follows in a book called "Health Education in Schools", which was co-edited by one of the Health Experts from across the sea. This expert played a key role in getting Health Education into Ireland. The book states, and I quote: "...(health education) seeks to venture into the 'soft' areas of values and feelings. It invades areas which many see as the preserve of parents or psychiatrists: it seeks to change attitudes and modify behaviour: This is not surprising given the World Health Organisation's (WHO 1984) definition of health as not merely absence of decease but mental, physical and social well-being..." How many of you realised that Health Education sets out to target your child's attitude to modify his or her behaviour? You are probably wondering how could somebody change your child's values and attitudes. First of all the children are encouraged to enter into a contract with the teacher, that what goes on in the Health Education--Lifeskills Programme, should not be discussed with anyone outside the classroom. So most parents don't know that their children are taking part in these classes.

Most parents teach their children very early on the difference between what is right and what is wrong; to have respect for their parents and for their elders; to develop virtues; and they help their children to reason things out against the ten Commandments. The decision making--values clarification technique encourages children to set themselves up to decide on important moral issues by basing their answers on their own reaction with a strong emphasis on what they feel, without any guidance from parents or teachers.

This takes place in groups in the classroom and through the use of the especially developed psychotherapeutic techniques, the children's values, attitudes and beliefs on moral issues are targeted for change and their behaviour is targeted for modification. The programmes actually state the students can change their values in the light of the experience of their peers and that they can use the peer group "as a practice arena within which he can first try out new kinds of behaviour" (The Social and Health Education Programme, 1982). The children are told that there is no such thing as right or wrong. How many parents want the peers of their children having such an influence on their moral formation?

Most parents think that peer pressure just happened. They are unaware of the fact that it plays a key role in IPPF's activities. I'll just give you an example of how the Decision Making technique operates as related to me by two young teenagers who learned the skill in their Pastoral Care class.

I was told, first you are given a moral dilemma, say the boat is too small, who do you throw overboard, or some such dilemma. I was informed that one considers each choice and the consequences of each choice and one acts on what one feels comfortable with. I suggested "Suppose you make the wrong choice"? The reply was "Right or Wrong don't come into the Decision Making Skills". I said, "What about God's laws, the ten Commandments"? The reply was, "No, they are not part of the decision Making technique". I said, "You know about 'Honour your father and your mother'. What do you do if your mother requests you to do something"? The reply was, "You use the Decision Making skills exercise and if you are prepared to take the consequences you would refuse her request". I enquired if they discussed Abortion or Euthanasia, and was told "Yes; abortion and 'mercy killing' are discussed in RE. and at least half the class favours both in certain circumstances".

If your child wants to lie, steal, cheat, have sex with his next door neighbour, and if his feelings say 'yes', then he is free to go ahead. Right and wrong don't come into the decision Making--Values Clarification.

You may be asking what role does the teacher have in all this. His--her role is clearly defined. First he--she must be "processed" into a non-directive facilitator of groups of pupils in the classroom. All of the psychotherapeutic methods developed by humanistic psychologists will have been brought into play during the psychologists training session, while the teacher is having his values, attitudes and beliefs clarified. He will have been instructed that he must not attempt to teach values. He must not moralise. After he has undergone the "process" he will be equipped to design his own Sex Education and the Health Education Bureau will have familiarised him with its lists of resources. A government publication in In-service Training states that: "In-service study should...demand a widening of interests and a conversion to new values and attitudes. This challenge to lifelong assumptions and the need to unlearn cherished routines with all the personal trauma involved demands psychological preparedness..." Students, we are told in a Social and Health Education Programme dated 1976. "At the start he may be unable to tolerate his new-found independence and some may regress to almost primitive reactions. These will include hostility, aggression and even rejection of the change of teacher's attitude. The student may not be mature enough to tolerate the disruption of the authority-dependence relationship. Early sessions may promote continuation of primitive type behaviour, but if the teacher recognises these new attitudes and understands them, then the learning experience will ultimately become very meaningful"!! (Page 8- this programme carries the endorsement of a high ranking member of the Roman Catholic Church).

Health Education---Personal Development---Lifeskills Programmes set out to make pupils autonomous and self-empowered: the influence of the Church and the Home is minimised and even ridiculed in the Health Education programmes.

Parents' attempts to communicate their moral standards to their children are portrayed as negative pressure which the students will be encouraged to overcome.

The programmes put the children through certain exercises that help the child to ease off the values that his parents would wish him to have. In the Social and Health Education Programme, known throughout Ireland as the Cork Programme, there is an exercise called "Those Significant Others", and one of the objectives is "to enable them (The Children) to deal constructively with the feeling that others are imposing on them an alien self-image through their expectations and sanctions". You see, in order for the child to become autonomous and empowered the child must cast aside his parents' influence and he is shown how to do this through role-play. An important point to remember is the fact that the Health Education Bureau's Teacher Training Manual states that Role-play is a major tool to bring about a change in behaviour.

LEARNING FOR LIFE

Some of you will have heard of a programme called "Learning For Life", which was developed by the Health Education Bureau, the Mid Western Health Board and the Tipperary NR Vec, and includes a credit to the Department of Education UCD.

The programme consists of a Tutor's Guide for the Teacher and three books for the student. A resource recommended in the Tutor's guide called "Taught not Caught" strategies for sex education is recommended by the developers of this programme as an aid for the teachers, who have already undergone the special Teacher Training Programme, when designing their sex education programmes.

This book carries the recommendation of the UK Family Planning Association; it was written by a charity collective who "believe that moral stands such as the elimination of racism, sexism, exploitation and oppression should be propounded in all work with young people, and who some years ago "were employed by a family planning agency which had established an education unit to provide health and human relations education to schools, institutions and other community groups".

The teaching methods described in this book are those which are demonstrated on Education Training Courses for Teachers held in the UK by the UK FPA, according to the British Family Planning Association's literature.

The book states: "The choice of sexual preference, to be Homosexual, Heterosexual or Bi-sexual, is one which can be reassessed from time to time. For some, however, it will be a permanent decision". The book states that if Self Esteem is a concept about self which incorporates how a person feels about her or his body and the pleasure that can be derived from it. It warns that if you want to persuade or convince that rape is wrong, then don't use Values Clarification. You should know that the book thinks it is okay to use values clarification when discussing pre-marital sex, homosexuality etc., but because the book is written by feminists who hold strong views on rape but not on other moral issues, they give the warning about the use of values clarification.

Economics Professor J Kasun, in the June-July 1989 issue of Economic Affairs, states that the Population Control Movement's strategy is the same in every country. The first line of attack is Sex Education to accustom children to be trusting and confiding in their teachers rather than their families, as it consciously engineers the reconstruction of humankind. **(Direction).**

THE IRISH FAMILY PLANNING ASSOCIATION

The IFPA has confirmed that it was involved in piloting the Lifeskills, Personal Development Programmes and that the UK Family Planning Association trained its tutors who in turn trained some of our teachers. It targeted the Primary Schools for Sex Education in the eighties and it also targeted Parents for "Parenting Courses". It has stated that it designed courses for parents, second level teachers, primary teachers, community training workshops staff, public health nurses, youth club leaders, health education staff, social workers, carers of the mentally handicapped and rape crisis centres councillors.

It had a member of its executive working for the Health Education Bureau training teachers. This gentleman is a key member contracted to the body that replaced the Health Education Bureau, namely the Health Promotion Unit in the Department of Health. He is acting on getting Social and Health Education into the Primary schools, and he was jointly responsible for the very controversial Aids Programme. The IFPA supplies resources on **Child Abuse**, Personal Development, Health Education, Career Guidance, Sexually Transmitted Diseases, Aids, Sexuality, Relationships Lifeskills, Personal and Social Education.

Remembering that IPPF has stated it works through the United Nations because the UN can influence governments through Charters and Declarations, I'd like to suggest that you obtain a copy of Ireland's First Report to the UN on measures adopted to give effect to the provisions of the Convention on the Elimination of All Forms of Discrimination against Women and also request a copy of the UN's response. You should also examine the Charter for children's rights.

I will end with a quote from the Humanist Magazine Jan-Feb. 1983: "I am convinced that the battle for humankind's future must be waged and won in the public school classroom by teachers who correctly perceive their role as the proselytisers of a new faith; a religion of humanity that recognises and respects the spark of what theologians call divinity in every human being.

"These teachers must embody the same selfless dedication as the most rabid fundamentalist preacher, for they will be ministers of another sort, utilising a classroom instead of a pulpit to convey humanist values in whatever subjects they teach, regardless of the education level - pre-school, day care, or large state university.

"The classroom must and will become an arena of conflict between the old and the new-the rotting corpse of Christianity, together with all its adjacent evils and misery, and the new faith of Humanism.

The Humanist Manifesto states that the next century can be and should be humanistic century. **Are you as a Christian prepared to stand aside?**

In this address I can see everything predicted by Weishaupt and the Protocols. This must answer many unanswered questions you have in your mind relating to the education and behaviour of your children. Now armed, you can make your presence felt by lodging complaints with your Child's school, Board of Governors, and the Local Education Authority. Ask questions about all these forms of so called

Education. If enough of us complain we can change attitudes. If we ignore this warning you may not get another chance.

We must also campaign to bring back our National Religion (religion accepted as the countries national religion) into school education and remove general religious education (a broad education covering all religions) from the curriculum. Remember the aim of Marxism-Illuminati is to remove religion from our thoughts as it is a stabilising effect on our lives. (General religious education is to remove the child from attachment to any one religion as a half way stage to removing religious education all together. They also wish to lower moral and sexual standards through education and through this, break up the family unit. Just look back 30 years and you will see how this policy is succeeding. We can reverse it and we must do so.

PROTOCOL SIXTEEN

BRAINWASHING

In order to effect the destruction of all collective forces except ours we shall emasculate the first stage of collectivism--the Universities, by re-educating them in the new direction. Their officials and professors will be prepared for their business by detailed secret programmes of action from which they will not with immunity diverge, not by one iota. They will be appointed with special precaution, and will be so placed as to be wholly dependent upon the government.

We shall exclude from the course of instruction State Law as also all that concerns the political question. These subjects will be taught to a few dozens of persons chosen for their pre-eminent capacities from among the number of the initiated. The Universities must no longer send out from their halls milksops concocting plans for a constitution, like a comedy or a tragedy, busying themselves with questions of policy in which even their own fathers never had any power of thought.

The ill-guided acquaintance of a large number of persons with questions of state creates utopian dreamers and bad subjects, as you can see for yourselves from the example of the universal education in this direction of the goyim. We must introduce into their education all those principles which have so brilliantly broken up their order. But when we are in power we shall remove every kind of disturbing subject from their course of education and shall make out of the youth obedient children of authority, loving him who rules as the support and hope of peace and quiet.

Classicism, as also any form of study of ancient history, in which there are more bad than good examples, we shall replace with the study of the programme of the future. We shall erase from the memory of men all facts of previous centuries which are undesirable to us, and leave only those which depict all the errors of the government of the goyim. The study of practical life, of the obligations of order, of the relations of the people one to another, of avoiding bad and selfish examples, which spread the infection of evil, and similar questions of an educational nature, will stand in the forefront of the teaching programme, which will be drawn up on a separate plan for each calling or state of life, in no wise generalising the teaching. This treatment of the question is specially important.

Each state of life must be trained within strict limits corresponding to its destination and work in life. The occasional genius has always managed and always will manage to slip through into other states of life, but it is the most perfect folly for the sake of this rare occasional genius to let through into ranks foreign to them the untalented who thus rob of their places those who belong to those ranks by birth or employment. You know yourselves in what all this has ended for the goyim who allowed this crying absurdity.

In order that he who rules may be seated firmly in the hearts and minds of his subjects it is necessary for the time of his activity to instruct the whole nation in the schools and on the market places about his meaning and his acts and all his beneficent initiatives.

We shall abolish every kind of freedom of instruction. Learners of all ages will have the right to assemble together with their parents in the educational establishments as it were in a club: during these assemblies, on holidays, teachers will read what will pass as free lectures on questions of human relations, of the laws of examples, of the limitations which are born of unconscious relations, and, finally, of the philosophy of new theories not yet declared to the world. These theories will be raised by us to the stage of a dogma of faith as a transitional stage towards our faith. On the completion of this exposition of our programme of action in the present and the future I will read you the principles of these theories.

In a word, knowing by the experience of many centuries that the people live and are guided by ideas, that these ideas are imbibed by people only by the aid of education provided with equal success for all ages of growth, but of course by varying methods, we shall swallow up and confiscate to our own use the last scintilla of independence of thought, which we have for long past been directing towards subjects and ideas useful to us. The system of bridling thought is all ready at work in the so-called system of teaching by object lessons, the purpose of which is to turn the goyim into un-thinking submissive brutes waiting for things to be presented before their eyes in order to form an idea of them... In France, one of the best agents, Bourgeois, has already made public a new programme of teaching by object lessons.

COMMENT

Here we see Weishaupt's plan to use University professors as his spearhead to brainwash students to their ways. We have many examples of this already happening as far back as Cecil Rhodes and his complete dedication to Professor Ruskin, followed by many others under Ruskin's spell. (see chapter 5 Part 2) It would be wrong to say that they are Communists, because Communism probably never came into the equation. They were simply, and cleverly, brainwashed.

We see indirect mention of the corruption of education that directly explains the moves you have seen in the last example of educational hijacking by the Liberal destroyers of morality and society who are the unknowing army (following Liberal policies that hand the agenda to moral and social decline required by Weishaupt's world order.) that is helping the planners of world domination to achieve their ambitions. The most sinister fact that has come from this plan is the participation of The United Nations and all its agencies. We will learn more about that in chapter thirteen. In the meantime consider the brainwashing that they have introduced into education that this well researched lecture by Elizabeth Surgrue has uncovered, it must give us pause for thought.

CHAPTER SEVEN, PART SIX.
THE LAW AND WHERE IT LIES.

The legal system in England, has, in the past, been copied by many countries in the world. It is based upon natural law going back to the Magna Carta. The strength of the system is the precedent built up over centuries that is used in judgement and although not perfect, has proved to be the most practical system in use today.

It may therefore surprise you to learn that it is now firmly in the past because when we signed the Treaty of Rome, followed by the Maastricht Treaty, we relinquished our right to control our law.

Our legal system, despite the lies we have been fed by politicians and bureaucrats, is subservient to Brussels. The Treaty that our politicians signed forfeits our right to pass law that cannot be overturned by the European Union. It states quite clearly "European Law, shall be binding in its entirety and directly applicable to all member states".

The European Court of Justice made the position absolutely clear, "Every national court must apply community law in its entirety and must accordingly set aside any provision of national law which may conflict with it, whether prior or subsequent to the community rule". This has been confirmed repeatedly by British judges who say that the treaty, once signed, made European law the "Supreme law of this land" **so we have lost sovereignty over law.** If this is the case, why do we continue to have a Parliament to create laws which can be overturned? Even worse, **is the European system democratic?** To answer this we need to know who makes law in Europe? Is it politicians? No. The law is made by un-elected EU representatives, otherwise Brussels bureaucrats who belong to the European Commission.

Our judges interpret that law, the European Court of Justice, which is a political court with a political agenda, based on the principles of Karl Marx and Weishaupt, make it. Its political aim is to create a Federal Europe as a half way measure to world government and it is used to punish Countries that get in its way. This is why Britain has found itself the target for its wrath. It has used its power to attack our freedom to punish the IRA for its campaign of terror by overruling judgements which have suited their political masters; the IRA being a weapon in the Marxist war as is the European Union. A significant pointer to the political thinking of those who drive the European Union towards Federalism is that the man who held the top job at the time of most significance to our membership, Jacques Delors, was a self confessed Marxist.

If the European union was a genuine effort to unite European nations, none of the routes to union would be one way streets. But the whole scheme planned originally by Jean Monnet has been set as a gradual entrapment to hold nations in place until they are completely subservient and denial of this is a blatant lie.

Proof of entrapment came from Helmut Kohl when he said "The future will belong to Germans...when we build the house of Europe"...."In the next two years, we will make the process of European Integration irreversible. This is a very big battle but worth the fight".

Right up till today politicians have led us on to believe we had and would keep sovereign power over our affairs. This proves this to be a lie and now I will prove the lie was quite intentional. Sir James Goldsmith studied the private papers of Jean Monnet **(172)** (The founding father of the European Union). This evidence comes from a speech given by Sir James Goldsmith to the Federation of Small Businesses, at Newcastle upon Tyne on Tuesday 27th. June 1996. He found writings that proved Monnet rejected the idea of sovereign states. Monnet believed that Europe should be a Federal Super-state into which all its ancient nations would be "fused". **This communication was made in 1952.** Monnet believed that Europe's nations should be guided towards the super state without their peoples' understanding what was happening. He recommended disguising each step with an economic purpose until the end result would be Federation. (Pure Weishaupt, using Illuminati tactics). **I believe Blair has the same purpose.** On May 6th. 1970 Monnet explained the deception to Edward Heath **(173)** and added "I told Heath how we had proceeded from the start, step by step, and how in this way we had gradually created the Common Market and today's Europe and I was convinced that we should proceed in the same manner". (Otherwise lie to the people of each nation about sovereignty).

Despite knowledge of Monnet's explanation Heath had this to say at the run up to Britain's entry to the European Union; "There are some in this country who fear that in going into Europe, we shall in some way sacrifice independence and sovereignty...these fears, I need hardly say, are completely unjustified..." Seventeen years later, in November 1990 when asked by Peter Sissons **(174)** on BBC television if, when he took us into Europe, in truth, he really had in mind a United States of Europe, with a single currency in essence opposite to what we had been told by his government, Heath answered; "Of course, yes".

This remains the main reason today why we should have another referendum to give the people a chance to vote on the loss of sovereignty, law enforcement, Tax collection, and Defence, to a body of un-elected Bureaucrats following Marxist policies and using Weishaupt's deception to hide the truth.

In my opinion this act of Heath's was treasonous and must put a question mark over his real political agenda. Heath and his gang of Europhiles interestingly have all taken lucrative rewards from Merchant banks and Multinationals like GEC and Anderson Associates and even Kissinger Associates, and Lord Carrington is Chairman of the Bilderberg Group which I deal with in chapter sixteen.

The reason for including this evidence in the law section is to make a very serious point. Take the hypothetical case of treason that is proved in the English courts, that is only relevant to Britain. Would the European Court of Justice be able to overturn this decision? **The answer is YES.**

PROTOCOL SEVENTEEN
ABUSE OF AUTHORITY

The practice of advocacy produces men cold, cruel, persistent, unprincipled, who in all cases take up an impersonal, purely legal standpoint. Their inveterate habit is to refer everything to the defensive value of its properties and not to the public welfare of its results. They do not usually decline to undertake any defence whatever, they strive for an acquittal at all costs, cavilling over every petty crux of jurisprudence and thereby they demoralise justice. For this reason we shall set this profession into narrow frames which will keep it inside this sphere of executive public service. Advocates, equally with judges, will be deprived of the right to communicate with litigants; they will receive business only from the court and will study it by notes of report and documents, defending their clients after they have been interrogated in court on facts that have appeared. They will receive an honorarium without regard to the quality of the defence. This will render them mere reporters on law-business in the interests of justice and as a counterpoise to the proctor who will be the reporter in the interests of prosecution; this will shorten business before the courts. In this way will be established a practice of honest unprejudiced defence conducted not from personal interest but by conviction. This will also, by the way, remove the present practice of corrupt bargaining between advocates to agree only to let that side win which pays most....

We have long past taken care to discredit the priesthood of the goyim, and thereby to ruin their mission on earth, which in these days might still be a great hindrance to us. Day by day its influence on the peoples of the world is falling lower. Freedom of conscience has been declared everywhere, so that now only years divide us from the moment of the complete wrecking of that Christian religion. As to other religions, we shall have still less difficulty in dealing with them, but it would be premature to speak of this now. We shall set clericalism and clerical into such narrow frames as to make their influence move in retrogressive proportion to its former progress.

When the time comes finally to destroy the papal court the finger of an invisible hand will point the nations towards this court. When, however, the nations fling themselves upon it, we shall come forward in the guise of its defenders as if to save excessive bloodshed. By this diversion we shall penetrate to its very bowels and be sure we shall never come out again until we have gnawed through the entire strength of this place.

The King of the Jews will be the real Pope of the Universe, the patriarch of an international Church.

But, in the meantime, while we are re-educating youth in new traditional religions and afterwards in ours, we shall not overtly lay a finger on existing churches, but we shall fight against them by criticism calculated to produce schism...

In general then, our contemporary press will continue to criticise State affairs, religions, incapacities of the goyim, always using the most unprincipled expressions in order by every means to lower their prestige in the manner which can only be practised by the genius of our gifted tribe...

Our kingdom will be an apologia of the divinity Vishnu, in whom is found its personification--in our hundred hands will be, one in each, the springs of the machinery of social life. We shall see everything without the aid of official police which, in that scope of their rights which we elaborated for the use of the goyim, hinders governments from seeing. In our programme one-third of our subjects will keep the rest under observation from a sense of duty, on the principle of volunteer service to the state. It will then be no disgrace to be a spy and informer, but a merit: unfounded denunciations, however, will be cruelly punished that there may be no development of abuses of this right.

Our agents will be taken from the higher as well as the lower ranks of society, from among the administrative class who spend their time in amusements, editors, printers and publishers, booksellers, clerks, and salesmen, workmen, coachmen, lackeys, et cetera. This body, having no rights and not being empowered to take any action on their own account, and consequently a police without any power, will only witness and report. Verification of their reports and arrests will depend upon a responsible group who will control police affairs, while the actual act of arrest will be performed by the gendarmerie and the municipal police. Any persons not denouncing anything seen or heard concerning questions of the state will also be charged with and made responsible for concealment, if it be proved that he is guilty of this crime.

Just as nowadays our brethren are obliged at their own risk to denounce to the kabal apostates of their own family or members who have been noticed doing anything in opposition to the kabal, so in our kingdom over all the world it will be obligatory for all our subjects to observe the duty of service to the state in this direction.

Such as organisation will extirpate abuses of authority, of force, of bribery, everything in fact which we by our counsels, by our theories of the superhuman rights of man, have introduced into the customs of the goyim....But how else were we to procure that increase of causes predisposing to disorders in the midst of their administration?...Among the numbers of those methods one of the most important is--agents for the restoration of order, so placed as to have the opportunity in their disintegrating activity of developing and displaying their evil inclinations--obstinate self-conceit, irresponsible exercise of authority, and, first and foremost, venality.

COMMENT

We can see the legal system changing and moving into the hands of political control in Europe, a step along the road to their type of politically controlled law that can be used to crush opposition to their dictatorship.

Once again they confirm that religion must be infiltrated and corrupted from within. Exactly what we have already experienced within the World Council Churches. It also confirms that they will re-educate youth to their religion without touching the churches. We have seen they are doing this through the research of Elizabeth Sugrue, using mind-bending methods to programme children away from family religion and community, to adopt their New World policies, policies that break up the family by teaching the children false powers to alienate the family strengths, from their thoughts, so that the state can control their direction and influence their actions. This down-grades the parents from their traditional right as the line of guidance for the child's well being. It would be a monstrous act of state interference and therefore we should fight this to our last breath.

CHAPTER EIGHT
PART ONE
THE EUROPEAN UNION, A STAGING POST TO GLOBALISM.

The dangers to democracy that the world is facing today is largely unknown, but very real, and set to succeed unless the Democrats of the world wake up to the creeping con-trick being assembled under many false reasons to explain the European Union's actions.

That this is being planned and executed by un-elected power groups with immense financial power is open knowledge to anyone who cares to research the **DIRECTION** of the world because direction gives up the Bankers secret as a watertight proof of their intentions. It is also possible to identify the organisations under the control of the International Finance Capitalists by the programmes and policies that leak out of their water tight security on information, so our first concern is to identify the sources of undemocratic power that are moving the world to Global Marxist Dictatorship.

The Liberty Lobby published a thorough report by Trisha Kitson on the organisations that hide their intent behind good inter-trading relationships that all countries need to control importation of foreign goods.

The first is the General Agreement on Tariffs and Trade (GATT). This treaty was first ratified in 1947 and was, along with The World Trade Board, later to become the International Trade Organisation and then the World Trade Organisation 'WTO'. At the same time the UN charter was partly written by Alger Hiss, (revealed as a Soviet spy by a young congressman named Richard Nixon.). It was the brain child of Harry Dexter White, Assistant Secretary to the Treasury, a Soviet spy, high up within the American administration.

By 1994 the WTO was given more power. The act contains 26,000 pages which on estimate occupied 1500 people for seven years. The size is such that no politician or journalist is likely to have read it or even a small part of it and therefore its contents are highly dangerous to democracy.

Trisha Kitson, in her article, claimed that from the 1994 GATT agreement signed by 125 nations on April 15th. 1994 at Marrakesh, Morocco, that through this World Trade Organisation, "A central trade authority which will be the most powerful economic and political body in the world", was formed. She goes on to say that it advances the Council for Foreign Relations and the Trilateral Commission's objective of a World Government. (These two organisations being firmly under the control and influence of Rockefeller). As the International Monetary Fund virtually dictates fiscal policies of nations down to a nations' tax level, so GATT will regulate how much duty each nation may levy on imports, removing the nations power to control imports.

Daniel Esty, of the Council for Foreign Relations claimed, "The WTO was created to get around congress---by enshrining the principle of Liberal trade in the international regime, the creators of the GATT elevated the commitment to freer trade to a nearly constitutional level, thereby limiting the power of governments around the world (And legislatures in particular) to give in to the pleadings of domestic special interests seeking to hide from the rigors of the global market place".

This statement is confirmed by Article XV1-4: "Each member (Nation) shall ensure the conformity of its laws, regulations and administrative procedures with its obligations as provided in the annexed agreements".

Looking forward, if we sign up for Federal Union in Europe it requires federal governments to "Form, regulate and implement positive measures and mechanisms in support of the observance of the provision by other than central government bodies". This means clearly, if we sign up to a Federal Europe and Federal Europe signs the act then we as a state or local area in Europe even if the EU has no legal right to control the state or local area, it is obliged to force compliance on that state or local area.

Another provision of the WTO act is to outlaw acts of national promotion like 'Back British Industry' or Buy British, which could be construed as unfair to other countries and could result in trade sanctions.

It is designed to make nations draft their laws to suit GATT and WTO. The WTO has been described by the New York Times as the third pillar of the World Order, along side the United Nations and the International Monetary Fund, but the true focus of GATT and the WTO is a **Hidden Agenda.** The main aim, hidden from America is to reduce wages in developed countries to a world wide norm, to produce higher profits for the ruling elite, the International Finance Capitalists, who have funded the research into GATT and the WTO through the powerful charitable trusts in America such as the Ford Foundation, the Rockefeller Foundation, and other trusts. The think tanks, that are free from tax, are controlled by the financiers, and this is where they plan the destruction of our democracy for their final target; complete financial and political control, otherwise, **ultimate power.**

Already in America the real wages of 80% of the workers have declined by 20% in real terms since 1973. To show how far wages may have to go, China can supply skilled labour at a fraction of Western costs.

The result of this is already being practised by multinational companies who walk over national governments to gain the cheapest labour costs. A typical example of this was recently witnessed in England by the actions of British Airways, who under Ayling's orders sacked a part of the staff at Manchester and Heathrow and moved the entire operation to India to reduce costs. This is a classical example of why Multinationals like 'World Order'; the reason, so they can ignore local regulations and follow their global policy for cheap production and cheap labour. GATT and WTO give them this freedom.

On December 6th. 1993 the Washington Times interviewed Sir James Goldsmith. In his interview he said, "Global free trade will force the poor of the rich countries to subsidise the rich in the poor countries. What GATT means is that our national wealth accumulated over the centuries will be transferred from a developed country like Britain---to developing countries like China, now building its first ocean going navy in 500 years".... "We have to rethink from top to bottom why we have elevated global free trade to the status of sacred cow or moral dogma

It is a fatally flawed concept that will impoverish and destabilise the industrial world while cruelly ravishing the third world".

However he failed to expose who was behind this policy, after all they were his former colleagues, so his integrity is praiseworthy.

So we can now identify three organisations that are behind the drive to Globalism:-
1. The United Nations. Formed by Alger Hiss, a Communist and controlled by a - Communist spy ring.
2. The International Monetary Fund. Controlled by the International Finance Capitalists, and planned by Harry Dexter White, a Communist.
3. The World Trade Organisation (WTO)-General Agreement on Tariff and Trade (GATT) controlled by a consortium of International Finance Capitalists and World Order politicians like Dr Henry Kissinger and Lord Carrington.

Their increasing powers through military control as in Iraq; Tariff control as in GATT; and World Trade as in the WTO, is alarming, and governments must re-think their policy of allegiance to these groups, loosely under UN control, in light of their undemocratic drive towards World control.

So that is part of the global power house, un-elected, and set on achieving their aims by deception. As time is not important to them, a creeping change allows them to go forward unnoticed accept by a few. That is classical Illuminati-Communist policy.

Now let us examine what C. Gordon Tether had to say on the 4th. January 1993. **(175).**

CREDIT ORGY IS RUINOUS

(OR, WHO IS TO BLAME FOR THE MESS THE WORLD IS IN?)

Where does the blame lie for the entire world being now bogged down in a recession of such a deep seated character that doubts are being expressed as to whether it will end before 2010, if at all? There is only one conclusion any impartial examination of this phenomenon could reach:

The main culprit is to be found in the orgy of bank credit creation which the central bankers of all the major countries presided over during the 1980's. This has left consumers everywhere so heavily in debt that normal spending patterns have been lastingly distorted out of all recognition, and very much for the worse.

In a nutshell, it was the deregulation of financial activity throughout the industrialised countries that opened the door to this vast and evil monetary explosion. And it was the central banking fraternity that sold the politicians the idea that such deregulation was a good thing of which no country could possibly have too much.

It may seem surprising at first sight that, so many seemingly solid members of society, as central bank governors, should be prepared to behave in such an irresponsible manner. But they have always tended to identify themselves with the interests of their fellow bankers in the commercial sector rather than with those of the general public.

In other words, to adapt an old saying, banking blood is almost invariably found to be thicker than democratic water.

A striking illustration of the serious nature of this weakness in the arrangements for ordering mankind's affairs has been provided during the past year by the investigation into the factors behind the collapse of the Bank of Credit and Commerce International (BCCI).

The official reports on this scandal have demonstrated that the Bank of England--perhaps the most renowned of central banks, seeing that it has been on the scene for 300 years--stood idly by while BCCI's criminal management perpetrated, under its very nose, the biggest swindle in the world's history. BCCI was also linked to The Federal Reserve Bank and several of its directors.

What emerges from all this, is that the central banking community cannot be trusted to behave in anything approaching satisfactory fashion, in either of the two fields that are supposed to be its special concern.

Its failure to prevent the well-being of the global economy being sacrificed on the altar of commercial banking greed shows that it would be extremely unwise to allow it to continue playing the large part it has of late in shaping global and national economic management policies. The Central Bank's failure to avert the tragedy that has overtaken millions of BCCI customers is equally eloquent in relation to its other main task: ensuring that the commercial banks in its care are properly disciplined.

What makes it vitally important that the lessons taught by the sins central banks have been perpetrating, should be learned, and the morals they taught promptly acted upon, is that a campaign is being waged by the international lobby to give them an even greater say in the economic management business than they have already. It has not yet surfaced to any appreciable extent in the United States. But the opposite is very much the case on the other side of the planet.

AFFRONT TO DEMOCRACY

In Britain leading members of the business community have been openly arguing that the battle against inflation and such other worthy causes would be better served if the Bank of England was given freedom from all forms of political control and influence in executing its monetary policy functions. For example, the central bank should control such matters as the manipulation of interest rates and the containment of credit creation.

The fact that such an innovation would be an affront to even the most basic forms of democracy does not seem to bother its exponents.

An even more ambitious project of the same kind is at the heart of the drive that the European Community "visionaries" have embarked upon to bring about the complete political unification of its 12 member countries. For, as envisaged in the recently much-debated Maastricht Agreement, this would entail effective control of many of the key aspects of the economic management of the proposed new super-state being entrusted to a new super central bank answerable to nobody but itself.

POLITICAL STORM

It is because many British Members of Parliament perceived, in the Maastricht agreement, an implicit threat to the survival of their country's national sovereignty, that Prime Minister John Major's efforts to speed the pact's passage through the Westminster Parliament generated such a massive political storm.

It is obviously a good thing that a spoke has been at last put in the wheel of central banker ascendancy and a brake placed thereby on the onward march of world government. But it would be a mistake to imagine that the fight to stop globalisation in its tracks is on the way to being won.

In short, no country, including America, that continues to value its right to rule itself, can afford to stand aside from the debate on the future of the independence to be "enjoyed" by central bankers.

It is important to remember at this point that the International Finance Capitalists control the media and book publishing, so to get you these facts is all the more difficult; but as you read this, we have succeeded. Please help us spread our message because the media will ignore this catalogue of facts, for the fiction they would have you believe.

Now let us again reflect on the words of Arnold Toynbee, who in 1931 promoted the idea of a United Europe. You will see in his mind the unification of Europe was only a first stage to world government.

"Really, the present economic unification of the world was implicit in the first circumnavigation of the globe, more than four centuries ago, by Western navigators". He went on to say, "I will merely repeat that we are at present working, discreetly but with all our might, to wrest this mysterious political force called sovereignty out of the clutches of the local national states of the world. And all the time we are denying with our lips what we are doing with our hands, because to impugn the sovereignty of the local national states of the world is still a heresy". This shows **Deception** and the aimed destruction of sovereignty, **a pre-requisite to federal government** and the hub of the proof that the European Union is only a part of a far larger plan for world domination. Deception is classical Weishaupt-Illuminati-Communism and **federalism is the death of sovereignty**.

Sovereignty within a nation state is a basic right that is not negotiable. It is the character, originality, and conscience of a nation state that no man can break without a natural spontaneous reaction.

The European Union, as stated by Jean Monnet, its adopted founding father, is heading to 'fusion' of nations. This is a federal state that will, out of necessity, kill sovereignty. Any politician, that says differently is naive or a liar.

No person in his right mind would vote to lose sovereignty to a union that is to strip it of character, originality, and conscience, less still to a group of politicians and bureaucrats who refuse to discuss their aims. It is equivalent to entering a black hole, not knowing what is on the other side.

It is now clear for all to see that European Union is a stage in preparation for World Government from where our laws, our money control, our food supplies, our army, our police, our courts, our wages, and our livelihood will all be controlled by this non-elected world government, headed by International Finance Capitalists and

controlled by Marxist policies. Within this, freemasonry will be banned and secret societies outlawed, according to the Protocols. Do you want all this, you Masons?

To prove this, the political drive in Europe has come from two men who have had a large part to play in the planning and direction. One was Altiero Spinnelli, the Communist leader and godfather of Europe. He was the true architect of the Maastricht Treaty. **(176).** The other was Jaques Delors who admitted to being a Marxist.

As evidence of intent of the European Union I am reproducing part of a speech by Sir James Goldsmith **(177)** made to the Federation of Small Businesses in

Newcastle-Upon-Tyne on Thursday 27th. June 1996. In his speech he shows clearly how our sovereignty has already been whittled away without publicity from our media, our so called protector.

SIR JAMES GOLDSMITH

"So how far have we already drifted towards federalism? How much power has already been abandoned, usually without the electorate being informed? The answer is a great deal. Let me give you just a few examples I will start with the right of parliament to pass new laws which cannot be overturned by anybody outside the country.

According to the treaty to which we have been committed, European law, I quote, 'shall be binding in its entirety and directly applicable to all member states". The European Court of Justice interpreted this very clearly. It stated: "Every national court must apply Community law in its entirety and must accordingly set aside any provision of national law which may conflict with it, whether prior or subsequent to the Community rule". British judges have confirmed this ruling. They have concluded that, I quote, "the treaty is the supreme law of this country taking precedence over Acts of Parliament".

There it is. It is now absolutely clear that parliament has surrendered its sovereignty on an ever increasing range of issues. European law has become the 'supreme law of this land'.

Who makes that law? Principally, the European Commission which consists of un-elected bureaucrats. Who interprets that law? The European Court of Justice, which is a political court with a political agenda. Its agenda is to create a Federal Europe and its
    judgements are made within that framework.. (We have Jean Monnet's words to Edward Heath to prove this statement within this address).

We should ask ourselves the question: If our MP's can no longer pass laws which are binding, what can they do? Why do we need them? What is the purpose of a general election?

Now let us turn to our economy. Is our government allowed to run it for the principal benefit of the nation? The answer is 'No'. It gave away that right when it signed the Treaty of Maastricht, as a result of which, we became committed to phase 1 and phase 2 of European Monetary Union.

The famous and much publicised 'Opt-out' of the single currency negotiated by John Major is largely cosmetic. It refers to stage 3. This is not an opt-out from our commitment to accept the obligations of phase 1 and 2. They (the opt-out clauses)
    stipulate that Britain will remain bound to, I quote, 'conduct its economic policies with a view to contributing to the achievements of the broad objectives of the Community'. This is part of article 102a of the Treaty. In other words, the government cannot conduct economic policies simply with British interests in view.

Britain is also obliged, I quote, to 'regard (its) economic policies as a matter of common concern and shall co-ordinate them within the council'. That is article 103(1). This means that the government has to satisfy the EU's objectives, not Britain's interests. Britain also has undertaken to, I quote again, 'treat its exchange rate policy as a matter of common interest'. That is in the article 109(m). So we will no longer be free to modulate our own exchange rates to reflect the needs of our own economy.

Finally, Britain is obliged to submit its economic plans to Brussels. Article 109e (2). That is Brussels' way of making sure that we are properly submissive. And if there is any disagreement about what we are doing, who will decide what is right? The European Court of Justice.

The whole of the spirit of the Treaty of Maastricht and the way it has been sold to us has masked the true meaning of almost all its principal elements.

Consider the case of 'subsidiarity'. We have been told by European leaders and by our own government that 'subsidiarity' is a form of decentralisation which ensures that power is not concentrated in Brussels. But when you study the terms of the treaty, you find that yet again we have been duped. In fact, subsidiarity does not apply to those powers already transferred to Brussels. According to the Treaty, these cannot be touched. Apparently, the Brussels bureaucrats own these powers for ever. In the vernacular of Brussels, powers that have already been centralised are known as 'acquis communautaire'. They are sacrosanct. In the European Union, you are only allowed to move one way: towards federalism. That is why the two key words of the Eurocrats are 'irreversible' and 'fusion'.

So when, according to the Treaty, can subsidiarity be applied? The answer is when it is deemed that a particular action cannot be carried out 'sufficiently' well at the national level and that, I quote, "it can be better achieved by the Community".

Note the words "sufficiently" and "better". Who is empowered to deem whether the member states can "sufficiently" achieve the proposed action or that it can be "better" achieved by the Community? Why, the Brussels Commission, who judges the issue? Why, the European Court of Justice, of course. So subsidiarity, far from ensuring that power is not concentrated in Brussels, has the opposite effect. It places all the power irreversibly in the hands of the Brussels bureaucrats.

In any case, the whole concept of subsidiarity is flawed. **In a true democracy, it is the people who decide which powers to lend to their leaders. In a false democracy, it is the leaders who decide which freedoms to lend to the people.** In the European Union, it is twenty un-elected bureaucrats who decide which freedoms we are still allowed to enjoy.

Now you can clearly see the similarity to the plans laid down in the Protocols to the make up of the Power inside the European Union; a power that is undemocratic and easily convertible to dictatorship. This should be enough to worry you.

NATIONAL AND GLOBAL CONTROL OF FOOD SUPPLIES

One of the tentacles of Globalism is to gain control of the world food supplies. The simple reason for this is that when control is fully in the Bankers hands they can starve nations who do not comply with their wish. The evidence that they are pursuing this policy is formidable.

The 'evil empire' of multinational companies has moved in to dominate agri-chemical and pharmaceutical industries in line with the plans of the global elite and their desire to control the world through food supply. To this aim they must reduce the world farming industry and dependency on land so they can take the initiative, buy up surplus land and then control production, leaving millions of farm workers without work, forcing them to retire to the cities for work, (this fulfils Marxist policy) where they leave the uncontrolled land culture for the tightly controlled city worker culture. (Remember Marxist policy requires land to be in state hands).

Unfortunately this policy only half worked. Our farmers were swamped with offers of financial assistance from the banks, quite often through machinery or chemical fertiliser or seed representatives who seemed to have the ear of their local bank. Many good farmers were tempted into this trap and banks seemed over-keen to oblige.

Then came the EU common agriculture policy, which at a stroke clamped down on yield quotas. This was followed by a reduction in the value of agricultural land which was the basis of the farmers' guarantee to the banks. So the banks demanded repayment of the loans which in turn bankrupted many farmers or left them with no capital to buy their seed and chemical fertilisers as they found they had no credit terms to alleviate their cash crises as the terms had been withdrawn by the bankers.

They had to sell their land at a fraction of the cost just to clear debts. This was one of the most deplorable periods in banking usury, displaying how the International Finance Capitalists control the banking industry as well as the seed and Agri-chemical multi-nationals. So what is the reason for all this when in general the world is short of food to feed its increasing millions? Quite simply the Multi-National grain and Agri-Chemical companies know their future lies in genetically engineered crops (the manipulation of the organic structure) in this field. The average earth farmer has no part to play, as he feels responsible for the husbandry of the land he owns. He is being made redundant, to make way for the land destroyers; the Agri-Chemical culture; who gain high profit from chemicals and seed sales.

There is a rush to invest in this field brought on by the vast resources. Lord Victor Rothschild invested in this future industry. He became chairman of Biotechnology Investments in 1981, a company registered in the Channel Islands. The 1996-97 reports show investment in forty quoted and forty-one un-quoted Biotechnology and health care enterprises. The management follows the customary pattern. The chairman now is Lord Armstrong of Illminster, a Rothschild man and director of the Bank of Ireland. British Biotech, founded in 1986 with Rothschild finance, by Dr Keith McCullagh and Sir Brian Richards, has a recognisable line of influence. Chairman John Raisman is on the board of Lloyds-TSB and formally of Shell UK and Glaxo Wellcome. Marius Gray is on the board of the Daily Mail. Henry De Ruiter holds three separate directorships in Shell companies. Keith

Merrifield was a director of Wellcome and David John was formally with Rio Tinto Zinc (then RTZ).

So now we see where the power comes from that is de-stabilising our agricultural production to force the Agri-Chemical culture's dubious production methods on the farming world. If Biotechnology is allowed to control our farm products they will be spoiled for good and a system the bankers control will replace good farming practice. This is for the banker's profit, not for our good.

Remember, Victor Rothschild was deeply involved in the Agricultural Research Council from 1948-1958. As chairman he was a member of the Advisory Council for Science and Technology (1969). He was a director of Shell Oil Company, founded by Marcus Samuel, the first Lord Bearstead. Victor Rothschild headed the Central Policy Review Staff, the Heath government 'Think Tank' 1971-1974. It was from these positions he master-minded the run down of scientific research and development, a direct reason that the research on Scrapie in sheep was closed just as they were to expand their research to cattle in 1981, under Mrs Thatcher's government. So you see a pattern that spreads over this catalogue of facts to add to the knowledge we already have, that Victor Rothschild was also the controller of a spy group in Cambridge and another in Oxford Universities that were Communist cells within a strong framework of Marxist led revolutionaries. So you can see these events are not isolated mistakes by government, or individuals, but carefully planned and expertly executed attacks on our society: by people in high places around government. A similar story covers America's declining agricultural business.

A report by Nexus Magazine **(178)** in their August-September Edition 1994 explains how the world seed market is in the hands of a few Multi-Nationals financed by Rothschilds and others within International Finance Capitalism.

SEEDS – SURVIVAL OR SERVITUDE

Total control of the world's seeds – and ultimately the survival of mankind itself--is now in the hands of an elite cartel of multinational corporations. Complicitous governments world-wide are enacting Plant Breeders' Rights legislation to enforce the seed monopolies, with six-month jail terms and fines of £250,000 for breaching patents or not paying royalties. Global diversity is under grave threat as genetically engineered seeds – tolerant to herbicides, 'designer-gene' and primed for profits – replace heritage seeds. 'Seed-saver' networks and conservationists in many nations are fighting a grassroots action to protect natural and regional plant varieties from extinction and to alert the world to the threat of control of the world's food supply, genetic manipulation, and laws that will allow the process of patenting of all plants, animals, genes and viruses.

The world's seed market today is worth $28,000,000,000, yet only a handful of major players--mainly petro Agri-chemical multinationals – will reap the rewards. Less than 20 major corporations now control global seed supplies; many are seeking patents on any newly-developed hybrids or those produced by transgenics (i.e., by genetic engineering). Multinationals have acquired 1,000 seed and plant-breeding companies since 1970; in the 1980's alone they invested a staggering $10,000,000,000 on company acquisitions. The world's largest seed company, Pioneer Hi-Bred International, holds 40 per cent of the United States market in hybrid corn seed, around 50 per cent of the markets of Spain, Austria and Italy, and 90 per cent in Hungary and Egypt. Pioneer Hi-Bred also leads the seed market in Brazil, Thailand, the Ukraine and a large number of developing countries. Imperial Chemical Industries, (ICI), is the largest chemical conglomerate in the United Kingdom, and is now one of the world's biggest seed-suppliers. ICI became one of the major players in the United States market in just five years. With the assistance of fellow United Kingdom giant British Petroleum, ICI swallowed up eleven of the largest seed companies from 1985 to 1990.

W R Grace, Dekalb, Shand, Monsanto and Cargill control the majority of other seed and plant-breeding companies in the Americas. French seeds giant George Limagrain competes for European seed domination with ICI., Ciba-Geigy (now Novartis), Shell, Rhone-Poulenc, Bayer, Pfizer (linked with DeKalb), Hoechst, and Pioneer Hi-Bred International. In Australasia and Oceania, ICI (Pacific Seeds), does battle with Pioneer Hi-Bred, DeKalb, Shand, Cargill, Agseed (a Limgrain company), Yates, New World Seeds and Seedco. Asia and Africa are also in the hands of the major United States and European Multinationals. Intense lobbying by the seeds cartel at the Uruguay round of negotiations of the United Nations General Agreement on Tariffs and Trade (GATT later The World Trade Organisation; WTO), paid off; countries under the protection of the International Convention for the Protection of New Varieties (U.P.O.V.), are enacting Plant Breeders' Rights (P.B.R.), bills and launching them on unsuspecting communities around the world.... The patent laws will demand royalties from growers, while the seed companies have the ultimate powers over what we eat, when we eat-or if we eat at all.

In 1968, at a meeting of the Bilderberg Group in Canada the debate showed how the multinational or Trans-National Corporations, financed by the International Finance Capitalists, were already more powerful than individual national governments, even that of the United States.

The power house of the International Finance Capitalist has been National debt loans and oil production. The Zionist overlords have forced America and Britain to war in the Gulf to protect their rights against Saddam Hussein, using the United Nations as a pretend cover. (This will be shown later).

You might well ask how is it that our politicians do not understand what is going on and stop the dictates of the bankers? I answer this by simply asking you to look at the Rothschild sphere of influence, where it reads like a Who's Who from parliament. In short its where the gravy train is standing.

This leads me to my last point, bringing the debate back to Europe but showing the global policy of Marxism to bring Britain to its knees.

I refer of course to BSE (Bovine Spongiform Enesphalopathy) and its alleged connection to CJD (Creutzfeldt-Jacob Disease). I do not wish to go into the raging debate of what is at the heart of its cause except to say that in fifteen years it has killed some fifty-four people in this country. Although one death is one too many from any disease it has to be taken in context. Lung cancer kills about 140,000 people a year in Britain alone. Have we banned smoking, or more to the point has the government even admitted the main cause of lung cancer is Diesel Fumes? The answer is, "no", despite two reports hidden from public view, through the power of the fuel lobby. These reports go back to the sixties. So why has the event of fifty-four deaths in fifteen years destroyed our beef industry when they don't even know its cause? The answer is, oil is owned by the bankers and farming isn't yet. But beware, they are after it and bankrupting farmers makes their job of acquisition easier and cheaper.

To understand the moves more clearly, part of the answer lies in the European Union's bureaucratic system which makes political decisions that suit the world policy of Karl Marx and the International Finance Capitalists, to destroy our food capability, to entrap us in the Federal Union. A large part of Britain's industrial base has been destroyed since 1945; our shipbuilding industry, our car industry, (Now even Rolls Royce), our nuclear power industry, our fishing industry, all destroyed by linked planning from the International Finance Capitalists, the European Union and the global elite, controlled by Marxism, and now our farming.

As I have stated before, the banks tried to break the farmers backs but only partially succeeded. When BSE came along it was the golden opportunity to finish the job. The EU took the initiative and banned only British beef for export. It did not ban any other country in Europe or impose the tight restrictions on any of them, just Britain. It has however been proved that most European countries had experienced similar attacks. So why was Britain singled out for special concern?

Quite simply Britain's agriculture was the most advanced in Europe and was causing the Agri-Chemical companies concern from farmers' resistance to genetic and chemical farming. It had to be broken up, for the multinationals future plans to work, and it suited the power crazy bureaucrats of Europe to teach sceptical Britain a firm lesson on who rules. So they have ordered the slaughter of millions of cattle. The result, in April 1998 alone, 16 farmers, out of total despair committed suicide, which exceeds the deaths from CJD, in one year, in only one month. That is the criminal stupidity of this trumped up exposure that was so adequately taken up by the puppets of the Finance Capitalists, the Media. The question is, can we trust the so called experts to give us truth that is not slanted to the needs of finance when they have ignored the damage to health of diesel emission?

About secret testing of dangerous substances Nexus Magazine, of February-March 1998 had this to say.

NEXUS MAGAZINE

For decades, Western democratic nations, the avowed champions of the civil society, freedom and human rights, have been using their own citizens as human guinea pigs in experiments involving radiation, biological and chemical weapons, psychotropic drugs, vaccinations and sterilisations...

Millions of citizens living in Western democracies are casualties of experimentation by the state. Some are ordinary citizens who served as unwitting guinea pigs, many more are people who are devalued, disenfranchised or discriminated against...The governments that pay lip service to freedom, justice and individual rights have preyed upon the powerless, the weak and the helpless, in what can only be described as Crimes against Humanity...The United Kingdom Ministry of Defence conducted its own top-secret germ warfare tests from 1964 to 1977. Stimulants, including Bacillus Globigii, Serratia Marcescens and E. Coli-162 were sprayed in public places including Waterloo Bridge and the Thames Embankments. Reportedly, 'massive quantities' of Biological warfare stimulant were also launched off the Dorset coast...Germ warfare agents were sprayed around the British biological and chemical weapons facility at Porton Down, as well as in London's West End, central Southampton, Portland Bill, Maiden Castle near Dorchester, Osmington Mills near Weymouth, and the Lyme Bay area in Dorset...Many tests involved direct spraying of stimulants into the air from vehicles, ships and aircraft".

This must make us think quite seriously: "Can we trust a word we hear from governments, bureaucrats or our media"?

A fourth pillar of world government is now in the preparation stage, where secret talks are taking place between twenty nine member nations of the Organisation for Economic Co-Operation and Development (OECD). These talks take place in complete secrecy, by press agreement, indicating they will discuss matters that will offend the peoples of member states and therefore the likelihood of them being aligned to the global movement is convincing.

The subject of discussion is the Multinational Agreement on Investment (MAI). Behind this grand name is yet another body that will give Multinational and Transnational corporations the ability to transcend the interests of national democratically elected governments. This has worrying implications for agricultural production and self sufficiency practised by farmers in the light of the developments by the Agri-Chemical and food marketing conglomerates. Despite the fact that there are no constraints on publicity the press have dutifully refrained from comment. This is their way of allowing these matters to pass into operation without comment and without general knowledge. If our politicians sign these agreements they are betraying their people.

The agreement will give un-elected corporations authority to overrule elected national governments thus rendering government impotent and meaningless. It would mean governments could no longer put constraints on products and marketing of multinationals if they considered them unsafe or unsuitable. Where is the big cry by our media? Does parliament know the implications? If you want to stir up some trouble write to your MP and lets start to oppose this folly.

Now let us take a look at the European Union through the eyes of an insider. A high ranking member of Jaques Delors team to establish a single currency; he is a highly trained financial expert, who was head of the Commission unit responsible for monitoring and servicing the system. He was respected within his field for his straight thinking and talking. As his knowledge of the European Union increased so did his misgivings consolidate.

He began to realise that the European Union was not in the best interests of Europe and was being run undemocratically under Communist type controls from Jaques Delors' office, for the benefit of the International Finance Capitalists and the Multinational companies. At first he tried to open an internal debate on the way forward but it was stone walled. After many attempts that were all ignored, he decided to write a book "The Rotten Heart of Europe" **(180)** His name is Bernard Connolly and his book is well worth reading to get an inside view of the European Union. In his opening words he states;

"This book tells the true story of the Exchange-Rate Mechanism, the ERM. It is about why the mechanism is a bad thing – Economically perverse and politically perverted--and why so many politicians, bureaucrats and commentators have fought so hard to hide this reality – the authorities did not want its (ERM) true story to be told, for the myths, misconceptions and taboos that sustained the ERM are exactly those that underpin the relentless drive towards monetary union and **a Federal Super State in Europe** – I came to realise that the mechanism was part of a programme to subvert the independence – political as well as economic--of Europe's countries – I was convinced the mechanism, together with the EMU it was intended to produce, was a massive lie". (Introduction page XI-XII). He goes on to say;

"My own decision to write this book in the way I have done was borne first of incredulity at the hundreds of 'Black is White' statements made about the ERM, and then of anger at the treatment given to anyone who tried to point out these lies".

His comment about Delors's office is a leader to show the **Direction** of the European Union, "----David Williamson, in theory the most senior of all commission officials, complained of, 'The KGB (Members of Delors' cabinet, or private office) looking over his shoulder' during the Maastricht negotiations and preventing him from doing his job professionally". (Introduction page XIV).

He describes the central core of his book in a surprisingly bold manner illustrating his reasoning; "My central thesis is that ERM and EMU are not only inefficient but also undemocratic: **(Direction)** A danger not only to our wealth but to our freedoms and, ultimately, our peace. The villains of the story--some more culpable than others – are bureaucrats and self-aggrandising politicians. **The ERM is a mechanism for subordinating the economic welfare, democratic rights and national freedom of citizens of the European countries to the will of political and bureaucratic Élite's whose power-lust, cynicism and delusions underlie the actions of the vast majority of those who now strive to create a European Superstate. The ERM has been their chosen instrument, and they have used it cleverly". (Introduction XVI).**

What we understand from these short extracts is that European Union is not democratic--it has no sound logic behind its policies--and it is being run for an Élite body of power brokers behind a hidden agenda. Do you want to risk being ruled by such a group?

He describes how Tory MEPs and Tory Europhiles joined together with Jaques Delors to have Mrs Thatcher removed from office as she alone stood against Britain's full participation. (Later you will learn where the order to remove her, originated, the Bilderberg Group, who decided she was a hindrance to progress and thoroughly planned her removal). First the papers started to blame Mrs Thatcher for Britain's woes led by Sam Britton in the Financial Times. Sir Jeffery Howe sided with Delors in a behind the scenes operation to oust Mrs Thatcher. Back home the split with Nigel Lawson's obsession with monetary union was widening gradually. Mrs Thatcher was isolated in her own party by a bunch of traitors. Traitors to her and above all traitors to the people of Britain. The overall power was too much even for Mrs Thatcher's iron will. She was ousted by a mealy mouthed bunch of her so called colleagues who took orders from the Bilderberg Group rather than fulfilling their duty to their electorate. By mid 1989 Mrs Thatcher was politically dead, the great fear is that British freedom and independence died along with Thatcherism.

Delors, the Corporatist (A true Marxist platform, but also a platform of the International Finance Capitalists) had won the day and Britain would now submit to the European Union politically but still the people of the country were not enthusiastic.

Kohl has always been a mystery to me, but Connolly points out that he was also a corporatist and therefore, I feel, must have some Marxist sympathy within his

political make-up. (Corporatism being sympathetic to collectivism and a destroyer of Smith's Capitalist, free enterprise of market forces, and competition).

In Mr Connolly's book, he gives highly technical details of the history of the ERM and EMU and blow by blow accounts of the day to day manoeuvres that only an insider in a high position would be party to. It is a story on its own. But it gives a very good lead as to how the bankers control the union, and the politicians, who rely on the bankers for state funding and therefore, toe their line. His conclusion is that the European Union, and the monetary section in particular, is undemocratic, with bureaucrats and senior politicians making decisions outside political control, leaving the council of representatives as an uncritical rubber stamp.

That this system can be allowed to ruin the economies of the weaker nations gives us **Direction** to their aims to subordinate states into submission to their undemocratic rule. He shows, with painstaking detail, how some countries (France and Germany) are more equal than others; how Britain had to come out of the ERM and how our economy, when released from the unworkable restraints of ERM, quickly recovered and grew enough to say that the system was flawed by the purpose from the start to hold nations down while federalisation overtook monetary events; a **Grand Deception**.

He states, "--the increasingly evident success story of British monetary policy outside the ERM led to vituperation from those who felt most threatened by it--the commission, the French government and, not least, Tietmeyer. It threatened to expose the theatre of cruel **Deceit** in which the ERM story was still playing. Somehow, the ERM myth had to be maintained". **(Page 165-6)**.

This proves **deception,** the policy that runs through Marxism.

As a clear message to the community and its peoples Connolly had this to say which goes a long way to attack the lack of democracy within the European Union. "Clearly, anyone genuinely interested in the economic well-being of the world as a whole, or even of a region of the world such as the community, should prefer countries that needed real depreciations to obtain them through nominal depreciation rather than through 'competitive disinflation'". **(Page 174).**

This is the key to understanding that monetary union is a diversion not an honest policy. It is a disabling mechanism to nations intent on retaining sovereignty over their own economy, so federalism can be swiftly introduced. Then there is no going back. Europe must wake up to this deceit, before it is too late.

Bernard Connolly goes on to state, – "there can be no doubt that a Maastricht European Central Bank would be a very different animal from the central banks with which Anglo-Saxon financial markets have had a symbolic relationship since the first World War. This is an important consideration in assessing the degree of damage that would be done to the city of London by British membership of an EMU".

He goes on to say, that the Maastricht philosophy is not designed to protect members against the arbitrary exercise of coercive power but an instrument to enforce that power. **(Page 249).**

In his summing up Connolly has this to say, "What does it mean to say that the Nation-State is no longer an economically viable unit? What implications might there be for 'Europe'? The most careful historical research into the development of the EU shows that the community has, up to now, been a mechanism for preserving those features of regulatory state power that Liberals find objectionable. It is this feature of Europe that has made it attractive to socialists and corporatists in national governments and the commission. Only their insistent propaganda has created the Myth that 'Europe is about an ever closer union of peoples'". **(Page 379).**

Firstly, this proves European Union is designed for the far left as it is collectivist, and secondly, as collectivism falls in line with the International Capitalists and Multi-Nationalists' policy, it suits the international set, which shows how the two opposites, Capitalism and Communism meet on the higher road to an eventual dictatorship through world government.

Thirdly it shows how the bureaucrats are prepared to pull the wool over our eyes by promoting it as 'An ever closer Union of Peoples' which is false and a **diversion** in Weishaupt's style, from the true agenda.

As a reason why the states of Europe cannot be compared to the joining of the fledgling states of America he had this to say, "Europe (that is to say, the democracies of Western Europe) was a collection of states all of which not only had their own linguistic and cultural identities but, after the short period of post-war reconstruction, enjoyed reasonable economic prosperity and political legitimacy (apart from Italy and Belgium and late comers Spain, Portugal and Greece). For them to surrender sovereignty to 'Europe' could only happen as a reaction to external pressure that threatened that happy state of affairs". **(Page 381).** (By whom? The International Finance Capitalists?).

As a possible reason for German participation he said, "Many Germans, particularly the older generation, want to avoid sounding nationalistic at almost any price. So they keep their uneasiness and doubts about the troubling aspects of Franco-German relations under wraps –"

"The French prime Minister, Pierre Bérégovoy has made it clear that the overriding French goal of monetary union is to end France's politically embarrassing dependence on the Bundesbank. The implication is that the Germans must sacrifice their currency so as not to damage Franco-German relations---" **(Page 384).** This clearly shows how Germany and France are jockeying for pole position and the rest of member countries are also rans'.

In sarcastic tone he says, "as one highly placed Énarque has recently put it: 'Of course we want monetary union. Ninety per cent of the élite want it. There is a little danger because the people don't want it: But we will take care of that'. **(Page 389).**

So much for the French élite and democracy. Obviously the people of Europe don't come into the reckoning of the elite; what arrogance.

Speaking of the French idea of monetary union Klaus Engelen had this to say, "The French idea of monetary union can only damage the 'ever closer union' of the peoples of Europe". Connolly adds, "What he might also have said, however, is that the same is true of the German idea. Maastricht, with monetary union at its heart, is not the natural competition of the treaty of Rome; instead it is a manifesto of division and conflict in Europe". **(Page 390).**

Connolly goes on to say, "The monetary union, now so fervently wished for by the French élite, would not restore legitimacy in France. Instead it would be the one thing most likely to re-awaken 'old demons' in Germany because, if it were run to suit France, however unlikely that seems, it would interfere in the ordering by Germans of their own domestic affairs. In other words, it would destroy political legitimacy in Germany, just as the Franc Fort policy and the drive to 'Europe' has done in France". **(Page 390).**

On the French attitude he says, "The technocrats have a contempt both for history and for democracy so total that the present tactic of the French

administration seems nonetheless to be, to go hell for leather for monetary union. The 'Grandiose failure of perception' seems likely to be theirs. Once again, economic perversity, legitimacy and stability of the European countries and amity among their peoples will be put gravely at risk. The history of the ERM is one of repeated rejection of the basic requirement of monetary union. That the people in every country should be prepared to let governments and central banks care more about economic conditions in the community than in their own country In short, the ERM story showed that 'Europe' is **not** a nation". **(Page 392).**

On Jaques Delors, "Jaques Delors was a federalist for less than totally praiseworthy reasons - a desire to comfort the Anglo-Saxon world and 'Anglo-Saxon' market economics combined with a compulsion to expiate the French shame of 1940 and 1983 - but at least he saw what federalism implied. His decision not to run for the French presidency, and his last, defeated speech to the European Parliament as commission President, expressed his realisation that the requirement for Federal Europe could not be met". **(Page 392).**

So maybe in the end Jaques Delors came to his senses. Who knows?

Then as if to extract Britain alone from the chaos called 'Europe' Connolly says, "– Britain is not at the heart of Europe, it never has been and it never will be". **(Page 393)**. This is a justifiable warning to our politicians to step back and look carefully at Europe's future before further 'harmonisation' as they call it, traps us for ever.

Now comes Connolly's most important comment which should make us all think twice about voting to go into a single currency;

"First, there is no reason to believe that sterling would depreciate rather than appreciate if it remained outside a single currency. The Swiss Franc **Appreciated** at the end of 1992 when the people of Switzerland voted against their country's incorporation into the European economic area, Ante-room to the European Union. Long term interest rates in Switzerland fell, and consumer confidence started to improve, more than a year ahead of any improvement elsewhere in continental Europe". As a sad side note to this he adds, "Despite all this, it is still the intention of the Swiss politicians to push the country into 'Europe' at some point in the future". **(Page 394)**.

A simple fact of mathematics is made clear; "The ERM could not profit one country without simultaneously harming others. Ultimately it hurts everyone. Fixed exchange
rates transform domestic policy questions from low politics (What gets done?) to high politics (Who decides what gets done?). The struggle for control of monetary policy becomes all-important, to the enormous detriment of economic and political health--- It would certainly be best for everyone if it did not happen (Single currency). But if it did, it would certainly be best for Britain not to be part of it". **(Page 396-7)**. These words come from an insider and must be of high significance.

Turning to Mrs Thatcher Connolly states, "One of Mrs Thatcher's ambitions was for Britain to have both its major parties support the capitalist economy. The conversion of Tony Blair to so many of Mrs Thatcher's policies means that her ambition is on the way to being realised - as long as Blair himself can be rescued from his infatuation with 'Europe'". **(Page 397)**. To this I would say to Mr Blair, look around you, and see who advises you. Are they not largely Internationalists? If so, in light of the evidence think again. Their hidden agenda is a federalised Europe and the single currency is their trigger.

To sum up his compulsive book he says, "Many of the single-currency zealots in Europe know all this perfectly well. This is why so much of the commission's propaganda effort has been directed-via its contacts with and subventions to organisations like Christopher Johnson's AMUE (Association for the Monetary Union of Europe) - towards fooling people into believing exactly the opposite. On this question, as on every other question about the ERM and monetary union, the propaganda steamroller attempts to flatten analysis. For analysis can only mean dissent, and dissent cannot be tolerated". **(Page 400)**.

This book is essential reading if you want a inside story of European politics, and a unique prospective of its un-democratic composition. It shows the all important **direction** of the European Union.

CHAPTER EIGHT, PART TWO.
EVIDENCE OF ZIONIST MARXIST INFLUENCE

So far in this discussion I have talked about Zionist influence within the International Finance Capitalists. It is now time to define this, as it is important, to understand the origin of the bankers and their associates, to realise how they have deceived their traditional race as well as the world. It is a fact that the bankers and directors of multinationals are dominated by people of Zionist origin and have adopted Zionism as a convenient link. I am aware that this is a generalised statement and there is a minority of people who might object to this analysis but it is true.

These men in the main are internationalists who are Zionists, because Zionism is the grouping of followers with international identity, hrough their belief in the higher road of Communism. The Zionist movement was founded by Rabbi Moses Hess, as was Zionism.

But Moses Hess was also the original founder of Communism which in its upper level was international collectivism. This became the creed of the International Finance Capitalists, who's only God was money and power, and they (Led by the Rothschilds) funded Communism **(181)** as a means of capturing the wealth and the political power in the world today, so they were using Zionism to hide their real hidden agenda, but in doing so created a promised land of Israel that must be an enigma to the Rabbinical order.

To understand this we must once again go back to biblical times. There were twelve tribes. Ten of these Israelite tribes dispersed, spreading out in all directions, some linking up with local tribes to form the Gentiles of the world. Two Judean tribes, Judah and Benjamin, which developed Judaism were left. It was from these two tribes the Jewish faith was carried to the corners of the world.

From their emigration, the ten tribes that dispersed, spread out over Europe and it is quite possible most gentiles are partly Semitic from this wide emigration.

Conversely the Jewish émigrés who spread North, intermarried and their Jewishness was gradually mixed with the gentiles of Europe. The Sephardic Jews,

the Israelites, dispersed along the North African coast and into Europe; from the South into Spain and Portugal, and from there to Brazil. Then to the West Indies, America and India following the trail of diamonds, precious metals and slaves. They too became superseded by the Ashkenazi group from Europe. **(182) (183) (184).** From this it can clearly be questioned; at what period of race mixing does a person pass from one religion to another and go even further and ask "What is there in a name?"

To add to the confusion of the Jewish race I have to add the Khazar factor which is a subject most Jewish writers try to side step because it is a hot potato. The Khazars existed as a powerful group between the seventh and fourteenth centuries AD, and are commonly called the 13th. tribe, **(185),** being enterprising and commercial, they dominated a area North of the Black and Caspian Seas.

At different times they have been called Tartar, Turko-Mongolian, Judeo-Mongol. In fact they were not born Jewish but rather adopted and adapted Judaism.

Secondly, and of most importance is when the Khazar tribe eventually dispersed in the 14th. century they went West to Europe and North towards the Baltic. So when the Talmudic government was transferred from Spain to Poland in the 15th. century they were well placed to influence it. Later the massive emigration from Russia and Eastern Europe, and the founding of political Zionism in the 19th. century by Rabbi Moses Hess formed the centre of modern Jewish power. **(186).** (This book is an excellent insight into the progress of Jewish History.). It was from this group of adopted Jews, who had no claim to land in Palestine that the bankers of Europe appeared, the Rothschilds being just one example. It was these adopted Jews that quickly and clinically spread their banking system all over Europe to England, to Africa, to America and Canada, and Australia, tying nations into debt and building up the power of industry till they became Multinationals and linked into their drive to world government. From this, several important points must be made. Adoptive Jews from this area have no legitimate claim to Arab lands whatsoever. In biblical terms Judaism, if I understand its Semitic origins, would be a veneer only.

The Khazars were not in any sense of the word 'Chosen People', as their practices were the very reason why the Jewish race was originally banished from its lands by God in the first place, as we will see in a moment.

The final truth is that the Khazars were simply not Semites; so to express unapproving views of their behaviour, then and now, is not anti Semitic.

As an example of proof of my argument I have the words of Bishop Montefiore, a Sephardic Jew who wrote in the Church Times of 24th. January 1992 **(187);** "In fact 'Cap'n Bob', (The late Robert Maxwell) like most Jews, probably did not have much more than a fluid ounce of Jewish blood in his veins. Anti-Semitism is built on a powerful racial myth, accepted by Jews and anti Semites alike---"Anthropology concurs with history in refuting the popular belief in a Jewish race descended from the biblical tribes", wrote Arthur Koestler in "The Thirteenth Tribe"; but his words were as distasteful to Jews as to their enemies. Shamir is busy peopling the West bank with Russian Jews of non Semitic origin. Russian pogroms were against people of Khazar-Turkish stock, Hitler's holocaust was a massacre of non-Semites".

What this all goes to prove, is that the adopted Jews are not Semitic and should not therefore come under the umbrella of protection from criticism that Semitic Jews enjoy. At this point I must say I am not in any way criticising the Jewish race in this book. I am distinguishing Zionists, whose aim is to have their own land, from a group of people, who are predominantly of adoptive Jewish background, who are not nationalists, but internationalists, who want to control the whole world, to satisfy their lust for total power. I believe that not only is this a just argument to present, with the wealth of evidence available, but an essential one, if open debate is to take place. It is above all, in the interest of the vast number of Semitic Jews in the world today and a debate that would finally clear the air from all the undertones that make Judaism for many, uncomfortable. The Jewish race has provided the world with remarkable talent culturally and practically, but among this talent is a minority that wishes our world wrong. These few have cunningly linked their hidden agenda with the Zionist movement and therefore used Zionism to silence the world against their hidden plans. It is time the Jewish people spoke out boldly against them and this is the reason why.

Zionism has led the Jewish people against their own religion as laid down in the Torah, and these are not my words but those of a distinguished Rabbi. Under the title, "The Torah Will Never be Changed" **(188),** Rabbi E Schwartz wrote about

Judaism and Zionism, "Today the Zionists celebrate the 42nd. year of the existence of the state and we Jews are in mourning for the 42nd. time. That is why we want to state the Jewish belief and to clarify misconceptions.

"Zionism says that we were exiled because of our military and economic weakness. But the Torah says: "Umipnay chatoenu golenu mayartsenu". Because of our sins we were exiled from our land. Only through repentance will the almighty alone, without any human effort or intervention, redeem us from exile'. At that time there will be universal peace. This will be after the coming of Moschiach and the prophet Eliyu'.

Since the inception of Zionism, all the leading Rabbis were staunchly opposed to Zionism, "because it is against our Torah and belief". For instance, the Lubavitcher Rebbe, Rabbi Shulem Dov Ber Schneerson---, one of the greatest Rabbis of that time, wrote that even if the Zionists were Torah observant we must still oppose the concept of the state for we have been forsworn by the almighty 'not to use human force to bring about establishment of a state, not to rebel against the nations, nor to leave exile ahead of time. To violate the oaths would result in your flesh being made prey as the deer and the antelope of the forest'. (Talmud Ksubos IIIa). We must oppose the state especially because it is against our real hope and belief and that only G'd alone will redeem us from exile when he sends Moshiach."To disobey these oaths will delay the coming of Moshiach. Whoever helps Zionism in any way will be accountable to G'd because he strengthens the hand of those who lead masses of people astray. Who ever is faithful to G'd and his Torah should not cooperate with or have contact with Zionists. On the contrary it is necessary to oppose Zionism in every way possible. So wrote the late Lubavitcher Rabbi---, over 90 years ago. Another party, Agudas Yisroel, was also established 78 years ago for the purpose of fighting Zionism.

"Gradually lured by money and honour they sold out to the golden calf of Zionism. Those who wanted to maintain their faith and continue the struggle against Zionism, dissociated themselves from those parties.

"The Zionist state employs a set of 'chief rabbis' and uses 'religious parties' to ornament their state with a clerical image. They study the Torah with commentaries altered to clothe the words with nationalistic nuances.

"The true Jews remain faithful to Jewish belief and are not contaminated with Zion.

"The true Jews are against dispossessing the Arabs of their land and homes.
"According to the Torah, the land should be returned to them.
"Jews are not allowed to dominate, kill, harm or demean another people and have nothing to do with the Zionist enterprise, their political meddling and their wars.

"The world must know that Zionists have stolen the name 'Israel' and have no right to speak in the name of the Jewish people."

Those are the words of a Rabbi E Schwartz. **(188).** From this viewpoint it seems Judaism has been high jacked by International Zionism just as Russia became hijacked by Marxism-Communism and the source of both was Rabbi Moses Hess and the funders were the Rothschild sphere of influence. If this is true, the authentic Jewish race should open up a debate world-wide to re-establish the faith in their Torah.

There is also an important point that he has declared as the law of the Torah and that is "Jews are not allowed to dominate, kill, harm or demean another people". If that is true, International Zionists are breaking this rule every day in their political manoeuvring as this book catalogues.

In studying the rise in Anti-Semitism, it is interesting to note how its increase was almost exactly in line with the growth of International Zionism. Going back to the first chapter, one of the first families to adopt International Zionism was the Rothschilds. Gradually International Zionism gained the upper hand, forcing Jewish nationals to adopt dual loyalty, one of the many causes of anti-Semitism.

The President of the board of Deputies of British Jews in 1934, Neville Laski KC, warned the colonial office of the International Zionists' covert intentions to establish the 'State' of Israel. Fifty years later Laski was declared a traitor. This shows how International Zionism hijacked the Jewish cause. Now the World Jewish Congress and World Zionist Organisation, both International Zionist controlled, dominate Jewish thinking but worse than that, with no more than sixteen million Jews world wide, control of world thinking is operated through systematic purchase of all media. It is the leaders of this group we are concerned with, not the normal Jewish family that only wishes, like most of us, to be left alone in peace. This proves that International Zionism is intent on dominating the world.

Today the world is held to ransom by a group of three-hundred bankers and an entourage of International Zionists and other money worshippers, mostly connected through Masonic membership, who are high in office in government and the Multinational companies, and leading the world to a global dictatorship. Now is the time to debate this one way road to ruin. Real Judaism must make itself heard above the clangour of International Zionism, to protect its faith in the writings of the Torah.

But the final diversion of this tentacle is that Zionism is but a tool to be used by the International Zionists while blame goes to true Zionists, the fall guys for the bankers plan, whose aim is to make the whole world their state with Communist rule. **Do you want that? If not help Judaism to assert itself over the bankers money power.**

CHAPTER EIGHT, PART THREE.

THE PUBLIC AND WORLD REVOLUTION

War is what is happening in Western society. A war, few recognise, as it is a ideological struggle in peacetime; a psychological form, which hides the direction of the
agenda towards world domination; It is a war we must recognise and win, if we are to hold on to the democracy we have, which has been, and is being whittled away by a invisible aggressor, that is a generally unknown force, controlled by International Finance Capitalism; a force that embraces International Zionism for global government using Communism, bred from the Illuminati of Weishaupt, which originated from Rabbi Moses Hess and spread world-wide through the Masonic movement. I have only shown the tip of the iceberg that proves this statement. Numerous writings exist to prove its progress, all of which are marginalised by our media throughout the world. I could produce a whole welter of evidence, that the Zionists, controlled as they are by the International Finance Capitalists; would immediately discount as anti-Semitic. What I have to say is not

anti-Semitic but anti International Finance Capitalist, the usurers, the very people who had the Jewish race exiled from their land of origin for their usury.

I support a peaceful return to their lands for Judaism, but not through falsification by atheistic Jews, who worship only one God, money, and one power, ultimate.

Our protector, the media, is in the hands of the enemy, the enemy within, that programmes our thought, and influences our governments towards their goal.

The war of ideology was a concept developed within the Communist state of Russia and perfected by the KGB. Whereas the armed struggle was open for all to see, the psychological war (Within peacetime) was only understood by a few whose work was quickly silenced by a media under enemy control, for that is what our media is.

The West has been systematically programmed to think of a cold war between East and West while an entirely different programme was being secretly carried forward. It was a programme where Western technology and research was flowing freely to the Soviet Union from Western capitals, in particular Washington and London. This was a **deception** of gargantuan proportions that the media, in full knowledge, failed to advise us. The forces that are subjecting us to their ideology are not Zionists, as they wish us to believe, but Atheists and Communists.

As proof of this complicity just study British government command papers and you will see collaboration with the Soviet Union in Science, Technology, Industry and Education. Take a look at the so called Guerrilla wars in Angola and you will find Soviet trained Cuban troops guarding oil installations owned by Western oil companies under International Finance Capitalist control.

In 1980, while the British Shipbuilding industry was near collapse a ship building agreement was made with Communist Poland worth £152,000,000.

Communist agitators were allowed to participate in the destruction of the British motor industry. You will remember 'Red Robbo'. A Communist, Reuben Falber had channelled funds from Russia to finance the operation against British

Leyland. When this was exposed by the Telegraph it barely made a ripple, Falber was not arrested as an enemy agent, and the matter, thanks to our press, passed by.

The Financial Times journalist C Gordon Tether was one of the first to expose the centralisation of power by the 'elite'. This earned him early retirement from his paper. Another writer who dared to expose the global elite, Dr Antony Sutton, was also marginalised. **(189).** Sutton's books make essential reading if you wish to understand this complex deception on the world. By this point in the book you may already question the news you read. I find that I can now see through the media news and nearly always guess the real agenda. It is a welcome relief to be able to understand each action and know its objective, although hidden.

As a footnote to this part of chapter eight I would like to introduce the words of Malcolm Muggeridge, a intelligence officer and one time editor of Punch; a late convert to Catholicism. What he says is highly significant to what I have just written.

"It is difficult to revise the conclusion that there is a death wish at work at the heart of our civilisation whereby our banks promote the inflation which will ruin them, our educationalists seem to create the moral and intellectual chaos which will nullify their professional purpose, our physicians invent new and more terrible diseases to replace those they have abolished, our moralists cut away the roots of all morality and our theologians dismantle the structure of belief they exist to expound and promote".

Given that he did not have the knowledge of the hidden agenda this is an accurate description of what has been happening.

CHAPTER EIGHT, PART FOUR.

DECLINE OF OUR AGRICULTURAL AND FOOD GATHERING INDUSTRY

Britain's greatness in the Industrial Revolution came from its self contained power. We had a dynamic steel industry, a adequate fuel industry (Coal) and a modernised and economic agricultural industry that added up to self sufficiency. Today our steel industry has been weakened, our coal industry reduced to one quarter of its original size and even our nuclear power industry hijacked by France when it was producing safer and more efficient power stations.

We have to ask, "Why?" "Have our government and industrialists got it wrong?" "Has demand caused these seismic changes in our industries?" When you study all three industries you find two common factors that have influenced their decline. One, without doubt is the dictates from the European Union, and the second and more surprising is the connection between the Rothschild group and our core industries, surprising because you might assume they had interest in preserving their industries' power and position.

But when you look at the Rothschild's broad spread of power, if they purposely run down industry in one country, so they can boost it somewhere else; in the case of the Nuclear Power Industry, in France, and of course they control French nuclear power. So they don't harm their overall power, in fact in controlling it in France, they gain power, this is why part of our industry has been disassembled and moved to France. This was done with the approval of the European Union whose nuclear energy policy is designed to make all member nations dependent on nuclear power from their approved source. What it does not state is, how France and the Rothschild group in particular have gained from the policy. The more cynical side to the whole affair is that the Rothschild influence now owns the majority of all power sources in Europe and, given a few more years, will have total control. It is from this point on that they can control industry which needs energy to survive.

The explanation of this leads into the farming and food industry. Simply without food people starve to death. So if the supply is controlled by multinationals outside the reach of national government they (The Multinationals and their masters) can control the food supply business and starve the people who do not obey their **direction.** Their direction to global control.

But two countries in particular had efficient farming industries. Industries that were capable of self sufficiency, they were America and Britain. Their farming was also in the hands of landowners which made them independent of the constraints that banks put on industry with debt control. First the bankers tried to put farmers out of business by debt loading them, just before legislation in Europe was introduced, the set aside policy, to reduce yield. This sent land prices plummeting down. This failed. They decided to go for the throat of farming.

There are many reasons they want traditional farmers out of the way. But the most important, is they are an independent body that traditionally is wary of change brought about by the Agri-Chemical Multinationals like Monsanto Chemicals and ICI. They have realised that the benefits of chemical farming are sometimes outweighed by the disadvantages such as pollution. Being mindful of husbandry, the traditional farmer does not wish to veer too far from nature's ways. This is a sound and balanced view.

However, we find the Agri-Chemical multinationals lead the bankers drive towards total chemical answers, with gene implanted seed, that will produce large profits for the seed industry, a multi-billion pound business. Who do we find at the spearhead of development? Non other than Biotechnology, a company formed by Victor Rothschild in the 80's while he was involved in running down our Agricultural watchdogs and research facilities, as already described. The very facility that was about to enlarge its research into Scrapie and to include cattle. This could have been a ghastly mistake or a well planned move to assist his future business. It certainly had an effect on research into BSE in relation to beef.

The researchers knew little about the disease of CJD and how BSE played a part. In those circumstances a responsible unit and government department would remain silent to avoid public outcry. But an unusual situation complicated the formula. The committee (SEAC) responsible for the research in Edinburgh, according to the Sunday Telegraph, 31st March 1996, had to face funding cuts and redundancies. The SEAC committee leaked a statement that started the scare.

The timing gave the EU the opportunity to attack the British farm industry alone, almost immediately, at the Inter-Governmental Conference only nine days later. In an article by Alistair D McConnachie **(190)** he suggests a reason for the EU's swift action, "The EU, believes the UK is standing out alone against moves to weaken the national veto, extend majority voting and give greater power to the European parliament. The EU ban is a straightforward attempt to put the screws on". This is a serious accusation so what proves its validity?

Simply, all meat producing countries of the EU should have faced the same ban. They all had CJD in cattle at approximately the same level. However the EU levelled its power against Britain alone, which has devastated our beef and milk industry, causing imports from far less controlled herds from Argentina, and other countries.

Although the EU did not start the scare they used it in a sinister way to whip the government of Britain. It also banned the world wide exports of a host of bye products and generally interfered in areas which none of us knew they had authority to control.

The EU also managed to do what the banks failed to accomplish. The decimation of our farming industry. I have to ask the question, "Were they doing the bankers bidding?" If the EU was genuine, it would have banned all beef until a cause was known.

Above all this it proved for all to see that the EU had the power to halt our trade with the rest of the world. That the BSE crises was used politically is certain. Can we trust the civil servants of Europe if this is the manner they consider opportune to further their undemocratic rule?

Banning beef was a heavy price to pay for a disease that is not understood. The cost to British farmers is crippling. Yet we have no movement towards banning

Diesel fuel now that it is clearly known it contains cancer forming particulates. There is a big difference. 147,000 people a year die from lung cancer, yet the fuel cartel has managed to hide this information from us for three decades till recently an American report gave positive evidence which the media hardly covered. The fuel cartel is controlled by the International Finance Capitalists. So is the media. Am I being cynical in thinking that this could be the reason for lack of action?

The CJD-BSE link has killed about one hundred and fifty-four people in fifteen years, yet beef was banned. This proves the political motive and the priorities of the men behind the government.

As a footnote to this section I must remind you that Karl Marx-Weishaupt policy required the destruction of the farming industry and confiscation of land from the bourgeoisie. This policy, which I have gone a long way to show is political, fulfils this condition of Communism, towards its goal of world dictatorship; for the farming land relinquished by our farmers will end up in the hands of the multi-national Agri-Chemical giants and the International Finance Capitalists, unless we act to halt them.

CHAPTER EIGHT, PART FIVE.
THE EUROPEAN UNION
A GRAND DECEPTION

To show how the power brokers of Europe have planned deceit from the start, let us return to Sir James Goldsmith's speech to the Confederation of Small Businesses. We hear the arrogant statements of leading politicians of EU countries and the reason we need another referendum.

"To understand how we could have been so deceived, we need for a few moments, to return to the history of the construction of the European Union. The founding father of the EU was a Frenchman called Jean Monnet, who, to this day, is revered in Brussels as a sort of patron saint.

"I recently studied his speeches and private papers as well as those of his closest colleagues. This is what I found. Monnet rejected the idea that Europe should consist of Sovereign nations. He believed that Europe should become a Federal Superstate into which all its ancient nations would be fused. "Fused" was the word that he used in a communication dated 30th. April 1952.

"His plan of action was just as clear. He believed that Europe's nations should be guided towards the superstate without their peoples understanding what was happening. He felt that this could be accomplished by successive steps, each disguised as having an economic purpose, but which, taken together, would inevitably and irreversibly lead to federation.

"The process proposed by Monnet was described by a Frenchman, Robert Marjolin, who served as the vice-president of the European Commission from 1958 to 1967. Marjolin, Monnet's close associate, also described the views of Walter Hallstein, the former German Minister who became the first president of the European Commission.

"The idea, Marjolin explained, was that after pooling Europe's coal and steel production, which was agreed in 1951, we were to co-ordinate Europe's atomic programmes. This became the Euratom Agreement. The next steps were the common Agricultural Policy, and the free trade area or Common Market. The single currency was to follow and so on.

"Monnet and his disciples forecast that these successive moves would necessarily lead to a fusion, (that word again), of economic policies because quite

obviously a single currency would make it necessary to have a single economic policy. And, I quote, "this fusion would compel nations to fuse their sovereignty into that of a single European state".

"So there it was. The leader of Europe consistently but quietly had always planned the fusion of the nations into a single European state. Heath's assertion that we were creating a family of sovereign nations was never part of the plan.....

"Mr Claude Cheysson, former French Foreign Secretary and member of the European Commission, stated that the Europe of Maastricht "could", I quote, "only have been created in the absence of democracy". He went on to explain that public debate would be counterproductive.

"Mr Raymond Barre, former French Prime Minister and also a former Commissioner, said, when discussing the construction of the EU: "I never have understood why public opinion about European ideas should be taken into account".

"But in September 1994, there came a defining moment. A leading German politician came out of the closet and told us the truth. He was Karl Lamers, the foreign policy spokesman for Chancellor Kohl, and he made public the thoughts of Germany's ruling coalition.

"Its proposals called for a European Superstate which would have one Parliament, one government, one Court of Justice, and single currency. In this way, the European Union would become what he subsequently called a "country" into which all existing nations would be fused. He could not have been more straightforward. He even added that national sovereignty "has long since become an empty shell".

"This opened the floodgates. Government after government publicly called for a federal Europe. They were joined by the European institutions. A document published by the European Parliament on the 8th. of December 1995, under the title "Summary of positions of the member States of the European Union", illustrates the degree of consensus which exists among the European political caste. They want a Federal Europe.

"The individuals then spoke up. The then French Minister for European Affairs, Alain Lamassoure, described one of the purposes of the current Intergovernmental Conference in this way: "The Treaty of 1996 must do for defence and foreign policy what Maastricht did for the single currency".

Here is how others describe what monetary union and the single currency will do:

* Jean-Luc Dehaene, Prime Minister of Belgium: "Monetary Union is the motor of European integration...".

* Otmar Issing, Chief Economist of the German Central Bank: "There is no example in history of a lasting monetary union that was not linked to one state".

* Hans Tietmeyer, Governor of Germany's Central Bank: "A European currency will lead to member-nations transferring their sovereignty over financial and wage policies as well as in monetary affairs..." "It is an illusion to think that states can hold onto their autonomy over taxation policies".

* Karl Lamers, Chancellor Kohl's spokesman: "Economic and monetary union is the central part of the project for European unification". It is, "of course, the highest and purest form of integration".

* Theo Waigel, the German Minister of Finance: "Germany as the biggest and most powerful economic member state will be the leader, whether we like it or not".

"And what does our own Chancellor (Written in 1996) of the Exchequer, Kenneth Clarke say? As usual, he misleads us or perhaps himself. He tells us, and I quote: "It is quite possible to have monetary union without political union. It is a mistake to believe that monetary union needs be a huge step on the path to a Federal Europe. The idea that it is in itself some threat to the nation state is wrong". It seems that Mr Clarke is either singularly ill-informed or that he has remained a devoted disciple of Monnet and his methods.

"To sum up, here are some quotes from Chancellor Kohl and from the leader of his opposition in Germany, Oskar Lafontaine, Chairman of the Democratic party:

* Kohl: "The future will belong to the Germans... when we build the house of Europe". "In the next two years, we will make the process of European integration irreversible. This is a really big battle but it is worth the fight".

* Lafontaine: "The United States of Europe has been the aim of the Social Democratic Party all the time".

Having described the £200 million budgeted for promoting Europe, Sir James goes on to say:

"The official European report explains the purpose of the information in the following words: "it is one of the instruments for citizens to think along European lines,. and to Shape public opinion because the general public...is not yet sufficiently committed to the European Ideal".

(All this should make you shiver")...

"It is time that we faced up to the fact that, like thieves in the night, the Eurocrats and their collaborators, have stolen our sovereignty and our freedom".

This adequately shows the commitment of the politicians of all parties in Europe who have no regard for the views of the nations' voters or democracy. Their arrogance is staggering. That they should have to spend a fortune on a publicity campaign of lies and half truths is in keeping with their Make-up and false doctrine.

We must make sure we get a referendum and that we vote to end the European Single Currency which is the one way road to loss of sovereignty by federalism.

From this chapter it is clear to see how Globalism is eating away at our sovereignty because the European Union with the Eastern block coming in behind Europe will form one of the three regional governments for global dictatorship; the other two being The America's and the Pacific Rim. We must thank Sir James Goldsmith for his eloquent exposure.

PROTOCOL THREE
METHODS OF CONQUEST

Today I may tell you that our goal is now only a few steps off. There remains but a small space to cross of the long path we have trodden before the cycle of the

Symbolic Snake, by which we symbolise our people, will be completed. When this ring closes, all the States of Europe will be locked in its coil as in a powerful vice.

The constitutional scales of these days will shortly break down, for we have established them with a certain lack of accurate balance in order that they may oscillate incessantly until they wear through the pivot on which they turn. The goyim are under the impression that they have welded them sufficiently strong and they have all along kept on expecting that the scales would come into equilibrium. But the pivots-the kings on their thrones-are hemmed in by their representatives, who play the fool, distraught with their own uncontrolled and irresponsible power. This power they owe to the terror which has been breathed into the palaces. As they have lost contact with their people, the kings on their thrones are no longer able to come to terms with them and so strengthen themselves against seekers after power. We have made a gulf between the far-seeing sovereign power and the blind force of the people so that both have lost all meaning, for like the blind man and his stick, both are powerless apart.

In order to incite seekers after power to abuse it we have set all forces in opposition one to another, breaking up their liberal tendencies towards independence. To this end we have stirred up every form of enterprise, we have armed all parties, we have set up authority as a target for every ambition. Of states we have made gladiatorial arenas where a host of confused issues contend... A little more, and disorders and bankruptcy will be universal.

Babblers inexhaustible have turned into oratorical contests the sittings of Parliament and Administrative Boards. Bold journalists and unscrupulous pamphleteers daily fall upon executive officials. The abuse of power is the final lever preparing all institutions for their overthrow, when everything will fly skywards under the blows of the maddened mob.

All people are chained down to heavy toil by poverty more firmly than ever they were chained by slavery and serfdom; from these they might free themselves, one way and another these problems could be overcome, but from want they will never get away. We have included in the constitution such rights as to the masses appear fictitious and not actual rights. All this so-called "People's Rights" can exist only as an idea which can never be realised in practical life. What is it to the proletarian labourer, bowed double over his heavy toil, crushed by his lot in life, if talkers get the right to babble, if journalists get the right to scribble any nonsense side by side with good stuff, once the proletariat obtains no other profit from the constitution, save only those pitiful crumbs which we fling them from our table in return for their voting in favour of what we dictate, in favour of the men we place in power, the servants of our agentur...Republican rights for a poor man are no more than a bitter piece of irony, for since he is obliged to toil almost all day, on the one hand, he is unable to use them, and on the other, they rob him of all guarantee of regular and certain earnings by making him dependent on strikes by his comrades or lockouts by his masters.

The people under our guidance have annihilated the aristocracy, who were their one and only defence and foster-mother for the snake of their own advantage which is inseparably bound up with the well-being of the people. Nowadays, with the destruction of the aristocracy, the people have fallen into the grips of merciless money-grinding scoundrels who have laid a pitiless and cruel yoke upon the necks of the workers.

We appear on the scene as the alleged saviours of the worker from this oppression and we suggest that he should enter the ranks of our fighting forces -- Socialists, Anarchists, Communists -- to whom we always give support in accordance with an alleged brotherly rule (of the solidarity of all humanity) of our social masonry. The aristocracy, which enjoyed by law the labour of the workers, was interested in seeing that the workers were well fed, healthy and strong. We are interested in just the opposite--in the diminution, the killing out of the goyim. Our power is in the chronic shortness of food and physical weakness of the worker because by all that this implies he is made the slave of our will, and he will not find in his own authorities either strength or energy to set against our will. Hunger gives capital the right to rule the worker more surely than it was given to the aristocracy by the legal authority of kings.

By want and the envy and hatred which it engenders we shall move the mobs and with their hands we shall wipe out all those who hinder us on the way.

When the hour strikes for our sovereign Lord of all the world to be crowned it is these same hands which will sweep away everything that might be a hindrance thereto.

The goyim have lost the habit of thinking unless prompted by suggestions of our specialists. Therefore they do not see the urgent necessity of which we, when our kingdom comes, shall adopt at once, namely this, that it is essential to reach in national schools one simple, true piece of knowledge, the basis of all knowledge-- the knowledge of the structure of human life, of social existence, which requires division of labour, and, consequently, the division of men into classes and conditions. It is essential for all to know that owing to difference in the objects of human activity there cannot be any equality, that he who by any act of his own compromises a whole class cannot be equally responsible before the law with him who affects no one but only his own honour. The true knowledge of the structure of society, into the secrets of which we do not admit the goyim, would demonstrate to all men that position and work must be kept within a certain circle, that they may not become a source of human suffering, arising from an education which does not correspond with the work which individuals are called upon to do. After a thorough study of this knowledge the people will voluntarily submit to authority and accept such position as is appointed them in the state. In the present state of knowledge and the direction we have given to its development the people, blindly believing things in print, cherishes - thanks to prompting intended to mislead and to its own ignorance - a blind hatred towards all conditions which it considers above itself, for it has no understanding of the meaning of class and condition.

This hatred will be still further magnified by the effects of an economic crisis, which will stop dealings on the exchanges and bring industry to a standstill. We shall create by all the secret subterranean methods open to us and with the aid of gold, which is all in our hands, a universal economic crisis whereby we shall simultaneously throw upon the streets whole mobs of workers in all the countries of Europe. These mobs will rush delightedly to shed the blood of those whom, in the simplicity of their ignorance, they have envied from their cradles, and whose property they will then be able to loot.

Ours they will not touch, because the moment of attack will be known to us and we shall take measures to protect our own.

We have demonstrated that progress will bring all the goyim to the sovereignty of reason. Our despotism will be precisely that; for it will know how to pacify all unrest by wise severity's, to cauterise liberalism out of all institutions.

When the populace has seen that all sorts of concessions and indulgences are yielded it in the name of freedom, imagining itself to be sovereign lord it has stormed its way to power, but, naturally, like every other blind man, it has come upon a host of stumbling blocks, it has rushed to find a guide, it has never had the sense to return to the former state and it has laid down its plenipotentiary powers at our feet. Remember the French revolution, to which it was we who gave the name "Great"; the secrets of its preparations are well known to us for it was wholly the work of our hands.

Ever since that time we have been leading the peoples from one disenchantment to another, so that in the end they should turn also from us in favour of that King-Despot of the blood of Zion, whom we are preparing for the world.

At the present day we are, as an international force, invincible, because if attacked by some we are supported by other states. It is the bottomless rascality of the goyim people, who crawl on their bellies to force, but are merciless towards weakness, unsparing to faults and indulgent to crimes, unwilling to bear the contradictions of a free social system but patient unto martyrdom under the violence of a bold despotism - it is those qualities which are aiding us to independence. From the premier - dictators of the present day the goyim peoples suffer patiently and bear abuses for the least of which they would have beheaded twenty kings.

What is the explanation of this phenomenon, this curious inconsequence of the masses of the peoples in the attitude towards what would appear to be events of the same order? It is explained by the fact that these dictators whisper to the peoples through their agents that through these abuses they are inflicting injury on the states with the highest purpose - to secure the welfare of the peoples, the international brotherhood of them all, their solidarity and equality of rights. Naturally they do not tell the peoples that this unification must be accomplished only under our sovereign rule.

And thus the people condemn the upright and acquit the guilty, persuaded ever more and more that it can do whatsoever it wishes. Thanks to this state of things the people are destroying every kind of stability and creating disorders at every step.

The word "freedom" brings out the communities of men to fight against every kind of force, against every kind of authority, even against God and the laws of nature. For this reason we, when we come into our Kingdom, shall have to erase this word from the lexicon of life as implying a principle of brute force which turns mobs into bloodthirsty beasts.

These beasts, it is true, fall asleep again every time when they have drunk their fill of blood, and at such times can easily be riveted into their chains. But if they be not given blood they will not sleep but continue to struggle.

COMMENT

The very first paragraph predicts the clamping of Europe into the clutches of the Symbolic snake. Otherwise in the trap of European Union, **Federalisation.** The snake is interesting. If you trace it back in history it was the snake from the garden of Eden that tempted Adam and Eve. It was the devil in disguise. This shows that this evil group that is pushing the world towards world government through dictatorship, is linked to Satanic power and use its symbols with ease.

It is also interesting to note that they think they have parted the people from their Monarchs and by doing so set all forces against each other. If you look back in Europe's history, that, to a large extent, has been fulfilled with one or two notable exceptions; Britain being one. Yet the press recently has done its best to part the people from their Queen and degrade the Royal Household. Is this surprising? The press is their tool. **Our Monarch is our best guard against the evils of this group of devil worshippers, this unholy Atheist group of Usurers and we must protect the monarch from their evil desire.**

The Protocols predict that all people will be chained down by poverty; the poverty of usurers debt. They claim to have killed off the aristocracy, who were the only group that could defend the mass against their power, then they give a false carrot to the workers to join their ranks of Socialists, Anarchists and Communists, to lead them to their own destruction as Communism has always done.

They state that they will use hunger to rule the mob. Remember the warning in this chapter about the food production industry passing into the hands of the Multinationals, Agri-Chemical and International Finance Capitalists. This is in preparation for this policy. Through starvation they can defeat even the most resilient foe.

They go on to describe the collapse of the financial markets in Europe and this is true of Germany in particular. The collapse of the Deutschmark, brought about by the Versailles agreement, that was planned by government advisors that can be traced back to the International Finance Capitalists as you will see in chapter ten (Harry Dexter White). They go on to explain how Hitler came to power through the mob and explain that their property would not be harmed in the violence. This was found to be true in Germany.

They go back to the French Revolution and once more to take credit for its "Great" victory, but they disclose that the people following them will turn to a greater despot, prepared by them, the Sole dictator of the world, and Zion.

This Protocol fits this chapter like a glove and must really make us think, Where did they come from?

CHAPTER NINE

THE SYSTEMATIC DESTRUCTION OF BRITAIN AND THE COMMONWEALTH

"So you see.... That the world is governed by very different personages from what is imagined by those who are not behind the scenes".

Words written by Benjamin Disraeli **(191)** in his novel 'Coningsby' the story of a banker, a fiction, that may have given a coded warning about the power of bankers; (because fiction is sometimes based on facts that can't be printed), certainly very relevant today. His inside knowledge of power behind politics would have influenced his writings and the Rothschild power over government at the time could have been his inspiration. It remains very true to this day; the hidden hand that rules. As then, it is still bankers, but with a far greater power from Internationalism brought about by money creation and global movement; a power greater than the National state.

We have already dealt with the Tonnage Act of 1694, which has held Britain in the slavery of debt to an elite group of merchant bankers. They surround the Bank of England and create money out of print cost alone for government's need to increase the money supply. Then at the mere cost of printing, charge the government between eight-ten percent interest on new money created, until the gilt edged government bonds are paid off by the treasury. This is the ultimate usury by bankers, taking no risk and becoming rich beyond belief. It is those bankers, mostly now International Finance
Capitalists, who hold the world to ransom today. **I must once again ask why do we let them do this to us when the government can produce its own money at no interest charge and save 24 billion pounds a year to spend on its political choices, better schools, better health care, a decent pension system, or whatever is needed? It is a pure folly to allow usurers to continue to rob us because politicians are too scared of losing their gravy train, offered as bribes to them when they are in office.**

The merchant banks have always argued that money creation is not safe in the government's hands. I say twenty four billion pounds a year interest on usury money is not a safe investment for money printed without the backing or support of gold or silver. It is the reason why all countries are held in the bondage of debt, and can be manipulated to suit the financial elite who now control politics throughout the world, by debt. It is also the reason why no country in debt to bankers can control its own economy, and this leads to the power of International Finance Capitalism which can and does manipulate finance to achieve global aims, hence the flood of our money that is now pouring into the Pacific Rim, where labour is cheap, and, therefore, putting our workers out of their jobs.

These are a few of the concrete reasons we must take back money creation (printing money) from the bankers. This applies to nearly every country in the world today.

There is no doubt in my mind that this is the central issue in the world today. It is the reason that people feel trapped in a financial spiral of borrowed money, both national and private. They no longer seem able to get out of debt: because when they do, the financial elite turn the screws again. This, maybe, by increasing interest rates or by using their lapdog, George Soros to bleed a country of its financial savings. It might even go to the extreme of robbing pensioners (Robert Maxwell) of their retirement savings (We are told by an ex-Mossad agent, that he robbed his pension funds to bankro Mossad) without compensation, and no support from the other 'Elite's' lapdog, the media. The interest charge for debt alone on created money (money printed by the merchant banks for the cost of printing and loaned to government for interest) costs us all about twelve pence of the twenty four pence tax on a pound of taxable income, a situation that is unsustainable.

The second major issue is that for true democracy, not a mimic of the elite, all countries should regain the freedom for their national media and the big global consortiums like News International should be broken up to allow freedom of national thought, in all its voices, to be heard. To make it representative, the media should all be controlled so that no minority group in the country can dominate its ownership and dictate its policy.

Through hard work and adventure, Britain, during the nineteenth century, was on top of the world as one of three major powers. It ruled over an Empire (Later the Commonwealth) of nations that encompassed the world of some 1,000,000,000 people; a powerful nation and, in many ways, a responsible nation, although some policies can be critically questioned. So how, at this point at the end of the nineteenth century could Britain start a free fall through the twentieth century to become an ordinary nation in debt and no longer a world influence. Well, debt has played a major part, but it has been accomplished by other destabilising factors which have all been planned thoroughly to reduce Britain to a hard up Island economy, dependent on outside help for most things that self sufficiency used to cover. Why was this planned and who planned it? It was planned as an essential move to gain power over a once powerful nation, a world exporter. A country with a large merchant fleet to carry its goods world-wide; whose power was its trade.

It was a necessary objective of the International Finance Capitalists because Britain's strength could block their plan for world domination that lay behind, and controlled the agenda of, every so called democratic country of the West, and even more totally the Soviet bloc.

In line with the International Finance Capitalists, their political wing, the Communist International has long since advocated a Federal Europe as a first stage to world domination through a three stage plan.

1   Socialise the economies of all nations.
2   Form regional groupings and intermediate federal governments.
3   Bring together the federalised governments under a world wide union (Dictatorship).

Weishaupt, Moses Hess, and Karl Marx all described similar policies and the European Union is fulfilling number two in readiness to introduce number three. But the essential watering down process of Britain had to come first.

All historians will agree that Britain's fall from a world power to another ordinary state this century, was dramatic, although they may all differ on the cause, but only one explanation fits the facts of what has happened. That is the Communist policy which was funded and masterminded by the International Finance Capitalists and carried out by infiltration of our government and political parties to such a degree that it makes mockery of our democracy and freedom. Of course I realise this could not have taken place without considerable funding from the bankers and assistance from the International Zionist, and Masonic movements.

The sharpest decline in Britain's fortunes has taken place since the two world wars, one leading to the other because of the overwhelming burden of the Versailles Treaty on the German people.

Weishaupt, Karl Marx and Communism all claim that wars drive the world further towards Communism. The Protocols predict that only one more world war will take place before Communism rules, or at least **'they' Weishaupt's Guardians'** rule. (The International Finance Capitalists, the same thing).

There is no doubt that the second world war brought dreadful hardship to Britain, for we as a country, having hocked our silver to America (Wall Street Bankers) to sustain a six year war against Germany, found the price was crippling.

Lets take a look at the words of C H Douglas in 1936 about this subject referring to the First World War; "Just as the banks created money out of nothing, so they bought the war debt for nothing, and our income tax, surtax and death duties are what we pay them for having created and appropriated for their own use, the national debt.....Taxation is legalised robbery". **(192).**

Yes we were in hock, not to America, as the media have led us to believe, but to the Wall Street Bankers, greedy to reduce Britain's world power to suit their agenda. With this debt they would have succeeded; except that Britain had hidden assets which for that moment kept us afloat. However another war could end all pretensions and eliminate a possible recovery.

Therefore to enter a single currency agreement with Europe is the height of political folly, tantamount to diving into the deep end of a swimming pool blind, not knowing if there is water in place.

It is also a folly because the European Union is a fake system without democracy or true representation, manned by highly paid europhiles who follow the International Bankers' agenda.

We have already seen how our government departments, the BBC and MI5 were infiltrated by a group of University Communist sympathisers, who played an active part in keeping Moscow informed of our every move. I refer to the group of Cambridge undergraduates who belonged to a Communist cell, financed and controlled by Cambridge Undergraduate Victor Rothschild: Antony Blunt, Guy Burgess, Kim Philby, Guy Liddell and Tommy Harris, known as the 'Ring of Five'. All these graduates took Communism seriously and remained set on helping Russia to make progress in its world revolution. They were all traitors to Britain's sovereignty, helping Communism to infiltrate our seats of power and set in motion the decline of Britain as a world power, both politically and financially. This was but one group that is known.

Another group was to be found at Oxford, this was a study group in the Oxford University Labour Club, highly secret till now, little has been spoken about its activities, but today a student from those days (1940) who attended meetings held by this group can give us first hand experience. She was a student studying Chemistry. Her name is Dr. Kitty Little.

She attended two meetings of this subversive organisation, but the one in question took place at University College, Oxford in October 1940. The script is from Dr. Little's memorandum submitted to the Royal Commission on Criminal Procedure in 1978. **(193).** You can read this evidence now realising Communism from Russia was a tool of the International Finance Capitalists.

TREASON AT WESTMINSTER

I first became aware of some of the problems that could be posed by the infiltration of subversive organisations into parliament when I attended a meeting of one such organisation in University College, Oxford in October 1940. For convenience I will call it the Soviet Subversive Organisation, although the leader of its political section, who spoke at that meeting, explained that it had not been given a name, and was not to be given a name, because without a name it would be more difficult to prove that it was a definite organisation. He also said that members had been instructed to leave the Communist party, or refrain from joining it, partly because their activities could then be blamed on the Communist party, while they would be able to show that they themselves were not Communists. (Note: this idea has since been extended, and the KGB has functioned almost as a publicity organisation, to claim and accept responsibility for the USSR acquiring information forbidden under the Official Secrets Act, and responsibility for a variety of other events that come under the heading of, "Unlawful". In parallel with this a number of self-appointed anti-subversive groups have been set up whose primary objective would seem to be to blame the KGB for almost anything and everything).

Despite this superficial vagueness we were given a precise account of the structure of the subversive organisation. It was in three main sections, the Political, Economic and Biological, together with a smokescreen of fringe left-wing organisations, of which the Communist Party was, at the time, the most prominent; that was to help conceal the existence of the three inner groups. The membership and structure of these three inner groups was definite, with the head of the biological section the overall head of the organisation. His name was Victor Rothschild.

We were also given a detailed account of the intentions and ultimate objectives of the political section. The majority of members were to infiltrate the Labour Party, while a smaller number were to infiltrate the Conservative and other parties. The Civil Service was also to be infiltrated. Infiltration was to be at, and from the top, so that the speaker had no doubts that when the time was ripe he himself would become Prime Minister. He even went as far as to say that when conversion to an absolute dictatorship was completed at the end of the 70's, he had been promised that he would be our first Marxist Dictator. If Labour had not a sufficient majority at the time of the last election that it intended should take place to retain effective control of the government, then members of his organisation - the Labour Party (now New Labour) - were to join with the members who had infiltrated the Conservative Party to form a 'National' Government. Any effective opposition would thus be destroyed.

He stated that in his opinion the British people would naturally oppose any form of extremism, and so the members of his section were being instructed to pose as 'Moderates', whether in the Labour or Conservative Parties. This would make it easier for them to join together as the 'National' Government. People with extreme left-wing views would also be encouraged to join the Labour Party, so that normal Conservatives who opposed the concepts of loss of personal freedom, national identity, and submission to a Marxist dictator, could later be equated with them as 'extremists', and be described as 'Fascists' or whatever the equivalent current term then would be. (Note: it is probable that some of those infiltrators who have in the last twenty years reached the top of the Labour and Conservative Parties, had formal training in the art of concealing their true opinions. Fuchs has described his formal instruction in what he called 'Controlled schizophrenia', and even boasted that when drunk he could retain his assumed character with the political opinions of those with whom he worked. Similarly another member of the organisation, Philby, (My Silent War) wrote "I will conclude by mentioning a factor which has unnecessarily puzzled some Western commentators on my case. That was the liberal smokescreen behind which I concealed my real opinions. One writer that knows me in Beirut has stated that the liberal opinions I expressed in the Middle East were 'certainly' my true ones. Another comment from a personal friend was that I could not have maintained such a consistently liberal-intellectual framework unless I had really believed in it. Both remarks are very flattering. The first duty of an underground worker is to perfect not only his cover story but also his cover personality").

Having dealt with their organisation and intentions the speaker went on to describe the detailed objectives of members of his political section. As well as giving the necessary assistance, by means of introducing legislation or otherwise, to plans of the economic and biological sections of the subversive organisation, one of their primary objectives was so to alter the laws and institutions of the country as to build the framework of an absolute dictatorship. **The members of his group who infiltrated the conservative party, along with members of the economic section, were to be primarily responsible for the economic smokescreen, now known as the EEC, that was to conceal the final stages of the transition to the Soviet dictatorship.** (Heath concealed the truth of the European Union from the people of Britain).

Among the other details he specified were the neutralisation of Britain and India; the elimination of our defences; the handing over of strategic bases to the Soviets, in particular Aden, Malta and Gibraltar; the destruction of Rhodesia and the subjection of South Africa; the abolition of the house of Lords; the destruction of all things traditional. The reorganisation of the army to eliminate existing regiments in order to do away with the traditional pride in their history was one of the suggestions made. But even at that stage in October 1940, he said that the top priority, the single most important thing they had to do, was to ensure the total destruction and elimination of **Rhodesia.**

At that time, in wartime Britain, such scheming and objectives might have seemed to be the temporary enthusiasm of a group of the type that in the 1919 White Paper on Russia were described as the 'fanatical young' in Russia who, along with foreigners and foreign agents and bribed bureaucrats, formed the five percent of the population that supported the Bolsheviks and enabled them to retain their stranglehold on the country. In 1941 I had the opportunity of going through all the papers of the Nazi group in Oxford, and the contrast with the activities of the Soviet group was striking. The activities of the Nazi group showed a minimal political content, and it could best be described as a glorified keep-fit organisation.

Given that they are agents of an alien-inspired organisation, aiming to bring Britain under Soviet control as a satellite dictatorship, it would seem that many of the actions of those who have infiltrated into successive governments are not only subversive, but have also offended under the Treason and other Acts, and therefore criminal. Here I shall confine my comments to some examples of direct aid to the Soviet military machine, with its objective of subjecting Britain and other nations to Soviet rule and domination".

In 1977, Dr. Little's evidence at the Windscale enquiry put this evidence into the public domain. However in that evidence Dr. Little did not name the leader of the political section that claimed at the meeting that he would become Prime Minister. (This statement is complete arrogance or certain knowledge, based on a sure, well planned route to power). That must frighten us all. I am able to disclose his name as Harold Wilson, in his address to the meeting he was helping to destabilise the United Kingdom in readiness for an eventual Marxist dictatorship. Dr. Little was present at the meeting.

For many years the press and media have hinted at his political secret. This is now proof of his allegiance to Communism and **Direction** of actions will now uphold this statement of fact.

On April the 9th. 1964 Harold Wilson won a tight majority to become Prime Minister. Immediately he surrounded himself with rich International Zionist advisers who also funded his election. They were rewarded with honours despite the fact they were all Armenian Zionists. It is noticeable how, politicians pushing Britain towards Global government are surrounded by International Zionists. Bill Clinton, in America, is another top politician in a similar position and his policy is pushing America into Globalism.

The signs that prove Wilson's allegiance were not slow in coming.

1   The first priority was to provide adequate technology and support for industry to modernise Soviet military strike force. Linked to this was a covert operation to run down British armed forces and strike power.

2   Running down vital strategic industry, and break up Britain's Shipbuilding industry, and destroy its rule over the sea. To force Britain out of its bases all over the world.

3   The destroying of the British Commonwealth.

4   Control over all forces opposed to Communism (Through the office of the United Nations), thus neutralising opposition but gaining support against their enemies. (This has been allowed by the agreement of senior Ministers in Britain and America. This has led to the SALT agreement which gives Soviet control over Britain's and America's foreign policy. It is from this we see Britain being pushed unwillingly towards global Communist control.

5   Control of all the worlds minerals and fuel supplies through the International Finance Capitalists (Funders of Communism). The destruction of Rhodesia and South Africa (Both rich in minerals, both now in the hands of Communist rulers). That these plans are clearly in progress, and had been, before Harold Wilson became Prime Minister shows that he was by no means the only planted Communist to reach high office. In studying facts before me I know of at least two other Prime Ministers who, if you follow the **Direction** of their legislation they were either duped into anti-British pro Soviet policies or actively sympathisers of International Finance Capitalism or indeed Communism. Libel will not allow me to name names but the circumstantial evidence is quite strong.

Now let us look at the parliamentary legislation that has progressed the Hidden Agenda of the Communist revolution against the interests of Britain and its wealth and sovereignty. A similar state of Communism has crept over America under many guises of radical Liberalism which we can see developing in chapter ten.

I turn again to Dr. Kitty Little's research to show with extreme accuracy the acts that have handed over our technology to Russia, while the world media told us we were deep in a 'Cold War' created by Winston Churchill's speech in America. It was a false cold war because as you will see from the following list through its entire length, until the collapse, Britain and America were actively collaborating with the Soviet Union to build up its industry and strengthen its military might. The real traitor in this story is our press, who in full knowledge of the facts, told us nothing, but fed us lies. Hear is the proof of the government's covert operations.

1.
THE PROVISION OF TECHNOLOGY AND INDUSTRY FOR SOVIET MILITARY REQUIREMENTS.

(194) "This is something that covers a far wider range of materials and products than just guns and weapons. The necessary power supplies, all forms of transport, machine tools, electrical equipment and a host of other items are just as important; no, more important.

The first of the post-war Agreements was the 1947 Trade and Finance Agreement (Command 7439, 1948. Published by Her Majesties Stationary Office), under which a railway system and power stations, together with the equipment required for its operation, were exchanged for a certain amount of grain. The Agreement contained the phrase 'such further goods as may be agreed'. Those further goods included Rolls-Royce Derwent and Nene engines, copies of which, were used in the Chinese air force planes in the attack on Korea a few years later. The inclusion of such open-ended phrases has been a constant feature of British Agreements with the Soviet Union ever since.

The main series of Agreements commenced in 1959. Between then and 1968 surreptitious help was given to the Soviet military and industrial build-up under cover of these agreements. From 1968 this assistance became blatant, while from May 1974 onwards the forms of the Agreements are consistent with Britain being treated as already a Soviet satellite state. Both the Agreements of 6th. May 1974 (Command 5659, 1974) and of 17th. February 1975 (Command 5924, 1975) specify 1984 as the end of the current phase of activity. (In 1984 the European Parliament passed its draft treaty establishing 'European Union' by a large majority. This was thwarted by the UK, and in the Autumn of 1984 we had the Brighton bomb at the Conservative Party Conference).

From the Soviet point of view the Agreement on Co-operation in the fields of Applied Science and Technology, signed by Fred Mulley and Antony Wedgwood Benn on the 19th. January 1968 (Command 3710, 1968) was crucial. All the statements in it are open-ended and far reaching. It has paved the way for the transfer of virtually the whole of Britain's science and technology to the Soviet Union-including previously classified information. (The USSR had 'Exchange of Information' agreements with France whereby that information was passed on to France).

Together with the long term Trade Agreement (Command 4132, 1969) it provided for industrial development to go into Soviet strategic industries instead of into British strategic industries. The scrambling of our major industries with those of the Soviet Union and other Soviet states, and the take-over of British companies by multinational corporations co-operating with the Soviets was encouraged.

British companies and industries have been nationalised where the subsequent change of management assisted greater Soviet involvement.

In the Agreement signed by Peter Shore and Goronwy Roberts on 6th. May 1974 (Command 5659, 1974), as well as the usual open-ended commitments, Britain was tied down to a list of projects that specifically included the setting up of industrial complexes and the modernisation of existing industrial enterprises in the USSR. The Soviet Union does not pay for the greater part of this help, although the excuse given to the public is that it is a part of Britain's export drive.

In the 1974 Agreement, under the heading of 'Research, development and joint activities' there is a long list of items that as well as computers, machine tools, electric power, oil, coal, and mining industries, containerisation, long term transport problems, chemical and petrochemical industry, etc., etc., includes copying machines. This particular item is of interest. Machines have now been developed that allow photocopies of documents to be transmitted by telephone, and the gift of the know-how to build and use these machines was followed by - the inauguration of direct dialling to Moscow. A relevant fact is that Government departments, together with other government - or Union sponsored - organisations now demand a great deal of technical information that is in no way required for them to perform their official functions efficiently - even lists of all files held in Government Research Establishments are demanded by Whitehall.

Several other factors have been introduced that assist in the mechanics of the process of transferring information. Thus, the powers of the Security Services, particularly where senior officials are concerned, have been limited so that, for example, they cannot prevent Ministers from 'declassifying' anything they wish; the Employment Protection Act protects suspects working in classified areas from being easily dismissed or transferred to harmless jobs; the Health and Safety at Work Act can be used as an excuse for outside Union officials to demand classified information; Soviet inspectors have been allowed to go to all factories from which goods are sent to Soviet countries; and so on.

The United States faces similar problems. Transfer of goods and information has been carried on since the last war, and the situation deteriorated drastically after the commencement of the SALT talks, that cover a good deal more than discussion about strategic arms limitation.

The next agreements, signed by Harold Wilson on the 17th. February 1975, on the occasion of a visit by himself and James Callaghan to Moscow, went a great deal further, and when fully implemented will make Britain entirely dependent on the Soviets in the fields of trade and industry.

There has also been very considerable assistance from Britain for the Soviet biological warfare effort. Under Agreements in the Early 60's (Command 1375, 1961; 2059, 1963 etc.) Soviet scientists were given the techniques for mutating viruses, bacteria and other organisms. They have since been given live samples of different strains of Foot and Mouth disease and a wide range of other agricultural diseases and pests (Command 2648, 1965; 6044, 1974). The 1975 Agreement (Command 5924, 1975) also agreed on collaboration on problems associated with influenza and other communicable diseases. (Under the provisions of the Science and Technology Act of 1965 the DHSS were enabled to institute research programmes at Porton). Under an environmental Agreement (Command 5778, 1974) signed by Antony Crosland and David Ennals, the British government has also undertaken to let them have full details of Britain's water supplies and consult with them over any changes that are made. It is since that Agreement was signed that a Minister for Water was appointed to the control of the country's water supplies which was brought under central control. Already the number of diseases with the characteristics of laboratory - induced infections is multiplying.

2.
THE ELIMINATION OF BRITAIN'S DEFENCES.

The elimination of Britain's defences has involved a great deal more than just running down the three services, though that has been taking place at an accelerating pace during the last twenty years.

Agents in the government have taken steps to ensure that a rapid build-up of military hardware, such as took place in the early war years, will not be possible. As the services have contracted, ships, aeroplanes, and other equipment have been disposed of. Sometimes this has been by means of physical destruction, as in the case of the TSR2, when not only the aeroplanes, but also the jigs and tools used in their manufacture were destroyed. Sometimes aircraft and other equipment have been sold abroad, under circumstances where they might in due course be used by Britain's enemies. To replace them a necessary component in the production of the high grade metals chromium is required, for which Rhodesia was the main supplier of high purity ore, although the Soviet Union has supplies of lower grade chrome ores. By no means the least of the reasons for the Rhodesian sanctions was to deprive Britain of this essential mineral. (Rhodesia, now Zimbabwe is a Communist controlled State).

Britain's industrial capacity is also in the process of being run down. This affects the defence position directly, in that in an emergency she will not have the capacity to manufacture ships, aeroplanes and military hardware. It also affects it indirectly, in that in the past Britain has relied on her strategic industries to provide the earnings to keep her economy viable. But while her industrial capacity is being reduced at an accelerated rate, the national debt is being increased by huge loans. This extra money is being used to pay inflated wages not only to workers in productive employment, but also to those in unproductive dead-end jobs in the civil service and elsewhere, and to pay for unnecessary projects that are not in themselves in the national interest. A considerable proportion of the extra loans are being passed on to countries that have come into the Soviet sphere of influence and are buying weapons and other equipment to use on behalf of the Soviet Military effort. All this means that although Britain is paying for weapons and military hardware to be used against her or her interests, using borrowed money for which she takes the responsibility for interest and repayment, because of her debts she will not herself be in a position to buy such equipment for her own defence against Soviet aggression.

The EEC is being used as a cover for further increasing the technical difficulties of rearmament. Industries are being scrambled within the EEC, with components for each item being manufactured in several different countries, so that in the event of even one country capitulating the whole industry would be put out of action. The EEC Commission is arranging that the greater part of its major industrial sites shall be in France - a country that is not in NATO but has close military ties with the USSR. (This is the pure folly we see within the European Union, and another pointer is that it is Communist inspired).

2a.
THE ELIMINATION OF BRITISH INDUSTRY

The agreement signed by Harold Wilson on 17th. February 1975, included several pages listing goods that by 1984, Britain will be committed to buying from the USSR, instead of selling on the world market - goods that Britain would normally rely on to manufacture and export, to keep her economy viable. The list included; power-generating equipment including complete equipment for steam electric stations and hydroelectric power stations; electric equipment including electric motors; electric welding and gas welding equipment; mining, crushing and grinding and dressing equipment; oil drilling equipment; material handling and road building equipment; laser equipment; metallurgical equipment; metal working equipment, printing industry equipment; food industry equipment; pump and compressor equipment; communication equipment; certain electronic components; ships and marine equipment including hydrofoil ships; tanks (reservoirs) for oil and oil products; aircraft and helicopters; tractors and agricultural equipment; trucks and cars; metallurgical industry products; enrichment of uranium in the Soviet Union from the raw material of British customers; chemical goods, window glass; canned fish; carpets; consumer durables (photographic cameras; movie cameras, watches, clocks, tape recorders, musical instruments, refrigerators, and other miscellaneous goods.

As the relevant Soviet industries reach the necessary output, their British counterparts are run down and eliminated, the process being scheduled for completion by 1984. The methods by which entire industries are being eliminated are complex, with the various strands in the progress carefully co-ordinated. The strike organisation, for example, is given precise dates for each strike for which excuses have to be found or created eighteen months or more ahead of time. Such precise co-ordination of apparently independent actions could not possibly have happened by chance.

The best known strand is trade union activity, and for many years trade unionists have been given immunity from a number of laws. But before the take-over of union leadership was completed, nearly all strikes were planned by an organisation (The 'Economic Section' of the subversive organisation) the most senior of whose members were not trade unionists, and who were presumably acting illegally. Many strikes are still planned by that organisation and are later made 'official' by the unions. Legislation has been introduced with the specific purpose of increasing the power of union leaders, so that they could blackmail both ordinary union members and also management. One such law has been that enforcing the closed shop. Another has legalised strikes in hospital and other essential services. And so on. One can observe that only certain industries have been dealt with by strike action. For other industries, such as the electrical industry, different methods have been employed.

Another strand has been complex and excessive taxation. This has served a number of purposes. It has reduced profits and so made necessary capital investment more difficult. It has contributed to the tendency to appoint people with financial rather than technical knowledge to senior decision-making positions, and this in turn has contributed to a tendency to look to short-term profitability, with the partial or complete elimination of high quality products together with the fundamental research that should lead to future developments.

Taxation difficulties have encouraged take-overs and mergers, that almost invariably lead to a reduction in the variety and quality of goods produced. This in turn has encouraged the take-over of firms by multinational corporations, while some British firms have been encouraged to open factories overseas. The latter removes work and technology from Britain and is only profitable in the limited financial sense. In the case of the take-over of British factories by foreign firms, they are often converted to components factories unable to manufacture completed products - and ready to be closed down if union activity alienates the management. On the propaganda front, concentration on the financial aspects has helped disguise the real decrease in technical capability.

Similar to mergers and take-overs in its effects, has been nationalisation, either complete or partial. Here it may be noted that the industries directly involved with commitments entered into agreements with the Soviet states, have been the primary targets for nationalisation.

Union action combined with excessive taxation and inefficient management alone has driven some factories out of existence, but another very effective cold war weapon has been the prices and incomes policies of the recent years. These have provided the excuse for Union and Government co-operation that has had the effect of rendering major industries insolvent, so that money taken by the government as tax can then be loaned back to the companies by the government to enable them to carry on. As the time approaches for the different industries to be closed down in accord with the Agreements with the USSR, these loans can be withdrawn.

The type of tactics that are being used to cripple and destroy British industry are the cold war equivalent of bombing raids".

We all know how effective this policy has been. It has had two main effects, reduced our self sufficiency and made us dependent on imports by weakening our industrial base. Secondly it has made us look misguidedly to Europe to save our future. But Europe is the future trap of those who have brought about our decline.

Not even content with the damage they wrought in the fifties, sixties, and seventies, they also attacked our Commonwealth that had for them both financial and political strategic interest. Dr. Little continues:

3.
THE DESTRUCTION OF THE COMMONWEALTH.

Orders were given by Soviet leaders that the power and influence - and the example of co-operation between free nations - of the old Commonwealth were to be destroyed.

Various steps were taken to weaken Commonwealth links, including a massive propaganda drive against certain Commonwealth countries - those richest in essential minerals - by the media and the press, while psychological warfare experts have rewritten much of the Commonwealth history to mislead people. To create the illusion that the Commonwealth still exists as a force in world affairs, small countries and territories have been 'Liberated', most to be immediately handed over to Marxist dictators supported by the Kremlin.

In 1959 Harold Macmillan visited Russia, a visit that saw the beginning of the series of Agreements that were to transfer Britain's science and technology to the Soviets. The following year he embarked on his 'Wind of Change' tour of Africa. The central African Federation, expecting soon to be granted Dominion status, was broken up, and, in one fragmented country after another, the elected leaders of the African people were replaced by men apparently arbitrarily chosen, but who were prepared to function as Marxist dictators.

With hindsight, we can see that the most important development was the take-over of mines and companies handling essential minerals, with which the Old Commonwealth is richly endowed, and the buying up of vast tracks of land by representatives of companies and international corporations co-operating with the Soviets.

The final stage in the destruction of the Commonwealth was initiated by Edward Heath who at the 1971 Commonwealth Conference took the lead in throwing out the Balfour formula which defined the theoretical basis for the Commonwealth Association at the Imperial Conference of 1926. This concept of mutual co-operation was replaced by that of mutual hate:

"Each of us will vigorously combat this evil within our own nation. No country will afford regimes which practice racial discrimination assistance which, in its own judgement, directly contributes to the pursuit and consolidation of this evil policy".

Following this, Britain in 1973 terminated the Trade Agreements with Australia, Canada, India, New Zealand, Pakistan and South Africa (Command 5404, 1973).

The 'evil' referred to by Heath has come to mean 'racist', and now in 1978 practising anti-racists, from the Foreign Secretary to the anti-racist knife and boot gangs, are making it abundantly clear that even when black and white are on excellent terms with one another, both are to be described as 'racist' if they are not also pro-Marxist. It also involves denial of the genetic fact, that racial characteristics additional to the external appearances that cannot be disguised, are different, and the latest Race Relations Act would seem to go as far as to make writing or speaking the truth about such matters an offence". (Since this was written both Rhodesia and South Africa have fallen into the hands of Communist governments).

Dr. Kitty Little goes on to show how British Bases all over the world have fallen into the hands of Marxist influence and those that are left are still under threat. This has dealt a severe blow to our control of the seas, that helped us trade throughout the world.

Put in these terms as accurate fact you can see how we have been deceived. But then came Mrs. Thatcher with new ideas and new promises. Her first big task was to neutralise Arthur Scargill, which she did clinically. Then she started a massive programme of De-nationalisation of our state industries, helped by the Rothschild bank and its sphere of influence. (Mrs. Thatcher blocked attempts to commit us to the single currency. It was because of her opposition to that and to the concept of Federal Europe that at the 1989 Bilderberg meeting that British Conservative agents were ordered to 'get rid of her.').

Why so hasty? Simply because it was a pre-requisite of the requirements of the European Union before they take over our mechanisms of government; tax, financial control, law etc., you notice how the Rothschild consortium get into everything.

So, can we trust Blair? Well he has made a bad start. He is surrounded by International financiers led by Hart, and Internationalist advisors led by Lord Simon, ex Chairman of BP, a multinational company, in sympathy with global government.

That all these reversals in fortune could have happened by bad decisions from politicians is unacceptable, so the all important **direction** now, proved by executive legislation listed in this chapter, must have been planned by people who do not honour the British agenda. In the past they were called traitors and with regret I must conclude, in my opinion, this title fits their acts.

There are the three other elements that have assisted the Marxist Psychological attack on Britain:

1   The media being in the hands of the International Finance Capitalists can marginalise any news they do not wish us to hear or discretely tamper with news to suit their agenda.

2   The use of Liberal forces throughout the world are destroying religion as we have already seen through the World Council of Churches.

3   The planned decline of moral standards, even backed by legislation, fought for by the Liberal element, that has had a large hand in destroying morality throughout the world, and the assistance of Internationalist officials who have controlled our censorship offices and turned them into a licence to film pornography and other distasteful footage.

All this the British people have had to endure because the politicians and our media have failed to protect us. Now is the time we must call a halt to this planned decline and show the world a lead, out of the grips of Marxism.

CHAPTER NINE, PART TWO.
THE USE OF THE IRA TO DISRUPT AND BREAK UP THE UNITED KINGDOM

On a building, in the Falls Road in Belfast, there is living proof that the IRA are linked with the Communist dominated ANC from South Africa, a link that tells the truth that the IRA are controlled by Communism and in the forefront of the hidden agenda to destabilise Britain. A mural adorns the wall, linking ANC and the IRA in the army of revolution. South Africa is now in the grips of the ANC and is therefore a Communist dominated state.

To clear up a misconception, the IRA's campaign of terror linked to the Sinn Fein's (Political Wing of the IRA) political campaign to use press coverage to its advantage, is levelled as much at the mainland, England and Southern Ireland as it is at Northern Ireland.

Unfortunately the people of Ireland still, wrongly, see the war of terrorism as a sectarian battle, not the ideological battle that it really is, which shows once again deception by the IRA - Sinn Fein leaders; leaders who have direct links to International Zionists.

As long as this prevails there is no chance of solving the Irish problem, but with the march of the European Union, time is short for continued terrorism, the IRA and Sinn Fein must fall in behind the European Union and the merging of the old Soviet bloc with Europe. Their job is all but done and they will lay down arms and get a hero's welcome into the community. That this is wrong will be forgotten.

Just to remind you, Karl Marx recommended a subversive war in Northern Ireland as a way to destroy the United Kingdom.

So like many of Marx's directives it has been proved effective, although it has not destroyed the United Kingdom yet.

Marx saw Ireland as the 'soft point' that could be used to destabilise Britain's resistance to revolution. If you study Karl Marx's policy 'Armed Insurrection' (196) you will see that IRA - Sinn Fein have stuck rigidly to his policy.

Von der Heydte showed with great accuracy the difference between revolutionary aims of organisations like Sinn Fein - IRA, and simple transgressions of law and order, "Irregular warfare is, by nature, mostly illegal combat, i.e., in violation of norms of law - but by no means is it an illegitimate form of combat, i.e., not just by the idea of law. It occurs largely outside prevailing law, particularly outside every codified or contracted law, even if it is waged for a just cause - which is certainly possible, and often is the case.

Its essential illegality, but its possible legitimacy, shows that there is a relationship between the phenomenon of irregular warfare and the phenomenon of revolution. Like revolution, irregular warfare, if victoriously waged, can lead to the emergence of new law on account of its success, despite its initial illegality; irregular warfare is war, real war, and every war can lead to new developments in law and new legal institutions. Like revolution, irregular warfare has a certain significance for law, because of this possibility of the emergence of new law.

Despite their original illegality, neither revolution nor irregular warfare can be viewed only as violations of law; were they only common violations of law, new institution could not develop from them". **(197).**

From this short description we can clearly see that the IRA- Sinn Fein is part of the International Socialist Revolution, and is involved in revolutionary war, with the aims and objectives put forward by Von der Heydte.

The correct response against such hidden warfare should be a military one but all along, governments in Britain and Southern Ireland have treated it as criminal terrorism and used ineffective forces to combat its source, added to which they have lost the propaganda war, so cleverly used by Gerry Adams. What was needed was a military initiative against what was quite clearly irregular warfare employing guerrilla tactics; but it is now too late to eliminate this enemy within. It is not surprising to learn therefore that the IRA are but one component in the International Socialist Revolution against Western Society.

But our society uses kid-gloves and tries to negotiate with terrorism, a sure recipe for disaster. Today it seems that terrorism has won unless Trimble says NO.

So we see a formidable array of covert force against us that has made life for some unbearable and for the rest of us uncomfortable. Now we can clearly see the source, it may be too late to start a fight back, at least against this target. (IRA).

PROTOCOL SEVEN
WORLD WIDE WARS

The intensification of armaments, the increase of police forces - are all essential for the completion of the aforementioned plans. We desire that they should be in all the states of the world, besides ourselves, only the masses of the proletariat, a few millionaires devoted to our interests, police and soldiers.

Throughout all Europe, and by means of relations with Europe, in other continents also, we must create ferments, discords, and hostility. Therein we gain a double advantage. In the first place we keep in check all countries, for they will know that we have the power whenever we like to create disorders or to restore order. All these countries are accustomed to see in us an indispensable force of coercion. In the second place, by our intrigues we shall tangle up all the threads which we have woven into the cabinets of the states by means of the political, by economic treaties, or loan obligations. In order to succeed in this we must use great cunning and penetration during negotiations and agreements, but as regards what we called the 'official' language', we shall keep to opposite tactics and assume the mask of honesty and compliancy. In this way the peoples and governments of the goyim, whom we have taught to look only at the outside of whatever we present to their notice, will still continue to accept us as the benefactors and saviours of their human race.

We must be in a position to respond to every act of opposition by war with the neighbours of that country which dares to oppose us: but if these neighbours should also venture to stand collectively together against us, then we must offer resistance by a universal war.

The principle factor of success in the political is the secrecy of its undertakings: the word should not agree with the deeds of the diplomat.

We must compel the government of the goyim to take action in the direction favoured by our widely-conceived plan, already approaching the desired consummation, by what we shall represent as public opinion, secretly prompted by us through the means of that so-called 'Great Power' - the press, which with a few exceptions that may be disregarded, is already entirely in our hands.

In a word, to sum up our system of keeping the governments of the goyim in Europe in check, **we shall show our strength to one of them by terrorist attempts** and to all, if we allow the possibility of general rising against us, we shall respond with guns of America or China or Japan.

COMMENT

This shows that the protocols belong to the International Finance Capitalists as they say they own all the national debts and have nearly all the media under their control.

Again they state Weishaupt's policy of deception by stating,, 'the word should not agree with the deeds of the diplomats'.

They will use the press to drive governments into their agenda.

They will show the strength of their power to one government in Europe by terrorist attempts. This is what has happened to England, using the IRA as the terrorist persuasion. This clearly shows **Direction**, that gives up the secret of intention.

CHAPTER TEN

AMERICA, THE BASTION OF CAPITALISM?

PART ONE

DOLLAR SLAVERY

Throughout our lives we have been led to believe that America was the country fighting to protect the free world from Communism. Whenever Communism advanced, Americans would be there fighting back the forces of evil, selflessly giving up their lives to make the world a safer place.

Our newspapers were full of the war of words between Washington and Moscow through several Presidents from both sides of the political divide; a war of words our press insisted, put the world in extreme danger, even on a war footing. Remember Cuba?

It might therefore be surprising for you to learn that all through this period of the 'Cold War', America and Britain were supplying Russia with technology to modernise, not only its domestic industry, but also its defence industry and biological and chemical industries. They both passed developments, classified as top secret, to their counterparts in Russia, not only during the Second World War, which could be understood, as Russia was a so called ally, but well into the cold war period, which meant that American designed weapons and technology were used by the Vietnamese forces against American troops; a situation that is particularly hard to believe. (I will be citing the sources of these statements in this chapter).

Needless to say, the Media, all through this period knew what was going on, but chose to remain silent because it suited their owners cause, the cause of International Finance Capitalism.

While America was throwing away the lives of its citizens for no gain, in fact a loss, the International Finance Capitalists were building up Russia's industry and passing on top secrets. It is a nightmare scenario that is so hard to come to terms with until you understand how the world is governed. When you accept that the Internationalists govern the world through the power of finance, you realise that the borders of the world are very different to the ones we are led to believe.

America, is today, and has been for most of the last century, the most powerful nation in the world. This has been brought about by, the desire of the American people to succeed; the good fortune of their emigration policy that attracted those who wanted a new start, and a country blessed with abundant liquid gold (oil) reserves; a combination that has made a rich country that is united in its parts by a Federal Government, but a Federal Government that was in place during its infancy.

Despite all this, two percent of the population control ninety percent of the wealth of America.

So how did this happen? Who are the two percent? and what is their money used to achieve?

The two percent are the International Finance Capitalists and oil barons. How this happened is the story of the early days of America; and their money is being used to obtain absolute power, political as well as monetary.

Let us go back to the early days to get an idea of the rapid expansion of a young and growing community.

Money was created in the first place to ease the problems found in bartering and act as a transfer system for land deeds and the like. It was considered illegal to gain benefit by lending money for gain, as money was considered a mere medium of convenience. But like most things in life, the power of money corrupted some who became money changers for great profit. It was these money lenders who saw the wrath of Jesus Christ in the temple when he, in rage, overturned their tables, and chased them out of the temple.

This practice was named usury and was outlawed in many places. Throughout history many famous people and governments have condemned usury. We can see many references in the bible; Ezekiel: Chapter XXII **(198)**, Leviticus: **(199)**, Deuteronomy 23 **(200)**, Ezekiel 18,**(201)**, Ezekiel 22 **(202)** are just a few. Even the great philosopher, Aristotle voiced his opinion firmly against usury (Encyclopaedia Britannica). Julius Caesar, in 48 BC removed money creation from the rich families and restored it to the government. For this he was murdered. But as a need existed for loans, so the business, however seedy, flourished. The great exponents of usury have been the Khazar adopted Jews who between the seventh. and fifteenth century spread all over the world, following the news of new territories of fortune to establish their banking systems in readiness for their master plan to control the world through debt. One such family that we have already seen was the Rothschilds.

Because the group had been around so long they had developed a system of money lending that was far in advance of the ordinary bankers. They traded through each other by letters of credit enabling large sums to be collected in foreign countries without the fear of robbery. We have already seen this used by the Rothschilds to pay Wellington's troops. We have seen Rothschild finance governments for wars and make rich profits for his efforts. We have even seen him fund two sides of a war, showing that morality is measured by profitability. We have also seen them make money out of supplying military needs.

So this new country of America was an ideal place to be for a banking concern with its eye upon control of finance and eventual enslavement of its government and peoples by debt slavery. Getting in early, on the ground floor, made the corrupting of its legislature an easy task for these skilled and highly trained bankers, and this they did as we will soon see.

A book that I recommend to understand the money lending history of usury is 'Lincoln Money Martyred'. **(203)**. It shows how a definite cycle occurs, where money is taken in by the bankers and made scarce to increase interest and lower wages and supplies, till a program is started against the usurers. They are eliminated and the money goes back into the people's pockets and the phase all starts again until the bankers lend to government and control politicians. It is then that wars occur instead of programs. The most famous example of this being the second world war after the financial collapse 1929-31 which triggered world recession.

What this creates for bankers is the war bond business, which forces a participating country into debt for a prolonged period, and is the most profitable debt they can obtain. This is why bankers have created and encouraged all the wars in the last two centuries, while countries could only stand by and pay up.

The greatest enemy of democracy is not Communism, which is a mirror hiding the truth, but debt enslavement. Britain and America are now completely in the banker's power and now do what they say, and this is how it happened.

We have seen, in the reign of William III, how the Bank of England, (note the deceptive name) founded by John Thompson, was formed to lend £1,500,000 to the King to fight a war against France. William Patterson, a banker and advisor of this private bank, was prompted to say, "The bank hath benefit of interest on all moneys it creates out of nothing". This was the start of Britain's debt slavery; a system that promises to deliver us, without political outrage, to our fate under the Communism of the International Finance Capitalists. (These Bankers are our real enemy and only a brave government can alter that by taking money creation back into government control where it belongs). The date was 1694 and the act was, "The Tonnage Act". Since then the Stock Exchange represents this debt through Government Gilt Edged Bonds, listed in our daily press. It is a debt for which we now pay half our income tax to service the interest charge alone, to enrich private bankers who created the money loaned out of nothing. They charge at least 8% interest to governments on outstanding loans. This is so ridiculous, when governments can do the same thing at no charge, but it seems that no politician dares to challenge the usurers and bring money creation back where it belongs, under government control.

What this early victory did was quickly grasped by the growing army of bankers searching the world for new lucrative colonies to move into and dominate. Such were the new colonies of the Americas; a large and widely spread territory that had all the potential for future wealth and rapid development which was encouraging people from foreign lands to start a new life in a unhampered colony, loosely controlled by British interests.

One of those bankers who had his eye on the Americas was Rothschild. Through the close contact he had with the King and government, in the second half of the 18th. century, he was well placed to obtain sensitive reports on developments, and as an advisor to the government, he was in a powerful position when necessary to influence the government to get his way. So why, at this stage, was a man so openly referred to as a usurer, allowed to influence money matters in such a manner?

The Rothschild Bank had helped the government to transfer money to Wellington for his wars, doing well out of the deal, but more importantly, in the words of Dr. R.E. Search' "The Jewish usurers revived their age old practices of collusion with and bribery of lawmakers or public officials, who accepted bribes or loans of money in exchange for influence or privileges of usury". **(204).**

This is true today; just look at the politicians and civil servants listed in the Rothschild sphere of influence. But the bankers had in those days a very fast and safe way of transferring money; namely credit transfer, between banks, this attracted governments to their door as journeying with money was thought to be too dangerous.

It was these very bankers in the second half of the 18th. century, led by Mayer Amschel Rothschild, who were beginning to look towards America as a future market. In 1790 he proclaimed, **"Permit me to issue and control the money of a nation and I care not who makes the laws". (DIRECTION).**

The next year, 1791, saw with his help, the first 'United States Bank'. (Notice the deception of the name which infers a government body. It wasn't, it was private, and still is.).

So how did the banking Internationalists of Europe capture, lose, and regain the rights to create money in America? Well, their first aim was to establish a bank that looked and sounded like a government organisation. The country was developing fast and money supply was in a critical state with a poor supply being chased by a ready market; ideal to be tamed.

But the laws for establishing a bank in order to create money were hotly opposed by Edmund Randolph, the Attorney General and Thomas Jefferson, Secretary of State. The man the bankers chose to put their point over forcefully, was Alexander Hamilton, who had changed his name from Levine before immigrating to America. The change of name was probably because Jewish applicants at that time were not given citizenship. This leads us to believe once more, deception was used by those bankers who wanted the American banking action badly. After much debate and strong opposition "The Bank of the United States" was given a charter for twenty years 1791-1811, with a capital of 10,000,000 dollars and immediately succeeded in a money hungry market.

By charter renewal time, once again Thomas Jefferson, still deeply concerned with the powers given to the bank, opposed the renewal, with these words, "I believe that banking institutions are more dangerous to our liberties than standing armies. Already they have raised up a money aristocracy that has set the government at defiance. The issuing power (of money) should be taken from the banks and restored to the government and to the people to whom it belongs". **NOTE "TO WHOM IT BELONGS".** This says it all, and is as true today as it was then, but in contrast to now, the newspapers, still free from banker control and influence from large advertisers, referred to the bank as a Viper, a Cobra, and a Vulture.

We also saw congressmen stand up for the interests of their voters, kill the renewal bill and close the 'First Bank of the United States'.

In revenge, the bankers switched their policy from good times (Times of plenty of money) to a policy of hard times, (Times of money famine) with high interest rates. In effect this took money out of circulation accept from state banks, who were, at this time small and easily out-manoeuvred by the private sector bankers. So through strain of withdrawals nearly all the state banks closed.

At this point Nathan Rothschild, in England, who controlled the English money changers and whose money started the bank in America, commanded his political allies in England to teach the 'Upstarts' a lesson and stated, "Either the application for renewal of the charter is granted, or the United States will find itself in the most dangerous war".

But Andrew Jackson stated, "You are a den of thieves - Vipers -- I intend to rout you out, and by the eternal God, I will rout you out". After this speech Rothschild issued orders, "Teach those impudent Americans a lesson. Bring them back to colonial status". So the war started between England and the United States one year after the bill was killed, in 1812.

But Andrew Jackson beat off the invaders and gave them a bloody nose. Still the Rothschild led bankers persisted and in 1816 once again were given a charter to start the 'Second Bank of the United States'. This time it had thirty five million dollars behind it which was the original stake of ten million dollars plus profit from its earlier trade. Not a bad business, but nothing to compare with what was to come, through the misguided handing over of money creation to this private bank. A policy that now enslaves America as well as the rest of the world.

The next challenge to the bank's future came with the election of Andrew Jackson as President in 1828. He immediately removed government money from the 'Second Bank of the United States' and deposited it into state banks.

The President of the Second Bank of the United States confided in the President, Andrew Jackson, that if they were allowed to open branches in the major cities of all the states they could control the policies of the whole country. He misjudged the President. Andrew Jackson vowed to fight the bank charter extension. Biddle, the President of the bank replied he would fund the opposition to prevent Andrew Jackson's re-election. For that moment the bank lost to democracy. However the bank's bribe fund reached out to enough congressmen to ensure Jackson's victory was short lived and Congress passed the bill but, Andrew Jackson, using his power as President, vetoed the bill and it expired in 1836.

This precipitated a short boom followed by a deep recession in 1837. A few years later the gold boom brought added prosperity to America and an influx of Jewish emigrants chasing the gold trail, not least bankers themselves.

But a far greater threat was looming on the horizon, a threat to the stability of the nation, a political divide between North America and the Southerners, who lived a life on huge plantations, served by slaves bought in the notorious slave markets was about to erupt. This divide was to seal America's fate as a nation, and this is how it happened.

Abraham Lincoln was elected President of the whole Union only to find that the Southern States wanted to break away to form their own government. The South seized Fort Sumpter and government arms stores. This to Lincoln was a declaration of war.

History relates that when Lincoln saw the situation in perspective he realised that the government would need finance to win a war, so he approached the big banker to fund his war; Appleton Cyclopedia 1861 states "The money kings wanted 24% to 36% interest for loans to our government to conduct the civil war". **(205).**

Lincoln, shocked and angry at the insult of extreme usury refused. The bankers chided that they would offer it to the Southern Confederacy. There is evidence that Rothschild's agent in the South did exactly what was threatened. **(205a)**

But Abraham Lincoln, in 1862, played a master stroke, suggested to him by his old friend Colonel Dick Taylor. He, in full conformity with the provisions of the United States constitution, produced $450,000,000 of debt free 'Greenbacks' to be issued to conduct his war. In this way he was competing with the bankers for money creation with this difference, there was no interest charge to the nation, but his Greenback was fully supported by silver, something the banks just could not match. A stroke of genius that should have succeeded but for the devious minds of the usurers. Lincoln's letter of thanks and appreciation to Colonel Dick Taylor was printed in the New York Tribune. **(206).**

"My Dear Colonel Dick: I have long determined to make public the origin of the greenback and tell the world that it is Dick Taylor's creation. You had always been friendly to me, and when troublous times fell on us, and my shoulders, though broad and willing, were weak, and myself surrounded by such circumstances and such people that I knew not whom to trust, then I said in my extremity: 'I will send for Colonel Taylor; he will know what to do'. I think it was January, 1862, on or about the 16th., that I did so; you came, and I said to you: 'What can we do?' Said you, 'Why, issue treasury notes bearing no interest, printed on the best banking paper. Issue enough to pay off the army expenses and declare it legal tender'. Chase thought it a hazardous thing, but we finally accomplished it and gave the people of this Republic the greatest blessing they ever had - their own paper money to pay their own debts.

It is due you, the father of the present Greenback that the people should know it, and I take great pleasure in making it known. How many times I have laughed at you telling me plainly, that I was too lazy to be anything but a lawyer.

Yours truly,   A. Lincoln.

But the victory of the Greenback was short lived as Dr. Search relates in 'Lincoln Money Martyred', although it won the battle against the Southern Confederacy it lost the war against the power and deceit of the bankers. **(207)**.

"The money changers had been able to fool and hoodwink England, and keep her in bondage for 168 years, and they wanted to very much continue, and to add the balance of the world to their conquest; making the people everywhere economic serfs, working for them. They did not intend to give up such a juicy plum without a 'scrap'.

"So they began to polish their weapons of warfare, namely-bribery, corruption of law makers, deception, make-believe, political pull, economic pressure, and all the rest; all tied up nicely with what propaganda they could make use of, and commenced their battle for world domination through the power of gold".

The idea of money printed by government as full legal tender was poison to the bankers. They must kill it at all cost. First, directed by Nathan Rothschild, from England, a campaign was mounted against the American greenback dollar. A campaign that deviously spread rumours, quite unfounded, that it was a 'Fraud' and not 'Sound' money. Just to confuse the masses.

The following editorial appeared in the London Times from an article by C.K. Howe, **(208)**; "If this mischievous financial policy which has had its origin in the North American Republic (Greenback issue of money) during the late (civil) war should become indurated down to a fixture, then the government will furnish its own money without cost. It will pay off its debts and be without debts. It will have all the money necessary to carry on its commerce. It will become prosperous beyond precedent in the history of the world. The brains and wealth of all countries will go to North America. That government must be destroyed or it will destroy every monarchy on the globe". So nearly did America escape the bonds of financial slavery.

The Rothschilds instigated the Hazard Circular, a devious work that stated; "Slavery is likely to be abolished by war power, and chattel slavery abolished. This, I and my European friends are in favor of, for slavery is but the owning of labor, and carries with it care of the laborers, while the European plan, led by England (The Rothschilds), is that capital should control labor by controlling wages.".

"The great debt that capitalists will see to is made out of the war (Our own civil war) must be used to control the value of money. To accomplish this, the government bonds must be used on a banking basis.

"We are now waiting for the Secretary of the Treasury of the United States to make this recommendation. **It will not do to allow greenbacks, as they are called, to circulate as money any length of time, as we cannot control that, but we can control the bonds and through them the bank issues**".

Their aim was to kill the greenback and bring money creation back under their usurious control. Dr. Search **(209)**, looking back at this time had this to say;

"Crooked? Criminal? Unconstitutional? Well, look around you today and see what the consummation of their activity at that time has accomplished, for right there began one of the blackest pages ever to be written into the history of our glorious country, binding our people link by link with a diabolical chain of economic slavery that can well be called the direct cause of all the grief, suffering, poverty, loss of homes, farms, business, and all the widespread unemployment we are laboring under today". Turn back and see what Thomas Jefferson, one of the men who helped to frame the constitution, had to say about private banks issuing money.

It was Congress that, through the influence of the Hazard Circular, and bribery and corruption by the bankers, won an amendment in the form of an Exception Clause passed on the 25th. February 1862 which classed the Greenback: Good for all debt both public and private **Except** duty on imports and interest on government debts. So it showed the government refusing its own money, making it 'unsound money' and congress passed the amendment with banker pressure hidden from view. **Deception.**

Lincoln, was forced to state that he "could not fight two wars at the same time; the Confederates at the front, and the bankers in the rear, and of the two the Confederates were the most honourable".

Senator Thaddeus Stevens had this to say; "Mr. Speaker, I have a very few words to say. I approach the subject with more depression of spirit than I have before approached any question. No personal motive or feeling influences me. I have a melancholy foreboding that we are about to consummate a cunningly devised scheme, which will carry great injury to all classes of people throughout the Union". He later stated; "We had to yield; we did not yield until we found that the country must be lost or the bankers gratified".

For the bankers to have done this to Lincoln at such a time showed that they only cared for gain not for principle. They showed their true hidden lust for power over politics and proved they were and are today unworthy of our trust in any form. We get a rare insight into the movement behind the scenes in this letter printed in 'Lincoln Money Martyred' by Dr. R.E. Search **(210)**. It is a letter from the Rothschild Bank in London.

Messrs. Ikleheimer, Morton, and Vandergould,
No 3 Wall Street, New York, USA.

Dear Sir: A Mr. John Sherman has written us from a town in Ohio, USA as to the profits that may be made in the National Banking business under the recent act of your Congress, a copy of which act accompanied his letter. Apparently this act has been drawn upon the plan formulated here last summer by the British Bankers Association and by that Association recommended to our American Friends as one that if enacted into law, would prove highly profitable to the banking fraternity throughout the world.

Mr. Sherman declares that there has never been such an opportunity for capitalists to accumulate money, as that presented by this act, and that the old plan of the state banks is so unpopular, that the new scheme will, by contrast, be most favorably regarded, notwithstanding the fact that it gives the National Banks an almost absolute control of the National Finance. "**The few that can understand the system**", he says, "**will either be so interested in its profits, or so dependent of its favors that there will be no opposition from that class, while on the other hand, the great body of people, mentally incapable of comprehending the tremendous advantages that capital derives from the system, will bear its**

burdens without complaint and perhaps without even suspecting that the system is inimical to their interests".

Please advise fully as to this matter and also state whether or not you will be of assistance to us, if we conclude to establish a National Bank in the city of New York. If you are acquainted with Mr. Sherman (he appears to have introduced the Banking Act) we will be glad to know something of him. If we avail ourselves of the information he furnished, we will, of course, make due compensation.

Awaiting your reply, we are

Your respectful servants,
"Rothschild Brothers".

This letter shows without doubt the Rothschilds deep involvement in the corruption of the American banking system. We see, through bankers' pressures, organised by Rothschild and the British bankers, The National Bank Act went before Congress and not only did it want, as in England, to have power to print its own money and redeem it themselves but they also wanted its redemption guaranteed by the United States government. Because the nation was young, at war and lacking in deep experience, its two advocates, Senator John Sherman in the Senate, and Congressman Samuel Hooper in Congress and all the behind the scenes bribery and corruption that took place, gave the bill a fine two vote majority in the Senate. Afterwards the Secretary to the Treasury, Salmon P Chase remarked; "My greatest financial mistake of my life. It has built up a monopoly that affects every interest in this country. It should be repealed, but before this can be accomplished, the people shall be arrayed on one side and the banks on the other in a contest such as we have never seen before in this country".

It is fitting now to remember the words of America's greatest President at the moment of his Gettysburg address. **(211).**

LINCOLN'S GETTYSBURG ADDRESS

"Four score and seven years ago our fathers brought forth on this continent, a new nation, conceived in liberty, and dedicated to the proposition that all men are created equal.

"Now we are engaged in a great civil war, testing whether that nation or any nation, so conceived and so dedicated, can long endure. We are met on a great battlefield of that war. We have come to dedicate a portion of that field, as a final resting place for those who here gave their lives that that nation might live. It is altogether fitting and proper that we should do this.

"But, in a larger sense, we cannot dedicate - we cannot consecrate - we cannot hallow - this ground. The brave men, living and dead, who struggle here, have consecrated it far above our poor power to add or detract. The world will little note nor long remember what we say here, but it can never forget what they did here. It is for the living rather to be dedicated here to the unfinished work which they who fought here have thus far so nobly advanced. It is rather for us to be here dedicated to this great task remaining before us - that for these honored dead, we have increased devotion to that cause for which they gave the last full measure of devotion - that we here highly resolve that these dead shall not have died in vain -

that this nation, under God, shall have a new birth of freedom - and that government of the people, by the people, and for the people, shall not vanish from the earth".

Its aspiration and wish should be a spur to Americans all over to rid their land of **usurers** and move forward to prosperity and self achievement by pushing hard for government change to Lincoln's ideals of government financial control and bring back the definition in their constitution over money creation, taking it out of the hands of the usurers for good by creating a **irreversible act of government control of our paper money**.

Let us look back and reflect on Benjamin Franklin's reply while in England, when asked why the American colonies were so prosperous (Before the bankers controlled money supply). He replied "That is simple, in the Colonies we issue our own money, it's called colonial scrip. We issue it in proper proportion to make the products pass easily from the producers to the consumers. In this manner, creating ourselves our own paper money, we control its purchasing power, and we have no interest to pay to no one".

This speech warned the bankers to act to halt diversion from their policy and Rothschild, within one year, forced debt money on the colonies, reducing the money available and reversing the state of prosperity.

Our text books have lied to us about the cause of the Declaration of The War of Independence of 1776, blaming it on tea tax and the famous Boston Tea Party, Franklin said; "The colonies would gladly have borne the little tax on tea and other matters had it not been the poverty caused by the bad influence of the English bankers on the parliament; which has caused in the colonies hatred of England and the revolutionary war".

The founding fathers of the United States, in 1776, mindful of the turmoil and disruption created by the International Bankers, made sure in their constitution, signed in Philadelphia, Article 1, section 8, paragraph 5; "Congress shall have the power----to coin money and to regulate value thereof".

It is this very article that should have protected the United States against the bankers, but Rothschild's plan, through the war in 1812 was to impoverish the United States to such a degree they would be forced to renew the charter for the Bank of the United States. Thousands died, but this mattered little as long as Nathan Rothschild could achieve his objective. In 1816 he did.

But then came Abraham Lincoln, whose experience led him against the bankers. He tried his best, in midst of war, to fight the evil usurers but could not fight an enemy at both doors at the same time.

After the civil war of 1862 the bankers caused a deep recession. Business failures grew, and only the bankers, in the know, flourished. They of course did it by creating currency scarcity. By 1874 the signs of a boom gradually appeared but business still failed. Dr. Search **(212)** claims; "It is our selfishness and criminal legislation that has overwhelmed us with these alarming conditions".

Currency contraction between 1865 and 1877 fell from $1,651,282,373 to $696,443,394 with an increase of population from 35 million to 48 million and a per capita figure from $47.42 to $14.60. From there on in the bankers seemed to have enough ears to bend to introduce legislation as they wished. The only unknown was Abraham Lincoln.

He then made a famous public utterance that would seal his fate, already under advanced planning from England, by a Jewish group who had moved to Canada to fulfil their plan. Lincoln said; "I see in the near future a crisis approaching that unnerves me, and causes me to tremble for the safety of my country. As a result of war, corporations have been enthroned and an era of corruption in high places will follow, and the money power will endeavour to prolong its reign by working upon the prejudices of the people until all the wealth is aggregated in a few hands, and the republic is destroyed. I feel at this moment more anxiety for the safety of our country than ever before, even in the midst of war. God grant that my forebodings may be groundless".

It was clear then that Lincoln was set on finally destroying the bankers grip on money creation. So on the 14th. of April 1865 at Ford's Theatre, while the theatre was crowded, and in the middle of a performance, a man hired by the plotters, called Booth, slipped into the box occupied by Lincoln and his party, pointed his pistol at close range at Lincoln's head and fired. With this tragic episode America finally, and increasingly, fell into the grips of the bankers, led by Nathan Rothschild, and have remained in their bondage till today, a bondage that holds America in debt slavery. Yet most Americans know little of this. Amazing what a controlled press can do. Confusion and deceit was used to cover up the leader of the assassination which enabled him to cross the border into Canada and safety. Unfortunately for him he drank poison set up for another plotter and died. America, on the day of Lincoln's death, was robbed of its freedom so boldly fought for by Lincoln.

Finally on December 23rd. 1913 Congress voted in the Federal Reserve Act, which finally took the power of money creation from government and handed it over to the Federal Reserve Bank, a bank not owned by the state, as widely believed, but privately owned by a group of International Finance Capitalists, with no national loyalty, such as the Rothschilds and Rockefellers.

This bill prompted Charles A. Lindbergh Senior to comment; "This act establishes the most gigantic trust on earth. When the President (Woodrow Wilson) signs this bill, the invisible government of monetary power will be legalised----The worst legislative crime of the ages is perpetrated by this banking and currency bill".

The bankers had won and had a free run without serious challenge till John F. Kennedy challenged the power of the Federal Reserve Bank through Executive order 11110. In an article; "President Kennedy, the Federal Reserve and Executive order 11110" an explanation is shown of Kennedy's clear intention to reclaim the power of money creation back into government hands where it belongs. It was published in the 'Final Call' **(213).** Remember The Kennedy's were rich and therefore less corruptible.

THE FATAL CHALLENGE OF PRESIDENT JOHN. F. KENNEDY

On June 4th. 1963, a little known attempt was made to strip the Federal Reserve Bank of its power to loan money to the government at interest. President John F. Kennedy signed Executive Order No. 11110 that returned to the US government the power to issue currency without going through the Federal Reserve.

Mr. Kennedy's order gave the treasury the power "to issue silver certificates against any silver bullion, silver, or standard silver dollars in the treasury". This meant that for every ounce of silver in the US Treasury's vault, the government could introduce new money into circulation. In all, Kennedy brought nearly $4,300,000;000 in US notes into circulation. The ramifications of this bill are enormous.

With the stroke of a pen, Mr. Kennedy was on his way to putting the Federal Reserve Bank of New York out of business. If enough of these silver certificates were to come into circulation they would have eliminated the demand for Federal Reserve Notes. This is because the silver certificates are backed by silver and the Federal Reserve notes are not backed by anything.

Executive Order 11110 could have prevented the national debt from reaching its current level, because it would have given the government the ability to repay its debt without going to the Federal Reserve and being charged interest in order to create new money. Executive Order 11110 gave the US the ability to create its own money backed by silver.

After Mr. Kennedy was assassinated just five months later, no more silver certificates were issued. The Financial Call has learned that the Executive Order was never repealed by any US President through an Executive Order and is still valid. Why has no President utilised it?

Virtually all of the nearly $6,000,000,000,000 debt has been created since 1963, but if a US President had utilised Executive Order 11110 the debt would be nowhere near the current level. Perhaps the assassination of J.F.K. was a warning to future Presidents who might think of illuminating the US debt by cancelling the Federal Reserve's control over the creation of money.

Mr. Kennedy challenged the control of money by targeting the two causes of the increase of debt; war, and the creation of money by the privately owned banks. His efforts to have all troops out of Vietnam by 1965 and the execution of Executive Order 11110 would have severely cut into the profits and control, of the New York banking establishment.

As America's debt reaches unbearable levels and a conflict emerges in Bosnia and Afghanistan that will further increase American debt, one is forced to ask, will President Clinton have the courage to consider utilising Executive Order 11110, and, if so, is he willing to pay the ultimate price for doing so?

That Kennedy died for this cause is the most plausible explanation of his death, and it follows a list of Presidents who crossed the money barons. The most urgent cause in the world today is to neutralise the International Finance Capitalists.

CHAPTER TEN, PART TWO.
THE TRUTH OF OIL AND IT'S POWER THROUGH WEALTH

Without doubt, oil has been the power behind the formation of political boundaries in the last one hundred years. Behind this power are two governments, first Britain and, shortly afterwards, came America. At the end of the last century Britain was considered the main power in the world. Today America, now in control of the largest supply of oil, is the country controlling the world, and this progression of oil wealth from one country to another has been no mere chance; each inch of the way has been commercially and physically fought for and won.

In the early days of the liquid gold rush, real gold was considered to be the measure of a nation's strength, under the ever watchful eye of the Bank of England and the Rothschilds. Oil made the pound sterling an international currency that every trader craved for, and the gold pouring into the banks' coffers from all over the world was considered to be its guaranteed support.

This was the position at the beginning of the 1800's with Britain stretching out all over the world and extending credit to build ports, rail links and communications to help trade in remote areas, yet oil was not yet the new gold. But Britain's credit extension was having the effect at home of depriving British manufacturers and exporters of sufficient capital to extend and increase their foreign trade and maintain their domestic base.

So Britain, while building up its markets abroad was setting a limitation for its performance for the future at a time when its competitors, particularly America, could step in and take over the ground it had prepared.

But at this time Britain remained unchallenged, with the largest world fleet of ships controlling the seas, one of the three pillars of Britain's strength within the Empire and no one to challenge them.

Because of this strength, world traders were obliged to use British Insurance (Through Lloyd's) and banking facilities to undertake their particular trade. In this way the banks and Insurance houses of the City of London grew and prospered. The banks led the way; Barings, Hambros and Rothschild, who manipulated gold reserves to maintain world superiority. So banking again was forging the future which would not remain unchallenged for long.

Britain's third pillar of strength was its domination of the world's raw materials, coffee, tea, metals, cotton, and by the end of the 1800's a new future star, petroleum, not yet in mass use but geared to develop rapidly as the major, and vital, raw material. Then came an Act of Parliament that was complete lunacy. The Repeal of the Corn Laws, which effectively removed protective barriers to trade. The farmers were the first to suffer with their crop protection removed. In fact the only winners were the international traders (now the Multinational companies) and the bankers involved in exports and imports who flourished. Britain began to be flooded by cheap imports from India, Turkey, and China as well as others. It was an act to encourage the use of cheap labour, wherever it came from, much as the MAI agreement being discussed at this moment is a move to release Multinational companies from national control to follow the same course, which is against the interests of all individuals.

It has been argued, and there is evidence to show it to be true, that the first World War was a result of the repeal of The Corn Laws and the effect it had on Germany's trade. It is without doubt that the British Merchant Banks created large profits from this Act particularly in trade with Turkey, India, and China and especially in opium, a banned substance today. (Heroin.). This whole surge towards cheap imports was creating a problem at home; lack of investment. The capitalists learned that they could play the world, and their origin demanded no loyalty. The only loyalty they showed was to money, and money was to be made at that time in the Middle and far East. Home industry was being starved of modernisation and, indeed, funding. This was evident at the International Exhibition of 1867 from the exhibits of the English manufacturers compared with those from Germany and the Continent.

By the end of 1890 Britain no longer could claim to rule the world even though the bankers maintained their profits from the Empire. Their investments were now geared to their advantage, not necessarily England's. Internationalism was now under way and Britain was to be reduced gradually over the next one-hundred years to a ordinary nation by the powerful play of International Finance Capitalism, and it was heralded by the Great Depression 1873 to 1896. This could all have been avoided if parliament had not succumbed to the will of the bankers who demanded the Repeal of the Corn Laws.

Britain was now faced with a dilemma. How to remain powerful and influential in a changing world? The answer, for many, was oil, introduced as early as 1882. For Britain's role in oil supremacy, Britain's naval supremacy was vital.

Two events in Europe were to worry the banking elite and those few in the know about industry and its essential services that make it thrive. First Germany began to build a modern navy and merchant fleet to compete against Britain's superior rule of the sea.

The second warning of Germany's intentions were their railway link between Berlin and Baghdad, joining Germany with a rich market in Southern Europe and the Ottoman Empire.

This linked with Germany's policy of breaking away from Adam Smith's policy of free trade to a more balanced policy of Friedrich List, of protection for local national industries which proved a unstoppable formula for Germany, but worried Britain. Prussian technical education and superiority became evident in the Franco - Prussian War of 1870. This made England fearful and led to movements of reform in the English Education system. (Education act of 1870).

A measure of Germany's success can be simply shown by its steel production, between : 1880 and 1900 it increased 1000%. Farming too was making large progress, by 1913 Germany was 95% self sufficient in meat production while Britain imported 45% of its requirement at this time. So with everything going right for Germany by 1914 it was not surprising to find Germany's merchant fleet was second only to Britain's and showed German traders the way to soaring profits, but it also sparked the desire to remain dominant. War was already looming. It was by 1910, that petroleum became a grand player in the 'Push for Power' game and the bankers were to be seen jockeying for position.

It was a Berlin lamp manufacturer named Stohwasser who first used the black sludge that seeped through rock as a fuel for lamps. By 1870 John D. Rockefeller gave birth to the Standard Oil Company to promote oil for lamps and oil as a medical cure for skin ailments.

By 1882 Admiral Lord Fisher, was so impressed by this oil, that he saw a whole new way of powering ships and pushed hard for his naval fleet to be oil powered as it would give Britain an advantage at sea. He stated that it would reduce visibility of smoke trail which could be seen 10 kilometres away and it would allow ships to gain full speed in thirty minutes against four to nine hours required by coal fired ships. The production of oil fuel was most economical, twelve men could provide fuel for twelve hours use, while coal took five hundred men five days to produce the same. Fisher was indeed before his time, but only just.

Herr Daimler produced a petrol engine for a car by 1885 and the realisation of petroleum potential grew during the next twenty years.

In 1905 British Intelligence, with collaboration with the bankers around the government, decided that petroleum would be critical to Britain's future. But no deposits of crude oil had, at this time, been found in Britain.

So the search was on for a supply that would be safe in a time of war, from areas considered neutral. To facilitate this policy Sidney Reilly, the notorious double agent (Born Sigmund Rosenblum, in Odessa, Russia who Rakovski named as a agent of the Bankers was employed to gain access to the oil wells of Persia, the rights to which had been given to an Australian, William Knox d'Arcy for services rendered to Persia in modernisation by Railway and industrial development. William d'Arcy was given a sixty year lease on the land for a mere 20,000 dollars plus 16% royalty on extractions.

Reilly, knowing William d'Arcy's religious leaning, approached him in 1905, just before he signed a contract with the Rothschild Paris branch and persuaded him to sell to a 'Good Christian Company' Anglo - Persian Oil Company. Needless to say the British government's involvement was kept a secret as was the banker's Jewish connection. This was Britain's first source of oil and would be a major factor in her future as well as a major source of income for the British Rothschild bank.

Germany continued to attempt to get Britain involved in its Berlin to Baghdad railway but the English parliament wanted to delay the progress till they had control of the whole oil supply of Persia and Kuwait. By 1907 Sheikh Mubarak Al-Sabah, suitably bribed with rifles and gold, signed Kuwait's oil rights over to the British political agent, Major C.G. Knox and by 1913 the Sheikh signed an agreement not to sign over other land without British consent. They had the area covered, but the Berlin Baghdad railway was still a threat to Britain's command of the world markets by superior sea power. So Britain persuaded Kuwait's leader to allow the port of Shaat Al Arab to become a British protectorate. In this way the Germans were denied access to large areas of the Persian Gulf and beyond, maintaining Britain's superiority.

But Germany negotiated and gained a two kilometre strip each side of its railroad to Baghdad where it had the right to drill for oil. Up to this time Rockefeller's Standard Oil Company Trust controlled Germany's supply of oil. This could make Germany independent from American supply and delivery by sea. However the First World War came before this was possible.

Meanwhile, Britain, having realised the advantage of oil, was hard at work now under the New First Lord of the Admiralty, Winston Churchill, establishing a commanding position in this new trade, by buying a major shareholding in Anglo

Persian Oil (Now British Petroleum); from this moment oil was the centre of British strategic interest.

So the position at the start of the First World War was that although Germany had potential in what is now Iraq, it had no production, relying on America for supply. At this time (1912) America supplied 63% of oil available for world markets Russia 19% and Mexico 5%, most of which was under the control of Rockefeller.

Britain's power barons by now knew the only way to stunt Germany's successful economic and political growth, which was a threat to Britain's authority world-wide, was to manoeuvre Europe into war. To that end the King and his foreign minister Edward Grey met the French President Poincare in Paris along with Isnolski, Russia's Ambassador to France, prepared a secret alliance against Germany which wove a net of states around Germany that if attacked would bring Britain, France and Russia to their support. **(214).** This became known as Britain's 'Pro Russian and Anti German Alliance'.

So oil was already a political consideration of government in Britain through Rothschild's advice and finance. America in turn was being advised by Rockefeller, who at that time was ahead in the race to control oil and its sphere of influence. But Britain's reason to control oil was far more political than America's. Britain's agenda was domination of Europe and its target was Germany as the biggest challenge to Britain's authority. Oil was to be the new revolution, to replace the industrial revolution, and Britain must win. Germany and the Deutche Bank had other ideas, however they had to be shelved when World War One broke out.

Helfferich, brings to us a statement made by Bismarck in 1897 to illustrate the unfortunate difference between Germany and Britain, "The only condition that could lead to improvement of German - English relations would be if we bridled our economic development, and this is not possible". **(215).**

On July 28th. 1914, Archduke France Ferdinand, heir to the throne of Austria, was assassinated in Sarajevo by a Serb, which in turn set a process in motion which brought about the First World War. That this had been arranged by the bankers keen to stunt Germany's advancement has been a matter for debate but Rakovski confirmed the plot in his prison discussion. **(See page 108).**

To add trouble to Britain's already declining wealth the Declaration of War with Germany came at a time when the treasury was bankrupt. To prove this a treasury official for Sir George Paish, Basil Blackett, drafted a memorandum to Lloyd George referring to the effect of war on the gold reserves. He said; "It is of course impossible clearly to forecast what would be the effect of a general European War in which most of the continental countries as well as Great Britain were engaged, leaving only New York as neutral among the big money markets of the world available from which gold could be attracted to the seats of war". **(216).**

Sir George Paish himself, the same day wrote to Lloyd George; "The credit system upon which the business of this country is formed, has completely broken down, and it is of supreme importance that steps should be taken to repair the mischief without delay, otherwise, we cannot hope to finance a great war if, at its very commencement, our greatest houses (Banks) are forced into bankruptcy".

So payments in gold and silver were immediately suspended and the Bank of England notes were handed out in their place. As a consequence the bank vaults filled with gold and silver in time to fight the war.

The First World War was to prove that liquid gold (Oil) was the tool of the future and a successful military advance in mobility and speed of attack. But as war developed the use of the oil grew for ship power and plane power as well as land mechanisation and logistics of war material supply at point of use became critical. But the modern surge of mechanised power brought its terrible reward, some 18 million deaths, 10 million of which were civilians. Behind this policy of carnage were the merchant bankers, who pushed Britain to crush Germany and control the world through the supremacy of oil, towards a British led World Order called "The Great Game".

The blow that finally ended the First World War was the blocking of Baku on the Caspian Sea to the German General Staff, denying them vital oil supplies to continue the war. This was the last blow to an exhausted Germany. Peace followed within weeks.

It was an immoral war as far as Britain was concerned, as its main endeavour was to crush Germany's chance to establish a safe oil supply, so they would be independent of Britain or America. For this extravagance millions lost their lives while the International Finance Capitalists of the City of London gained a foothold in the oil business that would dominate future world development through the control of resources like oil. To these men of money, death was of little consequence. That the British government, even then, did their bidding, is totally relevant to the history of power. **(217).**

Britain's intent in the First World War shows itself quite clearly if you study the position of confrontation they adopted, quite often far from the concentration of action, but almost always with an end target to protect, oil rich areas. An example of this was the British campaign in the Dardanelles with its horrific defeat, which was an effort to secure the oil supplies of the Baku region, belonging to Russia, which they did for the crucial weeks, denying Germany access and creating oil starvation and eventual surrender. Oil defeated Germany, at least the lack of it.

France, in 1917 appealed to America to send oil as they could not continue war if oil was not sent immediately. Rockefeller's Standard Oil Group came to their rescue. Oil was now vital and supply routes critical. This was the lesson of World War One.

The most striking example of opportunism shown by England during that war was while France was energetically defending territory along the Maginot Line, Britain moved some 1.4 million troops into the Mediterranean and Persian Gulf, not for the reason they gave, to assist Russia, but to position themselves in readiness for the victory of peace and the prize of war, the control of the Basin of Oil in the area.

Control it they did, at the demand of the bankers of the City of London, the proof of which was exposed when a secret agreement was found by the Bolsheviks in 1917 on taking power, that the area had been divided up by the allies with Britain gaining the best part of the oil rich areas of the Ottoman Empire.

Only one major oil area today was not included in this carve up and that was Britain's big mistake, Saudi Arabia. But it retained Jordan, most of Iraq and Kuwait and important ports of Haifa and Acre. So Britain's stake today shows a large section of Middle East oil under its control; in reality under the control of the bankers.

Not only were the British well placed for rapid oil supremacy through this agreement but they had an army of one million well placed troops to protect their interests against any aggressor and they tricked the Arabs with promises of Independence to join forces to protect their territories; a trick which Lawrence of Arabia was to bitterly regret in his memoirs. **(218).**

Now came three events that shaped the course of the century. At the end of the war the treaty for peace was signed at Versailles. A treaty so terrible in its contents that it was difficult to see how any country could survive under its conditions. It was a treaty purposely designed to halt Germany's rapid growth and its authors could well be found in the City of London. The treaty, which gave France reparations for war far in access of its legitimacy, guaranteed Germany's demise and almost certainly laid the ground for a Second World War, to break out of the bonds of eternal slavery.

Just before the end of the war Russia was seized by the Bolsheviks and power was gradually secured; Russia was in the hands of Communism. (Founded by the Rothschild sphere of influence already discussed).

The third act came from Gentile Zionists (Gentiles that support Zionism) **(218a)**. In a letter from the British Foreign Secretary, Arthur Balfour to Lord (Walter) Rothschild a national homeland for the Jewish people was promised. Lord Rothschild was a representative of the English Federation of Zionists. **(219).**

From this tentative letter the course of Middle East politics was to erupt. Even in Jewish circles, the Zionist method of return to the Promised Land would be described by traditional Jewish Rabbi's and others as an act against all the teaching of the Torah, because of the violence involved and because the Messiah had not arrived to lead them back to their Promised Land. But here we had a member of the group that caused their expulsion in the first place (Usurers) forcing a solution against all the commands of the Torah. It was a sad day for Judaism, it showed that International Zionism was taking over its agenda.

Both Balfour and Lord Rothschild had a goal; a goal already being energetically pursued by Ruskin's disciples, whose founder, Cecil Rhodes, set in motion, what became the Round Table, a very anti German Pro Empire group; a group that replaced its idea of military presence with a Commonwealth of Nations, supported by a pretence of self-government; a group that had a grand illusion of independence. Such names as Albert Lord Grey, The Times Newspaper, Arnold Toynbee, H.G. Wells, and Alfred Lord Milner (Cecil Rhodes's mentor) were involved. It was not long before the League of Nations took up the call and the first soundings of a New World Order, a Global order, were made.

The strategic design was to link England's Colonial list of dependencies from the gold and diamond mines of Cecil Rhodes, Rothschilds gold fields in South Africa, the shipping routes around Kuwait, Persia and Eastwards, through the Suez Canal, giving the power of shipping from the Cape to Cairo. This would be a route controlling the world's most valuable assets, gold, the standard of the World's money, and oil, the mobility of the future. This added up to power and control and to gain this wealth Cecil Rhodes instigated the Boer War (1899-1902) a war financed by Rothschild. Finance to secure the wealth of the Transvaal, at the time, controlled by the Dutch Boer immigrants.

Again we see wars taking place to steal wealth from the occupiers of valuable territory. Again we see the hands of the Rothschilds influencing the outcome. **(220).**

Britain, more correctly, the Rothschilds, now controlled South Africa. While at this point the Rothschilds were rich beyond compare, Britain was still bankrupt, after the war in 1920.

In fact the debt by today's standards was small, a mere 4.7 billion, but in those days it was formidable. It was the bank J.P. Morgan and Co. of Wall Street who financed Britain's war. The total debt was 7.4 billion pounds. This was the period that heralded the take-over of banking power by Wall Street from Britain's sick economy. The powers of Britain, its pillars of strength, were now being strenuously attacked; Control of world money (banking), world sea power, and control of strategic raw materials. It was to be a heated financial and industrial battle between a unexpected pupil America and Britain. Surprising perhaps because we are constantly reminded of the 'Special Relations' we have with America. But as we have already seen, the news we read is increasingly controlled by the financiers who in turn control every move we have so far discussed, so it is not surprising that some of the facts you now read contradict the news you have read.

As you have seen, J.P. Morgan, acting as sole agent controlling war loans for Britain, at great risk, held the master card for America's future plans. Firms like Du Pont, who helped Morgan, grew into the Multinational companies they are today through their help.

Morgan could hold Britain down after the war, while America pushed forward. As a result Wall Street took over as financial centre of the world. Strictly speaking this was an illegal operation as all the neutral countries are bound to have no part in war supplies. By 1917 Morgan was only saved from bankruptcy when a American ship, carrying oil to Europe for the war, was sunk and America joined the war on April 2nd. 1917.

Now comes a staggering figure that heralds the future thrust of banking. Due to the World War the national debts of the world rose to a unprecedented two hundred and ten billion dollars, a rise of 475% in six years. The Wall Street traders and banks took the lion's share of this market in war related bonds. It is from the reparations of the Versailles Treaty that the truth of power is shown, whereby the Bankers wrote the figures and called the tune and the British and US Governments just complied. **(221).**

It was at this point that the Guardians of the Illuminati, at this time in the guise of the Round Table, formed a semi-official body called the Royal Institute of International Affairs, controlled by Lional Curtis. It was funded by Thomas Lamont, J.P. Morgan's partner. It was here we first see Arnold Toynbee, take the stage as its first paid staff member. (Toynbee went on to make his famous speech).
. At the same time a similar grouping of Illuminati was formed under the name of the New York Council for Foreign Relations (Now just the Council for Foreign Relations). In both groupings its members were continuing the policy of Weishaupt via Ruskin Via Cecil Rhodes along the lines of Marxism's high road through Finance, Masonry and International Zionism. **Direction.**

As this group wrote the official history of the Versailles Treaty it glossed over the probable disaster of the treaty to Germany and Europe, as the bankers used it to make money from the war and ruin Germany's chance of further expansion in trade. It has generally been accepted by unbiased historians that it was the eventual cause of the Second World War. This was the bankers' cream on the cake, as wars make them money, as Morgan found to his great advantage. But Germany, as losers had a war debt in reparations of $132 billion gold marks and worst still the occupation of the Ruhr valley, the heart of German industry. This was the price Germany paid for being a challenge to the bankers' supremacy. The most important shock to Germany's independence was the seizure of all its colonial possessions which included its share in the Middle East oil rights which was handed to France by Britain.

War debt overwhelmed the world with nations' debts to America and above all Germany's reparations. By 1929 realisation brought the depression which was again engineered by a small powerful group of bankers who avoided loss and moved money to safe areas while cashing in on the profits of recession, for one man's loss, played correctly, can be another man's gain. For greedy bankers Europe, leading up to and even during the recession, was a haven of plenty, with America's interest rate held down by Morgan and his man Benjamin Strong, at the Federal Reserve. They cashed in on the lucrative European high risk market, with high interest rates, cutting deep into Britain's traditional market and taking over the supremacy of the financial market while Britain was disabled by war debts. Increasingly the world was being run by financiers and politicians were becoming their puppets. **Direction.**

In the twenties Rockefeller realised, that while he developed his oil interests a whole world of lucrative speculation was passing him by. Even in oil, while he concentrated on US oil, Britain and its financiers had gained some of the richest oil wells in the world. In Britain, Rockefeller had been excluded from the drive for oil by his banking colleagues and also from the spoils of war.

Britain, through the bankers, interests, had developed Royal Dutch Shell and Anglo Persian Oil (now BP) without including Rockefeller in the deal.

In March 1921 Winston Churchill convened a meeting in Cairo that cemented the British bankers' supremacy of the Middle East oil, and Anglo oil officials took over effective administration of Iraq, with British Air Force planes based in Iraq, and denying America a chance to get a foot in the door. This ignited the flames of an Anglo American war for the control of new oil fields, as the Americans and particularly Rockefeller felt Britain was gaining the high ground for world oil domination.

Mexico became a battle ground for control but Britain's interests, headed by Weetman Pearson, (Later Lord Cowdrey) the Mexican Eagle Petroleum Company, was sacrificed by Britain because the prospect of a war with Germany was looming. So Rockefeller's Standard Oil Company ran guns and money to subvert the Mexican government and place their man Carranza in power. But Carranza turned his thoughts to national interests and a decision was made that he must go. He was assassinated in 1920, but he left his nation a legacy of control over its mineral and oil deposits by passing a law that excluded foreign sources from the right to use their mineral wealth for personal gain. You could say that this was a, "last laugh at the bankers".

Deterding's Royal Dutch Oil Co. Ltd., realising oil without transport was worthless at a very early stage merged with Shell Transport and Trading Co. owned by Marcus Samual (Lord Bearsted). Quickly, they became the world's most powerful oil based trust and challenged Rockefeller's Standard Oil in his home territory through its acquisitions, Roxana Petroleum and California Fields Ltd. The oil fortune of this marriage produced a protected trust that is today one of the most influential corporate groups, The Pearson Group, owners of the Economist, and Financial Times, as well as the merchant bank of Lazard Freres. Once again we see oil, bankers, and the media in an unhealthy alliance. **Direction.**

So through these and other concessions, Britain, who had 12% of oil produced world-wide in 1912 was, by 1925 controlling the major part of the existing oil fields and their future supply. The oil war was brought to a sudden halt by Germany in 1922, and the Rapallo Treaty was the reason.

To the astonishment of those present, the German Foreign Minister, Walter Rathenau announced that Russia and Germany had come to an agreement by which Russia would forget Reparations in exchange for industrial technology. Britain's bankers feared Russia would also include oil rights for Germany in the deal. So they pursued the oil rights for Baku with all their devious ability. But a relatively small group, the Sinclair Petroleum Company, negotiated an agreement with the Russians to develop Baku oil fields on a 50-50 joint venture agreement. However it was a deceit because Harry Sinclair was in fact a middle man for Standard Oil Company and his company had some interesting directors, Theodore Roosevelt Jr., son of the former President. Archibald Roosevelt, Vice President, his brother, and William Thompson, director of Rockefeller's Chase Bank. Sinclair's offer included a $115 million investment and a large loan to the Russian government. The loan overcame its main hurdle as Sinclair had close contact with President Harding. Russia was given diplomatic recognition despite the Bolshevik take-over of government by force with only 5% of the population of Russia supporting the Communists.

Deterding's Shell Group, incensed by the outcome, helped to spread a rumour of scandal involving grants of oil leases that resulted in a Congressional inquiry. It became headlines in the Wall Street Journal and within a year Harding died mysteriously and Coolridge, his successor, cancelled Russian Diplomatic recognition and the Sinclair deal died. Such were the wars for control of the oil fields that did not even respect Presidents.

In the chaos of this warfare Germany pulled a flanker and signed a deal for technology in exchange for oil from Baku, allowing Germany to escape the ravages of taking oil from Britain or America.

Germany soon had an answer to the Rapallo agreement with Russia; on the 22nd. of June 1922 Walter Rathenau, Germany's foreign minister, was assassinated outside his home, and it was passed over as a right wing anti-Semitic act; it was the murder of one of the Illuminati Guardians, their own top men; which shows that they can kill their own for money. But the murder has been challenged since, and it has been suggested that those who gained from the death were in fact Britain's oil barons; an in house murder.

The murder of Rathenau started the slide of financial affairs in Germany, and the reparations committee, led by France, trumped up a shortage in reparations from Germany to France and ordered the occupation of the Ruhr. This brought Germany's industry to a halt as they refused to co-operate with the occupation.

Germany, to continue payments to England, printed money, causing inflation. They withheld payments from France, Italy and Belgium, being part of the occupation. Britain outwardly objected to this course. In consequence, Germany's currency was ruined, the savings of all Germany were laid to waste. The entire structure of Germany by the middle of 1923 was in ruins.

Germany was forced to concede to France and its occupiers. But America took over the initiative and the Dawes plan was the result of the Anglo American banking communities effort to stabilise the reparations and force financial control on Germany. For the next five years Germany paid reparations under the Dawes Plan but by 1929, owed more than when they started because Dawes and his London and New York bankers ran a scheme of usurious looting. The bankers then worked a scheme to lend money to Germany causing an enormous International Credit Pyramid, benefiting the London and New York bankers. In 1929 the Pyramid collapsed and the credit flow to Germany stopped. The bankers had pulled the plug. **(222)**.

The other war between America and Britain for oil supremacy had to come to an end, and in 1927 the Anglo American oil cartel, now known as the 'Seven

Sisters' was formally constituted at a shooting estate owned by Shell's Sir Henri Deterding, between Shell Oil, Anglo Persian Oil (BP), and Rockefeller's Standard Oil (Exxon). This formally ended the trade war by accepting the existing market shares enabling them to form a secret world price cartel that would fleece the world for all its worth. Any threat to break this cartel has been met with violence as we will soon see. By 1932 the other major oil companies joined the cartel Esso, Mobil, Gulf Oil, and Chevron. Together this formed the most powerful cartel the world had ever known. That it was also controlled by two of the most powerful banking families in their world, the Rothschilds and the Rockefellers, is a matter that should cause deep concern to us as collectivism and price fixing is the high road to a corporate control by Communism. **Direction.**

By October 1929, Montague Norman, governor of the Bank of England, requested the governor of the Federal Reserve Bank, George Harrison, to increase the interest rate. He did, and caused a gigantic financial collapse in America.

Ripples were felt in Europe when the Austrian Credit Anstalt Bank, through justifiable rumours, had a run on its deposits and became the largest bank failure in Europe. This started the collapse of the house of cards as Austria called in all funds from Germany to cope with the collapse. The effect was felt throughout Europe, but in Germany particularly, who only needed slight ripples to topple its fragile balance in its economy, under siege from reparations.

A decision to cut all credit lines to Germany made the situation worse and capital flowed out of Germany. Germany was bankrupt, but cynically bankrupted by the bankers intended plan.

Then came an attempt by a Swedish industrialist, Ivar Kreuger, through his American bankers, Lee Higginson, to make a loan offer to Germany in early 1930. But it was against Montague Norman and his banking friends long term plans and the loan was turned down by the Reparations Committee. Some months later Kreuger was found dead in his Paris hotel. Swedish inquiries found he had been murdered. The people who had most to gain from Kreuger's death were bankers in London and New York.

Schacht, who resigned as President of the Reichsbank had been busy. He had been backing the NSDAP party of Adolf Hitler since 1926. Now he promoted Hitler as the strong man of Europe. Montague Norman, and his banking friends, knowing exactly the direction Hitler would go, helped persuade the New York bankers, led by Paul Warburg, **that he would be a buffer in Europe that would stabilise Russia's uncertain action** (See Rakovski's interview page 108) **as Stalin had snatched power after Lenin's death. This decision was made by International bankers in full knowledge of Hitler's likely course including his anti Jewish policy. This policy set off a most despicable roll-call of support and appeasement.**

The truth was that Russia, controlled by the Bolsheviks, who in turn were funded by the Rothschilds, had lost control of Russia when Lenin died and Stalin snatched power. Stalin was not under the Guardians influence, which was a major set back to the Rothschilds' revolution. So through their influence in England and America, they set about installing a strong man in Europe to act as a buffer. Hitler was their choice. The English political world under Rothschild's influence complied with their wish.

Neville Chamberlain, Britain's prime minister, even eased Hitler's passage to war, and his advisor, Lord Lothian, actually backed the Hitler project as did Lord

Beaverbrook, a press baron of the time, and King Edward VIII, king of England, was an admirer of Hitler. (The Duke of Windsor after his abdication).

On January the 4th. 1932 Baron Kurt Von Schroeder, Adolf Hitler, Von Papen and the bankers from Cologne, Von Schroeder, agreed the financing of Hitler's NSDAP and by January 30th. 1933 Hitler became Chancellor of the German Reich. Financial support from Deterding's Dutch Shell followed for Hitler. This was followed by a visit to Germany by Montague Norman in 1933 when he arranged credit for Hitler's government and again in 1934 to stabilise loans. **(223).**

So International Bankers continued to fund Adolf Hitler, but more surprisingly they were led by International bankers from Wall Street and London, despite full knowledge by this point of Hitler's Jewish policy which although not generally known was known by the banking circles.

War from this point on was inevitable, and the bankers had engineered it into this impossible position for their own gain with no regard for death and financial ruin their actions would cause. Their object was to move the world towards revolution, a Marxist revolution. **Direction.** (See Rakovski interview pp108).

The Second World War lasted six years and over 55 million people lost their lives. A horrific story that should move the hardest person. Not so the bankers. They only used selective details from these statistics to silence anyone who criticised their actions. But they were partly responsible for the mass murder of these unfortunate people on all sides of the war.

The war had brought other realities. Britain was hard pressed to exist let alone control and mind over its Empire. Its trading routes were shattered and its whole structure required attention, even the population was exhausted by war..

It needed America's help to exist. America, seeing its chance to develop where Britain left off, encouraged Britain's dependence and used its expertise to take over the dream of Ruskin and Cecil Rhodes for a New World Order, a supreme world government. Little did they realise that this dream had been fed to them by disciples of Weishaupt, the world Masonic Movement, and the Internationalists led by the world bankers with clout from the media, under their control. They had carefully placed their two channels of communication and propaganda in position earlier in the century, the Royal Institute of International Affairs and its equivalent in New York, The Council for Foreign Relations. This, and America's war time security link between the American Office of Strategic Services, OSS and Britain's Special Operations Executive (SOE) developed into a collaboration, after the war, between MI6 and the CIA and the FBI and MI5. The game, Churchill's big gamble. His Iron Curtain speech on March 5th. 1946, spread a false belief that Russia, under Communism, was our enemy, which ignored America's continual and increasing efforts to modernise and finance Russia's stagnating industry and defence ability. America, and particularly Zionist bankers were financing the modernisation of Russia while the world thought, through the media's lies, that the world was in danger from the 'Cold War' and Russia did everything to encourage this as it helped to build up its defences and act as a mirror to hide a Marxist policy towards a world revolution, which their agents in America were actively preparing..

Meanwhile Anglo American Co-operation in oil policy was paying handsome dividends to the small group of bankers and businessmen involved. Rothschild and Rockefeller being the two banking giants with most to gain, both committed to promote a movement to a New World Order and the target, A World Government that was controlled by their agenda, outside democracy.

So enter left, Harry Dexter-White, assistant US Treasury Secretary. After discussions with Lord Keynes, he formed an agreement in 1944 named the Bretton Woods Agreement, the forerunner to the United Nations. It was accorded much publicity and explained as a benefit to nations through its three pillars of support.

Its member state contributions would act as an emergency fund for countries with balance of payment problems. A World Bank, which would fund member countries for large public projects, and the third pillar was a General Agreement on Tariff and Trade, GATT, to promote free trade. Oil revenue would fund the World Bank. It seemed a selfless scheme to help the Third World countries, but much would develop to show it was nothing of the sort, but an audacious scheme to enslave the third world countries with difficulties, and rob them of their mineral deposits while overwhelming them with national debt.

The first hint of something wrong came when Harry Dexter White was accused of passing American secrets to a foreign power. He was accused of being a Russian agent as you will see later.

Britain and America had voting control of The International Monetary Fund and the World Bank. All currencies were to be pegged to the dollar and the dollar was set against gold at $35 per ounce.

Of course the dollar had been the strongest world currency since the war, as the Wall Street bankers had gained fortunes from war bonds and loan repayments. No country could challenge the dollar. It was further strengthened when Winston Churchill allowed Saudi Arabian oil deposits to slip out of Britain's hands and into America's waiting grip of Rockefeller's Standard Oil and the Mellon family's company, Gulf Oil. This was America's first step to control foreign oil but by no means the last. It would become a cornerstone of its future power.

Coupled with this, the New York Federal Reserve Bank cornered the lion's share of the gold reserves during the Second World War, leaving America with a strong economy while just after the war, Britain suffered from six long years of conflict, no money, and a mountain of debt. All this and other events led to America taking over the world initiative and leadership from a crippled, but victorious Britain. This must pose the question whether being a victor is any better than being the vanquished when such decline in status is the end result.

The Marshall Plan was also to rob Britain of part of its oil market as oil supply (At a price) was part of the plan to help Europe recover from war. It would be American oil not British in a market Britain considered its own. **(224).** In every direction America was taking over the initiative from Britain.

Then came two more events that would seal the fate of Britain's decline and bolster the American bankers' prestige world-wide which finally handed the world agenda over to the bankers of Wall Street.

The first issue to present itself was the result of the bad handling of Iranian diplomacy by Britain at the demand of the bankers who owned the oil rights. Britain had pulled out all the stops to get the Iranian oil rights, but needed Stalin's help to protect them against the falsified claim that German oil experts were already encamped in the neutral zone. Russia sent its troops into Iran in 1948 and immediately started a systematic campaign of robbing the Iranians of the little food they had to feed their people. The result was tens of thousands of the Iranian people died while the Russian and British troops, with a small American contingent, were well fed. To add insult to injury, by sequestration of the Iranian Railroad the Anglo-American force, blocked the urgent transport of food and particularly heating oil in the winter of 1944-45, which killed thousands more Iranians, just to supply

Russia with lend-lease goods from America. This gave the Iranians just cause to hate the English, American, and Russian occupiers who were only there to protect their oil rights owned by not the countries, but the bankers.

After the war the politicians of Britain, America and Russia placed a mirror in front of the true agenda when Churchill, Roosevelt and Stalin signed an agreement to restore Iranian sovereignty.

Behind this erected mirror Britain demanded further oil concessions for Royal Dutch Shell, and Russia demanded a large exclusive right on the Northern territory, bordering Azerbaijan.

It was at this moment that Dr. Mohammed Mossadegh introduced a bill in the Iranian Parliament to prohibit any oil rights being negotiated by foreign countries. However this did not include the Anglo Iranian Oil Company concession, which was to be debated separately. This action, taken to the new United Nations, finally forced the foreign troops from their land, but the economy of Iran was still under British control through the Anglo Iranian Oil Company. As an example of the profit the Anglo Iranian Oil Company made out of Iranian oil, in 1948 it was $360 million and they paid Iran $36 million. Iran justly claimed they were being underpaid for their precious commodity and Britain's response was faked news reports by the BBC against Iran, designed to weaken its government's resolve. In the lead up to the election in 1951, both Britain and American propaganda claimed Mossadegh was a puppet of the Tudeh Communists, Russia and many other extreme elements, but he was a patriot to his country, and an enemy of Russia. On March 15th. 1951, the Iranian parliament, the Majlis, voted in Mossadegh's nationalisation plan for Anglo Iranian oil and on April 28th. 1951 Mossadegh was asked to form a government. This was seen as treason by Britain. (That means the bankers). Britain responded by a military exercise based at Basra (Iraq) a British controlled port.

Britain canvassed support from the Seven Sisters and started the strangulation of Iranian oil sales which bankrupted Iran. Mossadegh, in desperation, went to the UN for help to no avail, as the agenda was firmly with the bankers and then to Washington to be met by a stone wall of oil interests led by Averill Harriman. Yet Iran was fully in its rights to nationalise a company on its soil which was harvesting Iranian assets, provided Iran paid compensation which the Iranian government had already agreed to honour. So you see the combined power of banking and the oil cartel with their accomplice the United Nations brought a country to its knees. Britain, under Churchill, and America under Eisenhower, joined forces and planned Mossadegh's downfall with the co-operation of the Shah and his Generals, who wished to regain power. The CIA and the British SIS formed a joint operation code named 'Ajax' to overthrow Mossadegh and by August 1953 he was ousted from power, for oil, for power of oil, and for money, not for Britain, America, or right. The mirror of Communism was used to accomplish this infamous act. So many future battles, would reflect the same diversion from truth. The truth was that wars are to protect the banking and oil cartel against loss of its dubious rights.

Following on from this, revenge was also wreaked upon those who offered Mossadegh a life line while his oil was banned from the world markets by Britain and America. One such man was Enrico Mattei, the head of Agip. His job, as head of Agip was to build up an energy policy for the future, from an economy in ruins from the war. His first task was to find oil and gas supplies. He found gas and oil at Cortemaggiore in 1949. Mattei was a staunch nationalist, the enemy of bankers and Multi Nationals, who do not approve in national power. Oil companies do not like upstarts who find oil and rescue their country from the burden of imports. This is exactly what Mattei did for Italy. He also built a 2,500 mile pipeline to take the gas reserves to industry. This brought the wrath of the Cartel named by Mattei, 'The Seven Sisters'. His policy was to produce oil at the lowest price. In this he also crossed the Seven Sisters and their lapdogs, the Governments of Britain and America.

He accused the Seven Sisters of controlling production to maintain a high price and pressed on developing Agip along his own lines. He built Agip into a powerful player in oil and by 1958 Natural Gas sales topped $75 million, but, more important, it was to save dollar imports and rescue a beleaguered Italian economy. In the fifteen years after the war no man did more for Italy's economy. But no man annoyed the banking and oil cartel more, especially when he broke their blockade of Iran.

Meanwhile, the owners of Anglo American Oil changed its name to British Petroleum and were given 40% of the old concession with Royal Dutch Shell with a further 14%, giving Britain over 50% of oil production in Iran. American, oil companies, mostly owned by Rockefeller, got 40% between them, and France 6%.

Mattei, rejected by the 'Seven Sisters' when he applied to have a part of the Iranian oil concession, made a quick, quiet deal with Nasser, to extract oil out of Egypt around the Sinai Peninsula and to refine it at the ENI refineries for Italian consumption, again without having to pay in dollars and becoming a dollar slave.

His confidence growing, Mattei threw down the gauntlet to the oil cartel in 1957. He negotiated an agreement with the Shah of Persia that gave Iran 75% to ENI's 25% to develop 8,000 square miles of Northern Iran not allocated to other agreements.

At home he also attacked the cartel's pockets by underselling them at the pumps and forcing them to compete. The gainer, Italy's consumers and transport structure.

The negotiations with the Shah were a red rag to the Seven Sisters, Britain, and America. On the one hand, if the Seven Sisters let Mattei into their exclusive cartel the German and French and others would all want to be in and they would begin to lose control of power. So instead they protested to the Shah against Mattei's deal, but the deal was signed in August 1957, and SIRIP, the joint venture between Italy and Iran was under way.

Mattei, making his presence felt, began a new policy to develop smaller oil fields, which the Seven Sisters had rejected as unworkable. He negotiated to produce refined oil on the spot, building local refineries and breaking a golden rule of the Seven Sisters.

But the final blow to Britain, America and the Seven Sisters was when Mattei arrived in Moscow in October 1958 and signed an agreement with Russia that would enlarge Russia's capacity to deliver oil to its satellite countries, countries that the Seven Sisters considered their patch. The deal simply swapped oil for a much needed pipe line to deliver oil and gas around the satellites. Russia had no facility for such a pipe. It was a stroke of genius by Mattei, that cost him the ultimate price.

On October 27th. 1962 Enrico Mattei's work was brought to an abrupt end when his private plane crashed on take off from Sicily, killing all three on board. So ended many lives of people who got in the way of the Seven Sisters and the bankers. Needless to say no proof of murder was found, but it wouldn't be, given the circumstances. Two others who preceded him, Abraham Lincoln a United

States President, and Ivar Kreuger, a Swedish financier, both drew swords with the banking and oil barons and both ended up dead in suspicious circumstances.

Immediately the Media **(225)** gave us a story of a clandestine magnet that was a secret Communist. This was of course a lie. A lie used so often by the media under the bankers control when they, themselves, financed and controlled Communism from the start.

Mattei did more for post war Italy than any other Italian industrialist of the time. He was a patriot and a nationalist, and as such, was the most dreaded enemy of Communism. At the time of his death Mattei was arranging to meet John F. Kennedy to discuss detente with the Seven Sisters.

It was a little over a year after Mattei died that John F. Kennedy died also and in all the disinformation that has been spread by the Media, the poodle of the bankers, we will find lacking the most obvious reason for his assassination that fits all the main criteria, including, who gains?

The late 50's and 60's brought a bonding between Germany and France, Adenauer and De Gaulle. A bond that now rules the EU policy. This sent shock waves through England and particularly America, as a challenge to its strength, especially as De Gaulle had opted out of NATO to form his own defence and nuclear capability. It was attacked as a wild cat in a stabilising world. As a counter attack on the strong Europe of De Gaulle and Adenauer, Kennedy's team proposed a Europe along the lines of Jean Monnet, a market that would open its doors to American imports and be a strong member of NATO, dominated by America and Britain, and incidentally demanded that Britain should be a member of the then six nations of the Common Market. De Gaulle opposed Britain's entry. Just as Adenauer was about to complete his life's work of the French-German accord, and following external pressure from America, Adenauer was de-selected and replaced by Ludwig Erhard, in April 1963. Erhard was a fierce opponent of De Gaulle and favoured the American style Common Market with British participation. Even though the Adenauer-De Gaulle accord was ratified it was shelved. Britain and America satisfied themselves they had blocked a dangerous move to strengthen Europe.

It was at this time that a Harvard Professor, Dr. Henry Kissinger, became inter-linked with the Rockefeller Group. (Very important **Direction**, he is a key player).

Kissinger was under John J. McCloy, who brought him into his team to draft policy at 'The Council for Foreign Relations', a radical liberal group controlled by the Rockefellers. In fact at the time McCloy was a top lawyer and Chairman of the Chase Manhattan Bank, the oil barons' bank. The overall view was clouded by their wealth. They viewed the world as their sole market and interference as a dispensable irritation. (Like Mattei).

From 1957 we see the media under the control of this oil cartel coming into play, and moving the debate in the media towards the international banks of Manhattan and Wall Street, through national newspapers' and television's selective coverage, moving the debate away from the interests of the country as a whole, towards the narrow interests of the bankers linked to radical liberal policies.

Directly from the radical liberal thinking, of which Kissinger was a part, America stepped away from heavy investment in local industry, which as Henry Ford once stated, would make him the richest man alive, to a policy of foreign investment in the cheapest labour areas. A buy cheap, sell dear policy.

This banker-led dumping of local labour, led to the collapse of pride in production, which has led to poor quantity both in Britain's and America's remaining industrial base. Meanwhile the traitorous bankers continue to make a killing. Industry in this way started to cut corners, to compete, and standards fell, while car accidents and deaths rose in proportion to falling safety design, to cheapen production costs. To prove this in 1955 the American car industry used 19 million tons of steel. By 1958, three years later, this had fallen to 10 million tons for a similar output.

All this was inflicted on industry and the people, to suit the bankers' lust for profit, with no loyalty to national pride, something the bankers didn't understand and wouldn't accept. This was followed by the exodus of investment in America in the late 50's led by the New York bankers, who looked for fast profits (High interest rates) in Europe, the Pacific Rim and the Third World, to exploit cheap labour. The British bankers had already gone this way after the Second World War, leaving industry without much needed modernisation and development capital, the policy named 'Monetarism', and practised by all Multi-nationals today. **Direction.** So money flooded out of America and England to where it could double its profit from financing public works and modernisation ignoring the home market. The end result of this was that the home based multinationals were to look for cheaper labour and moved their factories to locations where cheap labour existed like the Pacific Rim.

It would not have been so bad for America if only the dollar left their shores but the banks, to suit their policies, exported gold as well, which, by the end of the 50's was spelling trouble for the Briton Woods Monetary System, the heart of the post war American success story.

The trouble came as gold value throughout the world established a 'Gold Exchange Standard' through Briton Woods for all members of the International Monetary Fund, not a national currency link to gold direct but through the dollar value of gold; the rate to the ounce was $35. This was set by Roosevelt in 1934, during the depression, with no account or change for war or post war conditions. Now this was all right if the dollar remained the only strong currency, but by the early sixties Europe was economically outshining the USA and conflict was certain with dollar exchange due to Europe's strong currency, and a re-appraisal of the set dollar-gold ratio was badly needed. But Washington, now completely controlled by the Wall Street bankers, failed to expose the danger.

The bankers of New York, thinking they controlled the system, saw nothing wrong in their policy. As International Bankers, they saw no national danger as the world was now their state. The result was that the stronger currencies kept overheating the system and the New York bankers, making huge profits from external investments (Between 10-14%), would not forsake their gravy train for the sake of the dollar, causing increasing international monetary crises. Behind the scenes they even lobbied Washington to leave them alone, causing the formation of what became the Eurodollar market of which British oil markets were a sizeable part, while America, through the greed of its bankers, spread its domestic inflation around the world.

President Kennedy, realising the danger that the bankers' power and position was causing to the domestic base of America's economy sought to redress the situation by taking back money creation into government hands and accordingly, after secret discussions with several top advisors, passed Executive order 11110 (as referred to in part one of chapter ten) to take back money creation from the private banking system of the Federal Reserve Banks, in order to control and manage domestic money supply without interference and more importantly influence from the New York banking power lobby. It was a brave attempt to right the wrongs the bankers had imposed on the American domestic economy and return money creation to its proper place, the government, not commercial private control.

Kennedy paid a high price for his betrayal of banking power. Six months after passing his Executive order 11110 he was shot dead by a gunman while travelling in an open car through Dallas. The media, the poodles of the bankers, sprang into action with ids-information theories; it was the Mafia, the Cubans, The Right Wing, The Unions, you name it, everyone he had annoyed. But no one in the press mentioned this Executive Order and its consequences for the bankers. If they had, the old question asked by criminologists 'who gains' would be answered, **"the bankers"**. It followed a long list of deaths of people who crossed their path like Matte. It is also the most logical explanation for a reason for his murder. It was another highly professional hit, a very expensive contract.

On November 22nd. 1963 Linden B. Johnson succeeded Kennedy. With Kennedy's death, died hopes of rescuing America from its bankers, its only **real** enemy.

LBJ, as he became known, wasted no time in cancelling Kennedy's policy of money creation; but to this day the Executive order 11110 has not been rescinded and therefore a bold President could use it again. Alas LBJ was a man controlled by the bankers.

LBJ put his energy into opening up the Vietnam conflict from a 'Technical Advisory Roll' to a full scale conflict, pouring half a million soldiers and billions of dollars into a war he could not win, but that would make huge profits for the bankers through the arms trade. They actually started to invest again in arms related home production to grab the high returns, showing their fickleness where greed rules the conscience and marginalises moral right.

Again, the bankers forced war on America to develop, for profit, the arms trade, helped by politicians who are under their influence. The result of this terrible time was called 'The Age of Aquarius', when the hippie movement was formed. But little known is the secret work carried out by the CIA and British and American scientists code named Mk-Ultra **(226)** which carried out experiments on mind altering drugs and sent home, from Vietnam, a whole generation of youth from a immoral war, if they were lucky enough to survive, to be alienated by the experiments that their country saw fit to expose them too. It created a culture of drug crazed hippies who have led a moral decline, ever since their creation within our society. Not content with this, the corporate scientists went to work on middle management within industry, using psychologists from national training centres to give them 'Sensitivity Training', brain washing them to accept corporate changes and most importantly blurring their notion of national pride.

In 1968 Robert Kennedy made his play for power. He was not under the bankers influence and was deemed to be a danger as was his brother, so before he could be elected he was killed by a lone assassin in Los Angeles. Was this again a convenience killing? Shortly afterwards, civil rights leader Dr. Martin Luther King died outside his Memphis Hotel. He was there to lend his office to try to stop the bankers using the South as a cheap labour area. He too was treading on the bankers toes. He too died.

Industry in the North started to move to the South to chase cheap, non union labour. Unemployment grew in the North with all the city decay and depravation that followed. But the bankers and their companies made greater profits while disinvestment in US industry began to show real effect while even the blue collar workers were drawn into the skirmish for jobs. This was all part of President Johnson's 'War on Poverty', a policy which created more unemployment to break resistance to the wage shrinkage to follow for the whole of the American population, using the rage card as a tool to success.

They successfully broke the back of labour unions as well as weakening political lobbies while the liberal media, under bankers' control, spread the word of **Radical Liberalism,** till people started to believe black was white. So confused were the people that the bankers could do anything they wanted. So they moved industry to cheap labour areas or abroad and continued disinvestment in America. They re-invested in Asia or South America, betraying their fellow Americans. (But you must remember the agenda was firmly in the hands of International Bankers that did not accept America as their nation, rather the whole world as their state).

So who is our enemy? **The Vietnamese or the Bankers?**

The truth is that while America was depicted in the press as the capitalist state holding back Communism in Vietnam, it was at the time, within its nation, pitting workers against workers, to benefit the bankers of Communism; the Wall Street gang of Traitors; the Guardians.

The fact that the media portrayed America as their hero against Communism, was all part of the mirror of deception, hiding the true agenda, **preparing America for the world government revolution, based on Communism, led by the Guardians.**

I know this is hard to grasp as the media has consistently told us differently, but this is the **hidden agenda** of the media who are controlled by the bankers and maintaining the bankers deception. **Direction.**

Another important **Direction** we find when analysing this history of events is that the bankers create the agenda, while the politicians just go along with the result, but the media falsely lead us to believe decisions are political. (An exception of course was Kennedy who was free from corruption by money. He paid the price of opposing the bankers).

Vietnam was a disgraceful war, created by bankers who wanted to boost arms sales. It was never the threat to the world depicted by our media. The American people should be worried how such a small minority group, however powerful, could influence the political agenda to such a degree. We will see later how deceit and corruption rose to the top of the political structure, encompassing Presidents and even to top civil servants with an anti-National agenda.

In chapter ten part four we will see how America supplied arms and technology to Russia which were used against their own troops in Vietnam. You have also seen how the troops were prepared for battle by cynical drug use and abuse, making them brave for battle but leaving them afterwards, to survive, dependent on the drug culture. (That the enemy within could influence the government into experiments on people with drugs to change attitudes and create a new culture of hippie New Age people is frightening, but the CIA did just that with project MF-Ultra). It is a disgraceful episode in American history and its source must be neutered for Western Democracy to survive. We must turn and oppose the real enemy; the enemy within, who, to further their aim, think nothing about death and destruction involved in conflict.

Once more the City of London bankers moved to take advantage of the flow of dollars out of America. They set up a Eurodollar market to compete and outstrip Wall Street, money dependent on Eurodollar oil sales forming a chest of money in the region of $1.8 trillion of hot money that was handled off shore to avoid national taxes, attracting all the criminal wealth to invest in the Eurobonds as no name was attached to these bonds.

Ironically, in the sixties, British industry was sick and its decline started to put pressure on Stirling, one of the pillars of the Bretton Woods. Coupled with the dollar's exodus from America at an alarming rate. (Due to the bankers policy). The Bretton Woods agreement was facing collapse. The British bankers were also exporting Stirling abroad, leaving British industrial base starved of much needed investment capital for modernisation and development. It was not helped by the maintenance of high interest rates by the banks themselves to attract the flow of cash to London markets.

By 1967 France, under De Gaulle, withdrew from the world gold pool, fearing an imminent collapse.

First Britain devalued by 14%. But America refused to devalue the dollar and the result was rapid, a surge in demand in payment in gold which depleted gold stock to an all time low of $12 Billion.

This couldn't go on. A meeting of the holders of gold was held in Stockholm and the Special Drawing Rights (SDR) agreement was signed.

However at the IMF meeting a month later France blocked this move.

Retaliation was swift; London and New York bankers started a panic run on the Franc and the bankers were helped by the media who promoted their cause. The French student riots were a direct response to the bankers but in the panic of 68 France's gold resources were reduced by 30%, creating a serious financial crisis. Within a year De Gaulle was ousted and once again the Anglo American Bankers won another victory.

In 1968 South Africa, being one of the large gold mining countries, rebelled against the pegging of gold to $35 an ounce. A boycott on South Africa followed, outwardly blamed on racial problems for public consumption; it was once again a mirror deception of the true reason that the bankers were quietly cornering the world gold stock.

So, you can see how the bankers deal swiftly and decisively with anyone who gets in their way. The Guardians control all the gold in the bank vaults. **Direction.**

The result of the bankers' policy in the sixties and the reluctance of political will to correct the gulf between the gold value and the dollar, and tame the Eurodollar reaped its tragic reward in the seventies; apart from the continual outflow of dollar capital from America, the recession brought endless hardships and panic. Something had to be done, gold reserves only covered one quarter of the official liabilities, leaving America technically bankrupt on paper if a run on gold should occur.

So, on August 15th. 1971, advised by his close aid, General Shultz, and a treasury official, Jack F. Bennett, (Later made a director of EXXON) Paul Volker, and Richard Nixon, shocked the world by suspending the dollar conversion into gold, putting the world onto a direct dollar standard, with no gold to back it. This plucked the heart out of the Bretton Woods agreement but for America, more importantly, foreign investors in Eurodollars could no longer ask for gold in exchange for their dollars.

Then came the fight for a reasonable devaluation of the dollar to gold around $70 an ounce, but the bankers wanted no change while gold flowed their way.

It has been suggested that the men behind Nixon's decision to suspend dollar conversion were London Merchant bankers, Sir Siegmund Warburg, Edmund De

Rothschild, Jocelyn Hambro and others, so that London could capture the Eurodollar initiative and regain a world status. **(227)**.

From this point on, America's policy was to control not to develop economies throughout the world. A policy devised by Dr. Henry Kissinger. (A major player in world government).

By 1972 Nixon once more devalued the dollar to $42.22 an ounce and from this move developed a more flexible 'managed float'. Still the dollar lost ground, dropping 40% one month against the Deutschemark. The bankers' greed has all but ruined the world's strongest currency. That the political agenda was controlled by the bankers comes over clearly when you study events leading up to 1973 when positive proof of where the power lay was first disclosed.

In May 1973 at Saltsjoebaden, in Sweden, 84 of the worlds most powerful bankers and their trusted political insiders met under the Chairmanship of Prince Bernhard's Bilderberg group. This group met in total secrecy and has been doing so since 1954. **Direction. A meeting called by the Guardians.**

This particular meeting was addressed by Walter Levy, who discussed a plan to increase oil prices by 400% on OPEC petroleum revenues. This was not a meeting to prepare the world's response to the OPEC price increase but to plan it before presenting it to OPEC. It was a planning meeting to manage the flood of dollars that would circulate the world if left to roam and direct them back into investment in America. Among those present at the meeting **(228)** were Lord Greenhill, Chairman of BP, Sir Eric Roll from S.G. Warburg and the originator of the Eurobonds, George Ball of Lehman Brothers, Investment bankers who tipped off Sir Siegmund Warburg to go into Eurobonds 10 years before. David Rockefeller, of Chase Manhatten Bank, Zbigniew Brzezinski, later President Carter's national security adviser. Germany's Otto Wolff Von Amerongen and Italy's Gianni Agnelli. A regular attendee at the Bilderberg meetings is Dr. Henry Kissinger. (A name to watch as this story unfolds).

What you have just read has frightening implications for democracy. First of all our media led us to believe that the OPEC (Arab) countries were the villains in the 400% oil price increase. It was a devastating blow to all countries, especially the Third World countries that struggle to exist. It was not the OPEC countries. Instead, it was a group of oil barons, International Bankers and Politicians in their influence plus media magnates, who voted themselves a thumping 400% profit increase and to hell with the world at large.

Well that is what it seems; but it was far more sinister than that, for the story, as it unfolds, will relate. The meeting was held to move the floating power of world finance sharply back into the hands of the Anglo American power banking interests and everyone of those attendees paid loyalty to either the Rothschild or Rockefeller power structures. It was by majority a Internationalist controlled consortium of power brokers, deciding matters which democracy intends only governments to decide. The shock waves that the price increase caused around the world were immediate and in some cases disastrous.

But the bankers' consortium overruled national government and virtually controlled world development with one card; **'Oil'**. This was because the whole of the world's structure came to a standstill without it.

Suddenly, the London and New York markets for petro-dollars, two relatively small circles of intimate bankers, used their power to rob the world in a way no country could resist because of its dependence on oil.

It was an outrageous situation with an odd twist; all the blame was squarely placed on the greedy Arabs, or at least that is what the media, the bankers' tool of disinformation, led us to believe. Before we see the planning put into the result of this drastic oil price increase, I am going forward to 1987 to visit a prison, Sandstone Penitentiary, with the Reverend Lindsay Williams.

In 1986 the American newspapers were reporting an unusual case of bank fraud, by a Jonathan Michael May. **(229)** (Gibb Stuart, James. "Hidden Menace to World Peace' Ossian Publishers). May had reportedly issued cheques to around sixty five million pounds without funds to cover them. He was, at a less than perfect trial, sentenced to forty five years in prison. His motives and the case received international coverage. The farming community in Minnesota was in a financial straight jacket due to a drop in crop prices. Along came May and offered them an escape from debt with a billion dollar fund, to extract them from the grip of debt collectors. The farmers, desperate for an escape took up his offer. May told them it was the manipulation of interest rates by the Federal Reserve Bank that had caused their distress in the first place and it would put the entire country in debt.

His system was to work through a pledge on the creation of actual wealth, and, provided the wealth created was levelled at the correct ratio to the loan involved, no interest or repayment would be necessary. (Otherwise a loan system without usury) It was an innovation the farmers saw as their salvation against a banking system that wanted to bankrupt them. Unfortunately the Federal Reserve Banks did not see it May's way and had him arrested. It could have so easily remained the news sensation of 1986 had it not been for the Reverend William's insistence to interview May. Was he a crook? He tried to interview May in prison but was denied access. Eventually, after much effort he was granted a telephone link which he taped.

May was a very widely travelled man who had worked for several Multinational oil companies where he claimed he had learned the inside secrets of their power and global control. This phone link should alert us all about the global control practised by oil and banking wealth, so closely linked.

A prisoner, trying to justify his innocence, tries hard to convince anyone that is allowed to speak to him, that he did not commit the crime. Not so Jonathan May. He did not waste precious time on that escape. He, instead, told a story that had the Reverend Williams gasping in amazement. First he described the banking trusts of John D. Rockefeller, trusts which had since become illegal as unfair tax avoidance, but the law did not cover existing trusts.

The stewardship of these trusts was controlled by thirteen old established banking families, who in their own capacity controlled the central banks of the hard currency countries like Britain and America. The central banks in their turn controlled the prime banks, all of whom practised fractional reserve banking, which allowed them to lend up to twenty-six times the amount of their deposits at any one time. This, practised over a prolonged period had made this small bank grouping so immensely rich that a time could be seen when they would preside over the entire financial matters of the world and the aim was to complete this by global 2000 (This is why 2000 has been built into such an event by politicians. Orders from above.).

He said that oil wealth had joined with banking, ploughing money into Wall Street and London till oil and banking was in common hands. (Mostly under the influence of Rockefeller and Rothschild). This was to be essential knowledge to what was to follow.

He said that a technical official and three US government officials (Doing the bankers bidding) visited the Prime Minister of Nigeria and gave him a fifty million dollar bribe to double his price of light crude oil. (This was a benchmark crude for oil price fixing and therefore important to what followed).

George Bush (Later President Bush) was at this time, as a member of the Trilateral Commission, (Funded by Rockefeller) in the Middle East persuading OPEC to increase its prices. The deal was that the international oil buyers were willing to support a massive increase if the revenues were invested in the prime banks of the United States, as long term deposits (Otherwise bringing back the flow of dollars to America). As a simple minded, unsuspicious race the Arabs agreed as they saw immense profit without seeing the motive.

The New York bankers could now lend twenty-six times these deposits which over time became considerable.

May was told by Sheikh Yamani's nephew that it was only at the end of the eighties that the Arab oil ministers became aware that the prime banks and the oil companies were under the same management.

Then came the most amazing disclosure, (that had similarities with a television soap opera). In 1981 he had been contacted by the Hunt Brothers, (who formed the basis for Dallas). The Hunt brothers made their fortune through oil and, through Governor Connolly, decided that Texas, the oil rich state of America, should become independent of America by opting out of the American Union by refusing to renew the agreement. They thought they could side step the system, but like the Arabs they were not well enough informed; although they were billionaires, they were not in the same league as the Rockefellers. The Hunt brothers decided to opt out of the Federal Reserve to create their own money. To do this they decided to buy silver to support their new currency. They cornered the silver market but in doing so made a big mistake. Supported by Austrian and German bankers and by the Shah of Iran they used the same man to do both the buying and selling in the same markets, a mistake that exposed their scheme to the Federal Reserve Bank which moved to bankrupt them, which it did. At that time they were worth 16 billion dollars. Retribution took place. The German banker was murdered by European Terrorists. His Austrian associate was beaten up and spent the rest of his life in a mental institution. The Shah was forced out of his country and was brought to the USA to be held in protective custody at a US base. May says he was in good health when he left Iran but was soon to be officially diagnosed as having a terminal illness, after his entire fortune had been sequestered by American banks.

May went on to describe how he and his associates in 1983 were informed about a very secretive group of bank holding companies. They were obtaining loans from the prime banks and buying up agricultural and commercial land, that were linked to banks who forced foreclosures through the Federal Deposit Insurance Company. What they found was that the Federal Reserve Board was using its close intimate knowledge of the state of farming and industry to acquire farming land and industrial land on the cheap after they had instigated foreclosure procedures against the farmer or industrial land owner.

Then came his claim that, mixed up in this whole scam, was a second group of holding companies, operating with the first group, and arranging credit with the first group, to purchase the assets and liabilities which included the Arab oil deposits from the increase of oil prices (four-hundred percent) deposited in American prime banks. The assets they bought were loans that had been made to Third World Countries. May went on to state that the full picture became apparent when president Marcos, of the Philippines, approached him in urgent need of rescue. Marcos was in a financial straight jacket Tailor-made by the International Monetary

Fund. He was unable to service his previous loans for the Philippines by a group of American bankers. His only way to get more money was to integrate a radical sell out of his country's National Sovereignty, by becoming dollar dependent through Paul Volcker's Federal Reserve. It would mean cash would be eliminated and the whole country would go on a centralised credit card system, with the Philippines Central Bank just a wholesaler for the new bank of Paul Volcker. On top of this the IMF would require a lien on all the Island's natural recourses and to get in companies outside their jurisdiction to administrate their proper mining and excavation. For this they would get perpetual royalties. This, the IMF claimed, would bring the island prosperity. As a carrot, the IMF offered to drop all previous debt claims.

But Marcos was not deceived by the word 'Perpetual', and realised he would be signing away his country's independence. (As is the case in signing into the European Union).

He refused to sign and in revenge the props of his regime were removed and he was forced out of office by bankers with a greedy agenda. Then the press went to town to discredit him and his wife, to justify his removal, another clinical operation whose aim was to rob a third world country of its assets. This is how the IMF is used by the bankers, first, to give loans they know can't be serviced; then to move in and asset strip them in return for a image of a carefree future. But in reality the country, if it signs the agreement, is signing away its only chance of eventual recovery, its own mineral assets.

May's associates could not help Marcos but it did give him a valuable insight into the global 2000 policy to enslave the world in debt.

It also added a new dimension to their policy through the IMF and debt on. eradication. So what did this policy do for those secret holding companies that took on the Third World debt as an asset with the Arab oil states as their liability? If the third world swapped its debt for equity in its own assets what would happen to the loans? Default; that is what would happen; and who lost their shirt? Not the prime banks, not the first secret group of holding companies, but the second group went bankrupt, without assets and therefore the Arabs lost their investments in what they thought was blue chip investment, by a scam intentionally played on them by International Zionist Bankers, robbing the Arab's of their investment while buying land and investment in farming with the Arabs money. Property the Arabs could not claim. A world class rip off. These are the people that wish to rule the world, if we do not get together to stop them.

As a support to this statement let's refer once again to Professor Quigley's 'Tragedy and Hope' **(230)** "...The powers of the financial capitalism had another far-reaching aim, nothing less than to create a world system of financial control in private hands able to dominate the political system of each country and the economy of the world as a whole. The system was to be controlled in a federalist fashion by the central banks of the world acting in concert, by secret agreements arrived at in frequent private meetings and conferences". (Bilderberg and Trilateral Commission).

So is Jonathan May's story a fabrication or a brave attempt to warn the world of powerful manipulation by the super rich banker?

First we are informed that a Nephew of Sheikh Yamani, the spokesman for the Arab oil cartel, confirmed the story. What we are asked to accept is Nigeria's part in increasing their price for light crude, which on investigation they did.

But then comes the interesting part that supports May's version. There was no outcry by the International Markets, they just accepted a immoral increase. This shows they were part of the plan. We also know that the Arab cartel invested large sums of petro-dollars in American prime banks and became the main source of money for Third World loans through the offices of the IMF. We also know that the loans were made without safeguard for the lenders. Through corrupt, Third World governments, most of the loans were spirited away into private, off shore accounts leaving the second group of holding companies with bad debts. So in essence his story was true and quite possibly he was jailed to silence him. His sentence was harsh and the judge recommended psychiatric treatment, without any evidence of a troubled mind. This all adds up to a fixed trial to remove someone 'in the know' about the bankers **Global 2000 Plan.**

A book worth reading about the Arab loans to Third World countries is entitled 'Odious Debts' by Patricia Adams, which establishes that loans were made by the consortium with Arab funding with no concern as to whether the debts could be serviced or whether even the funds would be used for the purpose for which they were given. From all these sources we get a definite **'Direction'** that the world economy is being pushed towards a **Hidden Agenda** controlled, not by politicians, but by bankers who increasingly act outside political parameters.

What has become clear from this brief look behind the mirrors is that the International Monetary Fund and the World Bank operate for the benefit of the bankers and their greed, not to solve the very difficult problems the third world countries present, not least corruption by the countries' officials.

Where else can we see such financial corruption? They take on world problems and exploit them. The answer is to be seen in Jaques Delor's Report on economic and monetary union, which provides for a Central Bank which would be independent of political interference from member states, as they are to be controlled by appointees of the Regional Banks, who in turn are independent of governments.

Thanks to the warning we have had from Weishaupt, Karl Marx, Rakovski, Jonathan May and Patricia Adams, we can make an informed decision on the future power of the bankers, and take money creation back into National Government hands, where it belongs.

So it was the Kissinger plan to instigate the Yom Kippur war, which set in motion the four-hundred percent oil price increase over a period of fourteen months. The devious actions of Dr. Henry Kissinger, responding to plans set out by the Bilderberg Group in their meeting in May 1973, was using his high office as Secretary of State, in Nixon's government to adopt policies detrimental to the whole world except the bankers and oil cartels who were about to make massive gains while the world suffered and even went to war, a war blamed on the Arabs, but planned and schemed by Kissinger and his office.

That this was a forerunner for the Iraq conflict seems an unlikely comment but there is proof that Dr. Henry Kissinger was again the motivator of this conflict under instructions from the Bilderberg group. In chapter 16 we will be studying the Bilderberg Group in depth. **(231).**

So it can be seen, with these few examples, how the combination of oil and banking has taken over the political agenda of America and Britain. It shows how they either create political agenda or ignore national agenda at will. This is simply anarchy which must be stopped by controlling banking influence and controlling oil power for the good of all nations. Oil is, after all, a world necessity, not a means to a political aim as the bankers see it.

PROTOCOL TWENTY

Today we shall touch upon the financial programme, which I put off to the end of my report as being the most difficult, the crowning and the decisive point of our plans. Before entering upon it I will remind you that I have already spoken before by way of a hint when I said that the sum total of our actions is settled by the question of figures.

When we come into our kingdom our autocratic government will avoid, from a principle of self-preservation, stupidly burdening the masses of the people with taxes, remembering that it plays the part of father and protector. But as state organisation is costly it is necessary nevertheless to obtain the funds required for it. It will, therefore, elaborate with particular precaution the question of equilibrium in this matter.

Our rule, in which the king will enjoy the legal fiction that everything in his state belongs to him (which may easily be translated into fact), will have power to resort to the lawful confiscation of all sums of every kind for the regulation of their circulation in the State. From this it follows that taxation will best be covered by a progressive tax on property. In this manner the dues will be paid without straining or ruining anybody in the form of a percentage of the amount of the property. The rich must be aware that it is their duty to place a part of their superfluities at the disposal of the state since the state guarantees them security of possession of the rest of their property and the right to honest gains. I say honest, for the control over property will do away with robbery on a legal basis.

This social reform must come from above, for the time is ripe for it - it is indispensable as a pledge of peace.

The tax upon the poor man is a seed of revolution and works to the detriment of the state which in hunting after the trifling is missing the big. Quite apart from this, a tax on capitalists diminishes the growth of wealth in private hands where we have in these days concentrated it as a counterpoise to the government strength of the goyim - their state finances.

A tax increasing in a percentage ratio to capital will give a much larger revenue than the present individual or property tax, which is useful to us now for the sole reason that it excites trouble and discontent among the goyim.

The force upon which our king will rest consists in equilibrium and the guarantee of peace, for the sake of which things it is indispensable that the capitalists should yield up a portion of their incomes in order to ensure the working of the machinery of the State. State needs must be paid by those who will not feel the burden and have enough to take from.

Such a measure will destroy the hatred of the poor man for the rich, in whom he will see a necessary financial support for the state, and the organiser of peace and well-being since he will see that it is the rich man who will be paying the necessary means to attain these things.

In order that payers of the educated classes should not too much distress themselves over the new payments they will have full accounts given them of the destination of those payments, with the exception of such sums as will be appropriated for the needs of the throne and the administrative institutions.

He who reigns will not have any properties of his own once all in the state represents his patrimony, or else the one would be in contradiction to the other; the fact of holding private means would destroy the right of property in the common possession of all.

Relatives of him who reigns, his heirs excepted, who will be maintained by the resources of the State, must enter the ranks of servants of the state or must work to obtain the right to property; the privilege of royal blood must not serve for spoiling the treasury.

Purchase, receipt of money or inheritance will be subject to the payment of a stamp progressive tax. Any transfer of property, whether money or other, without evidence of payment of this tax, which will be strictly registered by names, will render the former holder liable to pay interest on the tax from the moment of the transfer of these sums up to the discovery of his evasion of declaration of the transfer. Transfer documents must be presented weekly at the local treasury office with notifications of the name, surname and permanent place of residence of the former and the new holder of the property. This transfer with the register of names must begin from a definite sum which exceeds the ordinary expenses of buying and selling of necessaries, and these will be subject to payment only by a stamp impost of a definite percentage of the unit.

Just estimate how many times such taxes as these will cover the revenue of the goyim States.

The State exchequer will have to maintain a definite complement of reserve sums, and all that is collected above that complement must be returned into circulation. From these sums will be organised public works. The initiative in works of this kind, proceeding from state sources, will bind the working class firmly to the interests of the state and to those who reign. From these same sums also a part will be set aside as rewards of inventiveness and productiveness.

On no account should so much as a single unit above the definite and freely estimated sums be retained in the state treasuries, for money exists to be circulated and any kind of stagnation of money acts ruinously on the running of the state machinery, for which it is the lubricant; stagnation of the lubricant may stop the regular working of the mechanism.

The substitution of interest-bearing paper for a part of the token of exchange has produced exactly this stagnation. The consequences of this circumstance are already sufficiently noticeable.

A court of account will also be instituted by us, and in it the ruler will find at any moment a full account of state income and expenditure, with the exception of the current monthly account, not yet made up, and that of the preceding month, which will not yet have been delivered.

The one and only person who will have no interest in robbing the state is its owner, the ruler. This is why his personal control will remove the possibility of leakages or extravagances.

The representative function of the ruler at receptions for the sake of etiquette, which absorbs so much invaluable time, will be abolished in order that the ruler may have time for control and considerations. His power will not then be split up into fractional parts among time-saving favourites who surround the throne for its pomp and splendour, and are interested only in their own and not in the common interests of the state.

Economic crises have been produced by us for the goyim by no other means than the withdrawal of money from circulation. Huge capitals have stagnated, withdrawing money from states which were constantly obliged to apply to those same stagnant capitals for loans. These loans burdened the finances of the state with payment of interest and made them the bond slaves of these capitals....The concentration of industry in the hands of capitalists out of the hands of small masters has drained away all the juices of the peoples and with them also of the states...

The present issue of money in general does not correspond with the requirements per head, and cannot therefore satisfy all the needs of the workers. The issue of money ought to correspond with the growth of population and thereby children also must absolutely be reckoned as consumers of currency from the day of their birth. The revision of issue is a material question for the whole world.

You will be aware that the gold standard has been the ruin of the states which adopted it, for it has not been able to satisfy the demands for money, the more so that we have removed gold from circulation as far as possible.

With us the standard that must be introduced is the cost of working-man power, whether it be reckoned in paper or in wood. We shall make the issue of money in accordance with the normal requirements of each subject, adding to the quality with every birth and subtracting with every death. The accounts will be managed by each department (The French administrative division), each circle.

In order that there may be no delays in the paying out of money for State needs the sums and terms of such payments will be fixed by decree of the ruler; this will abolish the protection by a ministry of one institution to the detriment of others.

The budgets of income and expenditure will be carried out side by side that they may not be obscured by distance one to another.

The reforms projected by us in the financial institutions and principles of the goyim will be clothed by us in such forms as will alarm nobody. We shall point out the necessity of reforms in consequence of the disorderly darkness into which the goyim by their irregularities they plunged the finances. The first irregularity, as we shall point out, consists in their beginning with drawing up a single budget which increases year after year owing to the following cause: this budget is dragged out to half the year, then they demand a budget to put things right, and this they expend in three months, after which they ask for a supplementary budget, and all this ends with a liquidation budget. But, as the budget of the following year is drawn up in accordance with the sum of the total addition, the annual departure from the normal reaches as much as 50% in one year, and so the annual budget is trebled in ten years. Thanks to such methods, allowed by the carelessness of the goy States, their treasuries are empty. The period of loans supervenes, and that has swallowed up remainders and brought all the goy States to bankruptcy.

You understand perfectly that economic arrangements of this kind, which have been suggested to the goyim by us, cannot be carried on by us.

Every kind of loan proves infirmity in the State and a want of understanding of the rights of the State. Loans hang like a sword of Damocles over the heads of rulers, who, instead of taking from their subjects by a temporary tax, come begging with outstretched palm to our bankers. Foreign loans are leeches which there is no possibility of removing from the body of the State until they fall off by themselves or the State flings them off. But the goy States do not tear them off; they persist in putting more on to themselves so that they must inevitably perish, drained by voluntary blood letting.

What also indeed is, in substance, a loan, especially a foreign loan? A loan is - an issue of government bills of exchange containing a percentage obligation commensurate to the sum of the loan capital. If the loan bears a charge of 5%, then in twenty years the State vainly pays away in interest a sum equal to the loan borrowed, in forty years it is paying a double sum, in sixty treble - and all the while the debt remains an unpaid debt.

From this calculation it is obvious that with any form of taxation per head the State is baling out the last coppers of the poor taxpayers in order to settle accounts with wealthy foreigners, from whom it has borrowed money instead of collecting these coppers for its own needs without the additional interest.

So long as loans were internal the goyim only shuffled their money from the pockets of the poor to those of the rich, but when we bought up the necessary person in order to transfer loans into the external sphere all the wealth of States flowed into our cash-boxes and all the goyim began to pay us the tribute of subjects.

If the superficiality of goy kings on their thrones in regard to State affairs and the venality of ministers or the want of understanding of financial matters on the part of other ruling persons have made their countries debtors to our treasuries to amounts quite impossible to pay, it has not been accomplished without on our part heavy expenditure of trouble and money.

Stagnation of money will not be allowed by us and therefore there will be no State interest-bearing paper (Bonds), except a one-per-cent. series, so that there will be no payment of interest to leeches that suck all the strength out of the State. The right to issue interest-bearing paper will be given exclusively to industrial companies who will find no difficulty in paying out of profits, whereas the State does not make interest on borrowed money like these companies, for the State borrows to spend and not to use in operations.

Industrial papers will be bought also by the government which will from being as now a payer of tribute by loan operations will be transformed into a lender of money at profit. This measure will stop the stagnation of money, parasitic profits, and idleness all of which were useful for us among the goyim so long as they were independent but are not desirable under our rule.

How clear is the undeveloped power of thought of the purely brute brains of the goyim, as expressed in the fact that they have been borrowing from us with payment of interest without ever thinking that all the same these very moneys, plus an addition for payment of interest, must be got by them from their own State pockets in order to settle up with us. What could have been simpler than to take the money they wanted from their own people?

But it is proof of the genius of our chosen mind that we have contrived to present the matter of loans to them in such a light that they have even seen in them an advantage for themselves.

Our accounts, which we shall present when the time comes in the light of centuries of experience gained by experiments made by us on the goy States, will be distinguished by clearness and definiteness and will show at a glance to all men the advantage of our innovations. They will put an end to those abuses to which we owe our mastery over the goyim, but which cannot be allowed in our Kingdom.

We shall so hedge about our system of accounting that neither the ruler nor the most insignificant public servant will be in a position to divert even the smallest sum from its destination without detection or to direct it in another direction except that which will be once fixed in a definite plan of action.

And without a definite plan it is impossible to rule. Marching along an undetermined road and with undermined resources brings heroes and demi-gods to ruin.

The goy-rulers, whom we once upon a time advised should be distracted from State occupations by representative receptions, observances of etiquette, and entertainments, were only screens for our rule. The accounts of favourite courtiers who replaced them in the sphere of affairs were drawn up for them by our agents, and every time gave satisfaction to short-sighted minds by promises that in the future economies and improvements were foreseen...Economies from what? From new taxes? - were questions that might have been put were not asked by those who read our accounts and projects.

You know to what they have been brought by this carelessness, at what a pitch of financial disorder they have arrived, notwithstanding the astonishing industry of their peoples.

COMMENT

In this Protocol we see a mirrored image of what has taken place financially this century. 'They' (The Bankers) say when 'they' come to power they will not burden us with excessive taxes. But the taxes that we pay today go largely to paying the loan debts our governments have built up by allowing the bankers to create money for our use and charge interest on money that has only cost the bankers the printing charge. Fundamentally this is so wrong and so unnecessary when our governments could print the money themselves without interest charge and leave us without national debt.

'They' say the ruler will have the power to confiscate anything we own, this is Communism. 'They' also make much play on the poor man and try to con him into believing 'they' are there for him. The fact is the poor man pays very little or no tax, it is the middle class that is clobbered at the moment and these pirates wish to remove the middle class from the formula, because they are the most likely to rebel against their authority and dictatorship. 'They' say that the government bonds put up by government as security for state loans has caused stagnation of economies. This is quite true. But you don't leap into the hands of dictators (The Bankers) to avoid this problem, you change the system of money creation. That is the sensible move and it would free the world's economies from debt slavery at a stroke. 'They' admit that they have produced economic crises within our economies. 'They' have been designed to move the system towards their rule . Every war, every financial crisis has been of 'their' making all of which have been 'their' plan to move us into 'their' trap of world Government. Because the movement in 'their' direction is little by little we do not notice the drift until you look at **Direction** and this gives away the truth of 'their' terrible plan.

'They' admit that 'they' caused the policy of lack of available money through the gold standard. 'They' admit 'they' removed gold from circulation to achieve this. 'They' go on to say that all the systems that 'they' have imposed on debt loan states will be abolished under their government. So what 'they' are saying 'they' have imposed systems on our governments that will drive us towards bankruptcy and into 'their' dictatorship.

'They' admit loans are like the 'Sword of Damocles' hanging over us. But everyone who has tried to correct this stupidity of government has ended up dead. 'Their' resolve to impose this dictatorship of money upon us is absolute and nothing gets in its way. Therefore it is only the people who can stop it as the politicians are long in 'their' camp. It is not the people who have built up the loan debt but the politicians and it is just that that has made them subservient to the bankers will.

They show us a simple example of debt interest to illustrate why debt bankrupts governments especially when they are foreign (e.g. Morgan's loan to Britain for the First World War) If we had printed our own money to cover war debts we would have come out of the war without debt. So why do we not wake up to reality? They will do away with state loans and interest bearing bonds. Again we could do this if we controlled our own money supply. 'They' have terrorised the political world into subservience only the people, you and me can now save the world from their dictatorship. Here we see their confession that they have infiltrated the seats of power to influence the direction of politics it is those traitors within that have left us near slavery, but our one power is the people who must sit up and listen before it is too late.

NOW STUDY THESE SAYINGS AND RELATE THEM TO WHAT YOU HAVE JUST READ.

ON MONEY CONTROL.

> "Permit me to issue and control the money of a nation and I care not who makes it's laws."
>
> Meyer Amschel Rothschild. 1790

ON THE PROTOCOLS.

> "Whence comes this uncanny note of prophecy, prophecy in part fulfilled in parts far gone in the way of fulfilment? Have we been struggling these tragic years to.... extirpate the secret organization of German world dominion only to find beneath it, another, more dangerous, because more secret? Have we...escaped a Pax Germanica only to fall into a Pax Judaeica"?
>
> The Times, London May 8th. 1920.

ON THE CONSPIRACY.

> "In the desires of a terrible and formidable sect, you have only reached the first stages of the plans it has formed for that general Revolution which is to overthrow all thrones, all altars, annihilate all property, efface all law, and end by dissolving all society".
>
> The Abbe Barruel 1797 writing on the Anti Christian Conspiracy.

ON COMMUNISM AND ZIONISM.

> "Unless Bolshevism is nipped in the bud immediately it is bound to spread in one form or another all over Europe and the whole world, as it is organised and worked by Jews who have no nationality and whose object is to destroy for their own ends the existing order of things".
>
> British Government White Paper, Russia No. 1 (1919).

ON THE ZIONISTS.

> "There is now definite evidence that Bolshevism is an international movement controlled by Jews; communications are passing between the leaders in America, France, Russia and England, with a view to concerted action."
>
> Directorate of Intelligence, Home Office, Scotland Yard, London, in a monthly report to Foreign Embassies, 16th July, 1919.

ON THE WORDS OF A FAMOUS MAN

"This movement amongst the Jews is not new. From the days of Sparticus – Weishaupt to those of Karl Marx, and down to Trotsky (Russia), Bela Kun (Hungary), Rosa Luxemberg (Germany) and Emma Goldman (United States), this world-wide conspiracy for the overthrow of civilisation and for the reconstitution of society on the basis of arrested development of envious malevolence, and impossible equality, has been steadily growing".

Winston Churchill in Illustrated Sunday Herald. February 8th. 1919.

ON THE TERRIBLE REALITY OF THE PROTOCOLS.

"Whosoever was the mind that conceived them possessed knowledge of human nature, of history, and of statecraft which is dazzling in its brilliant completeness, and terrible in the objects to which it turns its powers. It is too terribly real for fiction, too well sustained for speculation, too deep in its knowledge of the secret springs of life for forgery".

The Dearborn Independent, July 10th. 1920.

ON EVIDENCE OF THE UNITED NATIONS AS 'THEIR' POWER.

The United Nations is Zionism. It is the super government mentioned many times in the Protocols of the Elders of Zion, promulgated between 1897 and 1905".

Henry Klein, New York Jewish lawyer, in Zionism Rules the World, 1948.

ON HOW THE PROTOCOLS FIT THE WORLD MOVEMENT.

> "The only statement I care to make about the Protocols is that they fit in with what is going on. They are sixteen years old and they have fitted the world situation up to this time. They fit it now".
>
> Henry Ford, in New York World, February 17th. 1921.

The weight of proof given in this book demands that we take the evidence before us seriously before it is too late.

CHAPTER TEN, PART THREE.
FOUNDATIONS - A THREAT TO DEMOCRACY.

You have just seen how a small, but powerful group of bankers, surrounding the Federal Reserve Bank were controlling, not only America's policies, but world policies. This may seem odd till you realise that banking has moved onto an international footing and the same names surrounding Wall Street also control banking in Germany, France, England and as far as Australia and the Pacific Rim. Banking at their level has no national boundaries and therefore it is in their mind natural to want a world free from national boundaries and restrictions that interfere with their progress to move money. However, for the people of the world, this is just against all our interest, to have a fluid banking system where money can starve one country and move its assets to say another area where labour is cheaper, or close a plant because of labour problems which are instigated by a desire, by Multi-National Companies, to move elsewhere. Globalism to this extent, which is collectivism, is pure Communism, and is not in our interest.

America is the largest borrower by far, with a national debt in excess of the total of all other countries. That is why America cannot make a political move without the bankers consent. That is no way to run a country especially when those bankers represent a minority interest.

Dr. Quigley had this to say about the aims of these bankers; "....Nothing less than to create a world system of financial control in private hands able to dominate the **Political System** of each country and the economy of the world as a whole. This system was to be controlled in a feudalist fashion by the central banks of the world acting in concert, by secret agreements arrived at in frequent private meetings and conferences (Bilderberg meetings). The apex of the system was to be the Bank of International Settlement in Basle, Switzerland, a private bank owned and controlled by the world's central banks which were themselves private corporations. Each central bank, in the hands of men like Montague Norman of the Bank of England, Benjamin Strong, of the New York Federal Reserve Bank, Charles Rist, of the Bank of France, and Hjalmer Schacht, of the Reich's Bank, sought to dominate its governments by its ability to control treasury loans, to manipulate foreign exchanges, to influence the level of economic activity in each country, and to influence Co-operative politicians by subsequent economic rewards in the business world". **(232).**

If you study the inter-relationship between just one thread of the banking hierarchy you begin to see how it all ties into a privileged secret society. Dr. Quigley goes on to show how Benjamin Strong, the first governor of the Federal Reserve Bank was in close liaison with Montague Norman **(233)** of the Bank of England. Strong owed his position to Morgan Bank, whose Henry P. Davison made him Vice President of the Bankers' Trust of New York. His governorship of the Federal Reserve was nominated by Morgan and Kuhn Loeb in 1914, and maintained close co-operation between New York, London and Paris. **(234).** It is from this powerful position that they dictate and manipulate political movement and desire to control the political agenda through a World Government. So what they do behind closed doors will effect every one of us. Carroll Quigley, in "Tragedy and Hope", an admitted insider who approved of the bankers' conspiracy but not its secrecy, goes on to show us the goals of this super elite group that is pushing the world, little by little, towards a global, Marxist-Socialist Dictatorship, which goes against the human endeavour of the last thousand years to shake off the chains of slavery and move towards democracy, as well as going against the Capitalist endeavour, the creed of the super rich.

So why do these super rich want to destroy our property owning society? He answers this question by a statement that is at first so far fetched as to seem ridiculous. He states that this banking group of the super rich wants to take over the world within a socialist programme that will use Communism or revolution to further its aim.

But he side-steps some of the bankers attempts to cover their plans for control of policy in America, for example the Reece Committee, and its struggle to expose their findings as we will see later in this report.

Remember that Quigley was an academic supporter of the bankers' revolution, his only difference with the group was their secrecy and his book was to re-dress this matter. For this, his work, considered a major contribution to world political knowledge was marginalised. **(235).**

Quigley relates how this idea of world conquest was planted in the bankers' minds and how it spread to the academic world and outwards through the Universities. What he is disclosing is the history of Ruskin onwards, but he does not go back to the source, the Illuminati of Weishaupt which we have already discussed. The bankers (Rothschild) sponsored Weishaupt, from which came a policy (The Communist Manifesto) and within this policy was Weishaupt's seven pillars of revolution plus his way to revolution; to capture the source of education and control the media. This plan is today near completion.

We have seen how they encouraged academia into their movement and we have seen how the media has been gradually bought out by the bankers financial power.

With these two moves the bankers go a long way to gain control over our minds and that means, your mind, and mine.

Quigley points out that Ruskin was a visible result of mind controlling politics. He enthused his students into action about the moral issues within a socialist agenda. **(236).**

Kenneth Clark, (Ex Chancellor of the Exchequer and Europhile) in his book 'Ruskin Today' **(237)** says; "He saw that the state must take control of the means of production and distribution, and organise them for the good of the community as a whole; but he was prepared to place the control of the state in the hands of a single man....The peasant communes in China, in particular, are exactly on his model. He would not have thought the cure worse than the decease because he could not imagine a worse disease than the capitalist society of the nineteenth century. Clark goes on to say, "Ruskin derived his views from the profit of dictatorship, Plato, as did Weishaupt and Marx".

Plato advocated the complete destruction of existing government structures, the elimination of marriage, state confiscation of all children, women should be equal to men and therefore fight wars alongside them, and private property should be eliminated. This was Plato's message that Ruskin read daily.

He interpreted this into his mission so that the English privileged class should go out into the world and follow his creed that he dressed up as a high standard of education, rule of law, freedom, decency and self-discipline which he wanted to spread through the working class of England and throughout the world.

This was pure Weishaupt policy, dressed up in respectable clothing to deceive the potential initiate needed to spread his gospel. Like all evil policies stemming from Plato's philosophy, it was clothed in deceit, to hide Satanism.

Cecil Rhodes we have seen, was one of those initiates, in Ruskin's 'pure' world and along with other students, launched his long range policy to federate the world (Again Weishaupt's policy that shadowed Marxism), and who do we find along side him, none other than Lord Rothschild and Alfred Beit, helping him to finance De-Beers Consolidated Diamond Mines and Consolidated Gold Mines, which were used to finance his political goal of a world federation as Ruskin had preached about from his privileged seat at Oxford.

Then came the secret society, to cover up the real aim of his thrust, a new world order under dictatorship, a society to encompass all Ruskin's converts into a powerful academic force for revolution. This group used Rhodes's fortune after his death in 1902 to further Ruskin's and Stead's ideals. It was a lady journalist, Flora Shaw (Later Lady Ludgard) who, as head of the Colonial Department of the Times carried the banner of Rhodes into the British Empire helping to extend their influence and scope.

The secret society was formed, as with Weishaupt and Communism, with an inner circle. Rhodes was the leader, Stead, Brett (Lord Esher) and Milner formed a inner circle executive with Arthur (Lord) Balfour, Sir Harry Johnston, Lord Rothschild, Albert (Lord) Grey as inner members. Later, after Rhodes's death, Milner organised the outer circle, and the Round Table Organisation, who like Weishaupt's Illuminati were not given the whole truth about the objectives of their organisation.

Gradually this grew and multiplied. The Royal Institute of International Affairs (At Chatham House), financially supported by Sir Abe Bailey and the Astor family, was founded in 1919 and similar institutions were established in the Empire and the United States between 1919 and 1927 called The Council on Foreign Relations and in 1925 by the Institute of Pacific Relations which was set up in twelve countries on the Pacific Rim (The third regional area for world government) **(238).** All these

Institutes were inter-locking with one aim, moving the world towards dictatorial one world government. With their grandiose concept, derived from the privileged education and background these so called intellectuals could not see they were driving the world towards dictatorship, and amongst them, those financing them, International Bankers, were moving them towards Weishaupt's goal of a Communist led world dictatorship. Each group thinking they had the power and right on their side while in reality, as always, finance controls the agenda and the bankers can arrest control at their will.

The influence and power of the British grouping stemming from the Round Table was immense. They influenced 'The Times' till 1922 and thereafter under the Astor family's ownership controlled it. So the power of the quality press was their mouthpiece to influence the thinking man. They also established chairs at Universities, particularly Oxford and Aberystwyth. The group worked tirelessly to move the British Empire into a federal system, then confederate the whole grouping, under the United Kingdom. Stead (From Cambridge) wanted America included. Quigley had this to say; **(239)** "The American branch of this organisation (Known as the Eastern Establishment) has played a very significant role in the history of the United States in the last generation.... By 1915 Round Table groups existed in seven countries, including England, South Africa, Canada, Australia, New Zealand, India, and a rather loosely organised group in the United States (George Louis Beer, Walter Lippmann, Frank Aydelotte, Whitney Shepardson, Thomas W. Lamont, Jerome D. Greene, Erwin D. Canham of the Christian Science Monitor and others). The attitudes of the various groups were co-ordinated by frequent visits and discussions and by a well-informed and totally anonymous quarterly magazine 'The Round Table', whose first issue, largely written by Philip Kerr, appeared in November 1910".

Funding, for this group, up till then, came from the Rhodes Trust, the Beit Brothers, Sir Abe Bailey and the Astor Family. After 1925 large donations were made available from American Foundations and especially the International Banking Establishment, the Carnegie United Kingdom Trust, and other organisations associated with J.P. Morgan, Rockefeller and the Whitney Family, as well as Associates of Lazard brothers and Morgan Grenfell and Company. **(240)**

So the Anglo American secret society was formed, controlled and financed by powerful men, mainly in banking. Milner himself became a director of public banks, the London Joint Stock Bank, Corporate Precursor of the Midland Bank. From this, his influence, politically and financially was tremendous, and he placed his followers strategically in important posts throughout England. It was at this moment that England was secretively penetrated by an enemy within, the most dangerous enemy of all, to be compared to the wooden horse of Troy.

But in fairness to these people, they were driven by a false vision of good, built into their minds by the inner circle of the Round Table, who by now were following the bankers' dream of world domination, Weishaupt's policy. **Direction.**

So the Anglo American Society now had a firm grip on education through their influence at Oxford, Cambridge and other chairs of learning. The Society had spread internationally, and had infiltrated the civil service and politics through Milner's influence. The societies thinking controlled the Times and was spreading its control wider into the media thus controlling its power. The society was heading along the path to Weishaupt's required pre-conditions for revolution. The Royal Institute of International Affairs, led by Lionel Curtis, spread its influence around the British Empire and was building a firm base in America as the Council on

Foreign Relations. J.P. Morgan Associates, Beer and Lamont, all attended the Paris Peace Conference, where the plans for these groups were originally discussed.

A very important moment for the Anglo American Society was the introduction of the New Republic Magazine, founded by Willard Straight; it was a left wing Radical Liberal publication supported by a surprising array of wealthy Americans who used Capitalism to attain their wealth and supported Radical Liberalism to salve their consciences. Names such as Payne Whitney, the magazine's founder, John Hay, Secretary of State who pushed the 'Open Door Policy' in China, and Nelson Rockefeller were among its contributors. The paper's purpose was to herd its sheep quietly into a Anglophile association. **Direction. (241).**

This was a task given to an Internationalist, just out of Harvard, and a member of the American Round Table, Walter Lippmann. As an establishment journalist his columns, that appeared in hundreds of American papers, the copyright of which was owned by the New York Herald Tribune, which in turn was owned by Walter Whitney, completes the links back to the Round Table and Wall Street. Wherever you turn in this account the full circle brings you back to the International Finance Capitalists. This is penetration in true Weishaupt style. All these groups are a result of Weishaupt's policy through Communism, Radical Liberalism, Masonic lodges, and the Round Table. The whole is financed by the so called Super Capitalists, the International Finance Capitalists, an unbelievable combination until you know that Internationalists want to wreck our religion, our governments, our democracy, and our nationalism, to reach its goal: world domination, where the state is a federalised world. They no more believe in Communism than I do, they just use it as they use the Masonic movement, the Round Table, the intelligentsia, the Liberals and the politicians. Until we wake up to this they will continue to move the world towards their goal.

The bankers of New York (again in the true Weishaupt style) moved to influence academic institutions. They became the source of finance for what the Americans named the Ivy League of Internationalists. Because of the endowments, the Universities were in constant contact with Wall Street and became dependent on foundation funding to pursue their research. What this did in the end was to allow the foundations to influence research and subtly direct it towards its aims. By the thirties J.P. Morgan and his sphere of influence were the driving force behind Harvard, Columbia and shared Yale with Whitney, and the good old Prudential Insurance Company which dominated Princeton University. The important fact is that these Universities were dependent upon grants and became singularly minded in pursuing their donors wishes to obtain their grants.

Five American newspapers by the thirties led the way for the power grouping, the New York Times, New York Herald Tribune, Christian Science Monitor, The Washington Post and the Boston Evening Transcript. The editor of the Christian Science Monitor was also the anonymous editor of 'The Round Table' Lord Lothian, who was later the secretary of the Rhodes Trust and Ambassador to Washington. **(242).**

With this power base and financial carrot, this group took over Universities, heart and soul, which in turn influenced the press, University teaching, and the practice of foreign policy.

Also linked with both the bankers and foundations were a select list of lawyers, whose names were generally linked with bankers, the foundations and politics. Names like Elihu Root, the Dulles Brothers, Arthur H. Dean, and John J. McCloy.

So the team with all its expertise penetrated and eventually controlled the agenda of America in spite of the presence of a political system. They even arranged the appointment of their own men to Ambassadorial positions in London. **(243).**

From this structure of organisation by the Round Table inner circle, the Anglo-American secret society infiltrated the heart of British and American political and social life, moving their men into positions of power.

Dr. Quigley, (A supporter of the bankers' agenda) says that the International Bankers were confident they could buy into the Communist-Socialist agenda to move their agenda forwards to revolution. Ruskin, a socialist, had already persuaded the Round Table groups that socialism was the vehicle to use. By having property, industry, agriculture, communications, education, and politics controlled by a small group of political financiers they could organise the world to their order of things. Now this goes against everything we know about Capitalism. But Quigley found nothing wrong with the meeting of Capitalism. Collectivism is a basic policy of Communism but also a end goal of Multi-National Corporatism. Power attracts extra power as banking power attracts political power and the most attractive route to total power was by the overthrow of existing power, national power. (That is what we are seeing today in the European Union). It was only Communism, which was world-wide and positioned for revolution that could achieve this goal, so Communism was the chosen tool, chosen at an early stage by the Rothschilds.

By taking this path to world domination the bankers risk the possibility that Communism will not lay down its arms when the world is overrun by Communism, but will instead turn the guns on the bankers and their plotters. However the super rich elected to take this risk, in the knowledge that nothing works without finance, the strongest weapon in the armoury.

Dr. Quigley goes on to say that the semi-secret organisations were; "To work to maintain peace, to help backward, colonial, and underdeveloped areas to advance towards stability, law and order, and prosperity, along lines some what similar to those taught at Oxford and the University of London, especially the School of Economics and the School of African and Oriental Studies. Here we must be quite clear; Quigley is stating that bankers are taking the world down a Global Socialist path as advocated at those Universities. But he did not take account of the bankers' greed. We have already seen, that far from helping Third World countries, the bankers have placed them in debt slavery from which they may not recover. This does not level with Dr. Quigley's views. We also know that Communism came from the Illuminati and Weishaupt, so the New Socialist Movement was not the motor of the bankers but the deceit of Weishaupt's Communism funded by the Rothschilds that drove the bankers' wagon of revolution. Dr. Quigley even attempts to defend the bankers and their victories and defeats **(244)** by impassioned pleading which somewhat down-grades his efforts, which are considerable, as a historian.

Gradually we see this secret society of bankers and the Round Table using wealth and influence to support Communism. In the thirties Dr. Quigley said; "It must be recognised that the power that these energetic left-wingers exercised was never their own power or Communist power but was ultimately the power of the international coterie..." **(245).** What this means is that without the wealth of the bankers behind them, Communism was nothing as it was not people led. But Dr. Quigley, although he mentions the banking families' involvement, he carefully ignores the original funding of the Illuminati by the Rothschilds and then their involvement with Karl Marx and the Communist Party Manifesto.

Trotsky himself, in his biography, mentions the international banking families and their funding of the Russian Revolution. By 1907 the British financiers were lending money for a revolution. By 1917 Sir George Buchanan and Lord Milner (Member of the Morgan-Rothschild-Rhodes confederacy and Founder of the Round Table arranged major funding for the revolution that forced Bolshevism on Russia. Another banking source in America gave Trotsky and Lenin and others a twenty million dollar boost for their final success of Bolshevism in Russia; his name; Jacob Schiff of Kuhn Loeb and Company. Other international bankers lent a hand, Olaf Aschberg, of Bye Banken Stockholm, The Rhine Westphalian Syndicate, and a banker named Jivotovsky, whose daughter married Trotsky. The main funding came from Max Warburg of Germany, whose brothers controlled New York banking interests. So between Max Warburg (A Rothschild agent) and Jacob Schiff, the Russian Revolution was made possible only by their funding, which was on all accounts, substantial. **(246).**

By the late forties information was gradually leaking out about Communist infiltration deep into government and particularly through the tax exempt Foundations which largely controlled the Academic thinking which developed America's policies with the world. Deep concern was being shown that these privileged institutions were so controlled by a left wing Communist agenda that they were doing harm to America's image world-wide.

With this exposed in a democratic country, it would be investigated and if found to be substantially true, it would be corrected. A special committee to investigate the tax exempt foundations was set up in July 1953 under B. Carroll Reece of Tennessee. However the bankers moved to limit the investigation and newspapers, as the poodles of the bankers made it known they would not give any hearing adequate cover to arouse the mass of people. Politicians were also warned that their campaign contributions might be at stake if they supported a move to censor the foundations.

So the Reece report found immediate hostility to its endeavours. But in fairness, carried out its duty and reported. It found some of the larger foundations were consistently supporting left wing activity, especially in regard to donations to Universities.

A member of the committee, Rene A. Wormser produced a minority reply to the report that confirms the main report and adds well founded comment to its content. **(247).**

THE FINDINGS OF THE REECE REPORT

The country is faced with a rapidly increasing birth-rate of foundations. The compelling motivation behind this rapid increase in numbers is tax planning rather than "charity". The possibility exists that a large part of American industry may eventually come into the hands of the foundations. This may perpetuate control of individual enterprises in a way not contemplated by existing legislation, in the hands of closed groups, perhaps controlled in turn by families. Because of the tax exemption granted them, and because they must be dedicated to public purposes, the foundations are public trusts, administering funds of which the public is the equitable owner. However, under the present law there is little implementation of this responsibility to the general welfare; the foundations administer their capital and income with the widest freedom, bordering at times on irresponsibility. Wide freedom is highly desirable, as long as the public dedication is faithfully followed. But, as will be observed later, the present laws do not compel such performance.

1 The increasing number of foundations presents another problem. The Internal Revenue Service is not staffed to adequately scrutinise the propriety and legality of the work of this ever-enlarging multitude of foundations.

2 Foundations are clearly desirable when operating in the natural sciences and when making direct donations to religious, educational, scientific, and other institutional donees. However, when their activities spread into the field of the so-called "social sciences" or into other areas in which our basic moral, social, economic, and governmental principles can be vitally affected, the public should be alerted to these activities and be made aware of the impact of foundation influence on our accepted way of life.

3 The power of the individual large foundation is enormous. It can exercise various forms of patronage which carry with them elements of thought control. It can exert immense influence on educational institutions, upon the educational processes, and upon educators. It is capable of invisible coercion through the power of its purse. It can materially predetermine the development of social and political concepts and courses of action through the process of granting and withholding foundation awards upon a selective basis, and by designing and promulgating projects which propel researchers in selected directions. It can play a powerful part in the determination of academic opinion, and through this thought leadership, materially influence public opinion.

4 This power to influence national policy is amplified tremendously when foundations act in concert. There is such a concentration of foundation power in the United States, operating in the social sciences and education. It consists basically of a group of major foundations, representing a gigantic aggregate of capital and income. There is no conclusive evidence that this interlock, this concentration of power, having some of the characteristics of an intellectual cartel, came into being as the result of an over-all, conscious plan. Nevertheless, it exists. It operates in part through certain intermediary or organisations supported by the foundations. It has ramifications in almost every phase of research and education, in communications and even in government. Such a concentration of power is highly undesirable, whether the net result of its operations is benign or not.

5 Because foundation funds are public funds, the trustees of these organisations must conscientiously exercise the highest degree of fiduciary responsibility. Under the system of operation common to most large foundations this fiduciary responsibility has been largely abdicated, and in two ways. First, in fact if not in theory, the trustees have all too frequently passed solely upon general plans and left detailed administration of donations (and the consequent selection of projects and grantees) to professional employees. Second, these trustees have all too often delegated much of their authority and function to intermediary organisations.

6 A professional class of administrators of foundations funds has emerged, intent upon creating and maintaining personal prestige and independence of action, and upon preserving its position and emoluments. This informal "guild" has already fallen into many of the vices of a bureaucratic system, involving vast opportunities for selective patronage, preference and privilege. It has already come

to exercise a very extensive, practical control over most research in the social sciences, much of our educational process, and a good part of government administration in this and related fields. The aggregate bureaucracy can hardly be exaggerated. A system has thus arisen (without its significance being realized by foundation trustees) which gives enormous power to a relatively small group of individuals, having at their virtual command, huge sums in public trust funds. It is a system which is antithetical to American principles.

7   The far reaching power of the large foundations and of the interlock, has so influenced the press, the radio, and even the government that it has become extremely difficult for objective criticism of foundation practices to get into news channels without having first been distorted, slanted, discredited, and at times ridiculed. **Nothing short of an unhampered Congressional investigation could hope to bring out the vital facts; and the pressure against Congressional investigation has been almost incredible. As indicated by their arrogance in dealing with this committee, the major foundations and their associated intermediary organisations have entrenched themselves behind a totality of power which presumes to place them beyond serious criticism and attack.**

8   **Research in the social sciences plays a key part in the evolution of our society.** of **Such research is now almost wholly in the control of the professional employees the large foundations and their obedient satellites.** Even the great sums allotted by the Federal government for social science research have come into the virtual control of this professional group.

9   This power team has promoted a great excess of empirical research, as contrasted with theoretical research. It has promoted what has been called an irresponsible "fact finding mania". It is true that a balanced empirical approach is essential to sound investigation. But it is equally true that if it is not sufficiently balanced and guided by the theoretical approach, it leads all too frequently to what has been termed "scientism" or fake science, seriously endangering our society upon subsequent general acceptance as "scientific" fact. It is not the part of Congress to dictate methods of research, but an alertness by foundation trustees to the dangers of supporting unbalanced and unscientific research is clearly indicated

10   Associated with the excessive support of the empirical method, the concentration of power has tended to support the dangerous "cultural lag" theory and to promote "moral relativity", to the detriment of our basic moral, religious, and governmental principles. It has tended top support the concept of "social engineering" - that "social scientists" and they alone are capable of guiding us into better ways of living and improved or substituted fundamental principles of action.

11   **Accompanying these directions in research grants, the concentration has shown a distinct tendency to favour political opinions to the left.** These foundations and their intermediaries engage extensively in political activity, not in the form of direct support of political candidates or political parties, but in the conscious promotion of carefully calculated political concepts. **The qualitative and quantitative restrictions of the federal law are wholly inadequate to prevent this miss-use of public trust funds.**

12   **The impact of foundation money upon education has been very heavy, largely tending to promote uniformity in approach and method, tending to induce the educator to become an agent for social change and a propagandist for the development of our society in the direction of some form of collectivism.** Foundations have supported text books (and books intended for inclusion in

collateral reading lists) which are destructive of our basic governmental and social principles and highly critical of some of our cherished institutions.

13   In the international field, foundations, and an interlock among some of them and certain intermediary organisations, have exercised a strong effect upon our foreign policy and upon public education in things international. This has been accomplished by vast propaganda, by supplying executives and advisers to government and by controlling much research in this area through the power of the purse. The net result of these combined efforts has been to promote **"internationalism"** in a particular sense - a form directed towards **"world government" and a derogation of American "nationalism".** Foundations have supported a conscious distortion of history, propagandised blindly for the **United Nations** as the hope of the world, supported that organisation's agencies to an extent beyond general public acceptance, **and leaned towards a generally "leftist" approach to international problems.**

14 With several tragically outstanding exceptions, such as The Institute of Pacific Relations, foundations have not directly supported organisations which, in turn, operated to support Communism. **However, some of the larger foundations have directly supported "subversion" in the true meaning of that term, namely, the process of undermining some of our vitally protective concepts and principles.** They have actively supported attacks upon our social and governmental system and financed the promotion of socialism and collectivist ideas. **(248)**

From this summary of the Reece Report you may feel this investigation exposed the truth and the matter was dealt with swiftly and clinically. But you would be wrong. **The press gave it low key exposure, the bankers moved to spread disinformation and the politicians sat on their hands, while the radical left re-grouped, shifting their operators around so no action was taken. So while the American people thought their deepest fears of Communism had subsided it was in fact re-grouped and as active as ever with a stranglehold on the foundations, the heart of political thinking. The media played a very large part in calming the population who at this point nearly became awakened enough to blow the lid off the Communist deception. (direction).**

I know what you are thinking, how could capitalists like these bankers fund such left wing activity? Remember Rothschild and his funding of the Illuminati, then Communism. International Zionism sees Communism as a vehicle that will transport them to political power.

In the Morgan Bank the senior partners had their own political stance. Dr. Quigley gives us a rare view inside banking. Morgan and Dwight Morrow, belonged to the Republican party, Leffingwell to the Democrats, Grayson Murphy to the far right and Thomas W. Lamont was firmly in the left camp; so alliance to a stance was always a practical decision not political. It was driven by which political stance would advance their bank; not for national or sentimental reasons. Political alliances were left to the consciences of each director, so outwardly they left a public image of the establishment bankers, while in fact they joined the plan to use Communism for revolution to attain their own goal, complete political and financial control world-wide.

So we find, through the members of the Lamont family a channel of support for Communism set up, using bank funds. Quite remarkable, and the evidence for this is contained in the files of the House Un-American Activities Committee. Tom Lamont, his wife Fiona, and his son Corliss between them funded at least twelve left wing organisations including the Communist Party itself. One organisation, Trades Union Services, incorporated from New York City had Corliss Lamont and Frederick Vanderbilt Field as officers both linking back to Wall Street and the Communist Party. Field also was on the editorial staff of The Daily Worker and The New Masses, both Communist publications. He was also the Communist Party link with the Institute of Pacific Relations between 1929-1947.

Corliss Lamont was a leading member of The Friends of the Soviet Union, formed in the twenties, that reorganised in 1943, with Corliss Lamont as its incorporator, and renamed as the National Council of American - Soviet Friendship. **(249).**

Dr. Quigley goes on to say that Corliss Lamont, was fully supported by his parents; became one of the chief figures that organised the Communist Fellow Travellers and was often a spokesman for Soviet views. By January 1946 he was called before the House Un-American Committee to give an account of the agenda of the National Council of American - Soviet Friendship. He refused and was cited by the House of Representatives on June 26th. 1946. Despite this, his father retained him in his will as co-heir to a fortune. **(250).**

In 1951 the Senate Judiciary Sub-Committee on Internal Security proved that China was lost to Communism by academic experts and fellow travellers who worked for The Institute of Pacific Relations. At this time it was well known the IPR was controlled by a Communist and radical Liberal agenda. **(251).**

"In 1951 the Subcommittee on Internal Security of the Senate Judiciary Committee, the so called McCarran Committee, sought to show that China had been lost to the Communists by the deliberate actions of a group of academic experts on the Far East and Communist fellow travellers whose work in that direction was controlled and co-ordinated by the Institute of Pacific Relations (IPR). The influence of the Communists in IPR is well established but the patronage of Wall Street is less well known.

"The IPR was a private association of ten independent national councils in ten countries concerned with affairs in the Pacific. The headquarters of the IPR and the American Council of the IPR were both in New York and were closely associated on an interlocking basis. Each spent about $2.5 million dollars over the quarter-century from 1925 to 1950 of which about half, in each case, came from the Carnegie Foundation and the Rockefeller Foundation (which were themselves interlocking groups controlled by an alliance of Morgan and Rockefeller interests on Wall Street). Much of the rest (of the money), especially of the American Council, came from firms closely allied to these two Wall Street interests, such as Standard Oil, International Telephone and Telegraph, International General Electric, The National City Bank, and the Chase National Bank....

"The financial deficits which occurred each year were picked up by financial angels, almost all with close Wall Street connections. The chief identifiable contributions here were about $60,000 from Frederick Vanderbilt Field over eighteen years, $14,700 from Thomas Lamont over fourteen years, $800 from Corliss Lamont (only after 1947) and $18,000 from a member of Lee, Higginson in Boston who seems to have been Jerome D. Greene". **(252).**

"In addition, large sums of money each year were directed to private individuals, for research and travel expenses from similar sources, chiefly the great financial foundations.

"Most of these awards for work in the Far Eastern area required approval or recommendation from members of IPR. Moreover, access to publication and recommendations to academic positions in the handful of great American Universities concerned with the Far East required similar sponsorship. And, finally, there can be little doubt that consultant jobs on Far Eastern matters in the State Department or other government agencies were largely restricted to IPR-approved people. The individuals who published, who had money, found jobs, were consulted, and who were appointed intermittently to government missions were those who were tolerant of the IPR line. The fact that all these lines of communication passed through the Ivy League Universities or their scattered equivalents West of the Appalachians, such as Chicago, Stanford, or California, unquestionably went back to Morgan's influence in handling large academic endowments". **(253).**

Dr. Quigley admits that the Academics who became members of the IPR board formed the IPR Party line which had a resounding similarity to that of the Kremlin, on the Far East and the State department followed this line closely. Then in an attempt to cover what he had just said he declares; "There is no evidence of which I am aware, of any explicit plot or conspiracy to direct American policy in a direction favourable either to the Soviet Union or to International Communism. Efforts of the radical right to support their convictions about these last points undoubtedly did great, lasting, and unfair damage to the reputations and interests of many people". **(254).**

He can't have it both ways, either these people aided and promoted Soviet policy (which has been accepted they did) and therefore worked against the interests of the United States and the free world, or they did not.

Dr. Quigley's attempt to show Russian, IPR, and State Department policy as three policies that coincidentally agreed, failed, as he gives us the evidence of co-operation and once again this great historian fails to meet the challenge to tell the story as it really was. But you must remember his agenda is the banker's agenda.

Here we see quite clearly the conflict of American policy. While America and the media were telling the world that they were fighting back the advance of Communism, their State Department was dumping its allies in China and handing six-hundred-million Chinese to Communism and suppression.

To disprove Dr. Quigley's cover up, the Reece Committee had this to say; **"During the period 1945-1949, persons associated with the Institute of Pacific Relations were instrumental in keeping United States policy on a course favourable to Communist objectives in China. Persons associated with the IPR were influential in 1949 in giving United States Far East policy a direction that furthered Communist purposes". (255).**

The proof of Dr. Quigley's inconsistency comes on page 938 of Tragedy and Hope, **(256)** where he states; "Dean Rusk, Secretary of State after 1961, at Oxford (1931-1933), is as much a member of the nexus (the Communist infiltrators) as Alger Hiss, the Dulles brothers, Jerome Greene, James T. Shotwell, John W. Davis, Elihu Root, or Philip Jessup".

Dr. Quigley still insists that although some may be Communists, IPR seemed to be immune from compliance with Communist policies. **(257).** The Reece committee found "The IPR has been considered by the American Communist party and by the Soviet officials as an instrument of Communist policy, propaganda and military intelligence. The IPR disseminated and sought to popularise false information including information originating from Soviet and Communist sources..."

"Owen Lattimore was, from some time beginning in the 1930's a conscious articulate instrument of the Soviet conspiracy. Effective leadership by the end of 1934 established and implemented an official connection with G. N. Voitinski, Chief of the Far Eastern Division of the Communist International.

"The net effect of IPR activities on United States public opinion has been such as to serve internal Communist interests and to affect adversely the interests of the United States".

What Dr. Quigley knows but fails to make clear is the reason why the group and all Communist infiltrators were named but not shamed and that is because of the power and influence of the bankers who had their men strategically placed to cover such events and also controlled the press who ignored the conspiracy or wrote it up as another right wing scare story which it was not. From this brief history, all of which can be proved by evidence you can see how, from the early thirties, America followed a pro Communist foreign policy while the media sang their praises as the world champions against Communist expansion. That they fought the Korean war and the Vietnam War to uphold this mirror, should make America sit up and think. For their sons, who were killed for a false agenda the politicians and the media in particular, must take the blame; **they betrayed America.**

THE FORD FOUNDATION

Let me make it quite clear. In America there are hundreds of foundations, most of which have been set up to protect the wealth of rich businesses and their families from the burden of crippling tax brought about by the lavish expenditure of politicians using borrowed money. Most of them play no part in the Establishment Secret Society that is using Communism and Socialism to move the United States and the world towards global dictatorship. However, a handful of the richest foundations have totally abused their tax exempt status to attack from within the structure, Morality, education, media, communications and the public sector of government. Chief amongst those have been the Rockefeller Foundation, founded by a major player in the International Banking Group, the Carnegie foundation, and the Ford Foundation.

If you study the life of Henry Ford, you will find he set up his Foundation to stop the predators of Wall Street, like Rockefeller, from snatching the Ford empire from his family. It is therefore sad to find that in an attempt to gain the power of Ford's money the foundation ended up in the hands of a member of the Wall Street group, Paul G. Hoffman.

Paul Hoffman came up through the far left agenda. As propaganda Director of the Council on Foreign Relations and Trustee for the Institute of Pacific Relations, he was considered far left. He brought in Robert M. Hutchins, a well known global collectivist to assist him and between them went to work suppressing anti Communist feeling that exploded around Alger Hiss and Harry Dexter-White, exposed by Chambers as a ex-member of the Communist underground movement.

In 1953 the Ford Foundation paid Paul Hoffman and Hutchins fifteen-million dollars to set up a fund for a organisation called The Fund for the Republic, so they could be moved from their positions within the Ford Foundation to make way for family friends.

One of their first achievements for the revolution was to undo the elaborate defences set up to protect government against subversive employees. They spent $300,000 on a study of the effect of Communism on America and no other person than Earl Browner, the national secretary of the Communist party, was a member of the team.

The Fund for the Republic spent $150,000 to prove academic freedom was being suppressed by patriotic demand. Hoffman even went to the Ford Foundation for more money ($1,134,000) to fund a campaign to grant recognition to Communist China after the forced occupation by Mao's forces.

In this way he soon used up the funds available then married Anna Rosenberg, and took a job in the United Nations and helped get UN funds passed to Castro's Cuba. In the meantime Hutchins had re-organised the 'Fund for the Republic' into a radical left wing organisation and re-named it, 'The Centre for the Study of Democratic Institutions', still funded by Foundations, but the Ford Foundation would no longer admit it supplied the money, but it seems they did as the work carried on.

Up till 1956 the Ford Foundation had spent over one billion dollars on education designed to control thought in many Universities. In irresponsible hands this could be devastating to democracy. **The Reece committee found a large part of the Ford Foundation funding dangerous to America's constitutional democracy.**

By 1966 the Ford Foundation was placed in the hands of McGregor Bundy and almost immediately its funding swung into action to back the far left revolution. So where did McGregor Bundy originate from? The Council on Foreign Relations, the breeding ground for far left and Communist revolution.. He graduated from Yale, became a Dean of Harvard, then he became a top advisor to John F. Kennedy and Lyndon Johnson. Then he became head of the National Security Council, where he did untold damage to the security of the United States, especially in his handling of affairs in the Dominican Republic by supporting a top Communist, Antonio Gozman, as the leader. This led to the early end of his appointment but as usual the power structure had their man moved to the Ford Foundation just as they did with Alger Hiss. He was moved out of the State Department when his Communist background became clear and he was made President of the Carnegie Endowment for International Peace, as you will see later in this chapter.

McGeorge Bundy's first big funding was 'The Black Revolution', where he literally made them awash with money, pouring $160,000 into the hands of a black revolutionary Communist, Milton Galamison, for his revolution against the American establishment. (Part of Weishaupt's plan to break up democracy).

McGeorge Bundy hired another black revolutionary Communist, Herman Ferguson, while he was under suspicion of plotting the murder of senator Robert Kennedy, and he was still on the payroll when arrested. To illustrate how finance can change attitude the National Urban League, a black moderate organisation was directed into a violent agenda in favour of black power when it received a two billion dollar grant from McGeorge Bundy's Ford Foundation, shifting the power of revolution to a direct attack on the establishment and democracy.

One after another left revolutionary organisation were funded in an attempt to undermine America and its constitution.

In W. Cleon Skousen's book 'The Naked Capitalist' **(258)** a list appears of just a few of the far left organisations that the Ford Foundation funded all of which have been subject to scrutiny by the congressional Un-American Activities Committee.

Council on Foreign Relations.	$ 1,000,000.
Adlai E. Stevenson Institute of International Affairs.	$ 1,000,000.
Institute of International Education.	$ 1,625,000.
World Affairs Council.	$ 102,000.
The National Committee on U.S. - China (Red China) Relations.	$ 250,000.
The United Nations Association.	$ 150,000.
Foreign Policy Research.	$ 275,000.
American Friends Service Committee (Pro-Vietcong).	$100,000.
Southern Regional Council (Communist staffed).	$648,000.
National Student Association.	$315,000.
Southwest Council of La Raza. (Headed by a known Communist Maclevie R. Barraza).	$630,000.
National Educational Television and Radio Centre (N.E.T.)	$6,000,000.
Public Broadcast Laboratory.	$7,900,000.

Dr. Quigley could see nothing wrong with this one sided funding that gave the far left an inside advantage in thought manipulation and pro-Russian policy formulation.

The interlocking between the foundations, Wall Street, The Anglo - American Secret Society, the Round Table, International Zionism, the Masonic movement and Communism is completed by the centres of planning for world government, The Council on Foreign Relations, The Institute of Pacific Relations, and now the United Nations, with other secret planning forums assembling regularly to advance the revolution, like the Bilderberg Group. This power group is formidable. Its big weakness is its secrecy, essential to dominate the world outside democracy. This enemy within can be beaten by exposure.

So it can be seen that a minority of foundations, with the richest purses were targeted by the Anglo - American Secret Society to ferment trouble within the masses. (A classic Marxist tactic). But surely, you will ask, the politicians must have known and would have stopped it? So let us now discover what was going on inside the halls of power, both in the government offices, and the political minds.

INFILTRATION

On a cold spring morning in 1932, Whittaker Chambers, the Editor of The New Masses, a Communist, (already mentioned as a radical left magazine) received a phone call from Max Bedacht, a top ranking Communist. Twenty-four hours later he was a member of the Communist underground. Perhaps it was the chance purchase of a second hand, fire damaged copy of Lenin's 'A Soviet at Work' that brought him so abruptly into the Communist underground; he had certainly been impressed with it when he read it, who knows? Chambers was a deep thinking man, not easily won over by blind political propaganda, and as such had already learned, when he walked out of the Daily Worker Offices, that the people are not the party; they just exist at its pleasure. This thinking of Chambers would eventually be his downfall.

He was a romantic Communist as his stories portrayed. But as an underground worker he was involved in work between the open party and the International underground movement, which he came to know intimately. He joined the underground as a party courier, and on one occasion Chambers recalls at the Alger Hiss hearings that he went to San Francisco to deliver a money belt with $10,000 in it to further espionage work in the Pacific Islands (The Pacific Rim now being federalised).

A brief spell in Tokyo was followed by a shift in Moscow's policy from a frontal attack on Capitalism to a policy called its 'Third Period' and the start of the all embracing of 'Liberalism' which in typical deception mood they called the 'Popular Front'. Chambers was about to meet Alger Hiss for the first time.

At Harvard University, Hiss adopted Fabian Socialism from a stance that could only be described as collectivism. But was that stance just a front? At his previous academy, John Hopkins, he was at the top in everything he did but, to his bitter disappointment failed to get a Rhodes Scholarship, known well for its left wing teaching. But despite this one failure he was, in most of his quests, ahead of his rivals; a person to respect in your associations. Maybe his fate was sealed when he married a society rebel, Priscilla Fansler Hobson. They returned to Boston for a time where he took a job at the Wall Street legal firm of Cotton and Franklin, lodging near Columbia University.

This was the time of the depression (brought on by the bankers), a time that made many a good man ponder his future and think of some better way forward. Was it Socialism? Socialism, even Marxism was becoming popular amongst middle class Americans as an escapist adventure from the devil they knew; a dangerous departure from reality, as it has always shown in the fullness of light. Alger Hiss, led by Priscilla, was drifting into Communism.

They moved to New York and Hiss took up with his old friend from University, Lee Pressman (of Russian origin) from the Wall Street firm of Chadbourne, Stanchfield and Levy. A man intimately involved in the liberalised thinking of the New Deal (New World Order), a Socialist maybe, even a Communist, it was not clearly known at this time, (not till later), but his contact with Hiss was leading him down a path to extremism.

This was the time of leftism amongst undergraduates, and for students out of University, an agency existed, the Agricultural Adjustment Administration (the AAA), which propelled trained left wing graduates into government services at high levels. The AAA became known as the Greatest Intelligence Service in Washington. Gradually they were pushing out the traditional Democrats from government offices and replacing them with radical left students amongst whom were known Communists.

So a cell of like minded students, all of high intelligence and all radical and to the left were taking over important administrative and policy making groups within government, and, when in place, surrounding themselves with their own colleagues and cell members. What seems quite clear, it was Pressman who moved this group into Communism, with his certainty of decisions combined with the false promises of Communism to liberate the people from their problems of the time. Slightly ironical if you then realise that the economic slump of the time had been created by the very bankers who originally funded Communism.

Even then, Alger Hiss could have gone either way, but for the arrival of a top Communist International agent, Hal Ware, who was to decide which way he was to go. He joined the underground.

Meanwhile, despite fierce opposition Franklin D. Roosevelt recognised the Soviet Union in 1932, and diplomatic facilities were exchanged which led to a new era in spying through Embassy channels. Ware was given orders to create

Communist cells and get their agents assigned to government, banks and industry. The orders to infiltrate was given by the NKVD, who directed the plan, dividing cells and creating others, always moving their devotees into key positions in teaching, government offices and politics. They were even told to list key jobs so when they became vacant, their chosen candidate would have the best qualifications.

First to be put in place were lawyers and economists and then public relations like personnel director's assistants. From there they could make sure their chosen infiltrators were hired. (The enemy within). **Direction.**

So by the time the Second World War took place they had infiltrated the vital organs of decision and put their top men in place. They were assisted unwittingly by the curse of all nations, the liberal element that always has to meddle with every aspect of our life with endless change that eventually destabilises society. Hal Ware chose Lee Pressman's cell to supply some of his top men, and along with others, joined Washington cell number one.

Ware's men penetrated the State Department, the Treasury, the War Department, the Labour department, the Justice Department, and even the Emigration Department; even more amazingly the White House staff.

Mother Bloor, Ware's Communist mother said, "I find his boys and girls everywhere. It's my comfort".

Alger Hiss' first job in government was when he became a legal interrogator on the Nye Committee. He was an instant success. Russia was now influencing American policy. In 1934 Whittaker Chambers met Hiss for the first time. Whittaker Chambers, introduced to Hiss as Carl, struck up an immediate friendship, meeting at least once a month.

Chambers was to organise a new cell which eventually included Alger Hiss, and George Silverman. It was George Silverman who would introduce Chambers to Harry Dexter White, the special monetary advisor to the Secretary of the Treasury, Henry Morgenthau Junior. This became a special cell for underground workers in high government office.

So far the cells had only infiltrated important posts and massaged policies. Now came the inevitable change demanded of these idealists. In 1929 Russia stopped the NKVD from sending America a subsidy for its spying network. This forced the network to take up espionage to prove to Russia their worth, so their subsidy would be reinstated.

So Chambers set up the small cell in which Alger Hiss supplied the secret papers from his office. Chambers would photocopy them and return them to Hiss to take back to his office. Simple, by 1935 Chambers was feeding his contact Peters all the Nye Committee files; Russia was grateful, but saw their opportunity to influence American policy. Early in 1935 Hiss returned to the AAA just in time for a reorganisation. An attempt was made to purge the AAA from their left wing infiltrators. Hiss was ordered by the Communist party to side with the right wing element as they wanted him to remain inside. Hiss was not popular with his AAA friends but the party came first. By September 1936 Francis Sayre, one of Hiss' law professors at Harvard, asked him to be his assistant in the State Department. Now Communism had a man in place in the sanctum of government.

Alger Hiss would borrow papers from his office and Chambers would have them photographed and take the microfilm to his new controller, Bykov, a Soviet agent, and as before return the papers to Hiss to replace in the office.

Now the Soviets were getting highly sensitive inside material. Bykov's next move was to insist on paying his agents, to gain further control on his operators, and degrade their reason for helping the Communist cause. In that way he could exercise more power over his subjects. A rug, a form of payment, given to Alger Hiss, would feature in his trial. By 1937 Whittaker Chambers had reached the end of his honeymoon with Communism. Either, at this point, he would bluntly accept anything that Communism threw at the world or he would begin to question the realities of Communism.

As we have seen Chambers was a deep thinker and he was destined to follow the second path towards disillusionment and outright opposition to Communism that so many people captured by the deception of its powers had already taken. For Communism, however, this was a serious loss as he knew too much of the inside workings of the underground movement. All of a sudden the crimes of Communism took on a new light. The liquidation of the Kulaks, the Stalin planned Ukraine famine in which it was estimated twenty-two and a half million peasants starved to death, the largest man instigated holocaust yet imposed upon a people. Then the 1936 purge trials of the old Bolsheviks like Bukharin, Kamenev and Radek, the men of the revolution were accused of being traitors on trumped up charges by Stalin's terror police.

Yes, Communism had fooled him and many other good men, but he now knew what he must do. Chambers was later to write, "Experience and the record had finally convinced me that Communism is a form of totalitarianism, that its triumph means slavery to men wherever they fall under its sway and spiritual night to the human mind and soul....I resolved to break with the Communist party at whatever risk to my life or other tragedy to myself or my family". **(259)**.

He planned his exit well. He bought a farm house in Westminster to disappear to when he needed to hide. He started to retain documents that would prove Alger Hiss and Harry Dexter White's roll in espionage as an insurance policy; the very papers that would eventually nail the lies of the spying. Most of the evidence was held on microfilm which he hid in a pumpkin and left it in his wife's Nephew's house for safe keeping. Then in April 1938 he made his move to leave Communism. What happened next ended up in a prolonged effort to bring both Alger Hiss and Harry Dexter White to trial for espionage and expose the depth of Communist penetration into the American government?

That this process was so difficult and that obstructions were put in the way of progress indicated the depths to which government was penetrated, right up to executive level within the civil service and within politics. What was less certain was how much help was given by power structures like the bankers, industrialists and the Zionist movement, all of whom had invested interest in clouding the facts of treason. It was not till the middle of 1948, ten years later, Alger Hiss was to be interrogated for espionage, a delay that gave Communism a sufficient space to re-group. The courage and patience of Whittaker Chambers in pursuing his case against Hiss was perhaps the main reason the case was heard at all.

Chambers at first, was reluctant to expose his former colleagues, but the realisation began to dawn on him when Stalin came to make a pact with Hitler on August 26th. 1939 (See Rakovski Interview page 108) that he must disclose everything. This was the culmination of the bankers' plot to make sure that war was inevitable between Germany and the other Western powers instead of Russia, making another stride forward towards their goal of revolution and at the same time insuring the bankers enjoyed a large loan debt charge for future years. **(260)**.

What was an extreme possibility became a fact in this pact and to those few who knew its implications it meant that everything the Russian intelligence gleaned from its American spy ring would be passed on to the Gestapo. Whittaker Chambers realised this total horror scenario and it cleared his last doubts about what he should do; expose the entire spy ring. By the first of September 1939 Hitler invaded Poland (instead of Russia). Early on in Chambers' disclosures he expected to find the names he named would be removed from office. To his dismay they were not. Someone, or some strong force, seemed to be protecting them from such a course.

Later (1948), it was clearly stated that Berle, who took down Chambers' story of espionage cells within government had reported direct to Roosevelt, who had in no uncertain terms told him to, "Jump into the lake". This account was given publicity at the trial of Hiss in 1948. **(261).** But Berle turned out to be a turn coat, from his anti-Communist stance, power or something corrupted him, because at Hiss' trial he played down the espionage ticket for all it was worth. The fact was that Roosevelt and the State Department were putting all sorts of obstructions in the way and Chambers revelations were being swept under the carpet by Berle, the Communist hater and others involved. But Levine would not let go. He called in a press friend, Walter Winchell. Walter Winchell took the story direct to the President and found a similar response from Roosevelt.

By 1946, seven years after Chambers' first exposed the spy ring, Alger Hiss was still enjoying high office and after a recommendation by John Foster Dulles became the new head of the Carnage Endowment for Peace, and was instrumental in the formation of the United Nations, and making sure it would be controlled and run by Communist sympathisers.

So we get a picture that even when the Communist underground had sections of its operation identified by the system there were those in power that could ignore evidence and even destroy it to prolong the Communist penetration of government. (Classical infiltration by Weishaupt-Marxist forces). **DIRECTION.**

Hiss was able to become a presidential advisor and as such did immense damage to America and the world. He prepared the American policy that was presented at Alta in 1945. This was the disastrous policy that set up Unity governments in Poland and Eastern Europe that handed these areas to the Eastern block and Communism.

Take the moment that Russia demanded sixteen votes at the United Nations. Roosevelt (at this time a dying man), Hiss, Stalin and an interpreter were alone in conference while America's high brass was left outside. The result was Roosevelt struck a deal that Russia would have three votes to America's one. All Roosevelt could say was, "I know I shouldn't have done it. But I was so tired when they got hold of me. Besides, it won't make much difference". Hiss later was to hint that he was the one who "Got hold of me".

Even when his position was exposed in a Canadian dossier on espionage as a Soviet spy who was at the time an assistant to the Secretary of State, Edward R. Stettinius, his position was protected by the forces of evil within the State Department. **(262).**

Remember he was first cited by Chambers in 1939 as a spy, along with his other colleagues. So till he left the State Department in 1946 to join the Carnage Peace Foundation he had influenced State Department decisions to give Russia greater voting power in the United Nations, the conditions of the German reparations to make sure Germany could not recover, the cession of Sakhalin and the Churls to the Soviet Union, and the decision to turn over to the NKVD the refugees who had escaped the Russian terror. **(263)**. In doing this and many other services to Russia, Alger Hiss betrayed America and the free world.

Even then, John Foster Dulles was warned about Alger Hiss' record of Communism by Larry Davidlow, a lawyer, but once more Dulles rejected evidence. Were the American Politicians and top civil servants within the banking-Zionist-Masonic-Communist conspiracy? Well on 1st. February 1947, Alger Hiss became President of the Carnegie Endowment and straight away he was director and member of The United Nations, Chairman of the executive of the Citizens Committee for Reciprocal World Trade, Member of the American Geographical Society, a director of the Woodrow Wilson Foundation, not bad for a man known for treason. **(264)**.

At last, the road was coming to an end for Alger Hiss. Whittaker Chambers had testified before the Un-American committee and named him as a Communist. At last, nine dangerous years later for democracy Alger Hiss would go under the microscope. ("Seeds of Treason"; this book includes the details of the hearing). All through the hearing the press and the President tried to make out that there was no substance to Hiss' accuser's evidence. Truman even called the hearings a pre-election 'Red Herring'. The twists and turns in the procedure became epic. By November 17th. Chambers decided to use his hidden evidence, microfilm, hidden in a pumpkin, and the hearings took a dramatic turn.

Nixon, (Later President) the interrogator at the hearings, re-convened the Un-American Committee urgently as he was suspicious of the State Department's moves, who seemed more concerned to disgrace Chambers than bring a spy to justice. By May 31st. 1949 Alger Hiss was in New York's federal court; after a marathon hearing it became apparent, that Judge Kaufman, who was an appointee of the President, made sure that the jury were confused, and after two days' deliberation advised the judge they could not come to a unanimous decision. Immediately the judge was accused of prejudice towards the defence by Nixon.

Ironically, it was up to Senator John Foster Dulles to put the government boot into Hiss when his case became a lost cause. (Ironically, because he was one of the establishment politicians who so carefully protected him from exposure in the first place).

Hiss was found guilty on the first and second count. It was January 24th. 1950, eleven long years of spying after he was first brought to the governments attention. Eleven years of untold treason.

HARRY DEXTER WHITE

We have just experienced how Communism infiltrated government offices to spy. But by 1936 spying was not their only intention. With Roosevelt's recognition of Communist Russia a new era started and the cell that Alger Hiss and Harry Dexter White belonged to within the Communist underground was formed, not only to spy, but to get its men into high positions so it could influence America's foreign and domestic policies to help Communism to corrupt America and the World from within. We have seen how the spy ring worked. Now we must examine the policies of Harry Dexter White who was largely the architect of this cell so we can understand the level of damage this spy ring did to the world and America in particular.

We have already seen how Alger Hiss helped to word the policy that gave Russia most of its satellite countries at the Yalta talks along with the cave in on voting rights for the United Nations. Now let us examine the policies Harry Dexter White influenced, and their direction. This will deliver to us the verdict on his political position and from this his guilt or otherwise in regards to his position as a spy and traitor to his adopted country.

Harry White (Weiss or Weit) was born on October 9th. 1892 in Boston, Massachusetts. He was the youngest son of Jacob White and Sarah White, natives of Lithuania, Russia. It was not till later (1909) that he added Dexter to his name, probably to sound more American. In 1917 he volunteered to enter the army and as an officer was assigned to camp Devens to train new recruits. At thirty (1922), having married, he enrolled at Columbia University, studying government. By 1923 he had moved to Stanford University to study economics which he passed with distinction and went on to Harvard to take his PhD. A Professor who taught him confirmed he had no visible left wing tendency at this time.

He also took up a teaching job at Harvard. In 1930 he was awarded his PhD for his paper on "The International Payments of France 1880-1913". His work was awarded the Wells prize for a essay on specified fields of economics. But this alone did not bring him a boost in his position, and he continued to teach at Harvard and made money and banking his speciality. **Direction.**

In 1932 he left Harvard for Lawrence College where he was promoted to professor of economics. He was considered as Conservative as Adam Smith.

The big depression came next that would last in economic terms right into the Second World War. Was this the time Harry Dexter White looked around for new ways to run the economy? Was this the time he formed his political alliance with Communism?

Events were overtaking his politics. Jacob Viner, of the United States Treasury Department asked him to assist him in overhauling the monetary and banking legislation and institutions to produce a long term plan for its administration. White accepted (1934). At last he could come to practical grips with his chosen subject.

Soon he was promoted to Principal Economic Analyst in the Treasury's Research and Statistic Division. At this time Roosevelt brought in his old friend Henry Morgenthau Jr. as first acting then Secretary to the Treasury in January 1934. John Morton Blum once said, "Morgenthau's first joy in life was to serve Roosevelt, whom he loved trusted and admired". **(265).**

It was not long before Morgenthau saw the talent of Harry Dexter White and made him his Principal advisor. As such, he became perhaps the most powerful influence outside politics and only second to Harry Hopkins, Roosevelt's personal friend and advisor. This power was because Morgenhau had the ear of Roosevelt and relied on White to produce policies to present to the President. Morgenthau increasingly asked him to do work that was not strictly treasury responsibility at Roosevelt's request. So if at this point Harry Dexter White was a underground member of the Communist movement he could wield great power to help the Communist cause, but there is no hard evidence to prove that he was a spy by 1934, and if he was, he kept his secret close to his chest.

On December 8th. 1941 he was made Assistant Secretary to the Treasury by Henry Morgenthau. His duties encompassed all foreign operations of the Treasury; by 1943 he also was put in charge of the Treasury's relations with the Army and

Navy. He was at this point one of the most powerful civil servants within the American administration.

White's suggestions were included in the final ultimatum to Japan in November 1941, which ultimately ended up with the Japanese attack on Pearl Harbour. Many Historians since have critically attacked America's role at this point for making conditions that brought about a conflict which Japan was not seeking and could not win.

In 1942 White played a major role in establishing a post war policy for International finance. It was the White Plan which became the basic structure for the International Monetary Fund. Both White and Lord Keynes jointly controlled the Bretton Wood Conference in July 1944, when the International Monetary Fund and the International Bank for Reconstruction and Development were born. Since that time this bank, in league with the World Bank, both linked to the United Nations policies, has systematically attempted to use the bank to give inadequate assistance to Third World Countries while locking them into debt slavery, while the banks acquire the mineral rights to these countries' only assets. This policy, that only benefits the bankers, effectively puts these countries into debt slavery for the foreseeable future. It follows the banker's policy, to own all world resources, so they can control the world through their chosen policy, Communism. **Direction.**

So the bank that was portrayed as the friend of the Third World was cynically used to arrest their only assets instead of helping them to develop their economies for self sufficiency.

During the Second World War, White was deeply involved in the negotiations between the US government and Nationalist China. At first America needed Nationalist China to occupy the Japanese Imperialists in war. So they funded the Chinese Nationalists. China, whose economy was in chaos, needed financial support to continue its war with Japan and hold back Communist forces from the North? America agreed to help but White advised caution, and he only dribbled money to Nationalist China. Was this because he saw the main chance for Communist forces in the North to take over power? Or was it just frustration with the nationalist control of its finances? The fact, that when Nationalist China was no longer needed to occupy Japan in war, America reneged on its support for the Chinese Nationalist cause and therefore allowed Mao (the Communist leader) to make his long march to capture China's heart, is compelling evidence. This policy could be fairly levelled at White, because of his hesitant policy in helping the Nationalists solve their financial problems. But it could be argued that America became frustrated by the Nationalist blackmail to keep them in power. The final result, the victory of Communism in China, might give us a better insight into White's reasons for holding back Gold deliveries, if it could be proved White was batting on the Communist's side.

White "Participated in a major way" in preparing a policy for post war Germany, known as the Morgenthau Plan. From this paper the Quebec Memorandum was signed by Roosevelt and Churchill, at the September 1944 conference. This dangerous paper planned to turn Germany from an industrial leader into a agricultural and pastoral desert; planned for the bankers of Wall Street in retribution for a war the scheming of which their agents carefully planned and the bankers of New York and others, financed. The fact that these bankers were Internationalists, which indeed Harry Dexter White was, gives us a major lead to the direction of his thinking and his policies. That these very bankers also financed

Marxism and through it Communism gets us nearer to the truth. **A MAJOR DIRECTION.**

Held, in the Franklin D. Roosevelt library, Hyde Park, New York, is a copy of the original map on which Harry Dexter White planned the partition of Germany. **(266).** A plan that was to be presented to those present at Yalta. The first part of the plan, to remove all industrial capacity from Germany and turn Germany into a agricultural and pastoral land of food production for Europe, was a truly aggressive policy that was going to cause the other European countries all sorts of problems, nevertheless it was partly imposed but had to be removed when the rest of Europe suffered its knock on effects. However the partition went ahead effectively splitting Germany in two, with the Eastern part under Communist control from Russia. **Direction.**

Once more we find Harry Dexter White behind a policy that ends up giving a large area of Europe to Communism. This was not all, at Yalta a large part of Europe that became the Communist Satellite countries was handed to Stalin to control. Even the allied forces, chasing the German army back to Berlin, halted the operation for over a month to allow Stalin's troops to enter Berlin first as the victors, to bolster the case for handing the satellite countries to Stalin at the peace conference. So it seems the politicians, including Roosevelt, were already in a conspiracy to allow Communism to increase its influence, while the media told us a very different story. This plan was all part of Harry Dexter White's recommendations to Roosevelt before the end of the war. The result was that a large part of Eastern Europe was taken over by Communism. Was this a planned policy or an unfortunate consequence of war? The careful pre-planning, culminating at the Yalta agreement convinces me it was no mistake, but a hidden intention to allow Eastern Europe to go Communist, as part of the 'New Deal' world revolution so dear to Roosevelt. **Direction.**

There is no doubt that Harry Dexter White's proposals for Germany were designed to weaken the future power of Germany; quite in line with the wishes of the Anglo-American bankers. So was he a Communist or a channel used by the bankers to move their world revolution forward through a well placed official? Really at this point it does not seem to matter which grouping he is loyal to, as they both have the same aim. But a Communist he was declared.

In May 1946 Harry Dexter White became the first American Executive Director of "The International Monetary Fund". The appointment was made despite the FBI's file on him, which showed justifiable concern over his trustworthiness, and held enough evidence to charge him with spying. However the main damage he did to America was from within, planned by his NKVD controllers to move the world towards Communism. By the end of March the heat to prosecute him became powerful. He resigned from the International Monetary fund, but before he went he made sure it was organised to the liking of the power bankers and of course was manned by Communist sympathisers. This remains the case today. Shortly after he retired and between hearings that would have fully exposed his position, he suffered a heart attack in September 1947. By August 1948 he suffered a second, this time fatal heart attack, and died before his trial for spying had been completed.

Elizabeth Bentley's and Whittaker Chambers' damning evidence, equally if not more conclusive against White, than Alger Hiss, would most certainly have served to seal his fate. Death robbed America of this justice. Five years after his death the Attorney General, Herbert Brownell stated clearly, "Harry Dexter White was a

Russian Spy. He smuggled secret documents to Russian agents for transmission to Moscow".

We must ask serious questions. Why did nine years pass, with knowledge of his possible spying, handed from the FBI right into the President's office in December 45', without any action taken to remove him from office till those accusations were properly investigated?

Why did President Roosevelt and President Truman resist and rubbish all attempts taking place to remove him from office? Why was the knowledge of his Communist activities so carefully played down and swept under the carpet?

Why was Communism within government allowed to continue and develop even after Hiss was jailed? These questions cannot be answered by an argument of lack of awareness or even of error or mistakes, because Communism, quite rightly was fast becoming a dirty word in America and some politicians like McCarthy would continue where Nixon left off.

If we then study what happened to Senator McCarthy, and how the man was so viciously attacked by Politicians and in particular the media for trying to do his job as head of the un-American Committee, you realise that behind politics there is a hidden agenda so powerful that they control political action.

Having read many books on these years (Listed in the Bibliography of each chapter) I have come to the firm opinion that enough evidence exists to answer these questions fully and the answers are surprising.

I do not think that Harry Dexter White was just a Communist, even if he ever was one, but he was a Zionist. What he did believe in, was the 'New Deal', Roosevelt's plan for the World; what is now known as The New World Order (As shown on the dollar note, depicted by a pyramid with a broken top with Lucifer's eye and the Illumination 'Illuminati') He certainly followed the bankers' desires and could well have been their agent within government. Following their will would most certainly have involved helping Communism as the bankers financed Communism to achieve the target of 'World' domination. Nearly all his actions benefited the International Bankers. He was an International Zionist. As Communism existed only because this group of bankers funded it and spread it through the world by use of the Masonic movement, it is reasonable to believe that, as an agent of the bankers, he would help to promote their chosen political creed for world domination. Viewed in this light everything he did was sympathetic to the design for world government and as such, as an International Zionist, believing the world was their state, there was no conflict of interest in helping Communism from within the government. **(Unless we can understand who our real enemy is we will continue to fire our guns at the wrong target).**

It is the direction of events that tell us the hidden truth of politics. Direction never fails to disclose truth in hindsight.

But in saying all this, we have one more question to answer. Why did the politicians try to cover up the extent of Communist infiltration into the Civil Service, until the momentum of evidence became so compelling, that they had to at least sacrifice part of the Communist cell to quieten public opinion? To answer this we must study President Roosevelt, a most complex man.

FRANKLIN D. ROOSEVELT.

"Mankind in the gross, is a gaping monster, that loves to be deceived, and has seldom been disappointed". **Henry Mackenzie.**

It has been said that the words used by the men of power are frequently chosen to hide, rather than, disclose the truth. That Roosevelt was adept at this becomes so clear to me, when studying his political life. He was a complex man who hid his thoughts from one half of his political colleagues, while allowing those he liked to influence him unduly. Thus he became focused on a policy so narrow and so dangerous to America that it threatened it's constitution and it's very democracy. This was because the men who surrounded him, and whom he liked, were either Communist infiltrators, like Alger Hiss, or belonged to the International oil and banking group like Morgenthau. It would be wrong to leave it there without mentioning the third force, a single man with more power over Roosevelt than all his advisors, Harry Hopkins. General John Deane, head of the United States military mission in Moscow wrote of Harry Hopkins that he carried out the Russian Aid programme "With a zeal which is approaching fanaticism" **(267).** Harry Hopkins an untrained diplomat in a strange way guided Roosevelt into every traitorous act against America and the free world. Many historians have tried to unravel this complication of influence but much still remains hidden; however the books and diaries of those involved unravel most of the truth and it is from these I draw my conclusions.

We will see how Roosevelt, advised by Hopkins and Alger Hiss, a special advisor from the State Department, a Communist spy and traitor, ended up in the Winter Palace of the Czars by the Baltic sea, and how Roosevelt handed Eastern Europe and China to Stalin almost without pressure from Stalin.

But to understand this fully we must first of all deal with Roosevelt's early life and the conferences leading up to Yalta. We must appreciate that Roosevelt, through his devious use of the media, already partly controlled by the bankers, was able to shroud his policies in a mirror of what the people wanted to hear; as time went by, he could even call black, white, and not be questioned. He became a hero by telling the people of America that they would not join the war unless America was attacked, yet he spent the following years planning America's participation and was, against the recognised rules of neutrality, supplying Russia, Britain, and others with arms before America entered the war.

The Second World War was **three wars in one.** The first was the declared war against Germany. The second, the war against Japan. The third war was a hidden war, but the war that would decide the fate of Europe and the Pacific Rim, depending on its outcome. No one knew this better than Churchill and therefore he fought to establish the theatre of both wars in such a way that Communism would be held at bay after the peace of the first two wars. That Roosevelt thwarted his endeavours at every point will become clear as we proceed through the conferences leading up to Yalta. What we must try to answer is why Roosevelt gave Russia everything in exchange for nothing?

So what of Roosevelt's early informative days? He was borne into a family with security and position and grew up in an atmosphere of careful preparation for a life that only wealth and understanding combined can offer a child. So his education was carefully watched by his parents and his holidays were used to broaden his knowledge of the world through travel. His early hobbies were shooting and collecting stamps; the latter remained his hobby for life. His father, a country squire, was wealthy but a democrat, in contrast to his position. They lived at Hyde Park, on the Hudson River, on their estate, Springwood, some one hundred and ten acres; modest by Vanderbilt standards, but a retreat that Roosevelt junior would love dearly.

In Finis Farr's book **(268)** we are told that Franklin Roosevelt's half brother married Helen Astor, the daughter of the Astor's who were in publishing (Owned the Times) who originated from John Jacob Astor, a German, who arrived in New York in 1874. **DIRECTION.**

Franklin idolised his father and his mother almost in an obsessive way. His mother was a forceful character, and in a way, father and son stood together on occasions to defend their line. (This could be a indication to his later practice, during the Conferences to side with Stalin to defeat Churchill).

He was educated by tutors and his parents at home till the age of fourteen. In his early formative days, he was shielded from the problems of the outer world by a privileged position in a wealthy and protective environment. At the age of eleven he was taken to visit the World Columbian Exposition at Chicago, in 1893. This sight of America's progress and authority left a lasting impression on the young Roosevelt.

One day at home his mother scolded him for ordering his guests around. After considering, he replied that unless he gave some orders, nothing would ever get done.

At fourteen he was to experience his first big break with his sanctuary, Springwood. He was sent to Groton School, a boarding school on the Thames River near New London, Connecticut.

Suddenly he was filled with a feeling of fear, left in the company of boys he did not know, and whom his shyness forced him to ignore. He became inward thinking and never again would he reveal his emotions to anyone. It was as if he had been punished by this place for something, he did not know.

As the toughness of early life made strong Presidents like Lincoln; here we have the opposite, an almost idyllic childhood, spoilt when life's realities are presented at a school away from home, to a boy of fourteen who has never known anything but a home environment.

Arriving two years late at fourteen did not help, as the other boys thought there was something not quite right with him. He was bullied.

In this school, built on the snobbery of its entries, it would be the boys who would seal the fate of each entry. What this did to Franklin was to force him to adopt an ingratiating manner which he used in later life when confronted with problems.

During his debating at school he claimed Japan would never attack the Islands and that Pearl Harbour could be made into a good naval base if it was dredged. He went on to comment that the United States and Russia are the only two countries no part of whose territory can be cut off by a naval enemy.

By 1900 Franklin moved to Harvard for his university education.

Once again he tried hard to get recognition in sport but failed and this failure would also affect him down the line. Then in December 1900 his father died. His mother took a house in Boston to be near her son. After trying many ways to gain recognition at Harvard young Franklin earned his place on the Crimson, the college news sheet. But his work was classed as average C grade and his achievements were limited. His greatest disappointment was not to be invited to join the famous Porcelain Club. Rejection hurt him deeply.

So he left Harvard and discussed with his mother what profession to adopt and it was decided that law would be suitable.

What his mother did not know was he had already struck up a relationship with a distant cousin, Eleanor Roosevelt. She was, according to her own writing at this time, a forlorn and unhappy girl. She started a courtship with Franklin in 1903 while he was still at Harvard but he kept this from his mother. When he finally told her she could not believe how he had hidden his liaison from her for so long.

After Franklin's graduation he became involved in the inauguration of Theodore (Teddy) Roosevelt on March 1905. President Teddy declared he would destroy "Malefactors of great wealth" who plotted to rob the people. Like most politicians it was a statement full of hot air. But Franklin was studying his style closely.

Two weeks later he married Eleanor in New York on the 17th. March 1905, a wedding which the new President attended. Was it from this point that he was destined to go into politics? His law studies at Columbia failed in the meantime. But at the second attempt he passed his law degree and in 1907 took a job as a junior clerk in Carter, Ledyard and Milburn, perhaps because his wife was the President's niece. By now Franklin saw this as a passing phase as he had the top office in politics firmly in his vision. In the meantime, much to the distress of Eleanor, he lived in a mansion, on East 65th. Street, built by his mother for him, next door to hers.

By 1910 he left his job in law to concentrate on politics and at the first attempt to become a Senator, fought a strong Republican seat for the Democrats, and won by 1,140 votes.

From the start, his family fortune set him above his fellow Senators who in the main lived in dingy hotels or boarding houses. He had his mother's wealth to set him up in a superior position and his background to pull all the important strings.

Now comes an interesting question, "Why did Franklin Roosevelt go into politics?" It wasn't to obtain the political back hander that usually propel candidates to power. His family had all they needed. Finis Farr suggests it was to impress the head of his boarding school, Dr. Peabody. (Groton School). **(269).**

First he studied the relationship between the elected Senator and his voters. Then he practised popular politics by opposing Sheehan for popular acclaim. He was only a part of the, "Stop Sheehan Campaign", but later he would claim the glory. He came close to Woodrow Wilson, New Jersey's State Governor. Wilson expounded to him his policy of 'New Freedom' that became Franklin Roosevelt's New Deal, which is now known as the 'New World Order' depicted on the back of a dollar note, under Satan's eye. He watched and noted the power, the problems and the mechanisms that made power possible. Roosevelt was at last coming to terms with the mechanisms that would hold power and feed the adulation of the people, particularly the adulation. Franklin D. Roosevelt had an extreme fixation of his own importance.

Like Wilson with his father, Roosevelt was driven towards the Presidency in a desperate desire to please his mother, a very dangerous motive to use to propel him into such high office; dangerous for America and the world. Add a world war to this scenario and it fills you with fear, yet, that is how it was.

Wilson, it was, who showed that foreign travel was good for publicity and you will see how Roosevelt used this gimmick to perfection.

Roosevelt also saw Wilson take, General Edward House, a complete stranger, as his personal advisor, after a few cordial meetings, a person who would dominate Wilson. (Roosevelt would mimic this with his personal advisor, a complete diplomatic novice, and political newcomer, Harry Hopkins).

Now that emulation might just have been a coincidence but coupled with the next look-alike becomes a deliberate act of copy. Wilson appointed a naval doctor to be his personal physician. Roosevelt copied this as well.

It was during the First World War that Roosevelt learned the power of bankers. The Wilson years formed ideas in Roosevelt's mind that he would use himself, and the bankers who dominated power, would use their men to steer a weak President to fulfil their requirements. House was their man close to the President.

Roosevelt saw Wilson take America into a war that would see five million people die, needlessly, to satisfy the lust for power by bankers who set up the assassination of Grand Duke Ferdinand to start the war in the first place, because wars moved the world towards their aim, one world government, and made extra money through national loans from governments involved. (this we have already discussed).

Wilson, on his part, gave America a tirade of patriotic platitudes which sounded sincere but which were full of errors and lies to excite the vacant minds of the masses. He even declared taxes would be raised to fight for freedom. Whose freedom? Those sentenced to die to line the pockets of bankers? America was mesmerised by his lies and half truths and went into war with a patriotic suicidal fervour. Roosevelt listened and learned.

He failed to sign up for active service, preferring to stay at his desk in the naval office, and it is interesting to note that another future politician did the same, in the shape of Dwight Eisenhower, who preferred to lead from a safe office. Finis Farr goes as far as calling him 'Yellow'. **(270).** For Roosevelt , he missed a chance to become a war hero, opting for safer office, and betraying his position in society, not least himself.

Roosevelt's greatest lesson from the war was his insight into the gullibility of the American people, a lesson he would use to great affect.

The fact is that America did not win the war; they came in too late to claim that; they just tipped the scales of the numbers game to make Germany realise they could not win. Out of nearly nine million people who were dead on all sides only one hundred thousand were American servicemen. This did not stop Wilson claiming an American victory and heaping the praises on a hyped up nation.

Roosevelt, watched, spell bound, as Wilson, after peace was declared on November 11th. 1918, progressed towards a peace conference. In Paris, where Wilson paraded his ego before the world as a saviour, an insult to the many nationals who lost their lives in this unnecessary war, he held court. He was strongly advised not to attend but his vanity knew better, so Colonel House drew up a fourteen point plan for peace for Wilson to discuss. But the Colonel's time was running out. He had been too much in the news to Wilson's cost. He sacked him on March 14th. 1919, and set about a disastrous policy for Germany which culminated in the rejection of the peace treaty and the League of Nations, which had been slipped into the treaty. (The First attempt to establish a World Order.).

By 1920 Franklin Roosevelt had been nominated as vice President by the Democrats. Meanwhile Wilson was trying to sell his peace treaty deal over the heads of the Senate to the people, during which he suffered a stroke and never again recovered his faculties. At the following election, Harding and Calvin Coolridge beat the Cox-Roosevelt ticket in a landslide victory, putting Roosevelt out of office.

Then came a devastating blow for Roosevelt; he contracted Poliomyelitis which paralysed him and left him an invalid for the rest of his life. You might think this would be the end of his political career, but in a strange way it assisted his journey to the top, where sympathy played a major role. It was at this time that Eleanor began to take an interest in radical left politics, maybe to guide her husband in his political career. She was determined he should continue his path to the top office.

To make money in the meantime, apart from his job at the Fidelity Deposit Company, he began to play the high risk share market with the help of his financial friend Morgenthau, a German emigrant. (His son Henry a gentleman farmer, became a close friend and later Secretary to the Treasury).

Most of Roosevelt's independent schemes ended as failures. His financial worries were ended however when his half-brother died leaving him $600,000.

His first attempt to re-enter politics came in October 1928, when Al Smith proposed him to take over the Governorship of New York. At first he refused but after extreme pressure conceded. After a fight he gained victory and was once again heading for the number one post.

He started to gather friends of influence. Henry Morgenthau was appointed Chairman of the State Agricultural Advisory Commission. His friend Louis Howe, who had been his assistant since that fateful illness still managed his affairs and protected him from his political enemies. Eleanor Roosevelt took on an information gathering role in his political life and became his conscience within his administration and as such was potentially powerful. She carried out these duties along with all her other interests (A school, a furniture company and others). During his Governorship of New York he planned his final assault on the Presidency aided and abetted by his team.

But Roosevelt had to wait. Herbert Hoover was President and seemed to settle in well. But seven months into Hoover's term of office, Wall Street suffered a reverse with a massive collapse. America went from a boom economy to bust and Hoover was blamed for the massive unemployment that followed, and was brought down by the Bonus Expeditionary Force, when he over reacted to a determined demonstration. So in 1932 Roosevelt was nominated Presidential candidate for the Democratic party and won a landslide victory. He had at last reached his dream, despite his handicap; a remarkable effort, that would prove to be disastrous for America and the world.

From what you have just read you will get the impression of a very complex man. He was brought up in privileged surroundings till the age of fourteen when he was sent to Groton School, a very unfriendly environment. This produced two markers to his future. Firstly he became inward looking and self praising, and secondly his exam results were low, achieving a average C grade. Not what you would expect from a future President. At university he failed to excel and at law school he failed his exam first time and scrapped through on the second attempt. Without his family money and his mother's connections he would not have gone anywhere. But he had set his heart on the Presidency and his determination was absolute, despite his poor academic standard and then his crippling illness. It is plain that he became dependent on a handful of people throughout his political life; first his wife, who became his conscience. She was of radical Liberal persuasion. Secondly Louis Howe, who was his devoted friend and servant. Then in office

Harry Hopkins, who was his policy advisor and protector, who guided him down the path to Russia. Then his friend Morgenthau, a Zionist who was a gentleman farmer and later Secretary to the Treasury, who in turn relied on Harry Dexter White to produce his policies.

His Secretary of State, Stettinius, was also a man who leaned heavily on his deputy Alger Hiss. So you begin to see a pattern developing where Russian lovers like Hopkins and Russian Agents like Harry Dexter White and Alger Hiss developed Roosevelts's policies which he just signed. That is what happened under America's weakest President, surrounded by friends of Russia and a wife that saw nothing wrong in Communism. We, however were led to believe that Roosevelt was apolitical hero by our press. Now we will see this play in action during the war conferences, and see how dangerous it was for democracy.

CASABLANCA, 1943.

"I have a hunch that Stalin doesn't want anything but security for his country, and I think that if I give him everything I possibly can, and ask nothing from him in return, noblesse oblige, he won't try to annex anything and will work for world democracy and peace". **(271).**

President Roosevelt talking to William C. Bullitt, American Ambassador in Moscow. From 'How we won the war and lost the peace'. Life. August 30th. 1948.

This sums up Roosevelt's totally immature political thinking and his lack of will to understand the facts of politics from his security advisors. The naiveté is horrendous. He would only take on board what he wanted to hear, and did everything to hide his intentions from those who opposed him. He went on to say to Winston Churchill:-

"I know you will not mind me being brutally frank when I tell you that I think I can personally handle Stalin better than either your foreign office or my State Department. Stalin hates the guts of all your top people. He thinks he likes me better, and I hope he will continue to do so". **(272).**

Franklin D. Roosevelt. From 'The Hinge of Fate', by Winston Churchill.

This sets the scene for the six conferences where Roosevelt would dominate the result of the decisions by this naive and ill thought out policy.

Roosevelt, during 1942, while America was still mobilising, made his top priority to supply arms to Russia. Yet Stalin was in no hurry to meet Roosevelt. He was playing him like a fisherman plays a salmon. The more he refused his calls to meet, the more Roosevelt would aim to please. It must have been a horrendous sight for the patriots like Bullitt, that knew the truth.

The truth was that America was pouring weapons, aeroplanes, vehicles and even machinery for production into Russia with technical support provided; So much so, that Churchill had to plead for his deliveries to be met.

General John Deane, in his book 'The Strange Alliance' **(273)** had this to say about Stalin's opinion; "In Russian eyes, the war with Germany and Japan was only the first phase in the ultimate struggle between Communism and Capitalism." Meaning the next enemy would be the whole Capitalist world. By refusing to attend Casablanca, Stalin had in Roosevelt, a man that would achieve more for him than if he had attended. Such was Roosevelt's passion to please. So Churchill and Roosevelt met at Casablanca and two points were ironed out in favour of Stalin..

The first, Roosevelt rejected Churchill's desire to attack Germany from the Balkans. This was Churchill's considered way to halt the creep of Communism. In this way Roosevelt left Central and Eastern Europe open to Communism.

Roosevelt also announced 'Unconditional Surrender' as the only acceptable peace. This would leave Germany and Japan, once the strong nations, holding back Communism in Europe and the Pacific Rim. From the ravages of war and the terms of peace they would be incapable of carrying out the defence against Communism. This would greatly affect the security of the Western world.

In this way Roosevelt played right into Stalin's hands. This all happened because Roosevelt did not do his homework or take advice from anyone he did not like, or did not agree with his ideas. But Harry Hopkins, the Russian lover, was at Roosevelt's side throughout the conference.

By the end of 1942 the war could have been brought to an agreeable close if it wasn't for the terms of surrender about to be imposed by Roosevelt to please Stalin. Of course Churchill objected but he could not put undue pressure on Roosevelt as he needed Roosevelt's commitment to win the war with his military and financial aid.

It was clear by the end of 1942, just before the Casablanca Conference that even Hitler was looking for a way out and a group of high ranking officers even plotted to kill him to achieve this, but they needed help from outside but it never came. Why was this opportunity passed over? To follow a policy that would hand over large areas of the world to Russia and Communism? We can only guess. Even in 1942 Russia was trying to get title to part of Poland and Finland, Latvia, Lithuania, Estonia and Romania. It seems that Russia was not ready for peace and it may be that this influenced Roosevelt enough to persuade him to ignore the German soundings for peace.

At this time the American people were being led to believe that Japan was their cause of war not Germany and Roosevelt did nothing to discourage this thought. Public opinion would have been different if the truth had been known. At the time of the press conference, Roosevelt had quashed Churchill's desire to attack through the Balkans. But the unconditional surrender came as a complete surprise to Churchill as Roosevelt slipped it into the agenda without consultation as Churchill confirmed later. Even Roosevelt admitted that he just added it to the communiqué. What it did was to ensure that the war went on another three years and Russia gained the territory they desired, a result beyond their wildest dreams; handed to them by a dreamer.

Major General J.F.C. Fuller had this to say about its contents; "First, that because no greater power could with dignity or honour to itself, its history, its people and their prosperity, comply with them, the war must be fought to the point of annihilation. Therefore, it would take upon itself a religious character and bring to life again all the horrors of the wars of religion.

Secondly, once victory had been won, the balance of power within Europe and between European nations would be irrevocably smashed. Russia would be left the greatest military power in Europe, and therefore, would dominate Europe. Consequently, the peace these words predicted was the replacement of Nazi tyranny by an even more barbaric despotism". **(274).**

This dreadful decision heralded the last but greatest atrocity of the war, the Atomic Bombs dropped on a nation already defeated, at Hiroshima and Nagasaki. But Roosevelt had enjoyed his trip to the conference, perhaps reminding him of his family trips abroad while young. He was not a traitor but perhaps more dangerous, Naive, and puffed up by his own importance.

QUEBEC 1 - August 1943.

Roosevelt's first Secretary of state was Cordell Hull. I only mention this as he was never invited to plan war matters with Roosevelt; a typical example of the manner in which Roosevelt dealt with people he did not quite trust or would not agree with his views. But Harry Hopkins, who held no high office and had no qualifications, attended all his war conferences. This shows complete disregard for democracy. The reason was most likely that Cordell Hull was Anti Russian. The 'New Republic' **(275)** said, it was he who had stopped Stalin getting territorial gains in 1942 from Churchill. He had also made it plain to Roosevelt the ambitions of Stalin for territorial gains in Europe. He even told Churchill in 1943; "Its my opinion that if Russia should eventually come into the war in the Pacific, it will probably be two or three weeks before victory, during which time she can spread out over Manchuria and other large areas and then be assured of sitting in at the peace conference". This was actually a very accurate prediction. It happened almost to the word. This illustrates how Roosevelt moved the agenda to suit Stalin and marginalised his own team to do so.

However Quebec 1 was an exception for Hull; he was invited to arrive after the important decisions were made. Stalin had again rejected Roosevelt's invitation knowing Roosevelt would give ground he could not hope to claim.

The main discussion point was the invasion. Where should it take place? Roosevelt, Hopkins and Marshall, the President's military poodle, all voted against Churchill and in favour of a French landing in the spring of 1944, much to the disquiet of Churchill who knew that the war against Germany was already won but the secret third war against Communism would depend on positions held at the end of the conflict. However Roosevelt, who would not take advice from his Secretary of State, Hull, who knew this threat, moved to please Stalin and ignore the truth. This was becoming the pattern of his ill-informed Presidency. It is interesting to note that Roosevelt, at the final press conference said that there had been no disagreement over policy. In both Harry Hopkins' and Churchill's memoirs it states quite a different story of heated arguments. This shows how Roosevelt tried to hide his agenda from the public view by lies and withholding truth. It was only because the United States was putting up the bulk of the money and troops for the landing that Churchill decided to concede the point.

During this conference Harry Hopkins had in his pocket a top secret military document, considered very high level. How Harry Hopkins had this can only be answered by Roosevelt's trust of his judgement because he had no formal training or knowledge in this field. One paragraph explains its concern; "Russia's post-war position in Europe will be a dominant one. With Germany crushed, there is no power in Europe to oppose her tremendous military forces. It is true that Great

Britain is building up a position in the Mediterranean vis-à-vis Russia which Britain may find useful in balancing power in Europe. However, even here Britain may not be able to oppose Russia unless she is otherwise supported.

This quite clearly puts the future of Europe under the microscope. It defines the position of Europe after defeat and even suggests Britain may need support. It was a report that pre-empted the post war domination of Europe by Communism so that action could be taken.

Harry Hopkins' reply was, "The conclusions from the foregoing are obvious. Since Russia is the decisive factor in the war, she must be given assistance, and every effort must be made to obtain her friendship. Likewise, since without question she will dominate Europe on the defeat of the Axis, it is even more essential to develop and maintain the friendliest relations with Russia". What he was saying was Roosevelt's line; give Russia everything and hope she will be friends. I have got to question Harry Hopkins own integrity at this point. It is inconceivable that in light of all the warning signs available, Roosevelt and Harry Hopkins could not see the facts staring them in the face. He had intelligence reports; he had Churchill's warnings; he had warnings from his Moscow Embassy. How could Harry Hopkins take this line unless he was on Russia's side? Whoever wrote that report, Marshall, Roosevelt or Harry Hopkins was a traitor. One thing was sure; the American people didn't get to know the truth, Roosevelt was built as a hero, not as a Russian apologist.

General Albert C. Wedemeyer, in the Wedemeyer Reports, **(276)** states that General Marshall "Thus became a easy prey to Crypto-Communists, or Communist-Sympathising sycophants who played on his vanity to accomplish their own ends". That shows how Communism worked even within the military establishment. They targeted people and found their weaknesses.

At Quebec 1, Roosevelt decided to have American troops land in Southern France while the British contingent would land at Normandy. This assisted Russia to become dominant in Eastern Europe; it was left to Sherwood to fight against Roosevelt's plan to no avail. Once again Churchill gave in because he desired to stay on workable terms with Roosevelt.

To show a last glimpse of the absurdity of American foreign policy, Cordell Hull, the Secretary of State in Roosevelt's government till he resigned in 1944, stated in his memoirs that he was not told about the atomic bomb till it was dropped. Yet at the same time Klaus Fuchs, Harry Gold, David Greenglass, and the Rosenberg's all knew about it. They were all Communist spies. This only goes to illustrate how Communism had infiltrated the American defence system secretly, like a thief in the night. Those spies were all Internationalists, as were a large number of the Communist spies who have been named over the years.

CAIRO - November 1943.

At Cairo Roosevelt had his usual team of close advisors, led by Harry Hopkins and was due to meet Churchill and Chiang Kai-shek in Cairo and then to go on to meet the illusive Stalin in Teheran, the capital of Iran.

But Roosevelt was a ill man by this time and he began to show the strains and sometimes even hesitated over his work. Work, where a long line of blunders or illogical decisions crept into his decisions. Some of the historian apologists blame blunders on his illness, but history shows us clearly this was not the case for he sent

Harry Hopkins to Moscow in 1941, well before the strain of office took hold, almost with a blank cheque signed by Roosevelt, to fill in as he desired.

What in truth Roosevelt suffered from was the extraordinary effect of power over the world that captured the inadequate mind, giving him the equivalent of vertigo. He began believing he was the man sent to set the world to rights. A new peace. A new world. A **New World Order.**

The immediate problem at this conference was that China was becoming weaker, too starved of financial support to turn the tables on Japan let alone its Communist aggressors, led by Mao Tse-tung up North. China had taken the brunt of a six year war, occupying Japan in conflict so that America could concentrate its resources on Germany. All it wanted was help to prop up its falling currency. It could have scraped through if Japan had been its only battlefront. But Mao was threatening to march south and maintaining two fronts was bankrupting Chiang Kai-shek's Government. While the Nationalist forces held Japan's expansion at bay, Mao was making big inroads into China's Northern territory, armed and supplied by Moscow with US weapons. So Mao controlled the provinces of Chahar, Hopeh, Suiyuan, Kansu, Anhwei, Shensi, Shantung and the Northern part of Kiangsu. Soon Mao had an army of half a million soldiers, a very formidable force. The Communists were preparing for the end of hostilities between China and Japan when Chiang would be at his weakest, and powerless to defend his land. Chiang had no doubt who his real enemy was. He said; "The Japanese are only lice on the body of China, but Communism is a disease of the heart". Unlike Roosevelt, Chiang was worldly wise; he knew that China's long struggle was against International Communist revolution not the Japanese, who sealed their fate by attacking Pearl Harbour, as Roosevelt had enticed them so to do.

America's, China policy, under Roosevelt, was in every way against America's self interest. General Marshall, who commanded American troops in that region in 1945-6, has been blamed for blunders which left Communism the victor. But he was only obeying orders from the White House, It was Roosevelt's policy decision with advice from Hopkins and Harry Dexter White.

Once again we find a cell of Communists and fellow travellers within the administration conveniently placed to advise the President that it would be desirable to turn China over to Communism by forcing Chiang to make a treaty with the Communist rebels to protect China from Japan. These left wing advisors were Owen Lattimore, Lauchlin Currie, John Carter Vincent, and the Davies service group in the Foreign Service and we must not forget the highest ranking infiltrator of all, Harry Dexter White. Lauchlin Currie was also in a high position; he was an assistant of the President in the White House. When the heat was on in 1948 to find Communists within the administration he quickly disappeared to South America and gave up his US citizenship. It was this man who, with Harry Dexter White, gave references to Nathan Gregory Silvermaster to keep him in high office in government service, knowing him to be a leader of the Communist party and known by the security services.

So it was natural that Roosevelt took a line on China favourable to Communism. That Roosevelt and after him Truman would not listen to his security advisors about these infiltrators and held them in office is quite as remarkable as it is disturbing.

So here we had President Roosevelt at this conference notifying Chiang Kai-shek that he must take Communists on board in his cabinet if America was to help him. This was not noted in the communiqué after the conference, as this decision was completed in Churchill's absence, a measure of Roosevelt's deceitfulness.

Deep in his devious mind was how he could swing China into Communist control to please Stalin. In August 1942 he had sent Averell Harriman to ask Stalin if he would join the Japanese war when the time was right, he received back from the wily man a half promise. Later Hull extracted a promise from Stalin in 1943 that he would help defeat Japan after Germany was beaten. At this time wise council was cautioning the West to keep Russia out of the possible peace settlement, but ignoring this, President Roosevelt would invite and beg Stalin to come into the defeating army ranks and claim the spoils. So at Cairo, Roosevelt was preparing Chiang for his eventual fate; run out of his land by Communism.

To test the ground, Roosevelt suggested to Chiang that the port of Dairen should be handed to Russia. Chiang declined but it would become one of Russia's spoils later, offered to Stalin by Roosevelt.

Churchill, dissatisfied with the discussion about Japan, a battle in which British troops were not involved, turned the agenda to the Balkans once again. This time Roosevelt was not amused as this would upset Stalin, his friend, so it became a battle of wills.

At Cairo, Roosevelt agreed with Chiang to form a front in Burma and drive up to China, making a corridor to China. So Chiang went home happy only to find Roosevelt reneged on this agreement ten days later when he had talked to Stalin. The consequence was, Japan, happy at the outcome, mounted a defensive that drove deep into China. Chiang was holding on to power by a very weak thread. This was the beginning of the end for mainland Nationalist China.

As a parting sop to Churchill, Dwight Eisenhower was made Commander in Chief of OVERLORD (The move against Germany in France) much against, for once, the advice of Harry Hopkins, who preferred General Marshall. The meeting in Teheran followed immediately.

TEHERAN - November 1943

The disastrous result of Teheran came at the end of the war when General Patton was halted from liberating Czechoslovakia by General Eisenhower, acting on orders from Washington, because Roosevelt, with Churchill's reluctant consent, agreed that Stalin's red army should liberate it as agreed at Teheran and Yalta.

So Teheran handed the territories and lives of millions of people to the red butcher of Moscow. This was all done without press release. Czechoslovakia was not the only casualty of Roosevelt's generosity. Poland knew their case would be discussed but no Polish politician was invited; in fact the exiled government was not informed till six months later, in June 1944. This was because Roosevelt was going for a fourth term in office and no scandal over Poland should destroy his chance.

The partition of Poland had already been agreed at Teheran, in favour of Russia. This and many other actions of Roosevelt were in complete variance to the agreement of The Atlantic Charter, so easily forgotten by Roosevelt. The mere thought of millions of people of Europe who were condemned to Communism by the stroke of a pen by a brutal dictator, and an inadequate President and a regretful but compromising Prime Minister, worries my mind. What those people have suffered should be an enduring lesson to us to fight Communism as it is now confronting us.

Teheran was the time that Stalin took over the World agenda for peacetime, with a weak President agreeing to his every whim and an outvoted Churchill regretting everything he saw. It was at Teheran that Stalin plotted his great coupe that Yalta would deliver. In America, if the White House was keeping quiet about the Teheran agreement the American Communist party certainly was not.

Earl Browder, at that time the head man in the American Communist party, called a meeting in Madison Square Gardens, where he told fifteen thousand Communists that Teheran had supplied the course for the post war world. Earl Browder was released by Roosevelt from prison on a White House pardon and maintained a secret connection with Roosevelt through Josephine Adams, acting as a courier. At least forty contacts were made with Roosevelt in the three years preceding his death. This was later confirmed by Adams testifying under oath before a Senate subcommittee (February 26th. 1957). So has Browder confirmed it with some pride on his part? **(277)**

Roosevelt, while meeting privately with Stalin, suggested that after the war America and Britain would have more ships than they needed, and Russia might like to accept them as a gift to the Soviet Union. The bells of joy started to ring in Stalin's mind of power and strength that he would obtain from this inadequate man in his midst. He knew he could get more, so he made Roosevelt Chairman of the conference to feed his ego. Stalin discounted a Balkans invasion in favour of OVERLORD to occupy America and Britain while he occupied his agenda. Then Stalin turned to Japan and with overriding assurance declared; "We shall by our common front beat Japan". He went on to say at a dinner later that he would be keeping Latvia, Lithuania, and Estonia which he had already occupied..

Before the next session Churchill requested a meeting with Roosevelt but he declined preferring to meet with Stalin. At this secret meeting with Stalin a most extraordinary question was posed to Stalin. Would he care to discuss the future peace of the world? He agreed and it was as if Roosevelt had gone through all his handout routine to reach this rather remote and, at the time, irrelevant matter for this conference. So Roosevelt promoted vigorously his idea for **The United Nations Organisation** consisting of an assembly, executive committee, and his super policemen, the Four Power Policemen consisting of The Soviet Union, The United States, Britain, and China. Stalin, who saw the idea as a dream nevertheless encouraged Roosevelt and agreed to be one of the policemen.

Stalin's confidence lead to a clash with Churchill again over the Balkans but Roosevelt sided with Stalin and the matter was closed, when General Marshall, who had once suggested a military division should be placed in Southern France, sided with Roosevelt and Stalin.

If the note in Harry Hopkins pocket at Quebec was recalled, everything it forecast would be brought to life at Teheran. In a word Russia was to dominate Europe. But who wrote that note? Was it political or was it from the real power behind politics, the bankers? Perhaps we shall never know.

Stalin was ready with his plan for Europe in the next session. Eastern Germany, up to the Oder River was to be taken from Germany and given to Poland, while the land taken by Russia in 1939, while Russia was in league with Hitler, was to remain in Soviet hands. Churchill, abandoned by Roosevelt, once again could not win for the sake of his brave friends from Poland. The agreement was a betrayal of the Polish people and a monstrous violation of the Atlantic Charter, a charter which turned out to be a diversionary propaganda exercise.

Three men raped Poland, without Poland even being represented at the meeting, to the liking of Stalin but a devastation of democracy by the other two countries. (This is how Communism grows). It was known by the participants of this meeting that fifteen thousand Polish army officers had been brutally massacred by Stalin at Katyn Forest, yet they allowed this butcher to disenfranchise this proud nation, the nation which, when attacked by Hitler, brought Britain into the war.

When Stalin had won Poland he asked if there was any other business, Roosevelt, in haste, replied; "There is the question of Germany". **(278).** Stalin immediately replied he would like to see Germany split, Roosevelt, again in undue haste, agreed. In fact the plan came from Roosevelt which included the confiscation of the Ruhr, the Saar, Hamburg Port, and Kiel Canal, which were to be handed to the United Nations. It was a plan to reduce Germany to insignificance, luckily the plan was not settled but it would come up again at Quebec 2.

That the agenda of the World passed into Stalin's hands at this conference is hard to grasp and it is even harder to grasp the motives of the man who allowed it to happen, Roosevelt. At home Roosevelt broadcast to his nation, referring to Stalin he said; "He is a man who combines a tremendous, relentless determination with a stalwart good humour. I believe he is truly representative of the heart and soul of Russia; and I believe that we are going to get along very well with him and the Russian people--Very well indeed".

So he presented his weakness, as a man of the moment (deception), who had made a good friend, who was representing the 'heart and soul' of the Russian people. How can democracy survive with lies not challenged by the media?

QUEBEC 2 - September 1944.

Quebec 2 took place when the allied forces had successfully accomplished OVERLORD and were at the Siegfried Line. Russia had pushed the retreating German army off their soil. Victory was certain. The conditions of victory were yet to be voiced, although Stalin had his ideas firmly prepared to take advantage of the victory vacuum.

The Secretary of the Treasury, Henry Morgenthau, a Jew by birth with Zionist instincts, wanted to punish Germany for their callous treatment of the Jews caught in the war, and he was backed by those very bankers from Wall Street who contained, amongst their numbers, the Jewish bankers who funded Hitler throughout the war.

As Roosevelt was up for election for a fourth term, he bowed to pressure to allow Morgenthau to attend the conference, as he wanted to please the New York Jewish vote to damage his rival. Yes these decisions were made for all the wrong reasons.

But Morgenthau was not the problem, it was his Assistant Secretary to the Treasury, Harry Dexter White, who would prove to be a problem. His department was in charge of foreign affairs, so he was involved in foreign negotiations, particularly in China. His birth details show he was the son of a Jewish émigré from Russia, one Jacob Weit.

For Morgenthau, Harry Dexter White prepared a plan for Germany after the war, and Morgenthau, with his Jewish background, let sentiment rather than reason take over, and he agreed with White's plan. On September the 6th. the plan went before Roosevelt, Stimson and Hull. For the next days a frantic battle went on between Stimson and Hull on one side opposing the plan and Morgenthau supporting it.

The plan in brief was going to destroy Germany's industrial base and leave Germany as an agricultural and Pastoral desert. It was blind vengeance no better than Hitler's concentration camps. It was in the interest of the Western world to rebuild Germany quickly to act as a buffer to Stalin's plans. The plan also wanted to destroy Germany's coal industry which other European countries relied upon. This was the height of folly. It was clear that this plan was to please Stalin, but for all we know it could have been written in Russia, as Harry Dexter White was a Russian Agent through banking.

More worrying was Roosevelt's health. His Secretary of State, Stimson had this to say in his diary; "I have been much troubled by the President's physical condition...I rather fear for the effects of this hard conference upon him. I am particularly troubled...that he is going up there without any real preparation for the solution of the...problem of how to treat Germany. So far as he has evidenced it in his talks with us, he has had absolutely no study or training in the very difficult problem which we have to decide". **(279).**

Stimson knew as well as anyone who had studied Europe that it was essential to get this policy right for the future peace and prosperity of all Europe, and to treat it lightly or emotionally would be a disaster.

He also wrote in his diary that Roosevelt would go to Quebec without preparation and that he had; "Absolutely no study or training" in the matter.

Harry Dexter White was prepared, having received his orders from Jacob Golos, a high ranking Russian agent in America. Strangely, Hull and Stimson were both excluded from the conference. But before the conference Morgenthau put a document with the main features of the Morgenthau plan before Roosevelt, and he signed them with a brief acceptance; OK.

At the conference Churchill started in a manner violently opposed to the plan. But Morgenthau was prepared. **(280).** He told him Britain would gain from the destruction of the Ruhr and the second bribe was a six and a half billion dollar credit. So Britain was bribed to accept, a shame on Churchill's credibility; the plan was passed.

But after the conference, Hull, still worried by the terms of this terrible document would have on Europe, went to see the President and cleverly dropped a remark that made Roosevelt pause. He stated that if its contents got out to the press his election chances would evaporate. After consideration Roosevelt started to retract on the agreement, thus avoiding a disaster of world proportions, planned by Russia and planted on Roosevelt by a high government official, who happened to be a Communist agent through banking.

As Hull feared, the press got hold of the report through a leakage. (By a communist?). The immediate reaction came from Germany. Goebbels rallied his troops into a last resistance, instead of suing for peace, and the war lasted a further seven months. But essentially the plan was dead and Harry Dexter White went on to his next mischief where he played a leading roll in the Bretton Wood Conference and the setting up the International Monetary Fund shortly after this conference.

Roosevelt, through his policy of deceitful mirrors, policies that had a hidden agenda behind them, aimed to hide the truth in his policies, consequently he won a fourth term as President, on January 20th. 1945.

YALTA - February 1945.

By this time Roosevelt was very ill and all the President's advisors opposed his trip accept Harry Hopkins. He went with no strategy and no presentation, only his conviction that Stalin liked him. So would any child befriend a monster bearing gifts. It would be his last and fateful trip, because two months later on April 12th. 1945 Roosevelt died.

Just before leaving for Yalta, Roosevelt was informed that the secret manufacture of the Atomic Bomb was ninety nine percent certain and it would be available by August.

During the sea voyage, James Byrnes, who accompanied the President showed surprise at his lack of preparation for the conference, despite the library of information available on the ship. Back home Mrs. Roosevelt was wading deep in left wing politics. Roosevelt had nominated Henry A. Wallace to be Secretary of Commerce. This was a man with a proven open line to pro-Communist elements. Even Roosevelt's own party opposed it. So, Mrs. Roosevelt, proving her attachment to Communism, cabled the ship to advise Roosevelt what to do to get the nomination through the opposition **Direction. (Admiral Leahy. Memoirs 1950).**

Yalta was a favourite resort for the Czars, located on the Black Sea, with a back cloth of forests. Roosevelt's group were accommodated at the summer home of Nicholas II. The British group at the Villa Vorontsov at Alopka, twelve miles away. Beria's NKVD was everywhere hunting out clues for Stalin.

Roosevelt, once again demonstrated his theory that the Russian team, led by Stalin, with Beria, Vishinsky, and Molotov were nice people, by toasting them as emulating the atmosphere likened to; "That of a family".

This idea that Bolsheviks were good men must be understood to follow from Roosevelt's naive behaviour. But Roosevelt rejected all that was derogatory about Russia from his mind, for example like the Polish officer's massacred at Katyn.

This pro-Russian line was all over Washington because Franklin Roosevelt, Eleanor Roosevelt, and Harry Hopkins created a fairytale myth about Stalin as his friend, an image only the brave would challenge.

Although Secretary of State, Edward R. Stettinius was at Yalta, his presence was immaterial, but one of his assistants, Alger Hiss played a leading part; he was a Communist spy within the State department. Alger Hiss sat next to Harry Hopkins, and behind the President, once again feeding policy to Roosevelt to suit Russia.

The final list of decisions, not to be released to the press included;

1 The German nation would be divided. A large part given to Poland to compensate for the large part Russia held and would not return.
2 Königsberg was to go to Russia and East Germany was to go to Russia for communisation. (This was to be referred to as the greatest atrocity in world history. Millions of people were enslaved into Communism by this act).
3 Reparations were to be taken from Western Germany "in kind". (meaning whole industries and goods, even human labour. Bynes referred to this as forced labour).
4 Poland, a casualty of war, was to be cut up. Some ten million Poles East of the Curzon line were to be given to Soviet rule without a vote on the matter. This annexed nearly half of Poland

and at least a third of its population was given to Russia. This included the Drohobycz oil fields, essential to Poland's economy. A Communist puppet government was to be imported from Russia.

5   It was included in the agreement that the 'United Nations' would be unable to police the expanding Russian Empire and Roosevelt gave in to Stalin's demand that the Soviet Union should have three votes in the General Assembly of the United Nations. (Sitting behind Roosevelt at this time was Alger Hiss,
A communist, and one of two presiding officers at its organising convention to be held in the following April) (For Roosevelt the name, "The United Nations", put him on a cloud of joy. It was the culmination of his life's ambition, and here, in his dying hours he had achieved it. That the United Nations would turn out to be a fraud on all nations and a bed for Communist manipulation, never crossed his mind. He was ecstatic).

6   Stalin gained yet another promise from the conference. That all Russian nationals around Europe should be rounded up and returned to Russia by force if need be. The state department had decided to abide by the Geneva Convention but Roosevelt sent a message to them overriding the decision. (They were sent at bayonet point, by boxcars, to Russia. A unbelievable betrayal of freedom).

7   An agreement was made to allow Stalin to take his troops into Berlin and Prague first. This was despite the British and American troops arriving a month beforehand at the outskirts of Berlin and Bradley under order
from Eisenhower to wait. So was General Patton stopped on the outskirts of Prague so the Russians could liberate the city, thus taking two of Europe's gems plus, for good measure, the Skoda munitions works and Jáchymon Uranium deposits. (Churchill did his best to oppose this course but once again was ignored by Roosevelt. A regular pattern.
Churchill had this to say in his memoirs, "The United States stood on the scene of victory, master of world fortunes, but without a true and coherent design. Britain, though very powerful, could not act decisively alone. I could at this stage only warn and plead. Thus this...was to me a most unhappy time. I moved amid cheering crowds...with an aching heart and a mind oppressed by foreboding".) **(280)** (The integrity of the statesman allows no deeper comments.)

8   Then, alone with Stalin, and Roosevelt, excluding Churchill, the discussion, went further. What was about to receive the rubber stamp of Yalta had already been mostly conceded by Roosevelt. 3000 tanks, 75,000 motor vehicles, and 5,000 aeroplanes for Russia's Far East Force.
In the months ahead 860,410 tons of dry cargo and 206,000 tons of liquid cargo were sent to build up Soviet Military power and as they sat down to agree terms the cargo was already beginning to move.

But Stalin wanted more. He wanted the Communist conquest of China, no doubt so he could use it one day against capitalism. Russia was to annex South

Sakhalin and the Kurile Islands at Japan's expense. At the expense of China, Russia was to gain Dairen as a International Port and the naval base of Port Arthur, under a long lease.

The Manchurian railroads were to be under a Soviet-Chinese Company. At this point you might expect any self respecting politician to call a halt. Roosevelt didn't. He gave Stalin all he requested. None of it his to give.

Then Stalin agreed to enter the war (which he had already done anyway) three months after the German surrender. Russia actually entered it six days before Japan surrendered and two days after the atomic bombs were dropped. A horrendous price to pay for a army that had little part in this theatre of war.

William C. Bullitt, America's late ambassador to Moscow had this to say about Yalta;

"President Roosevelt broke the pledge which he had made to the Chinese government at Cairo and - secretly, behind the back of China - signed...an agreement by which the vital rights of China in Manchuria were sacrificed to Soviet imperialism. By this secret agreement Roosevelt gave to the Soviet Union not only "pre-eminent interests" in the great Manchurian port of Dairen and full control of the great naval base which protects it, Port Arthur, but also "pre-eminent interests" in the railroads which lead from the Soviet Union to Dairen and split Manchuria from the Northwest to the South.

In view of Roosevelt's Cairo pledge that Manchuria would be restored to China this secret agreement was entirely dishonourable. It was also potentially disastrous not only to China but also to the United States, because it gave Stalin a deadly instrument....

As an additional payment for this repetition of his promise to fight Japan, Stalin persuaded the President at Yalta to agree that the Communist state which he had set up in the Chinese province of Outer Mongolia should be permanently detached from China, and the Southern part of Sakhalin, and the Kurile Islands, which cut the great circle aeroplane route from Alaska to Japan, should be annexed by the Soviet Union.

The Agreement...was kept secret from the American people...not even Mr. Byrnes knew it existed. And the exhausted President returned from Yalta to Washington amid the most unanimous applause of his bamboozled fellow countrymen".

Since these terrible events it has been widely agreed that Japan was about to surrender before the Atom bombs were dropped. It has also been agreed, amongst high ranking military staff, that the events leading from Yalta, for the Asian continent, were a disaster that any strategists could have prevented. The world was unlucky enough to have a President who chased rainbows of fantasy to achieve his goal, "The United Nations" In the end it was all that really mattered to him. Roosevelt had this to say at the close of the conference;

"The Crimea Conference...spells - and it ought to spell - the end of the system of unilateral action, exclusive alliances, and spheres of influence, and balances of power...I am sure that - under the agreement reached at Yalta - there will be more stable political Europe than ever before".

That this statement could be so far from reality, time has proved.

Yalta was the culmination of Roosevelt's long, dangerous, and treasonous give-away to Stalin. Shortly after he returned to America; he suffered a stroke and died.

> "The United Nations is Zionism. It is the super government mentioned many times in the Protocols of the Learned Elders of Zion, promulgated between 1897 and 1905".
>
> **Henry Klein, New York Jewish Lawyer.** Writing in 'Zionism Rules the World. 1948.

PROTOCOL SEVEN
(REPEATED)
WORLD - WIDE WARS.

The intensification of armaments, the increase of police forces - are all essential for the completion of the aforementioned plans. We desire that there should be in all the States of the world, besides ourselves, only the masses of the proletariat, a few millionaires devoted to our interests, police and soldiers.

Throughout all Europe, and by means of relations with Europe, in other continents also, we must create ferments, discords, and hostility. Therein we gain a double advantage. In the first place we keep in check all countries, for they will know that we have the power whenever we like to create disorders or to restore order. All these countries are accustomed to see in us an indispensable force of coercion. In the second place, by our intrigues we shall tangle up all the threads which we have woven into the cabinets of all states by means of the political, by economic treaties, or loan obligations. In order to succeed in this we must use great cunning and penetration during negotiations and agreements, but, as regards what is called the "official language", we shall keep to opposite tactics and assume the mask of honesty and compliancy. In this way the peoples and governments of the goyim (Gentiles), whom we have taught to look only at the outside of whatever we present to their notice, will still continue to accept us as the benefactors and saviours of the human race.

We must be in a position to respond to every act of opposition by war with the neighbours of that country which dares to oppose us: but if these neighbours should also venture to stand collectively together against us, then we must offer resistance by a universal war.

The principal factor of success in the political is the secrecy of its undertakings: the word should not agree with the deeds of the diplomat.

We must compel the government of the goyim to take action in the direction favoured by our widely-conceived plan, already approaching the desired consummation, **by what we shall represent as public opinion, secretly prompted by us through the means of that so-called "Great Power" - the press, which with few exceptions that may be disregarded is already entirely in our hands.**

In a word, to sum up our system of keeping the governments of the goyim in Europe in check, we shall show our strength to one of them by terrorist attempts and to all, if we allow the possibility of a general rising against us, we shall respond with guns of America or China or Japan.

COMMENT.

This Protocol tells us the secret of their plans for power. They will increase armaments. The whole of this century the nations of the world have increased their stockpile of arms at the expense of the tax payers and encouraged by the bankers, who lend the nations the money to buy them in the first place, which in turn builds up the national debts of the countries. It is those national debts today, that hold nations in debt slavery. It is the bankers who gain, sometimes twice because of their relationship with the arms manufacturers.

We also see that they wish to increase the police forces. So it is not surprising we find in a survey of national police forces that nearly all countries in debt slavery have increased their police forces in the last forty years by at least fifty percent.

Then we see that they want to change the world into a global village by lumping ninety nine percent of us into a proletariat (A typical word under Communism for the masses) with a few chosen (and friendly to their cause) millionaires and a large army and police force to quell any attempt to revolt against their austerity.

We see they want to create ferment in Europe. They succeeded in two world wars, both funded and secretly planned by bankers to sell arms, and to move the world towards Communism, their goal. Although the general public have been ill informed about the hidden agenda by our media, which is not surprising, (as the bankers own the media) the people and politicians in power have always known who controlled the wars and why. Wars have many uses to the bankers not least to show those in power who controls them.

Then they suggest they will leave one item alone. National language. The reason is this would be outside their ability to control, because in this matter they would have to deal with the masses not the politicians whom they control, the public is more fickle.

They warn us that they will deal with anyone who goes against their will. We have seen Saddam Hussein do just that, and how the bankers have used the United Nations to halt his activities. But was it the United Nations, or was it America, Britain and Israel, controlled by the International Zionist bankers, using the United Nations as a cover to protect oil rights owned by the bankers? If nations should agree together to oppose the bankers' tyranny they will use the power of the United Nations to halt their actions.

They will compel us to do their bidding to further their plan for world government and they will use the tool of the media which they fully own or control to achieve this end.

They vow to keep the governments of Europe in check, and they will use terrorism to control one country (Britain with the IRA, a Marxist organisation). The whole idea of the European Union is about this control of Europe as it is the area that is most likely to oppose their endeavours. You then see that if Europe should rise up in its defence the guns of America, China and Japan will defend the bankers against Europe. America is particularly interesting as this is the centre of the bankers, and International Zionists control the American government.

So in this part you have seen how America, far from being the protector of the world against Communism has actively driven parts of the world towards

Communism. This process continued through Truman's and Eisenhower's administration, giving first part of Korea and then Vietnam to Communism and, although I have no space to prove this statement there is equal proof that America, while telling the world that it was the defender of the free world against the progress of Communism, was never serious about winning the wars. What I am saying was that after Roosevelt, the process of giving Asia to Communism continued.

CHAPTER ELEVEN
PART ONE.
COLLECTING OUR THOUGHTS.

"A Nation can survive its fools, and even the ambitious, but it cannot survive treason from within. An enemy at the gate is less formidable, for he is known and he carries his banners openly. But the traitor moves among those within the gate freely, his sly whispers rustling through the alleys, heard in the very halls of government itself. For the traitor appears no traitor, he speaks in accents familiar to his victims, and he wears their face and their garments and he appeals to the baseness that lies deep in the hearts of all men. He rots the soul of the nation; he works secretly and unknown in the night to undermine the pillars of the city; he infects the body politic so that it can no longer resist. A murderer is less to be feared".

Marcus Tullius Cicero, 105-43 B.C.

"Marxism, you say, is the bitterest opponent of capitalism, which is sacred to us. For the simple reason that they are opposite poles of the earth and permit us to be the axis. These two opposites, Bolshevism and ourselves, find ourselves identified in the Internationale. And these two opposites, the doctrine of the two poles of society, meet in their unity of purpose, the renewal of the world from above by control of wealth, and from below by revolution".

Quotation from a Jewish banker by the Comte de Saint-Aulaire in 'Geneve Contre la Paix', Libraire Plan, Paris, 1936.

These two quotations give us the warning of the hidden enemy, and the truth as to from where we can expect the attack to come. From these warnings we must take account of the facts that I am disclosing if we are to understand who our enemies are, and how we can prepare to remove the threat they pose.

These quotations, which I have already used, contain the method to be used to destroy Nations within the world to prepare the world for a federalised state, a world state, a world controlled by a minority group, the bankers, for selfish, power-mad reasons that will destroy democracy and hand the world to a Communist dictatorship.

We, among a group of Western Nations, believe, because our media have told us so, need no longer fear the threat of Communism; after all, didn't Russia and its satellites collapse under Communism? Isn't Communism a spent force? How can they harm us now? We only formulate these questions because our media have led us down this alley. What they have not told us is that Communism collapsed in Russia and its satellites because Russia and Communism chose it so to do.

Within the overall plan, Communism would be seen as a reason not to allow the Soviet Union and it satellite states access into a Federal European Union. However if they seem to have relinquished Communism, Europe would accept their membership and the people of Europe would not be suspicious. So this is why Russia and the Satellite States chose to abandon Communism till Europe is federalised. This we must resist with all our power. This use of a political distraction in Marxist terms is called 'Diversiya' or diversion because the collapse of Communism diverts our thought from Communism while it enters our cities and corrupts our systems as Cicero said, 'he (Communism) in this case, "rots the soul of a Nation", "He infects the body politic", and because he is unknown, he is hard to resist or combat. Diversion is not an alternative policy; it is a distraction. Until we understand this tool in the armoury of Communism we will not understand its method of warfare and alas Communism has made most of its progress in the world because the liberal establishment does not understand 'Diversion'. Diversion undermines our society through religion, politics, morals, Education, and by using Liberalism to do its work, through the insistence of Liberals to interfere in sensitive matters like Homosexuality, Lesbianism, Race Relations, and all the minority groups that solicit attention. By doing so the Liberals have successfully lowered morality and the media took no time in climbing on this bandwagon. Thus, through Liberal support, Communism attacks the very pillars of our society that hold us together. All these people, some who dislike Communism, unknowingly help it on its path to world government.

Diversion is used in secrecy, a clandestine conspiracy, that uses propaganda, agitation, public bombing, spread of diseases, terror, provocation, disinformation, and all subversive activities, to achieve its goal. We will see in the next section how Communism has used the IRA as a diversion to disrupt the United Kingdom, an aim that is a pre-requisite to forcing us into a Federal Europe. We can also see the war over Kosovo as part of the same diversion where the establishment in America, now controlled by the bankers controlling Communism, has to break nine hundred years of sectarian conflict to move Yugoslavia into a Federal Europe. Those who think that the IRA is about religion and Kosovo is about protecting the Albanians are focusing on the wrong target. It is this deception, that Communism relies upon to move its policy forward in a constant revolution. Remember, Communism is a constant revolution, a war. Diversion hides this from view except from those who understand its ways.

Communism's diversion is an exact science as is war. To Communism, boundaries do not exist, and you will find international Finance Capitalists have had the same approach, so they believe the world is the state and no Nation has boundaries.

Federalism is a staging post to achieve a Communist, "One World State". To achieve this, our roads to power have been infiltrated, including MI5, MI6, the CIA, the academic world and its agencies, that now control intelligence, and security and indeed strategic studies. We have seen how International Zionist spies have reached the top of America's civil service. So too have they achieved the same in Britain where Victor Rothschild was a prime example. At this level of entry the damage a spy can do to our democracy is immense. We saw it in America from Alger Hiss and Harry Dexter White. They were only two of many spies hidden in the administration. Many still exist today. We have also seen how a weak President was influenced by these Communist agents. In Britain they have even planted politicians in important posts as we have shown with Harold Wilson. Evidence, that cannot be printed, places at least two more recent Prime Ministers in the same frame.

There has been an almost suicidal attitude in America and the United Kingdom, in political circles, supported by the bankers and the bankers' press, that has refused to debate the issues that I disclose within these pages. The grip of the Masonic - Banker - Communist power house has gradually grown throughout this century. America came close to exposing the hard core of corruption when McCarthy exposed the 'Enemy within' but the Communists, financed by the bankers, and protected by the media effectively neutralised his attempts to warn America of the threat from Communist penetration in its society. Similar attempts were made to hide the early days of Harold Wilson at University, and other Communists like Victor Rothschild. The damage they did to our society was incalculable.

Diversion is part of the whole concept of revolution. It started, as we saw, with the French Revolution where Pre-Communism, under the Illuminati and Masonry, took over France. They went on to win the Bolshevik Revolution in 1917 and impose Communism on the Russian people. From Russia, through the Internationale, they have spread world-wide, corrupting democracy, morality, and religion in their wake, and, because they are let in the front door by International Bankers, we have not noticed their entry. This is the danger of the 'Enemy within' as Cicero so aptly wrote, even before Christianity gripped the world.

In diversion nothing can be taken at face value. Every action has a hidden agenda or put it another way a secondary motive. It uses 'Maskirovka", a screening (Mirror) as a cover, to hide its true purpose, and therefore nothing is what it seems. In a way it is like a continual conjuring trick that hypnotises its audiences..

A very clear example of this was exposed in Viktor Sovorov's "G.U.S.M. - **(281)**, where he showed that the International Ballistic Missiles deployed on military parade (May Day) were merely mock ups and not what the vision showed. Accordingly the West was forced to increase its weaponry (Increasing the bankers profits) to counter balance an incorrect assessment of what they saw. That was diversion in a simple form in action. That is revolution, and once again the bankers gained. But we saw it as a threat, and it is this deception that Communism relies upon to further its cause.

Now let us move this on a stage to less obvious diversions that seem to be more evolution of standards within our society. Liberals would argue that all reforms on the social level have been hard fought for and won by their dedication to represent minorities. So let us first remind ourselves of the evidence captured by allied forces in 1919 which laid down the grounds for Communist attack on all democracy throughout the world.

1 Corrupt the young. Get them away from religion. Get them interested in sex.
2 Make them superficial. Destroy their ruggedness.
3 Get people's minds off their governments by focusing their attentions on athletics, sexy books, plays and other trivialities.
4 Divide the people into hostile groups by constantly harping on controversial matters of no importance.
5 Destroy the people's faith in their natural leaders by holding the latter up to contempt, ridicule and disgrace.
6 Always preach true democracy, but seize power as fast and (As) ruthlessly as possible.
7 By encouraging government extravagance, destroy its credit. Produce fear of inflation with rising prices and general discontent.

8	Incite unnecessary strikes in vital industries. Encourage civil disorders and foster a lenient and soft attitude on the part of the government toward such disorders.
9.	By specious argument, cause the breakdown of the "Old moral" virtues – honesty, sobriety, self-restraint, faith in the pledged word, ruggedness.

If you study these requirements of revolution you will see that they were successful in reducing our moral, religious, educational and domestic standards to their present level. Liberals would claim that it is their hard work that did this as if these falling standards were a virtue. They aren't. The Roman Empire, perhaps the greatest Empire that ever existed, collapsed through its decline in morality.

Remember the words of Mikhail Borodin, spoken to Madame Chiang Kai - Shek; "In order to achieve a reversal of the declension of peoples under Western Socialism and Liberalism, and to achieve universal Communism, our methods are to work with religious organisations and with men and women who are leftist bent. For they are the least suspect and can best serve as our advanced troops.

Through our Socialist and Liberal friends we have used the legislative route - Parliament - to turn the countries in the direction we wish them to go by encouraging more socialistic legislation with spend, spend, spend as the motto. This would enable the national economic policy of the country to be acclimatised to deficit spending. (Borrowing. This is how they hold our politicians to ransom).

"Throughout the ages and from the experience and associations with Liberals around the world, we find that by and large because of their manifold ideas vectored in whichever direction, they cannot or will not follow a goal to a logical end. Call them fertile of mind, if you will, but having so many ideas they become self-contradictory in their thinking and with the many goals they wish to achieve they are automatically and mutually self-destructing.... In fact they are often very clever and ingenious; certainly they are necessary forward troops attired in camouflage to achieving success in world revolution... In other words, Liberalism must be made the spearhead for Communism... Liberals, Liberal intellectuals and intellectuals are all ready instruments to be used for the advancement of our beliefs and cause.

"These (Trades Unions) need not be Communist affiliated or Communist motivated nor need the union officials feel beholden to us for our help. We encourage these organisations to demand higher and even higher wages and peripheral benefits and fewer and fewer working hours which is always welcome to all workers. We help them financially whenever we can so they could strike and go on striking.

"To achieve the greatest possible dissemination of our ideology, we have to rely on the news media of the world".

This quite clearly lays down the programme that we have suffered from for most of this century. It shows that the Liberal and Socialist element are used by Communism to achieve its aims. You can see that bankers are behind this policy because we see deficit spending as a weapon in their armoury.

He spells out the illogical thinking of Liberals that suit their goal. He also shows how our Trades Unions have been used to achieve their aims, and shows how Communism (Through the Bankers) relies on the media of the world as a mask for their activities.

So the argument that our religious, moral and family decline is just evolution is shattered by this statement from such a high Communist agent and proves that decline is ordered by Communism. A Strategic **DIRECTION.** (Remember Direction proves movement towards its objective, Communism, and World Government; its aim, originating from Weishaupt's Illuminati, and cloned into Communism). If further proof is needed we have it from a Soviet defector, Tomas D. Schuman, in his famous, "Love Letters to America". **(282).** In a condensed form the targets he exposed were:-

Religion; politicise, commercialise, entertain, remove religious observance from schools. (The aim is to crush our religion).

Education; inculcate permissiveness and relativity. Changing history to suit the agenda. (Writing national figures, such as Shakespeare and Winston Churchill out of History and Watering down religion into a general study rather than a National religious education).

Media; monopolise, manipulate, discredit, focus on false or divisive issues, such as homosexuality, rather than to defend sexual morality. (The lowering of moral standards over the last twenty years).

Culture; create false heroes and role models. (Creating heroes of footballers and models rather than consistent achievers. The honours system can fairly be brought into this field).

Law and Order; introduce a legislative rather than a moral code. (The collapse of morals through legislative interference).

Social Relations; promote rights rather than obligations. (for minority groups such as homosexuals).

Security; Attack intelligence agencies, the police and armed forces. (Recent attacks on the police by the courts and the Brussels European Courts of Justice).

Internal Politics; generate disunity through party antagonisms. (Conservative party disunity).

Foreign Relations; repeated capitulation to Soviet strategies, and disharmony between Western powers. (Kosovo, Rhodesia, South Africa).

Family and Society; break up and induce disloyalty. (They aim to break up the family unit and the media is doing their part to bring this about as well as political legislation).

Health; promote sporting entertainment rather than individual participation, unrealistic ideals of socialised Medicare and junk food. (They wish to promote a unhealthy society).

Race; promote hatred and division through environmental rather than genetic arguments, and promotion of racial issues and enforced legislation. (We can see this in our papers and around us all the time).

Population; control through urbanisation, and eliminate patriotism and independence based on land ownership. (Blair's secret legislation to create twelve regions of Britain is the most ominous step to achieve this aim of Communism. This policy comes straight from Brussels where this is already a plan on a future map of what was Britain. We can only stop this by voting no to the Euro, so we can stop Federalisation of Britain and loss of our precious sovereignty).

Labour; pit trades unions against society. (This we have so vividly seen, culminating in the miners strike that caused the government to collapse. Margaret Thatcher redressed the balance but Blair, despite his rhetoric is gradually giving the unions back power to hold the country to ransom again. (Communism would not tolerate this but they use it to destabilise non Communist nations).

Read these and you will see it resembles, to the letter, what has happened in the Western world in the last seventy-five years. It is comfortable to believe that none of this is happening to our democracy, but Communism relies on this hidden reality to achieve its end, world control through an alliance of banking power, Masonic secrecy, Communist Diversion, and media deceit. Unfortunately senior civil servants and politicians of all parties collaborate with International Finance Capitalists. This full circle scenario leaves us isolated from power unless we use our only, and greatest power, the power of the masses, to change the direction, back to democracy.

Also, as proof of diversion, we have the historical accounts of a giant among historians, Carroll Quigley, who, despite his underlying agreement with the financiers and their plan for world domination, hated their secrecy and went about giving us an account of their planned take-over of world power in his book, "Tragedy and Hope." **(283).** In this book, covering 1814-1964, he shows how Capitalism went through three phases; mercantile, industrial and financial. Each phase superseded the previous one, until the final capitalism of financial origin which took decision making out of the hands of traders and manufacturers, where it belongs, and put it in the hands of bankers and financiers. Their aim was to have an international policy to suit their agenda of free flowing capital, which is in their interest, but not in the interest of nation states. That is why they approve Communism, as they wish to establish the world as a single state, which suits the bankers. A policy the same as Marxism.

Quigley shows us inside the establishment mind of the super rich by showing us the use of the foundations in America to protect their wealth from taxation and he shows us how they interlock with the banks and the multinational companies to form an enormous financial power structure to break down national interests. From this has flowed GATT and now the MAI policy. (Which we must stop at all cost).

He shows how Cecil Rhodes started the Round Table group and how, after his death, the control and influence was taken over by the bankers and their multinational industries, which, led by J.P. Morgan, into a secret society, working through the Institute of International Affairs. This society controlled and influenced the English speaking nations and even penetrated China.

Quigley also was honest enough to tell his readers which papers at that time were controlled by the Bankers and gave Anthony Sutton no coverage when he exposed his sensational testimony to the Republican Convention about America's roll in funding and supplying Russia with arms and technology; The New York Times, The New York Herald Tribune, The Christian Science Monitor, The

Washington Post, and the Boston Evening Transcript, and that Lord Lothian, who was the editor of the Round Table magazine, also wrote for the Monitor. Another case of closing the circle.

Alas, Quigley was marginalised by the very people whom he had supported. They stopped his book being distributed by its publisher who had to conform to the Bankers' will, censored by a hidden group of power brokers. It took him eight years to find another Non Establishment publisher to re-publish his work, a hard lesson he learned but we must be grateful he succeeded to get his work re-published as it gives us a rare insight into the hidden agenda within the bankers world. **DIRECTION.**

We have seen Rakovski's interview that took place inside the NKVD headquarters. Evidence that tells us of the upper road (higher level) of Communism, the real policy of Karl Marx and the Illuminati which is a policy of elitism, designed for the Rothschild Bank as a policy to create a world government.

What this means is that the Communism that was presented to the people, was a diversion. It presented a mask to hide the true policy of elitism to favour bankers and academia. Even within Communism the mask is used. But the bankers need this mask to achieve their aim. Rakovsky gave us this rare insight into the truth behind the mask. **DIRECTION.**

Rakovsky even gives names when challenged to identify the ruling elite amongst the bankers. He named Kuhn Loeb and Co. as a bank and the Schiffs, Warburgs, and Eastern Establishment men like Baruch, Lipperman, and Rothschild. It was Baron Lionel Rothschild who controlled Karl Marx and Herzen in the First International and financed the Communist Manifesto.

Rakovsky also tells us Trotsky was the Bankers' man in the Russian Revolution whose wife, Sedova, was an associate of the Warburgs and Jacob Schiff. We also learn that Archduke Ferninand, who died at the hands of an assassin in 1914, was killed with Trotsky's connivance, and probably ordered by his banking backers, an act which started the First World War, another diversion that moved the action in favour of the banking agenda. **DIRECTION.**

We have seen the evidence of Jonathan May, who exposed the plans of the American and British banking establishment that staged the four-hundred percent oil price increase in 1973 and then went about defrauding the Arab nations of their oil income. **DIRECTION.**

We have seen how banks have dominated national politics of most countries and even now the world as a whole, through the International Monetary Fund and the World Bank. We have also seen how third world countries are robbed of their only assets, their mineral reserves, by these banks, and we saw Delors form the European Central Bank in 1989, which will do exactly the same when the time comes in Europe. **DIRECTION.**

So what of more recently, April 99.. Well, in the Daily Mail **(284)**, we were told that our government, under the bankers' friend, Tony Blair, has deceitfully started eight new Regional Development Agencies to go with the four regions already given some form of self government; Scotland, Wales, Northern Ireland, and soon London under a Mayor. This policy is billed by the government and Media alike as giving self government to specific areas. This is a deception, a diversion, because along with the eight new regions; Northern, North West, Yorkshire and Humberside, West Midlands, East Anglia, South West, and South East, and London under the Mayor, it is preparing the United Kingdom for Federalisation in Europe, before the referendum, before we have joined the Euro, and without our knowledge of the intent; starved of information by the media except the Daily Mail. This has been done secretly, dividing the UK into twelve regions with assemblies by act of parliament. In Brussels they have maps showing the regions of Europe. These regions comply with these maps and correspond to Europe's twelve regions to replace Britain. Our inside man has studied these maps. **DIRECTION.**

Yes, replace Britain, as England will no longer exist. This is not a scare story, the legislation has gone through parliament and exists. The idea is that Europe, as it exists now will split into one-hundred and eleven regions of control, governed directly from Brussels. So if you don't believe we are losing control of our own affairs this is the time to start thinking before it is too late. Just look at Blair's Regional Development Agency Bill. You will see he is doing the Bankers Bidding. Deceitfully behind closed doors the European Commission Office in London helped to set up Regional Conferences. Behind closed doors just as the Bilderberg Group meets.

Each regional area has its own Agency and its own Chamber, (To replace parliament) seventy percent of the members are appointees, guaranteeing a non representative decision making body, avoiding democracy, and the others come from Europhile organisations like the CBI and the trades unions. **DIRECTION.**

This is going to be the Trojan Horse within our walls, locking us into Brussels whether we like it or not. So is Britain a nation of the past?

Well, if the latest BBC directive to its staff is anything to go by it is about to be banned **(285).** According to the BBC 'British' is an offensive word. It is ironical that this should come from the BBC, whose motto was "Nation shall speak peace unto nation", why they even say 'Nation' is also an insult. Wonder where they got that idea from? Could it be Brussels? So sorry Michael Fish, no more national weather and no more national news at nine. Just another hint to show us that Britain and its national assets are being rubbished by Blair and the BBC in a hidden agenda the people don't want. **DIRECTION.**

The protocols, a pertinent example of which is printed at the end of each section, have in their time provoked the most amazing reaction, especially after they were translated into different languages in 1920. As I have already stated, I do not wish to enter the argument about their authenticity, which has been well discussed and led to violent attacks by the Zionist authorities. Forged they are not. Because a forgery is a fake of a similar product. From their content you get three distinct impressions; the financial expertise, their accuracy, and Masonic content. To say they are anti Semitic is so far from the truth to be laughable. That they give the gentile a feeling of inferiority is nearest the truth which could cause resentment.

There is one truth that the Zionist movement never mentions; their accuracy in prediction. Everything of note that has happened this century is covered in their dialogue. It is almost impossible to believe that anyone could have predicted the future so accurately. But, turned into a thoroughly researched political plan, by a small group of the world's most powerful men, it is possible to see how their money creates the future agenda, and therefore the amazing prediction could be, in actuality, a thoroughly though out plan and the accuracy is their achievement of implementing their plan.

The International Zionists, funded and led by the International banking cartel, mostly of Khazar origin of middle Europe, have a very good reason to rubbish this document; because it exposes their hidden agenda towards a world dictatorship. So it is natural they must pour scorn on its authenticity, and they did it to a man.

In the book, "Holy Blood and the Holy Grail" **(286),** the Protocols are discussed but it strangely criticises them in their reference to a King, being the King of the Jews, who will be the real Pope. They go on to say Kings have not existed in Judaic tradition since biblical times.

What they have failed to acknowledge is that the Jews involved in the Banking world are adoptive Jews from Eastern and Central Europe and they did have a King in the Khazar region. The reference to Pope is to say that their King will be all things to all people including the Pope. You must understand that they wish to kill all religions save their own creed, based on a combination of atheism and Judaism, to suit the moment. Their religion will be the sole religion so a International church is referring to a world religion. The book concludes; that the Protocols of the Elders of Zion were based on an original authentic script. On this I agree. They go on to say it was not a Jewish but a Masonic oriented secret society which used Zion. Well here I disagree with their conclusion. Research would tell them that Bankers were an important part of the Masonic world. Part of the Masonic ceremony uses words and props from Judaism. There were also lodges that were primarily banking lodges dominated by Jews, so I stick to my previous guess that their origin was predominately Khazar Jewish, Masonic and controlled by financial expertise.

They claim, Nilus himself, who came across the script, radically altered it to achieve a point against his rivals within the court of the Czar. Well that is good stuff but no proof is offered, but it fits their story nicely. It is this sort of controversy that has succeeded in marginalizing the power of this remarkable script.

As I only offer it as an amazing prediction the rest is academic but it gives you an insight into the controversy it caused. Needless to say Zionists proclaim it was a forgery even today, but never have they proved what it was forged from or who forged it, only un-established theories have they used to try to kill its power.

PROTOCOL TWO

ECONOMIC WARS

It is indispensable for our purposes that wars, as far as possible, should not result in territorial gains: war will thus be brought on to the economic ground, where the nations will not fail to perceive in the assistance we give, the strength of our predominance, and this state of things will put both sides at the mercy of our international agentur, which possesses millions of eyes ever on watch and unhampered by any limitations whatsoever. Our international rights will then wipe out national rights, in the proper sense of right, and will rule the nations precisely as the civil law of states rules the relations of their subjects among themselves.

The administrators, whom we shall choose from among the public with strict regard to their capacities for servile obedience, will not be persons trained in the arts of government and will therefore easily become pawns in our game in the hands of men of learning and genius, who will be their advisers, specialists bred and reared from early childhood to rule the affairs of the whole world. As is well known to you, these specialists of ours have been drawing the information they need to fit them for rule from our political plans, from the lessons of history, from observations made of the events of every moment as it passes. The Goyim are not guided by practical use of unprejudiced historical observation, but by theoretical routine without any critical regard for consequent results. We need not, therefore, take any account of them - let them amuse themselves until the hour strikes, or live in hopes of new forms of enterprising pastime, or on the memories of all they have enjoyed. For them, let that play the principal part which we have persuaded them to accept as the dictates of science (theory). It is with this object in view that we are constantly, by means of our press, arousing a blind confidence in these theories.

The intellectuals of the Goyim will puff themselves up with their knowledge and without any logical verification will put into effect all the information available from science, which our agentur specialists have cunningly pieced together for the purpose of educating their minds in the direction we want.

Do not suppose for one moment that these statements are empty words: think carefully of the successes we arranged for Darwinism, Marxism, Nietzcheism. To us Jews, at any rate, it should be plain to see what a disintegrating effect these directives have had upon the minds of the Goyim.

It is indispensable for us to take account of the thoughts, characters, tendencies of the nations in order to avoid making slips in the political and in the direction of administrative affairs. The triumph of our system, and of the machinery of which it is composed, which may vary according to the temperament of the peoples we encounter, will not be assured unless its practical application is based upon a résumé of the lessons of the past in the light of the present.

In the hands of the state of today there is a great force that creates the movement of thought in the people, and that is the press. The part played by the press is to keep pointing out requirements supposed to be indispensable, to give voice to the complaints of the people, to express and to create discontent. It is with the press that the triumph of freedom of speech finds its incarnation. But the Goyim states have not known how to make use of this force; and it has fallen into our hands. Through the press we have gained the power to influence while remaining ourselves in the shade; thanks to the press, we have got the gold in our hands, notwithstanding that we have had to gather it out of oceans of blood and tears. But it has paid us, though we have sacrificed many of our people. Each victim on our side is worth in the sight of God a thousand Goyim.

COMMENT.

They claim that wars must not end in territorial gains, so they are kept on an economic level. This is to suit the greed of the International bankers with an added bonus of making countries involved more dependent on their loan services. So you see that they manipulate nations in order to create wars so they can benefit from the lucrative loan business during and after the conflict. Their aim is to make all countries dependent on their services. This part of their programme is almost complete, where nearly all countries of the world are in debt slavery.

They claim that when this programme is complete their (the bankers) international rights will wipe out national rights. We can see this already taking place in the European Union, where federalisation is the secret policy behind the undemocratic power, to remove nation status from its members in a secret plan towards world government where the European Union will be one of three regional governments. This is also why Blair has formed twelve regions of Britain to comply with EU policy; again at the directive of the Bilderberg committee, the planners for world government. They are the administrators that the bankers have chosen. They also claim that the new breed of politician has been hand reared by them (the bankers) to rule the affairs of the whole world. This is interesting when you study the way Clinton and Blair seem to do their bidding and must give us cause for concern as to how their democratic promises will be fulfilled in the light of their adherence to Bankers directives.

We learn that, they not only control the press, but they use it to push opinion towards their policies. I cannot underestimate the power this has in an information market that is controlled by a powerful small minority of world citizens. If people only see one side of an argument they will fall down on that side, right or wrong. That is what these evil men know will happen. They claim to have killed Royalty, and to a large degree they have, but let me warn them Britain will not allow them to kill our Royal family easily, despite Mr. Murdoch's prolonged attempt to finish it off. In Australia and Britain he will know who has our voice, and it is not him.

They claim to feed us plans that they wish to put into effect. This is true. The GATT agreement and now the MAI agreement are typical examples both good for bankers and multinational companies but both very bad for the people of the world.

At the end of this Protocol they tell us the truth about the press and the media. They own it all and use it to influence thought, while they stand aside but control its message from their secret centre of power.

CHAPTER ELEVEN, PART TWO.
THE IRA - A WEAPON FOR REVOLUTION.

"If England is the fortress of European landlordism and capitalism, then the only point from which a strong blow can be struck at official England is **IRELAND**".

Karl Marx. From a resolution on relations between the Irish and English working class. 1869.

Karl Marx, way back in 1869, realised that Ireland was the weak link in British defence and could be used in Communist Revolution terms to attack the strength of England.

However our media, with few exceptions, would have us believe Ireland is all about a religious divide and the entrenched positions of both sides that lead to, an impossible position. It is therefore not surprising that we have a mirror in front of our eyes that gives us a false image of the real truth; the truth that the troubles are about the destabilisation of Britain and not about a Roman Catholic and Protestant divide. This is only cunningly used by the IRA to ferment unrest and keep anarchy at a high level. The public agenda of the IRA is only used as a screen to hide the truth that they wish to kill all religion. The press has promoted the Sinn Fein - IRA campaign as a sectarian struggle which has been boosted by Sinn Fein - IRA propaganda, whereas it is part of a much larger organisation of world wide revolution. A struggle for world domination.

We find the roots of this world-wide terrorism in the centres planning one world government, New York, Moscow, Israel, and London. I have even been told, how true it is I do not know, that all terrorism world-wide is planned by a central planning office in London, the headquarters of a foreign security agency. Certainly we have seen co-operation between the IRA, the ANC and the PLO.

From the conflicts of the sixteenth and seventeenth centuries, history shows the world to arrive at a point of revolution that started in France, namely the French Revolution 1789, won by the new Republic with the Masons of Weishaupt in charge.

From this point on, the divide between the Roman Catholic and Protestant factions grew, and the Irish in general were to become the victims of the world revolution, and to be used as pawns in an endless battle to bring Britain to its knees. Its purpose was not to protect Catholics but rather destroy all religions and with it national identity, as I have already shown. (A policy that is included in the programme of Federalisation being forced on Europe with Bl air's assistance).

Archbishop le Febvre informed the world that numerous senior Roman Catholic churchmen in the Vatican were Freemasons yet in Ireland we have a divide that is meant to be between Catholic, non-Masons, on one side, and Protestant, Orange Order Masons, on the other. This is the front view they want you to accept.

Ireland Chosen to Lead the Revolution to Bring England to its knees.

In the dark age history, after the collapse of the Roman Empire the Celts used European tribes from mainly Germany to assist in protecting Britain from the Barbarians. This emigration gradually became known as the Anglo Saxon community, which in turn drove the Celts to the extremities of their land, Scotland, Wales, Ireland, and Cornwall. It was at this stage that latent hostility developed between England and its remote states. By the time of the French Revolution, and at the start of Europe's Revolution Ireland was already divided into two religious groups, the Roman Catholics, mainly in the South of Ireland and the Protestants in the North. From this divide there built up secret societies which, as in France, played a major part in influencing power. In France Freemasonry was the conduit through which these secret societies grew, using the rites, mainly from the discipline of the Grand Orient, whose power and influence throughout the world's Masonry is well documented, spreading to America in the guise of the Scottish rite, and secret societies such as the Carbonari of Italy that re-invented ancient conspiracy to use in the nineteenth century. Archbishop le Febvre showed us how many Roman Catholic churchmen in the Vatican became Freemasons which only adds to the complexity of the conspiracy but shows how Weishaupt's Satanic evil penetrated its enemies to corrupt from within. The Roman Catholic church in Ireland has openly been hostile to any form of Freemasonry, and quite rightly so because it is its intent to kill religion.

In Ireland the Roman Catholic church has stood firm against Masonry, mainly because the Protestant Orange Order is a Masonic society.

Up to the French Revolution the Roman Catholic and Protestant societies opposed each other within a controlled system of mistrust one against the other.

When Weishaupt started the Illuminati, **(287)** in 1776, and planned, and won the French Revolution through the two-hundred and sixty-six branches of the Grand Orient in 1789, he began to think of spreading his revolution to England and he considered Ireland as England's weak limb. The proof of this can be found in the Hon. Robert Clifford's translation of Abbe Barruel's "Memoirs Illustrating the History of Jacobinism" 1798, **(288)** and also in Lady Queenborough's **(289)** book where she quotes from the autobiography of Theobald Wolf Tone and Pollard's "The Secret Societies of Ireland" **(290)** who showed how the Irish secret societies were part of a larger conspiracy that encompassed Europe and America. (The World).

Pollard states; "These emissaries from France aimed at bringing England low, and spreading the doctrine of world revolution, by means of an alliance between the catholic malcontents of the South and the Republican Presbyterians of the North". This proves that the people of Ireland have been pawns in a game not of religious hatred but in a prolonged and determined attempt to bring England to its knees.

Hidden agenda.

Clifford's translation also states; "What unhappy deluded people then were the lower associates, (The Roman Catholic people of Ireland) who were informed of nothing, but were to be mere agents of rebellion and murder, and were hurried on into the abyss of horrors by a few political libertines who grasped at dominion, and wished to wade to the helm of the state through the blood of their countrymen". In those parts where the whole population was Catholic, hand bills were distributed, purporting to be the constitution of the Orange Men, which was death and destruction to every Catholic, for, if the common people could be once stirred up to rebellion, it was easy to turn their minds against government as the centre of the Orange Man".

The association mentioned in this passage was the Irish Brotherhood, later to become the United Irishmen, founded by Wolf Tone and Napper Tandy in 1791. Clifford also shows how contacts were in place with the Illuminated Jacobin Club in Paris, the Revolution Society in England and the Scottish Committee of Reform. So we have completed the circle that proves that the IRA, which developed from the United Irishmen, was a member of the Illuminati of Weishaupt through the Grand Orient lodges and it was started by Masons.

In 1796 and 1798 Tone made two unsuccessful attempts to land French troops on Irish soil. In 1857-1858, under James Stephens, the Fenian Society was formed, later to be known as the Irish Republican Brotherhood, and from its initial launch was linked to the European Revolutionary Movement. In 1865 they joined the group of secret societies under Karl Marx, the International Working Men's Association, founded in London one year before they joined.

From this point Lady Queenborough refers to them as a; "Definite element in the complex machinery of World - Revolution", making the point that they were not a revolutionary society for the purpose of establishing an independent Republican Ireland.

It is worth remembering at this moment that Karl Marx saw Ireland as the key to destroying England. Lady Queenborough confirms Pollard as stating; "Insurrection in Ireland is a just part of a larger revolution to destroy the existing social order". From this it is quite clear their aim is not just to break the bond between the Northern Irish community and England but to destroy the English and Southern Irish parliaments; "It is at all events clear that Marx knew, even if the mass of the Irish dupes did not, that the Irish revolutionary dream of the IRB and

Fenian leaders was not merely a Nationalist dream, but was to be a social revolution".

In 1896 the Irish Socialist Republican Party was founded by James Connolly and linked to the American based Industrial Workers of the World (IWW). In 1905 Sinn Fein was formed by Arthur Griffiths, later to be linked to the IRA. By 1917 the revolutionary leader Eamon de Valera took over the Sinn Fein and linked it to the Irish - American organisation Clan - na - Gael and the IRA was formed in 1916 to balance the UVF (Ulster Volunteer Force), the Protestant defence force.

Then to complete the Communist connection to Marx in 1920 the Irish Republican Brotherhood linked with the IRA and formed the Irish Communist Brotherhood, joining up with Communist revolutionary circles in America. All through this process the conduit for its logistics were the Masonic lodges of the Grand Orient.

As Clifford foretold the majority of Sinn Fein - IRA activists are sincerely committed to the furtherance of their own sectarian ideals, in this way the leaders have successfully set up a screen in front of our eyes, showing us a religious divide when the game plan is quite different. This is classic Communism in practice. **DIVERSION.**

So the Illuminati had, from the French Revolution, moved in on young America and built the seeds of revolution in Ireland and to aid and abet them was non other than our Prime Minister at the time, Lord Palmerston (Disraeli) a man of Jewish extraction but also a Grand Master of the Grand Orient Masonic Lodge.

According to Nesta Webster close links between the Irish Republican Brotherhood and the Ancient Order of Hibernians and Knights of St Columba, formed in 1882, exercised revolutionary influence over the Roman Catholic Church in Ireland. **(291).**

Europe in the nineteenth century was the centre of revolution. The Carbonari spread from Italy to France and the Grand Orient. **(292).**

The Italian revolutionary, Guiseppe Mazzini had close links with General Albert Pike, the Grand Master of the Scottish Rite in America, a self confessed Luciferian and the American leader of Weishaupt's policy, after Weishaupt's death.

The American Scull and Bones Society, founded in America in the thirties is linked to German Masonic Lodges most certainly Illuminated. It had among its members President George Bush (A ardent supporter of the New World Order) and McGeorge Bundy who in turn link with the Ford Foundation, the Carnegie Endowment for International Peace and the Aspen Institute all of which have funded research into world power. It was President Rowan H. Gpither, in 1954, in a statement from the Ford Foundation that let the true agenda of their direction within the power foundations become public; "To use our grant-making power so to alter life in the United States that we can be comfortably merged with the Soviet Union". If that wasn't a warning to take heed of, I don't know what is.

So we have seen how revolution fits into the agenda of the world movement and we can see now more clearly how revolution, organised by terrorists but controlled and financed by Communism and its bankers, has been used to push forward the boundaries of revolution, just one tool in Communism's armoury. The Irish destabilisation is a classic example. Now let's compare the problems in Ireland to those in South Africa brought about by the ANC in its progress to power.

Terrorism: the IRA and the ANC.

If we examine the evidence available we get a far different picture of the events in Ireland than the papers have presented to us over a long period. Take the account of a journalist, himself an Irish citizen. In Martin Dillon's book "The Shankill Butchers" **(293)** we find not only did the Ulster Volunteer Force (UVF) and the Ulster Democratic Alliance (UDA) co-operate in terrorism, **(Page 11-13)** but Spence, a UVF leader and intern in Long Kesh re-established his thinking along Marxist lines, so much so he installed a Socialist policy in his own brigade **(37-38)**.

We also learn from this book that none other than Harold Wilson was responsible for releasing Jerry Adams from jail when he wanted a deal. In hindsight we must ask if this was not just a hidden agenda to insure that he returned to his duties in organising the demise of Britain, the aim of the IRA; the task we know the Marxist IRA were set to achieve. **(Page 181)**.

We learn that the IRA set out in the seventies to demoralise the population of Northern Ireland and the government in England. **(Page 182)**. Now comes the crunch that tells us the truth about all Northern Ireland paramilitary UDF, UDA, and the Provisional IRA. Contact existed between these groups in the seventies to plan terrorism and apportion territories for the taxi and building scams they all used to fund terrorism. From this we see that they were at one in prolonging terrorism, and Marxism was their meeting point. **(Page 257)**. They also joined to plan the demise of Leone Murphy, who was a loose cannon within terrorism. **(Page 258-265)**. So what you see in our news is just a mirror of what they want you to believe. The facts behind the news are usually quite different. **DIRECTION.**

In Alison Phillip's book, "The Revolution In Ireland 1906-1923" **(294)**, he shows how atheistic Jews from Poland and Russia emigrated to Northern Ireland after the Bolshevik Revolution to influence and guide terrorism to destabilise England; "The 'Reds', too, seized their opportunity, so early in 1918 foreign Communists - notably Polish and Russian Jews from Glasgow - had been filtering into Northern Ireland in considerable numbers, and committees of the Third International, in touch with Moscow, were established in the principle cities. With the withdrawal of the British forces and the general collapse of administrative order, these groups began to show an ominous activity". The truth is, they infiltrated, took over, and controlled terrorism as a tool to de-stabilise England and they have controlled it ever since. That is why the real power behind the IRA, the Provisionals and Sinn Fein is never exposed, as it would be a give away to the source of terrorism, for which they wish religion's divide to take the blame, while they use religious extremism to hide the truth. (A typical Weishaupt ploy to use other names to hide his work from the public gaze). **DIVERSION.**

The IRA and ANC Link.

Henry Pike, in his "History of Communism in South Africa" **(295)** relates a parallel move to influence terrorism in South Africa. Although he does not mention Jewish involvement, it is well documented since the start of this century that SACP, (The South African Communist Party) was behind terrorism and the armed struggle, led by ANC (African National Congress) and the leaders of both organisations were both Communist and Jewish, names such as Joe Slovo, Ronnie Kasrils, and Albie Sachs, led both groups, the ANC being formed in 1984 to lead the terrorists in the final thrust to power in dictatorship.

It is not racial to state this information as it is a matter of fact; a matter of recorded history contained in Gideon Shimoni's book "Jews and Zionism: The South African Experience" **(296).** However to expose Jewish involvement in Communism is immediately jumped upon by International Zionism, using the Jewish good name to silence those who dare to speak.. We can see this quite clearly in the manner in which C. Gordon Tether was treated when he exposed the conspiracy of bankers and was immediately removed from mainstream journalism which cost him his financial column and his career.

Journalism, was either silenced, as in the case of C. Gordon Tether or bought out. Dr. Anthony Reilly, a Bilderberger and promoter of One World Government, owned the Dublin based, Independent Newspaper Group. (Owner of the Independent and the Independent on Sunday purchased 1997). In 1994 he took over the powerful Argus Newspaper Group in South Africa from Harry Oppenheimer and continued a policy of funding the Communist ANC. In such a position Dr. Reilly wields great power. Add to this his close relationship with Bilderberger Peter Sutherland of BP and Goldman Sachs, and Trilateralist Garrett Fitzgerald, former Taoiseach (Prime Minister of the Republic of Ireland) and you begin to see how they can be used to move the political agenda towards their revolution.

Searching a little deeper we find that the Hollinger - Telegraph Group, headed by Conrad Black, now resigned, a Bilderberger, has close links with Anglo American Gold and investments in South Africa. So when Andrew Hunter, Conservative member of Parliament, presented sensational evidence to the House of Commons that proved beyond doubt that the Sinn Fein, the IRA and the ANC were linked in terrorism, a disclosure that any journalist would like to be first to expose, the press gave it little attention and MI5 and Special Branch tried to silence Andrew Hunter. From this you can determine two important facts; the press, when called upon, does the bidding of the global elite. Politicians and highly placed civil servants also bow to their power but so does our secret service, so we get a sandwich effect, power from above and below, denying the public the free news they rely upon and deserve. In this position they form false opinions in their minds. That amounts to auto suggestion.

Just to illustrate the lengths this global elite go to, to get their way, the British Prime Minister, Margaret Thatcher, in 1987 accused the ANC of being terrorists, so the global Elite donated £75,000 to the hard up Conservative party, through Consolidated Gold Fields, linked to Harry Oppenheimer, and Anglo American Gold of South Africa. From that point comment was restrained to mild criticism. In a few words they use every tool in their armoury; a policy whose origin is in Communism. (Weishaupt). **DIRECTION.**

An investigation into Nelson Mandela's Communist controlled ANC in the lead up to the elections shows that Reilly's newspapers consistently attacked Nelson Mandela's rival, Dr. Buthelezi, spreading rumour and innuendo about his Inkatha Party, which upheld a democratic multicultural policy, yet praised the ANC at every opportunity, in the full knowledge that the ANC was controlled by the Communist - banker agenda.

Although Mandela was obliged to make Dr. Buthelezi, a democrat and friend of the West, a minister in his ANC - SACP dominated government, and despite the fact that Nelson Mandela, F. W. de Klerk and Dr. Buthelezi signed a solemn agreement that promised International mediation for regional government for the Zulu party of the IFP (Inkatha Freedom Party), once in power, Nelson Mandela blatantly ignored this agreement.

If you now look back at Ireland; a pre-condition in the present peace negotiations has been the ceasing of the armed struggle and the de-commissioning of all weapons. Sinn Fein - IRA have consistently declined to hand in arms with the result that the agreement has been ignored to keep the peace talks active. All this does, is give Gerry Adams another victory and gradually he is wearing down all opposition within government to these conditions. Yet a peace without the handing in of arms is unthinkable. It is also unthinkable that convicted terrorists from both sides should be let out of jail on a pretext of accord from a terrorist group that signed an agreement that included handing in arms and now refuses to do so. Yet that, as a present to terrorism, is exactly what our foolish government has done to expedite the agreement. To achieve this, parliament had to undo the wording of the peace agreement which stated that the release of prisoners was dependent on the handing in of arms by the terrorists, this Mo Molem did, thus betraying the moderate leader of the Ulster Unionists David Trimble, whose fragile balance with his own party is now upset.

What we have seen both in Ireland by the Sinn Fein - IRA and in South Africa by the ANC - SACP is the tactical use of the old Communist combination of armed and ideological struggle throughout negotiations. **South Africa has been taken over by an ANC council that had twenty-eight out of thirty-eight of its council members, known members of the South African Communist Party.** In the armed struggle between the ANC and mostly IPF supporters some 14,000 black South African citizens died, mostly Zulu supporters of Dr. Buthelezi. Amongst this was a cynical move to kill key figures in the IFP, where over 400 died by 1996. In Britain we were only allowed glimpses of ANC excess, mostly confined to Mandela's wife and her followers which he marginalised to isolate her in order to protect the ANC.

So our press in the mainstream were also responsible for hiding the true events that could prove the absurdity of the hand-over of power in South Africa to Communism, while a democrat like Dr. Buthelezi was passed over. In Ireland we see a similar pattern of internal discipline by the IRA, while a peace accord was on the table, which promoted headlines like; "IRA punishment squads step up the beatings", and "Godfathers of violence step up beatings to keep a grip on power". So it is not surprising that in a firmly Catholic street in Belfast a painted wall depicts the coming together of terrorism between the IRA and the ANC; a coming together that represents just one arm of the octopus of Communism's link to the powerhouse of International Finance Capitalism.

The leadership of both the Sinn Fein - IRA and the ANC - SACP are on record as Marxist, both organisations were trained and equipped by the Soviet Union and its satellites and they were both financed from abroad. What is so obviously excluded from this report is that the media, including the BBC never referred to the Communist affiliation of either the ANC or the IRA. From this we must conclude that our media is controlled by the same people who promote terrorism for their final aim; **World Domination by the International Finance Capitalist.**

What I have tried to show in this part of the chapter is how seemingly two different terrorist groups in two seemingly divorced territories of the World are linked by Communism, world finance, the Masonic Movement and International Zionism, and that these groups are, within a secret agenda driving the world towards

Communist Revolution, driven by the money of banking, the Atheist evil of Communism, and International Zionism, and the secrecy of Weishaupt's Illuminati within the Masonic Movement, and that they are assisted in their endeavours because the media is under the bankers influence. **DIRECTION.**

South Africa – The Transition From A Debt-Free State To Debt Dependency.

It would be wrong to think of South Africa in isolation. Since the Second World War the British and American Governments have collaborated with Russia and 'Iron Curtain' countries. We were informed that a cold war existed between our nations and America was holding back the march of Communism. Nothing could be further from the truth. If you study British command papers of this period, especially under Harold Wilson, you will find the hidden agenda was a policy to build up Russia's strength, modernise it and help them colonise areas of importance against the interests of the British people and the armed forces, Africa has, in the eyes of Russia, many advantages, not least its rich mineral reserves and the Communist think tank knew that if the Western World, and in particular Britain, was parted from Africa's resources, they would have won a major battle in their war. (Revolution).

So progressively Communism has infiltrated and controlled terrorism in Africa, not for the benefit of the poor Africans, but to cause maximum damage to the West and any democratic local opposition like Ian Smith in Rhodesia (now Zimbabwe) and Dr. Buthelezi of the Inkatha Freedom Party. Progressively government has turned a blind eye to Communism's progress and at times even acted to hide this knowledge.

Let us take an example of this disgraceful betrayal. In 1990 the member of parliament for Basingstoke, Andrew Hunter, revealed that the IRA collaborated with the Communist controlled ANC, whose thirty-eight member executive council had no fewer than twenty-eight known Communist members of the South African Communist Party as joint members.

Margaret Thatcher, Prime Minister at the time, Replied; "We never support armed struggle (by definition the Marxist - Leninist term for military action) no matter by whomsoever it is proposed, and the ANC stands for armed struggle and continues to do so". (Daily Telegraph 20th. April 1990). **(297).**

By May 1992 Hunter finished a 110 page report: "Twilight and Terror - Sinn Fein - IRA: The South African Dimension". **(298).** At that time Hunter was visited by Special Branch officers and an attempt was made to persuade Hunter not to continue with his investigations and he was indeed threatened it could damage his career.

On the 14th. May 1993 an Executive Intelligence Review report **(299),** on the murder of ANC leader Chris Hani had this to say; "Immediately after Hani's murder, the ANC called for outside investigators to oversee the murder inquiry. The British government in turn appointed the recently retired head of Scotland Yard's Anti Terrorist branch, George Churchill Coleman, formally responsible for co-ordinating police response to all acts of terrorism in Britain. Churchill Coleman is a **high level Freemason,** who, according to an intelligence source who knew him, quashed an investigation into relations between the IRA and the ANC. Here is proof of the ANC and IRA link, but more importantly how official police protection is given to hide the secret agenda of terrorism, and the ever present Masonic connection.

In Africa we have seen destabilisation by premature de-colonialisation where countries or large assets have been subjected to the forces of International Finance Capitalism by ruthless businessman like Tiny Rowland. The end result is that these countries are robbed of their precious minerals in exchange for a debt slavery that will ensure them third world status for the foreseeable future. Each time we see an African country get its so called independence, we see, when we research the circumstances that these very countries, with adequate wealth within their soil, end up in debt slavery to the International Monetary system while the International Finance Capitalists rob them of their birthright. We also find a few politicians who take over control of these countries move towards a single party state because Communism controls their politics. Communism does not help these people; it protects the dictatorship against the people. The take over of Rhodesia (Zimbabwe) was a classic example of this.

The declaration of Independence of Rhodesia by Ian Smith was tolerated by Britain till 1979, while terrorist groups prepared for the final move. It came in an unexpected way, at the Lancaster House Conference in 1980. At this conference control of Rhodesia was passed to a Soviet trained Marxist, Robert Mugabe, who, until a few months before, was not even in the running and the Nationalist leader Nkomo, up to then the front runner, was left high and dry.

During the whole procedure it was obvious that an Anglo - American and Russian agreement had been reached to hand over Rhodesia to a Communist dictatorship. What happened behind those closed doors? I am told, Nkomo would not sign Rhodesia's mineral rights over to the International Finance Capitalists so they could continue to milk the country of its natural wealth. So they used their great power to appoint a Marxist who knew the system and complied. In fact before the announcement was made Mugabe's signature was safely in their hands. The reason for this was to ensure they controlled the high grade chromium mining from Rhodesia, essential for modern weapons, as well as a bonus of the other minerals like gold and copper.

President Marchel of Mozambique, a Marxist, played a vital part in the negotiations and implementation of the Lancaster House Agreement on Rhodesia according to Richard Luce, MP, the Parliamentary Under Secretary of State at the Foreign and Commonwealth Office. Once again Marxists seemed to be controlling the actions of Western Governments; some hidden power. Once again the play was for the mineral wealth. So who were the British and American politicians responsible for the complete capitulation to Communism? Dr. Henry Kissinger, from Eastern Europe and leading Bilderberger. Lord Carrington, Conservative Foreign Minister and now Chairman of the Bilderberg Group. (He is also a partner of Kissinger Associates). The third man was Lord Soames. Kissinger and Carrington are both associated with every avenue to the super rich. Lord Soames was connected to the Anglo - American establishment through his directorship of N. M. Rothschild. So once again we see politicians becoming major players in the Anglo - American power establishment having done their duty to the establishment while in political office. A kind of reward for delivering the goods. That this delivery has cost the Western democracies dearly does not seem to be an issue as the press has failed to expose it, as they too are in the Anglo - American establishment.

So how did our so called uncommitted BBC behave during the build up to a capitulation to Communism in South Africa? Remembering that the BBC was meant to represent the Anglo Saxon Christian Society of Britain in its views to the world, we find the coverage very one sided when it covered views on South Africa; taking a very Liberal left wing position, ignoring other views almost completely. Radio serial transmissions featured Anti Apartheid fiction on a regular basis, and regular contributions included Nadine Gordimer and Janet Suzman who all gave a very one sided account of South African Affairs. In August 1992 a discussion on inter-White violence in South Africa on BBC World Service was one sided, giving the ANC view only from the Jewish Communist, Dennis Goldberg, an ANC terrorist training officer and ANC representative in London. My point here is that if you massage output to give just one point of view when it matters, people adopt that view. The BBC know that well. Their slanted media coverage was restricted to the area that they had targeted for Communist take-over of South and South West Africa, (Namibia), now both successfully in Communist hands. The hard pill to swallow; our media, our bankers, and our politicians and civil servants all took part in handing this area to Communism while our politicians and media gave us a very different story to hide their treachery.

The Media's line was quite simply the story of the darker side of Apartheid in South Africa; a cruel policy that no decent person could support. The media used this to convince the world the ANC had a just cause and to do so they had to lie and tell half truths about the ANC's opposition, the Inkatha Party. Nearly every story told about South Africa at this time blamed the Zulu Inkatha Party for the terrorism in South Africa. They were the evil terrorists. This of course was not true and is not borne out by the truth of South Africa. The Zulu race, under Dr. Buthelezi gave passive resistance to Apartheid and to the ANC. The ANC ran a campaign of violence against the Zulu tribes and against the white population, often twisting the truth about their activities to gain media publicity. Where else have we seen this? Northern Ireland of course. For example the 'Necklace of Fire' was a ANC weapon used against defaulters from their own ranks and against the Zulu tribesmen. In Ireland the IRA used knee-capping.

So let us get Africa first into focus. The continent of Africa is around eleven point eight million square miles containing fifty-five countries with a population of over four-hundred and ninety million people. Within this continent over two-thousand different tribes exist with different languages and different cultures. Most of Africa's problems stem from conflict between these tribes. Communism, to gain its hold over Africa has used the tribal differences to de-stabilise targeted areas for Communist gain. Therefore from the beginning of the seventies over five million black people have died, not by the hands of the minority white governments but by the tribal in-fighting, largely orchestrated by Communism. Although most African nations have undemocratic dictatorships, it is the tribal heads who rule Africa, many still using the power of the witch doctors to hold their tribes down and it is this problem that has built up the idea that the people have been held down. Most of them have been so restricted within the tribal system that they have little knowledge of Western Democracy. This makes the task of external influence by a group wishing to use their immaturity much easier and Communism has filled that roll although most of its victims do not even understand what they have agreed to support.

So why does Communism want Africa with all its problems? Certainly not to better the lot of the ordinary African. We only have to look at Russia, where Stalin killed twenty-two and a half million peasant small holders, to realise that people under Communism are totally dispensable.

They want South Africa to enable the Communist funding bankers to control the world supply of minerals. These figures suggest why:-

AFRICA'S SHARE OF WORLD PRODUCTION

Platinum Metals	86%
Chromium Ore	83%
Vanadium	64%
Gold	49%
Manganese Ore	48%
Uranium	17%

This shows quite clearly why Communism (of the bankers) must control Africa. By this they control the world resources, a part of their total aim. So Russia, since 1945, has gradually Communised thirty-seven countries in Africa, using all their tools, including the support of terrorist groups, and up to 60,000 red troops occupying territory like Angola, where the Cuban army has even protected Western oil facilities belonging to the International Finance Capitalists.

There is another reason why Communism wants control of South Africa; to control the Cape of Good Hope route for world trade and in particular, oil shipping. Whoever controls this route, controls the world oil supply. So you can see why Rhodesia, and in particular South Africa are so important to those who wish to control the world. Black power, used by Communism, is not delivering any benefits to the ordinary African, who has been betrayed by Communism, through the ANC and Black Power (A tool of Communism).

So behind an elaborate construction of mirrors of diversion and deception, and with the aid of media sympathetic to the International Finance Capitalists, South Africa, like Rhodesia (now Zimbabwe) before it, and some thirty-five other African states were guided, under this elaborate deception, towards Communism. The difference with South Africa is that Britain, not America, had a large vested interest in its wellbeing, and that this power game of Communism could take place beneath the surface of the disinformation that the press was feeding the world shows one telling fact; the British establishment was secretly supporting the move towards Communism. This is the only possible conclusion you can draw. It is not possible that the informed circles did not know what was happening and we must conclude that the power of banking has so much political leverage that they can control the body politic whenever and however they wish. **DIRECTION.**

Communism still hides behind the ANC, preferring to remain in charge behind the scenes (a typical Weishaupt policy). In May 1994, following the election, the Government of National Unity was formed under Nelson Mandela's Presidency. The ANC had a landslide victory, winning two-hundred and fifty-two seats. The former President F. W.de Klerk gained eighty two and the Inkatha Freedom Party forty-three seats with twenty-three seats to other minor parties. The South African

Communist Party did not contest the election, they did not need to. Fourteen out of twenty-seven cabinet appointments were known Communists. **DECEPTION.**

Communism under yet another name (ANC) controlled South Africa, a former friend of the West and a very important sea root for world shipping, captured by disguised Communists for the world revolution. It is true that nothing has been done to use their power yet, but it is there to use when needed.

One of the first acts of Mandela was to initiate a peace process, bringing in his rival Dr. Buthelezi; he also repealed the Ingonyama Trust Act, which took away from the Zulu population the right to self determination, and, as if to de-stabilise Dr. Buthelezi with his own party, the new 'Peace Party' of Mandela put a ban on the use of spears, a traditional ceremonial part of Zulu custom. A more appropriate ban on weapons in the hands of ANC members (former terrorists), such as Soviet made automatic guns, was not even considered. Every act was one sided, each taking away Zulu freedoms that they even enjoyed under Apartheid.

All this time the media, owned by the Anglo - American establishment (the bankers) blamed the Zulu people for terrorist atrocities which were mainly perpetrated by ANC terrorists. (Communist controlled). The only break in this pattern came when Nelson Mandela wanted to distance himself from his wife's activities, activities; that were commonplace right through the ANC in the form of small cells of organised terrorism to keep the masses in line. We have seen the same pattern in Ireland through IRA cell population discipline meted out to their own people who show dissent. This is Communist discipline in action.

In 1919, at the third Communist International, Communism made an important decision for the future. Their attachment to the Socialist and Working Man's Movement had been a failure. So although Moscow was the centre of Communism, Lenin clearly stated that this would only be a temporary measure while Communism spread and adapted throughout the world. The Comintern was the grouping of Communism and from this body spread the words of Marx to the four corners of the world.

Africa was particularly vulnerable as it had an immature political development or a minority undemocratic rule, both of which were an easy target for Communism. The immature states were unable to make democratic decisions, therefore they relied on tribal lords to make the decisions for them. So first Communism targeted tribal chiefs with promises of power and influence to get them elected; bribery and corruption is and always has been a way of life in Africa; Communism wasted no time in using it to its advantage.

So let us now review the passage of Communism, through International Zionism, to South Africa so we can understand the reasons for this progress of political conversion without a mention of Communism. **(DECEIT)**.

From the writings of J. A. Hobson (Fabian) and H. P. Cartwright we learn that the early exploration of Diamond and Gold mining in South Africa was financed mainly by Jewish Bankers from South Africa and abroad, mostly of Central European origin (Khazar Kingdom). **(300). (300A).**

From this early point a strong influence of International Zionist power over the media nationally and internationally is a straight forward matter of record of ownership which is well documented. However it remains unknown as an acute secrecy has prevailed, hiding the International Zionist domination of the United States foreign policy that has allowed the Anglo American establishment to develop Marxist policies in targeted areas. The evidence of history is very simple and an incontrovertible fact; Moses Hess, the 'Red Rabbi', converted Karl Levi (Marx) and his philosophy to Communism (Illuminati) as it became known. **(301)**. At this time a large number of 19th. century revolutionaries were Jewish **(302)**. The Bolshevik revolution was mainly masterminded by European and Russian Jews, and supported by European Jewish Bankers of the Khazar tribes from Europe and America such as Jacob Schiff. During Communist rule in Russia 1917 - 1989, Zionists have consistently filled upper and middle management posts in Russian affairs, even sensitive posts such as head of the KGB. Yuriy Andropov was a Zionist. During a visit to the Soviet Union by Nathan Sharansky, the Chairman of Moscow's Rabbinical Alliance, declared that; "More and more of Russia's business, media, and political leaders are very open about their Jewish origins".

Now comes a typical Communist twist in its direction; it supports Islamic Movements, which seem to defy its Jewish relationship until you understand the war of Communism that believes everything is correct if it moves Communism forward - this does, as it outwardly shows – and it becomes a counter balance to the United States foreign policy, dominated by the Zionist Agenda.

Fortunately quite a few Jewish intellectuals have written the truth about world affairs and the Jewish establishment. Men of the calibre of Professor Noam Chomsky, Alfred Lillienthal and Israel Shahak, have written objectively about Zionism. It was Rabbi Dow Marmur in 1982 who wrote, in reference to early Israeli settlements in Palestine, that; "Zionism had become a largely secular, Marxist movement". **(303)**.

In Pike's "A History of Communism in South Africa" **(304)**, he shows us that at the onset of diamond mining, Communism found its way to South Africa with direct family links to Marx himself. Although he denies the presence of Judaism, he goes on to list many Jewish names involved and it is a matter of record that most of the gold and diamond business as well as the media is in their hands there.

A true record of the immigration and settlement of the Jewish community and its activity can be found in Saron and Hotz in 1955, **(305)** and Shimoni in 1980, "Jews and Zionism: The South African Experience (1910-1967), **(306)** particularly shows the force of Zionism taking over the Jewish agenda. Shimoni was blunt about the Jewish control of the revolutionary movement and, like Pike, gave full details of the Rivonia Affair in 1963 that identified Nelson Mandela as a convinced Communist. It is interesting to note from these writers that immigration took place mainly from Central and Northern Europe and that these Khazar adoptive Jews played a leading role in Bolshevism.

Just recently we were informed that the Russian immigrants to Israel played a major part in the resulting Socialist victory in Israel (May 1999). (Again we see Khazar adoptive Jews from the same areas that the world bankers originated from in the 18th. and 19th. Century).

We have also seen ultimate complicity by successive British governments giving political asylum and sanctuary to Orsini, Mazzini and Marx in the 19th. century, followed by the South African Communists, Ronnie Kasrils, Albie Sachs, the Slovo family and Dennis Goldberg in the 20th. century, while their Communist terrorists in South Africa planned and executed many acts of terrorism. (In Communist terms armed struggle).

A mixture of Communist, Zionist, Liberal influence contained in our media, especially the BBC, allowed Dennis Goldberg, unchallenged comment on South African affairs on the BBC world service. Joe Slovo was at this time strongly suspected of being a high ranking KGB officer, and if so was hell bent on the destruction of our Western democracy, yet our media, of all shades of colour,

Conservative, Liberal and Socialist, was universally promoting the ANC, a Communist controlled organisation, intent on the destruction of our very democracy. All this must be appreciated when studying how Communism has crept into the lives of people through deceit and under hidden agendas, without them even knowing that Communism was behind their chosen politicians. **Deception.**

Since the French Revolution in 1789 the Illuminati who bred Communism through their member Karl Levi (Marx) then disguising its presence, spread Communism throughout the world under the hidden umbrella of the Masonic lodges of the Grand Orient and others. They were also responsible for the 1821 Dekabrist uprising by Czarist officers who returned from Europe brainwashed by Weishaupt's revolutionaries. This was a signal that Russia was on the agenda of world revolutionaries. History shows how 'Pilot' revolutions swept Europe in 1848 which were financed by European capitalist bankers. The 1905 Russo - Japanese war was part of the same movement and the first serious attack on Russia, which failed, was in the same year. Then, while Europe was pre-occupied in war, came the Bolshevik Revolution in 1917, which won Communism its first dictatorship. All these Communist (Illuminati) led revolutions were financed by the Anglo - American financial network, the same network that provided Trotsky and his revolutionaries with the money to launch the Bolshevik revolution that captured Russia with only 5% of the population supporting their cause. Finance powered them to victory by violence. Today we are being powered to a Communist future by the same Anglo-American banking establishment that funded the Bolshevik revolution, by creeping loss of our sovereignty that will lead to Federalism and then to a world government by the very same bankers and their 'Useful idiots' who help them in return for power and reward.

South Africa should be a lesson to us before it is too late. Africa is an area where they have used both the armed struggle, in Angola, and terrorism in Rhodesia and South Africa along with all the other weapons of Communism we have already discussed. They have also used biological warfare, in time of peace by Western standards, as described in Soviet papers found by the British security services in the hands of an IRA cell referred to in Hunter's evidence, already discussed.

By the fifties British Governments of both persuasions are shown by government command papers to have collaborated in vital fields of science, technology, industry, economics and nuclear energy, right through what our so called press was assuring us was a 'cold war with Russia'. This whole process also hid from view the preparations for Communist rule in South Africa. This is Communism in action, using disinformation as an International Hall of Mirrors, erected by the press, paid for by the bankers, and planned by Communists, all concealing the truth from us so we do not know what is happening.

I am not a supporter of suppressive regimes like former South Africa, but I would expect Anglo-American co-operation would have installed democratic, free, Western style democracy within Africa. Instead we have seen one state after another replace old Colonial regimes by corrupt, genocidal, one party Communist dictatorships, often torn by internecine strife. Some states, Angola, Ethiopia, Ghana, Mozambique are constantly in a state of internal conflict.

This in itself makes a lie of superficial Western concern for human rights. There only seems one set of rules for Africa, the agenda to make it a Communist federal state under a unrepresentative dictatorship. They rob the individual countries of their natural resources and lend them money so they remain in debt slavery to the bankers; the very bankers of the Anglo-American establishment that wish to control the world through Communism.

It is the media that allows them to get away with this secret plan. But they, the bankers, own the media. It is up to all of us to oppose this suicidal folly. The Fabian, Nicholas Murray Butler, in 1937, stated that Capitalism was the high road to Socialism while Communism was the low road. In fact Marx split Communism into two dimensions. The Communism of the working class, the visible Communism we know about that has been used as a mirror to hide the second type. The hidden agenda, hiding behind this mirror is the secret elitist Communism. This is the true Communism that Karl Marx (Levi) designed for the super rich bankers (At that time the Rothschilds) which is referred to by Butler as the high road to Socialism. I have always been curious to know why International Communists were so sure, that without them lifting a hand the world would one day be controlled by Communism, and they would only have to wait for that day. It seemed it would all happen without effort. Now I know why. They think that Capitalism, in its blind stupidity, is driving the world to Corporate Collectivism, which is Communism, and Karl Marx knew this. Therefore the words of J.P. Warburg become more plausible in this context, "We shall have world government, whether or not we like it. The question is only whether world government will be achieved by consent or conquest".

Power, under Communism in the Soviet Union was a triangle to establish equilibrium of rigid control; the Communist party, the armed forces, and state security, the KGB. We can now see by simple deduction how this has changed since the stage managed collapse of the Iron Curtain.

That power triangle has now passed to the International Finance Capitalists, in league with the Communist International, and political Zionism which encompasses organised world Jewry. In this grouping, money is the ultimate controlling power, so the bankers now hold the control and Wall Street and the City of London are the centres of that power. The rigidity of that early Soviet triangle has been replaced by a more flexible linkage which is more difficult to identify as it is mixed up in a complex of institutions and diversities of the financial world. The secretive agenda within our financial institutions is backed by politicians, bankers, diplomats, industrialists, and academics who all add up to a powerful momentum pushing the Communist ideal of world government forward without public debate or acceptance. Knowledge of their plan is what they fear; my task is to give that knowledge. The triangle is a rigid glance at the make up of the establishment. In practice it is more like an octopus, with tentacles creeping into all the control mechanisms of government. Tentacles that move freely to achieve their set goal, always connected to the main body but not always seeming to act in unison, nevertheless achieving their aim, **(DIRECTION),** before moving to another. They use people to achieve their goals without informing them of their objective, using the system to destroy the system and creating a constant momentum that is difficult to analyse or attack as one tentacle will act with complete freedom from another, only guided by **DIRECTION** to its end goal.

Communism believes everything is correct, as long as the result of action, political, psychological or military, moves Communism forward. Communist leaders like Stalin were only criticised when they failed to achieve this simple policy. What it means is that war, famines, holocaust, assassination, subjection of people to slavery, experimentation on human beings for test purposes and many other human atrocities are acceptable if Communism gains. **DIRECTION.**

The 19th. century military authority, General Carl Von Clausewitz wrote; "War is only a continuation of state policy by other means". **(307).**

The Communist system follows this statement precisely; the Western system, in military practice, complies with the political system; it does not function as part of it. As a direct result of these two definitions of war. and engineered by the international bankers, millions of people, in this century alone, have been sent to their deaths in wars financed by the bankers to move Communism forward. The people have been given all sorts of false propaganda to get their support, but never the truth. Millions of people have also lost their life savings by the peaceful manipulation of the money markets, again by the bankers, to move state control nearer to Communism, because each failure helps liberals reform our structure which in turn moves towards a dictatorial system of state control, and in Communist controlled countries, wealth confiscation. No better example of this can be found than in Stalin's holocaust, where twenty-two and a half million peasant land owners died as a direct result of his policies and his purge on the bourgeoisie, where he confiscated their bank balances, their property, and violated their privacy. Liberals are the forward troops of the socialist revolution. They prepare the ground for Communism to occupy. Rhodesia and South Africa are good examples of this policy in action where Western Liberals prepared the ground for a successful revolution.

The original tribes in South Africa, the Zulus are led by Dr. Buthelezi, a moderate democratic leader. While the Liberal element of the world clamoured to promote sanctions against South Africa, Dr. Buthelezi, although bitterly opposed to Apartheid, warned against sanctions repeatedly, as he knew they would have a devastating effect on his people and all the black emigrants who had come to work in South Africa. One of the 'Useful Idiots' from Liberal thinking, as Lenin called them, was Archbishop Desmond Tutu, who repeatedly promoted sanctions as a way to destroy South Africa's Apartheid. However Apartheid was not the real reason to introduce sanctions, it was to bring South Africa to its knees ready for a revolution, now complete.

But the Western press, which knew this well, promoted sanctions as a policy against Apartheid and according to Eric Butler, **(308)** the American Government made a statement from their information office in Johannesburg which claimed; "It is the view of the United States Government that the current problems and unrest in South Africa are not Communist inspired. The root cause of South Africa's problem is Apartheid". So this statement cleverly switched what the government knew to be the truth, the domination of the ANC by Communists, to a half truth about Apartheid, which gave the Liberals the lead to move the agenda on for Communism.

That Marxism controls the ANC is well recorded; less known is that the Congress of South African Trades Unions (COSATO) is also under Communist control. On the twenty-third of May 1996 'Business Day' advised the world of a document, 'Movement for Transformation', a Communist document, which had been adopted by the ANC and COSATO. **(309).** Another publication from the International Freedom Foundation (The SACP: Emerging from the Shadows?) gives a full account of how the ANC was infiltrated and then controlled by the South African Communist party **(310).** Incidentally, it also shows how the Communist party of Great Britain helped to move Communism forward in South Africa. So we must assume that Communism, far from being in its death throes since the collapse of Russian Communism, is healthy and moving forward. **DECEPTION.**

Now, looking forward, we will see South Africa move towards a one party dictatorship led by the Communist ANC, and this will come because the constitution allowed change, with a two-thirds majority, which was reached at the elections in May 1999.

So will this give the ordinary African joy or will he still be the loser in power politics? If we judge by the experience in Russia, the people will be worse off as Communism does not care about people, it only pretends to care.

Thabo Mbeki, now President of South Africa, was reported by Aida Parker in 1993, to be one of the South African Communist Party's authorities on Marxist Philosophy, and a student from the Lenin school in Moscow. She also wrote that he was recruited by the British Intelligence service MI6 while a student at Sussex University. This seems to show, along with Andrew Hunter's evidence, collusion between Capitalist and Communist States. The ironical thing about the Communist war is that this man, Mbeki, whose energy was spent in de-stabilising South Africa for Communist gain, is now involved in touring Western countries to drum up aid for the country he caused to collapse under sanctions, and he seems to have met with success. We must conclude therefore, that South Africa is firmly now in the hands of the International Finance Capitalists and their partner, Communism.

As South Africa was snatched from Western control by Communism after the staged demise of Communism in the Soviet Union we must take this as a warning, Communism is alive and moving forward to its goal; World Domination, with the financial blessing of a small group of very powerful bankers and their agents from politics and the media.

We have already covered the media, and we know that ninety-five percent of the media is owned or controlled by the International Finance Capitalists, who in turn have controlled Communism from its conception. This applies all over Africa. Right from the start in South Africa the press was in the hands of International Finance Capitalists, the Oppenheimer's Argus Newspaper. (Now sold to Anthony O'Reilly, a One World advocate). A family among the super rich of the world. This press influence spreads through the Masonic movement all over the world and can influence what is said in their papers at any important moment of time when the right articles can influence the path of decisions made by their 'Useful Idiots' (The politicians). For example our news has played down the Communist affiliation of the motivators within the ANC such as the Slovo family, Maharaj, the Lithuanian, Albie Sachs, and Ronnie Kasrils also Lithuanian. Once again we see the Siamese twins appearing in every revolution, International Zionists who are Communists. This is no coincidence.

After learning about the direction of South Africa it is not surprising to learn that Russia funded South Africa's ANC to the tune of over two and a quarter million pounds a year in what was classed as humanitarian aid. What is surprising is that America, that had no historical connection to the area was funding the Communist sponsored ANC to the tune of ten million pounds annually, as well as consolidating its presence in South Africa. **(311).**

This heralded all the signs that the super rich bankers were moving in to consolidate their assets and grab what was going. Companies like Anglo American, RTZ, and De Beers led the field at that time. Patti Waldmer of the Financial Times **(312)** stated that the South African Government was holding talks with credit bankers in London and by May the Financial Times advised that the World Bank was to make a loan of six-hundred million pounds for development in South Africa. South Africa, at a stroke, went from a debt free country to a country plagued by debt bearing interest. The bankers had won the big prize - South Africa went into debt slavery like the rest of us, despite the natural wealth of the country. Why? Because the natural wealth of the country was not in the hands of the nation but in the hands of companies owned and controlled by the Rothschilds, the Oppenheimers and a handful of wealthy Bankers who also have interest in the World Bank.

We must also look at the prizes for faithful politicians. Dr. Chester Crocker, who was the Under Secretary of State for South African Affairs found himself on the board of Minorco (Oppenheimer Company). Cyrus Vance, the United Nations representative imposed on South Africa, is linked to the Federal Reserve Bank, the Rockefeller Foundation, and the Ditchley Foundation. Lord Carrington, for his part in handing over Rhodesia to a Communist dictator is Chairman of the Bilderberg Group and Director of Dr. Henry Kissinger's World power based, public relations company; all part of the Anglo American Establishment, to name but a few. This is the way the establishment rewards outsiders who do its bidding.

So did this sudden interest in South Africa develop from the eighties on? No. To understand this we must look back in history and follow the trail of the gold and diamond emigration and examine who were the gainers. In the late 19th. century the European bankers moved in on the mineral wealth of South Africa and Rhodesia (Zimbabwe) Barnato, Beit, Eckstein, Oppenheimer, Philips, and Cecil Rhodes led the field of mainly Jewish emigrants who sought a new source of wealth. De Beers Consolidated Mines was formed in 1888. 1893 saw the Rothschilds join the race. They formed Rand Mines with no less than three Rothschilds involved, Lord Rothschild, Leopold De Rothschild, and Alfred De Rothschild. Then came the Anglo American Corporation, owned by the Oppenheimer family in 1917. A large immigration of Indian and Chinese labour followed to fill the need for miners and labourers. **(313).**

Lord Milner, the British High Commissioner, was deeply involved in fermenting the war of 1899-1902, to capture the agenda from the Boers. This is described in Ivor Benson's book **(314).** It describes how a new Afrikaner moneyed class took over the power in South Africa from the Boers. This pattern, Benson claims, is followed throughout the world. He shows how the Anglo American establishment and a new comer, Tiny Rowland, flourished even after trade sanctions, and how Oppenheimer's Central Selling Organisation collaborated with Russia to control the diamond market, at the very moment when NATO forces faced the might of the Warsaw Pact. At this time Tiny Rowland had a personal link with the ANC President, the late Oliver Tambo, and Anglo American executives met regularly with the ANC leaders. All this, while the armed struggle was in full swing and the South African Communist Party, and the African National Party, were banned.

Now lets follow some of these players through to find out the true motivation and from where the thrust derives. Oppenheimer's man, Julian Ogilvie Thompson, was a director of Consolidated Gold Fields as was Sir (Chips) Keswick. He is also chief executive of Hambros Bank, a member of the Court of the Bank of England and on the boards of De Beers Consolidated Mines and Anglo American Corporation of South Africa. His brother Henry is a director of Rothschild's Sun Alliance Insurance and Rothmans International, a group with strong links in South Africa. As we have heard, Chester Crocker, who brought about the Namibian Peace Accord in 1990, was invited to join the board of Oppenheimer's Minorco. From 1987-1991 the British Ambassador to South Africa was Sir Robin Renwick. In

1996 he joined the board of Robert Fleming with investments in Hong Kong and South Africa.

Henry Keswick's wife has been a Director of the Conservative party's centre for policy studies. The Keswick family is also closely associated with the Jardine Matheson Group (Hong Kong) and Henry Keswick is also a director of the Telegraph newspaper in England which along with its partner the Hollinger Group of Conrad Black brings linkage to Dr. Henry Kissinger, Lord Carrington, and Paul Volcker, the shakers and movers of World Government. What we must realise is that we are dealing with very powerful people who are completely ruthless when it comes to attaining their goal, world dominance. This is the Anglo American Establishment at work. You might well ask why the people who owned the wealth of South Africa needed to go to these lengths to continue in business.

We only have to go back to the hand-over of Rhodesia to black rule and you will see that they rescued Rhodesia from a Nationalist Nkomo, who wanted quite rightly, to use the wealth of Rhodesia for the benefit of his people. He was replaced by a Marxist dictator trained in Moscow, Mugabe, who signed away the wealth before gaining power. The ANC, to gain power, did a deal with the capitalists, again allowing them to keep their mineral monopoly and even agreeing to debt dependency; a fatal mistake. But we know Communism is using Capitalism to gain world power.

Now we have gone full circle back to the Capitalists and learn that money dictates the agenda. Without it, Dr. Buthelezi could not match the highly funded ANC. Without press support he could not even get his democratic message heard while the media and the money are at the disposal of Communism, and a minority group with money power, making sure democracy will continue to lose. Therefore it is in our interest to make sure our press is fair and democratic and not at the disposal of a minority group's **HIDDEN AGENDA.**

PROTOCOL FIVE.

What form of administrative rule can be given to communities in which corruption has penetrated everywhere; communities where riches are attained only by the clever surprise tactics of semi-swindling tricks; where looseness reigns; where morality is maintained by penal measures and harsh laws but not by voluntarily accepted principles; where the feelings towards faith and country are obliterated by cosmopolitan convictions? What form of rule is to be given to these communities if not that despotism which I will describe to you later? We shall create an intensified centralisation of government in order to grip in our hands all the forces of the community. We shall regulate mechanically all the actions of the political life of our subjects by new laws. These laws will withdraw one by one all the indulgences and liberties which have been permitted by the Goyim, and our kingdom will be distinguished by a despotism of such magnificent proportions as to be at any moment and in every place in a position to wipe out any Goyim who oppose us by deed or word.

We shall be told that such despotism that I speak of, is not consistent with progress of these days, but I will prove to you that it is.

In the times when the peoples looked upon kings on their thrones as on pure manifestation of the will of God, they submitted without a murmur to the despotic power of the Kings: but from the day when we insinuated into their minds the conception of their own rights, they began to regard the occupants of thrones as mere ordinary mortals. The holy unction of the Lord's appointed has fallen from the heads of Kings in the eyes of the people, and when we also robbed them of their faith in God, the might of power was flung upon the streets into the place of public proprietorship and was seized by us.

Moreover, the art of directing masses and individuals by means of cleverly manipulated theory and verbiage, by regulations of life in common and all sorts of other tricks, in all of which the Goyim understand nothing, belongs likewise to the specialists of our administrative brain, reared on analysis, observation, on delicacies of fine calculation; in this species of skill we have no rivals, no more than we have in the drawing up of plans of political action and solidarity. In this respect the Jesuits alone might have compared with us, but we have contrived to discredit them in the eyes of the unthinking mob as an overt organisation, while we ourselves all the while have kept our secret organisation in the shade. However, it is probably all the same to the world who is its sovereign lord, whether the head of Catholicism or our despot of the blood of Zion! But to us, the chosen people, it is very far from being a matter of indifference.

For a time perhaps we might be successfully dealt with by a coalition of the Goyim of all the world: but from this danger we are secured by the discord existing among them whose roots are so deeply seated that they can never now be plucked up. We have set one against another, the personal and national reckonings of the Goyim, religious and race hatreds, which we have fostered into a huge growth in the course of the past twenty centuries. This is the reason why there is not one state which would anywhere receive support if it were to raise its arm, for every one of them must bear in mind that any agreement against us would be unprofitable to itself. We are too strong - there is no evading our power. The nations cannot come to even an inconsiderable private agreement without our secretly having a hand in it.

Per me reges regnant. "It is through me that Kings reign". And it is said by the prophets that we were chosen by God Himself to rule over the whole earth. God has endowed us with genius that we may be equal to our task. Were genius in the opposite camp it would still struggle against us, but even so, a newcomer is no match for the old-established settler: the struggle would be merciless between us; such a fight as the world has never yet seen. Aye, and the genius on their side would have arrived too late. The wheels of the machinery of all states are moved by the force of the engine, which is in our hands, and that engine of the machinery of the states is - Gold. The science of political economy, invented by our learned elders, has for long past been giving royal prestige to capital.

Capital, if it is to co-operate untrammelled, must be free to establish a monopoly of industry and trade: this is already being put in execution by an unseen hand in all quarters of the world. This freedom will give political force to those engaged in industry, and that will help to oppress the people. Nowadays it is more important to disarm the peoples than to lead them to war; more important, to use for our advantage the passions which have burst into flames, than to quench their fire; more important to catch up and interpret the ideas of others to suit ourselves than to eradicate them. The principal object of our directorate consists in this; to debase the public mind by criticism; to lead it away from serious reflection calculated to arouse resistance; to distract the forces of the mind towards a sham fight of empty eloquence.

In all ages the people of the world, equally with individuals, have accepted words for deeds, for they are content with a show and rarely pause to note, in the public arena, whether promises are followed by performances. Therefore we shall establish show institutions which give eloquent proof of their benefit to progress.

We shall assume the liberal physiognomy of all parties, of all directions, and we shall give that physiognomy a voice in orators, who will speak so much that they will exhaust the patience of their hearers and produce an abhorrence of oratory.

In order to put public opinion into our hands, we must bring it into a state of bewilderment by giving expression from all sides to so many contradictory opinions, and, for such length of time as will suffice to make the Goyim lose their heads in the labyrinth and come to see that the best thing is to have no opinion of any kind in matters political, which it is not given to the public to understand, because they are understood only by him who guides the public. This is the first secret.

The second secret, requisite for the success of our government, is comprised in the following: to multiply to such an extent national failings, habits, passions, and conditions of civil life, that it will be impossible for anyone to know where he is in the resulting chaos, so that the people in consequence will fail to understand one another. This measure will also serve us in another way, namely, to sow discord in all parties, to dislocate all collective forces which are still unwilling to submit to us, and to discourage any kind of personal initiative, which might in any degree hinder our affairs. There is nothing more dangerous to us than personal initiative: If it has genius behind it, such initiative can do more than can be done by millions of people among whom we have sowed discord. We must so direct the education of the Goyim communities that whenever they come upon a matter requiring initiative they drop their hands in despairing impotence. The strain which results from freedom of action, saps the forces when it meets with the freedom of another. From this collision arise grave moral shocks, disenchantments, failures. By all these means we shall so wear down the Goyim that they will be compelled to offer us international power of a nature that will enable us without any violence to gradually absorb all the State forces of the world and to form a Super-Government. In place of the rulers of today we shall set up a bogey which will be called the Super-Government Administration. Its hands will reach out in all directions like nippers and its organisation will be of such colossal dimensions that it cannot fail to subdue all the nations of the world.

COMMENT.

Well, this does not need much comment. We can see most of what is covered in this Protocol happening all around us today. But remember this was written at the turn of this century. Quite amazing really. You can observe all the tricks they use in their endeavours. It is quite shattering how evil can have such careful planning, but here is the proof of it in writing.

You will notice how personal initiative is their greatest fear. So we must make sure they have their cup full of our initiative.

CHAPTER TWELVE
AUSTRALIA - ALL ABOARD THE GLOBAL ONE-WAY TRAIN.

South Africa and Australia are very similar in as much as they have a vast territory with a relatively small population. They are both blessed with abundant natural resources and vast agricultural potential. So we can see why they both attracted the attention of a emigrant population seeking a new life. They both attracted the Khazar tribes from middle and Eastern Europe that adopted Judaism.

Despite this, in the early part of this century the banks were still in the hands of government, and the government owned Commonwealth Bank was founded in 1912. At this time they were able to finance the Australian people independently of the private bankers' usurious services. They, as in America, served the largely emigrant population well, despite continual pressure to change the system in favour of debt usury.

The first big test of the Commonwealth Bank was to fund the Australian Government's $700,000,000 loan to fight World War One and would have gone further if it had been needed. After the war it went on to fund the completion of the Trans-Australia Railroad. After these two expenses Australia was not in debt slavery, unlike the private sector where the bankers imposed usurious terms on the private sector or indeed government, if they got the chance.

The sudden death, in 1923, of the Commonwealth Bank's first head, Sir Denison Miller, paved the way for take over by the private bankers, who moulded it to their usurious ways, and it is now regarded as an enemy of the Australian population.

Regardless of this, the Australian Government helped to form The Reserve Bank of Australia, which played a major part in financing the Australian contribution to the Second World War. This bank was led by H.C. Combs. In this way, Australia, unlike Britain was able to self-finance its war efforts over two major wars and end up with little debt as no interest was charged for created money, needless to say, this put Australia in a healthy position after the war.

Unfortunately this bank too has been corrupted by Finance Capitalism and is now in the hands of private bankers who charge the government interest on money created from nothing.

At the heart of the world's troubles is this privatised usury orchestrated throughout the world by a small group of bankers who create money for governments from nothing (Just the cost of printing) and charge 8 -10% interest on their free money (USURY). This is legalised robbery because our law perceives no crime.

C.H. Douglas had this to say; "Just as the banks created money out of nothing, so they bought the war debts for nothing, and our income tax, surtax and death duties are what we pay them for having created and appropriated for their own use, the National Debt (Taxation) is legalised robbery". **(315).** Even the Economic Research Council has deep reservations about the private bankers' powers to create money and charge interest. The Council's 1981 report had this to say; "It is apparent that no new (credit) money can be created except through the banking system, which issues it as interest bearing debt owed to them (the bankers) by the nation. The result of this has been the piling up of an enormous burden of debt on which succeeding generations of our people will have to pay huge sums each year in the form of interest and sinking fund.

"As the banking system, in creating this money, is merely using the Nation's credit by liquefying it, the right of the banks to treat such created credits as a loan and to receive payments of interest thereon is unjustifiable, and it is therefore submitted most strongly that they are not entitled to anything more than an agreed fee based on the extra work devolving upon them by the handling of these funds". **(316).**

So, although Australia put up a strong fight against control by private bankers, as usual, the bankers did their preparations thoroughly and made sure they had their men in place in the important posts before they moved to take over Australia's banking. Now they control it fully.

The Institute of Economic Democracy **(317)**, in its 1981 edition of The History of Commonwealth Banking had this to say; "The federal government could direct the reserve bank to adopt a completely different policy to that which results in ever-escalating debt, crushing taxation and insidious inflation. For example, **interest rates could be reduced to the point where they were sufficient to meet the administration costs of creating and administrating credit. New money could be made available as credit, instead of debt, for financing consumer discounts as a major part of an anti-inflation policy. But none of these and similar steps will be taken until a more enlightened public insists that the disintegration of Civilisation can only be halted by a reversal of present credit policies". This means that institutions that are not under banker control are prepared to come forward and tell the truth. But alas the media did not give it space to develop.**

Australia has had the good fortune to have a ardent campaigner for social and financial justice in Eric D. Butler of the Australian League of Rights (founded in 1946), a strong advocate of the Social Credit philosophy of Finance, and fiercely opposed to debt usury as used by the private banking circle. In a publication in 1947 he dealt with the power of the International Jews and exposed their control of International Finance, and Globalisation which is so obvious today. To understand the path of banking history, it is recommended that you should read this book. **(318).**

Lord Tankerville also published a very interesting book about capital flow and its affects, entitled "Poverty Amidst Plenty" **(319),** a very apt coverage of the poverty caused by a bankers' created world depression. Even at this early stage he saw globalisation as a national enemy as he describes the large divide between the Anglo American establishment elite (Bankers) and the ordinary people who were experiencing their agricultural businesses run down or sold off to International Capitalists due to an imposed shortage of money in circulation caused quite purposely by the private banking section.

This was the forerunner to a collapse of the Australian agricultural economy as an important part of preparing Australia to be both the centre of the Pacific Rim for global, Regional control and at the same time compliant, by means of introducing imported goods to feed the population. The idea of the global capitalists is that no area will necessarily maintain self sufficiency as this leads to rebellion against their diktat. A starving people will comply. These are the sort of terrorists that we allow to control our finances. All this has been preparation for the next move to

Federalisation of the Pacific Rim to include Australia as the Management control centre just like Brussels. To this effect you already see the movement of the main players into position in Australia.

But Australia is at last waking up, thanks to the Australian League of Rights **(320),** in their Intelligence Survey of May 1998 they had this to say; "The social tensions generated by blind faith in 'The Market' which dominates the thinking of the economic rationalists are becoming more and more a factor in social welfare budgets. The pace of change is less important than the direction in which economic change takes us in the long-term....There is an awful lot of poly-speak about these days. But it will take more than sweet words to diminish wide public concern at a crumbling health service, a cash strapped police force, a confused education system, a languishing rural sector with its small towns evaporating and its youth fleeing, and a whole bag of other social woes... Of course, there is a lot more, such as Australia's tax-weary middle class, the continuing strain on family structures and the widening gulf between rich and poor...But such (Welfare) cases are all the periphery of a terrible and undeniable hardship, and this should never be forgotten. For thousands upon thousands of Australian workers, for example, their only crime has been to be in the wrong job amid the capricious economic shifts that bring "downsizing" and all the other job-stripping devices in the rush to 'rationalism', globalisation, privatisation and 'Asian enmeshment'".

The following notes from On Target 6th. to 20th. June 1998 are interesting in the light of the last quotation. "Japan's recession forced almost a million people out of work in April, triggering its highest unemployment in the post-war period and signalling new depths for the Asian crisis". **(324).** With thirty thousand workers displaced every 24 hours throughout April in Japan, the pressure on Asian economies is being geared up to new levels of intensity. There will be no debt relief until every Asian government is on its knees, surrendering control of its economy, and laying out the red carpet for the entry of the multinationals to take over local industries. **(321).** It is clear that major planning has gone into preparing for future mergers and take-overs throughout Asia. On April 14th. the Financial Review **(322)** reported that one of the biggest investment banks in the world, Goldman Sachs, was gearing up in Australian facilities.... (Liberal Government) Prime Minister John Howard has made it clear that he welcomes the idea of Australia becoming the financial centre for the Asia-Pacific region. Goldman Sachs is taking him at his word: 'Goldman Sachs' Australian target is to generate the same share of business as it enjoys in other markets. In 1997 Goldman Sachs topped the international league table in mergers and acquisitions (On Target June 5th. 1998)".

While John Howard (Prime Minister), Peter Costello (Treasurer) and Tim Fischer (Trade), doggedly hold that there is no real alternative to the course they are following, they are accepting the philosophy of economic determinism which, they may be astonished to know, has been the basic philosophy of Marxism, a philosophy which is still prevalent in spite of the collapse of formal Communism. Australia's allegedly conservative political leaders are telling the Australian people that they have lost the control of their own destiny; which clarifies the basic issue now confronting the Australian people. A warning from Wall Street international giant, Citibank, that Australia would be on a danger course if it turned its back on Internationalism, is an indication of the type of international pressure being applied to the Howard Government".

Just as in Britain, the people are being told that they would be ill-advised to turn their backs on internationalism. Yet Internationalism should be for the people's interest not to scoop the world further into the hands of the super rich International Bankers, who create slavery for the rest of us. The form of Internationalism on offer is disastrous for the Nations' people, disastrous for the nations and their sovereignty, but suits the bankers and multinationals because it allows them to move manufacture and food production to where it is cheapest. We are simply being manipulated by bankers using politicians to give use meaningless clichés that misrepresent the bankers evil intent. We must halt this process before it goes any further. In Australia, at least, there is a spirited fight back against Globalism. The Australian Prime Minister, John Howard, who ousted the notorious Labour Party Prime Minister, Paul Keating in 1996 conceded, in the words of Eric Butler, that he; "Was not his own man". **(323).** He admitted to the difficulty of being in government in a globalised economy where there is loss of sovereignty and..."Simplistic answers win the hearts of the hard pressed", and that "he had no choice but to continue as he was".

"There is always a discontent with the prevailing political establishment and somebody new always has some superficial attraction. We are going through globalisation; there is a lot of economic change. There is a lot of people being knocked around by it and who feel threatened by it and I understand that". (from a speech, Queensland State Election in June 1998).

John Howard's lack of thought for his nation state, his people and his conscience, was served a timely blow in the form of a unknown, Pauline Hanson, a Independent candidate in a new One Nation Party, taking 23% of the vote and very nearly holding the balance of power in the Queensland Parliament. A remarkable effort. So what was her message? Simply to honour the nation and halt Globalism and its dreaded fear of swamping Australia with Asians. What it said loud and clear was that elected governments no longer represent the people but are ruled and controlled by Globalism and the International Bankers and Multinational companies.

If we look back in politics we can see a time when the policies of major political parties were distinct and different, offering the voter a real choice. Today in Western politics, the political choice has gone. All parties, to get into office, have no choice but to follow the agenda of the real power, the bankers, as they finance government expenditure, through national loans. This is how, relatively unknown politicians, like Blair, who was by no means the front runner for leadership end up in the top job, because of their relationship with the bankers, and you always see a bankers' man as a controller, in this case Mendelsohn. Gone are the days of choice, this is why people are saying; why vote at all. This is where we must be very careful. But I must say, that with the vast majority of people feeling that politicians of all parties are not representing them, this dangerous attitude will prevail. This is why an unknown party, representing the people's wish to leave the European Union, as it is, a dangerous association of politicians driving Europe to a remote, un-representative, un-democratic Federation, won three seats in the European parliament, much to the dismay of the major parties. Political parties must decide who they represent, and be open and honest about it.

At least John Howard was honest about it. Either politicians represent the people who elect them, which is democracy, or they give in to minority pressures of banking and turn democracy into Autocracy, and eventually dictatorship. Those are the two paths forward, at this time politicians are treading the path to Autocracy while pretending to dispense democracy and this is why, increasingly, the electorate is becoming isolated.

Socialism went down this path when it abolished Clause Four of state socialist ownership and control. This shows how even the main plank of Socialism was destroyed to suit the bankers agenda in an attempt to control the debt usury escalation of private money creation bearing interest which is a charge on taxation. All this is to push Globalism; beginning at the European Union and going down as far as Australia and the Pacific Rim.

So it is no coincidence that what is happening in Europe is also happening in the Pacific Rim. It is all part of the same bankers' plan for Global Autocracy. What Howard said was that he could no longer make a choice. He was wrong. The choice for nations wishing to maintain their Status Quo is quite simple. They must take the power of money creation out of the hands of private bankers and place it in the national domain where it rightfully belongs, with adequate safeguards to stop politicians misusing their power. When we take this road the nation will be safe and so will democracy. While we follow the path of Globalism, we will only witness our cherished democracy crumble into the chaos of the European Union in Brussels and the same applies to Australia. It will slide into the grasp of the Federal Pacific Rim.

Australia has been fighting back and the surprise in 1998 was when Pauline Hanson took 23% of the vote in the Queensland parliamentary elections. Shock waves went through the Anglo American establishment; the Financial Times of the 15th. June 1998 wrote of it as a threat to Australia's future; "The strong performance of an extremist political party in state elections in Queensland could push the Australian dollar to new lows, and force the central banks to raise interest rates, economists warned last night". Now that is a loaded article. First, Pauline Hanson was just one of millions of people in Australia who felt they had lost out on democracy, they weren't extremists; they followed the traditional fear of an Asian invasion because of the sparse population of Australia, but more importantly they opposed Globalism and the federation of the Pacific Rim. So the organ of the bankers (The Financial Times) attacked Pauline Hanson, accusing her of being an extremist, which she is not. (This word is used by a lot of the bankers' press to rubbish people who pose a threat to their plans. They went on to say; "and force the central bank to raise interest rates". A clear indication to legitimise a move of usury by private bankers.

The second example of the bankers press was in the Daily Telegraph, a Conrad Black publication, under the caption; "Far right party's success raises fears of an investment backlash". "The success of Pauline Hanson's One Nation party in the Queensland state election will hurt Australia's reputation and could damage its financial markets if reflected nationally, political leaders claimed yesterday.... Blue collar workers and farmers in Queensland's rural seats have rallied round Mrs. Hanson's seductive message that Australia can revisit its post-war glory days, when a wall of tariffs protected businesses. One Nation tells them that globalisation is not an economic necessity but a international conspiracy, founded on Asia's desire to get its hands on Australia's vast open spaces and natural wealth". Again the far right label, a press assumed label, that is far from the truth. Then the threat to worry the people; 'Will hurt Australia's reputation' and 'could damage its financial markets', then a total distortion of the truth that it was an international conspiracy, which it was not, then they mix it up with party aims to say; 'Founded on Asia's desire to get its hands on Australia's vast open spaces a natural wealth'. In this way they shift blame before the reaction.

The issues of Globalism and Asia's emigration are two separate issues both equally able to destroy Australia if allowed to run their course.

The plain truth is that Pauline Hanson is a danger to Globalism and must be stopped. Trashing people who get in the way is part of the globalists' expertise (remember Senator McCarthy).

What they feared was, for once, what a politician was saying; that jobs should be protected, farmers should not be bankrupted and rural communities destroyed, as was happening in England and America, and that the traditional family should not be attacked by destructive legislation, as it is in the United Kingdom, and that multinationalism should not be imposed on an unwilling indigenous population. (The traditional fear of a Asian take-over of Australia, not Racism).

Why should pig farmers be put out of business by subsidised meat from Canada? Indeed, why should each country not consume its own agricultural produce? All this is an anathema to the destabilising tactics of the global elite on the course to a new world order.

The fight back in England is small but strong, and growing. The UK Independence Party being just a small part of the campaign to bring back true democracy to a disenfranchised electorate.

So Australia is no different to England, South Africa, America, or indeed most countries in the world who are in debt slavery. They are no longer able to fulfil their desired programmes as they are forced, by finance, to install the destabilising programmes of Globalism into the heart of our society; programmes that make us dependent on other countries for food; programmes that force farmers to use chemical farming methods and introduce GM modified seed. Programmes that destabilise the family unit and lower moral standards. Legislation that takes away our national identity and changes our regional political boundaries till we feel we no longer belong to any country or area and with this lose, pride in our surroundings. These are but a few of the massive legislative programmes that Globalism is forcing on national governments, the last of which will be the death of the nation, replaced by remote federal control by the bankers' chosen agents, just as the protocols predict.

So who are these faceless bankers changing the layout of Asia? Well, we have seen financial collapse in Asia recently. What is happening is that the industrial base in Asia is being gradually bought out by the bankers, as this is the area they have chosen to be their factory for the world. So we find the Rothschilds well established in Australia through Rothschild Australia and Rothschild Australia Capital Investors, also E.L. and C Baillieu (Edward Latham Baillieu, formally deputy Grand Master of the United Grand Lodge of England) and Rio Tinto Zinc, and the latest and very forceful banker Goldman Sachs; they lead a group of International bankers and investors that is preparing the Pacific Rim for federalisation as the third region of a world government. What I see resulting from this world-wide, is the disintegration of humanitarian relief and well-being of the people. Globalism is oppressive, and genocidal. Hiding behind politics, it operates by harnessing the armaments and agro-chemical industries in order to achieve its aims. It is aware that agriculture is vital to the world's survival.

So Pauline Hanson's brave thrust has driven a stake right into the heart of Globalism. But she has paid the price, properly set up. If we stop now, the wound will heal and the monster resume its course; we must continue to drive stakes into its heart until it lies dead before us. We cannot expect our politicians to change without our encouragement so we must guide them to the people's will. Only the people are a greater force than finance capitalism.

When we examine the agricultural policy in Australia we become immediately aware of a underlying similarity between American and British agriculture, where the base of self sufficiency, the bedrock of agriculture, is being cynically destroyed. It is destroying rural communities. The reasons are both universal and cynical; they aim to create rudderless communities, devoid of national controls; where the multinational seed manufacturer can dictate what crop you buy, where you get your seed, and what chemicals you use to destroy your land. Farmers must realise this is the direction being dictated by the bankers driven by Globalism, where they control who grows what and where. By making former nations dependent on imported goods, they can starve whole areas in their proposed federations like Europe, if they do not comply with their will. Land and land ownership is the enemy of the globalist plan. Both Weishaupt and Karl Marx, in their plan for world control, recognised that landowners had to be destroyed, as they maintain pockets of self sufficiency, the second greatest enemy of Communism (religion being the first). That is why healthy self sufficiency is being crushed by, first, the attempted bankruptcy of farmers in the seventies and eighties, and now the meat scares of Salmonella then BSE, used selectively against Britain, as one of the strongest farming communities to break, and then as a final blow to farming a savage foot and mouth outbreak where over six million animals were slaughtered. and. This is not about health and care as it might seem but has been used as the mirror by the media to hide the truth. This is about the destruction of a system that gets in the way of what they (The bankers) term progress, but is in fact their war to win control of world food production for their profit. Every movement that they make can be seen in a new light when you know their agenda.

GM modified seed can be seen as useful to world food shortages, so the bankers have trained their media to push this line. But this is not the truth. Behind the mirrors of yields and pest controlled seed is a far more cynical story. They are trying to kill off varieties available to farmers to lead them down a path of no return, where a reducing number of seed manufacturers control the market with seed that produces crops that are infertile, so farmers are forced to buy seed from the seed manufacturers, and the suitable chemicals from a linked source. Farmers, particularly in Africa, rely on setting aside part of their crop for re-seeding, which saves them a major part of their costs and keeps prices down. The seed manufacturers, led on by bankers' pressure, want this practice to stop; yet this is just one example of farmers self sufficiency which should be encouraged.

GM modified seed is praised as being a high yielding and a pest resistant seed. Yet in one of the first independent reports to surface, the US Department of Agriculture state these claims have been proved to be false. The US Department of Agriculture claims they positively do not produce a greater yield. In their tests, 12 out of 18 areas tests showed no increase in yield. They also found on a controlled farmers test that seven out of twelve areas used the same amount of pesticides. This effectively disproves the claim that plants designed to contain pesticide control, need less chemical spraying. So Monsanto, Zeneca and the other seed giants' claim to a new deal for a hungry third world is a false mirror to hide their true aim towards a world controlled food market of which the big chain super markets are a part. That is why we see their reluctance to make sure products containing GM source are properly marked. But luckily people power, a force we must never underestimate, is winning.

Recently I have had the privilege of visiting an organic farm to find out for myself the practicality of a policy that would bring back traditional farming with modern methods.

The Dutchy Farm, in Gloucestershire, is pioneering modern organic farming, and passing on its knowledge and methods to any farmer interested in converting back to organic production. Far from being an old fashioned romantic dream, it is a practical, highly technical and largely successful attempt to show that traditional farming can be beneficial to the market and, if widely practised, would produce products with more taste and with less dangerous chemical content, and that, if practised by a majority of farmers, would compete in price if it had a good market management.

The advantages of organic farming are numerous to a nation state. We could take the initiative back from the enemy of the nation state, Globalism. We would be back on track to self-sufficiency in production (most of what we buy now in supermarkets is imported). We would get back to tasty food, full of natural goodness. Our land and rivers would not be polluted by poisonous chemicals being forced on farmers. This in turn would make sure that the habitat would remain secure for the host of nature that makes up the countryside.

Farmers would regain their own control of their destiny and the rural decay that is devastating our countryside would be halted and once again rural communities would thrive as the food centres of our community.

All these things would reverse the relentless onslaught of the bankers agents, the globalists, whose task it is to decimate our chance of self sufficiency. The proof of this policy is in the writings of Weishaupt, Karl Marx (Levi), the Protocols, Lenin, Zionism and the whole trail of linkages we have already discussed that lead us to the final aim, world government, by un-democratic control. It is still in our hands to change direction, but we have not got that long left to reverse our fortunes. We must act now.

So what we have just learned is completely in line with the aims and aspirations of the International Zionist; where all policy moves are hidden behind a wall of mirrors to fool our understanding. This is pure Illuminati policy from the evil mind of Weishaupt through Karl Marx, passed round the world by a substantial part of the Masonic movement and funded by International bankers. This is an extraordinary story of evil intent. It shows how a world population of only seventeen million Jews, have in their midst a evil core of about five thousand, mainly Khazar Kingdom Zionists who are a substantial part of the organisation behind this evil endeavour and how the majority of Jews, who, to a large extent, do no approve of the power and direction the bankers ruthlessly follow, however sit on their hands rather than oppose and liberate themselves from the bankers agenda. They need help to come out of this hell the bankers have planned for the world and we must on no account blame the Jewish race because a very powerful handful of adoptive Jews have taken over the Jewish agenda and rule it with a rod of iron. That same group also wants to control us all through their hidden moves towards global power. We must realise that a sizeable number of us function wittingly or un-wittingly, even at high levels, in business or public life, in a complaisant and at most times, mutually profitable liaison with the powerful core of what Winston Churchill called; 'International Jews'. The cross the Jewish race has had to bear is its isolation. They have been isolated by centuries of prejudice and statelessness; therefore they have learned well to sit on their hands. They must wake up to the fact that organised Jewry is the tool of the International bankers who are as much their enemy as they are the enemy of the world's gentiles, religions, and democratic freedom, and are leading them down a path opposed to their Torah.

In 'On Target' **(324),** we have this important statement to consider; "There is no doubt in history from the Illuminati in 1776, the French Revolution 1789, or the founding of the Rothschild Empire in the same time warp, that leading Jews were at the forefront of revolution and secret societies of the 19th. Century. History also relates that Communism throughout its history was financed by firstly European and later American bankers. There is no doubt, either, that organised Jewry has been, and remains a key element in International Finance Capitalism, and this is well documented in contemporary records. The same records reveal compellingly that under the influence of subversive, mainly Marxist Jewish, factions were influential in government circles during the 1939-45 war, British and American governments in particular collaborated officially with the Soviet Communist regime from the end of the war. Karl Marx (Levi) was Jewish, Moses Hess, who shaped the philosophy of Karl Marx into what came to be known as Communism, was also the founder of modern Zionism. Both men lived in nineteenth century Germany and experienced the disabilities - restrictions - imposed on Jews. Robert Wilton, correspondent of the Times in Petrograd, wrote with some sympathy of similar disabilities endured by Jews in Poland and Russia. But Wilton also wrote how Jews rose to occupy a very high proportion of key positions of influence in Russia, including virtual control of the press. He also wrote of the move of extremist Jews (Zionists) in revolutionary activities; of the leading role played in the Bolshevik Revolution of 1917 and that they continued to be dominant in the Soviet Hierarchy. **(325).**

That eminent and responsible individuals such as H.G. Wells, T.S. Eliot, and Hilaire Belloc wrote of this growing Jewish power has been deliberately forgotten by media today, where Jews are identifiably dominant, and is now instead reflected in persistent attempts at character assassinations with accusations of "Anti-Semitism".

George Orwell wrote that; "Those who control the past control the future, and those that control the present control the past".

In the United States it is well known that to oppose the power of Jewry is almost certain political suicide. Through the America-Israel Public Affairs Committee (A.I.P.A.C.), the B' nai B'rith and Anti Defamation League (A.D.L.) the massive resources of organised Jewry are promptly brought ruthlessly to bear, to vilify and eventually unseat politicians. **(326).**

In Orwellian terms, you could suggest that organised Jewry currently controls the past, the present and, it is intent on controlling the future. This power of evil suppression of free speech must be halted by the people's power. From this short summery of power we can see where our evil enemy lies. It is up to all of us to take action to minimise their success.

We cannot expect help from our media as it is all under the control of these power seekers who force them to comply with their wishes as they do to our politicians. We are on our own, but people do have power to make change. The force of the Zionist power through money has overtaken the reason of the Jewish race and eclipsed it. The only power that can change this is the power of the people.

So we can now clearly see the pattern being used by the Anglo-American establishment to move in and take over the agenda of territories all over the world. We can see how terrorism is linked into this evil plot, while the world believes terrorism is local reaction to a local issue. We must come to terms with these unquestionable facts if we are going to counteract terrorism and the plan for World

Government. We must support the Jewish population when they question their banking benefactors about their Jewish credentials, especially their commitment to the Torah.

PROTOCOL TWENTY-TWO.

THE POWER OF GOLD.

In all that has so far been reported by me to you, I have endeavoured to depict with care the secret of what is coming; of what is past; and what is going on now; rushing into the flood of the great events coming already in the near future, the secret of our relations to the Goyim and of financial operations. On this subject there remains still a little for me to add.

In our hands is the greatest power of our day - gold: in two days we can procure from our storehouses any quantity we may please.

Surely there is no need to seek further proof that our rule is predestined by God? Surely we shall not fail with such wealth to prove that all that evil which for so many centuries we have had to commit has served at the end of ends the cause of true well-being - the bringing of everything into order? Though it be even by the exercise of some violence, yet all the same it will be established. We shall contrive to prove that we are benefactors who have restored to the rent and mangled earth the true good and also freedom of the person, and therewith we shall enable it to be enjoyed in peace and quiet, with proper dignity of relations, on the condition, of course, of strict observance of the laws established by us. We shall make plain therewith that freedom does not consist in dissipation and in the right of unbridled licence any more than the dignity and force of a man do not consist in the right for everyone to promulgate destructive principles in the nature of freedom of conscience, equality and the like. The freedom of the person in no wise consists in the right to agitate oneself and others by abominable speeches before disorderly mobs, for true freedom consists in the inviolability of the person who honourably and strictly observes all the laws of life in common, and human dignity is wrapped up in consciousness of the rights and also of the absence of rights of each, and not wholly and solely in fantastic imaginings about the subject of one's ego.

Our authority will be glorious because it will be all powerful, it will rule and guide, and not muddle along after leaders and orators shrieking themselves hoarse with senseless words which they call great principles and which are nothing else, to speak honestly, but utopian.... our authority will be the crown of order, and in that is included the whole happiness of man. The aureole of this authority will inspire a mystical bowing of the knee before it and a reverent fear before it of all the peoples. The true force makes no terms with any right, not even with that of God: none dare come near to it so as to take so much as a span away from it.

COMMENT.

So they confirm they control the power of gold. Well, it could be that the importance of gold has been overrated in the past and the correction of this could make a lie of this statement. They talk of God, but their God is the God of the Devil, a satanic God of Usurers.

Be well aware they promise to rule with undemocratic despotism. Can the funders of all the wars in the last two hundred years be trusted to run our world for good? I think not and these Protocols should be a chilling warning to us all.

CHAPTER THIRTEEN
THE UNITED NATIONS.

> "The United Nations is Zionism. It is the super government mentioned many times in the Protocols of the Learned Elders of Zion, promulgated between 1897 and 1905".
>
> **Henry Klein, New York Jewish Lawyer,** writing in 'Zionism Rules the World' 1948.

The United Nations **(327)** was launched with a fanfare of trumpets that proclaimed that, after the Second World War, which was a terrible world disaster the United Nations was 'The last hope' for mankind. It was launched as a world organisation that would knock heads together to prevent war. It was a world wide peace organisation. Since then the world has looked upon the United Nations as an International World Body that seems to be unable to organise its forces to control local troubles, and has a top heavy administration when action is required.

In short it frustrates an expectant world. This public image is a diversion. Its message, after the terrors of war, was received with relief and hope by a war-torn world, which did not want to hear the fears of the dissenters. In fact the United Nations was a plan, hatched by a group of Communist infiltrators inside the American Civil Service, supported by the Anglo American Establishment (The bankers) and was the brainchild of a dedicated group of top advisors inside the American administration. The list of participants involved in the post war foreign policy preparation for the United Nations were; Alger Hiss, Harry Dexter White, Virginius Coe, Noel Field, Laurance Dugger, Henry Wadleigh, John Carter Vincent, Nathan Silvermaster, Harold Glasser, David Weinroub, Irving Kaplan, Solomon Adler, Victor Perlo, William Ullman, Abraham Silverman, William Taylor, and John Foster Dulles. All but John Foster Dulles were later shown to be Communist agents within the American administration and nearly all were of Eastern European extraction. Even John Foster Dulles' sympathies seemed to fall on Communist ground, as he was Stalin's legal representative in America, and a close friend of J.P. Morgan, the banker.

So it was that the deceit of America's hidden agenda, a move to establish a One World Order (Government) was born in the shadow of a horrific war and heralded as a move by world leaders that was a 'Last Hope'.

It was perfect timing for the promoters. Communism was to gain. Stalin immediately requested that the headquarters should be in America and the ever willing Rockefeller obliged by providing the land for his dream of world power. Everything for Communist advancement, under a new name. Again, (remember Weishaupt), Communism was pushing deeper into the capitalist strong hold, this time being invited in by a group of traitors within America's power house.

That this deceitful move, with the connivance of the President's office, and supported from within his administration, could ever have happened, should send the American people into a determined course of action to rout out and destroy the offenders, but, although this did happen with Alger Hiss, and Harry Dexter White at their trials, a programme of damage limitation was put into action by the media to hide the full impact of Communist penetration from the people. Now you can see how the press is used. They totally demolished Senator McCarthy as an advocate and as a person. That is the power of the Bankers, and Communist collaboration with their two powerful weapons of control, money and the media. McCarthy was marginalised and the attack on Communism died from lack of media exposure.

This power within didn't just happen; it had been building up steadily, positioning itself since Weishaupt's Illuminati established themselves under the control of General Pike in the 19th. Century. Remember they did the same thing in France prior to the French Revolution.

By the early part of the 20th. Century the power base of the Illuminati-Masonic infiltrators was impressive. In education they had a commanding position. In politics they had infiltrated all major parties and in government administration they were building up a sizeable army of administrators in key positions who were reflected in the trials of the forties and also exposed in the Reece Committees' Report.

It was just after the First World War that they made the first move to establish the 'New World Order'. (Shown on the circled Pyramid with Lucifer's eye on a broken tip, surrounded by light 'the Illuminati' and the words in Latin 'Novus Ordo Seclorum' which translated mean New World Order. This copy of the seal of Independence on the one dollar note proves the presence of the Illuminati as the date in Roman numerals is MDCCLXXVI (1776), not just the date of the Declaration of Independence as some American's think but the date of the birth of the Illuminati. This insignia gained Masonic authority when the Illuminati merged with the Masonic movement at the congress of Wilhelmsbad in 1782. Take a look at a dollar note. This proves Illuminati's power in America then, in the early days of America, and today.

President Woodrow Wilson, with his advisors Paul Warburg, his faithful Colonel House, Thomas Lamont, and others, went to Paris with hopes of establishing their plan, originating from Weishaupt, for a New World Order (as displayed on the seal of the Declaration of Independence). What we must learn from this is that the American structure of power had been deeply infiltrated by a Satanic-Masonic group at a very early stage of its development.

The forerunner of the United Nations, the League of Nations, was to be the organ for a World Order; however, Congress on their return from Paris, and after a strong reaction against the plan by the people, rejected it.

But as we have already seen, when the Illuminati loose a battle they re-group to make sure it does not happen again, as they did in 1905 after the first attempt at overthrowing the Tzar of Russia. In the second attempt in 1917 they (the Bolsheviks) succeeded.

In the 1920's the Internationalists formed a series of groups all over the world to promote their plan for a One World Government. In America this organ of planning was called the Council on Foreign Relations (CFR). Today you will find the American Administration, as well as other planning groups like the Bilderberg Group and the Trilateral Committee are strongly attended by today's members or ex-members of the CFR.

Another powerful group that developed through the Education system (Weishaupt's first target) was John Dewey and his 'Frontier Thinkers', the Foundations sponsored by such establishment figures as Rockefeller, Carnegie and others, whom we have already examined.

The purpose of these Radical Liberal (Communist) sponsors was to pass on information designed to direct and influence teaching and therefore future social legislation, and channel the pattern of behaviour of the population in the future.

Dr. Harold Ruggs, one of Dewey's followers, had this to say which epitomises Communism, "A new public mind is to be created. How? Only by creating tens of millions of new individual minds and welding them into a new social mind. Old stereotypes must be broken up and new climates of opinion formed in the neighbourhoods of America". **(328).** In other words brainwash American youth, with out and out Communism. (Called Radical Liberalism). This forced education is now used throughout the world as we have already seen (on religion), enforced by the United Nations.

The CFR now felt strong enough by the late 30's to start to plan their 'New World Order'. The US Secretary of State, Edward Stettinius, reported to the President, "With the outbreak of war in Europe, it was clear that the United States would be confronted, after the war, with new and exceptional problems". So at the suggestion of the CFR, 'The Committee on Post War Problems' was set up and all but one sole member came from the CFR, now recognised as a government body despite their Radical Liberal approach.

The plan of this new breed of Academic American, led by powers of the Illuminati, was to destroy standards of Religion and Morals that had evolved through national experience, and fill their minds with Humanistic ideals that always flow readily from ultra Liberal thinking. Firstly by destroying the pillars that held up the temple of society, and secondly by moulding the minds of the future generation, to accept without question, the destruction of the social order and the introduction of the One World Philosophy; a philosophy they would not ever be able to promote without **deceit.**

So it was a complete post war policy that was set up and running before 1939 and the start of World War Two was activated. It was a policy that would drive America into a World Communist Organisation, (The United Nations), set up by their own politicians, who were in turn advised by mainly Communist infiltrators within sensitive government posts, but that fed the mass of America a generally Anti-Communist message, so much so that they became in their deceit, in national and international terms, the world police against Communist expansion. It is a remarkable story of **deception** but everything that happened during and after the war shows how Roosevelt and his advisors drove Communism forward to a world power, while publicly claiming to be the controller of Communist expansion. If you now re-study all Roosevelt's moves as previously reported, **DIRECTION** shows a uniform and one way move to surrender to Communist power. Why? Because America was controlled by bankers, who in turn financed Communism and Russia and controlled the education through Foundations; the sensitive administration through infiltration; the money through the power of money creation and loans; the media through acquisition, and in doing all this they could actually control the minds of the people, using this power to destroy those who tried, like Senator McCarthy, to warn America of their **Hidden Agenda.** The facts of this story I have already reported and used adequate reference to prove the **direction** of movement which is diametrically in contention with the media message, proving media compliance to the power of the bankers.

So it was, that in 1942 the representatives of twenty-six nations, none of which truly knew the driving force of the CFR, issued a 'Declaration of the United Nations'. From that moment the allied powers were sidelined by this new, and ill considered, plan. But the world was knee jerked into this **deceit** for very pressing reasons; the CFR well knew that it would draw American support from domestic voters and condition the minds of the world to favour a Weishaupt master plan for world domination without telling them the truth of his Satanic plan. This is, of course, all the more important in America where Religion is widely practised.

In fact the use of the 'United Nations' name was premature because it had not at this point, in 1942, been officially opened, yet we have seen how Roosevelt, tossing aside Churchill's warnings, gave Stalin, at the Yalta meeting, three votes on the General Assembly to America's one, and a veto was also written into the mechanisms at the request of Stalin.

It was not until April 26th. 1945 that the United Nations Charter was adopted, before forty-six Nations of the world, all equally in the dark about its true aim, to bring 'One World' government under Communism to the world. A significant statistic produced by a researcher, Robert W. Lee, shows there were forty-two members of the US delegation to this inaugural meeting in San Francisco who were CFR members (Council on Foreign Relations). **(328a).** The custodian of this conference's minutes was none other than Alger Hiss (Communist agent). **(329)** He was responsible for having it ratified by the Senate.

So we begin to see the early day planning and the abnormality of this **deceitful** monster. The Anglo American Establishment in league with Communism, pulled out all the stops to get this project through America's lawmakers. So the media was drummed up to give popular support as disclosed in the official theoretical journal of the Communist Party. (April 1945). "Great popular support and enthusiasm for the United Nations' policies should be built up, well organised and fully articulate. But it is necessary to do more than that. The opposition must be rendered so impotent that it will be unable to gather any significant support in the Senate against the UN Charter and the treaties that will follow...." **(330).**

So it was that the bankers unleashed the powers of the Media to do just that, flooding the population with pro UN stories of the aims and the promises of a new beginning, but, hiding its true agenda, a 'Universal Socialist World'. What also was hidden from view was the $65,000,000 loan, interest free, from the American taxpayer.

In this way the formation, of the 'United Nations', which we thought was a organisation formed by world frustration with war, was in fact a cynical plot of the Illuminati and its followers to control the world through Communism, and was to be driven through the Senate on a fanfare of false hope and a background of **deceit**. You may say, "This is not true", but remember that the media formed your opinion.

John Foster Dulles had this to say in a speech in April 1952; "The treaty-making power is an extraordinary power, liable to abuse. Treaties make International Law and they also make domestic law. Under our constitution, treaties become the supreme law of the land. They are indeed more supreme than ordinary laws, for Congressional laws are invalid if they do not conform to the constitution. Whereas treaty laws can override the Constitution. Treaties, for example, can take powers away from the Congress and give them to the President. They can take powers from the States and give them to the Federal government, or to some international body, and they can cut across the rights given to the people by their Constitutional Bill of Rights". He, John Foster Dulles, a lawyer by profession, spells out clearly how American opinion can be ignored by a future world government.

No nation has ever been so **deceived** by its elected representatives; hooked on power and the gravy train of the power elite, or just plain ignorant, as so many political representatives have become in a world of **Hidden Agendas.**

If anyone cares to examine the Constitution of the USSR and compare it with the Constitution of the United Nations all doubts about the similarity and purpose of the 'Trojan Horse' within our walls will be dispelled; even down to the UN seal designed by Carl Aldo Marzani, a Radical Liberal.

So it was, and is today, that the United Nations hides its One World goal of Communist rule, behind a flood of propaganda about peace and justice, freedom and human rights, none of which it has even begun to achieve, nor will, as it is weighed down by hidden power and agendas that, for instance, allow Israel to decimate Palestine territory while Anglo American oil rights are given full military might, as against Iraq, for very dubious, media promoted reasons that actually add up to oil right protection, with no care for the protection of the Iraqi people.

The same of course, can be voiced about the battling warriors, Clinton and Blair, through NATO, whose real agenda is getting Yugoslavia ready for Federal Europe, not as our media has promoted, coming to the aid of the ethnic Albanians. Never in the life of war and strife has any large nation gone to war for purely selfless ideals. Behind every conflict lies a Hidden agenda most often to protect banker interests. They cause wars, they fund wars, and they reap the world's money for so doing.

In the United Nations; **(330)** America's United Nations Ambassador even openly asked the press to misled the public by saying; "Help us create the sense of our over-riding human concern. Interpret us to each other not as plotters (which they were) or as war mongers, or as demons or demigods, but as puzzled yet aspiring men and women struggling on the possible brink of Armageddon to achieve a common understanding and a common purpose. We are not like that, I have no doubt. But I believe the majority of our delegates would accept such a description of their attitudes. The whole press corps working at the United Nations has a unique part to play in projecting this picture". **DECEPTION.**

Here you clearly see a servant of government, the so called guardian of the people, quite clearly, encouraging the press to lie to the people about the purpose and intent, while the true agenda is to drive the world unknowingly towards a Communist, One World Government, Weishaupt's original plan, funded by bankers for bankers; a plan which will finally take away our precious democracy and replace it with **PURE DECEIT.** This is George Orwell arriving late.

Now lets see what this charter has to say about peace-keeping at the heart of its promised charter; it claims it is; "Determined to save succeeding generations from the scourge of war". (So do the Protocols) and; "To reaffirm faith in fundamental human rights of men and women and of nations large and small". This comes in the introduction to the charter.

So how have they honoured this commitment? In the fifty years of UN presence there has been more than seventy substantial outbreaks of violence, starting in Korea, Vietnam and going right up to Kosovo. During this period over one billion people have been enslaved by Communism. Yet the UN has never lifted a finger to intervene or halt the march of Communist Tyranny. So liberty, heralded as its sword of justice is not one of their aims after all.

But when Iraq challenged Kuwait, for drilling in its territory to steal oil, this all-powerful monster, supported by its puppet states, raised high their principles and fed the press a host of patriotic lies to bounce nations into action; and for what? Not save the poor Iraqi's from their leader, no!. To protect oil rights, that is all. Remember the Rothschild and Rockefeller families control 80% of oil that comes out of the earth, and that includes a large part of oil in Arab lands.

As soon as the oil was secured and the territory made safe, the so called United Nations' forces retreated, leaving the Iraqi people to fend for themselves. But President Bush, an ardent advocate of the New World Order, openly claimed in public it was not to right wrongs but to; "Advance the cause of the "New World Order". (Remember he was Grand Master of the Grand Orient Masonic order in America).

The press, whose job it is to hunt out and expose hidden agendas sits on its hands, as the same bankers control them. So the people are left in a truth vacuum.

That puts paid to another claim of the United Nations as a peace-keeping organisation. In article 55 of the UN Charter it refers to the "Self determination of peoples". To most of us that means us, but you would be wrong; they refer to peoples as a collective group; under Communism the person does not come into the picture.

If you first study Weishaupt's policy, which we have, then read the Communist policy and aims. Then compare them with the high words of the UN Charter; you will know you are reading a continued policy. Remember, Weishaupt said, when his Illuminati was threatened with closure, that within a year he would be back again, stronger than ever, under a new name. The United Nations is one of its many names, as is Communism.

Now if you look at the battles fought by the United Nations you will see another staggering statistic. Bear in mind that when you think of the United Nations' action you talk about America supplying the largest section, with Britain second, and maybe small contingents from a handful of other countries. America and Britain supplying cutting edge technology from the period of conflict.

Firstly, you would expect a force of this pedigree to be superior to any third world army and also to be well informed about conditions and local opposition. So, in the light of this, let us assess the pattern of success and let us list the winners and the losers. Remember one isolated statistic does not prove **Direction,** but a continuing pattern does.

On June 30th. 1960, after a massive anti colonial campaign against the powers of Europe with interests in Africa, the Congo was given independence from its Protectorate, Belgium. Immediately it split into two power groupings. One led by Patrice Lumumba, a Communist, with a link to Moscow; and Moise Tshombe, the son of a local business man, a strong anti Communist, and believer in free enterprise, who wished to establish an American style of government.

Soon the Congolese military rebelled against their Belgium officers and Lumumba fired them, promoting the rebels into high office they were not trained to hold. The result was that they went on a orgy of raping and plundering. European nationals fled in terror. Belgium, to protect its nationals, ordered its army back to the Congo to protect its people. Lumumba declared war, and asked the United Nations to intervene.

Belgium asked America to assist, so it could not be accused of trying to influence the Congo. Tshombe, who stayed loyal to Belgium, was refused aid by America who suggested the UN should solve the problem.

At the UN however, the US delegate sided with Russia in condemning Belgium and Tshombe, and decided to send in UN troops to help Lumumba. Belgium withdrew its troops, leaving Lumumba to continue his rape and pillage. In one disgusting incident his mob army forced Nuns to dance naked and sing hymns about their Messiah, Lumumba; they were then raped.

One week later UN troops by the thousand arrived but nothing was done to quell the mob army. The UN sat back and watched Communism take over in anarchy. The UN, instead of even-handedly enforcing peace stood aside and watched Lumumba's mob army continue their anarchy. It frustrated Moise Tshombe to the extent that he led the Katanga province to break with the central government of Lumumba. In his public statement he declared; "I am seceding from chaos".

Tshombe used Belgium's help to control the mobsters of Lumumba and he re-organised his army successfully with help from Belgium. Still the UN stood aside.

Then the interior minister of Katanga, Godefroi Munonga, made a statement; "I want my country, Katanga, to be a bastion of Anti Communism in Africa. I detest Communism and will not alter my opposition to it. Katanga will stay independent, no matter what. We will not give in". Now if the United Nations were the last hope of mankind and even-handed, they should have welcomed this statement from a country now at peace, with a federal policy in mind for the Congo. The United Nations however attacked Katanga but met solid resistance. So the United Nations' forces unleashed mercenaries who systematically started to murder and rape the civilian population and burn their properties and steal their belongings. An official figure released showed that 90% of buildings destroyed by the UN army were civilian properties. Even the white population helped to hold back the UN forces and a week later the UN ordered a cease fire. Katanga was once again freed from war and Communism.

As in all wars, truth was the first casualty, and the UN spread a tissue of lies to hide their true agenda, to deliver Communism to the Congo. But some of the pressmen were so horrified by what they saw, and they were backed by graphic newsreel coverage, that some honest reports avoided the bankers' censorship. With hindsight, a year later, an internal memorandum, within the UN, found its way to the American Committee for aid to Katangan Freedom Fighters. This memorandum set out a plan for a second attack on Katanga and stated; "The US will judge itself bound, as in the past, by UN decisions and will supply the necessary transport aircraft, and later on aircraft". It then went on to say; "The State Department has based its policy on the UN and it will in no circumstances disregard its obligations to the UN". That makes it clear that the US Government, even if it wanted to help Katanga, would not risk its position with the United Nations.

So on December 29th. 1962, the so called 'Peace Keepers' from the UN, with fresh American equipment, made their second attack on the freedom loving Katangans, and their freedom was crushed. Why? If the UN was for peace and freedom, this attack would have been out of the question. If America and Britain had chosen to support freedom against Communism this would not have happened. But, as we have seen the bankers control America and Britain through National debt, and therefore, control political action. The bankers also control Communism, the vehicle they chose to dominate the world. The United Nations are their army to achieve this goal. Without the press, they could not get away with this, but as we know, they own and control most of our press, world-wide.

So we have a United Nations victory, on the second attempt, and a hand over to Communism **Direction.**

It is not the people on the ground who are Communists; they aren't; but Communism has its ways of manipulation as we will now see. What we have not been told by our media is that the Under Secretary for Political and Security Affairs at the UN has always been a Member of the Soviet Union's delegation ever since 1945. He in turn is a senior advisor to the Secretary General and as such is able to give Moscow immediate sight of all plans of activity by UN troops in advance in all conflicts in the world.

With this in mind it isn't surprising that in the next two conflicts we see once again a similar pattern as in the Congo, but Communist gains by defeat.

Colonel E.P. Farrell, of the USAF, who served in both Korea and Vietnam, wars, had this to say, "All of our military operations had to be forwarded by radio to the Soviet Commander of the United Nations Security Council.....before our forces went into action....The Soviet Commander delayed the battle plans until he had relayed our battle planning information to Moscow.

"The enemy then relayed these battle plans to their Communist forces in the field. They knew beforehand when we were coming and how many of us there were. The enemy knew our every move at all times. Our troops were led like sheep to the slaughter in both Korea and Vietnam.

"Every President and every Congressman since Truman has been aware of this treason by the United Nations Security Council against our military forces. The deaths, suffering and wounded - and prisoners of war - are to be laid at their feet. This is treason at the highest level".

General Mark Clark commented, "Perhaps Communists had wormed their way so deeply into our Government on both the working and the planning levels that they were able to exercise an inordinate amount of power in shaping the course of America in the dangerous post war era.

"I could not help wondering and worrying whether we were faced with open enemies across the conference table and hidden enemies who sat with us in our most secret councils". **(331).**

These two comments lead us into the same direction and General Douglas McArthur's remarks, "I was.... worried by a series of directions from Washington which were greatly decreasing the potential of my air force. First I was forbidden 'Hot' pursuit of the enemy planes that attacked our own. Manchuria and Siberia were sanctuaries of inviolate protection for all enemy forces and for all enemy purposes, no matter what depredations or assaults might come from there. Then I was denied the right to bomb the hydro-electric plants along the Yalu. The order was broadened to include every plant in North Korea which was capable of furnishing electric power to Manchuria and Siberia. Most incomprehensible of all was the refusal to let me bomb the important supply centre in Racin, which was not in Manchuria or Siberia, but many miles from the border, in Northern Korea. Racin was a depot to which the Soviet Union forwarded supplies from Vladivostok for the North Korean Army. I felt, that step - by - step my weapons were being taken away from me". (McArthur, General Douglas.). **(332).** This completes a very sad episode of treason against the American people as well as all the other troops who risked or lost their lives for the freedom of others. In hindsight we now know they were betrayed from above. Lives wasted, (58,000 dead in Vietnam alone, for bankers and their hidden agenda once more).

I could cite many more important statements by senior officers on both sides to give more evidence in the same direction. But it only confirms what we have already learnt.

So in Korea the United Nations troops lost to Communism. In Vietnam a similar pattern also occurred, where Vietnam was captured by Communist Forces against what should have been an unbeatable force of UN Troops. Not only did the UN (America) loose but they left the Communists their equipment to use against anyone who chose to attack the new Communist State of Vietnam. **Direction.**

Two more Communist gains by defeat this time. Since 1945 the world has seen over seventy major outbreaks of violence. This includes Hungary, where freedom from Communism was crushed. The UN did not lift a finger to assist the cry for freedom; the same applies in the Middle East, where Palestinians were brutally treated by Israel without UN intervention.. Tibet, where a whole nation was ravaged by Chinese Communist aggression without UN help to stop the Chinese power. (Communist gain).

Then we come to today's wars. The first Gulf War, where Saddam Hussein was attacked by the full force of modern weaponry, coming in the disguise of the United Nations. The UN makes great play of its 'equal rights' and 'self determination of peoples' but they are empty words and the UN record of disgraceful, one sided action, proves this. While the UN publicity machine churned out its message of restraining a wild card (Iraq), George Bush himself was more forthcoming when he stated quite clearly at this time that, "They were going to war to advance the cause of the "New World Order". It was not for the people at home, but it was to do with the power balance in the Middle East; even this was not the whole truth; the elite Anglo American Establishment (The Pilgrim Society) in 1897 agreed to aid the British Crown when required. In this instance they jumped to rescue Rothschild's oil interests in Kuwait, using the UN umbrella as a cover. The reason why the American political sector complies is quite simply that they owe the Rothschild controlled bankers $3.4 trillion dollars in national debt.

So the UN battle, promoted as a battle to come to the aid of an Arab country was a screen to hide the real agenda, protecting bankers' interests; the other reason the UN forces are used on a regular basis. If it had been an honest attack to free Kuwait and save the people of Iraq, Saddam Hussein would have been removed from power.

In Africa we have seen State after State fall to Communism, aided and abetted by American and British governments doing the biding of the bankers. Now thirty-seven out of fifty-five states in Africa have fallen to Communism. We have studied the Congo, Rhodesia (Zimbabwe) and South Africa and it becomes clear that there is an overall plan to move Africa to Communism, using a hidden agenda inside the American and British administration and when resistance occurs, like the Congo, even force is used by the United Nations. So who pays this monster of deceit, the United Nations? Well America foots the largest part of the cost, which is unknown to many Americans, and the General Assembly judges how much America pays. That means that the American taxpayers **(333).** Starting off at 50% of the budget it is now down to 25%; the other members pay according to their ability.

So what does Mr Average America get for his hard earned cash? A Trojan Horse within their walls. A Communised spy centre and Communist support centre to promote World Communism and **One World Government.** Every move they make, every policy they announce, is designed to move the One World Government nearer.

So what of the UN organisations UNICEF and UNESCO. Behind their caring images, promoted by our unfaithful media, lies the same history. This article in Congressional record should expel any doubt (Proceedings and debates of the 87th. Congress, second session. Paul Harvey's article on UNESCO).

CHAPTER THIRTEEN, PART TWO.

UNESCO: Communism's Trap for our Youth. Extension of remarks of Hon. James B. Utt of California in the House of Representatives Tuesday, September 4th. 1962.

Mr. Utt. (334) Mr Speaker, under unanimous consent to insert my remarks in the appendix of the record, I wish to insert an article by Mr Paul Harvey, news analyst, American Broadcasting Network, entitled "UNESCO: Communism's Trap for our Youth".

I have long contended that UNESCO posed a threat to our American Youth by imposing international control of our curriculum by an international organization which does not embrace the American ideals, liberty and freedom.

This article points out the fact that UNESCO is not tolerated in the Communist countries, as these countries do not accept the precept of UNESCO. Therefore, this program is simply preparing the youth of the free world to the subjugation of International Communism I hope that every parent who has children at school will read this and demand that the UNESCO program be forbidden in our American schools.

THE ARTICLE FOLLOWS.

When your child comes home from school parroting some phrase about the "world society of the future--" are you going to tell him it's wrong for him to "love his neighbor"?

When he comes home talking of world brotherhood, are you going to contradict the Christmas message of peace on earth and tell him that all men are not brothers?

Now wait a minute.

When your child goes from house to house for UNICEF, collecting coins for underprivileged children overseas, are you prepared to tell him he should not be charitable to those who have less?

When his elementary school textbooks indoctrinate him with the philosophy of world government are you prepared to insist that world war is preferable?

Are you against world government just because the American Legion is against it? I have been wrestling with these questions and seeking answers for several weeks.

I told you there was evidence that UNESCO was brainwashing patriotism out of our youngsters and substituting the United Nations for God.

I said if I found fire where I'd smelled smoke we'd go into it further. Well, I have gone into it further, I have burned a lot of late night nights digesting and analyzing all the evidence pro and con, concerning UNESCO, and I have reached a conclusion which I want to discuss with you, but you are going to have to wade with me through some of the preliminary evidence.

UNESCO is the United Nations Educational, Scientific, and Cultural Organization. It is an organization with thousands of publications, too vast to enumerate.

UNESCO booklets are distributed through the National Education Association and the PTA to teachers and students.

UNESCO literature is issued through programs, newspapers, magazines, civic groups, government agencies, but mostly directly or indirectly, it's philosophy of one-world government is aimed at the classroom.

Twelve persons connected with the administration of UNESCO have been identified in sworn testimony before congressional committees as Communists.

Seven have been connected with Soviet espionage.

Six others refused to appear before Government loyalty boards.

But now we are not challenging the loyalty or the motives of this organization. We are seeking to determine whether, whatever their intentions, a whole generation of young Americans is getting brainwashed for their own good or somebody else's.

Sometimes the defenders of the citadel, when they get desperate, become as vicious as the attackers.

The critics of UNESCO have sometimes let themselves get so worked up that they start flailing their arms, swing in all directions, becoming at once ineffectual and slightly ludicrous.

Let us instead, suppose that the world government idea is a good one.

Let us admit that all God's children would be better off living together than fighting and that the next generation of children all over the world should be reared to this understanding.

That national boundaries are not something to fight over and that a United Nations is the way to discuss our disagreements.

That it is unnecessary to spill any more blood defending the American flag if we all pledge allegiance to the UN flag.

That is what the UNESCO disciples believe.

They are not all Communists. They are decent citizens who are convinced that this is the better way and that is why they are indoctrinating your child today through UNESCO literature and UNESCO influence in his elementary school classroom.

But this is the rest of the story:

Russia is not thus indoctrinating Russian children.

This is the larger issue. This is the point well-meaning veterans organizations, and others have missed. While we are allowing our youngsters, thus, to have their American allegiance brainwashed away, so they do not consider Americanism worth fighting for anymore, the Russians in their schools (and I wouldn't say this if I couldn't document it with current evidence) continue to preach and teach their elementary school children that Communism is the only efficient government.

That God does not exist.

That Russia one day will rule the world.

Now wait a minute.

I'm talking now to the mostly good American parents who have been convinced that UNESCO was the proper way to prepare the next generation of world citizens to live together.

Don't you see what is happening?

Through UNESCO-American school children are being influenced away from their national allegiance.

American school children are being indoctrinated with world government ideals while the Russians prepare their children to run that world government.

They are softening the patriotism of our next generation, while hardening their own. The end result of this lopsided indoctrination is too obvious to require elaboration.

Ex-Senator William Benton, speaking to UNESCO, said, "We are at the beginning of a long process of breaking down the walls of our national sovereignty. In this, UNESCO can be, and indeed must be, the pioneer".

But Red Poland has pulled out of UNESCO. And Red Hungary. And Red Czechoslovakia.

They will not use this "break down the walls" and love everybody stuff in their schools.

They will love Communism and teach Communism and only we, the United States of Americans will dilute our patriotism until the American flag is a faded rag not worth fighting for.

You may have difficulty getting your school administrators to admit that they are using UNESCO materials even if they are. The best test is to learn directly from the students, if they are being taught that "collectivism is inevitable". That "polygamy is acceptable". That "private property has no place in the new order". That "we are all citizens of the world with allegiance to all nations and to no one nation".

School teachers are vulnerable.

The President of the National Education Association, Dr. Lyman Ginger, says Russia "Has an excellent school system". The basis for his judgement is that the Russian teacher is paid one and a half times as much as the Russian skilled worker. Of course, that fact loses its lustre when you realize that the Russian factory workers have to work eighty hours and forty-nine minutes to buy one pair of shoes.

Yet many American teachers have felt that in adopting the international outlook, they were being modern and imitating what their NEA President calls the Soviet Union's "Excellent school system". Though Russia's schools are not teaching internationalism.

Communism over God. Russia over all.

Ask Mrs. Eleanor Roosevelt about her recent visit to Russia. Are Soviet schools incorporating the UNESCO program? Certainly not.

Are Russian schools teaching that one nation is just like any other nation and that we must all live together under a United Nations? Certainly not.

Our UNESCO literature is indoctrinating American children with the idea that we should have an international anthem. Would Russian schools thus teach Russian children? Certainly Not.

Mrs. Roosevelt found the Russians demanding an indelible allegiance to their own country. Seeking in every way to strengthen their own country. Teaching their children, by the Pavlovian reflex method, precisely and only what the Soviet state wants them to believe. As Pavlov taught his conditioned dogs, they teach their children to hate the United States.

Is there nothing to encourage international peace in their curriculum? Nothing. The classroom is a nationalistic weapon of the Kremlin.

The UNESCO Seminar - which guides American teachers - states, "One of the chief aims of education everywhere is to develop those qualities of citizenship which provide the foundation upon which international government must be based". No, not "everywhere".

So before we rewrite our textbooks, as the UNESCO Seminar recommends, "On a view to improving them as aids to international understanding". Let's be sure everybody else follows suit or the implication is obvious. We grow nationally soft while they grow hard and strong. Only a Russian citizen or Soviet subversive would want that.

Now please don't come back at me with the many old pro-and con arguments that have been weighed by the American Legion and the VFW and countries civic and discussion groups for years. I have, I believe, seen them all and I am not concerned with more hash from these leftovers.

We are not debating whether UNESCO's philosophy is good or evil.

We are not opposing the United Nations. We are not denouncing international co-operation.

We are not challenging the rightness or the wrongness of editing textbooks to put the UN in and rewriting history, to take the United States out and coaching our teachers to erase national boundaries from the minds of the next generation.

I only object to this one fact. It is not who is right that is of greatest importance, but what is right.

That while we are thus conditioning our children to salute a mongrel flag; Russia is conditioning her children to salute only the hammer and sickle.

Suppose you and I were trainers, training professional fighters and you taught yours to fight and I taught mine to dance the minuet. We'll have a real happy party. But Russia is training fighters.

Now you say, what can you do?

If you are concerned with preserving patriotism in the next generation of Americans, then the youngster first must hear it at home.

Dad's constant complaining about unfair taxes and "crooks in Washington" does little to instil faith and confidence in our Government. It must be counterbalanced with a respect for the strengths of our nation, rather than a constant exaggerated emphasis on its weaknesses.

After the youngster has heard a little star-spangled conversation around the house, it's time for the parents to attend PTA meetings and to take an active, intense, personal interest in what the school is teaching and what it is not teaching.

If you don't others will.

If you figure you can stay home, and play cards on PTA night, and "Let George do it", you'd better expect the worst, because George doesn't always agree with you.

The FBI has established that the Communists in the United States, under orders from Moscow, are making a concerted effort to work through respectable forums, including PTA groups. If you can't take an interest in directing your child's education, they will.

They are; right now.

Much has been said about what Americans stand for. Equally important are the things Americans won't stand for.

And for goodness sake, understand this: Everybody who subscribes to the UNESCO philosophy of education is not a Communist. He may unwittingly be their tool, but a host of them are decent, honorable, entirely sincere parents, like yourself, who believe this is the best way to prepare their children for a future day, when they must live with others in peace, or perish in an atomic ash pile.

Don't try to shout them down, but try patiently to help them understand that Russia, as usual, is not keeping her part of this co-operative bargain.

Russia permits no UNESCO indoctrination of her youngsters.

Russia teaches "Communism without compromise", and unless we prepare young Americans to believe in freedom without compromise, so that they will keep it strong and defend it against all enemies (foreign or domestic), we are dooming tomorrow's Americans to the fate of today's Hungarians.

But if we can revive in America's youth, some of the faith of our fathers, then this will again become the land of the free, and the home of the brave, and strong enough to keep your enemies at arms length which is quite enough to hope for in our time. (Article by Paul Harvey, News Analyst, American Broadcasting Network. Entitled UNESCO: Communism's Trap for our Youth. Reprinted on Page 157-159 'Fourth Reich of the Rich' by Des Griffin. Emissary Publications, 1976.).

This article, now enshrined in the archives of the House of Representatives, shows quite clearly how the Communists work within our society, to bring it down, and how we, through perfectly sane and honest reasons, allow institutions like UNESCO and the United Nations to undermine our very strengths of freedom without responding to their treason within our society. **(335).** UNESCO today is still moving our children's education towards Communism. What must be done to stop this? Quite simply we must demand our governments stop the interference by the United Nations and UNESCO with our Education system. If we shout loud enough, we will be heard. We are already having good effect on governments over genetically modified crops. Let this spur us on to face this threat to our freedom.

Now you are beginning to get a full picture of the **Hidden Agenda.**

Foot Note.

In the United Nations building in New York, in the main lobby, stands a naked figure of Zeus, the Greek God, the supreme God of the pagan Pantheon. He represents Satan, the God of the world. **(336).**

Up stairs there is a 'Meditation Room'. The floor plan is in the shape of a truncated Pyramid, a symbol of the Illuminati. (As on the back of a one dollar note). On the back wall of the meditation room, over one-hundred occult symbols are displayed from various organisations including Masonry, Spiritism and all the ancient fertility cults.

In the centre of the room is a large polished black block. This is the Ashlar, representing Freemasonry. The rough block represents humanity being formed and polished by the use of the compass and the square into a smooth, finished, even, rectangular block which is fit for use in a building. This symbolises Masonry taking the masses of humanity and forming them into a finished block under their control, thus building their **New World Order.** (Again modern day Illuminati of Weishaupt).

Over the top of the black block is a single floodlight. This projects a shaft of light onto the block, symbolising the sun, sending its semen to fertilise the earth. (Weishaupt Illuminati). The United Nations is a fraud, a deception. We must all consider whether it should not be disbanded. **(337).**

> "The world is governed by very different personages from what is imagined by those who are not behind the scenes".
> **Benjamin Disraeli, from his book; 'Coningsby' Page 233.**

The ambition of those behind the scenes (The Bankers) is made crystal clear by Carroll Quigley **(338)**; their aim is, "Nothing less than to create a world system of financial control in private hands to dominate the political system of each country and the economy of the world as a whole. This system is to be controlled in feudal fashion by the central banks of the world acting in concert, by secret agreements arrived at in frequent private meetings and conferences". (Tragedy and Hope"). Later on we will study in depth one of these secret committees, and their equally secret conferences; the Bilderberg Committee.

PROTOCOL NINE
RE-EDUCATION.

In applying our principles let attention be paid to the character of the people in whose country you live and act: a general, identical application of them, until such time as the people shall have been re-educated to our pattern, cannot succeed. But by approaching their application cautiously you will see that not a decade will pass before the most stubborn character will change and we shall add a new people to the ranks of those already subdued by us. (Fits the UN).

The words of the Liberal, which are in effect the words of our Masonic watchword, namely, "Liberty, Equality, Fraternity", will, when we come into our kingdom, be changed by us into words no longer a watchword, but only an expression of idealism, namely into: "The right of liberty, the duty of equality, the ideal of brotherhood".

That is how we shall put it--and so we shall catch the bull by the horns....De facto we have already wiped out every kind of rule except our own, although, de jure, there still remain a good many of them. Nowadays, if any states raise a protest against us it is only pro forma at our discretion, and by our direction, **for their anti-Semitism is indispensable to us for the management of our lesser brethren.** I will not enter into further explanations, for this matter has formed the subject of repeated discussion amongst us.

For us there are no checks to limit the range of our activity. Our Super-Government (The United Nations) subsists in extra-legal conditions which are described in the accepted terminology by the energetic and forcible word -- **Dictatorship.** (From the Horse's mouth). I am in a position to tell you with a clear conscience that at the proper time we, the law givers, shall execute judgement and sentence, we shall slay and we shall spare; we, as head of all our troops, are mounted on the stead of the leader. We rule by the force of will, because in our hands are the fragments of a once powerful party, now vanquished by us. **And the weapons in our hands are limitless ambition, burning greediness, merciless vengeance, hatred and malice.**

It is from us that the all-engulfing terror proceeds. We have in our service persons of all opinions, of all doctrines, restoring monarchists, demagogues, socialists, communists, and utopian dreamers of every kind. We have harnessed them all to the task: Each one of them on his own account is boring away at the last remnants of authority, is striving to overthrow all established forms of order. By these acts all states are in torture; they exhort to tranquillity, they are ready to sacrifice everything for peace: **but we will not give them peace till they openly acknowledge our international Super-Government,** and with submissiveness.

The people have raised a howl about the necessity of settling the question of socialism by way of an international agreement. **Division into fractional parties has given them into our hands, for in order to carry on a contested struggle, one must have money, and the money is all in our hands.**

We might have reason to apprehend a union between the "clear-sighted" force of the goy kings on their thrones and the "blind" force of the goy mobs, but we have taken all needful measure against any such possibility: between the one and the other force we have erected a bulwark in the shape of a mutual terror between them. In this way the blind force of the people remains our support and we, and we only, shall provide them with a leader and, of course, direct them along the road that leads to our goal.

In order that the hand of the blind mob may not free itself from our guiding hand, we must every now and then enter into close communion with it, if not actually in person, at any rate through some of the most trusty of our brethren. When we are acknowledged as the only authority we shall discourse with the people personally on the market places, and we shall instruct them on questions, of the political in such wise as may turn them in the direction that suits us.

Who is going to verify what is taught in the village schools? But what an envoy of the government or a king on his throne himself may say, cannot but become immediately known to the whole State, for it will be spread abroad by the voice of the people.

In order not to annihilate the institutions of the goyim before it is time, we have touched them with craft and delicacy, and have taken hold of the ends of the springs which move their mechanism. These springs lay in a strict but just sense of order; we have replaced them by the chaotic licence of liberalism. We have got our hands into the administration of the law, into the conduct of elections, into the press, into the liberty of the person, but principally into education and training as being the corner-stones of a free existence.

We have fooled, bemused and corrupted the youth of the goyim by rearing them in principles and theories which are known to us to be false although it is by us that they have been inculcated.

Above the existing laws, without substantially altering them, and by merely twisting them into contradictory interpretations, we have erected something grandiose in the way of results. These results found expression first in the fact that the interpretations masked the laws (legal jargon): afterwards they entirely hid them from the eyes of the governments since it had become impossible to understand the tangled web of legislation. This is the origin of the theory of arbitration.

You may say that the goyim will rise upon us, arms in hand, if they guess what is going on before the time comes; but in the West, we have prepared against this a manoeuvre of such appalling terror that the very stoutest hearts quail -- the undergrounds, those subterranean corridors, before the time comes, will be driven under all capitals, from whence those capitals will be blown into the air with all their organisations and archives.

COMMENT

Well here we have the inner thinking of the planners of World Government letting out some of their secrets. We learn that Anti Semitism is essential to the management of their own brethren, this is at the heart of the International Zionist's system to control their own people. This is interesting as it has been used to silence the world about all Jewish matters as well, which is unhealthy for the free world. We must have, in a democracy, the chance to criticise any minority when we think they are causing us injustice. That is what this discourse is all about. It relates to this well planned plot to bring the world to **DICTATORSHIP** and exposes the plotters who happen to be predominantly of international Zionist origin, but mainly adoptive Jews, but the core of this plot is controlled by no more than five thousand people, people that have only one 'God', money and one purpose **World control.** To finally face up to this plot is as much in the interest of the world Jews as it is in our interest as Christians. It is a Satanic plot and every other connection is subordinated by this fact. If the Jewish people honour their belief in the Torah they will understand why we must honour ours.

It shows once again how they have corrupted youth through education into a selfish, self seeking, mob, we see today, every day. But they are mistaken if they think all youth is like their loutish models. I can see a whole new awakening beginning that is questioning why our society is declining and they are determined to do something about it.

CHAPTER FOURTEEN
PART ONE
THE COUNCIL ON FOREIGN RELATIONS.

It is now the turn for the Council on Foreign Relations to come under our scrutiny. The Council on Foreign Relations (CFR) was founded in 1921 under the control of Colonel E. Mandell House, when America decided against joining the League of Nations, an early abortive attempt to move to global control. The top figures behind its formation were John D. Rockefeller, J.P.Morgan, Paul Warburg, and Jacob Schiff, a re-run of the very people who created the Federal Reserve System in 1913 and the graduated income tax system in the USA in 1916. **(339)**.

Colonel House produced an anonymous book 'Philip Dru - Administrator' **(340)**. In this book House details a plan for the creation of a one world totalitarian government, along the same lines as Karl Marx.

It was not till 1928 that the CFR started to be a force, when Rockefeller's Foundation and later the Ford Foundation, and the Carnegie Foundation began to fund its activities.

It was with Rockefeller money that they bought their present building, the Harold Pratt House, 58 East 68th. Street, New York City **(341)**.

Carroll Quigley confirms their make up in 'Tragedy and Hope' **(342)** by saying "The CFR is a front for the international bankers and elitist insiders, and is linked to the Institute of International Affairs in England and other similar groups world-wide". Its status as a secret organisation was established in its 1966 annual report; "It is an express condition of membership in the council, to which every member accedes by virtue of his membership, that unless expressly stated by an officer of the council to the contrary, all proceedings at the council's afternoon and dinner meetings as well as study and discussion groups are confidential, and disclosure or publication of statements made at such meetings or attributions to the council of information, even though otherwise available, is contrary to the best interests of the council and may be regarded by the board of directors in its sole discretion as grounds for termination or suspension of membership pursuant to article 1 of the by-laws".

So how do we know the CFR is part of the undemocratic move to global government? Well you don't have to look far. The 1959 Study, **(343)** 'Basic Aims of US Foreign Policy' stated, "The US must strive to build a new international order". (To include Communists). The same report suggested that the United States should, "Maintain and gradually increase the authority of the United Nations" and "Make more effective use of the International Court of Justice, jurisdiction of which should be increased by withdrawal of reservations by member nations on matters judged to be domestic".

This same study, from way back in 1959 also called for secret talks with Russia about disarmament and recommended talks with China; this when America was in a so called 'Cold War' with both countries. **(Hidden Agenda).**

What we have here is an unofficial body with no government approval making decisions behind closed doors that can influence the world agenda by the pure power of the selected attendees. This is pure anarchy. The fact is that these powerful secret groups only get away with it because they contain the shadowy figures who control politics.

The last glimmering of doubt is expelled from your mind when you learn the CFR's declared policy aim is a "New International Order" so close to Weishaupt's "New World Order" and the United Nation's "One World Order".

The next point that becomes so obvious as you study leading politicians and civil servants is how many of them were initially trained for their position within the CFR. So much so it led Congressman John Rarick to claim, "The CFR is the establishment. Not only does it have influence in key decision making positions from above, but it also finances and uses individuals and groups to bring pressure from below to justify the high-level decisions for converting the United States from a Sovereign, Constitutional Republic, into a servile member state of a one world dictatorship". **(344).**

Fortunately we have had a very informed and detailed description of the CFR from an insider, Rear Admiral Chester Ward, who wrote a condemning account of CFR activities in conjunction with Phyllis Schlafly, his co-author, entitled "Kissinger on the Couch**". (345).**

In this book he claims that he did not agree with the CFR policies; he stayed in the organisation for sixteen years because his, "access to 'confidential sources' can provide more significant intelligence information than can be secured from the reports made available....from our (USA) $6 billion a year intelligence community". Given his first hand knowledge of the minute details of the complete operation of the CFR, this comment should make us all concerned, "Previous attempts to document the CFR's influence have been ignored or smeared by the Liberal press as exaggerated. This is to be expected, considering the beach head that key CFR members hold in all parts of the media, and especially because any attempt to tell about the power and activities of the CFR is bound to sound exaggerated.

"Actually, however, all the published accounts this far have understated the CFR's influence, just as all previous accounts of Henry Kissinger's power vastly underestimate him**". (346).**

We also have the words of a paper (before its purchase by the power block) the Chicago Tribune **(347)** with a stinging attack on the CFR's part in two wars, "The members of the council are persons of much greater than average influence in the community. They have used the prestige, that their wealth, their social position, and their education have given, them to lead their country towards bankruptcy and military debacle. There is blood on them - the dried blood of the past war (1941-45) and the fresh blood of the present one". (The Korean War).

In Des Griffin's 'Fourth Reich of the Rich' **(348)** it becomes clear that CFR members have taken over the media, politics, the civil service, the Foundations and are at the moment within the United Nations and the Bilderberg group, and that two main sources provide the funds to exercise the power behind this entourage of Liberal, one world, humanistic, socialist government: the Federal Reserve Bank, controlled by the Rothschilds and the Rockefeller Foundation.

Griffin states **(349)** that the CFR are in flagrant violation of the Logan act which forbids American Citizens;

A. Without the permission or authority of the government;
B. Directly or indirectly;
C. to commence or carry on any verbal or written correspondence or intercourse with any foreign government or any officer or agent thereof; OR
D. To counsel, advise or assist in any such "correspondence", i.e. in any verbal or written correspondence by a United States citizen with any foreign government or...agent thereof;
E. With the intent to influence the measure or conduct of any foreign government or any officer or agent thereof in relation to any disputes or controversies with the United States, OR
F. With the intent to defeat the measures of the government of the United States.

He goes as far as to say that the CIA is the enforcement arm of the CFR, and cites Allen W. Dulles as first head of O.S.S. operations in Switzerland during World War Two and later President of the CFR then ending up as the head of the CIA.

He also shows proof that the CFR would lie to cover up its connection to the Rothschild's Federal Reserve Bank. **(350).**

(351) Griffin shows systematically that members of the CFR and Bilderberg organisations are in **Direct Violation** of their oaths when they are sworn into public office, if they attend secret, clandestine meetings that discuss the 'Dissolution of national sovereignty and the creation of Adam Weishaupt's 'New World Order'.

He then cites article 3 section 3 of the United States Constitution, "Treason against the United States shall consist only in levying war against them, or in adhering to their enemies, giving them aid and comfort...".

Griffin then goes on to prove that the CFR's secret planning breaks the Constitution. What we see in America, we also see in our own political system in Britain. We are, like America, under siege by a hidden group of dedicated people who intend to overthrow our society to install their world dictatorship in its place.

People who meet in secret, to undermine our way of life, developed over the centuries, and aspire to interfere with our property, our prosperity, our family, our institutions, our education, and our religion, and every avenue that is built up to make our society whole, fair and prosperous, should be brought to task as the enemy within, whatever their power or position, for they corrupt our life and lower our moral standards, to achieve their **Hidden Agenda, World Control,** with us as their slaves.

FOUNDATIONS:
A Source of Funds for Subversion.

Foundations found their ultimate power in funding the research into America's foreign policy. It has to a large degree ignored the American people's opinion and developed an extreme Socialist international policy for America. The research, funded by the Foundations, that bring the policies forward is predominantly controlled by Radical Liberals (Communists) and is guided by the policies drawn up by Weishaupt over two-hundred years ago.

The organs of research are the Council on Foreign Relations, as we have already discussed, The Foreign Policy Association, The Institute of Pacific Relations, (The body preparing the Pacific Rim for federalisation as a regional government), the United Nations Association and a host of Universities that hold seminars on international relations that, in general, vie with each other to be the most radical in their deliberations.

Nowhere can be seen, in this array, one single organisation that opposes Globalism, or indeed that opposes the United Nations, the centre of the 'New World Order'.

That this funding, directed in a narrow channel towards a single objective, world domination, by a small group of powerful and rich bankers, whose foundations are used to promote a type of Socialism that will enslave the world, must worry us all.

That this small group should be able to influence policy to such a degree shows us all how, by careful planning, that group has so infiltrated our offices of government that politicians and the democratic system is powerless to act without their support, or the support of the media, on one hand, or the public on the other. The media, being in the hands of the planners of Globalism, which is seen quite clearly when you study the list of CFR members that are journalists, will not act against the bankers cause, so it is left to us to shout about it. We must spread the truth and force our politicians to listen. It is only the 'People', who can change the course of the world now.

It is almost impossible to find a Foundation supported organisation of any size which does not support the United Nations or its list of global schemes. The organisations like the CFR force Americans to support the outright interference of the internal affairs of other nations, using taxpayers money to promote and introduce Communism to the third world, when Communism is the last thing they want. We have already seen South Africa as a typical example where vast amounts of American taxpayers money was handed to the ANC even while it was still a terrorist group and controlled by Communists. At this point maybe we should stop and take stock on our barometer, **'Direction'**, to advise us if we are paranoid about Communism.

What we have so far found, in our whole study, is that every battle, every negotiation, every political action, especially by the American government has led to political gain by Communism, or bankers gain (as in Kuwait), or both; the duo, both on the same side, in the ball game of politics. It is a one way street to Communism with no exceptions. This, when America, as it would have us believe, as the most powerful nation in the world, genuinely was fighting against Communism, to hold back its advance. The facts are plain, American and British political agenda has been hijacked by banker power linked to Communism. Their hidden agenda is being pushed forward under other press pretences, while we are being told lies, or being diverted by other matters, such as diversionary promotion of sport and sex to distract our minds, while they complete their hidden agenda to enslave the world.

Within this scenario the Foundations play a dominant role in developing US and United Nations policies. This they have achieved because within the Radical Liberal control of Foundations, there is no funding for opposite views. It is therefore one sided funding towards Marxism. (Illuminati).

The influence of the Radical Foundations, and their drive towards Globalism has penetrated deep into the State Department and Congress with well placed CFR members in key positions to make policies flow smoothly. To accomplish their aims they dominate public opinion by use of academic journals covering international learned affairs, and it is from this source that most of the national press get their leaders when writing on the subject of foreign affairs, or their other source, State Department officials, who in turn move on to top Foundation jobs. There is a return movement of Foundation employees who become top officials in the State Department, ensuring complete control by the Globalists.

In England the Rhodes Scholarship fund of Great Britain, created by the 'Rhodes Trust Group', to promote internationalism, is a prime move centre in America for British (Rothschild) ideas. A steady flow of young Americans gain scholarships through the Rhodes Trust Group (President Clinton being one example) who go back to America to take top jobs in administration, legislation, and education, having been illuminated in global policies. They form a tight network of hidden power. Dr. Frank Aydelotte, in his book "The Rhodes Trust, **(352)** had this to say, "The influence of this group on American Education practice and particularly on the rapidly increasing maturity and breadth of methods of instruction in American institutions of high learning, has been immense. The number of them going into government is constantly increasing".

By 1953, out of a total of 1,372 American Rhodes Scholars, 431 held high teaching posts (including 31 College Presidents), 113 held government positions, 70 held press and media positions and 14 were executives in Foundations. The Rhodes Scholarship within its programme, developed its scholars around the policies of Weishaupt and his New World Order. So you can see how gradually America has been hijacked by Globalism against the American Constitution and the interest of the American people.

In 'Foundations' by Rene A. Wormser **(353)** a list of high achieving Rhodes Scholars is presented and Wormser points out that Cecil Rhodes, who created the funding of this scholarship was a close friend of Andrew Carnegie, the founder of the Carnegie Endowment for International Peace, a Foundation that has had a huge impact on America's foreign policy. The other Foundations with equal power are the Rockefeller Foundation and the Ford Foundation. They in turn organise conferences on international affairs and forums on global matters but as they are controlled, organised and promoted by converted Globalists no proper free debate takes place, instead most of the conferences, like the Bilderberg Group or the Trilateral Commission debate behind closed doors, attendance by invitation only, so any decisions made will always favour globalist views and therefore the impact on foreign policy in America becomes one sided and against America's interest and contrary to the aspirations of the American people. It is only because the media present it in a plausible manner that Americans are not awakened to the treason within.

The conferences being so predictably one sided, monotonously recommend aid for under-developed countries with no strings attached. The aid to come from the American taxpayers but paid out through the United Nations rather than American agencies. Thus setting the scene for the bankers to tie up the third world into debt slavery, while they hold their mineral wealth as collateral.

The conferences also, to show their political colours, constantly applied pressure for recognition of Communist China and its aspiration to join the United Nations (now achieved) and American abandonment of Atomic Weapons on a solely unsatisfactory basis of unilateral disarmament. Thus, through their monopoly of discussion, they in turn have recognition by the government as an academic think tank, that government does not need to fund.

Thus Radical Liberal ideas are promoted, as well debated ideas, within the official government thinking, when in fact they are only debated by promoters of the Communist thinking of these bodies, while opponents get no funding to oppose the Radical Liberal thinking; a loaded ball game.

When it came time for the Reece Committee to report their findings into Foundations they had this to say of the Carnegie Endowment for International Peace: **(354).**

"An extremely powerful propaganda machine was created. It spent many millions of dollars in:

The production of masses of material for distribution;

The creation and support of large numbers of international policy clubs, and other local organisations at colleges and elsewhere;

The underwriting and dissemination of many books on various subjects, through the "International Mind Alcoves" and the "International Relations Clubs and Centres" which it organised all over the country;

The collaboration with agents of publicity, such as newspaper editors;

The preparation of material to be used in school text books, and co-operation with publishers of text books to incorporate this material;

The establishing of professorships at the colleges and the training and indoctrination of teachers; the financing of lectures and the importation of foreign lecturers and exchange professors;

The support of outside agencies touching the international field, such as the Institute of International Education, the Foreign Policy Association, The American Association for the Advancement of Science, the American Council on Education, the American Council on Learned Societies, the American Historical Association, the Institute of Pacific Relations, the International Parliamentary Union and others, and acting as mid-wife at the birth of some of them". **(355).**

From this it is easy to see the power of money being used to promote a very complete saturation of both individual and group thinking through its wide forum from learning to foreign affairs. A term the Foundations would use publicly to describe their aim was, "The Education of Public Opinion". That is not the same as public education, but the moulding of public opinion to their way of thinking. The Reece Committee, in its report made it Crystal clear that no private group should wield so much power to influence what is read or taught in American schools and colleges. Yet that is exactly what this private group sought to do and were not curtailed by the Reece report which was largely ignored by the American government, through pressure from the Anglo American (bankers) Establishment.

In a year book by the Carnegie Endowment for International Peace in 1934 it described Nationalism as, "Violently reactionary" in America but went about supporting mainly Communist regimes that showed "Violently reactionary" attitudes in support of Nationalism, quite often against America's interests.

The Rockefeller Foundation showed its colours in supporting Globalism by saying, The challenge of the future is to make this world 'One World' - A world truly free to engage in common and constructive intellectual efforts that will serve the welfare of mankind everywhere".

The Reece Committee had this to say about the aims of certain Foundations on a one track path to Globalism; "The weight of evidence before this Committee, which the Foundations have made no serious effort to rebut, indicates that the forum of Globalism which the Foundations have so actively promoted and from which our foreign policy has suffered seriously, relates definitely to a collectivist point of view. (Collectivism being a main plank of Communism). Despite vehement disclaimers of bias, despite platitudinous affirmations of loyalty to American traditions, the statements filed by those Foundations whose operations touch on foreign policy have produced no rebuttal of the evidence of support of collectivism". **(356).**

Rene Wormser states; "In an affidavit filed with the Reece Committee, Dr. Felix Wittmer, former Associate Professor of Social Studies at the New Jersey State Teachers College, described his experiences as the adviser to one of the International Relations Clubs founded by The Carnegie Endowment.

"Dr. Wittmer said that there were about a thousand of these clubs and that, as a result of association with them, a great proportion of the student members had acquired strongly leftist tendencies. **(357).** At regional conferences, said Dr. Wittmer, "a large majority of those students who attended, favored views which came close to that of the Kremlin".

"Speakers were provided by the Carnegie Endowment. Among the speakers supplied to the club at New Jersey Teachers College was Alger Hiss. When Dr. Wittmer protested against receiving Hiss as a speaker, the secretary of the Endowment, said Dr. Wittmer, reminded him, in no uncertain terms, "that" our club, like all the hundreds of other clubs, was under the direction of the Carnegie Endowment for International Peace, which had for years liberally supplied it with reading material, and which contributed funds to cover the honoraria of conference speakers".

"Radical infiltration in the club of which Dr. Wittmer was adviser became so pronounced that he resigned his position.

The Foreign Policy Association was supported by the Carnegie Endowment whose research director was Vera Micheles Dean. She gave an address to six-hundred students at Vassar College with a strong Plea for Socialism", supporting Communism. **(358).**

The Council On Foreign Relations, being financed by both the Carnegie Foundation and the Rockefeller Foundation, pushes Globalism for all its worth. Yet this agency became for all intents and purposes part of the American Government when World War Two started. The Rockefeller Foundation funded the "War and Peace Studies", then the State Department took them over with all their personnel from the CFR. Once again Radical Liberals penetrated the State Department and influenced its thinking towards Communism. After the war the CFR went about a comprehensive selective manipulation of the history of World War Two which they claimed to be "Debunking Journalism". **(359).**

Professor Harry Elmer Barnes, in his book, "The Historical Blackout and the Perpetual War for Perpetual Peace" **(360),** describes it as a conspiracy to prevent the American people from learning the truth. (Hidden Agenda). When you realise that our media, including the published word, and its distribution, is owned and controlled by two spheres of influence, that of the Rothschilds and Rockefellers, the Anglo American Establishment, and they in turn control Communism, the Foundations, The Council on Foreign Relations, the Trilateral Commission and others, you can easily understand how they wield so much power. From this chapter you now see that this power is directed solely towards the one world Communism of Weishaupt without the knowledge of the people of America and the world.

A considerable part of Foundation funding is done without due attention and monitoring by the funding Foundation; so the McCarran Committee report claimed. They concluded; "The net effect (referring particularly to the Institute for Pacific

Relations) of IPR activities on United States public opinion has been Pro-Communist and Pro-Soviet, and has frequently and repeatedly been such as to serve International Communist and Soviet interests, and to subvert the interests of the United States". **(361)**.

Yet, some of the trustees of the IPR were men of unquestionable reputation. So how could its staff turn its drive to Pro-Soviet policies? Professor David N. Rowe, a member of the Yale Committee on International Relations, and an expert on 'The Far East' was a director of the IPR who resigned when he found, as a director, he had no power to guide research. The directors were just respectable figureheads. Professor Rowe testified to the Reece Committee that on one occasion the executive refused to advise the board the names of applicants for a executive secretary. It was this issue which led to his resignation, as he did not want to lend his good name to the IPR to mislead people about its political standing.

The Rockefeller Foundation, despite clear evidence from Alfred Kohlberg, a director of the IPR, that the IPR was a Communist front organisation, continued to fund the IPR which must cast doubt on the ability of the trustees of the Rockefeller Foundation to vet the recipients of funding from their source or the overall motives of the foundation. It was a disastrous result for America and freedom, tying them into the bonds of Communism. It was the organisation (IPR) that influenced the American Government to abandon Mainland China to Mao's Communist troops.

The American people were probably fooled into accepting the course of events because of the long list of famous names adorning the boards of these institutes and Foundations, according to Professor Kenneth Colegrove. In his testimony to the Reece Committee he had this to say; "The large number of famous names on the list of trustees is due to an old superstition that our institutions must be headed by famous groups of men. And I will say frankly, it is to impress Congress as well as the American people; to impress public opinion as much as possible. It is an old superstition. It is not necessary at all". **(362)**.

This leaves the Foundation Bureaucrats solely in charge of decisions about where the funding goes. Add to that the infiltration of Communist influence into Foundations in the 30's and early 40's, and you get a very dangerous situation where, the reports that governments rely upon for policy decisions, can be doctored to suit a minority view. That is exactly what we have seen as we dig deep into the structures of these dangerous think tanks.

Professor Colegrove continued; "In the aggregate, the officers of these Foundations wield a staggering sum of influence and direction upon research, education, and propaganda in the States and even in foreign countries".

When you then realise, that out of over four-thousand Foundations, the big six held in excess of $4,000,000,000 in assets, you begin to realise the power of this monster in the wrong hands. At least three of the six big foundations are giving Communism an untold fortune to use for its political aim, Global Government, under Marxism.

René Wormser, in 'Foundations : Their Power and Influence' shows how Foundations promoted 'Globalism' **(363)** the major aim of Marxist policy, while ignoring American interests. Professor Kenneth Colegrove testified to the Reece Committee; "In my opinion, a great many of the staff of the Foundations have gone well beyond Wendell Wilkie with reference to Internationalism and Globalism.... There is undoubtedly too much money put into studies which support Globalism and Internationalism. You might say that the other side has not been as fully developed as it should be". **(364)**.

An American Diplomat Mr. Spruille Braden, a former Assistant Secretary of State commented; "I have the very definite feeling that these various Foundations you mention very definitely do exercise both overt and covert influences on our Foreign Relations and that their influences are counter to the fundamental principles on which this nation was founded and which have made it great". (The Foundations referred to were the Carnegie Endowment, The Rockefeller Foundation, The Ford Foundation and The Rhodes Scholarship Trust. It equally applies to the Foreign Policy Association, The Council on Foreign Relations, The Institute of Pacific Relations, and The United Nations Association, the very grouping that the majority report of the Reece committee called a 'Concentration of Power'.

In fact if you study the books and papers promoted by the Carnegie Endowment through The International Relations Clubs and Centres they are, Globalist, Marxist, or plain out and out Communist propaganda, but it is being used to educate the aspiring world managers. The end result is Communism, as an accepted philosophy for Global control, through lack of comparison to other ways forward, friendly to sovereign nations.

The Reece Committee actually makes this point, stating that it would be amazing if the modern expert had any other view to Globalism, as the money was all backing this policy. This is not just a chance funding, but a dedicated drive to exclude any other sentiment other than global control entering the Arena and it has been these listed Associations and Foundations that have controlled the agenda towards this goal. The Average American is both Patriotic and proud of his nation and its constitution. This dedicated group of Foundations, driven by the Marxism of Weishaupt's origin, funded by the super rich and largely manned by Zionist Internationalists, wish to destroy American Patriotism, and confuse their Religion while effectively by-passing the American Constitution. Americans would be wise to spend some time to help themselves understand this political agenda hidden from us all.

The United Nations has taken over the Foreign Policy of the United States, which is the territory of the State Department; this is against the terms of the American Constitution, leaving a very dangerous situation which allows the American foreign policy to be manipulated by forces controlled by minority groups that in turn guide and create the policies of the United Nations. So we see those that fund the Foundations, the super rich bankers and their associates, through money, control the direction of foreign policy research and decide who receive grants. We have seen how those grants have been almost exclusively given to Radical Liberal research. (Communist). We have also seen the policies they have created for the promotion of one world collectivism, that is the main plank of Communism.

But how have they been able to pull this political coupe off, under our very eyes without detection? Well of course, they have been detected by a very concerned collection of people around the world who have written about it and spoken about it. But they lack the backing of the one force that counts; our media, who can, and do feed us what their masters, the bankers, wish us to hear and exclude the truth from their accounts of events. This is why the success of this account is so vital to us all, as it informs the world of the true agenda, hidden by press censorship.

Let us, once again, examine the way the press and media behave. Let us study their policy towards the United Nations. In a free press, you would expect articles for and against, critical and supportive.

So it is not surprising to find that the Council on Foreign Relations, Foundation funded, has been involved in re-writing history to give a partial 'History Blackout'. Evidence to this effect was given to the Reece Committee. **(365).**

The hope was that criticism of the main players in the Second World War like Franklin D. Roosevelt and his team of Radical Liberals would escape critical analysis. Professor Harry Elmer Barnes, in his book 'Historical Blackout and Perpetual War for Perpetual Peace' **(366),** shows the details of a conspiracy to hide from the American people the truth of America's political agenda under Roosevelt's leadership. The result of the Foundations desire to hide the true agenda was a three volume history of the war, funded by the Rockefeller Foundation, who gave $139,000 to cover its production costs.

We see at the Carnegie Endowment and its linked line of funded groups, its one sided uncritical promotion of the United Nations. René Wormser states, "Nothing else could explain the truly intemperate propaganda which has been launched to indoctrinate our people into blind support of the United Nations. There has been no disposition whatever to be objective; to criticise what is fallacious and what is dangerous. There has been no debate on merits. There has been only propaganda in support". **(367).**

He goes on to say how the group of Foundations, led by the Carnegie Endowment, spends millions of dollars on propaganda to support the United Nations, claiming it to be the light and our saviour. But any contrary view by eminent Americans receives no similar coverage by this group or indeed the media.

The UN is a busy agency, attempting to gradually take over the core decisions now being made by Nation States. Some of its work is useful to our community, but much of its meddlesome work, dangerous to Nation States and their freedom of decision. A typical example that needs a Committee of Investigation is the demand for Nation States to subordinate their economic welfare to the UN and the world in order to have peace. This dangerous idea would mean no nation could make its own economic decisions for the good of its own people. That all decisions should be made Globally; but in who's interest? Industrially, the MAI agreement is pushing this line for all its worth. The benefactors are the bankers and multinational companies. The losers are all the people of the world.

Although the American taxpayer funds twenty-five percent of the cost of the United Nations, its people know little of its workings. UNESCO has funded a series of books on the Social Sciences, the second policy they have chosen to indoctrinate the world. This is why, behind the scenes, the Foundations are so involved with Social Science research. They use their funds to establish a pattern of thought amongst the young to establish a friendly environment for their future global socialist society through Marx and Weishaupt's teachings. The former socialist Prime Minister, Mendès - France, wrote a book on economics, which is now the official UN book on the subject, which is an extreme, collective, left wing work which will leave anyone other than Communists and extreme Socialists horrified at its conclusions. Yet this book is the official work on this subject, economics, promoted by UNESCO. It has also been financed by American Dollars.

We do not know what is being planned by the UN agencies, despite our membership and position, and their think tank, the Foundation, funded research units for our future, but if it is anything like what we have already seen, our future as free thinking Nation States is about to disappear for ever.

We have already seen how the UN has interfered in our Schooling throughout the world. They are responsible for removing National religion from our school's programme and replacing it with a general religious study.

They are also behind all sorts of teaching that ultimately removes parental authority over our children.

Globalism is their goal and we now see Globalism being promoted vigorously in posters and the media, wherever we look. It seems that we are getting near the heart of the Global planner's secret power house, but we are not quite there yet.

Very few people would object if the United Nations was an even handed, neutral world organisation, holding together nation states that aspire to fair dealing and peace with support for small nations threatened by neighbours or aggressors, an organisation that wanted nation states to live in peace and prosperous harmony.

But, although this is the picture we have been given of the UN, it is far from any of this simplistic ideal. It was formed by a Communist agenda to promote Communism and protect Zionist interests. Its agenda is not controlled by Nation members but by a hidden agenda within a minority group of bankers and their associates to promote a 'One World Order' that puts money, resources, and political power, under the control of a International Zionist banker cartel, the dangers of which I cannot begin to estimate. Now, I feel, the UN has gone beyond the point where we can re-direct its power and purpose, as it is so infiltrated by radical destroyers of National identity, it is practically beyond reform. It should therefore be replaced by an organisation that will remain neutral and honour the "Nation States"of the world.

CHAPTER FOURTEEN, PART TWO.

THE INTERNATIONAL MONETARY FUND.

In 1946 the Radical Liberal element of America's administration was busying itself in implementing the plans it had laid to engulf America, and through it, the United Nations and the world, in radical Socialism; the Weishaupt plan. The UN, already formed, was the centre of 'One World' planning now referred to as 'Globalism and all around it were Foundations and Research Groups planning and promoting their own contribution to enslave the world in International Zionist Communism.

On the 23rd. of January 1946 President Truman nominated Harry Dexter White as the first Executive Director of the International Monetary Fund, and in February, despite protests, White was confirmed as its first Executive Director for two years. His contribution to setting it up in the first place was considerable. He had been at the head of the planning stage and guided American support behind the UN and International Monetary Fund. Previously he had been involved in the whole concept of the Bretton Woods planning from his position as deputy to Morgenthau at the Treasury Department. Later the Treasury would bring in the Marshall Plan, put forward to help Europe recover from the war and make America's bankers rich while doing so.

It was a time for all sorts of international fly traps to be erected. In October of the same year the preparatory meeting to discuss a International Trade Organisation (ITO), then the World Trade Organisation (WTO) took place in London.

As the International Monetary Fund was to be a organisation that would develop from Bretton Woods, a problem arose immediately which brought Harry Dexter White and his counter part from Britain, Keynes, to bitter disagreement. The stumbling block, according to Richard Gardner, was, "Were the Fund and the Bank purely financial institutions whose direction could be entrusted to a group of international civil servants? Or did their operations have such economic and political implications as to require close control by member governments? The articles of agreements signed at Bretton Woods made no clear choice for either alternative. It remained for the Savannah talks to decide between them". **(368).**

At Savannah it became obvious from the start that the International Monetary Fund would be an instrument of American power politics, while embarking on an international identity. **DECEPTION.** Each point of dispute was won by the Americans, much to the frustration of Keynes, as was its positioning in Washington under the political eyes of the US and the civil service. Richard Gardner wrote, "An important victory for the idea of close national control of the Bretton Woods institutions. It was to have a profound effect on their future development". **(369).** At the end of the conference at Savannah it was clear that America had achieved a tight control of the fund. The fund was outwardly to be a devise to help nations move goods around the world without currency problems and to assist trading, especially in the third world. As such it would be a temporary fund by nature, requiring earlier settlement than with loans.

A revealing memorandum amongst Harry Dexter White's papers at Princeton University showed his position clearly. After stating that international relations had deteriorated sharply since Roosevelt's death he went on to say, "The major task that confronts American diplomacy - and the only task that has any real value in the major problems that confront us - is to devise means whereby continued peace and friendly relations can be assured between the United States and Russia. Everything else in the field of international diplomacy pales into insignificance besides this major task. It matters little what our political relationships with England become or what happens in the Balkans or the far East if the problems between the United States and Russia can be solved. Contrariwise, if we cannot discover ways to assure sincere friendship and military alliance between those two countries, the international manoeuvring in the Balkans, the Far East and in Europe can only accentuate the fear of war, and if anything enhance the chances of major conflict. Let us therefore examine the situation anew...". **(370).**

This short passage gives us a firm idea where his loyalty lay. (Russia). It exposes everything he thought. When we study his work in high ranking positions in America's administration; White was the Bretton Woods power behind the policy, which encompassed America's post war monetary policy from the International Monetary fund to the World Bank. It was the White - Morgenthau ticket that won all the discussions and the way forward for America's future within the 'New Deal'; the drive for a One World Government, a Communist policy backed by Morgenthau (A Zionist) and White, a Zionist and possibly a Communist.

Churchill, in a speech at Fulton Missouri in March 1946, made his famous 'Iron Curtain' speech **(371),** which began a slow process of conversion to direct support for Britain in America, but, to counter balance this, Moscow was beginning to flex its muscles over the Black Sea and Northern Iran.

Gradually Churchill's warning began to demand a new honesty in politics, at least in the realms of the public awareness of the threat of Communism, but alas with hindsight, it has proved to be another mirror, erected by the power brokers, to hide their secret agenda. It was at this time America should have been rescued from its corrupt civil service, and its power politicians, who had aligned themselves with the bankers. But their will and their finance was not equalled by the Anti Communist lobby, and the great betrayal of America by the media was responsible for the failure of the Anti Communist lobby to get its message across.

In the complexities of Communism however, the beginning of the end was in sight for Harry Dexter White. As early as August 1945 Miss Bentley, a Ex-Communist agent, went to the FBI building in New Haven and gave evidence of a Communist spy ring within government that included Harry Dexter White.

By November 1945 Hoover, the head of National Security, sent a letter to General Vaughan, which included a list of suspects.

Hoover's letter to General Vaughan reads as follows:-

"As a result of the bureau's investigative operations, information has been recently appeared, from a highly confidential source, indicating that a number of persons employed by the government of the United States have been furnishing data and information to persons outside the Federal Government, who are in turn transmitting this information to espionage agents of the Soviet Government. At the present time it is impossible to determine exactly how many of these people had actual knowledge of the disposition being made of the information they were transmitting. The investigation, however, at this point has indicated that the persons named hereinafter were actually the source from which information passing through the Soviet espionage system was being obtained, and I am continuing vigorous investigation for this purpose of establishing the degree and nature of the complicity of these people in this espionage ring.

The Bureau's information at this time indicates that the following persons were participating in this operation, or were utilised by principals in this ring, for the purpose of obtaining data in which the Soviet is interested...".

Second on the list was the name of Harry Dexter White, yet he remained in office for a further eighteen months before finally being forced to resign. In that time we can only imagine how much damage he did to America and how he arranged, when he was forced to resign, that adequate safeguards had been installed to make sure Communism held on to its gains, and consolidated its position, which it did in a most extraordinary way.

At this point we must ask why the President did not have all the named spies suspended from duty and removed from all sensitive posts? He didn't. He allowed Harry Dexter White to become the Executive Director of the International Monetary Fund which, financially, could ruin world trade.

It was not until the end of 1946 that Silvermaster resigned from government service, followed by Ullmann and Perlo in March 1947 and Glasser at the end of 1947.

Harry Dexter White was allowed to resign by President Truman on March 31st. 1947. He would die before the court would deliberate on his spying charges. The heritage of his work has brought the world to the brink of Communism behind a screen of the United Nations, the International Bank for Reconstruction and Development, (Now the International Monetary Fund) and the World Bank; all of which were the special interests of the spy Harry Dexter White.

Thanks to Churchill's intervention at Fulton, Harry Dexter White wrote in May 1948 **(372);** "I doubt if any responsible official of the member governments in spring of 1944 believed that by 1948 - only three years after the cessation of hostilities - the tensions between certain of the major powers would have been so pronounced and that the world, instead of drawing together during these years, would have moved so precipitously towards a split...".

Now we come to the extraordinary way that Communism held on to the agenda of the International Monetary Fund and the bank. In June 1946 the headquarters of the International Monetary Fund, which had been initially at the Washington Hotel, in Washington, the seat of politics, was moved to 1818 H Street, New York, where it shared premises with the International Bank for Reconstruction and Development.

Glasser (another suspected spy) at the Treasury meanwhile organised the removal of a large consignment of files claimed to be needed by White at his new offices. Now this might have, on the face of it, seemed a perfectly logical move to take the fund to the centre of banking, New York. But it had another slant. By this time White knew his days were numbered. With the backlash from his pending trial, it would be reasonable to assume every effort, politically, would be made to distance the fund from Communism while it was located at the seat of government in Washington. It was vulnerable to political tides created by his trial. The logic, though there is no proof of its correctness, is that Harry Dexter White moved it to New York under the protection of the International bankers, who funded Communism, to protect its future; that is both logical and probable. (When White finally resigned, the control of the fund was indeed taken on by bankers). **(373).**

Politically, America began to realise that Churchill had been right about their dubious ally (Stalin) during World War 11. America politically knew they must somehow control the spread of Communism. But at this time they were deeply penetrated by Communism, and to hinder this aim America's wealth was being used by International Zionists to build Russia into a formidable world power. These same bankers had under their control the Media, as we have already seen, the Academic force, and selected, bought politicians. So America would struggle, as a bastion against the spread of Communism, but with its penetration, was destined to fail in every theatre of conflict. That is how we have seen the world's greatest power fail in its attempts to halt Communism's gradual advance, where the enemy within (remember Cicero) has corrupted the ability to succeed and even its ability to cleanse its ranks of infiltrators. Cicero, quite rightly said, all those years ago, that a traitor within; "...Rots the soul of the nation; he works secretly; an unknown in the night, to undermine the pillars of the city; he infects the body politic so it can no longer resist. A murderer is less to be feared". **(374).** So nothing really changes, history carries many warnings and answers to our problems.

White was to see his carefully laid plans for China start to bear fruit when in January, 1947 the Communist army of General Lin Piao started its offensive that would capture Nationalist China for Communist domination.

The Stage was set for the biggest confidence trick yet on the people of the world. The false cold war between Russia and the West that was to see millions die in wars and terrorist action, funded by the bankers and planned by Communists to bring their revolution nearer to their goal, 'One World Government'. During this so called 'Cold War' the bankers were pouring billions of dollars into Russia to build its industry and fund its armies. As we have already seen, American made war weapons and transport, were used by the North Vietnamese against America's own soldiers. This alone should make every American soldier determined to rid its government of every Communist infiltrator.

But to do so now would require a well founded and sustained attack on the American Administration and a campaign against International Bankers interference in government.

In David Rees' book on "Harry Dexter White" **(375)** we begin to see how the world Bank fell into the hands of private investors. After the war there were few countries able to act as guarantor for loans as the national budgets were diminished by war. So the World Bank turned to private investors, mainly from Wall Street sources. In 1947 a Wall Street Lawyer, J. McCoy became President of the World Bank and in March 1947 the Wall Street financier, Eugine R. Black was appointed as the new American executive of the Bank.

It was at the end of March that Harry Dexter White wrote his letter of resignation to Truman **(376)**:

Dear Mr. President,

I am writing to submit my resignation as US. Executive Director of the International Monetary Fund. I have for some time cherished the idea of returning to private enterprise but did not want to leave the Government until the Bretton Woods organisations, in which I am so deeply interested, were well launched. The work of the fund is now off to a good start. The period of active operations is just beginning, and this is an opportunity for my successor to take over.

In the absence of Mr. Gutt, who is in Europe on business for the fund, I am acting Chairman, and have promised to remain until he returns in the early part of May.

I want to thank you, Mr. President, for your confidence in me and for the opportunity you gave me as US. Executive Director of the Fund, to help bring the Bretton Woods proposals to realization. I shall continue to follow their work closely and will of course be glad to help any time I am called upon.

It has been a source of satisfaction and encouragement to me to know of your keen interest in the Fund and your policy of bending every effort towards achieving a stable and prosperous world economy. I shall always remember with pleasure my connection with your Administration.

Please accept my warm personal regards and good wishes. Respectfully yours,

Harry D. White.

As you can see he made sure his men (The bankers men) were in place before he left; in this way the system (Bretton Woods) would move forward under guidance from Wall Street and their World Agenda. It was that simple.

At White's last public appearance on April 3rd. 1947, he made sure that one part of his Bretton Woods plan, an International Trade Organisation would be accepted as an independent part of his complete plan. **(377).** (This is the forerunner to the World Trade Organisation 'WTO').

White's successor at the International Monetary Fund followed the same pattern as the bank. Andrew N. Overby, a former assistant Vice President of the Federal Reserve Bank of New York and the Irving Trust Company of Number 1, Wall Street.

Although White's fund and bank (The International Monetary Fund) became almost redundant after his departure, it was coincidental. It was because Bretton Woods did not offer solutions to war depression and insolvency felt by Britain and

Europe that the Marshall Plan was developed to help German industry recover, which offered better terms and future results, something White fought against while in office, reflected in his plan for Germany after the war.. In his opinion Germany should have been crushed. Luckily American politics decided differently.

One more agreement was signed in October 1947 at Geneva at the second attempt, that is now considered the most troublesome piece of international entente ever ratified, the General Agreement on Tariffs and Trade (GATT) so frequently the source of friction between America and Europe.

A setback occurred in August 1947 when the conversion agreement was cancelled, because Britain entered a period of serious balance of payment problems, and the multilateral agreements of Bretton Woods seemed to be in tatters. The loan from America quickly changed the course to rebuild Western Europe, recognising Britain was no longer a force in the top league. (This of course does not include the City Establishment who by then were international players largely divorced from political interference).

White in the meantime had moved on and was now a financial consultant. One of his clients was the Council of Jewish Federation and Welfare Fund, where he worked on a committee to outline specific types of additional studies that would be most appropriate and helpful to the projected Institute of Overseas Studies. **(378).**

It was to be twenty years, when the fund introduced drawing rights, that the fund would slowly build its potential to satisfy multilateral demand. White's proposals were never delivered, they included a plan to increase world liquidity through 'Trade Gold', sponsored by the fund. In doing so he was admitting Bretton Woods had been very disappointing.

One of White's last thrusts at America came in his support of Henry Wallace as a third party candidate in the 1948 Presidential elections. Henry Wallace had been sacked by Truman (asked to resign) because of a Madison Square Gardens speech supporting a pro Russian policy. White by now had suffered his first heart attack, yet ahead of him was the Grand Jury. **(379).**

Miss Bentley, at the hearing, admitted as a Communist, of being in contact with the spy ring in which Harry Dexter White, Silvermaster and others were involved. She also said "White would also help to get people of Communist sympathies into government employment". This she stated was second hand information given to her by Silvermaster.

Chambers, in his evidence, as an Ex-Communist, admitted he could not say if White was a card member of the Communist Party. However it is well known that people in his position (White) often avoid joining the cause they support, to make identification more difficult when exposed.

White, despite his health, put up a vigorous defence and denied knowing Chambers.

Before the hearing could reach a conclusion Harry Dexter White died of a heart attack on the afternoon of August 16th. 1948 at his home at Blueberry Hill, leaving a incomplete trial and a debate that would live on.

Today, of his guilt, there is no doubt. Though of his sincerity as an International Zionist, he saw the world as his state, as Weishaupt before him. This could be described as a greedy goal for such a minority group, but behind them then and today, they have money power, bought political power, the media and a whole host of Radical Liberal institutions like the Council on Foreign Relations, the United Nations and the Foundations, and, above all, they control money creation throughout the world, which brings them great power and profit. However this is their Achilles Heel, that we can use to advantage to halt their progress.

Perhaps the final official words on Harry Dexter White came from the Attorney General, Herbert Brownall, at an address given to the Executive's Club in Chicago **(380)**: "Harry Dexter White was a Russian spy. He smuggled secret documents to Russian agents for transmission to Moscow. Harry Dexter White was known to be a Communist agent by the very people who appointed him to the most sensitive position he ever held in Government service".

"...I can now announce officially, for the first time in public, that the records in my department show that White's spying activities for the Soviet Government were reported in detail by the FBI to the White House...in December 1945. In the face of this information, and incredible though it may seem, President Truman subsequently on January the twenty-third, 1946, nominated White who was then Assistant Secretary of the Treasury, for the even more important position of Executive Director for the United States in the International Monetary Fund".

That was a condemnation of those who had appointed him to high office, but it is also a warning to us to be more careful in choosing our political representatives. It seems only when the news of White's activities could no longer be hidden, Truman did something about it, which puts into doubt where his sympathies lie.

Without a doubt, White's combined policies, while in the Treasury Department and later in the IMF, encompassing Bretton Woods' Three Point Plan for a Multinational Controlled World, have dominated American politics since the Second World War albeit with ups and downs.

Today the International Monetary Fund still exists along with the World Bank, and GATT is still causing friction between Europe and America. The United Nations is the centre of 'One World' planning and is now policing the World, preparing it for Federalisation as we have seen in Kosovo and now in East Timor. What we must realise is that this is nothing to do with coming to the rescue of ethnic minorities as our politicians try to instil into our minds, but it is a ruthless attempt to prepare Europe and the Pacific Rim for Federalisation as Regional Governments within a 'One World Order'; Weishaupt's plan. So unless you want to see Communism taking over our lives we must act now to stop Federalisation of Europe and the Pacific Rim. In Britain we must say **NO** to the single currency as this will block and delay Federalisation. In the Pacific Rim we must make sure that the Governments know the agenda that awaits their surrender.

Without White's dedicated work and planning, the world would today be a far safer place. But we cannot go back and cancel a part of history, we must, even at this late hour, learn lessons and start the fight back.

The Globalists are building their World Government before our eyes, bit by bit, driven by planning from the Foundations for the Council on Foreign Relations who control the direction of the United Nations and also the foreign policy of the United States. Let us remind ourselves who funded the Council on Foreign Relations; not Government, but J.P.Morgan, John D. Rockefeller, Paul Warburg (Rothschild's agent in America), and Jacob Schiff; the very same group of banking barons who forced the Federal Reserve Bank system on a reluctant Government in 1913, and who were also responsible for introducing the graduated income tax to America, to pay for the interest charged on created money, a tax that goes totally into bankers' pockets for creating new money for the minimal cost of printing; a rip off that continues today all over the world. To realise the significance of this move to central banking and graduated income tax, both central banking and graduated income tax are major policy pillars of the Communist Manifesto published in 1848, and appear in Clinton Roosevelt's book "The Science of Government Founded on Natural Law". **(381).** So we can see the early connection to the Illuminati, who, through Karl Marx, created Communism.

Colonel House, President Wilson's close advisor, wrote an anonymous book, "Philip Dru - Administrator" **(382),** in which he discussed plans for a 'One World Totalitarian Government' along the lines of Karl Marx. (Page 45). So the planning towards Globalism was thorough, going back to Weishaupt's presence in America under General Pike (The evil Lusifarian) preparing the ground for insiders like Colonel House to be in position by the beginning of the 1900's. Remember what Carroll Quigley said in "Tragedy and Hope" **(383)**; "The CFR is a front for the International Bankers and the elitist insiders". As documented earlier, the Council On Foreign Relations is the American branch of the Institute of International Affairs in England. So we can see from this that the bankers who control American and British politics, control the two major money markets in the world, and from this point can dictate policies. So it is no surprise that from within this network of power we are being forced into agreements that suit the bankers and multinational companies but are nothing but bad news for Nation States and their peoples.

Let's take a brief look at some of the international agreements that have been forced upon a largely ignorant world.

CHAPTER FOURTEEN, PART THREE.

THE GATT AGREEMENT.

GATT is short for General Agreement on Tariffs and Trade. It is an international trade agreement that controls the moving of goods and services across national borders, by requiring countries to reduce tariffs. Recently they have extended their power to include non tariff barriers to trade, to include regulations and subsidies.

It was first introduced in 1947 at the Uruguay round of the Multilateral Negotiations and it was signed by representatives of 125 nations embodying the 'Final Act' in Morocco on April 15th. 1994. This act contains 26,000 pages, insuring no politician or any pressure group could read, let alone understand, its contents. An abridged version of 500 pages has proved unobtainable to most applicants.

As we have already seen, the World Trade Organisation was given a kiss of life by GATT, elevating it into a central trading authority which will become the most powerful economic and political body in the global world of the power barons.

The proof of this came from Daniel Esty of the Council on Foreign Relations in a November issue of the CFR Journal 'Foreign Affairs' **(384).** "....by enshrining the principle of Liberal trade in the international regime the creators of the GATT elevated the commitment to freer trade to a nearly constitutional level, thereby limiting the power of governments around the world to give in to the pleadings of domestic interests seeking to hide from the rigors of the global market place". The dangers of this are great, as we are now seeing where Europe does not wish to import hormone fed beef, but may be forced by GATT to do so, even though they do not consider this practice to be safe.

GATT goes on to say in article XVI-4; "Each member (Nation) shall ensure the conformity of its laws" (Just like the EU is demanding). Thus GATT can override our National Laws. Where have you seen that before? From the European Courts of Justice and EU law. Now can you see how the EU is just a part of the global plan?

So GATT forces nations to drop their national law to comply with an almost world wide agreement. This is preparing the world for a system where the bankers and multinational companies (Heading for collectivism which is Communism) can move production at will and ignore national interests and laws. This is bad news for employment, and bad news for the Sovereignty, of a Nation, and is devastation for us, its peoples.

A strong national economy is totally dependent on producing its own needs, food and consumer goods. When a nation becomes dependent on foreign imports, it is vulnerable to pressures to accept laws that are not good for its national well-being. All policy accepted by nations should bear this in mind. (Information from the Social Creditor Vol. 74 no. 6, November-December 1995).

MAI AGREEMENT.

(NOT YET SIGNED).

The MAI agreement is the 'Multilateral Agreement on Investment'. It has been discussed, behind closed doors since 1995 in Paris by twenty nine of the worlds wealthy nations that belong to the OECD, the 'Organisation of Economic Co-operation and Development'.

Why is it secret? Because Clinton and his Radical Liberal administration and advisors don't think Congress or the people of the world need to know. But the Multinationals know about it; they have been consulted and asked to contribute policies that suit them. But Unions and Environmental and Community Groups have been excluded.

MAI is designed to multiply the power of corporations over local government and to eliminate policies that could restrict the movement of factories and money around the world. It places corporate profits above all other values. (For the bankers no doubt). If introduced in its present form, the MAI would radically limit our ability to promote social, economic and environmental justice. In other words it puts our democracy at risk.

The MAI by-passes our democracy by empowering foreign corporations to sue governments directly for cash compensation for failure to enforce MAI.

Taxpayers would be required to pay this fine. We must stop this act at all costs if we care for our social structure and our environment.

The MAI would set strongly enforced global rules limiting governments' rights and ability to regulate foreign investors and corporations. Specifically, it would;

* Empower foreign corporations to sue the federal government over federal, state and local laws, which could force governments to pay damage and - or overturn their laws. (Investor to State Dispute Settlement).

* Require governments, as a result of binding arbitration, to compensate foreign corporations for laws that could limit corporate profits, such as environmental, human rights, labour, public health, consumer protection and local community development standards. Believe it or not, this would even apply to government policies that could limit future profits. (Establishes a global "regulatory takings" law.).

Prevent governments from promoting local businesses by requiring that foreign corporations be treated at least as favourably as domestic companies. Foreign corporations could be treated better than domestic companies, however. (National Treatment).

Require countries to treat investors from any country in the same manner, preventing any country or state from using human rights, labour or environmental standards as investment criteria. (Most Favoured Nation).

Keep governments from requiring foreign corporations to meet certain conditions, such as maintaining and investment in a community for a set amount of time, using recycled or domestic content in manufacturing, or hiring local workers even if the same requirements are applied to domestic investments. (Performance Requirement).

Include a bag of tricks such as roll-back and stand still that further advance economic deregulation.

Bind all signatory countries to these obligations for a minimum of 20 years.

> **We are writing the constitution of a single global economy.**
>
> **Renato Ruggerio, Director General of the World Trade Organisation (WTO), October 8th. 1996, speech presented to the UNCTAD Trade Development Board.**

WHAT DOES THIS MEAN FOR OUR COMMUNITY?

It means your community could not require a foreign corporation to hire local people, use recycled materials, use parts made in Britain, or enter into joint ventures as a condition of operating in our community. (That applies to every nation that signs the agreement).

If your community wanted to give a low-interest loan to a local company, it would have to offer the same low-interest loan to a foreign corporation.

If your community tried to enact these or similar measures, foreign corporations could sue your government for interfering with their right to profit that is assured by MAI. The foreign corporation could choose the forum for the lawsuit, including the International Chamber of Commerce. The community would not be able to represent its interests in these disputes when brought before such private groups. Rather, the federal government would defend the case behind closed doors.

> This (MAI) could well be the most anti-democratic, anti-people, anti-community international agreement ever conceived by supposedly democratic Governments.
>
> David Korten, Author "When Corporations Rule the World".

Does this seem far fetched? It isn't. Already using an MAI-like provision of NAFTA, the US-based Ethyl Corporation has sued the Canadian government for $251 million in damages related to a public health and safety law. This law effectively bans a gasoline additive (MMT) produced exclusively by Ethyl Corp. MMT has been banned in many US states because it harms cars' pollution control systems and is a suspected toxic substance. Ethyl says it should be compensated under NAFTA because the Canadian law will hurt its potential future profits and harm its reputation. This pending case is just a preview of coming attractions if the MAI goes into effect.

The MAI is a wolf in sheep's clothing. Its proponents insist that it is just trying to get the same treatment for all investors and their assets. In fact it is threatening our democracy. With the MAI in effect, Congress, a State Legislature, or a Town Council, considering a new law would have to worry about whether some foreign company might sue them for cash compensation.

ITS A BAD DEAL FOR ALL WORKING PEOPLE.

The MAI would establish and consolidate extensive rights for investors and corporations while limiting existing protections for labour. As a result, the standard of living and the rights of the working people in the United States and world-wide would be threatened in a number of ways. Here are a few:

Foreign corporations would be exempt from many national, state and local initiatives that promote local employment and investments because the MAI bans performance standards and other policies that target specific kinds of development such as small business.

No one would be able to require foreign firms to hire a certain percentage of local residents. They could not be required to use domestic materials, which create local jobs.

The MAI makes it easier for corporations to move capital where and when it is most profitable with little accountability. This would accelerate plant closings and job loss in the US as corporations seek lower wages and labour standards, especially as developing countries are pressured into signing the MAI.

As has already been shown, corporations can use the threat of moving to other countries to diminish union organising power. The MAI would dramatically increase their ability to use this threat.

IT'S AN ENVIRONMENTAL HAZARD.

The MAI would pose an immediate threat to environmental protection. Regulating business operations is vital to controlling environmental damage. The gravest threat to government's power to regulate is in the MAI's provisions on expropriation, and the ability of foreign corporations to sue governments if policies undermine planned profits.

By allowing foreign corporations to challenge environmental and health regulations in special 'Corporate Courts', the MAI would arm investors to:

Halt future government actions for a safe and healthy environment. Here's how:

TOXICS: If the MAI becomes law, many federal, state and local laws governing toxics would be endangered. Foreign companies could claim that the value of their investments would decline due to policies restricting toxic emissions or disposal practices. As in the Ethyl case just cited, investors are already trying to intimidate governments and forestall regulation by suing for large sums.

PROCUREMENT: Federal, state and local governments are at last beginning to introduce social concerns into how they spend taxpayers' money. An executive order directs federal (America) agencies to buy 'Green' products, such as those made with recycled content or using renewable energy. Cities and counties are moving in this direction too. These good efforts would run foul of the MAI which would ban any performance requirements; for instance, offering priority to companies using best environmental practices.

SUSTAINABILITY AND NATURAL RESOURCES: The MAI clashes with the move towards a more sustainable future, which many believe should be built on small-scale enterprises and local control of resources. The MAI would also guarantee large multinational corporations with new rights to establish mining, timber or other natural resource-exploiting investments. The MAI could be used to overcome moratoria on such destructive activities. The planet simply cannot afford to be bound by the MAI rules for twenty years. (Maybe after twenty years the bankers dictatorship will rule the world unless we stop it).

This act we must stop at all costs if we care for our social structure and our environment.

O.E.C.D. AGREEMENT.

O.E.C.D. is the Organisation for Economic Co-operation and Development. It is a intergovernmental organisation representing twenty nine advanced economies from Europe, North America, and the Pacific Rim. (The third area being federalised for world government). The O.E.C.D. is a collection centre for data and performs economic analysis, (slanted towards global government). It is considered the 'Think Tank' of the industrialised world. The MAI agreement is its first major attempt to introduce binding international rules. Funded by bankers for their benefit and the benefit of multinational companies.

WTO.

The WTO is the World Trade Organisation, which was formed by the 1994 Uruguay round of GATT negotiations to oversee and enforce GATT trading rules. In 1996 WTO established a trade group to consider if and how the WTO should regulate foreign investment. Potential WTO investment rules are called Multilateral Investment Agreements (MIA), not to be confused with the MAI that is being negotiated at the O.E.C.D.

So you can see that the Anglo American banking establishment has put in place a whole mechanism of undemocratic authority funded largely by their own sphere of influence or by our tax contributions. It is designed to side-step national sovereign interests (our interests) to create a world where a small group of bankers and industrialists, (through collective Communist practice) can ignore national working practice, stop national subsidies for national industries, move work around the world to the cheapest areas like China, ignore national currency laws, ignore local environmental law and generally limit a nations ability to promote social, economic, and environmental justice. In effect it puts our democratic process out of business. **Do YOU want that?**

(This information comes from a group in America set up to fight the MAI agreement. Take a look on their website;

http:www.greenecon.org/MAI/index.html). (386).

The history book shows that the World Trade Organisation was first the brain child of none other than Harry Dexter White, (Communist) under the name of the World Trade Board, and born from discussion at the Bretton Woods conferences. It was later named the International Trade Organisation (ITO); finally to take on its present name, World Trade Organisation (WTO) in 1994. The New York Times actually described it as the 'Third Pillar of the New World Order' along side the International Monetary Fund and the United Nations, all of which Harry Dexter White played a major role in creating.

This of course, is the behind the scenes work, going on to move the world to a one world, global government, controlled by Communist policies from Weishaupt and Marx for the benefit of the Anglo American Establishment, dominated by Internationalists and multinational barons who see Communism as their future. The men controlling the scheme are called the Guardians. Unfortunately the people do not come into their consideration as you can see when studying the MAI agreement alone.

We must now look back at the words of the awakened financier, Sir James Goldsmith, who was at one time in the camp of the elite but was converted to realism by a patient brother. He said in an article in the Washington times (387); "Global free trade will force the poor of the rich countries to subsidise the rich in the poor countries. What GATT means is that our national wealth, accumulated over the centuries will be transferred from a developed country like Britain... to developing countries like China, now building its first ocean-going navy in 500 years".

"China can supply skilled labour for a fraction of Western costs. (Confirmation where production will go). It is quite amazing that GATT is sowing the seeds' of global social upheaval (MAI) and it is not even the subject of debate in America...(It is now, thanks to Goldsmith and many others). If the masses understand the truth about GATT, there would be blood in the streets of many capitals. **A healthy national economy has to produce a large part of its own needs.** It cannot simply import what it needs and use its labour forces to provide services to other countries". (That means we must produce our own food and a large part of our own consumer goods).

"We have to rethink from top to bottom why we have elevated global free trade to the status of sacred cow or moral dogma. It is a fatally flawed concept that will impoverish and destabilise the industrial world while cruelly ravishing the 'Third World'. (previously shown but reprinted to remind us of this plot to enslave mankind).

The truth is out, from the brave words of a Jewish Financier. Words that would damage his former associates but nevertheless bravely spoken. It is the truth we must take on board.

PROTOCOL THIRTEEN
DISTRACTIONS.

The need for daily bread forces the goyim to keep silence and be our humble servants. Agents taken on to our press from among the goyim will at our orders discuss anything which is convenient for us to issue directly in official documents, and we meanwhile, quietly amid the din of the discussion so raised, shall simply take and carry through such measures as we wish and then offer them to the public as an accomplished fact. No one will dare to demand the abrogation of a matter once settled, all the more so
as it will be represented as an improvement...and immediately the press will distract the current of thought towards new questions. Have we not trained people always to be seeking something new? Into the discussions of these new questions will throw themselves those of the brainless dispensers of fortunes who are not able even now to understand that they have not the remotest conception about the matters which they undertake to discuss. Questions of the political are beyond the comprehension of any save those who have guided it already for many ages, the creators.

From all this you will see that in securing the opinion of the mob we are only facilitating the working of our machinery, and you may remark that it is not for actions but for words issued by us on this or that question that we seem to seek approval. We are constantly making public declaration that we are guided in all our undertakings by the hope, joined to the conviction, that we are serving the common weal.

In order to distract people who may be too troublesome from discussing questions of the political we are now putting forward what we allege to be new questions of the political, namely, questions of industry (GATT, WTO, MAI etc.). In this sphere let them discuss themselves silly! The masses agree to remain inactive, to take a rest from what they suppose to be political activity, in which we trained them in order to use them as a means of combating the goy governments, only on condition of being found new employments, in which we are prescribing them something that looks like the same political object. In order that the masses themselves may not guess what they are about, **we further distract them with** amusements, games, pastimes, passions, people's palaces....Soon we shall begin through the press to propose competitions in art, in sport of all kinds: these interests will finally distract their minds from questions in which we should find ourselves compelled to oppose them. Growing more and more unaccustomed to reflect and form any opinion of their own, people will begin to talk in the same tones as we, because we alone shall be offering them new directions for thought...of course through such persons as will not be suspected of solidarity with us.

The part played by the liberals, utopian dreamers, will be finally played out when our government is acknowledged. Till such time, they will continue to do us good service. Therefore we shall continue to direct their minds to all sorts of vain conceptions of fantastic theories, new and apparently progressive: for have we not with complete success turned the brainless heads of the goyim with progress, till there is not among the goyim one mind able to perceive that under this word lies a departure from truth in all cases where it is not a question of material inventions, for truth is one, and in it there is no place for progress. Progress, like a fallacious idea, serves to obscure truth so that none may know it except us, the chosen of God, its guardians. (Their God is Satan, their hidden truth **Deception).**

When we come into our kingdom our orators will expound great problems which have turned humanity upside down in order to bring it in the end under our beneficial rule.

Who will ever suspect then that all these peoples were stage-managed by us according to a political plan which no one has so much as guessed at in the course of many centuries?

COMMENT

Now we see the policy of distraction. We see it every day in Soaps on television, in the way sport is being produced. Politics is put in the background, sex is promoted and the decline of moral standards is on display daily on the television and in a large range of magazines and papers, all of which are in the hands of the global promoters, the Bankers and their sphere of influence.

They show how they will control our minds, a policy that was perfected by the KGB in the Soviet Union, part of the global plotters.

They confirm their tight hold on the press.

They claim they are chosen by God. The god they refer to is Satan, the god that descended to earth not the true God of Heaven. They are, if not practising, using Atheism to take charge of our souls and our mind and corrupt us in Satan's path.

If we are to halt this monster, all religions must come together in a holy combat against this evil scheme that has been, over the years, hidden from our view by the press, the traitors to our democracy.

CHAPTER FIFTEEN
PART ONE.
THE BILDERBERG GROUP.

Politically denied by officials throughout Europe and America, the Bilderberg group meets once a year, to discuss international politics, and move the global aspirations of bankers and Communism forward towards their intended goal, 'World Government'.

Those who attend the meeting are invited by the steering committee, and are chosen because they have shown sympathy towards the policy of collectivism on a world scale; so leaders of multinational corporations, international bankers, politicians, media magnates, high ranking military and academic figures are included in the guest list.

The meetings, once a year since 1954, have been held in different countries; on each occasion under tight security, enforced by the top national security of that country with help from the CIA. So secret are these talks that no participant can speak about them, no press release is prepared after they finish, and no press articles appear in the national news despite the fact that the media can claim between 20 and 25% of members.

The driving force who started the Bilderberg group was Joseph H Ritinger, a man with a remarkable address book full of top members of European and American society, probably prepared for him by the bankers behind the society, (Rothschild and Rockefeller). The Rothschilds in particular, nearly always installed a trusted front man to promote their will rather than appear as the promoters themselves. Examples of this can be found in the Civil War in America where their interests were served by August Shoenberg in the North, and Judah Benjamin, the Secretary of State for the Confederacy. Another example was Paul Warburg, a Rothschild agent who set up the Federal Reserve Bank system for the Rothschilds, the power behind the money creating banking monopoly in America. This was brought to public notice by Colonel Ely Garrison, financial advisor to Woodrow Wilson and Teddy Roosevelt when he said; "Paul Warburg was the man who got the Federal Reserve Act together after the Aldrich plan aroused such nation-wide resentment and opposition. The mastermind of both plans was Baron Alfred Rothschild of London". **(388).**

It is therefore not surprising that we find that our two prime world banking families have hosted the Bilderberg meetings in America at the Woodstock Inn in Vermont and Williamsburg, Virginia, both owned by the Rockefellers. We also find the same in Europe at the Hotel d'Arbois at Megeve in the French Alps, owned by the Rothschilds. Another world billionaire Wallenburg was the host at Saltsjobaden in Sweden. What we are beginning to see is that a small group of very powerful, rich men are trying to move the politics of the world to suit their aims to not only control the world financially, but to by-pass national politics and control the world through global law, global banking, a global army (the United Nations), and only three regional governments; Europe, The Pacific Rim and the Confederate States of America. (North and South including Canada).

If we now look at just a few of the regular participants we begin to see a super power structure of banking, political, and media power. The present Chairman is Lord Carrington, Margaret Thatcher's Foreign Minister, a banker, and Director of Kissinger Associates. Henry Kissinger, Nixon's Secretary of State and director of Kissinger Associates along with Lord Carrington. John R. Galvin, who was Supreme Allied Commander of Europe. Queen Beatrix of the Netherlands whose husband Prince Bernhard was the first Chairman. Queen Sophia of Spain. The famous Liberal media mogul, Katherine Graham, Chairwomen of the Washington Post. Robert Bartley, editor of the Wall Street Journal. Giovvanni Agnelli, Chairman of Fiat. David Rockefeller, head of the Chase Manhattan Bank. A past regular member was Bill Clinton while he was Governor of Arkansas. We also find politicians littering the invitation list, who must first prove their support for a one world government, such as Gordon Brown, Tony Blair and the previous Conservative Chancellor Kenneth Clarke. Yet we find that political, media and government sources deny that these meetings exist.

In Des Griffin's book he goes as far as to say that there will be; "A global army at the disposal of the United Nations, which is to become the world government (George Bush's New World Order) to which all nations will be subservient by the year 2000" (But like all plans running late). **(389).** The date might be a little out, like Orwell, but the process is moving on a pace. We see the United Nations meddling in everything that disrupts the path to Globalism already. The United Nations is seeking enforcement powers to act globally without individual members giving their consent.

This is what a prime mover, Dr. Henry Kissinger said; "A UN army must be able to act immediately, anywhere in the world, without the delay involved in each country making its own decision whether to participate, based on parochial considerations...." **(390).**

An interesting statistic which Des Griffin brings out **(391)** is that nearly every member from the United States who attends the Bilderberg meetings is or has been a member of the Council on Foreign Relations, a Weishaupt influenced organisation, that controls America's foreign policy.

Another interesting piece of the puzzle is that Kenneth Clarke, a former Conservative Minister, wrote a book on Ruskin, the arch disciple of Weishaupt who brought his policies into the twentieth century through Rhodes and his backers, led by the Rothschilds. So linkages begin to appear from strange directions and not from where you might expect them to appear.

I will be approaching the research on Bilderberg in what may seem a rather haphazard manner, dealing with evidence outside a strict historical order. For this I make no apology as I find that by dealing with it in this manner it becomes clearer why the Bilderberg Group was formed in the first place, and why, for those who control it, its content must remain a secret, denied by governments and power barons alike.

If we go back to **(392)** Arnold Toynbee's speech at the fourth annual conference of the Institutions for the Scientific Study of International Relations in Copenhagen June the Eighth-tenth, 1931, and promoted by the League of Nations, you begin to hear the words of Weishaupt given public airing and debated by semi-official organisations that now control foreign policy in the world. This meeting was the source that built the power structure that has rejected all democratic input to promote its narrow undemocratic single course to its aim, one world control through undemocratic methods. We see in Toynbee's speech that his perception of human affairs is that even in 1931 they were all international. Was this true or just a dream of internationalists? Ample evidence, already presented shows that internationalism is driven, not by the people of the nations, but by a small group of international bankers and multinational corporations intent on by-passing national sovereign laws for their own profit.

Toynbee tries to excuse his ideas as a matter of history and lays the end result on the sailors who circumnavigated the world. What utter arrogant convenience to find an innocent scapegoat. In fact the internationalists were very busy at this time establishing their structures, always semi-official, to move the world from nation state status to world control under a federalist, collective system. (Communism **DIRECTION**). Examples we can find are numerous; the Covenant of the League of Nations, the Multilateral Treaty of Paris for the Renunciation of War as an Instrument of National Policy, the Statute of the Permanent Court of International Justice, the General Act of Arbitration and Conciliation, the World Disarmament Conference and so on. It was a time to globalise everything that moved. Luckily, through the sense of the American Senate, who at that time were highly suspicious of Globalists, the League of Nations was rejected, only to find that the Communists, led by Alger Hiss and Harry Dexter White were to set the stage for the United Nations, its successor, at a time when the world was weary of war and therefore vulnerable.

Toynbee, like all Weishaupt's disciples, used deceit to achieve his goals quite clearly laid before the assembly in these words; "In the spirit of determination which happily animates us, we have no inclination to under-estimate the strength of the political force which we are striving to overcome. What is this force? If we are frank with ourselves, we shall admit that we are engaged in a deliberate and sustained (Weishaupt style) and concentrated effort to impose limitations upon the sovereignty and the independence of the fifty or sixty local sovereign independent states which at present partition the habitable surface of the earth and divide the political allegiance of mankind. The surest sign, to my mind, that this fetish of local national sovereignty is our intended victim is the emphasis with which all our statesmen and our publicists (The media) project with one accord, and over and over again, at every step forward which we take, that whatever changes we may make in the international situation, the sacred principle of local sovereignty will be maintained inviolable….. It is just we are really attacking the principle of local sovereignty that we keep on protesting our loyalty to it so loudly. The harder we press our attack upon the idol, the more pains we take to keep its priests and devotees in a fool's paradise".

Here we see quite clearly the Weishaupt policy to kill national pride and the sovereign state. This is also the aim of Communism. It is also the hidden aim of the European Union, an even though we hear official protest, federalism is to take over from sovereignty and already is eating away at the nation state. Toynbee tells us they lie to hide the truth; Edward Heath, according to the Referendum Party, did exactly that over sovereignty, **(393)** when advised to do so by Jean Monnet, the so called godfather of the European Union.

To accept Internationalism you must also accept your own loss of national sovereignty, whatever country you live in. You must be prepared to have your law administered from a remote, unrepresentative body, divorced from your National interests, who look to global rulers for their guidance. Your taxes will be fixed to suit a third of the world, not your own nation with its own problems, often so different from other nations. (Once tax collection goes to Federal Europe, it has gone for good under internationalism). Your defences will again rely on a World Task Force who will not see events as your National Army would, within a democratic government system.

Worst of all Globalism will allow international companies to ignore local health and environmental laws at their will. (One of the aims of the MAI agreement). Finally you must accept Communism as the only world political movement. Can you accept any of these? You might say, What is this to do with the Bilderberg Group? Everything.

At the end of World War II we saw another dramatic change in the content and ownership of our media and national press. During the War, while we were fighting for our very existence, the Globalists were plotting their coupe and the first mechanism that they thrust upon us was the United Nations.

As we have already seen, the United Nations, was planned during the war and in the planning, was the knowledge that the launch of the new world organisation was to be timed to use the vacuum of war weary nations directly after the trauma of the war years. It was to be gut reaction that drove nations to sign up to this 'Last Chance for Mankind', without proper examination of the plans or the caution of in depth research into the movement's origin.

Meanwhile the media was changing; changing hands and changing its direction. Items which had been treated up to this point as mainstream middle of the road, began to have a new label, suddenly they were being described as right wing, not just by the socialist media but by the so called conservative tabloids as well. So we found that institutions of our establishment that were considered national cultures, including morals were gradually being shifted to a false labelling of right wing thinking on the fringe. This pattern change in the media is shown in Colonel Turner's brilliant analysis. **(394).** The change that Colonel Turner reports, is from an industry that represented all political wings in many publications, highly controlled by its new owners, the bankers, but still outwardly diverse in politics to suit the mirror they want us to believe, while behind the scenes they reserve the right to silence any news that goes against their goal for world government. This effectively produces a one sided debate from which we form our opinions. (Remember, on the whole, we form our opinions from the contents of our media).

Two Royal Commissions on the media in 1947-1949 and 1961-1962 failed to redress the problems of who owned the press and the dangers of the press passing into the hands of a small group of powerful people whose aims were anti national and intent on destroying the ordered democracy of national sovereignty. Big empires were growing up that breached national boundaries to become global media cartels with immense power at their finger tips to control the minds of their sphere of readership. We see the Canadian based Hollinger Group, with a turnover of over seven-hundred-million dollars, owning over 200 newspapers and magazines in the USA and Canada as well as in the UK (where they own the Daily Telegraph, a right wing quality paper). On their board of directors we find Lord Carrington and Dr. Henry Kissinger, both leaders in the Bilderberg Group (Lord Carrington being Chairman), Peter Bronfman, Paul Reichmann, and Sir Evelyn de Rothschild.

Conrad Black, the Chairman of the Hollinger Group is a member of the Institute for Strategic Studies, the Trilateral Commission, and the steering committee of the Bilderberg Group. (The Inner planning council).

The second big, and empire was Rupert Murdoch's News International. This was financed by Edgar Bronfman, Harry Openheimer, the Rothschild family and the late Armand Hammer, of Occidental Petrol. Murdoch made massive purchases, beyond the ability of any single unsupported media mogul.

Murdoch bought newspapers, magazines, publishing houses, film studios, television, media distribution companies and newsprint in a big way.

In London alone he controlled the Times and Sunday Times, (quality papers) the Sun, Today, and the News of the World, (mass media) and although this concentration of ownership passed through the control system, it was against all the guidelines laid down to prevent this happening. Even more sinister was Murdoch's move into children's publishing and Television and its influence on education. **(395).**

Murdoch is now truly global with media in Europe, Australia, The UK, America, and now the Pacific Rim.

Robert Maxwell was, till his death, another chosen developer of banker power media, financed and controlled by the bankers' agenda for world control. We saw in his portfolio of purchases the same domination of media, including children's publishing and an added speciality, data control. Companies included Global Analysis Systems, the government agency Professional and Executive Recruitment, the publisher Macmillan and Co. of New York, (the publisher of the original 'Tragedy and Hope' by Carroll Quigley) which included BRS Technologies, another data base company.

What should horrify us all about this drift of media and information data into a small minority group's hands with an endless money facility, is that influence can, and is, being used by these media groups to channel opinion towards global government, while still seeming to represent the broad mix of political opinion, which is another mirror in front of our eyes, hiding their true intent.

We should also make sure the watchdogs do more than lip service when protecting our democracy from minority monopolies like these.

Watchdogs are expensive, and are a waste of money, if, as the end result, they do nothing to protect us from media purchase by the Globalists or other minority interests.

Their appointment should be thoroughly researched to avoid appointing a member of, in this case, the globalist sphere of influence, or any other similar group.

From this learning exercise outside the Bilderberg Group, you will have seen the tentacles of their influence spread; controlled by the power structure of Globalism that joins in the planning of global manipulation of nation states, by their own media, and their own bankers; both of them have long since sold out to international global dictatorship while protesting their allegiance to national sovereignty. They are the traitors within our gates.

"Spotlight" is the publication from Washington DC that has highlighted Bilderberg Group meetings and published names of participants as well as details of content. It listed fifty leading media representatives that were also members of the Council on Foreign Relations, many of whom were regular participants at the Bilderberg Group and the Trilateral Commission. This shows how these groups spread their sphere of influence, and control America's, and Britain's, foreign policy through a handful of powerful, non-government, pressure groups, well funded and established to develop and control the world movement to global dictatorship.

A strong offensive against the movement to Globalism cannot be found anywhere in America and Britain. The agenda of the media was all tied up with the

International Finance Capitalists, so they could not find the means and financial support to promote a counter offensive against the destroyers. The International Finance Capitalists alone are our true enemy within, not Communism. Communism is just one of their instruments used to promote their will. So too is Liberalism, although most Liberals would adamantly deny this truth.

By the early 50's it became apparent to the bankers that their efforts were getting lost because of lack of co-ordination. It was decided by David Rockefeller and others that a planning group should be formed to co-ordinate their efforts towards a global world economy. A steering committee was formed and Dr. Retinger, through his impressive list of contacts, asked Prince Bernhard of the Netherlands to be its first chairman. (The Bankers usually chose people to front their groups who have a questionable background. All the secret work was decided behind closed doors by the steering committee, a group of trusted devotees of the Bankers, such as Conrad Black of the Hollinger Group. Dr. Retinger was already involved in the ACUE, The American Committee on a United Europe, formed at a luncheon in honour of Winston Churchill. From this movement the development of the Bilderberg Group was proposed. The ACUE's chairman was William Donovan, a former Director of the Office of Strategic Services (USA). The Vice President was Allen Dulles, Director of the CIA and its secretary was George Franklin, Director of the Council on Foreign Relations and later Co-ordinator of the Trilateral Commission. It was one of the main funders for the European Movement of which Retinger was the Director General. So America secretly funded and influenced the pro European Movement, the planners of the European Union; another piece of the puzzle that proves that the European Union is in place to suit the American Bankers plan for Global government). **DIRECTION. (Today, Europe's top man, Romano Prodi, was also an Italian member of the Bilderberg Group).**

The steering committee, who debate policies and make decisions, to be reported to meetings without debate, were all trusted global power enthusiasts from five main groups; Bankers, the media, multinational industrialists, top public servants and politicians. The known activists all played an internal part in the Bilderberg Group while an organisation, known as Friends of Bilderberg were participants by invitation only. It is an invitation to be withdrawn at the slightest hint of leaking information. In a curious way these participants were the reason for Bilderberg; the bringing together of finance and politics under a secret cloak that enables the politicians to open up and deliver their political ideas rather than be tied to party thinking. Most invited attendees were well vetted before attending with a few errors taking place, Margaret Thatcher being one exception.

An uncanny record rapidly built up when matters discussed at Bilderberg meetings would be executed shortly after the closed discussion. Right from the first meeting this was apparent; Eringer quotes George McGhee, the former US Ambassador to West Germany as saying that the Treaty of Rome, which created the European Common Market, had been, "Nurtured at Bilderberg" proving that the European Union is a mechanism of the power barons, not a natural association of like thinking nations. That is why all decisions are made behind closed doors, by an un-elected bureaucracy, not National Representatives, as it is the only way the power barons can insure obedience.

So you begin to see a false facade erected around the European Union which lies to the public about its true purpose and its ultimate **direction, a One World Government**.

At the very first meeting in 1954 an American delegate (and we must realise here that nearly all American delegates are members or have been members of the Council on Foreign Relations) openly forecast, that Senator Joe McCarthy would either be totally marginalised or even taken care of (killed?) by the time the next meeting came around. We have already seen how the press and media totally discredited him for telling the truth. They performed the most complete character assassination ever undertaken by a so called free press. Why? Because Senator McCarthy and Nixon had got within reach of totally exposing the whole secret truth about Communist penetration of the American administration and their foreign policy, a policy supported by the bankers, and the policy makers within the Bilderberg Group. The bankers whole secret plan could fall if McCarthy was allowed further time to expose the direction of the Globalists, including their bankers, who funded the course of treachery against **America's Sovereign State and its Constitution.**

The media caused his downfall by labelling him as an extreme right wing fanatic and, because the press all repeated this lie, the people believed the lying press. McCarthy in fact underestimated America's infiltration by Communism and was only trying to wake up an ill informed nation, betrayed by its own guardian of democracy, its press. Today the control of America is firmly in the hands of the globalist traitors but the people misguidedly still listen to those who would betray them. America must wake up to reality before the final hour of no return.

So it was, that at the first meeting at the Hotel Bilderberg at Oosterbeek, in Holland eighty invited participants decided that "insufficient attention had so far been paid to long term planning, and to evolving an international order which would look beyond the present-day crisis, "When the time is ripe, our present concepts of world affairs should be extended to the whole world". This statement shows us clearly **DIRECTION** 'A World Order'. Weishaupt's Satanic plan still ringing out after so long; a policy that never died with its originator. The participants at these meetings can be likened to Weishaupt's early recruits who only knew a user friendly enlightened part of his plan and promoted it with enthusiasm. They were brainwashed by an ideal without knowing its evil control. So Bilderberg is planned along Masonic lines of gradual expansion of the end goal if its member responds positively to each stage. Its secrecy also comes from the Masonic method but secrecy is democracy's enemy, usually used by those who want to deceive, and I think we have adequately proved that Weishaupt and deceit have ruled the execution of the policy that takes this shameful path to global dictatorship.

In Robert Eringer's book **(396)** he produces a list of some of the world's top press participants at the Bilderberg meetings **(Page 34)**, some of whom are even members of the steering committee. Names like, William Rees-Mogg, ex editor of the Times and Rothschild Director. Frank Giles from the Sunday Times, Andrew Knight of the Economist and News International. Conrad Black of the Hollinger Group (Telegraph in Britain) and on the steering committee of the Bilderberg Group. Theo Sommer, of Die Ziet (Germany). Michel Tatu of 'La Monde' (France). Carlo Sartori 'La Stampa' (Italy). Niels Norland 'Berlingske Tirende' (Denmark). Hedley Donovan, Henry Grunwald, and Ralf Davidson of 'Time' (USA). Asborn Eliot, former editor 'Newsweek' (USA). Arthur Sulzberger of the 'New York Times' and a string of political columnists.

Yet with this wide range of press attendance only a Conservative columnist, William F Buckley dared to write a rather negative report, "Guests of the Bilderberg society are bound by the same rules as members of the Bilderberg society - not to write about the proceedings". Even with this general report Buckley has not been invited back to Bilderberg meetings. Let us remind ourselves of several passages in the twelfth Protocol. **(397).**

"We shall deal with the press in the following way: what is the part played by the press of today? It serves to excite and inflame those passions which are needed for our purpose or else it serves selfish ends of parties...

"Not a single announcement will reach the public without our control. Even now this is already being attained by us inasmuch as all news items are received by a few agencies, in whose offices they are focused from all parts of the world...

"We shall have a sure triumph over our opponents since they will not have at their disposition organs of the press in which they can give full and final expression of their views..."

Our own Cecil King, Chairman of IPC wrote to his publishers that on no account should any report or mention of Bilderberg conferences be printed. We also come back to evidence relating to the determined journalist of the Lombard column in the Financial Times, C. Gordon Tether, who believed no meeting that planned the future of the world should go without public knowledge as it was anti democratic to do so. His editor, Max Henry Fisher, moved in the elite circles of Bilderberg and tried to censor Thether. When he found he couldn't he sacked him. Yet all Thether was trying to do was the job he was paid to do, open up a debate publicly in the interests of open democracy. So let us remind ourselves again what a top manager in the media had to say at a closed meeting of the press.

NOW READ THE BOX ON THE NEXT PAGE.
IT TELLS YOU THE TRUTH ABOUT OUR SO-CALLED FREE PRESS AN EXPOSES WHERE THE POWER LIES TODAY.

FREEDOM OF THE PRESS

"There is no such thing...as an independent press...There is not one of you who dares to write your honest opinions, and if you did, you know beforehand that it would never appear in print. I am paid weekly for keeping my honest opinion out of the paper I am connected with. Others of you are paid similar salaries for similar things, and any of you who would be so foolish as to write honest opinions would be out on the streets looking for another job...

The business of the journalist is to destroy the truth; to lie outright; to pervert, to vilify; to fawn at the feet of mammon, and to sell his country and his race for his daily bread...what folly is this toasting an independent press? We are tools and vassals of the rich men behind the scenes. We are the jumping jacks, they pull the strings and we dance. Our talents, our possibilities and our lives are all the property of other men. We are intellectual prostitutes".

John Swinton, former chief of staff to the New York Times, in a toast before the New York Press Club in 1953. **(398).**

What Bilderberg tries to do is discuss matters privately and use its participants (between 80-100 each meeting) to go out into the world and try and impose their decisions on the world in a deceitful way.

A very clear example of this was when Dr Henry Kissinger met with the Arabs (OPEC) to encourage them to increase the price of their crude oil by four-hundred percent and invest the extra profit in America. In this way the plan, that started in Bilderberg was blamed on the Arabs by the world-wide press.

The promoters of Bilderberg would have us believe that the meetings are just important people letting their hair down. One report even suggested that it was a session of drinking and fornication, but we must ask this very important question; Would international bankers, leaders, media magnates and academics, travel half way round the world to meetings in-between a heavy schedule to cavort? The answer is NO. They would only go for something they believed was important and that is precisely what they think it is. These men and women are not indoctrinated in Weishaupt's ways. They truly believe, in their ignorance, they are saving the world. Weishaupt magic! They are the useful pawns in the game. Their reasoning for doing it can be diverse. Innocent belief, Political or career gain, curiosity, or political acceptance of world power being the right road forward. What they don't know is what awaits them at the end of the road. World slavery to a banking cartel dictatorship through Communism, Weishaupt's policy for the Rothschilds. How am

I so sure? By now I have studied all aspects of Globalism for five and a half years and I am convinced the world is being steered towards a global dictatorship, and **DIRECTION throughout my history of Globalism proves this momentum.**

If Bilderberg is of no importance as the promoters claim, why do troops from America and Britain mount security guard at each venue and turn the hotel into a fortress?

Why are the hotel residents removed and all the staff replaced by Bilderberg staff?

Why are all the rooms used for their conferences de-bugged before each session?

The answer is that we are not meant to hear tomorrows news, today, because we might influence it. It is a planning group for the future, i.e., the European Union; the Pacific Rim; The spread of Communism in Africa; the downfall of McCarthy; the hijacking of oil prices; the Gulf War; the removal of the Right Honourable Margaret Thatcher as Prime Minister; the planning of a republic in Australia; the Stabilisation of Serbia for the Federalisation of Europe; the Independence of East Timor to enable the Federalisation of the Pacific Rim. All these and many more have been the subjects of debate within Bilderberg and its sister, the Trilateral Commission. The job of the Bilderberg Group is to identify anything getting in the way of Globalism and to eliminate it. It is also a forum to discuss what is needed to establish Globalism in Europe, like further power to the un-elected executive of the European Union, and in the world, the need for a global army through the United Nations; again, an un-elected executive body with immense power. We must start to recognise these changes for what they are and oppose them.

At this point it might be wise to remember the words of Benjamin Disraeli in his book 'Coningsby' which gives us a coded insight into the world of the Bilderberger and their masters, the money creators; "The World is governed by very different personages from what is imagined by those who are not behind the scenes". **(399).**

Professor Carroll Quigley, a free mover inside the power elite of the bankers, who wrote 'Tragedy and Hope' is perhaps in a better position than most to tell us the inside story. In his book he had this to say about the power seekers from banking. Their aim is; "Nothing less than to create a world system of financial control in private hands to dominate the political system of each country and the economy of the world as a whole. The system is to be controlled in feudal fashion (Communism) by the central banks of the world acting in concert, by secret agreements arrived at in frequent meetings and conferences". (Bilderberg and other groups). **(400).**

Well, there in a paragraph, you have the game plan. A undemocratic, anti nation, anti sovereign, state, privately planned by bankers who already have money power but now want political control as well; it amazes me that someone of Carroll Quigley's intelligence could support such a group of power bandits.

What this clearly shows is that the aim of the inner circle of the Bilderberg Group is nothing less than the New World Order, first planned by Professor Weishaupt of Ingolstadt University for Mayer Amschel Rothschild. A plan that spread throughout the world through the Masonic Lodges and incorporated the spread of a political force to bring it about; Communism.

Now let us see who has really betrayed us all this century. In David Rockefeller's speech to the 1991 Bilderberg meeting he said this to the assembled Bilderbergers; "We are grateful to the Washington Post, The New York Times,

Time Magazine and other great publications whose directors have attended our meetings and respected their promises of discretion for almost forty years..."

This is betrayal of everything the press is meant to represent, not least its readers. The press magnates have failed to honour their reason for existing; to inform the public, its readers, of everything they can discover, to protect us, their readers, against any conspiracy. Here we see them deeply involved in conspiracy, and in doing so, betraying their readership, even to the point of lying.

The reason came out later in David Rockefeller's speech; "It would have been impossible for us to develop our plan for the world if we had been subject to the bright lights of publicity (What he means by this is the spotlight of democracy, as his plan would never have seen the light of day) during those years". It is only Satan and his followers who are fearful of light. This shows this plan as Satanic; the true God, and democracy welcome openness and light.

We must go back to the total blackout on information from the content of Bilderberg meetings. We have been told there is little discussed of interest to us. Can we believe this, having learned of some of the activities of the Bilderberg Group? I think not. If there is nothing to hide, why, tell me why, do they spend so much on security before and during a meeting? The answer is that they do discuss things that we just must not get to know about. They depend on secrecy and deceit.

Proof of this came from the 1989 Bilderberg meeting on the Spanish island of La Toja. At this meeting they discussed how best to remove Margaret Thatcher from power in Britain as she was interfering in their European policy and causing a lot of trouble and delay to their schedule. The following report was printed in 'Spotlight' on the twenty-ninth of. May 1989 **(401)**; entitled "Thatcher - Targeted by Elite", "The Bilderberg group was discovered hiding out on the Island of La Toja, off the Atlantic coast of Spain (near Pontevedra), during the weekend of May 11th.-14th., plotting the political assassination of British Prime Minister Margaret Thatcher".

The meeting was confirmed by Miguel Garzon of the Spanish Embassy in Washington. Garzon said that King Juan Carlos and Primer Minister Felipe Gonzalez of Spain attended but would have nothing to say.

The meeting was also confirmed, in a negative way, by an associate of Henry Kissinger who refused to deny that the secret meeting had taken place.

Kissinger, a top officer of both the Bilderberg and its brother group, the Trilateral Commission (TC), is known to have attended.

Except for the SPOTLIGHT, the Bilderberg group succeeded in maintaining an absolute news blackout. A computer search for the word 'Bilderberg' showed that it had not been used, during the first fifteen days of May, by the Associated Press, United Press International, the New York Times, the Los Angeles Times, the Washington Post or any of the major magazines.

Extract from Spotlight newspaper of the 29th May, 1989.

The interesting point here is that Margaret Thatcher had attended a previous meeting in Turkey in 1975, and had even been photographed with some of the banking set. This was well before she became Prime Minister and long before Nigel Lawson ruined the British economy. By 1989 she was in trouble politically, not least with the pro Europe 'wet' group led by Edward Heath and it was a simple matter for the Bilderberg agents to convince them she should be ditched. But the decision was made in Bilderberg, divorced from British politics and secret from the world.

Those British Bilderbergers that complied with this, committed treason against our Sovereign State. Undoubtedly it was Her Bruges' speech in the summer of 1988 that set the seal on her fate, when she stood up against the thrusts of federalism from the United States of Europe. Once again it proves Europe's policy is planned by the banking elite and is not a policy born and bred in a Democratic Europe; and they have no intention of making it democratic.

Let us now turn our attention to what is quaintly named 'The Friends of Bilderberg'. The organisers, led by David Rockefeller, knew well that they needed contact with the political and management movers around the world from the Media, Politics, Academic circles and power groups like NATO and the European Union. This was where Bilderberg met the outside world on their terms to move its agenda forward. Those who were invited were thoroughly vetted to make sure they held similar views so their plans and secrets would be safe. As we have seen, a few errors were made. Mrs Thatcher was invited to attend the 1975 conference before she became Prime Minister, and through her husband's connections in business, it was perhaps wrongly assumed she would be firmly on their side and cause no ripples. She respected their silence, so it seemed she was a convert. So when she stood up for Britain's rights during her Bruges speech in 1988 the Bilderberg Committee and indeed the so called 'Wets' in the Conservative Party were dismayed. The Bilderberg Group could not let this powerful defence of Sovereignty delay or reverse their plans, so action was taken. This was gross interference in what we believe to be the sovereignty of a national state and clearly identifies the course that the Globalists are taking, that is hidden from our view. It also shows the power they have to mobilise enough Conservative support to achieve their aim. Those Conservatives, in following instructions from a private body outside Britain, were all committing treason against the sovereign state; in doing so they were also supporting federalism against **the National Sovereign State.**

The Bilderberg Group's headquarters in New York are called 'The Friends of Bilderberg, Incorporated' and can be found at 39 East 51St. Street. It is contained within the offices of a public relations firm called Murden and Company. One of Murden and Company's clients has been the Trilateral Commission. Murden was also involved with forming the Inter-American Relations; a group dedicated to bring about the eventual federalisation of South America and Canada to North America as one of three regional powers in the plan for **World Government.** The setting up of this group corresponds to a discussion within the second Bilderberg meeting in 1955, and the Chairman of the new group was David Rockefeller and its two Vice Chairmen Emilio Collado and Arthur Taylor, who are three of the inner committee of Bilderberg.

The founder of Murden and Co. has an interesting history. He was an assistant to Henry Ford II, liaising with Foundations, International Groups, and managing public and government relations for Ford; Internationally. **(402).** He moved to Exxon Corporation (Oil) and in 1962 set up his own company of public relations.

The Bilderberg Group, the chief benefactor of funding from both Exxon and the Ford Foundation, is therefore not surprisingly under his organisational control. The usual linkage you find to organisations driving the world to federal monopoly.

The Ditchley Foundations.

The story would not be complete unless it had the final linkage in place. Murden and Company were also the American Ditchley Foundation, which links to the British Ditchley Foundation, found in a stately home buried in the Cotswolds and heavily guarded and surveyed by closed circuit television. This linkage brings into play the connection between the Anglo and the American establishment, behind the global planning.

Ditchley was bought in 1953 by David Wills, of tobacco fame, and he developed it around a tax exempt foundation (American style). It is yet another secret meeting point for establishment figures such as government advisors, bankers, businessmen from both sides of the Atlantic (Anglo and American) to meet and discuss in secret their plans towards Globalism. **(403)**.

Because Ditchley (Traditionally Churchill's safe-house during World War II) was also used by government for conferences, the toing and froing of officials was not considered unusual; a perfect secret retreat.

On both sides of the Atlantic, the Ditchley Foundation organises conferences and meetings that promote Globalism internationally. These conferences could well be described as treasonable as they conspire to plan to destroy the National Sovereign State of America and Britain behind closed doors and the press, if in attendance, say nothing. The conference facilities are under the protection of MI5 and Special Branch from the Thames Valley Police.

The board of Governors at the Ditchley Foundation have included Lord Hume (Dec), Ex-Chairman of the Bilderberg Group, Lord Roll, Bilderberg inner Committee member and Chairman of NM Rothschild bank, Henry Heinz II, of the Bilderberg inner Committee, and George Franklin, the co-ordinator of the Trilateral Commission, plus at least ten other Bilderbergers. So we can see that from this grouping, decisions at meetings are passed up to the Bilderberg Group.

Unlike Bilderberg they have about twelve meetings a year each on a set subject from the Media to the balance of power in the Pacific, NATO to the prospect for Religion. Their important conclusions then become papers to be delivered to the Bilderberg meeting once a year.

So you can see three important results, all of which lead us to conclude these discussions are against the interests of democracy.

Firstly they are secret. Only those who wish to impose their will deal secretly.

Secondly they are selective. Only those bent on supporting Globalism are invited.

Thirdly, in the case of the Ditchley Foundation only groups that follow the Federal Global path can book their facilities.

So we have debate being driven towards a federal Globalism because other alternatives are not even given an airing. Why does this happen? The answer lies in the people who organise this power group. You see the same names cropping up in all these groups, David Rockefeller, Rothschilds or their agents and lesser men like Lord Carrington and his partner Dr. Henry Kissinger and many others.

Now let's take a look at three lists of Bilderbergers. The first is the list of the members at the first Bilderberg Conference in May, 1954.

Bilderberg Conference 1954.

CHAIRMAN: Prince Bernhard of the Netherlands

VICE-CHAIRMAN: John Coleman and Paul Van Zeeland

Addressed By
George Ball, USA.
Etienne de la Vallee Poussin, Belgium
Barry Bingham, USA
H.M. Hirschfield, The Netherlands
Hugh Gaitskill, UK

David Rockefeller, USA

Paul Nitze, USA
J.D. Zellerbach, USA

Participants
Robert Andre, France
Ralph Assheton, UK
G. de Beaumont, France
Pierre Bonvoisin, Belgium
Sir Robert Boothby, UK
Max Brauer, Germany
Irving Brown, USA
Raffaele Cafiero, Italy
Walker Cisler, USA
Gardner Cowles, USA

Clement Davies, UK

Jean Drapier, Belgium
R. Duchet, France
M. Faure, France
John Ferguson, USA
John Foster, UK

Participants Cont.
Sir Oliver Franks, UK
G.P. Geyer, Germany
Sir Colin Gubbins, UK

Dennis Healey, UK

Henry Heinz, USA
Leif Hoegh, Norway

H. Montgomery Hyde, UK
Charles Jackson, USA
Nelson Jay, USA
P. Kanellopoulos, Greece
V.K. Koningsberger, The Netherlands
Ole Bjorn Kraft, Denmark
P. Leverkuehn, Germany
Giovanni Malagodi, Italy
Finn Moe, Norway
Roger Motz, Belgium
Rudolph Mueller, Germany
George McGhee, USA
George Nebolsine, USA
H. Oosterhuis, the Netherlands
Cola Parker, USA
George Perkins, USA
Sir Harry Pilkington, UK
Alberto Pirelli, Italy
Ludwig Rosenberg, Germany
Paolo Rossi, Italy
Denis de Rougemont, Switzerland
Paul Rijkins, the Netherlands
Ernst Schneider, Germany
W.F. Schnitzler, Germany
Joseph Spang, USA
M. Steenberghe, the Netherlands
Terkel Terkelsen, Denmark
Herbert Tingsten, Sweden
H. Troeger, Germany
Vittorio Valetta, Italy
Andre Voisin, France
M. Waldenstrom, Sweden
H.F. van Walsem, the Netherlands
Jean Willems, Belgium
Tom Williamson, UK
(404). (Bibliography).

The second list shows the members of the inner steering committee as at April 20th. 1980.

Officers and Directors of the American Friends of Bilderberg Incorporated.

PRESIDENT AND TREASURER: Henry Heinz II.
SECRETARY: Paul Finney.
ASSISTANT SECRETARY: Charles Muller.
DIRECTORS: Jack Bennett, **David Rockefeller,** Arthur Taylor.

Members of the Steering Committee, 1980.

CHAIRMAN: **Walter Scheel.** Former President of the Federal Republic of Germany.
HONORARY SECRETARY GENERAL FOR EUROPE: Victor Halberstadt, Professor of Public Finance, Leyden University.
HONORARY SECRETARY GENERAL FOR THE UNITED STATES: Paul B. Finney, Executive Editor, Fortune Magazine.
TREASURER: Willem F. Duisenberg. Deputy Chairman Executive Board, Central Rabo Bank.

NATIONAL MEMBERS

Austria Hans Igler. President, Federation of Austrian Industrialists.
Belgium Daniel Janssen. Chairman, Belgium Federation of Chemical Industries. **Member of the Trilateral Commission.**
Baron Lambert. Chairman, Groupe Bruxelles Lambert, S.A. **Member of the Trilateral Commission.**
Canada Donald S. Macdonald. Senior partner, McCarthy and McCarthy.
Denmark Niels Nørlund. Editor-in Chief, 'Berlingske Tidende'.
France Thierry de Montbrial. Director, **French Institute of International Relations:** Professor of Economics, Ecole Polytechnique.
Ernest-Antoine Seillière. Deputy Director General, Compaignie Générale d'Industrie. **Member of the Trilateral Commission.**
Federal Republic of Germany Alfred Herrhausen, Managing Director, Deutsche Bank A.G.
Theo Sommer. Editor –in-Chief, 'Die Zeit'. **Member of the Trilateral Commission.**
Greece Costa Carras. Member of the Board, Union of Greek Shipowners.
International Christoph Bertram. Director, the International Institute of Strategic Studies.
Italy Romano Prodi. Professor of Industrial Economics, University of Bologna, Former Minister of Industry. **(Now EU Commission President).**
Stefano Silvestri. Vice-Director, **Institute International Affairs.**
Norway Niels Werring, Jr. Senior partner, Wilhelm Wilhelmsen, President of the Norwegian Shipowners Association.
Sweden Björn Lundvall. Managing Director Telefonaktiebolaget LM Ericsson.
Switzerland Franz J. Lütolf. General Manager and member of the executive board, Swiss Bank Corporation.
Turkey Selahattin Beyazit. Director of Companies.
United Kingdom Alistair Frame. Deputy Chairman and Chief Executive of Rio Tinto Zinc.
Andrew Knight. Editor, 'The Economist".

United States of America Jack F. Bennett. Director and senior **Vice President, Exxon Corporation.**
Theodore L. Eliot, Jr. Dean, Fletcher School of Law and Diplomacy, Tufts University.
Murray H. Finley. President, Amalgamated Clothing and Textiles Workers Union.
Vernon E. Jordan, Jr. President, National Urban League.
Henry A. Kissinger. Former Secretary of State. **Member, Trilateral Commission.**

Winston Lord. President Council of Foreign Relations Inc. Member, **Trilateral Commission.**
Bruce K. MacLaury. President, the Brookings Institution. **Member, Trilateral Commission.**
Arthur R. Taylor. Managing Partner, Arthur Taylor and Company. **Member, Trilateral Commission.**
Marina vN. Whitman. Vice President and Chief Economist, General Motors Corporation. **Member, Trilateral Commission.**
Joseph H. Williams. Chairman and Chief Executive Officer, the Williams Companies.
Charles W. Getchell, Jr.

(405). (Bibliography).

The third listings show:

Draft Agenda for Bilderberg June 6th - 9th. 1991, Baden Baden.

DEFINING DEVELOPMENTS FOR THE ALLIANCE. (405)

Session 1 and 2.	**The Middle East: Political Fallout and Future Prospects.**
	Panel: Lawrence Freedman (UK)*
	Tugay Özceri (TURK)
	William Quandt (US)
	Patrick Wright (UK)
Session 3.	**Eastern Europe: Economic Prospects.**
	Panel: Jean-Louis Cadieux (EUR. COMM)
	Thomas W. Simons, Jr. (US)
Session 4.	**Developments in the Soviet Union: Political and Economic Impact on the Alliance.**
	Panel: Jack F. Matlock (US)
	Volker Rühe (FRG)
	The Practical Agenda for the Alliance. *
Session 5.	**Basics of Transatlantic Relationship.**
	Panel: Henning Wegener (NATO)
	Robert B. Zoellick (US)
Session 6.	**Do we have the Institutions to deal with the Agenda?**
	Panel: Robert D. Blackwill (US)
	Ruud F.M. Lubbers (NETH)
	Manfred Wörner (NATO
Session 7.	**Economic and Financial Threats to the Relationship.**
	Panel: Panel: Michael J. Boskin (US)
	Karl Otto Pöhl (FRG)
Session 8.	**Current Events.**

* Background Paper.   May 10th. 1991

Provisional List of Participants.

Chairman. Lord Carrington. Chairman of the Board, Christie's International plc; Former Secretary General, NATO. British Cabinet Minister.
Honorary Secretary General for Europe and Canada. Victor Halberstadt. Professor of Public Economics, Leiden University.
Honorary Secretary General for USA. Theodore L. Eliot, Jr. Senior Research Fellow, Hoover Institution on War, Revolution and Peace, Stanford University.
Honorary Treasurer. Conrad J. Oort. Adviser to the Board of Management, Algemene Bank Netherland NV; Professor of Money and Banking, University of Limburg.
Austria. Peter Jankowitsch, Minister in State in Charge of European Integration and Development Cupertino.
Guido Schmidt-Chiari, Chairman of the Managing Board, Creditanstalt Bankverein.
Franz Vranitzky, Federal Chancellor.
Belgium. Etienne Davignon, Chairman, Sociét Générale de Belgigue; Former Vice Chairman of the Commission of The European Communities.
Jean-Louis Cadieux, Deputy Director-General for Foreign Affairs, European Community.
Wilfried Martens, Prime Minister.
Guy Spitaels, Chairman Socialist Party, Minister of State.
Canada. Conrad Black, Chairman, The Daily Telegraph plc.
Jean-Claude Delorme, Chairman of Caisse de dépôt et placement du Quibec.
Marie-Josse Drouin, Executive Director, Hudson Institute of Canada.

Anthony G.S. Griffin, Director of Companies.
John Polanyi, Professor of Chemistry, University of Toronto.
Michael Wilson, Minister of Industry, Science and technology and International Trade.
Denmark. Ritt Bjerregaard, Labour member of Parliament; Chairman of the Labour Group.
Aage Deleuran, Editor-in-Chief, "Berlingske Tidende".
Nils Wilhjelm, President, Industrial Mortgage Fund; Former Ministry of Industry.
Finland. Aatos Erkko, Publisher, "Helsingin Sanomat".
Jaakko Honiemi, Managing Director, Council of Economic Organisations in Finland, former Ambassador to the United States of America.
France. Bertrand Collomb, Chairman and Executive Officer, Large Coppée.
Claude Imbert, Chief Editor "Le point".
Marc Ladreit de Lacharrière Chairman Fimalac.
André Lé-Lang, Chairman, Compagnie Financière de Paribas.
Thierry de Montbrial, Director, French Institute of International Relations; Professor of Economics, Ecole Polytechnique.
Michel Noir, Mayor of Lyon, Ex-Secretary of State Foreign Trade.
Federal Republic of Germany. Christoph Bertram, Diplomatic Correspondent, "Die Ziet".
Hans-Otto Braütigam, Minister of Justice of Brandenburg.
Birgit Breuel, Member of the Board, Treuhandanstalt.
Werner H. Dieter, Chairman of the Board, Mannesmann A.G.
Björn Engholm, Prime Minister of Schleswig Holstein, and Chairman of the SPD.
Dieter Kastrup, Director Political Department, Minister of Foreign Affairs.

Hilmar Kopper, Spokesman of the Board of Managing Directors, Deutsche Bank A.G.
Kurt Lauk, Vice Chairman of the Management Board, Audi A.G.
Karl Otto Pöhl, President, Deutsche Bundesbank.
Volker Rühe, General Secretary Parliamentary Party CDU.
Heinz Ruhnau, Chairman of the Board, Deutsche Lufthansa A.G.
Thëo Sommer, Editor-in-Chief, "Die Zeit".
Erwin Teufel, Prime Minister of Baden-Würtemberg.
Otto Wolff von Amerongen, Chairman and CEO of Otto Wolff Industrie-Beratung und Beteiligungan GmbH.

Greece. Costa Carras, Director of Companies.
Efthymios Christodoulou, Minister of Economic Affairs.
Minos Zombanakis, Chairman, Group for International Study and Evaluation.
Iceland. Bjöorn Bjarnason, Member of Parliament, Independence Party.
David Oddsspon, Mayor of Reykjavik, Chairman Independence Party.
International. Arthur Dunkel, Director General G.A.T.T.
John R. Galvin, Supreme Allied Commander Europe, SHAPE.
Max Kohnstramm, Former Secretary General, Action Committee for Europe, Former President, European University Institute.
Helga Steeg, Executive Director, International Energy Agency.
Henning Wegener, Assistant Secretary General for political affairs, NATO.
Manfred Wörner, Secretary General of **the North Atlantic Treaty Organisation.**
Ireland. Peter D. Sutherland, former member, **Commission of the European Communities, Chairman, Allied Irish Bank Group.**
Italy. Giovanni Agnelli, Chairman Fiat S.p.A.
Giampiero Cantoni, Chairman, Banca Nationale del Lavoro.
Gianni De Michelis, Minister of Foreign Affairs.
Mario Monti, Rector and Professor of Economics, Bocconi University, Milan.
Virginia Rognoni, Minister of Defence.
Paulo Zannoni, Senior Vice President for Defence and Space, Fiat S.p.A.
Luxemburg. Jaques Santer, Prime Minister.
Netherlands. Ernst H. van der Beugel, Emeritus Professor of International Relations, Leyden University; Former **Honorary Secretary General of Bilderberg Meetings for Europe and Canada.**
Ben Knapen, Editor-in-Chief NRC Mandelsblad.
Pieter Korteweg, President and CEO of the board Committee of the Robeco Group.
Ruud F.M. Lubbers, Prime Minister.
H.M. the Queen of the Netherlands.
Norway. Arne Olav Brundtland, Senior Research Fellow, **Norwegian Institute of International Affairs.**
Per Ditlev-Simonsen, managing Director, Sverre Ditlev-Simonsen and Co.
Niels Warring, Chairman of the Board, Wilh Wilhelmsen Limited A/S.
Portugal. Francisco Pinto Balsam, Professor of Mass Communication, New University of Lisbon; Chairman Sojornal Sarl; Former Prime Minister.
Carlos A.P.V. Monjardino, President of the Fundaçao Oriente.
Carlos Pimenta, Member of the European Parliament, Former Secretary of State for the Environment.
Spain. Jaime Carvajàl Urquijo, Chairman and General Manager, Iberfomento.
Jordi Pujol, President, Generalitat de Catalunya.

Narcis Serra, Deputy Prime Minister.
H.M. The Queen of Spain.
Sweden. Stan Gustafsson, Chairman of the Board of Directors, AB Astra.
Lars Jonung, Professor of Economics and Economic Policy at Stockholm School of Economics.
Bo C.E. Ramfors, Managing Director and Group Chief Executive of Skkandinaviska Enskilda Banken, Board Member of several Companies.
Switzerland. Fritz Gerber, Chairman of the Board of F. Hoffmann- La Roche AG.
Alex Krauer, Chairman and Managing Director, Ciba-Geigy Limited.
Michael Ringier, Publisher, Chairman of the Board of Ringier Inc.
Turkey. Selattin Boyazit, Director of Compa.
Vahit Halefoglu, Former Minister of Foreign Affairs.
Tugay Ozçeri, Under Secretary, Ministry of Foreign Affairs.
United Kingdom. Gordon Brown, Member of Parliament. **(Now Chancellor of the Exchequer).**
Lawrence Freedman, head of Department of War Studies, Kings College.
Christopher Kogg, Chairman of Courtaulds plc.
Andrew Knight, Executive Chairman, **News International plc. (Rupert Murdoch).**
Lord Roll of Ipaden, President, S.G. Warburg Group plc.
John Smith, Dec., Member of Parliament, Shadow Chancellor of the Exchequer.
Patrick Wright, Permanent Under Secretary of State and head of the Diplomatic Service.
United States of America. Paul Allaire, President and CEO of Xerox Corp.
George W Ball, Former under-secretary of State.
Robert L. Bartley, Editor, "The Wall Street Journal".
Robert D. Blackwill, Lecturer in Public Policy, John F. Kennedy School of Government. Harvard University; former member National Security Council.
Michael J. Boskin, Chairman, President's Council of Economic Advisers.
Nicholas F. Brady, Secretary of the Treasury.
John N. Chafee, Senator.
Bill D. Clinton, Governor Arkansas. **(Now President of the USA).**
Charles H. Dallara, Assistant Secretary for International Affairs.
Kenneth W. Dam, Vice President, Law and External Relations, IBM Corp. Former Deputy Secretary of State.
Diane Feinstein, Former Mayor of San Francisco.
Katharine Graham, Chairman, **The Washington Post Company.**
Maurice R. Greenberg, Chairman, American International Group Inc.
J. Bennett Johnston, Senator (Democrat).
Vernon E Jordan, Partner, Akin, Gump, Strauss, Hauer & Feld (Attorney at Law) Former President, National Urban League.
Henry Kissinger, Former Secretary of State; Chairman, Kissinger Associates, Inc.
Charles McC. Mathias, Partner, Jones, Day, Reavis & Pogue; Former US Senator. (Republican).

Jack F. Matlock, Jr. Ambassador to the USSR.
William B. Quandt, Senior Fellow, the Brookings Institute.
John S. Reed, Chairman Citicorp.
Rozanne L. Ridgway, President, The Atlantic Council of the United States.

David Rockefeller, Chairman, Chase Manhattan Bank, International Advisory Committee. **Active in Council on Foreign Relations, Bilderberg Group, and the Trilateral Commission.**
John S.R. Shad, Director and Philanthropist.
Thomas W. Simons, Jr, **Ambassador to Poland.**

John C. Whitehead, Former Deputy Secretary of State.
Brayton Wilbur, Jr, President and CEO, Wilbur-Ellis Company.
Lawrence Douglas Wilder, Governor of Virginia.
Lynn R. Williams, International President, United Steelworkers of America.
James D. Wolfensohn, President, James D. Wolfensohn, Inc.
Robert B. Zoellick, Counsellor and Under Secretary Designate for Economic Affairs.
Rapporteur. Grant F. Winthrop, Partner Milbank Wilson Winthrop, Inc.
Alice Victor.
In Attendance. Maja Banck (NETH). Executive Secretary, Bilderberg Meetings.
Felicia Cavasse, Organiser, 1992 Conference. (FRA).
Günther F.W. Dicke. First Vice President, Deutsche Bank A.G. Organiser, 1991. (FRG).
Veronique Morali, Organiser, 1992 Conference. (FRA).
Charles W. Muller, President, Murden and Company; American Friends of Bilderberg, Inc.
(406). (Bibliography).

Now re-study this list of proposed participants. I have printed in bold the important names. Pay particular attention to their position in politics, the civil service, in academia or business, and you begin to realise that for a private meeting these members combine to represent not people power but position power that can seriously alter the power structure in the world today. We see everyone from Presidents down, people who should respect their National Duties, plotting to undermine those very duties for a utopia they perceive as a last chance. A last chance for what? Well they may well see a light in the tunnel of deceit, but they should know the fraud being played on their enthusiastic ignorance.

Notice how David Rockefeller is once again on the list. He is in fact one of the original founders of the group, like the Bilderberg group before it, and his name, was also associated with the Council on Foreign Relations. It seems he was buying his way to his dream of global government. The Rothschilds were also represented, but, in their way, by agents like Lord Roll, this being their way of standing back from the limelight.

Now you can see linking between groups. You can also see how the moneyed power elite have paid for their own agenda, using the political movers of the world as pawns, moving towards the bankers final aim, **World Government. DIRECTION.**

PROTOCOL EIGHTEEN
ARREST OF OPPONENTS.

When it becomes necessary for us to strengthen the strict measures of secret defence (the most fatal poison for the prestige of authority) we shall arrange a simulation of disorders or some manifestation of discontents finding expression through the co-operation of good speakers. Round these speakers will assemble all who are sympathetic to his utterances. This will give us the pretext for domiciliary perquisitions and surveillance on the part of our servants from among the number of the goyim police....

As the majority of conspirators act out of love for the game, for the sake of talking, so, until they commit some overt act we shall not lay a finger on them but only introduce into their midst observation elements...It must be remembered that the prestige of authority is lessened if it frequently discovers conspiracies against itself: this implies a presumption of consciousness of weakness, or, what is still worse, injustice. You are aware that we have broken the prestige of the goy kings by frequent attempts upon their lives through our agents, blind sheep of our flock, who are easily moved by a few liberal phrases to crimes provided only they be painted in political colours. We have compelled the rulers to acknowledge their weakness in advertising overt measures of secret defence and thereby we shall bring authority to destruction.

Our ruler will be secretly protected only by the most insignificant guard, because we shall not admit so much as a thought that there could exist against him any sedition with which he is not strong enough to contend or from which he is compelled to hide.

If we should admit this thought, as the goyim have done and are doing, we shall ipso facto be signing a death sentence, if not for our ruler, at any rate for his dynasty, at no distant date.

According to strictly enforced outward appearances our ruler will employ his power only for the advantage of the nation and in no wise for his own or dynastic profits. Therefore, with the observance of this decorum, his authority will be respected and guarded by the subjects themselves, it will receive an apotheosis in the admission that with it is bound up the well-being of every citizen of the State, for upon it will depend all order in the common life of the pack.

Overt defence of this kind argues weakness in the organisation of his strength.

Our ruler will always be surrounded among the people by a mob of apparently curious men and women, who will occupy the front ranks about him, to all appearance by chance, and will restrain the ranks of the rest out of respect as it will appear for good order. This will sow an example of restraint also in others. If a petitioner appears among the people forcing his way through the ranks and trying to hand in a petition, the first ranks must receive the petition and before the eyes of the petitioner pass it to the ruler, so that all may know that what is handed in reaches its destination, and that, consequently, the ruler himself is subject to control. To exist, the aureole of power requires that the people may be able to say "If the king knew of this", or "The king will hear of it".

With the establishment of official secret defence the mystical prestige of authority disappears: given a certain audacity, and everyone counts himself master of it, the sedition-monger is conscious of his strength, and when occasion serves watches for the moment to make an attempt upon authority.... For goyim we have been preaching something else, but by that very fact we are enabled to see what measures of overt defence have brought them to.

Criminals with us will be arrested at the first more or less well-grounded suspicion; it cannot be allowed that out of fear of a possible mistake an opportunity of escape should be given to persons suspected of a political lapse or crime, for in these matters we shall be literally merciless. If it is still possible, by stretching a point, to admit a reconsideration of the motive causes in simple crimes, there is no possibility of excuse for persons occupying themselves with questions in which nobody except the government can understand anything.... And it is not all governments that understand true policy.

PROTOCOL NINETEEN

RULERS AND PEOPLE.

If we do not permit any independent dabbling in the political we shall on the other hand encourage every kind of report or petition with proposals for the government to examine all kinds of projects for the amelioration of the condition of the people; this will reveal to us the defects or else the fantasies of our subjects, to which we shall respond either by accomplishing them or by wisely rebutting them to prove the short-sightedness of one who judges wrongly.

Sedition-mongering is nothing more than the yapping of a lap-dog at an elephant. For a well organised government, not from the point of view of the police but of the public, the lap-dog yaps at an elephant entirely unconscious of its strength and importance. It needs no more than to take a good example to show the relative importance of both and the lap-dogs will cease to yap and will wag their tails the moment they set eyes on an elephant.

In order to destroy the prestige of heroism for political crime we shall send it for trial in the category of thieving, murder, and every kind of abominable and filthy crime.

Public opinion will then confuse in its conception this category of crime with the disgrace attaching to every other and will brand it with the same contempt.

We have done our best, and I hope we have succeeded, in preventing the goyim from adopting this means of contending with sedition. It was for this reason that through the Press and in speeches indirectly - in cleverly compiled school-books on history, we have advertised the martyrdom alleged to have been accepted by sedition-mongers for the idea of the commonweal. This advertisement has increased the contingent of liberals and has brought thousands of goyim into the ranks of our landstock cattle.

COMMENT

Here we see the lengths that they will go to control the people's minds and actions. No dissent will be allowed. Political opposition will be dealt with by the harshest punishment, similar to theft or murder. This is complete dictatorship, where the 'Granny' state knows best. This is Communism being used to follow the death of Capitalism, the bankers' false standing, because Capitalism is driven by competition not robbed of it, as the Multi-Nationals intend to do.

CHAPTER SIXTEEN.
THE TRILATERAL COMMISSION.

The idea for the Trilateral Commission was the natural continuation of Bilderberg, (which was mainly a planning committee for the federalisation of East and West Europe). Its purpose was to move the three laterals, Europe (East and West), the Pacific Rim (Including China), and America (including South America and Canada) into controlled federations as a first step towards regional Government, a step before world government.

It is therefore not surprising to find three dedicated One Worlders planning its launch. Firstly the funder, David Rockefeller (Chase Manhattan Bank Chairman). Secondly, Henry Owen, at that time the director of Foreign Policy Studies at the Brookings Institute and thirdly, the acknowledged brains behind the commission, Zbigniew Brzezinski, the Head of Russian Studies Department, at Columbia University; (Later to become a close White House advisor). His idea was in line with his book 'Between Two Ages' (Published 1970) where Brzezinski promoted a body of developed nations, to contain chaos in global politics in particularly the third world. At this point I must make it quite clear that these were the ideas of Brzezinski, and the Owen's Institute financed his research.

However we must query the agenda of David Rockefeller, who seems to be motivated by balance sheet politics and what will eventually benefit his banking and Insurance Group. He has devoted a large part of his life to One World Politics and his wealth could force his totally narrow sighted policies on an unsuspecting world.

So Brzezinski, funded by the Brookings Institute, came up with a plan for a high powered Commission of developed nations to add strength to the world economic community, but as the research has all been done along the narrow thinking of One World dogma, so the idea and possibilities appealed to David Rockefeller, particularly as it brought together North America, Europe and Japan, the three highly developed areas of the world. Rockefeller in particular saw it as an opportunity to influence the foreign and economic policies of the world.

It was at the 1972 Bilderberg meeting in Knokke, Belgium, that David Rockefeller outlined the plans for a Trilateral Commission, and Brzezinski was at hand to promote his case. Bilderberg welcomed it.

By May 1972 Brzezinski sent George Franklin, his close friend who happened to be the Executive Director of the Council On Foreign Relations, (the breeding ground for One Worlders') to Europe, according to an internal memo, to "Explore there, both degree of interest and possible participants".

In June, Franklin and Rockefeller went to Japan to gain recruits.

In July a Trilateral planning group was formed, meeting at Rockefeller's mansion in New York, including Henry Owen, McGeorge Bundy, Robert Bowie, C Fred Bergsten, Karl Carstens, Guido Colonna de Paliano, Bayless Manning, Rene Foch, Francois Duchene, Max Kohnstamm, Saburo Ikita, Kiichi Miyazawa, and

Tadashi Yamamoto, representing Europe, Japan and America, but all privately, not officially; from there on Rockefeller funded its pre launch until the Kettering Foundation took over. By January 1973 Gerard Smith (North America) was elected Commission Chairman, and Max Kohnstamm (for Europe), and Takeshi Watanabe (for Japan).

Brzezinski was made the Director and his friend Franklin the North American Secretary. Again internal Commission records show that approvals came from "The highest political and financial circles". This is where the political power colludes with the financial private power of banking.

By 1973 the Tripartite Committees had been formed:

United States. I. W. Abel, President, United Steelworkers of America.
Harold Brown, President, California Institute of Technology.
Patrick Haggerty, Chairman, Texas Instruments.
Edwin Reischauer, Harvard University Professor and former Ambassador to Japan.
David Rockefeller, Chairman, Chase Manhattan Bank.
William Roth, Roth Properties.
William Scranton, former Governor of Pennsylvania.
Paul Warnke, Partner, Clifford, Warnke, Class, McIlwain & Finney.
Europe. Klaus Dieter Arndt, Member of the German Bundestag.
Kurt Birrenbach, Member of the Bundestag.
Francesco Compagna, Member of the Italian Chamber of Deputies.
Marc Eyskens, Commissary General of the Catholic University in Louvain.
Mary Robinson, Member of the Senate of the Irish Republic.
Otto Grieg Tidemand, Shipowner, former Norwegian Minister of Defence; former
Minister of Economics.
Sir Kenneth Younger, Former Director of the Royal Institute for International Affairs.
Sir Philip de Zulueta, Chief Executive, Antony Gibbs and Sons (Merchant Bankers).
Japan. Chujiro Fujino, President, Mitsubishi Shoji Kaisha.
Yukitaka Haraguchi, President, All Japan Metal Mine Labourer's Union.
Kazushige Hirasawa, Editorial Writer, the Japan Times.
Yusuke Kashiwagi, Vice President, Bank of Tokyo.
Kiichi Mijazawa, Member of the Diet.
Kinhide Mushakoji, professor, Sophia University.
Saburo Okita, President, the Overseas Economic Co-operation Fund.
Ryuji Takeuchi, Former Ambassador to the United States.
(407).

So on the 1st. July 1973 the Trilateral Commission was officially opened but secrecy was again its code. Only official releases gave just the minimum of information and among its Commissioners some surprising names appeared; Jimmy Carter, then Governor of Georgia, John B. Anderson, a member of the House of Representatives, Hedley Donovan, at the time editor of 'Time, Inc.', the late Reginald Maudling, Sir Eric (now Lord) Roll of the Rothschild Bank, Alastair Burnett, Editor of the Economist and Broadcaster, Giovanni Agelli, Fiat President, Denis Healy, former Chancellor of the Exchequer, Edward Heath, Member of the British Parliament and former Prime Minister, Raymond Barre, (French) Vice

President of the Commission of European Communities, Dr. Henry Kissinger (The Fixer) and Baron Edmond de Rothschild. (This is just a few of a formidable bunch of private citizens taking action; but we must ask, how much rubs off on their public life and influences their policy decisions towards the trilateral aim of One World Government?). I suspect they all promote the aim of the One Worlders' to their best ability, which puts a question mark against their integrity.

The first public statement to be made after the first meeting held in Tokyo on October 21st.-23rd. 1973 stated; "It will be the purpose of the Trilateral Commission to generate the will to respond in common with the opportunities and challenge that we confront and to assume the responsibilities that we face".

"The Commission will seek to promote among Japanese, West Europeans and North Americans the habit of working together on problems of mutual concern, to seek to obtain a shared understanding of these complex problems, and to devise and disseminate proposals of general benefit".

"The co-operation we seek involves a sustained progress of consultation and mutual education, with our countries coming closer together to meet common needs. To promote such co-operation, the Commission will undertake an extensive program of trilateral policy studies, and will co-operate with existing **private institutions** as appropriate".

At this point it might be asked, Why waste money on two groups when Bilderberg could be opened up to the Trilateral Grouping? Robert Eringer gives us some idea.

1 Bilderberg is bilateral and does not include Japan.
2 Bilderberg is ad hoc while the commission maintains a formal membership.
3 Bilderberg is primarily concerned with East-West political relations while the Trilateral Commission is more interested in North South economic relations.
4 The Trilateral Commission publishes a magazine called 'Trialogue' (but it only gives a rather romantic gloss to their work).

To this list I would add that the Bilderberg Group discuss agenda that should not be heard outside their meetings and certainly not by a competing power group. (The reason for their tight security).

The Trilateral Commission also publishes documents presented to government for consideration so their secrecy is partly a myth; but they still hide behind closed doors for debate which maybe, unfairly, gives them a reputation like Bilderberg.

The Commission has produced reports like "The Crisis of Democracy", by Samual Huntington, later to become Co-ordinator of Security Planning at the National Security Council. This was an attack on the Pillars of our democracy. They have recommended the sale of official gold to private buyers, now being followed in Britain by Gordon Brown, which removes an important reserve that is a standby in an emergency. (Report by Professor Richard Cooper of Yale University, later to become Secretary of State for Economic Affairs). (It is interesting to note that all these policies are funded by American Foundations and the Authors are nearly all Illuminated Professors, (Weishaupt's Disciples) and also go on to big government jobs at a later stage.

A report "Energy: Managing the Transition" made a case for higher energy cost. Its author, John Sawhill, went on to become Deputy Secretary of the Department of Energy. We have to wonder what part his thoughts may have played in the oil price increase of 400%. Who were the gainers? The bankers of course, like Rockefeller. (Remember the Protocol that claims that all the Gold is in their hands).

Another report "The Reform of International Institutions" was written by C. Bergsten, who went on to become Assistant Secretary to the treasury for International Affairs.

Like the Council on Foreign Relations, which is known as the Centre of Foreign Policy for America, although it is a privately funded group with foundation participation, its members spread themselves out into all corners of America's administration, carrying with them their narrow, one world views, so the Trilateral Commission does the same, also with a fully focused narrow view, the one world view as its goal. Now America's administration is dominated by people from these groups to such an extent, that other paths forward, to a democratic future, are being closed and debate stifled, by the mere presence of surrounding power of the disciples of One World Dictatorship. The total power of these groups and their disciples is known as the Shadow Government.

Now lets take a look at some of the politicians who have joined the Trilateral Commission and found that they have suddenly achieved meteoric rise to fame, and position of power.

The first candidate must be Jimmy Carter. A peanut farmer from Georgia and Governor of his State. In October 1972 he was invited to lunch by David Rockefeller and Zbigniew Brzezinski at the Connault Hotel in London. Carter impressed the two plotters, having opened trading offices in Brussels and Tokyo, for the State of Georgia. This fitted the ideal of Trilateralism perfectly. Avrill Harriman, had already recommended Carter, as a potential President, to Rockefeller.

First he was enlisted as a Trilateral Commissioner and was dedicated to its cause, using its facilities as a learning exercise on the subject he was, to say the least, not very well briefed upon; Foreign Policy.

Soon, from nowhere, Carter was suddenly thrust into the race for President, so much so, that headlines in the papers began to ask, "Jimmy Who?" Gradually, thanks to an almost unanimous press promotion, Jimmy Carter started to look like a winner, and his first success was his win in Iowa State Caucus in 1975. While the press promoted the 'Come on', "Jimmy Who?" none of its journalists bothered to ask the question about the Trilateral Commission, which he openly voiced as his source of education on foreign policies. No one asked, where his campaign funds came from? Meanwhile, he was talking Rockefeller's language. In a speech to the Foreign Policy Association he proclaimed; "We must replace Balance-of-Power politics with world order politics", just what Rockefeller wanted to hear.

From there on, he began to rise as if from nowhere; but of course he had the best PR money could buy. He was now one of their pawns and they wanted him in office. 'Time' Magazine, headed by Trilateralist Hedley Donovan, led the PR push for Carter. They had all the expertise within the Trilateral Commission to promote a Peanut for President, if they so wished.

Every Trilateralist played his part and soon, people began to believe Carter was the unaffected new-comer, unaffected that is by the very power that was promoting him; as the press told them, so the people believed the press. But we now know who owns the press. They cannot be trusted.

Brzezinski assumed the role of Carter's Foreign Policy Expert, writing, in the end, all his speeches. So it was that Jimmy Carter, from nowhere was forced onto America, because money power bought his Presidency.

Trilateralists, naturally were put in place around him. Walter Mondale, Vice President; Cyrus Vance, Secretary of State; Harold Brown, Secretary of Defence; Zbigniew Brzezinski, National Security Advisor; Warren Christopher, Deputy Secretary of State; Anthony Solomon, Deputy Secretary of State for Monetary Affairs; Richard Cooper, Under Secretary of State for Economic Affairs; C. Fred Bergsten, Assistant Secretary of the Treasury for International Economic Affairs; Andrew Young, Ambassador to the United Nations; Robert Bowie, Deputy Director of Central Intelligence; Richard Holbrooke, assistant Secretary of State for East Asian and Pacific Affairs; Graham Allison, Assistant Secretary of Defence for Planning; Lucy Benson, Under Secretary of State for Security Assistance; Samual Huntington, Co-ordinator of Security Planning at the National Security Council; John Sawhill, Deputy Secretary of Energy; Paul Volker, Chairman, Board of Governors, US Federal Reserve System (Privately owned); Hedley Donovan, Senior White House Advisor; Lloyd Cutler, Council to the President; Sol Linowitz, Panama Treaty Negotiator and Middle East Negotiator; Henry Owen, Economic Advisor for the London Summit; Leonard Woodcock, US Permanent Representative to Peking; Paul Warnke, Director, Arms Control and Disarmament Agency; Gerard Smith, Ambassador-at-Large for Nuclear Issues; Elliot Richardson, US representative to UN Law of the Seas Conference; and Richard Gardner, Ambassador to Italy.

It could be called a Trilateralist's victory, and Power Grab. But if that was the Trilateralists idea, Carter had others. As his confidence grew he dumped his new advisors and listened instead to his own Georgia Mafia. Carter turned out to have a mind of his own.

But those who created him could also destroy him. Theo Sommer (of 'Die Ziet' from West Germany) a member of the Trilateral Commission and the Bilderberg Group, started the decline of Carter on a decision, made against Trilateralist advice, not to deploy the Neutron Bomb for NATO forces.

Carter further dug his grave when he refused to support the Shah of Iran. Rockefeller had a very large investment in Iran to protect. Kissinger, on behalf of Rockefeller persisted in putting pressure on Carter's administration till the Shah was allowed refuge in America, which upset the new rulers of Iran, as the CIA had already advised. So the power of the Trilateralists was immense, even though Carter stepped back from their force.

What should be a warning to us is that an un-elected body of private individuals, because that is what they are, when attending Bilderberg or Trilateral meetings, can command the affairs of the world which will effect us in our entirety.

In case you might think that this was an exception let us now study George Bush, a politician from the other side. (Republican).

After briefing Jimmy Carter on the world situation, George Bush, head of the CIA, tendered his resignation. Several weeks later he was, like Jimmy Carter, asked to join the Trilateral Commission by David Rockefeller. Bush, describing the Trilateral Commission as a, "Very worthwhile organisation", accepted. Bush was now being considered as the replacement for Jimmy Carter, who at that time was considered a liability by David Rockefeller. Rockefeller must have been impressed with George Bush as he took with him a small cheque towards his fighting fund, with a promise of more to come, including a Rockefeller fund raising dinner. Now, you ask yourself, how is it Rockefeller funds a Democrat one moment and a Republican the next? The answer is of course that to Rockefeller, at his level, there is no difference; the real test is how pliable the candidate is, and how hungry he is for power. When they are hungry for power they can be moulded and manipulated with greater ease. Bush was very hungry, and through his Masonic links was already a converted 'One Worlder', an almost perfect start for a malleable President as far as Rockefeller was concerned.

During his time as a Trilateral Commissioner, George Bush attended two full scale Commission conferences in Bonn and Washington, and smaller meetings around North America. Prudently, in October 1978, he resigned from the Commission before he set up his 'Bush for President' campaign committee. The campaign under way, began to show the same signs of support from the press and funding from the power bankers that Carter's earlier campaign had received. It was money power buying political power. Carter knew straight away he was being pushed aside by his former sponsors. Rockefeller had judged the mood of America, and put up a candidate to the so called right, who vowed to, "Strengthen our Intelligence", words the people wanted to hear. Now we must realise that parties don't matter; it is the people behind politics who control the agenda and buy who is elected.

George Bush was rich, having made his fortune in the 50's from Texan oil, but he also cherished his East Coast contacts, which fared well for him because for the first time, the Texan oil magnates and the East Coast Establishment agreed on the same candidate, George Bush.

Having won the Iowa State Caucus, just like Jimmy Carter, he rapidly became a front runner from an outsider position at 50-2. Once again 'George Who?' was the call, and once again no member of the press asked about his two year membership of the Trilateral Commission.

But his luck was to change when William Loeb, a publisher, outside the control of the establishment, started a fierce campaign against Bush and his connection to the Trilateral Commission and its backer Rockefeller. Loeb started to promote Ronald Reagan, putting Bush down as the lackey of the 'Liberal Establishment' of 'One Worlders'.

Bush was ousted in New Hampshire by people power, which shocked him considerably, because of the size of the defeat.

The word was out, Bush would not recover. As we know, Ronald Reagan won and made George Bush his Vice President, but Bush would succeed an old, tired, Reagan and become another pawn in Rockefeller's game plan.

A third name that also rose rapidly was that of John B. Anderson, another member of the Trilateral Commission. This gives us a detailed insight that shows how money power corrupts the democratic system. Our aim should be to change election rules to remove the possibility of money power corruption and media controlled interference because it is these two powers, both in the same hands, that endanger our democracy.

So now let us turn and look at the man himself, David Rockefeller. He went into banking in 1946 after a education at Harvard and the London School of Economics. He was a man who believed in secret agendas along the narrow agenda of the radical Liberal desire for One World Government. He is a man who believes that he has a right, as a private citizen, to manipulate political power with money. He is a man who believes the world should move to an undemocratic World Government, controlled by bankers and their followers, multi-national corporate companies. David Rockefeller is the undisputed, and un-elected head of the world banking system. He has spent an abnormal part of his life pushing for his self financed groups to take over the high ground of American foreign policy. To do this he formed the Bilderberg Group. He was also involved in the Council on Foreign

Relations and was the original funder of the Trilateral Commission. His friend, Retinger, a Communist, was funded to develop the Bilderberg Group. He has funded all ideas that further the 'One World Government' cause.

So, where does he get his money from to substantially fund so many groups and foundations that move his baby, 'Globalism' forward?

As head of the Chase Manhattan Bank Rockefeller controls seven financial institutions, four banks and three major insurance companies; The Chase Manhattan Bank is the largest and most powerful bank in the world, doing business with over six-thousand banks all over the world. He also controls The First National City Bank, and the First National City Bank of Chicago. His Insurance Companies are; Metropolitan Life, Equitable, and New York Life.

His oil assets include working control of; Standard Oil of New Jersey; Standard Oil of California; Standard Oil of Indiana; Mobil Oil and Marathon Oil.

As if that is not enough he also has controlling interest in industry; Pan American Airways, Eastern Airlines, United Airlines, International Business Machines, American Telephone and Telegraph, Allied Chemicals, Anaconda Copper. Columbia Broadcasting System, Atlantic Richfield, Honeywell, CPC International, Safeways, Motorola, Borden, Kimberly Clark, and Domino.

He controls 20% of US banking (by far the biggest); 20% of American Industry; Half of the total production of US oil, and 25% of US investment.

By 1960 he became President of the Chase Bank and by 1968 he was appointed Chairman of the board of the Chase. Now came his initiation into the secret world of foreign policy planning. He was elected as a member of the 'Council on Foreign Relations', a secret forum for government foreign policy decisions and a debating society for the direction of government policies. It was also a recruiting ground for sensitive government positions and it is interesting to note once again that David Rockefeller's father donated the offices, Harold Pratt House, to the council as a gift.

Joseph Kraft, in the July 1958 issue of Harper stated; "It is undeniable that the council, (The Council on Foreign Relations acting as a corporate body), has influenced American policy with wide ranging effects upon the average citizen. Set against the total public, the council can hardly be called a representative body, its active membership is, by force of circumstance, Eastern, and, by any reckoning, either rich or successful. Its transactions are remote from public scrutiny". So this shows that it is undemocratic and possibly Anti-American, with its Eastern influence, which we find has a hidden agenda.

Rockefeller came to depend on the Council on Foreign Relations for advance information on world events, according to Peter Collier and David Horowitz, in their book; "The Rockefellers".

In 1964 Rockefeller gave 500,000 dollars to the Council on Foreign Relations; he was a major backer with foundations and this proves that the council was controlled by finance to produce policy in line with global strategy.

By 1972 Rockefeller was elected chairman of The Council and, by achieving this post, could directly influence American foreign policy, although this body, considered a government think tank, was in fact a private organ of the Rockefeller Empire and all its policies prepared for government were policies of the One World strategy, which Rockefeller used his power of money to promote. He is a man with a personal card index of thirty-five thousand 'friends' in high places. This assumed supremo status, self created by massive wealth, is today a direct challenge to democracy and National Sovereignty.

In Robert Eringer's book **(408)** he concluded, that he could not agree that the evidence he found added up to a conspiracy; yet he clearly shows how two groups, plus Rockefeller's Council on Foreign relations now create America's foreign policy. I have to say that his book, was written in 1980 and therefore I have been able to show a considerable number of policies created within these groups that have since come to light; for example Bleiberg's decision to have Lady Thatcher removed from office and the plan for the Gulf War. With hind sight these policies may have changed his conclusion. I believe I have clearly shown the path of conspiracy over 200 years and how it relates to these two organisations as well as the Council on Foreign Relations. I also think that the following list of Council members of the Trilateral Commission show how industry, banking, academia and the press are behind secret planning for our future world; and that it links to the original Weishaupt plan of 1776. (Note how many Ministers of Foreign Affairs attend these groups).

Many of the people listed as members are not aware of the motives of these groups. This is the danger of secret organisations. They believe they are helping the world to peaceful prosperity. They are, but the people they help are the bankers and Multi-National Corporations, not the mass population. For them the future is bleak unless we reverse the drift to Federal Globalism. Their participation can be likened to the original novices of the Illuminati, who were told enough to make them enthusiastic and nothing to make them suspicious.

(November 20th. 1979).
Georges Berthoin, European Chairman.
Egidio Ortona, European Deputy Chairman.
Martine Trink, European Secretary.
Takeshi Watanabe, Japanese Chairman.
Nobuhiko Ushiba, Japanese Deputy Chairman.
George S. Franklin, Co-ordinator.
Tadashi Yammoto, Japanese Secretary.
David Rockefeller, North American Chairman.
Mitchell Sharp, North American Deputy Chairman.
Charles B. Heck, North American Secretary.

NORTH AMERICAN MEMBERS.

David M. Abshire, Chairman, Georgetown University Centre for Strategic and International Studies.
Gardner Ackley, Henry Carter Adams University Professor of Political Economy,
University of Michigan.
Doris Anderson, President, The Canadian Advisory Council on the Status of Women;
Former Editor, Châtelaine Magazine.
John B. Anderson, US House of Representatives.
J. Paul Austin, Chairman, Coca-Cola Company.
George W. Ball, Senior Partner, Lehman Brothers.
Michel Belanger, President, provincial Bank of Canada.
Robert W. Bonner, QC., Chairman, British Columbia Hydro.
Robert R. Bowie, Harvard Centre for International Affairs.

John Brademas, US House of Representatives.
Andrew Brimmer, President, Brimmer and Co, Inc.
Arthur Burns, Distinguished Scholar in Residence, The American Enterprise, Institute for Public Policy Research; Former Chairman of the Board of Governors, US. Federal Reserve Board.
Philip Caldwell, Vice Chairman and President, Ford Motor Company.
Hugh Calkins, Partner, Jones, Day, Reavis & Pogue.
Claude Castonguay, President, Fonds Laurentien; Chairman of the Board, Imperial Life Assurance; former Minister in the Quebec Government.
Sol Chaikin, president, International ladies Garment Workers Union.
William S. Cohen, United States Senate.
William T. Coleman, Jr., Senior Partner, O'Melveny & Myers; former US Secretary of Transportation.
Barber B. Conale, Jr., US. House of Representatives.
John Cowles, Jr., Chairman, Minneapolis Star & Tribune Co.
John C. Culver, United States Senate.
Gerald L. Curtis, Director, East Asian Institute, Columbia University.
Louis A. Desrochers, Partner, McCuaig, Desrochers, Edmonton.
Peter Dobell, Director, parliamentary Centre for Foreign Affairs and Foreign Trade, Ottawa.
Claude A. Edwards, Member, Public Service Staff Relations Board; former
President, Public Service Alliance of Canada.
Daniel J. Evans, President, The Evergreen State College; former Governor of Washington.
Gordon Fairweather, Chief Commissioner, Canadian Human Rights Commission. Thomas S Foley, US. House of Representatives.
George S. Franklin, Co-ordinator, the Trilateral Commission; former Executive Director, **Council on Foreign Relations**.
Donald M. Fraser, Mayor of Minneapolis.
John H. Glenn, Jr., United States Senate.
Donald Southam Harvie, Deputy Chairman, Petro Canada.
Philip M. Hawley, President, Cartert Hawley Hale Stores, Inc.
Walter W. Heller, Regents' Professor of Economics, university of Minnesota.
William A. Hewitt, Chairman, Deere & Co.
Carla A Hilla, senior Resident Partner, Latham, Watkins & Hills; former US. Secretary of Housing and Urban Development.
Alan Hockin, executive Vice President, Toronto-Dominion Bank.
James F. Hoge, Jr., Chief Editor, Chicago Sun Times.
Hendrik S. Houthakker, Henry Lee Professor of Economics, Harvard University.
Thomas L. Hughes, president, Carnegie Endowment for International Peace.
Robert S. Ingersoll, Deputy Chairman of the Board of Trustees, The University of Chicago; former US. Deputy Secretary of State.
D. Gale Johnson, Provost, The University of Chicago.
Edgar F. Kaiser, Jr., President and Chief Executive Officer, Kaiser Resources Ltd.,
Vancouver, and Kaiser Steel Co., Oakland.
Michael Kirby, president, AFL-CIO.
Henry Kissinger, Former US. Secretary of State.

Joseph Kraft, Columnist.
Sol M. Linowitz, Senior Partner, Coudert Brothers; former US. Ambassador to The Organisation of American States.
Winston Lord, President, **Council on Foreign Relations.**
Donald S. Macdonald, McCarthy & McCarthy; former Canadian Minister of Finance.
Bruce K. MacLaury, President, The Brookings Institute.
Paul W. McCracken, Edmund Ezra Day professor of Business Administration, University of Michigan.
Arjay Miller, Dean Emeritus, graduate School of Business, Stanford University.
Kenneth D. Naden, President, National Council of Farmers Co-operatives.
Joseph S. Nye, Jr., John F. Kennedy School of Government, Harvard University.
David Packard, Chairman Hewlett-Packard Company.
Gerald L. Parsky, Partner, Gibson, Dunn & Crutcher; former US. Assistant Secretary of the Treasury, International Affairs.
William R. Peterson, Chairman, Lehman Brothers.
Edwin O. Reischauer, University Professor and Director Japan Institute, Harvard University; former US. Ambassador to Japan.
John O. Rielly, President, **The Chicago Council on Foreign Relations.**
Charles W. Robinson, Chairman, Energy Transition Corporation; former US Deputy Secretary of State.
David Rockefeller, Chairman, The Chase Manhattan Bank N.A.
John D. Rockefeller, IV, Governor of West Virginia. Robert V. Roosa, Partner, Brown. Bros., Harriman & Company.
Eilliam V. Roth, Roth Properties.
William V. Roth, Jr., United States Senate.
Henry B. Schacht, Chairman, Cummins Engine Inc.
J. Robert Schaetzel, Former US. Ambassador to the European Communities, Ambassador to the United Nations.
Mitchell Sharp, Commissioner, Northern Pipeline Agency; former Canadian Minister of External Affairs.
Mark Sheperd, Jr., Chairman, Texas Instruments Incorporated.
Edson W. Spencer, President and Chief Executive officer, Honeywell Inc.
Robert Taft, Jr., Partner, Taft, Stettinius & Hollister.
Arthur R. Taylor, Chairman, the American Assembly.
James R. Thompson, Governor of Illinois.
Russell E. Train, former Administrator, US. Environmental Protection Agency Assistant Secretary of State for Economic Affairs.
Martha R. Wallace, Executive Director, The Henry Luce Foundation Inc.
Martin J. Ward, President, United Association of Journeymen and Apprentices of the Plumbing and Pipe Fitting Industry of the United States and Canada.

Paul C. Warnke, Partner, Clifford and Warnke, former Director, US. Arms Control and Disarmament Agency and Chief Disarmament Negotiator.
Glenn E. Watts, President, Communications Workers of America.
Caspar W. Weinberger, Vice President and General Counsel, Bechtel Corporation.

George Weyerhaeuser, president and Chief Executive Officer, Weyerhaeuser Company.
Marina v.N. Whitman, Vice President and Chief Economist, General Motors Corporation.
Carroll L. Wilson, Mitsui Professor Emeritus in Problems of Contemporary Technology, School of Engineering, MIT; Director, World Coal Study.
T.A. Wilson, Chairman of the Board, The Boeing Company.

Former Members in Public Service.
Lucy Wilson Benson, US. Under Secretary of the State for Security Assistance.
Harold Brown, US. Secretary of Defence.
Zbigniew Brzezinski, US. Assistant to the President for National Security Affairs.
Jimmy Carter, President of the United States.
Warren Christopher, US. Deputy Secretary of State.
Richard N. Cooper, US. Under Secretary of State for Economic Affairs.
Lloyd N. Cutler, Counsel to the President of the United States.
Hedley Donovan, Special Assistant to the President of The United States.
John Allen Fraser, Canadian Postmaster General and Minister of the Environment.
Richard N. Gardner, US. Ambassador to Italy.
Richard Holbrooke, US. Assistant Secretary of State for East Asian and Pacific Affairs.
Walter F. Mondale, Vice President of the United States.
Henry Owen, Special Representative of the President for Economic Summits; US. Ambassador at Large.
Elliot L. Richardson, US. Ambassador at Large with Responsibility for UN Law of the Sea Conference.
John C. Sawhill, US. Deputy Secretary of Energy.
Gerard C. Smith, US. Ambassador at Large for non-proliferation Matters.
Anthony M. Solomon, US. Under Secretary of the Treasury for Monetary Affairs.
Cyrus Vance, US. Secretary of State.
Paul A. Volcker, Chairman, Board of Governors, US. Federal Reserve System.

European Members.
Giovanni Agnelli, President Fiat.
P. Nyboe Anderson, Chief General Manager, Andelsbanken A/s; former Danish
Minister for Economic Affairs and Trade.
Luis Maria Anson, Presidente de la Agencia EFE, Madrid; Presidente, Federacion Nacional de Asociaciones de la Prensa.
Giovanni Auletta Armenise, Chairman, Banca Nazionale dell' Agricultura, Rome.
Piero Bassetti, Chamber of Defence, Rome.
E.K. den Bakker, Chairman of the Board, Nationale Nederlanden.
Georges Berthoin, President, European Movement.

Kurt H. Biedenkopf, Deputy Chairman, Christian Democratic Union, Federal Republic of Germany, Member of the Bundestag.
Claudio Boada, Chairman, Altos Hornos de Vizaya; former Chairman, Instituto Nacional de Industria Madrid.
Macel Boiteux, Chairman, French Electricity Board.

Henrik N. Boon, Chairman, Netherlands Institute for International Affairs; Former Dutch Ambassador to NATO and Italy.
Guido Carli, President, Confindustria; former Governor , Bank of Italy.
Hervé de Carmoy, Président du Directoire, Midland Bank, Paris.
Jaime Carvajal, Chairman, Banco Urquijo, Madrid.
Jean Claude Casonova, Conseiller auprès du Premier Ministre; former Professor of Political Science, Institute of Political Studies, Paris.
José Luis Cerón, former President of the Spanish Board of Trade; Chairman of ASETA.
Willy de Clercq, Chairman, Party for Freedom and Progress, Belgium.
Umberto Colombo, President, National Committee for Nuclear Energy, Rome.
Guido Colonna di Paliano, Former Italian Ambassador to Norway.
Francesco Compagna, Chamber of Deputies, Rome.
Richard Conroy, Member of Senate, Irish Republic.
The Earl of Cromer, advisor to Baring Bros. & Co., Ltd.; Former British Ambassador to the United States.
Antoinette Danis-Spaak, Chairman, Democratic Front of French Speaking Bruxellois, Member of the Chamber of Representatives.
Paul Delouvrier, Former Chairman, French Electricity Board.
Jean Dromer, Président Directeur Général, Banque Internationale pour l'Afrique Occidental.
François Duchêne, Director, Sussex European Research Centre, University of Sussex.
Horst Ehmke, Deputy Chairman, parliamentary Fraction of Social Democratic Party, Federal Republic of Germany; Member of the Bundestag; Former Minister of Justice.
Pierre Esteva, Directeur Général, Union des Assurances de Paris.
Carlos Ferrer, Chairman, Spanish Confederation of Employers' Organisations; Chairman Ferrer International.
K. Fibbe, Chairman of the Board, Overseas Gas and Electricity Company, Rotterdam.
M. H. Fisher, Editor, Financial Times, London.
Garret Fitzgerald, Member of Irish Parliament and Leader of Fine Gael Party,
Former foreign Minister of Ireland.
René Foch, Conseiller Principal, French Delegation to the OECD.
Antonio Garrigues, Director, Association para el Progeso de la Direción, Madrid.
Michel Gaudet, Président, Fédération Française des Sociétés d'Assurances; Président,
Du Comité Européen des Assurances.
Sir Ray Gelds, Chairman, Dunlop Holdings Ltd.
Giuseppe Glisenti, President, La Rinascente, Milan.
Ronald Grierson, Director, General Electric Company Ltd., London.

Lord Harlech, Chairman Harlech Television; former British Ambassador to the United States.
Hans Hartwig, Chairman, German Association for Wholesale and Foreign Trade.
Denis Healy, member of British Parliament; former Chancellor of the Exchequer.
Edward Heath, Member of the British Parliament, former Prime Minister.
Terrence Higgins, Member of the British Parliament, former Minister of State and Financial Secretary to the Treasury.
Diether Hoffman, Speaker of the Board of Directors, Bank für Gemeinwirtschaft AG.,
Frankfurt on Main.
Jozef P. Houthuys, Chairman, Belgium Confederation of Christian Trade Unions.
Ludwig Huber, President, Bayerische Landesbank, Girozentrale Munich.
Horst K. Jannott, Chairman, Board of Directors, Munich Reinsurance Society.
Daniel E. Janssen, Administrateur Délégué et Directeur Général, Belgian Chemical Union.
Karl Kaiser, Director, Research Institute of the German Society for Foreign Policy.
Sir Kenneth Keith, Chairman, Rolls Royce Ltd.
Henry N.L. Keswick, Chairman, Matheson & Company Ltd.
Michael Killeen, Managing Director, Industrial Development Authority of the Irish Republic.
Norbert Kloten, President, Central Bank of the State of Baden-Württemberg.
Sir Arthur Knight, Chairman, Courtaulds Ltd.
Max Kohnstamm, Principal, European University Institute, Florence.
Erwin Kristoffersen, Director, German Federation of Trade Unions.
Jacques Lallement, Directeur Général du Crédit Agricole, Paris.
Giorgio La Malfa, Chambers od Deputies, Rome.
Baron Léon Lambert, Président du Groupe Bruxelles Lambert, SA.
Liam Lawlor, Member of the Irish Parliament.
Arrigo Levi, Columnist, La Stampa, Turin, and the Times, London.
Mark Littman, Deputy Chairman, British Steel Corporation.
Richard Löwenthal, Professor Emeritus, Free University of Berlin.
Evan Luard, Former Parliamentary Under-secretary of State for the British Foreign Office.
Roderick MacFarquhar, Former Member of the British Parliament.
Carlos March Delgado, chairman, Banca March, Madrid; Vice Chairman Juan March Foundation.
Robert Marjolin, former Vice President of the Commission of the European Communities.
Roger Martin, Président, Compagnie Saint Goblin Pont-à-Mousson.
Haans W. Maull, Journalist; Writer, Bayerischer Rundfunk.
Pietro Merli-Brandini, secretary General, Italian Confederation of Labour Unions.
Cesare Merlini, Director, Institute for International Affairs, Rome.
Thierry de Montbrial, director, Institut Français des Relations Internationales, Paris.

Alwin Münchmeyer, Chairman of the Board, Bank Schröder, Münchmeyer Hengst & Co.
Preben Munthe, Professor of Economics, Oslo University; official Chief Negotiator between Labour Unions and Industry.
Dan Murphy, secretary –General of the Civil Service Executive Union, Dublin.
Karl Heinz Narjes, Member of the Bundestag.
Friedrich A Neuman, Chairman, State Association, Industrial Employers Societies, North-Rhine Westphalia.
Egidio Ortona, President, Honeywell Information Systems, Italia; Former Italian Ambassador to the United States.
Alfonso Osorio, Member of the Spanish House of Representatives; Former Vice President of the Spanish Government.
Bernard Pagezy, Président Directeur Général, Sociétés des Assurances du Groupe de Paris.
Antonio Pedrol, Chairman, Consejo General de la Abogacía Española.
Sir John Pilcher, Former British Ambassador to Japan.
Konrad Porzner, Parlamentarischer Geschaeftsfuehrer der Sozial-Demokratischen Bundestagsfraktion; Member of the Bundestag.
Jean Rey, Ministre d'Etat, Belgium; former President of the Commission of The European Communities.
Julian Ridsdale, Member of the British Parliament; Chairman, Anglo-Japanese Parliamentary Group.
Sir Frank Roberts, Advisory Director, Unilever Ltd., Former British Ambassador to Germany and the Soviet Union.
Mary T. W. Robinson, Member of the Senate, Irish Republic.
Lord Roll, Chairman, S.G. Warburg and Co. Ltd.
John Roper, Member of the British Parliament.
Franois de Rose, Ambassadeur de France; Président Directeur Général, Société Nouvelle Pathé Cinéma.
Baron Edmond de Rothschild, Président Compagnie Financière Holding, Paris.
Ivo Samkalden, Former Mayor of Amsterdam.
John C. Sanness, Professor, Norwegian Institute for Foreign Affairs.
W.E. Scherpenhuijsen Rom, Chairman, Board of Managing Directors, Nederlandsche Middenstandsbank, NV.
Erik Ib Schmidt, Permanent Under-secretary of State, Denmark; Chairman, Risø National Laboratory.
Th. M. Scholten, Chairman of the Board, Robeco Investment Group, Rotterdam.
Gerhard Schröder, Member of the Bundestag; former Foreign Minister of the Federal Republic of Germany.
Pedro Schwartz, Director, Instituto de Económia de Mercado, Madrid.
José Antonio Segurado, Chairman, International Relations Commission, Spanish Confederation of Employers' Organisations; Chairman, SEFISA.
Erik Seidenfaden, Editor, Directeur de la Fondation Danoise, Institut Universitaire International de Paris.

Frederico Sensi, Ambassador of Italy; Former Italian Ambassador to the Soviet Union.
Roger Seydoux, Ambassadeur de France; Président du Conseil d'Administration, Fondation de France.
Lord Shackleton, Deputy Chairman, Rio Tinto-Zinc Corporation Ltd., London.
Sir Andrew Shonfield, professor of Economics, European University Institute, Florence; Former Director, Royal Institute of International Affairs.
J.H. Smith, Deputy Chairman and Chief Executive Officer, British Gas Corporation.
Hans-Günther Sohl, Chairman of the Board, Thyssen A.G.
Theo Sommer, Editor-in-Chief, Die Ziet.
Myles Staunton, Member of the Senate, Irish Republic.
G.R. Storry, Professor, Far East Centre, St. Antony's College, Oxford.
John A. Swire, Chairman, John Swire and Sons Group of Companies.
Peter Tapsell, Member of British Parliament; Junior Conservative Spokesman On Foreign and Commonwealth Affairs; Former Conservative Spokesman on Treasury and Economic Affairs.
Niels Thygesen, professor of Economics, economic Institute, Copenhagen University.
Otto Grieg Tidemand, Ship-owner; former Norwegian Minister of Defence and Minister of Economic Affairs.
Ramón Trias Fargas, Member, Spanish House of Representatives; Chairman, Convergencia Democratica de Cataluña.
Sir Anthony Tuke, UK. Group Chairman, Barclays Bank Ltd.
Sir Mark Turner, Chairman, Rio Tinto-Zinc Corporation Ltd.
Heinz-Oskar Vetter, Chairman, German Federation of Trade Unions; Chairman, European Federation of Trade Unions.
José Vilá Marsans, Chairman, Sociedad Anonima de Fibras Artificiales; Director, Banco Central, Barcelona.
Paolo Vittorelli, member of the Italian Parliament, Director, Amanita.
Sir Frederick Warner, director Guinness Peat Overseas Ltd.; Former British Ambassador to Japan.
Luc Waiters, Chairman, Groupe Almanij-Kredietbank, Brussels.
Edmund Wellenstein, former Director General for External Affairs, Commission of the European communities.
Kenneth Whitaker, Member of the Senate, Irish Republic; former Governor of the Central Bank of Ireland.
Alan Lee Williams, Former Member of the British Parliament.
Otto Wolff von Amerongen, President, Otto Wolff A.G.; President, German Federation of Trade and Industry.
Sir Philip de Zulueta, Chairman, Anthony Gibbs Holdings Ltd.

Former Members in Public Service.
Svend Auken, Minister of Labour, Denmark.
Raymond Barre, Prime Minister and Finance Minister, French Republic.
Lord Carrington, British Secretary of State for Foreign and Commonwealth Affairs.
Michel Debatisse, Food and Agricultural Minister, French Republic.

Herbert Ehrenberg, Minister of Labour and Social Affairs, Federal Republic of Germany.
Marc Eykens, Belgium minister of Co-operative development.
Bernard Hayhoe, Parliamentary Under Secretary of State, British Defence Ministry.
Otto Graf Lambsdorff, Minister of Economics, Federal Republic of Germany.
Jean-Philippe Lecat, Minister of Culture and Communications, French Republic.
Ivar Nøgaard, Danish Minister of the Environment.
Michael O'Kennedy, Minister of Foreign Affairs, Irish Republic.
Henri Simonet, Minister of Foreign Affairs, Belgium.
Thorvald Stoltenberg, Secretary of State, Norwegian Ministry of Foreign Affairs.
Olaf Sund, Senator for Labour and Social Affairs, land Government of Berlin.
Michael Woods, Minister for State in the Office of the Irish Prime Minister.

(409).

When you study this list and analyse the positions held by the participants you begin to see a pattern. There is a large contingent of serving or past politicians. Amongst those politicians there is a considerable contingent from the foreign affairs section of government. There is also another section that can be traced by going back to the sphere of influence of the Rothschild bank (Report One; Volume One) and you will find, particularly in the English contingent that most of the members are also involved with this banker in some way or another.

There are two people in particular who are active everywhere the global movement appears; David Rockefeller and Dr. Henry Kissinger. Other names seem to be embedded in its centre like Lord Carrington, Raymond Barre, Paul Volcker, Zbigniew Brzezinski, and the elusive Edward Heath.

There is also a large contingent who attend these meetings that have been involved with the Council on Foreign Relations or the equivalent in other countries. This all helps me to decide that there is a proven conspiracy between these groups that goes back in history to the Rothschild involvement with Communism.

The following chart of the plan of conspiracy shows another very interesting fact that, until I made this flow chart, I confess I had not noticed. If you look at the chart it quite clearly shows how the Rothschild sphere of influence concentrated their resources on breaking down the 'Old World Order', while the Rockefeller family were largely involved in building up 'The New World Order'. Now we have come to the end. We are not able to speak about the Inner Group as there is practically nothing known about them accept they call themselves the Guardians. Suffice it to say that they hold their meetings in absolute privacy within the confines of their banking kingdoms or at their private estates, so no leakage has given us the chance to expose their names or their debates. But this is in a way not important. What is important is what we see to be happening and I hope you will help me give this proven fraud maximum publicity, because it is urgent that we act now to stop the drift to Globalism through Dictatorship

THE HIDDEN TREE OF POWER.

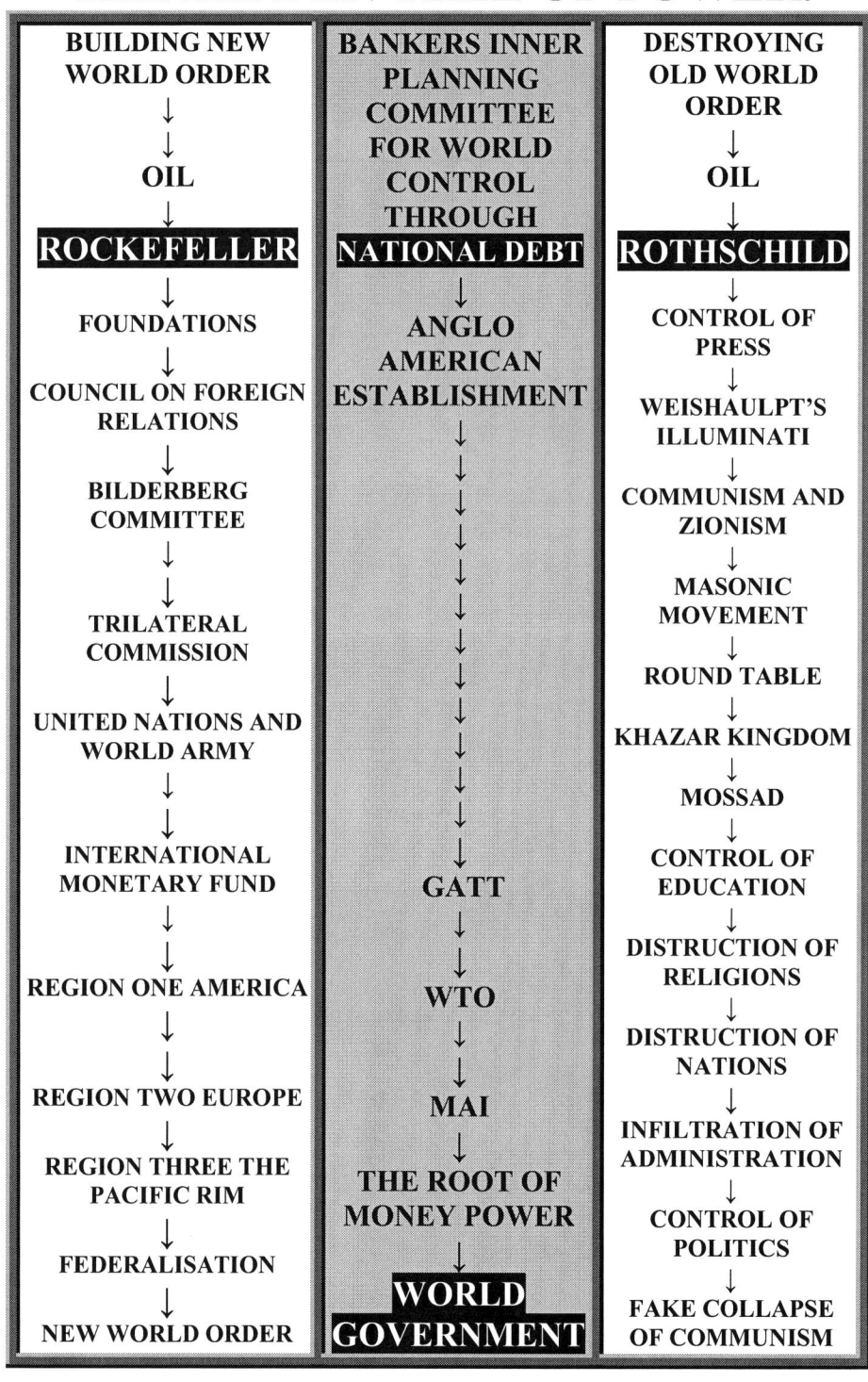

BUILDING NEW WORLD ORDER	BANKERS INNER PLANNING COMMITTEE FOR WORLD CONTROL THROUGH NATIONAL DEBT	DESTROYING OLD WORLD ORDER
↓	↓	↓
OIL		OIL
↓		↓
ROCKEFELLER		**ROTHSCHILD**
↓	↓	↓
FOUNDATIONS	ANGLO AMERICAN ESTABLISHMENT	CONTROL OF PRESS
↓	↓	↓
COUNCIL ON FOREIGN RELATIONS		WEISHAULPT'S ILLUMINATI
↓	↓	↓
BILDERBERG COMMITTEE		COMMUNISM AND ZIONISM
↓	↓	↓
TRILATERAL COMMISSION		MASONIC MOVEMENT
↓	↓	↓
UNITED NATIONS AND WORLD ARMY		ROUND TABLE
↓	↓	↓
INTERNATIONAL MONETARY FUND		KHAZAR KINGDOM
↓	↓	↓
		MOSSAD
↓	↓	↓
REGION ONE AMERICA	GATT	CONTROL OF EDUCATION
↓	↓	↓
REGION TWO EUROPE	WTO	DISTRUCTION OF RELIGIONS
↓	↓	↓
REGION THREE THE PACIFIC RIM	MAI	DISTRUCTION OF NATIONS
↓	↓	↓
FEDERALISATION	THE ROOT OF MONEY POWER	INFILTRATION OF ADMINISTRATION
↓	↓	↓
NEW WORLD ORDER	**WORLD GOVERNMENT**	CONTROL OF POLITICS
		↓
		FAKE COLLAPSE OF COMMUNISM

THE BRITISH AMERICAN PROJECT
FOR SUCCESSOR GENERATIONS.

In the last chapter we dealt with the power structure just below the bankers who are planning the gradual take-over of world power, such as the Trilateral Commission, the Bilderberg committee and the Ditchley Foundation. There are other layers of more localised groups that are preparing each developed country for the eventual move to a federalised regional grouping in readiness for world government. It would be interesting to briefly study one such group that is active in two regions, America and Britain. It is the 'British American Project for the Successor Generation'. In it you will find groupings that line up with and are complementary to their peers, the Bilderberg Group and the Trilateral Commission, and carry the work of these groups forward to the next stage of federal planning for the area they represent. (unofficially).

Perhaps I should make it crystal clear at this stage that each person is an individual who does not represent his employer although some are indeed the top executives or representatives of their companies. What they are preparing is the next layer down in readiness for regional government.

I have in my possession a newsletter of the British - American Project for the Successor Generation, from Spring 1987, listing members at the conference. It is marked Private, for circulation only among Alumni and other trusted friends. Each member has a phone number provided and in most cases a photograph. This newsheet was a supplement, listing the members of the 1986 conference. It was a special supplement to 'Signal' their in-house-magazine. I don't intend to print the entire list of attendees but just to mention one or two.

Christopher Beauman, Morgan Grenfell Investment Management Ltd.
Lt. Col. F.R. Dannatt MC, Ministry of Defence, Whitehall.
Alan Doig, SES Faculty Office, University of Liverpool.
Stephen Dorrell, Conservative MP.
Michael Elliott, The Economist, USA.
Daniel Franklin, The Economist, GB.
Gloria Franklin, Head of Political Studies, Ministry of Defence.
David Lipsey, New Society. London.
Kenneth Ludmerer, Washington University.
David Natzler, House of Commons.
Julia Neuberger, South London Liberal Synagogue.
Trevor Phillips, LWT, South Bank TV.
Stephen Quinn, Arthur Anderson and Co.
Paul Schulte. Ministry of Defence.
Sue Slipman, National Council on One Parent Families. Ex-communist.
Carole Stone, BBC Bristol.
Christopher Smith, MP, House of Commons
The Hon. Rupert Soames, GEC Computers Ltd.
Julian Target, Confederation of British Industry.

Michael Waldman, BBC Television.
Stephen Waley-Cohen, Jewish Leader.
Nicholas Wolfers, Midland Bank International.
Michael R. Zedek, Temple B'nai Jehudah, USA.

The meeting had eighty-five participants.

What you have seen from this small extract is a group, largely Jewish, which represents people from banking, Multinational Companies, the investment industry, education (particularly University), defence, the media, politics, local government, energy, civil service, and Jewish leaders.

These are in the main precisely the areas targeted for penetration to develop the revolution within our society and all the components must be considered to be well placed by now.

This group is a joint venture of the Royal Institute of International Affairs (Chatham House, London), a Institute set up by Cecil Rhodes' friends and the School of International Studies (SAIS) of the John Hopkins University of Washington DC. The Anglo American dream ticket to world domination without democracy by un-elected, self appointed, decision makers without a mandate from the people.

PROTOCOL TWENTY-ONE

LOANS AND CREDIT.

To what I reported to you at the last meeting I shall now add a detailed explanation of internal loans. Of foreign loans I shall say nothing more, because they have fed us with the national moneys of the goyim, but for our State there will be no foreigners, that is, nothing external.

We have taken advantage of the venality of administrators and the slackness of rulers to get our moneys twice, thrice and more times over by lending to the goy governments moneys which were not needed by the States. Could anyone do the like in regards to us?…Therefore, I shall only deal with details of internal loans.

States announce that such a loan is to be concluded and open subscriptions for their own bills of exchange, that is, for their interest-bearing paper. That they may be within the reach of all, the price is determined at from a hundred to a thousand; and a discount is made for the earliest subscribers. Next day, by artificial means, the price of them goes up, the alleged reason being that everyone is rushing to buy them. In a few days the treasury safes are, as they say, overflowing, and there's more money than they can do with. (why then take it?) The subscription, it is alleged, covers many times over the issue total of the loan; in this lies the whole stage effect – look you, they say, what confidence is shown in the government's bills of exchange.

But when the comedy is played out there emerges the fact that a debit, and an exceedingly burdensome debit, has been created. For the payment of interest it becomes necessary to have recourse to new loans, which do not swallow up but only add to the capital debt. And, when this credit is exhausted it becomes necessary by new taxes to cover, not the loan, but only the interest on it. These taxes are a debit employed to cover a debit.

Later comes the time for conversions, but they diminish the payment of interest without covering the debt, and besides they cannot be made without the consent of the lenders; on announcing a conversion a proposal is made to return the money to those who are not willing to convert their paper. If everybody expressed his willingness and demanded his money back, the government would be hoisted on their own petard and would be found insolvent and unable to pay the proposed sums. By good luck the subjects of the goy governments, knowing nothing about financial affairs, have always preferred losses on exchange and diminution of interest to the risk of new investments of their moneys, and have thereby many a time enabled these governments to throw off their shoulders a debit of several millions.

Nowadays, with external loans, these tricks cannot be played by the goyim for they know that we shall demand all our moneys back.

In this way an acknowledged bankruptcy will best prove to the various countries the absence of any means between the interests of the peoples and those that rule them.

I beg you to concentrate your particular attention upon this point and upon the following: nowadays all internal loans are consolidated by so-called flying loans, that is, such as have terms of payment more or less near. These debts consist of moneys paid into the savings banks and reserve funds. If left for long at the disposition of a government these funds evaporate in the payment of interest on foreign loans, and are replaced by the deposit of equivalent amount of rents. And these last it is, which patch up all the leaks in the State treasuries of the goyim.

When we ascend the throne of the world all these financial and similar shifts, as being not in accord with our interests, will be swept away so as not to leave a trace, as also will be destroyed all money markets, since we shall not allow the prestige of our power to be shaken by fluctuations of prices set upon our values, which we shall announce by law at the price which represents their full worth without any possibility of lowering or raising. (Raising gives the pretext for lowering, which indeed was where we made a beginning in relation to the values of the goyim).

We shall replace the money markets by grandiose government credit institutions, the object of which will be to fix the price of industrial values in accordance with government views. These institutions will be in a position to fling upon the market five hundred millions of industrial paper in one day, or to buy up for the same amount. In this way all industrial undertakings will come into dependence upon us. You may imagine for yourselves what immense power we shall thereby secure for ourselves...

PROTOCOL TWENTY-THREE

INSTILLING OBEDIENCE.

That peoples may become accustomed to obedience it is necessary to instil lessons of humility and therefore to reduce the production of articles of luxury. By this we shall improve morals which have been debased by emulation in the sphere of luxury. We shall re-establish small master production which will mean laying a mine under the private capital of manufacturers. This is indispensable also for the reason that manufacturers on the grand scale often move, though not always consciously, the thoughts of the masses in directions against the government. A people of small masters knows nothing of unemployment and this binds them closely with existing order, and consequently with the firmness of authority. Unemployment is a most perilous thing for a government. For us its part will have been played out the moment authority is transferred into our hands. Drunkenness will also be prohibited by law and punishable as a crime against the humanness of man who is turned into a brute under the influence of alcohol.

Subjects, I repeat once more, give blind obedience only to the strong hand which is absolutely independent of them, for in it they feel the sword of defence and support against social scourges.... What do they want with an angelic spirit in a king? What they must see in him is the personification of force and power.

The supreme lord who will replace all existing rulers, dragging on their existence among societies demoralised by us, societies that have denied even the authority of God, from whose midst breaks out on all sides the fire of anarchy, must first of all proceed to quench this all-devouring flame. Therefore he will be obliged to kill off those existing societies, though he shall drench them with his own blood, that he may resurrect them again in the form of regularly organised troops fighting consciously against every kind of inflection that may cover the body of the State with sores.

This chosen one of God is chosen from above to demolish the senseless forces moved by instinct and not reason, by brutishness and not humanness. These forces now triumph in manifestations of robbery and every kind of violence under the mask of principles of freedom and rights. They have overthrown all forms of social order to erect on the ruins the throne of the King of the Jews; but their part will be played out the moment he enters into his kingdom. Then it will be necessary to sweep them away from the path, on which must be left no knot, no splinter.

Then will it be possible for us to say to the peoples of the world: Give thanks to God and bow the knee before him who bears on his front the seal of the predestination of man to which God himself has led his star that none other but Him might free us from all the before-mentioned forces and evils.

PROTOCOL TWENTY-FOUR
QUALITIES OF THE RULER.

I pass now to the method of confirming the dynastic roots of King David to the last strata of the earth.

The confirmation will first and foremost be included in that in which to this day has rested the force of conservatism by our learned elders of the conduct of all the affairs of the world, in the directing of the education of thought of all humanity.

Certain members of the seed of David will prepare the Kings and their heirs, selecting not by right of heritage but by eminent capacities, inducting them into the most secret mysteries of the political, into schemes of government, but providing always that none may come to know the secrets. The object of this mode of action is that all may know that government cannot be entrusted to those who have not been inducted into the secret places of this art….

To these persons only will be taught the practical application of the a forenamed plans by comparison of the experiences of many centuries, all the observations on the politico-economic moves and social sciences – in a word, all the spirit of laws which have been unshakeably established by nature herself for the regulation of the relations of humanity.

Direct heirs will often be set aside from ascending the throne if in their time of training they exhibit frivolity, softness and other qualities that are the ruin of authority, which render them incapable of governing and in themselves dangerous for Kingly office.

Only those who are unconditionally capable of firm, even cruel, direct rule will receive the reins of power from our learned elders.

In case of falling sick with weakness of will or other form of incapacity, Kings must by law hand over the reins of rule to new and capable hands….

The King's plans of action for the current moment, and all the more so for the future, will be unknown, even to those who are called his closest counsellors.

Only the King and the three who stood sponsor for him will know what is coming.

In the person of the King who with unbending will is master of himself and of humanity all will discern as it were fate with its mysterious ways. None will know what the king wishes to attain by his dispositions, and therefore none will dare to stand across an unknown path.

It is understood that the brain reservoir of the King must correspond in capacity to the plan of government it has to contain. It is for this reason that he will ascend the throne not otherwise than after examination of his mind by the aforesaid learned elders.

That the people may know and love their king it is indispensable for him to converse in the market-places with his people. This ensures the necessary clinching of the two forces which are now divided one from another by us by the terror.

This terror was indispensable for us till the time comes for both these forces separately to fall under our influence.

The King of the Jews must not be at the mercy of his passions, and especially of sensuality: on no side of his character must he give brute instincts power over his mind. Sensuality worse than all else disorganises the capacities of the mind and clearness of views; distracting the thoughts to the worst and most brutal side of human activity.

> The prop of humanity in the person of the supreme lord of all the world of the holy seed of David must sacrifice to his people all personal inclinations.
> Our supreme lord must be of an exemplary irreproachability.
> Signed by the Representatives of Zion, of the 33rd. degree.

COMMENT.

So we see the end of the Protocols. I do not know whether they are a genuine document of historical importance or a skilful attempt to discredit the Jewish race. Either way they do not take away a word of the history of conspiracy that I have uncovered. As far as I am concerned, if they are genuine they relate accurately to the pattern of events that have taken place in the last century. If they are a deceitful plan to blacken the Jewish race they can only have been a remarkable account that has proved to have been prophetic and consistently accurate.

You must judge for yourself which they may be as the experts have been divided for a century. What is much more important is that what has been described as a conspiracy theory has now I think been shown to be a fact. We must carefully consider the implications of this as it will effect our children's future. Do we want them to live in a world of dictatorship from the men who have created every war there has been in the last two-hundred years?

Do we want our children to continue to live in debt slavery to the bankers? If not, I have shown you what we must do to beat the Guardians at their own game.

THE WORLD AND EUROPE
A HIDDEN AGENDA: BEHIND A HALL OF MIRRORS
SUMMARY

When I first decided to research the power behind the drive to a Federal Europe all I expected to find was the undemocratic manner in which the un-elected commissioners made the decisions about Europe. It was obviously being manipulated by some un-known force and I wanted to know exactly how this invisible control operated. It was therefore a complete surprise to me when I found that it had a history, going back two hundred years, and involving the whole world in a hidden plan for world government.

When I gradually came to terms with my research I knew I could not tell the history of Europe without the larger world influence. So I set about finding a certain way of logging the facts that I had found so that they would, despite my personal prejudices, and indeed the prejudices of the authors I quote, deliver a sound judgement on the pure historical content. The most effective and positive method I found was an analysis of direction, which, is used throughout the history. By direction I mean in which direction the initiative moved after a war, or peace treaty, or recession. I found, in testing this system over parts of history, that it was by far the most accurate barometer for accessing power; where it came from and to where it was going.

So you see throughout this history how direction plays the key role of delivering a positive answer as to whether the events are, as a collection, a factual truth (the continual one way direction bringing the positive proof) or just another theory as the bankers would have you believe. I claimed in the introduction to this series that it would turn everything we know through the media on its head and I think you will agree that it does when you read this summary; and remember it is just a summary of the complete work, so it has no bibliography as you find in the complete history. Now let us sit back and remind ourselves of some of the important facts we have learned during this history of power.

Our history begins with the birth of Meyer Amschel Rothschild in a rough tenement at the back of the Judengasse in 1744, the son of a Jewish merchant of Frankfurt.

When he eventually became a merchant banker he was introduced to the Masonic lodge of L'Aurore by Geisenheimer, a lodge connected to the Grand Orient. The whole history you will read, stems from this chance introduction to Masonry. .

His business was already providing food, and clothing, as well as being the paymaster to the Prussian troop). By 1807 he moved into the finance of governments to include war and army equipment.

In 1802, Solomon Rothschild, one of five sons, joined the Lodge of L'Aurore, already 'illuminated' by Weishaupt. Nathan was now in England developing his banking contacts and buying goods in England for sale back home in Frankfurt.

Mayer (Now changed in spelling to sound more German) Amschel Rothschild opened a school within his Jewish community that taught the Torah but also studied revolutionary literature like Voltaire, showing his interest in revolutionary teaching. This was not universally popular amongst his other Jewish compatriots.

His banking business was expanding, with a string of loans to Governments; showing his desire to reach the point where he could control politics through banking loans.

Meanwhile in London Nathan Rothschild was lending money to England for its part in the European theatre of war and was even able to bring news of the war to the government before its own couriers.

Because of conflicts, governments needed funding to go to war. Rothschild provided that funding; in some cases funding both sides through agents so they could not be found out in their disloyalty. The American civil war was one example as indeed we find their agents on all sides in the Second World War.

By the mid eighteen hundreds war and government loans were the bulk of their business, both very profitable, encompassing the financing of arms, army logistics, and pay-rolling. But unknown by most informed politicians there was a far more dangerous possibility from the gradual build up of debt owed by each country to one source and its agents. **(Direction).**

It was at this time that Solomon, the eldest son, became involved in the Masonic movement, which by chance was a lodge Illuminated by Weishaupt. From this moment on, revolution to kill Christian religion, confiscate land and property, including farmland, and move the world to a single dictatorship, was funded by the Rothschild bankers.

A policy was drawn up by a member of Weishaupt's Illuminati; one Carl Levy, (Later known as Carl Marx) entitled the 'Communist Party Manifesto'; a plan that without funding would have been dead and buried well before its author, but this evil policy, born from all the worst of Satan's devious plans, was an atheist platform that was deceitful to its supporters; but survived solely through funding. The working class was promised freedom from slavery and power over their lives. In fact the hidden policy of Communism was a plan to suit the rich and powerful at the expense of the working class. This was the hidden high road to revolution.

So Communism, which should have died, was carried forward by International Finance Capitalism, in secret, as a weapon of revolution to achieve total political and monetary control of the world. Weishaupt's 'New World Order'. **(Direction).**

The Rothschild bank was enslaving one country after another into debt by taking over and controlling money supply as we have seen. Let us at this point remember Mayer Amschel Rothschild's words, "Permit me to issue and control the money of a nation and I care not who makes its law". **(Direction).** Now if banking was just to increase his wealth he would not have made this remark. It was quite clearly a statement that by controlling money supply, he could control the politicians and that is exactly what we find happening throughout this history and you can see it happening today. **(Direction).** The bankers have increased their power as the debts rose until today where politicians give lip service to the electorate while bowing to the power of the bankers and Multinational companies. It is this fraudulent control over our lives we must stop at all costs. **This is our main target and the bankers are our only enemy not the multitude of aggressors that their system creates to** divert our attention from their usurious power. **(A horrific example of which we have seen in the dreadful attack on New York, but it is a direct result of not finding a solution to Palestine's problems).**

An important proof of the existence of a plan towards world government was the words of James P. Warburg who stated, "We shall have world government, whether or not we like it.... By conquest or by consent". (February 1950). It was his family, as Rothschild's agent, who funded Adolph Hitler in the run up to the Second World War.

We have seen Professor Robison's, (1798) and Abbe Barruel's, (1799) works on the Illuminati, both printed about the same time and both sounding the same warning about the Illuminati, yet neither of these two men had met or shared information. (Independent proof of the Illuminati and its funders).

The first big victory for the Illuminati (formed in 1776, the same year as the American Declaration of Independence was signed) was the French Revolution, organised by Weishaupt through the Grand Orient Masonic lodges of France in 1789, putting France under a revolutionary government, led by Masonic lodges; a control that still lies hidden today. (They won the French Revolution, and still control France, **DIRECTION**).

The aims of the Illuminati are;
1. Abolition of all National Governments. (Nationality to go, EU policy).
2. Abolition of private property.
3. Abolition of inheritance. (Tax is doing this job).
4. Abolition of patriotism. (By federalisation).
5. Abolition of Religions. (By UNESCO).
6. Abolition of family. (Through moral decline and break up of family).
7. Creation of New World Order. (World government by Dictatorship).

We have seen this policy carried forward till today by Communism (this is one way we know Communism is a disguise of the Illuminati). The Illuminati managed to spread its message by giving its novices only the feel-good policies to promote. So many of their supporters promoted it without knowledge of this evil content. **(Direction).**

It spread especially within the halls of learning (Universities and Colleges) and via the inter-linking orders of Masonry, throughout the world. More importantly through the secret banking network of International Finance. It was a meeting of high minds on the axis of power between Academia and Banking, hiding its evil Satanic greed to control the world and kill religions; all religions, and all Sovereign Nations, our two main props, our pillars we turn to in moments of need (as we have seen in New York). **(DIRECTION).**

We have learned from Ruskin, through Cecil Rhodes, how the Illuminati captured a banker funded drive to influence the British Empire and beyond, and Carroll Quigley, who supported their cause but not their secrecy, gave us an insiders account of the drive to world order. We have seen his views in action through Clinton, also initiated into a Illuminati scholarship, the Rhodes Scholarship; a thorough training in the art of the Illuminati's progress to One World Government, without full knowledge behind its evil intent. **(Direction).**

To understand how the Illuminati changes its name, like a Chameleon changes its colours, we have the words of Weishaupt himself who stated quite clearly that if the Prefect of Bavaria banned his organisation it would rise again, under another name, stronger than ever. **(Direction).** Through this history we have seen it rise under many names; German Reading Societies, Communism, Freemasonry, the

Round Table, Milner's 'useful idiots', International Zionism, The Anglo American Establishment, The Council on Foreign Relations, The United Nations, The Royal Institute of International Affairs, The School of International Studies, The Bilderberg Group, The Trilateral Commission, The Ditchley Foundation, Ruskin, Cecil Rhodes, The Rhodes Scholarship, to name but a few and linked to the bankers through the Bank of International Settlement, in Switzerland, and through the World Bank, the International Monetary Fund, and the Merchant and Credit banks of England and America. It now commands a strong position within world politics.

So how does that all link with today's world problems? One early warning of world domination through secrecy came from Arnold Toynbee, an Oxford graduate, who helped to write the fateful Versailles Treaty. At this conference, the League of Nations was formed, with the aim of creating a World Government as you will now see. (Weishaupt's policy).

In his address to the Institution of Scientific Study of International Relations Toynbee made clear that the intention was to move forward to World Government by depriving each National State of its Sovereignty but secretly (Weishaupt's policy), without the mass knowing the aim, as we see in Europe. **(Direction).** This is made quite clear; then he tells us who influences his thought, "Left alone from interference from behind politics from the bankers, the world would find peace and compromise as the economic reality". (From Toynbee's speech). Well that is exactly my point; left alone from bankers' influence over politics, the world would find a path to peaceful co-existence. Bankers should be banned from funding conflict for their profit. Their funding of war is the reason why we have seen so much conflict in the last two hundred years. What Toynbee fails to say is that the bankers are bankrolling the alternative, a World Government as a substitute. Would you trust the bankers knowing they have created every war in the last two hundred years for profit? I think not. Because their alternative peace is designed to make even greater profits than war. That is why we must fight European Federalisation as it is the next stage in the bankers' war within peace; their move towards a World Government. **(DIRECTION).** You will have noticed that the promoters of this Federal Europe deny it exists. Toynbee actually says they will deny loss of Sovereignty to Federalisation while actively supporting it. **(Direction).** We have also seen Edward Heath do the same.

If you want Federalisation of Europe, which brings loss of Sovereignty, (Control over our own affairs democratically) vote yes to integration with Europe; but be warned it is not democratic, (Answerable by elected members to their state and people) it is controlled by a Pro-Communist structure behind which the bankers control decisions. I cannot believe that this is what the vast majority of people want.

What we need to do is control our own (Each nation's own) money supply and restrict banking in its endeavours to create wars. This would solve the major world problem of war without losing our democracy.

We have learned from the Kaiser's banker, Walter Rathenau, who Rakovsky's names as one of 'Them', a Guardian, a member of the inner circle of bankers, that; "Three-hundred men, each of whom knows all the others, govern the fate of the European continent, and they elect their successors from their entourage". What he refers to is the group of bankers and others that is driving Europe to a hidden Federalisation as a region of a World Government.

The reason why Walter Rathenau was exposed by Rakovsky was because he had been assassinated. No living member of the inner circle is ever identified as all meetings are hidden behind banking work.

Rathenau's words were confirmed by a Jewish member of 'Israelite Universëlle', Jean Izoulet in 1931, when he said, "The meaning of the history of the last century is that today three-hundred Jewish financiers, all masters of lodges (The important Masonic link), rule the world". So we get a clear statement of the Masonic connection. We have further proof of the link between Masonic Lodges and Zionism all of which, as a collective, proves the very important linking and usage of the Masonic movement within the International Zionist movement towards World Government and also its desire to kill all Christian Religions. (Part of Weishaupt's seven point plan). These pages are very important in understanding the early history that moulded the conspiracy, from Socinus to Oliver Cromwell, in England, to the Duke of Orleans, who controlled the 266 Masonic Lodges of the Grand Orient, who in turn received Weishaupt's plan for the French Revolution, which handed France into the grip of the Satanic Illuminati.

The world Masonic Convent of Wilhelmsbad of 1781, spread the word of the Illuminati to the world, via the order of the 33rd. Degree, from which the plan to dissolve Christian Religions was carried World-wide as well as the later policy clone, from Illuminati to Communism. (Remember that when we mention Zionism, the members of this group are International Zionists, who are both atheists and one-world government supporters).

We learn how the bankers create war by funding, and how they use money to create the theatre for war.

By the early part of the last century the centre of power of the bankers moved to Wall Street. **(Direction).** We have learned how a group of bankers, led by Paul Warburg, financed Hitler's rise to power, which puts a very different picture on the position of International Zionists who insist that governments clamp down on all comment that offends the Jewish race. **(Direction).** This clamp on discussion is dangerous because from discussion the truth is found.

The bankers have gradually (Remember the whole policy is a creeping take-over of power, denying each step before it happens) taken over national debt and personal debt, binding the nation and its people into debt slavery, and I show how it all started with a loan to William III that created the Bank of England, **(direction)** and then Nathan Rothschild used the same policy to enslave the new independent colonies of America.

This debt slavery is so unnecessary, because if the government created new money itself, while printing it under a strict, impartial control, no national debt would be owed, and no interest charged on money created from nothing. (The national debt is currently running over two hundred and eighty billion pounds). Furthermore income tax and other taxes which cover the current interest bill of about 28 billion pounds could be reduced. (This is interest alone without re-payment). It would also leave a healthy sum to enable us to fund our National Health Service properly perhaps for the first time and other necessities. It makes sense to change to government control of money creation, and it will also stop the flow of funds to globalise the world. It needs guts and determination, but the prize is enormous.

Let us remind ourselves of the words of a banker so that we become certain that this whole conspiracy is a proven fact, and not just a theory. "Marxism, you say, is the bitterest opponent of Capitalism, which is sacred to us. For the simple reason they are opposite poles of the earth and permit us to be their axis. These two opposites, Bolshevism and ourselves, find ourselves identified in the International. And these two opposites, the doctrines of the two poles of society, meet in the unity of purpose, the renewal of the world from above by control of wealth, and from below by revolution". Here is your positive proof that the Capitalism of the bankers (Not Adam Smith's version) meets Communism in the Multinational Corporation whose desire is corporate collectivism which is Communism. **(DIRECTION).** What the banker ignores is that Capitalism's main plank is competition, which is excluded by corporate collectivism, so the multinational is breaking the main rule of Capitalism by its lemming like drive to be the sole supplier in his field for the 'God of corporate accountancy'; **profit.** I doubt whether this analysis has once been considered by Multinationals in their drive for ever greater profits but they are endangering the freedom of the world with their selfish blinkered view.

We must retain competition to contain collectivism and save capitalism and ourselves from the wish of the bankers, **the world's only powerful enemy**. One area we can make a start in is to stop the MAI agreement, now under discussion, before it is ratified by the nations of the world.

Two men tried to take back the creation of money from the bankers Abraham Lincoln and J.F. Kennedy, under executive order 11110. Their death, and now our knowledge of their sacrifice, should now make us determined to beat the bankers and take money creation back under our control.

The history tells us briefly how the media has gradually been bought up by the bankers and is now almost totally controlled, world-wide, by their agenda. **(DIRECTION)**. The demise of such journalists as Gordon Tether tells us the truth and the owners, support that truth. Their power in controlling minds is immense, especially when the control is co-ordinated by a single message. (Remember Murdoch's claim to have used his paper to elect Blair, who really came from nowhere And should go back there.).

We need transparent legislation to make sure our press is removed from minority control and made truly democratic and honest in representing the people's, not just the bankers' interest.

Weishaupt, who was brought up in a Jesuit Seminary, began to hate the Catholic order and reverted back to Judaism and then took on Satanism as a backcloth to his order of the Illuminati. **(Direction).** This departure from the church had a profound influence on the policy that followed. We have already seen his seven point plan, built from his five years study of all the depraved philosophies from Plato to Voltaire, but hidden from Weishaupt's novices giving them a false sense of well being and a feeling of pride of the superior knowledge they were to spread, like butter, over mankind. (Not knowing the evil intent behind his policy to destroy religion and turn the world into a form of slavery to serve the elite members of his Atheist club of superior minds). The motto of this club was 'Novus Ordo Seclorum' New World Order. **(Direction).** (This appears on the back of the one-dollar note and shows how his organisation controlled America at a very early stage, as this was used on the seal of the Declaration of Independence).

We learn that the Masonic Order in England has two headquarters. The second offices of the $4^{th.}$ to the $33^{rd.}$ degree and beyond is at Ten, Duke Street, St. James, London. This is where the Supreme Council, the top end of British Masonry resides.

It was, we learn, General Pike who named Illuminati's 23 Councils, the Supreme Councils of the World.

The British Museum holds a defining letter from Pike, the head of the American Illuminati and a self confessed Luciferian, to Mazzini, the man who took over from Weishaupt, as head of the Illuminati, Worldwide. This letter discloses that the

Illuminati will control the world after a third world war, when the Nihilists and Atheists will take part in the conflict and the world will fight to destroy these revolutionaries, and when the world succeeds all mankind will be in a vacuum, ready for Illumination. Is this the war we now see, as a result of the attacks inside America? To halt this possibility we must stand by our Christian Churches, and maintain world peace, but kill terrorism in its true form, not Bush's idea.

One of the two pillars of the Illuminati that had to be in place before they corrupted our society was the control of education by Weishaupt's novices. Lady Queenborough tells us just how important it is to control the educated mind. Ruskin was one of Weishaupt's disciples who cloned his recruits, in ignorance of their patron. He was building up a false utopia for privileged undergraduates which was the start of the New Illuminati under many other names as we have already seen.

Baron Lionel Rothschild, paid a member of the Illuminati to produce a policy to create a New World Order. Karl Marx (Levy) produced a policy based on the seven-point plan of the Illuminati. The funds of the Rothschilds and their banker friends, backed Communism and we learn from Rakovsky, that Baron Lionel Rothschild was probably the head of the first International. **(Direction)**.

Trotsky was behind the assassination of Arch Duke Ferdinand and the financiers were the paymasters. This assassination started World War One. We also see Lenin, Trotsky and the Bolsheviks start a International Zionist led revolution with only five percent of the people supporting their cause that handed Russia over to Communism. **(Direction)**.

Lenin died unexpectedly and Stalin snatched power, starting the largest Holocaust the world has known, where somewhere in the region of twenty-two and a half million peasant landowners lost their lives. A Holocaust that the bankers must have financed as they financed Stalin's Russia from the Bolshevik revolution to the collapse of Russia in 1989. We learn from the inside interview of Rakovsky at the NKVD headquarters. (Rakovsky was under arrest along with Trotsky's followers because Stalin feared their power). This document gives us a rare insight into Bolshevism and Stalin, and how Hitler, who dreaded Communism, was diverted from attacking Stalin and instead declared war on Poland to bring in the Allied Forces under agreements previously signed. A plan laid down by the bankers behind Rakovsky.

He (Rakovsky) discloses the details of the 'High Road' to Communism, **(direction)** the road the bankers use as their plan for world government. **(DIRECTION)**. Rakovsky reminds us of Marx's words, "Communism must win because capital will give it that victory". Today we see the multi-nationals doing just that. **(DIRECTION)**.

The five-point star used by Russia and Europe is the sign to say that the Nations are controlled by the Rothschilds' sphere of interest. (Each nation in the European Union is depicted by a five-point star representing the five sons of Mayer Amschel Rothschild.

We see Rakovsky showing how the Illuminati, funded by the bankers, planned and won the French Revolution and plunged the French into debt slavery under Masonic-Banker control. Rakovsky exposes how the bankers created 'Credit Money', a false money given a legal standing, otherwise usury. We also know the bankers control politics by the power of the national debt. **(DIRECTION)**.

He shows how the bankers accumulated so much money that they control stock exchanges world-wide, and national loans, world-wide, and that they can buy any country's debt without problem. This wealth then becomes anarchical with the possibility of severe moral and social influences available as weapons in revolution. **(DIRECTION).**

Rakovsky states that New York now pushes England along the path of revolution; not Moscow. **(While we aim our wrath at the mirrors around the deception we cannot and will not hit the right target). (DIRECTION guides us to targets).**

Trotsky stated correctly that the bankers, "Carry out irresistibly and unconsciously their revolutionary mission". I would add to them, the Directors of Multinational companies. Rakovsky says quite clearly that the bankers have ultimate money power and all they lack is political power; it is natural to assume this is their ultimate desire; therefore revolution to obtain it is a matter of using their money to make it happen.

Weishaupt was the founder of the first Communist International, the leader of the Illuminati and a Mason. He also used his position to implant Communism in France, through the Lodges of the Grand Orient. This confirms that Communism took over from the Illuminati when the Illuminati was banned in Bavaria. **(Direction).**

We learn from Rakovsky that Baron Lionel Rothschild was most likely the chief of the first Comintern. He also talks of evidence that Weishaupt's army of intellectuals helped the Rothschilds to develop their banks all over Europe, and that Disraeli's portrait in 'Coningsby of Sidona was in fact a portrait of Baron Lionel Rothschild. **(Direction).**

Evidence of the power of the Rothschilds came from Mayer Amschel Rothschild's wife; "If my sons want it, then there will be no war"; proof that their finance created or halted wars; a sobering fact. Rakovsky goes on to say, "Since that time every war is a giant step towards Communism". This links war to revolution which brings Communist domination nearer to reality, and this is exactly what our indicator, **DIRECTION** shows.

We are told by Rakovsky that the real enemy of Communism is the thinking middle-class. It is from this group that all reaction starts.

Trotsky was the Bankers' man of the Bolshevik Revolution; his wife was related to Jacob Schiff and linked to the Warburgs. Then comes the greatest surprise; Kerensky was a collaborator of not Lenin, but Trotsky, as the Bankers' representative. Rakovski names the financiers behind the Bolshevik Revolution; Jacob Schiff and Max and Paul Warburg. (These bankers are both Rothschild agents and belong to their sphere of influence. They funded Bolshevism till its planned collapse in 1989). **(Direction).**

Ninety percent of the leaders in Russia appointed after the revolution, came from the ancient 'Bund' of the Jewish proletariat. The 'Bund' had infiltrated all socialist parties. (A typical Weishaupt plan of preparation). **(Direction).**

Rakovsky claims that nearly all leaders of the Allied Nations were Masons. **(Direction).** Is this why our politicians do the bidding of the bankers, against national interests? Rakovski claims all Masonic organisations work for the triumph of the Communist Revolution but hide their intent behind their slogan 'Liberty, Equality, Fraternity'. The irony is that the Masons will be the first to die once the revolution rules the world; not my words; Rakovski claims it is the "Real secret of Masonry".

We find that Britain's Master spy, O'Reilly (Famous for his help in buying the oil rights in Persia) a spy in British Intelligence, was in fact a double agent under the bankers; his real name was Rosenblum, a Lithuanian Khazar Jew.

Then Rakovsky states that the Versailles Treaty was a 'decisive' move towards revolution. **(DIRECTION).** What this confirms once again is that the politicians and their advisers are so infiltrated, that they do the bankers' bidding. He claims this led to the Wall Street crash and the demise of the Deutschmark and a general world recession, which directly caused the Second World War. **(DIRECTION).**

Rakovski now names the bankers who negotiated a loan for Hitler to protect Europe from Stalin. (Not at that moment under the Bankers' control). It was the Warburg bankers who negotiated and loaned Hitler money, from Wall Street funds, **(direction)** to fund the National Socialist Party, and finance the elections, the SA and SS. They also arranged for millions of marks from German Financiers through Schacht. So we find that Jewish bankers funded Hitler. Surely this must change the censorship developed around Jewish matters since the Holocaust? (Because by funding Hitler's path to power and through the war they must have funded the Holocaust and therefore must take some blame for the horror it created through finance. To arrive at the truth of this matter it is not helpful to have serious evidence hidden from view to accomplish unjustified demands by International Zionists and their organisations that benefit by silencing truth).

According to Rakovsky, we interestingly find that Hitler took over money creation and this weapon enabled him to wipe out unemployment in Germany, (this is an important leader) Something the bankers certainly do not want us to know, and a reason to silence the truth.

Rakovsky gives us a very real cause to uphold when he tells us; "In reality Christianity is our only real enemy". **(DIRECTION).** This tells us that if we allow the modern way of life to kill our religion, Communism will win. That should make us determined to support our religion to our last breath.

Now comes the truth Rakovsky left to the end. The truths that we must take on board if we seriously wish to oppose the Bankers' secret move to Communist control. They have one aim; the triumph of Communism. He goes on to say, "It is not Moscow which will impose its will on the democracies, but New York". **(DIRECTION).** Yes, the bankers of Wall Street through money power.

He says, "The 24th. of October 1929 (Wall Street Collapse) will go down in the history of Communism as more important than October 1917 (The Bolshevik Revolution). **(DIRECTION).** Meaning that this was the Super Capitalists' master stroke to move forward the Communist Revolution, and when we study history from then to today all wars and financial crises have moved the agenda nearer to Communism; this our barometer, **direction** tells us.

Rakovsky lays down a path for Stalin to take, to move the war in a direction that will benefit Communism.

1. Stalin makes a pact with Hitler for the division of Czechoslovakia and Poland (preferring the later for first attack).
2. Hitler will accept.
3. The democracies will then attack Hitler not Stalin, as they will only take on one aggressor at a time.

This diversion was put to Stalin, and Stalin made a pact with Hitler, and Hitler attacked Poland instead of Russia, bringing in the allied forces. **(Direction).** All this in spite of Communism being Hitler's main enemy. By 1942 Stalin broke his pact with Hitler and joined the allied offensive in words more than spirit.

We learn how the lowering of morality has been used as a revolutionary tool to destabilise our society using minority pressure groups to approve alternative life styles that corrupt society. (The reason the Roman Empire fell so many years ago). **(DIRECTION).**

We are forced to receive pornography from European TV stations and we have been told by the European Union we cannot block them. Our media continues to lower its standard led by News International's 'Sun' newspaper right through a new breed of teenage magazines that encourage under-aged children into sexual experience before they are mature enough to handle the consequences. This is a planned assault on Western Society.

Lynette Burrows shows us how government is trying to take over the task of directing our children and in doing so removing parents' rights, under the guidelines of the United Nations, as a first step in the Marxist plan to break up the family unit. **(Direction).**

We see the course of social and moral destabilisation as a planned assault on Western society and the part played by the media. **(Direction).**

Christian religion has been infiltrated at the level of the World Council of Churches by Communist infiltrators intent on destroying religion. We have it within our power to reverse the decline of our religion by supporting our Church and its moral code. It is one of our staunchest pillars against Atheist evil, but is at risk when attacked from within.

On education, we find out how Weishaupt sent out two thousand trained Illuminati to take over the power of education through Universities and Colleges, world-wide. Ruskin influenced so many young men at Oxford University and formed a dedicated band of disciples, led by Cecil Rhodes and funded by a group led by the Rothschilds, who went out and formed the Round Table that spread Weishaupt's message throughout the Empire. When the task was completed, the power within publishing had all reference to Weishaupt and his Illuminati removed from history books and encyclopaedias, so his work would go on un-noticed. **(Direction).**

We learn why we find education is in a crisis in this informed age. Sex education in schools is being used to alienate children from their parents and traditional family values, (Clause 28 is just a typical example) and **direction** comes from the United Nations.

Elizabeth Surgrue describes how she set about finding the sources of legislation that forced schools to teach social sciences to pupils, a policy taken from the Humanist Manifesto, 1 and 2 of 1933 and 1973 and adapted by the United Nations as their policy. **(Direction).** It is a policy where Jesus Christ had no part and these Atheist, Anti Family policies were accorded recognition by 300 educationalists world-wide. We can clearly see from Elizabeth Surgrue's dedicated research that it is part of the plan to destroy Religion, the moral fabric of society, and the family unit. **(A major proof of religious and moral decline).**

Our legal system, developed over centuries, based on natural law, and supported by precedent, is all but destroyed by the European Court of Justice, which overturns, for political reasons, not legal, verdicts made in our courts. What this is gradually doing is making our legal system subservient to Brussels. **(Next the world. DIRECTION).**

Jean Monnet stated that Europe's nations should be guided towards the Super State (Federalisation) without people understanding what was happening. On May 6th. 1970 Monnet explained this deception to Edward Heath. He stated, "I told Heath how we had proceeded from the start, step by step, and how in this way we had gradually created the common market and today's Europe, and I was convinced that we should proceed in the same manner"; in other words, hide the truth about National Sovereignty. Heath must have agreed so he did; only admitting his deceit in an interview with Peter Sissons in November 1990. The reason why the people must have a chance to decide whether or not we wish to lose our sovereignty is precisely because Edward Heath hid the truth from the voters in the first referendum and on such a fundamentally important issue. I view this as treason against the Sovereign State. We must correct this vote at the first opportunity along with the question of the Single Currency, and the hidden policy towards Federalisation.

The European Union, the brain child of Communist infiltrators within the American government, is a staging post for Globalism, and the mechanisms surrounding the UN, the GATT Agreement (the General Agreement on Tariffs and Trade), the WTO (the World Trade Organisation) are all in position to move trading to a international level, ignoring national laws and requirements. The hidden aim of the GATT and WTO agreements is to reduce wages in developed countries to come in line with a world-wide norm. Sir James Goldsmith gave an endorsement to this when he said, "Global free trade will force the poor of the rich countries to subsidise the rich of the poor countries". We see these organisations controlled by the Banker – Communist ticket. **(DIRECTION).**

1. United Nations. Formed by Alger Hiss, a Communist, and controlled by International Zionists – Communist agenda.
2. The International Monetary Fund. Controlled by International Finance Capitalists, and planned by Harry Dexter White, A Communist sympathiser.
3. The World Trade Organisation (WTO) – General Agreement on Tariffs and Trade (GATT) controlled by a consortium of International Finance Capitalists and world order politicians like Dr. Henry Kissinger and Lord Carrington. The national governments must study the impact of these un-elected groups on our freedom and must act decisively to limit the damage that they can do to a nation state with their global solutions.

We see how Britain has drifted into the European Union bit by bit while the politicians deny our loss of sovereignty. Sir James Goldsmith told us bluntly just how much we have already lost through the European Court of Justice (A political court) where the treaty states; "European law shall be binding in its entirety and directly applicable to all member states".

Our judges now concede that British law is now subservient to European law which is now the supreme law of the land. **(Direction).**

But the European parliament controls the European Court of Justice which is a political court with a end aim; to create a Federal Europe.

Britain has to submit its economic plans to Brussels under Article 109E (2).

'Subsidiarity' is meant to be a form of decentralisation, but it does not apply to those powers already transferred to Brussels which cannot be touched. European law only allows movement on the way towards federalisation. Any other way is not recognised.

In a true democracy, it is the people who decide which powers to lend to their leaders. In a false democracy, it is the leaders who decide which freedoms to lend to the people. In the European Union, it is twenty un-elected bureaucrats who decide our fate.

We see the global control of our food. A policy to make every nation dependent on imported food, so a firm hold is exercised over the people of all nations. **(Direction).**

The seed manufacturers are trying to control farming through seed modification by removing the possibility of a farmer using part of his crop from last year to produce the current harvest, by making his crop infertile. This insures the farmer will have to buy fresh seed every year. This is particularly hard on the third world farmers who generally use this practice to save costs, and is a criminal assault on farmers and their control over their own destiny. **(Direction)**.

The European Union has used the BSE crisis selectively to devastate the British farmer. This is all part of the Marxist policy to destroy landowners and make people depend on other nations for their daily bread. If this is not true why is France excused the same treatment?

Then we learn the intention of the MAI agreement, a vicious anti people, anti nation law designed to give un-elected Corporations the right to overrule elected National governments, so they can do what they want, for example, disregard pollution regulations, national employment laws, and move money and even factories to the cheapest part of the world without recourse from the Nation State. It is the worst piece of anti-people legislation I have ever seen and we must stop it. **(Direction)**.

Bernard Connolly, an insider, and a senior financial expert, responsible for the ERM and EMU policy within Brussels bureaucracy, began to realise how the European Union was not in the best interest of Europe and was being run undemocratically. He claimed that the ERM, then the EMU, were bad both economically and politically and are a tool to underpin the relentless drive towards a **Federal Super-state** because it subverts the independence, both political and economic, of the Nation states within Europe.

I show how International Zionism linked with Marxism through Rabbi Moses Hess, founder of both movements, joined with the banking group (Rothschild) of International Finance Capitalists, to create a satanic alliance with the ultimate power of money. . .

Most of the motivators of One World Government originate; from the Khazar Kingdom, and were adopted Jews, and a majority of the bankers and supporters of One World Government originate from this Khazar tribe. History firmly shows them as the intruders into Judaism, but now we see how they have taken over the political agenda of Israel and, not only control it, but America's political policy as well as England's. They are the originators of the One World Order, Rabbi Moses Hess, Karl Marx and Professor Weishaupt all originated from the Khazar Kingdom as did Robert Maxwell and Dr. Henry Kissinger. **(DIRECTION)**.

This group (Khazar Kingdom) has worked against the strict command of the Torah which insists they return to the Promised Land in peace. I show how they force International Zionism onto Israel and its people.

The history relates how International Zionists are used to destroy the domestic structure of a nation state. The infamous 'Red Robbo' of British Leyland is an example who was in fact a planted Zionist Communist, one Reuben Falber. We record the decline of our agriculture and food gathering industry. We see how first the bankers tried to use financial loans to close farms. When this failed, the BSE story, which had been officially known for some time was used politically to ruin farmers and it has succeeded. If the EU had been even handed all over Europe, stocks of animals would have been subject to the same rules. But to show that the EU uses situations politically, only British beef was banned, not only to Europe, but to the whole world.

Gradually the truth is coming out and we find that France had BSE – CJD at around the same scale, but through secrecy and lack of official reporting, the result could well be ten times worse. The important point to bear in mind is the Karl Marx – Weishaupt policy called for the destruction of the farming industry and the confiscation of land. This is being done through bankruptcy. **(DIRECTION).** **Foot and Mouth is finally killing our farming industry.**

Once again we turn to Sir James Goldsmith and his speech to the Confederation of Small Businesses, to find a whole host of comment by Eurocrats and politicians which shows us quite clearly, that Europe is to be a Federal State, outside democracy, without recourse to public opinion.

Europe is to have just one parliament, one Court of Justice, and a single currency and if they have their way, (Prodi is already discussing this with the heads of the nation states) one Army. With this will also go one Foreign Policy. **(DIRECTION).**

You have to ask yourself; is this happening? All the proof says Yes, it is. Then ask yourself; do you want to lose control of your money, your tax collection, your justice system, your defence and your foreign policy? and if we do, why should we have a parliament at all. It then becomes quite clear that our parliamentarians, who support Federal Europe like Blair, are lemmings. Above all else we must make sure we get a referendum so we can kill any idea of a single currency and even more important a Federal Europe, the heart of the Un-Democratic movement which is part of the One World Government plan through the Bankers – Marx's secret agenda.

The systematic destruction of Britain and the Commonwealth was planned. **(DIRECTION).** Britain in the 19th. Century was the strongest nation in the world. To take over the world agenda the Finance Capitalists knew they had to crush the strength of Britain and bring it down to a second division player. This has largely been achieved by the International Finance Capitalists through the movement of money and the creation of wars. They starved Britain of finance after the war when they needed support. This was carefully planned by Wall Street bankers and has been assisted by the policies of the greedy multinational corporations chasing cheap labour; and of course the Euro Dollar market. A large part has been played by Wall Street, as they became the gainers in the ascendancy of the dollar over the pound. Ultimate power, came from this elite band of money creators, the Merchant and Credit bankers, who wielded unbelievable power over governments. It is this pincer movement between banking and political assault, on the Commonwealth of Nations, that has come from traitors within our gates, shown clearly by Dr Kitty Little's 'Treason at Westminster. We learn of Kitty Little's first hand knowledge of subversion while she was at Oxford University where she describes a Pro-Communist meeting she attended in October 1940 addressed by Harold Wilson, a student at Oxford and propaganda enforcer for the unnamed group. (To make it more difficult to label it as a Communist policy). So not only was Harold Wilson a Communist at Oxford, under the control of Victor Rothschild, as was the group of Cambridge spies, but in a convincing manner he went on, as Prime Minister, to hand over a large section of industry and technology to Russia. He was also surrounded and financed by a group of Armenians, more than certainly from the Khazar Kingdom. The proof of destruction of British industry, the removal of British defence and the destruction of the Commonwealth, all part of the major plan to destroy Britain, is explained on the following pages. **(DIRECTION).**

Once more we see the traitor within destroying our pillars of strength from government's highest office. This should make us all pause to think very clearly how to defeat such an enemy.

We see how the IRA is used to de-stabilise Britain and break up the United Kingdom. We uncover the IRA link to Communism through a mural on the Falls Road linking the ANC and the IRA into the army of revolution. **(Direction).**

That is why, no matter how much we give in to the IRA, they will always demand more. They are at war, perpetual war, in the Communist definition, and negotiation is as much part of that war as planting a bomb. This is a policy that Western military sources just don't, or won't, take on board. They will only cease when their war is won.

We begin to learn the complex web woven by Communism and the International Finance Capitalists in what we have perceived as the centre of Conservative – Capitalist thinking, opposed to Communism. **(Direction).** As America is now the recognised centre of world finance the importance of this knowledge is paramount. We learn, at a time when America, according to our so called free press, was holding back the march of Communism; that they 'America', and I must expand on that, through the power of International Zionism and Communist penetration of high government offices, were supplying North Vietnam with high technology weaponry through Russia, and the International Zionist lobby, controlled by Wall Street bankers, were the conduit. **(DIRECTION).**

We continue our learning curve through a short précis on how banking and International Zionism took over the agenda from the words of Rothschild, to R.E. Search's words.

Many American politicians like Thomas Jefferson, and Abraham Lincoln, fought tooth and nail to stop usury, but failed under the ultimate power of Nathan Rothschild, a remote banker from England. But Abraham Lincoln had his moment of glory when he created 'The Green Back' which freed America's money from usury; a moment of victory over bankerism, short lived, as Abraham Lincoln was Assassinated.

Rothschild crushed this rebellion. After more than a century of battling by 1913 the bankers won by bribery, (Politicians), and the convenient death of a President, Abraham Lincoln. Money power bought the right to create new money by private bankers, in this case the Rothschild Federal Reserve Bank. (The secret of money power used by bankers to insure the one way **DIRECTION).**

So why did Abraham Lincoln fight the Bankers? Because they wanted between 24-36% interest on loans to fund the civil war.

We learn why America's economy was so important. For one hundred and sixty-eight years the bankers had held the British people in debt slavery by interest charged on money loans created from paper. Yes, bankers were charging interest to governments (England) to create new paper money from nothing. (This is the central feature of this history we must re-address). The bankers used bribery and deception and lies to wrest the creation of money from American politics. At this point the initiative came from British bankers. Later, in the early years of the 20th. Century we see the power centre move to Wall Street, New York, and we also see the start of the demise of the British Empire. At this time the Rothschilds, who had been responsible for the destruction of the Old World Order had all but finished their task. Now was the time in the early 1930's to build the New World Order, a task given to Wall Street, led by the Rockefeller family who in turn, through the International bankers, Multinational Corporations and International Zionists, controlled America's foreign policy. (see the flow chart at the end of this summary. **(Direction).**

Why did the bankers control America's foreign policy? Let us go back to Abraham Lincoln's visit to England, where he said, when asked why the American colonies were so prosperous, "That is simple, in the colonies we issue our own money, its called colonial scrip. We issue it in proper proportion to make the products pass easily from producers to the consumers. In this manner, creating ourselves our own paper money, **we control its purchasing power, and we have no interest to pay to no one"**. This is at the heart of defeating our only enemy, 'The International Finance Capitalists'.

What I find in the history of International Banking, is that they cared little for the people who died to protect their cause, to fight off governments that wished to create their own money; indeed they forced governments into wars to gain for themselves control of money creation, regardless of death and destruction, all of which benefited bankers.

Now we jump a century and look at the next death of a President in suspicious circumstances. We move to the death of a President we knew, John F. Kennedy. Final Call tells us the circumstances involved in his death. We know from criminologists that the most important lead in a death like this is "Who gains?".

Kennedy, a rich man in his own right, was not controlled by the bankers. We find that Kennedy challenged the two causes that were of direct interest to the bankers, war debt, by moving to finish the Vietnam war, and the creation of new money; both a gold mine for bankers in the private credit banking business.

Kennedy moved to end the Vietnam War with an aim to move all troops out of Vietnam by 1965. He also began a secret execution of an Executive order 11110 (a privilege of the President to bypass Congress), which moved to take back money creation privilege into government hands, taking it away from the Wall Street bankers. **(Reverse direction).**

Five months after passing Executive Order 11110, he was assassinated. We have been fed many stories by our media, controlled by the bankers. But we ask, "Who gains?" The answer, with the knowledge we have must be The Bankers, and probably the most accurate answer to a problem with the hidden knowledge Final Call discloses. **(Direction).**

Going back, we learn that a new force was beginning to change the strength in the world. The product was oil, that would turn out to be a product as good as gold. So who moved into this new innovation? Why none other than Rothschilds and Rockefeller banks.

By 1880 Germany was moving into big Industry, Steel. It was beginning to challenge Britain's supremacy. A German was the first to use the black sludge that oozed out of rock, to light lamps. It did not take John Rockefeller long before he saw the potential of oil, and started the Standard Oil Company.

It was however, a British Admiral, Lord Fisher, who pressed for an oil-powered engine for shipping (1820) that started a new era. By 1885 Daimler produced a petrol engine and the oil revolution, slow to start, was never the less under way.

As soon as its potential was realised by 1905 the bankers latched onto the new gold and the Rothschilds and Rockefellers led the field. So supply was the main concern and the double agent for British Intelligence, Sidney O'Reilly, (born Sigmund Rosenblum) played a major role for the Rothschilds by wresting the Persian Oil Wells for England and in particular the Rothschilds. Today BP is a company under their control, originating from Sidney O'Reilly's astute negotiations.

So by the beginning of the First World War, Britain, although hardly recognised as an oil producer was building up its production. At that time America produced 63% of world oil with Russia producing 19%. What is important to realise is that Zionist bankers controlled nearly all oil production through financial power, the Rothschild and Rockefeller sphere of influence. **(DIRECTION)**.

By the time of the first World War, Britain was nearing bankruptcy through the continual practice of the, now international bankers, moving money around the world to chase higher and higher returns, starving the local economies of investment.

This was really the defining moment, when the bankers shed the nationalist cause for an international and global course and their dual nationality did not help. They were ruthless for money power and national borders got in their way**, so globalism was the new call and the policy of the Illuminati fitted their new revolution towards internationalism like a glove. (DIRECTION)**.

Britain went into the First World War bankrupt. Who benefited from the war? Bankers from Wall Street who eventually funded Britain's war. (They printed bank notes to replace gold and silver. This helped to fill the Bankers' vaults with gold and silver in time to go to war; at a price, war interest). Oil was the hero of war, as it mechanised the theatre of war and became the final victor against a German Command starved of oil by blocking off their main source, at Baku, in Russia.

We have learned how the Bankers' agent, Trotsky, was behind the assassination of Arch Duke Ferdinand. The bankers had a planned strategy to bring Europe to war to further the revolution towards world government. The strategy at the time, from within British banking circles was named "The Great Game". **(DIRECTION)**.

It was an unnecessary and immoral war, created for Bankers' gain while **eighteen million people of Europe died, of which ten million were civilians. (It is always the ordinary people that suffer most).** It was the Bankers' selfish greed that brought about a holocaust of the innocent, where governments became the slaves of the bankers. The only gainers were the bankers, who funded war for profit and for political gain. They achieved both, when their men virtually dictated the terms of the Versailles Treaty; today recognised as the cause of the Second World War, again part of the 'Big Game' of the Bankers' treachery. **(A prelude to DIRECTION)**.

So how are governments pushed into war? Britain had two reasons, debt slavery to bankers who control government action through debt. The second reason was to crush Germany's attempt to become a oil-producing nation, which would help to expand their steel industry and capture customers from Britain.. We talk of government, but oil was banker-owned but government inspired a kind of unholy partnership, hence British Petroleum, a deceit in the name; a typical Weishaupt ploy.

Just before the end of the war, while the world looked away to Europe, the Bolsheviks, led by Lenin and Trotsky, marched into Moscow as the victors of the Bolshevik revolution. It was funded by the Wall Street bankers, led by Schiff and the Warburg brothers, as agents of the Rothschilds, the funders of Communism. They knew that to fight during the war in Europe would give them a surprise element without full publicity. An ideal time to cause war. **(Direction)**.

The third act that almost went unnoticed was Arthur Balfour's letter to Lord Walter Rothschild which promised a national homeland for the Jewish population of the world. From this letter Middle East politics would erupt, but more importantly it was described by traditional Jewish Rabbis and other honest Jews as an act against the Torah, which it most certainly turned out to be. **(The Torah states quite clearly that the Jewish tribes of Israel will only re-enter the Promised Land when the Messiah comes to them and leads them back in peace. The Rothschilds were certainly not the Messiah. (Direction). Today's terrorist attacks are a direct result of not finding a solution to the problems of Palestine. (I am told that the leader of the Guardians will announce a solution to the Palestinian problem that will be acceptable to both sides in 2004).**

It was a very careful plan of International Zionism and government to block German ascendancy in Europe and build up the Commonwealth of Nations to replace the Empire. This shows, even at this time, how International Zionism was ruling the British government, and also the American government.

One banker, J.P. Morgan, acting as sole agent for Britain, used his banking skills to rescue bankrupt Britain and start the big switch of banking power from the City of London to the heartland of International Banking, Wall Street. After the war, the total national debts of all nations rose by 475% to a staggering 210 billion dollars with Wall Street as the big gainers. This movement of power from one continent to another demonstrates that the home of banking, like the home of Communism was not important to the International power, it could move anywhere it found greatest power. This goes a long way towards answering the presumed collapse of Communism in 1989. In fact its power moved secretly to Wall Street. **(DIRECTION).**

This was the era of the new driving forces towards globalism. (The new grouping of the Illuminati). Thomas Lamont, J.P. Morgan's partner, founded the Royal Institute of International Affairs, run by Lionel Curtis and staffed by Arnold Toynbee, the man who made that first sounding of global endeavour in 1931. They started to adopt new names as Weishaupt said he would.

American Bankers, led by the Rockefellers, funded their equivalent 'The Council on Foreign Relations', again a grouping of Illuminati, Weishaupt style, not officials of the American Administration, as most Americans have been led to believe. **(DIRECTION).**

By the early twenties Rockefeller was aware that Britain had stolen a march on his domination of oil power by developing Royal Dutch Oil and Anglo Persian Oil. (Now BP). Churchill had moved to cut off Persian oil from America by well placed military pressure in the Gulf. This set off a oil trade war. The first casualty was a man America installed in the Mexican Government, Carranza. He was assassinated in 1920 when he denied America oil rights for Mexican Oil, in favour of national interests. **(Once again a politician thinking 'NATIONAL' is assassinated to suit globalism.**

Back in England, Deterding, from Royal Dutch Oil Company, realising transport was essential to oil supremacy, joined forces with Shell Transport and Trading Company owned by Marcus Samual, (Later Lord Bearsted). Very quickly they were challenging Rockefeller in his own territory.

In 1922 Germany shocked the oil world by announcing at the Rapallo Treaty that Walter Rathenau, Germany's Foreign Minister, had come to an agreement with Russia to swap reparations for industrial technology. Baku once more was in the spotlight, as the Establishment feared that Russia would include oil rights. So Rockefeller, in disguise as Sinclair Oil Company put in his bid. The Bolshevik revolution was ignored, where profit was concerned; in fact some of the bankers involved funded Bolshevism.

But Germany pulled off their coup, including the oil deal. On the 22$^{nd.}$ of June 1922 Walter Rathenau was assassinated. **(Yet another assassination when Nationalism came first).** It was the British banker-oil interests that were the gainers and British Oil Barons, of which International Zionist Bankers were the masters. Germany was laid to waste by the Versailles Agreement, something the oil deal could have halted. Yet we learn from Rakovski, that Rathenau was one of the chosen men behind world government and banker control; one of 'them'. **(Reverse direction).**

So 'they' could be ultimately ruthless, even to their own, when their plan was put into jeopardy. **(Re-direction).**

This oil war was effecting the Bankers' plan for world government; it had to cease. So in 1927 the Anglo-American Oil Cartel was formed known as 'The Seven Sisters', a world-wide price fixing syndicate. (In line with collective corporatism, a part of Communism.). **(DIRECTION RESTORED).**

Once again we see a bank initiative, this time by Montague Norman (Bank of England), who upset the world money market by asking the Federal Reserve to increase interest rates, which caused the Wall Street collapse of 1929, which starting a deep world-wide recession. **(The final cause of World War Two, DIRECTION).**

Schacht, the banker who promoted Adolph Hitler as the strong man of Europe, with Montague Norman's help, persuaded Paul Warburg and his Wall Street Bankers, that Hitler would be a strong buffer in Europe, as Stalin had snatched power in Russia and was a wild card. So bankers, led by Paul Warburg, financed Adolph Hitler. The reason behind this funding was that Rothschild, who funded Lenin and the Bolshevik Revolution, had lost control of Russia when Stalin took over power. Stalin was not under the Bankers' control at first.

By 1933 Hitler became Chancellor of the German Reich. International bankers and oil magnates continued to fund Adolph Hitler. At this point we learn from Rakovski that Hitler, who hated Communism, was manoeuvred into attacking Poland by Stalin, instead of Russia, and that Rakovski, from jail, planted this plan into Stalin's mind. **(DIRECTION).**

So the war was not fought for the reasons given by our press. Behind the scenes a very different set of rules were being used to move Europe into a position that would cause a demand for a United Europe (The European Union), not the fight that Hitler really wanted, which was a fight to the death against Communism.

For this greedy desire of Bankers, **fifty-five million people died for their cause,** because of the hidden agenda of the power barons behind the Anglo American Establishment. This power was led by the Wall Street Bankers; only they gained from war, through loan interest and by moving their revolution forward. **(DIRECTION).**

Britain and the rest of Europe were served up with an undemocratic plan for the European Union with a hidden agenda to federalise Europe as a region in a World Government and it is that process that we can still**, and must stop.**

Churchill, after the war made the first comments about a dangerous future. He claimed that with war gains given to Stalin by Roosevelt, an 'Iron Curtain' had split Europe. **(Direction).** The Iron Curtain would serve to hide the biggest deception of history between governments, the media and their people, the people who have been constantly lied to about America's fight against Communism, while behind the scenes it promoted and fed Russia technology, as we have seen. So who was behind the deceit? The bankers of Wall Street and Oil Barons of course.

We must realise that today five hundred bankers (increased from three hundred) control the movement to the 'New World Order'; the Rothschild and Rockefeller led movement that funded International Zionism and Communism. Now International Zionism controls National Zionism and directs a large part of the Jewish agenda. **(DIRECTION).**

While the war was raging, a select group of American radicals and Communists from within America's administration, planned the agenda for peace to move their revolution forward. First we had the Bretton Wood Agreement of 1944, the forerunner to the United Nations, then the GATT Agreement, to promote free trade. Then a World Bank funded by oil revenue, designed to fund large national projects. So when peace came, it seemed a worthwhile alternative to war weary nations to support the United Nations. But as usual from the bankers, what you see is not what you get.

Britain and America (The Anglo American Establishment) had voting control over the World Bank and the International Monetary Fund and dominated the United Nations with Russia's help. All currencies were to be pegged against the dollar which in turn was set at thirty-five dollars per ounce of gold. The dollar was untouchable, as Wall Street's wealth mushroomed through war loans and recovery loans, and the Federal Reserve had most of the world's gold reserves. Conversely Britain's Economy was debt ridden having fought six long years of war.

What Britain and America did next I have shown; a far different account of Iranian politics than our press allowed us to read. A mirror was erected in front of the events and false news was given to the world by the press.

Iran was isolated and oil exports banned to the World. Mossadegh, after trying every avenue, was offered help by Enrico Mattei, the head of Italy's AGIP. AGIP was charged with building a energy policy of the future, to prop up a devastated Italian economy after the war. Mattei was a staunch nationalist, therefore the enemy of the Bankers and their cartels. Oil companies do not like upstarts who find oil and rescue their country from imports, but this is what Mattei did for Italy. He pressed ahead providing fuel at low pump prices and also developed natural gas, saving dollar imports and helping a floundering economy.

He did more for Italy than any other man, but annoyed the banking oil cartel when he broke the blockade of Iranian oil embargo by the oil powers. Mattei signed a big deal with the Shah which infuriated the Seven Sisters, but the final straw was Mattei's deal with Russia to swap oil to Italy for a much needed pipeline to deliver oil and gas to Russia's new satellite countries. This sealed Mattei's fate. On the 27th. of October 1962 Enrico Mattei was killed in a private plane which crashed on take off, killing all passengers. **Once again a man who crossed the cartel for NATIONAL reasons, died in suspicious circumstances. (DIRECTION).** Shortly after Mattei died so did John F. Kennedy when he planned to take back the power of money creation into government hands under executive order 11110. Again an assassination with no conclusion but a **NATIONAL** move, against **GLOBAL INTERESTS**. But on the basis of "Who gains" the Bankers must be the prime suspects. It is the Bankers who are America's real enemy. It was at this time that Dr. Henry Kissinger, a Harvard Professor, became linked with the Rockefeller Group through the Council on Foreign Relations. It was also at this time that the world press was used to move the agenda to world politics. **(DIRECTION).**

Monetarism was the Bankers' new pursuit and globalism was its space. Both British and American industrialism suffered from decline while industry in America first moved from the North to the South, chasing cheap labour; it then started the move to the Pacific Rim. A similar decline occurred in Britain, as industry was moved even to Russia as we have seen under Harold Wilson.

The International Finance Capitalists, who did not recognise boarders, controlled industries' decline and movement, in order to chase cheap labour.

While this happened we were fed stories of discord between management and unions causing the break-up of industries through financial withdrawal because of union militancy. Money in the meantime was chasing high profits in Europe and the Pacific Rim. The industrial unrest was organised by the bankers communist friends to further the bankers revolution.

Lyndon Johnson succeeded Kennedy and, as a Bankers' man, opened up a full-scale war in Vietnam, a continued war that would hand yet another territory to Communism. The war had a triple effect for bankers, it made money on loans; tested new military equipment and moved revolution forward for Communism as the end result attests. **(Direction)**. The most horrendous fact that came from this war was that, under Mk-Ultra, experiments were carried out by British and American Scientists on American troops using mind altering drugs, sending a whole generation of soldiers home from war (if they were lucky) as drug crazed hippies, who, in turn led a moral decline back home. (This helped the banker's revolution through a moral decline, but was a horrific disaster for the men involved.). **(A almost unbelievable DIRECTION).**

Hidden from America by their press was the disgusting truth that the arms industry under banking finance, was supplying arms to Russia that ended up in Vietnam, killing American troops, something that is difficult to believe but nonetheless true.

By 1968 Robert Kennedy made his play for power, but was killed by an assassin in Los Angeles. (KENNEDY WAS A NATIONALIST). Shortly after this, Martin Luther King, who opposed the use of cheap labour by industry moving south, suffered the same fate. (Was it the Bankers?). So who is our enemy; the Vietnamese or the Bankers with their poodle the media?

While America was depicted in our press as the Capitalist State holding back Communism in Vietnam, it was all the time, within its own nation, pitting workers against workers, to benefit the Bankers of Communism, the Wall Street International Finance Capitalists.

In 1968 South Africa complained about the pegging of gold at $35 an ounce, a pre-war price, which was deeply effecting them. A boycott of South Africa followed, outwardly blamed on racial problems; another classical Bankers' deception. So we see that the bankers act ruthlessly to deal with anyone who gets in their way, but always get governments to carry the blame.

By 1971 the dollar-gold standard value made America vulnerable to bankruptcy. America was put on a direct dollar standard, leaving Eurodollar owners unable to ask for gold in exchange for their petrol dollars. It was from this point forward, that American policy would control economies throughout the world, a policy that Dr. Henry Kissinger drafted. **(DIRECTION).**

In May 1973, in Sweden, eighty-four of the world's most powerful bankers and their trusted insiders met under the chairmanship of Prince Bernhard. As before, this group met in complete secrecy. No press reports were allowed to leak out. This meeting, addressed by Walter Levy, discussed a four hundred percent increase in OPEC petroleum revenues. It was discussed at the Bilderberg meeting not at OPEC. In fact no OPEC officials were present. The meeting was under International

Zionist control, yet OPEC, an Arab oil cartel was selected to carry the blame for the greed of the International Zionist bankers. **(DIRECTION).**

This policy was accepted in innocence by OPEC, but it was the plan of Bankers that forced the world to pay four hundred percent more for its crude. So the Arabs got their increase but were falsely blamed by the world press for their greed, which was not of their making, but placed at their feet by the trickery of the Bankers. We learn from the script of the Jonathan May's account what happened next.

The end result was that Dr. Henry Kissinger's plan to instigate the Yom Kippur War was used to trigger the four hundred percent oil heist. Here we see a Secretary of State instigating a war to promote a decision made in the Bilderberg meeting. **(DIRECTION).**

That this was a forerunner of the Iraq Conflict seems an unlikely comment but there is proof that Dr. Henry Kissinger was again the motivator of the conflict under instructions from the Bilderberg group.

So it can be seen how banking has taken over the political agenda of America and Britain. It is essential we regain the political agenda to save the world from anarchy.

In Chapter Ten Part Three, we learn about the charitable foundations and how their tax-exempt funds are being used to fund the organisations that are planning the destruction of democracy in America and Britain. **(DIRECTION).**

We see the Anglo-American (Secret) Society controlled and financed by powerful men; men belonging to the Round Table of Cecil Rhodes, linked to the most powerful bankers in the world, and the funds from their foundations, used to move the world to their false utopia, a World Government. (A world governed by Communism and controlled ultimately by power bankers, mostly within the Masonic movement; and under the control of Weishaupt's Illuminati). **(DIRECTION).**

So the largest of the Foundations in America, the Ford Foundation, the Carnegie Trust, and the Rockefeller Foundation, were used to fund research used by government to develop education, social policies, and foreign affairs. The wealth of these Foundations was channelled down a narrow path funding radical left wing research, that gradually introduced Weishaupt's policies to education while undermining moral and social policies, and delivering solutions to foreign affairs that moved America and the world towards, not away from, Communist control. **(Capitalist funds used to finance radical left wing policy. The hidden agenda. (DIRECTION).**

So much did the Universities depend on Foundation funding that their direction was trimmed to line up with the wishes of their source of revenue, which was down the path of the seven-point plan of Weishaupt's Illuminati.

Then we learn from Professor Caroll Quigley's history and it is very clearly stated; that the International bankers were confident that they could buy into the Communist-Socialist agenda to move their agenda forwards to revolution. Ruskin, a Socialist, had already persuaded the Round Table Group that Socialism was the vehicle to use. By having property, industry, agriculture, communications (media), education and politics controlled by a small group of political financiers they could organise the world to their order of things. **THE ULTIMATE DIRECTION). He goes on to say that collectivism is a basic policy of Communism, but is also an end goal of the Multinational Corporation. The most attractive way to total power was by the overthrow of existing power, National power. (That is why Europe is being federalised to kill national power).**

So through this power behind academic research, America was being moved forward in revolution by hidden forces, using secrecy and deception, but no war as we know it.

By 1953 the Reece Committee was set up to investigate the power of the Foundations and their tax exemption; tax exemption that was funding radical left wing research. Even then the Banker Power tried to kill off the committee before it started. They failed. The fifteen point summary of the Reece Committee shows clearly that a few, very powerful, Foundations controlled research that could lead to a policy of collectivism, leading to a World Government, and that the overall power of research was towards leftist policies, policies more in line with Communism. **(This official report warns America of DIRECTION).**

From the fifteen points it is made clear that the power of control of the Foundations is in the hands of a few very powerful people and the influence on education and foreign policy has been very great. **(Getting very near to the goal of total power. DIRECTION).**

This is the heart of Weishaupt's policy, to take over education and corrupt foreign policy from within, and it has succeeded, if you can believe the Reece Committee. We have seen how the Council on Foreign Relations, foundation funded, has moved the American Foreign Policy towards Communism. The other group is the Institute for Pacific Relations (IPR). It is a private Council of ten independent national councils that are concerned with the Pacific Rim, being funded by the Carnegie Foundation and the Rockefeller Foundation. In 1951 the Senate Sub Committee on Internal Security proved that China was lost to Communism by academic experts and fellow travellers who worked for the IPR. Professor Quigley even admitted that the academics of the IPR produced policies almost identical to the Kremlin's. **(DIRECTION).**

The Reece Committee found that the IPR was considered by the American Communist Party and Soviet officials as an instrument of Communist policy.

Although the groups of Communist infiltrators were named by Chambers, only Alger Hiss and a few others were finally found guilty. The others just moved on, or even stayed in their previous jobs. So while America was telling its people and the world, through the media, that they were fighting back the advance of China, they were actually reneging on commitments to the Chinese Nationalists and handing six-hundred million Chinese to Communism and slavery.. **(DIRECTION).**

The Ford Foundation funds Communism and its policies through their influence in many Universities. Under McGeorge Bundy, the funds were directed at the far-left revolution through the Council on Foreign Relations. We see a list of some funding by the Foundation. Whittaker Chambers, a self confessed ex-member of the Communist cell, that penetrated deep into government, fought for years to have the Communist cell exposed, and many times being ignored until the profile of his evidence became so great that action was forced on a reluctant President. Then every obstacle was placed in the way, including stonewalling from the Presidents office.

Alger Hiss gave sensitive papers to Chambers to photograph and return. It was in 1938 that Chambers left Communism and decided to betray his former spy ring. By 1946, seven whole years later, no trial or even arrest had taken place. Meanwhile Hiss had been one of Roosevelt's top advisors during the war and was with Roosevelt at all his meetings with Stalin. Alger Hiss was the man behind the Formation of the United Nations.

Hiss, as a presidential advisor, did immense damage to America and the World. (DIRECTION).

In 1949, nine years after Chambers exposed Hiss, he was at last taken to trial. It was to be eleven years before he was found guilty of spying. Eleven years of untold treason against America. But worse, his ex-friends in the Communist party remained in office to continue their work for Russia from inside. Alger Hiss made sure Eastern Europe was Stalin's prize.

A similar process was started against Harry Dexter White, again long after the FBI knew of his Communist sympathies. In 1942 White was the main author of the plans for the International Monetary Fund and the Bank for Reconstruction and Development, both linked to the United Nations.

During the war White was deeply involved in negotiations over China, and steered American policy towards handing China to Communism.

He was the major contributor to the Morgenthau Plan; a plan to turn Germany into an agricultural and pastoral desert, a plan of retribution to suit the Wall Street Bankers. (Luckily rejected, While they hid the truth of their part in Hitler's funding). He was also involved with Roosevelt's gift to Communism of Eastern European countries. **(DIRECTION).**

In May 1946 Dexter White was made the first Executive Director of the International Monetary Fund despite files held on him by the FBI detailing his part in spying.

The amazing part of this history is how the administration in America was so infiltrated by Communist and Bankers' agents that they could even delay such serious accusations for such a long period of time. Harry Dexter White was undoubtedly a highly intelligent person but he believed in the 'New Deal', Roosevelt's plan for the world, originally designed by Weishaupt's Illuminati. He was certainly a banker's man and his work proved that. He was also an International Zionist. (The world is their State). I show how I believe Harry Dexter White colluded with Communism through his beliefs. Harry Dexter White died of a heart attack before he reached his trial. (Unless we can understand who our real enemy is, we will continue to fire our guns at the wrong target).

We study the complex character of Franklin D. Roosevelt. It is a story of an inadequate man with a giant sized ego to hide his shortcomings. A man who fully accepted advice from the men he liked, like Alger Hiss and Harry Hopkins and rejected ideas from others like Churchill. We learn that the Second World War was three separate wars in one, first a declared war against Germany, second was the war against Japan, and the third was a hidden war that would decide Europe's fate and that of the Pacific Rim. We see how Roosevelt thwarted Churchill's attempts to make sure of the future freedom of Europe by mounting the European offensive to halt Russia's advantage. We have seen how Roosevelt gave Stalin the Eastern Satellite countries for his part in World War Two, much against the advice of Churchill. **(DIRECTION).** But Roosevelt's advisors, Alger Hiss and Hopkins were at his side at every meeting from Cairo 1 to Yalta, feeding him a Communist hit list to please Stalin. It was a remarkable act of betrayal that was hidden by the Western Press as tools of the bankers. Worse still, Roosevelt reneged on agreements with Nationalist China, allowing Mao Tse Tung to capture China for Communism, advised this time by Harry Dexter White, a Communist sympathiser. **(The Trojan horse inside, deciding DIRECTION).**

All through this period of deceit the media were full of praise for Roosevelt's democracy in handling Stalin. This double treason set Communism in a commanding position that the Western World has chosen to ignore, misguidedly thinking, it was a passing phase.

Evidence captured by allied forces in 1919 that outlines the thrust of Communism after the Bolshevik revolution.

1. Corrupt the young and bring them off religion and on to sex.
   Succeeded.
2. Make people superficial. Destroy self-sufficiency.
   Succeeded.
3. Focus on athletics and sex, divert minds from politics and government.
   Succeeded.
4. Set people against people, group against group. (A task for the press).
   Succeeded.
5. Destroy people's faith in leaders by ridicule, (the press) and disgrace.
   Succeeded.
6. Preach true democracy but grab power ruthlessly.
   Succeeded.
7. **Encourage State borrowing and destroy credit, using inflation.**
   Succeeded.
8. Incite strikes in vital industries.
   Succeeded.
9. Kill all moral standards, honesty, sobriety, and faith in the pledged word.
   Succeeded.

This shows one hundred percent movement towards Communism. (DIRECTION).

When you examine this list it has all come to pass. You must also compare modern society with the past Great Roman Empire which collapsed through moral decline; you see how Communism uses all proven methods to destabilise our society.

Michael Borodin confirms these nine objectives in what he had to say to Madame Chiang Kai-Shek; his comments were both controversial and a strong warning to Western democracy. What he clearly states is that our religious, moral, and family decline is not evolution but Communism's hard work and infinite planning in action. Please believe he is correct, as evolution of thought and Liberalism are the enemies of democracy. They are the easy answer of socialism for their penetration of our society, a penetration that is driving us today towards Communist revolution. This can even be recognised in the dreadful events on the eleventh of September 2001 in America.

Tomas D. Schuman confirmed these nine points, in his 'Love Letters to America' where he, almost to the dotted 'i', presented the points of world decline found by the allied forces way back in 1919. (Both Russians.). So these contributions are firm proof of Communist intention. **(The DIRECTION to the left is clear).**

Carroll Quigley tells us that Capitalism went through three phases, Merchantile, Industrial and Financial. It was the financial stage that took the decision making out of the hands of the industrialists, and moved their agenda to an International forum and because the International Capitalist wants borders of the nation state removed, he sees Communism as the political policy to produce this change to suit Multinational Collectivism, and their desire to move production to the cheapest point. That is what the MAI is all about; good for the Multinationals but disastrous for us. A pure Communist act of evil aggression against the Nation State, and capitalism. **(A DIRECTION that must be stopped).**

But his own men for exposing the truth of their policy marginalised Carroll Quigley. He was, as an intelligent and important historian, dispensable to the bankers for exposing their aims, as the bankers knew it would warn the world in advance, and ruin their plan for world control. So they had his book removed from circulation, despite the fact that it was an important contribution to history, and printed by a major publisher. This shows us that history is what they (the Bankers) want us to believe. **Censorship for DIRECTION).**

Banks dominate national politics, while third world countries are robbed of their assets and we have seen Jacques Delors form the European Central Bank which will do exactly the same in Europe in the future.

Our own Prime Minister Tony Blair has secretly moved to establish eight new regional development agencies in England to join the four regions already formed, in readiness for England to disappear replaced by the new agencies as zones of Europe. We learn that this is not to devolve government onto the regions, but to conform to a map already planned, that is held in the Brussels offices of the European Union, in preparation for Federalisation, a Federalisation without proper elected representation. Anarchy, where England no longer exists. **Do you want that?**

We read the words of Karl Marx, "If England is the fortress of European Landlordism and Capitalism, then the only point from which a strong blow can be struck at official England is **IRELAND**". So way back in 1869 Karl Marx realised that his revolution must use Ireland to destroy England. **(Important DIRECTION in understanding what the Irish problem is all about.**

The ANC, IRA, and PLO are linked in a world-wide organisation of terrorism. The IRA, like all the Marxist revolutionaries, wishes to destroy the Roman Catholic Church, but to use it to destroy Britain first, in typical Communist style. We know how successful they have been and even now are reluctant to hand over one piece of armoury to further peace. The reason is that they are fighting a war to destabilise Britain and their continued resistance to disarm is part of their war within International Communism to bring England to its knees. Their final aim, for any Roman Catholic who might doubt what I say, is to destroy the Roman Catholic religion, the very same aim as Communism. So be in no doubt; what you see, is not what you get with the IRA.

Ireland was chosen to lead the revolution to bring England to its knees. My short history of the IRA shows how Scottish Masons infiltrated the Irish Secret Societies and built up a revolutionary group that became the IRA and its political sister Sinn Fein.

We learn of the linkage of the revolutionaries to our British Prime Minister Disraeli, a Mason and Grand Master of the Grand Orient, an Illuminated lodge in England, that is linked through the Grand Orient to Weishaupt's Illuminati.

The American Scull and Bones Society, founded in the 30's, was linked to Illuminated lodges in America. Among its members was McGeorge Bundy, linked to the Ford Foundation and others, and President George Bush, also a Grand Master of the Grand Orient, and supporter of the New World Order. **(DIRECTION).**

Harold Wilson was responsible for releasing Gerry Adams from jail. Was this to further the revolution?

The IRA and its close links to the ANC and terrorism in South Africa tell us the story of the linking of all Terrorism.

The British Government and its security service tried to hide evidence of collusion between the IRA and ANC, brought to the public attention by Andrew Hunter, and we have seen how he (Andrew Hunter) has since been savaged by the press.

We have seen, in South Africa, how Nelson Mandela, a Communist, was chosen by the Bankers' media to be promoted as the first black President of South Africa. This, while Dr. Buthelezi's party was hammered by the South African press and the Argus Newspaper Group of Dr. Reilly, who financially supported the ANC. **(DIRECTION).** We have seen how powerful groups of associates, Peter Sutherland of BP and Goldman Sachs, Garrett Fitzgerald, Trilateralist and former Prime Minister of the Republic of Ireland, help to move the political agenda towards revolution.

In Ireland and South Africa the armed struggle and the ideological struggle were used to farther their cause.

The British, American, and Russian diplomacy handed South Africa to Communism, once the wealth of South Africa was safely in the Bankers' vaults. Immediately Mandela faced a debt dependency economy set up by the Bankers to rob the country of its freedom of decision. The people were and are still losing their birthright and are probably in a more desperate condition of despair than under the old system. That Britain and America allowed Communism to take over South Africa is a matter of shame. **(DIRECTION).**

Hunter tried to expose the ANC and IRA collaboration, but Hunter was visited by Special Branch to try to force him to suppress his report by suggesting it might harm his career. He didn't. It did.

African countries are gradually falling into Communist hands and one party dictatorship, while the BBC World Service has given the world a very one-sided account of the affairs. What we must take into account here, is that a totally undemocratic organisation like the ANC, committed to Communist solutions, was allowed to, and indeed funded, to eclipse the Inkatha Freedom Party of Dr. Buthelezi (the only true hereditary heir of South Africa) who was both democratic and pro West. This could only have happened under an administration in Britain and America that was lying to its people about its foreign policy. I think by now you have enough evidence to prove this to be true. In fact it is the Bankers who sway the governments and force their hands to help Communism, their political path to World Government. **(The bankers' power of forcing DIRECTION).**

The control of South Africa is so important to Communism. Africa's share of Chrome ore is 83% of the world total; Platinum 86%; Gold 49% and Uranium 17%. This shows quite clearly why Communism and the Bankers want to control South Africa. (Communism for political power and the bankers to control the resources).

The early settlers in South Africa contained a group of Central European Jews, largely from the Khazar Kingdom, who went to South Africa to dominate the Gold and Diamond industries; names like Rothschild, Oppenheimer, and Cecil Rhodes's Lord Milner. We learn another key to our understanding from a Jewish writer and Rabbi, Dow Marmoc, that **"Zionism has become a largely secular Marxist movement". (DIRECTION).**

We find more proof that Communism was carried forward by International Zionism and funded by International Zionists, who believe that the world is their state and we see how this movement links into politics today.

The Australian Banking system came through two World Wars without debt by creating its own money. But then the International Bankers targeted and bought out those banks to hold Australia in debt slavery ever since the Second World War. This clearly shows the advantage gained by a government-controlled currency, but fight hard you must, to create this advantage for your nation. Remember these bankers are ultimately ruthless. **(This clearly shows freedom from debt slavery as a weapon against DIRECTION).**

A global bank Goldman Sachs, has moved their big guns into Australia to establish their strength in the chosen centre for the Pacific Rim. **(DIRECTION).**

Just as in Britain, the people of Australia, and all over Europe, are being told they would be ill advised to turn their back on Internationalism and Globalism. So who is telling us this? The press of course, with a few exceptions, and our government, led by a Federalist Blair and an apologist in Australia, John Howard. We need people with the guts to stand up to the bankers and say enough is enough. **(We need a free press to reverse DIRECTION).**

What this really proves is that both Europe and the Pacific Rim are being Federalised for bankers interest not ours. We see that an Australian party, the One Nation Party, has challenged the establishment, and has had considerable success, the message being what the people want to hear. **(People are the power against the DIRECTION).**

Agriculture in Australia is also under attack to remove self-sufficiency from their choice of sourcing, the necessity for food will then drive the people into line over Global policies.

GM food and the seed policy of the Multinationals are the way they intend to progress by taking farming policy out of the hands of farmers and into the control of the International Finance Capitalists, so they can halt any national protest directed at their policies. **(DIRECTION). We must make our nations self-sufficient.**

Prince Charles is fighting back with a programme towards organic farming. A project well worth encouraging. We must examine the dangers from chemical farming and see if we can come to a compromise between chemical necessity and organic purity.

International Zionism with its banker support has hijacked the legitimate Jewish agenda, and now controls many of its National and International bodies. Communism, its political wing, has been promoted world-wide through the Masonic lodges of the Grand Orient and others.

The America–Israel Public Affairs Committee, the B' nai B'rith, and Anti Defamation League, use their immense power through money control to forge Agendas on the American political scene. **(Power-broking. DIRECTION).**

(Without a free media we can only try and get this true history to you direct. Because of the truth of this history, we will be excluded from bookstalls through the distribution system, all under the control of the bankers. We will also be excluded from media publicity and critic, so important in getting a new book promoted. We have two options, by the Internet, which we are using, and by word of mouth which means you. I hope you will help us bypass the Bankers' censorship).

The United Nations promoted as, "The last hope of mankind", was in fact a carefully planned fraud on the world that was to help Communism, and protect Israel from world criticism. All but one of the men within the American administration that prepared the United Nations project were known Communists or sympathisers.

From an early time in America the Illuminati appeared in symbol on the back of a dollar in the form of the seal from the Declaration of Independence, a broken top on a pyramid with Lucifer's eye looking out of the broken top surrounded by light, the Illuminati of Weishaupt. The words 'Novus Ordo Seclorum' translated to 'New World Order'. The seal shows, in Roman numerals the date of Independence which is also the date of the formation of the Illuminati, 1776. This proves the power of the Illuminati at a very early stage in the development of America.

The forerunner to the United Nations, "The League of Nations" was also an organ of world order but Congress killed it dead.

It was at this point that the One World Group formed the Council On Foreign Relations to plan America's move towards world order and it was in this group, funded by bankers, that the United Nations was planned before and during the second world war and promoted by Roosevelt to Stalin at Yalta. At this meeting we saw Roosevelt give Russia three votes in the General Assembly against America's one and a veto at Stalin's request was also included. So in April 1945 the UN charter was adopted before 46 nations of the world. **(DIRECTION).** Of the American delegates 42 were members of the CFR, the pro Communist planning group. Alger Hiss, a Communist agent, was the custodian of the minutes of the first meeting and responsible for having the minutes ratified by the Senate.

The constitution of the USSR and the constitution of the United Nations were identical. **It was the Trojan Horse within America. (A decisive DIRECTION).**

We have since seen, how the United Nations allow Israel to decimate Palestine and its people, while Anglo – American oil rights of Zionist companies are given full military support, as against Iraq.

Clinton and Blair, through NATO, used force against Yugoslavia to prepare the area for Federalisation within Europe, not to help the Ethnic Albanians. **(DIRECTION).**

In fifty years of the United Nations there have been over seventy substantial outbreaks of violence from Korea to Kosovo. During this period over one billion people have been enslaved by Communism. Yet the UN has never lifted a finger to intervene. **So Liberty is not one of their aims they have honoured. (DIRECTION).**

It claims to be a peacekeeper and it refers to **'The self determination of peoples'.** When you understand Communism, peoples is the collective not the individual, and people are completely dispensable under Communism. **Once more they have failed to observe this aim in article 58 of the charter. All these events show DIRECTION.**

While all this deceit surrounds us, the press sits on its hands and leaves us in a 'truth vacuum'.

The truth that is Weishaupt's policy, is seen in the Communist policy, and is refined into 'the United Nations' policy. This could have been analysed by any competent press, but alas, we are cheated of protection by their allegiance to Communism through their ownership by the Bankers.

The United Nations force, sent into the Belgium Congo, attacked the democratic forces of Moise Tshombe when he declared independence from the Communist State led by Lumumba. Eventually the UN crushed democracy and handed the Congo to Communism. **(DIRECTION).**

The Soviet Union had a man in a position of power within the United Nations. The Under Secretary for Political and Security Affairs at the UN has always been a member from the Soviet Union.

So Moscow has always had advance knowledge of all operations carried out by the UN. That means that in Vietnam all military operations were passed to Moscow and on to the Vietcong before attack. That also means that all American operations were compromised before they took place. **(DIRECTION).** This has not changed from Vietnam to today, despite many concerted attacks on the absurdity of the situation by American Generals.

If you study all the battles fought by the United Nations in the last fifty-five years, on each occasion, power has passed to Communism or oil rights have been protected, if they were part of the banker's assets. We have seen for instance thirty-seven out of fifty-five states in Africa alone handed to Communism. In Vietnam we saw 58,000 lives wasted only to hand Vietnam to Communism, to suit the Bankers' hidden agenda.

Yet when Hungary cried out loud to be freed from Communism the United Nations forgot its noble aim of "Self determination of the people" and allowed the USSR to crush their brave attempt to throw off the chains of enslavement.

The Gulf war was again a war to protect bankers' interests not to aid the beleaguered people of Iraq against its leader. Once again all this shows us **direction.**

There has been a concerted plan to turn over Africa to Communism. First the Congo and the UN's ill considered part in handing The Congo to Communism. The peaceful deceit of Britain and America in pushing Rhodesia (Zimbabwe) and South Africa into undemocratic Communist governments and a whole host of banker and business help (plus Tiny Rowland's support) for the ANC and other Communist terrorist groups; the secret conduit, through which aid to Communism passed in exchange for mineral rights. **(Bankers assets protected by handing over to Communism. DIRECTION).**

We get a frightening glimpse on how UNESCO poses a threat to our children by controlling the international Curriculum that excluded Liberty and Freedom. We read Paul Harvey's article that has been written into congressional records at the 87th. Congress, second session.

What this article shows is how Communism has imposed a softening of national pride into UNESCO directives, that are used selectively in Western society only, and do not apply to Russia, effectively softening Western views towards National pride and against religion.

Russia does not indoctrinate its children with UNESCO directives and Poland even pulled out of UNESCO.

Schools are reluctant to admit they use UNESCO literature or directives, but they all do, so you can start to use your parent power to halt this indoctrination.

What UNESCO, with its Communist agenda, is doing, is undermining our very strength of freedom. We must demand that the government stops interference from UNESCO in our internal affairs, and make fully public their plan, so we can see what they wish our children to learn. **(DIRECTION).**

The Council on Foreign Relations, founded in 1921 by Colonel House, Woodrow Wilson's personal adviser, took over the agenda of 'The League of Nations'; the first attempt to introduce a platform towards global control. We also see the very people who created the Federal Reserve Bank in 1913 become the top figures in the CFR, John D. Rockefeller, J.P. Morgan, Paul Warburg, and Jacob Schiff. It would be wrong to describe this group as Communists; but to achieve their aim, a World Government, they have funded Communism, and Wars. **(DIRECTION).**

The CFR is a privately funded organisation (by Rockefeller Carnegie and Ford Foundations) which has been used by the American administration to research and recommend America's reaction to world politics. The CFR policy is to create a

'New International Order', so close to Weishaupt's 'New World Order'. **(DIRECTION).**

Members of the CFR have spread out into the Media, politics and the civil service, moving their influence even further.

However their main power has been in preparing foreign policy for America in their move towards world government under Communism.

Des Griffin discloses how members of the CFR and Bilderberg Committee are in direct violation of their oaths when they are sworn into public office. He states that the CFR, through secret planning, break the law of the constitution and are therefore traitors to the American Constitution and their people. **(Hidden DIRECTION).**

We found that tax Foundations, free from tax collection, fund the narrow path to One World Government research, and help the system spread Communism to the third world through banking, and fund terrorists like the ANC.

The Rhodes Trust Scholarships train Americans to spread Radical Liberal ideas and it reaches the top. (President Clinton was a Rhodes Scholar). We find Cecil Rhodes was a close friend of Andrew Carnegie, one of the founders of the Trust that partly funds CFR research.

There is no counter balancing think tank to put up a case for National views that is funded. All funding goes one way towards Collectivism and One World Government.

The big six Foundations have in excess of $4,000,000,000 in assets, so you begin to realise the power they wield, and when you find that three of the big six Foundations give Communist organisations like the CFR and IPR huge sums of money to dress up America's foreign policy as devolution, when it is plainly a treasonable policy against the constitution and the American people, **you begin to wonder how this can possibly happen.** The reason is that the power of money, linked to the academic circle of learning, has created a unique power drive hidden by the deceit of Weishaupt, and spread world-wide by secret Masonic lodges, using Communism as a constant cradle for revolution. It is a power structure that is energised by the extreme opposites that meet in harmony on the axis of the extremes. This is the point where Capitalism of the International Finance Capitalist and represented by Multinational Companies, dissolve into collectivism which is Communism.

Multinationalism is the enemy of true Capitalism as it wishes to kill competition. Capitalism will only thrive with competition and therefore we must make sure the Multinational companies **abide by National Laws**. We must therefore oppose the MAI agreement to protect our National interests, and likewise oppose European Federalisation.

History has even been re-written to create historical blackouts. The absence of Weishaupt in history is an example, and criticism of the main players in the Second World War, like Roosevelt, is another.

So we have found the United Nations guilty of moving the world towards 'Global Communist Dictatorship'. We also find that it has interfered with our Children's education, taking our children away from Religious Study by teaching general religion without commitment. **(DIRECTION).**

The International Monetary Fund, is, like the United Nations, a tool of the Banker – Communist plan and is used to enslave the third world into the rigours of debt slavery and part with the rights of their minerals to a banking cartel of greed. **(DIRECTION).** Harry Dexter White was made the first Executive Director of the fund in January 1946 by Roosevelt, despite the fact the FBI had a catalogue of spying allegations against him. But Roosevelt and Morgenthau, the Secretary of State and a Zionist like White, protected White till his position was impossible to sustain; by March 1947 he resigned. He died before he could be tried for spying, but he left the fund, a Communist staffed organisation, like the United Nations, ready to go forward towards a Global future funded by the bankers and Foundations.

America set up the biggest confidence trick yet played by the politicians on their own voters. The "Cold War" was a scam to hide trade agreements; the supply to Russia of arms, a vast quantity of money and technology; and all this while our press promoted a false cold war.

The General Agreement on Tariffs and Trade (GATT) was signed in October 1947; a source of frequent friction between America and Europe ever since, and part of the Globalists' preparation for world government. It was signed but not understood by one hundred and twenty-five nations. GATT says "Each member (Nation) shall ensure the conformity of its laws", just like the European Union demands. In this way GATT can override our law, as indeed the European Union is already doing. **(DIRECTION).** This is all part of Globalism, taking away our rights to make our own laws to control our national state.

The MAI agreement is a tool of Globalism; good for bankers, good for Multinational Companies but bad for Nation-States and very much against the interests of the people of the world. **But it is not signed yet and we must continue the pressure to stop it being signed.**

Another mechanism of world power is the World Trade Organisation. Sir James Goldsmith said to the Washington Times, **"A healthy National Economy has to produce a large part of its own needs".** Both in America and England our industries have been decimated and exported to the third world and now even to China by the Finance Capitalists in search of cheap labour. This is a direct result of GATT and the WTO, encouraged by bankers' greed. (Here we see a ex-insider looking into his old domain and exposing part of the truth contained in this history for which I thank him).

We study the Bilderberg Group, the general planning forum for world government. If any of these groups were official inter-government forums, we would find they would be open, and the debate reported. With the Bilderberg Group, we find it holds top secret private meetings for Bilderberg members and their invited guests only. No debate is reported, despite the fact that some twenty percent of members are from the press. (Names like Conrad Black). **(DIRECTION).**

Started in 1954, it was formed to move the global agenda forward, without the knowledge of the people of the world. It is not surprising that we find Rockefeller, the builder of the New World Order, as the main funder with the Rothschild sphere of influence in the background, having all but completed their task of destroying the Old World Order.

Bilderberg is a group of very powerful men, who believe it is their right to take over world politics for their own benefit, and we have seen how they deal with politicians who get in their way. It is a super power structure of banking, political and media power, with academic support. The present chairman is Lord Carrington, a banker and director of Kissinger Associates; top members include David Rockefeller, Dr. Henry Kissinger, Katherine Graham, owner of the Washington Post, Robert Bartley, editor of the Wall Street Journal; Bill Clinton was a regular visitor while Governor of Arkansas.

All last century the press became increasingly owned by a few very powerful media moguls, funded by a small group of International Finance Capitalists and a half-hearted effort to halt this buy-out failed. So we have a handful of very powerful internationalists controlling our information.

Conrad Black is Chairman of the Hollinger Group; a member of the Institute for Strategic Studies; the Trilateral Commission, and the Bilderberg Group. Rupert Murdoch's News International, financed by Edgar Bronfman, Harry Oppenheimer, The Rothschild family and the late Arnald Hammar of Occidental Oil. Murdoch has made massive Media purchases beyond any unsupported publisher's ability. His Empire now is strong in America, Europe, and the Pacific Rim. (Bilderberg's three areas of regional government).

Robert Maxwell was doing the same till his sudden death. All of them support the cause of One World Government.

By the mid-fifties it became clear that energy was being lost because it was not being directed correctly. Hence the Bilderberg Group was brought in to concentrate energy effectively. The steering committee controls the group's policies. We find that, surprisingly, the Treaty of Rome, which created the European Common Market, had been 'Nurtured at Bilderberg', according to George McGhee, the former US Ambassador to Germany. So, the European Union was not planned by Europeans, but this un-elected group of power Barons, the Guardians, behind closed doors. This gives us a clue to the reason why the whole constitution of the European Union is Un-Democratic. It also gives us a reason why the politicians lie to us about our sovereignty, because we are meant to be locked into Europe before we learn that we lose our sovereignty. So we must say "**No**" to the Euro, to save our sovereignty, because the Euro is the locking in device.

The Bilderberg Group at their first meeting decided to be a long-term strategy-planning forum, to extend national planning to world planning. Remember that this group did not represent any nationally elected representatives; all attendees were purely private. They were taking up Weishaupt's plan for a world order in secret and deceitfully planning it.

The Amazing part is you see a list of press attendees at Bilderberg, yet we are told nothing of this evil planning that is taking place. This proves that the press is now controlled by the bankers group and no longer represents the people.

John Swinton, Chief of Staff to the New York Times, gives us the confirmation that all journalists are puppets to the rich men behind the scenes. He states that it is a journalist's job to destroy the truth. **(The truth about our media).**

The 400% oil price rise was first planned by the Bilderberg Group and Dr. Henry Kissinger met with the OPEC (Arab oil Group) group to encourage them to increase the price of crude by this enormous amount, and invest the profit in American prime banks. It was then seen by the world that Arab oil power had forced the price up but it was a Bankers plan from Bilderberg, and the press spread the lie even though they knew the source; to trigger the increase Dr. Henry Kissinger arranged the Yon Kippur war to help hide the truth.

Subjects that the Bilderberg group have discussed include the spread of Communism in Africa; since then thirty-seven out of fifty-five states have fallen to Communism; the downfall of McCarthy; the plan for a Gulf war and the removal of Margaret Thatcher as Prime Minister of Britain for interference in their European strategy; the planning of a Republic for Australia; the stabilisation of Serbia to make it ready for Federalisation and the same in East Timor for the Pacific Rim. All these policies stem from the Bilderberg Group of un-elected but powerful people with a hidden agenda, every event being thoroughly planned. **(DIRECTION).**

At this point we must recall Carroll Quigley's words that describe this group, in 'Tragedy and Hope', "Nothing less than to create a world system of financial control in private hands to dominate the political system of each country and the economy of the world as a whole. The system is to be controlled in feudal fashion (Communism) by the central banks of the world acting in concert, by secret agreement arrived at in frequent meetings and conferences". (Such as the Bilderberg Group and the Trilateral Commission). Well you can't have it confirmed more clearly, and it supports what I have said. **(This gives us a very fair idea of the DIRECTION that the world politics of the un-elected is taking us without our consent or even our knowledge).**

Another Foundation in both England and America used as a planning group towards globalism, is the Ditchley Foundation. On its board of Governors we find Lord Hume (Dec), ex-Chairman of the Bilderberg Group; Lord Roll, of the Bilderberg steering Committee and Chairman of N.M. Rothschild; Henry Heinz II, on the Bilderberg Steering Committee, and George Franklin, the Co-ordinator of the Trilateral Commission. So we see linkage between all their secret planning Committees. **(DIRECTION).**

We get a very good idea of the make up of the Bilderberg Group and who attends their meetings.

We learn about the second major Commission that is responsible for moving the Third area, the Pacific Rim, towards federalisation as a region within World Government with its headquarters in, possibly, Australia. We only have hints of this, like the build up of Goldman Sachs in Australia. **(DIRECTION).**

Zbkniew Brzezinski was the initial source of the idea for the Trilateral Commission, and it was quickly taken up by David Rockefeller to mould to his plan for a New World Order. It was funded again by private money, the Bookings Institute. The idea was to bring together North America, Europe and Japan, the three laterals of high development to which could be attached the other nations of the world in Federation.

Amongst its members we again see a spread of bankers, high national officials and academics of the Illuminati and of course the Press. As in all other groups we see David Rockefeller; Sir Kenneth Younger, former director of the Royal Institute of International Affairs, and amongst its attendees has been Jimmy Carter, who was promoted as a Presidential Candidate by David Rockefeller's funding. **(Politicians that broke their allegiance to America and Britain to attend these secret meetings).**

When in office Jimmy Carter surrounded himself with Trilateralists with Brzezinski writing all his foreign policy speeches. You see the list of Trilateralists around him.

Another President, George Bush senior, was also funded by Rockefeller. He joined the Trilateral Commission before he was promoted by Rockefeller, under a "Bush for President" campaign. What we see here is money buying political power and it was only Rockefeller who had unlimited finance to accomplish a continuing funding for his political aspirations. We see where the Rockefeller power is based. On top of this he funds many groups dedicated to one world politics as we have seen.

Apart from David Rockefeller, who plays a large part right through the sphere of global power, we see once again Dr. Henry Kissinger as a Commission member;

Casper Weinberger; Warren Christopher; Jimmy Carter; Hedley Donovan; Walter Mondale; Cyrus Vance; Paul Volker, Chairman of the Board of Governors, Federal Reserve Bank; The Earl of Cromer, former British Ambassador to the USA, Denis Healy, Edward Heath, Lord Roll, Chairman S.G. Warburg, Baron Edmund de Rothschild, Lord Shackleton, Deputy Chairman Rio Tinto-Zinc Corporation Ltd.; Gerhard Schroder, Chancellor and former Foreign Minister of FRG, and Lord Carrington. All have attended Trilateral meetings. All are major players in politics, finance, or industry and members of the Anglo – American establishment. **(They all seem prepared to destroy democracy and openness to support this secret group that wishes to kill the democratic right of the people).**

We now have reached the time for a conclusion but first I would ask you to take a look at the flow chart of The One World Government.

What this has shown, a fact that had not presented itself to me before, is that the Rothschild sphere of influence mainly organised the destruction of the old world order and as such has all but completed its job, and the Rockefeller sphere of influence has been in charge of creating 'The New World Order', a task yet to be concluded. So it is at this side of the chart that we must act, to stop this plan that depends on secrecy.

COMMENT

We have travelled through two hundred years of history; the true history of the world, undiluted by any agenda from any direction. It is a history that I discovered, told in parts, by many distinguished authors, politicians and honest Jewish historians, which is, as a collective work, an almost unbelievable 'Hidden Agenda', yet we must believe our only real guide to true history when we study the **DIRECTION** that the political takes after every event in history that leads us to the true agenda. That is what this analysis of history is all about. It is to find the truth within all agendas.

Now we must apply this lesson to Europe because it is where Britain, as a Nation, can play a vital roll in leading the world out of debt slavery and Federalisation into a European Union of Sovereign National States trading economically and forming a powerful trade base for world trade; this is precisely what the Hidden Agenda has falsely led us to believe it was doing and is the agenda the bankers would fear most. I have spent five years researching and writing this history; when I started, I was only interested in the European Union, as I could see it was deceitfully promoted and definitely undemocratic.

I did not seek, or even intend, to get involved in any form of racial or political witch hunt; but when I found the truth of the history, I was determined to identify those involved as they are trying to gain control of our lives in a dishonest and immoral manner and we must stop this for the sake of our National Democracies.

You may ask, why should we stop the European Union developing, why not just change it? We can't alone. There are too many gainers now to stop this totally corrupt system that Europe has produced through non-representative decision-making inside an elite group of Federalist Zealots like Prodi, and the President of the European Bank.

The European Union has moved gradually into the hands of the Bankers' delegates and now is so undemocratic that even staff, who try to discuss its democracy, are sacked and replaced by friendly Federalists, as in the case of Bernard Connolly.

Remember the propaganda passed on to us by Edward Heath, that our Sovereignty would not be effected by our membership of the then Common Market. It is a whole catalogue of un-true statements by politicians and others, especially the press, which have led us along a road of no return. There is an added fear of the Eastern Block dragging down the standards of the top achievers like Germany and Britain when they gain entry to the Federal State of Europe.

So why should Federal Europe be stopped? Because we will lose our national control over our affairs to an un-democratic body of Eurocrats that has been placed in position by the power of Bankers, whose Hidden Agenda is to destroy the Nation State; our State; our England. What does Europe offer us in place of freedom to choose? The chance of joining a collapsing economy with a drastically falling currency.

So if everything goes wrong who will sort it out? Well if Mr Prodi has his way, our army will be integrated into a European army controlled by Brussels.

Surely we can control expenditure through our internal tax system? No. If Mr. Prodi has his way, tax harmonisation will be controlled by Brussels, and we will have to pay more and comply.

Well, if that fails, surely we will have recourse to right wrongs in our courts? No; Brussels will ultimately control all national law, or override national law if it so wishes, not by Natural Law but by political law. The law of dictatorship, the only law it observes. It is the law based on the Bankers' wishes.

Well what about the education of our children? They will become increasingly fed programmed education from the Humanist education system adopted by the United Nations, that is intent on killing Religious Education and promoting all sorts of anti-family programmes that we have already discussed. The European Union naturally supports this way forward, which incidentally hides the history of people like Professor Weishaupt.

In the year (December 2000) 2000, we were asked to relinquish our veto in Europe, that allows us to halt legislation we know to be wrong. This would have happened in the European Treaty in which Prodi planned to settle Europe onto a Federalist path once and for all. It has been temporally halted. Do you want Federalism? If not, help us stop their scheme.

What we must remember is that the Bankers' way is to creep legislation onto us so that we do not realise what is happening. We have past reminders. The European Union has killed our domestic nuclear business, in favour of a less reliable French reactor and even made sure our nuclear business secrets are handed to France. (Owned by the Rothschilds).

It has decimated our fishing industry, and handed our fishing zones to foreign fishermen who abuse the rules. (Especially the Spanish Fishermen. Weishaupt's food dependency policy).

It has selectively attacked our farmers when the whole of the European Union farming community has BSE and CJD problems, which is now coming to the attention of the public. Why should our farmers be singled out to be the only ones to observe very strict safety laws when France and others by-pass safety and sell their stock for consumption? The reason is quite simple. Every country in the world must be dependent on other states for food according to the Bankers' policy created by Weishaupt. (formally Britain was largely self sufficient.) If **your Nation** depends on food imports it can be starved into recognition of the rules of

World Government. If you don't think this is honest comment, study Communism in Soviet Russia. It will soon convince you.

Federalisation is a process to level down developed countries to the lower standards of, in Europe's case, so called Ex-Communist states. Do you want to be down levelled to help Communism? If not, fight to save our Sovereign State; say no to Federalisation.

We have been told that the European Union is good for us. Yet consistently we have sold less to Europe each year of our membership than Europe has sold to us; twenty-five percent less on average; a deficit we have to make good by sales to the rest of the world. So Europe needs us. We don't need Europe, and don't let anyone tell you differently. We have a widening balance of trade with Europe, and this is against our interests.

So who benefits from European Rule? Some countries that are small or lacking in commercial power, like Greece, Spain, and Southern Ireland. The Ex-Soviet block hopes to fall into this category if they are accepted. Where does this leave us? Permanently in a far-left Socialist Europe, controlled by collective political policies. Do you want that? Remember Socialist and Communist policy is, and has been, controlled by finance from the Bankers.

Increasingly we learn of new mechanisms that the Bureaucrats of Brussels have devised to hold us into their web of control while they remove our democracy. First it was the farming policy of the GAP; a policy to remove self sufficiency and replace it with a subsidy policy which, when collapsed, will kill all traditional farmers; the new breed of chemical dependent farmer, using modified seed from multinational corporate collective co-ops will take over; under the control of the banker-multinational cartel. The use of the BSE to CJD scare, has been part of this policy to destroy Britain's strong farming community.

We have seen a failed attempt to control our economy through the ERM (Snake) in the Common Market. Luckily it had such a devastating effect on the economy that we were forced to pull out of monetary union, and we have prospered ever since.

ENTRAPMENT THROUGH THE EURO

So the EU set up a second plan to entrap the states that came out of the ERM; the introduction of the EURO. Britain and two other states opted to remain outside the Euro on its introduction, and our economy has gone from strength to strength. This country was offered a Referendum before we entered the Single Currency thanks to the pressure applied by the Referendum Party, led by Sir James Goldsmith, a honourable Jewish gentleman, and so it stands today.

So why is the Euro such a problem? It is not because of the loss of our pound. It is because it has been designed to lock each country into the European monetary system while they Federalise the system. At that point we will lose our Sovereignty and control over all our domestic affairs. **So we must say 'NO' to the Euro to halt the process to Federalisation.** Most of the British electorate would gladly be a Sovereign State within Europe, but would almost unanimously reject a Federal Europe. I myself, would welcome a close trading agreement between

Sovereign states, but the bankers want a world with no borders or rules to curtail their drive to move the world towards their goal, and it suits the multinational corporations as well. That is what we must stop.

We have even been warned that the Euro can go against our interests by Eddie George, Governor of the Bank of England, when he said that thousands of jobs would be at risk if the politicians get the decision of entry to the Euro wrong. But we will lose jobs if the International Bankers get their way and we are federalised, because jobs will increasingly go to low cost labour areas of Europe and the third world.

Back in 1996 Jacques Delors stated, to the dismay of the Euro elite, that the Euro, the key to Federal Europe was in doubt, "It will be difficult to achieve economic and Monetary Union within the agreed timetable". (His timetable and his hidden agenda for Federal Europe were passed down to him by Monnet). These were the words of a arch architect of Federalism speaking, and it started hysteria within Brussels' corridors of power.

The announcement that BMW have reneged on their promise to re-build the Rover Group must be a warning that foreign intervention in our business base is unreliable and can only be regarded as a passing bonus, and realise that we can in the long run only rely on our internal economy to support our life style. (This is also confirmed in the latest crisis in the steel industry). This alone should make us think about foreign intervention from all directions, and shows that European co-operation is fictitious, a dream of Empire builders, encouraged by the Bankers' agenda.

The Europhiles would have us go into monetary union at any cost, but is this practical? The Euro, since its introduction in 1999, has fallen in value by as much as thirty percent. That means that so have the countries that have tied their currency to the Euro. We have not yet, and I hope we will continue to move with caution. But our Prime Minister, the Right Honourable Tony Blair, is an out and out Federalist, and will rush us in if he possibly can; that is why he has made arrangements to prepare our currency and our establishment for monetary and Federal Union. Only a concentrated mass of people power could possibly change a hardened political mind. We must apply that pressure to him direct and to our MP.

The Euro is not welcomed by the people of Europe, or by small and medium sized firms, and even with many of the European Governments; so the European Commission found from its latest research. Europeans on average pay only 0.8% of their bills in the Euro and companies using the Euro in transactions were a low 1.9%. This sad reflection goes against the predictions of the former EU Commissioner Ives Tilbault de Silguy, who predicted it would take over all transactions in the Euro Zone. In Britain it is only the Multinational Corporations that wish to join the Euro. Medium and small businesses show a majority that wish to stay out. Why? Because Britain has a healthy economy with the rest of the world; now nearly sixty percent of our world trade; while our trade with Europe is a growing deficit and has been since we joined the market.

Therefore to base our future on Europe, when Europe will use our success to fund the entry of Soviet bloc countries into the European Union, would be a catastrophe that would finally submit Britain to total debt slavery for the foreseeable future. **That is what the bankers want.**

Europe is a mismanaged Socialist nightmare of gigantic proportions, like the Soviet Union. Its inefficiency has been well catalogued by the press over three decades of farm subsidy. The GAP has been well criticised for its corruption and its waste, yet it has never been a serious subject for reform within the Union. Why?

Because there are too many gainers and because they need it intact to kill off the traditional landowner farmer and replace him with the chemical zombies who will do their bidding. **That is what the bankers want.**

We have even seen corruption inside the Commission, forcing the entire Commission to resign. Why is this? When a corrupt, undemocratic, system is used, we have seen that the Bankers prefer to have their front men corrupt, because in this way, they can use their past demeanours to force them to follow their policies. That is why we see so many officials exposed for past excesses, and anti democratic practices. You will find all undemocratic control in history acts in this way. (Power is having a hold over people).

So it is not surprising that when it became necessary to replace Jaques Santer, through his corrupt commission we found Romano Prodi's name put forward as a Mr. Clean, when in fact his name was linked with the most corrupt political system in Europe, (That of Italy) and as a former Prime Minister, he would have been intimately involved in collusion between business and politics. The surprising factor is that Tony Blair actively canvassed for his acceptance. (Maybe this is because Prodi is a Federalist Zealot and so is Tony Blair. We also find Prodi was a consultant for Goldman Sachs, a prime mover in World Government and a close associate of the bankers behind it). Mr Prodi was also an attendee of the Bilderberg committee. So from this you once again see the linking that tells the truth about the intentions of the European Union.

FEDERAL EUROPE.
THE HIDDEN AGENDA.

Prodi has openly stated that he wants to "Move beyond" the nation states and create "A political Europe". That means that he wants to kill the nation state and introduce a Federal State of Europe in its place. Make no mistake; that is where Europe is heading, without a vote cast by the people of Europe, unless we can change this by voting against the single currency.

The last audited annual report of the Court of Auditors, the European Union's financial watchdog, claimed that £2.81 billion pounds were wasted last year through bad book keeping and fraud. That is 5.4% of their total budget of £52 billion. The court for the third year running would not certify their legality. Britain is claimed to finance around 20% of the EU budget. So what will it be like, with the old eastern block joining and doubling its size? Remember it is for these reasons that our tax burden keeps rising, especially indirect taxes like VAT.

IMPOSED LAW WITHOUT JUSTICE.

Our legal system has always been based on Natural Law and a person has always been deemed innocent until proved guilty. Now with the increase in the power of the European Court of Justice, (A political Court) this no longer applies. A whole string of cases taken to the European Courts have been reversed, an example is sex discrimination at work, led by the Ministry of Defence case, paying out more than fifty-five million pounds for pregnant women discharged from the forces, even though they signed contracts agreeing to this if they became pregnant, and all because the burden of proof is on the employer to prove his case for dismissal. This has opened a whole can of worms waiting to be claims.

At the same court, Britain was fined one hundred million pounds for protecting its fishing industry against pirate fishermen from mainly Spain, who broke quota regulations imposed by the EU. Spain used a loophole in the EU law to Quota hop some of the British Quotas by flying the British flag on Spanish owned boats registered as British; thus stealing our quota. The Thatcher government responded by passing an act to halt this abuse, excluding nearly a hundred 'Spanish Flag' boats. Spain claimed that British Law and Britain had no right to exclude anyone from applying for British Quota on grounds of nationality. The EU found for Spain and the fine was levied. **(Federalism was given legality over the nation** fishing **state).** Yet the British quota was stolen from an already depleted British industry. It has been estimated that British fishermen have lost four billion pounds worth of fish since this political decision was made in Brussels with no basis in natural law.

British fishing fleets in this period have seen over three-thousand boats decommissioned, yet our taxpayers had to pay this fine, and part fund a programme worth £894 million to buy fishing rights for Spain and Portugal to fish off the coast of West Africa. **(This was a gross injustice against the hard pressed British fishing industry).**

What does this say? British law and its parliament are subservient to every political law Brussels cares to saddle us with. This is our inheritance from Edward Heath and today Tony Blair seems set on the same course.

We have also seen the reversal of British court rulings too numerous to mention. But IRA terrorists have had a great run of compensation, unlike their poor victims, from the political courts of Europe. This just adds to proof of their agenda.

As a footnote to this, an amusing article was published in the Daily Mail on Saturday July 24th. 1999 written by the British MEP Nigel Farage (Of the UK Independence Party) which was full of humour about the non functioning, and the shambles of the new EU Parliament in Brussels, and he poses a quite serious question; "If the bureaucrats cannot run a building efficiently, how can they claim to run an increasing number of national states within Europe?". Britain pays over a million pounds an hour to belong to this corrupt and disorganised club, so that MEP's can wallow in comforts and claim massive expenses, and for what? To have our industry and our nation ruined by laws and prejudices we can no longer act against. Now is the time to say **'NO MORE'**.

THE EUROPEAN UNION P.R. GOES INTO OVERDRIVE TO CLAIM BLACK IS WHITE.

In Europe, if the concept of union was accepted by the people, the Commission would not be spending £180,000,000 on highly selective propaganda to boost their cause. But that is what Brussels has set aside; our money to promote something we do not want. £120,000,000 of this money is to promote the sagging Euro. All this should please those of us who wish to stop Federal Europe, because it shows that Brussels is realising it is losing the PR battle and Europeans are generally becoming disillusioned.

Meanwhile surveys show an increasing number of Europeans dissatisfied with the European Union. The teachers in Britain have hit at the European Commission, accusing them of producing "Blatant and misleading propaganda" in the literature for 11-14 year olds. They complain that the case against the European Union has not had a fair hearing. It was selected propaganda, not an educational guide, and as such should not be part of a balanced learning course. A pole in Germany showed 84% did not want the Euro.

Europe has always maintained that British industry backed the European Union. But in an ICM survey for Business for Sterling an overwhelming 63% of businesses wish to keep the pound with only 32% of businesses backing the Euro. So that shatters Europe's claim to have British Industry on board. The gainers are Multinational Corporations, led by the CBI, and it is them that seem to welcome the Euro and Federalisation, as a move towards world government.

In the war of words the people are confused by scare tactics from the commission. Europe claims more than half Britain's trade is with Europe. This is wrong. Nearly sixty percent of all British trade is with the rest of the world according to official figures.

Employment worries are targeted by saying three and a half million jobs depend on trade with Europe. Well more European jobs depend on trade with Britain, remember we import 25% more from Europe than we sell to them. Therefore that trade will continue what ever happens but if it should stop, Britain would be a net gainer.

Europe is a huge market of three hundred and seventy million people. So what. The world is a much larger market of Six Billion people.

British membership of the European Single Market led to the scrapping of ten million customs forms, saving one-hundred and thirty-five million pounds a year. This is typically selective and ignores the mountains of red tape with which Eurocrats have burdened business. These are just some of the claims of 'Britain in Europe' a European friendly group that seems to wish to hide debate and present a European distortion to fool the electorate. Statistics can indeed be distorted, Europe stretches this art to its limit.

The truth behind this entourage of fudge is that Britain has a very good future in remaining in the world market, because we have, thanks to Mrs. Thatcher, moved on from the remnants of the industrial revolution, to the technical electronic revolution and service industry, and we are well placed to succeed in this field.

But if Tony Blair has his way, Britain would be broken up into the twelve regions (Already planned) for England, with England disappearing all together, and all nations converted into the single state of Europe. (This would mean the end of our Union Jack the Same Union Jack that the British tourist authority has decided to drop in all its literature, as it is too 'Triumphalist' in response to focus groups). We have seen the result when Mr. Ayling, a dedicated One Worlder, removed the Union Jack from the tail fins of British Airways planes, and now he has lost his job, partly through pressure from BA's shareholders and customers; quite rightly so. But they now claim to be a 'One World Airline'.

We can all write to our MP's and political leaders. They are swayed by a continual flow of mail on one subject.

My fear is that under this Labour government we are being pushed, gradually into a position of no return. I believe that Mr. Blair and Mr. Prodi have planned a side stepping advance for after the December 2000 Governmental Conference that will by pass the Euro and its promised referendum and land us, unknowingly, into a Federal Europe without return. So we must be vigilant.

1. We must press hard for a Referendum that also asks if we want a Federalised Europe, with all the loss of Sovereignty that will follow. That sovereignty that Edward Heath told us would be safe if we went into Europe.
2. We must continue the battle for our pound, in case the Euro is still used to deliver us to Federalism.
3. Britain must not sign the New European 2000 Treaty at the International Governmental Conference in December 2000. (As this conference failed to agree we have a breathing space till the next meeting).

Remember, we are surrounded by global talk. Global logistics and Global Communications. There is not an inevitable link between this and a single Global Government, especially if that government is forced upon us without a vote and devoid of democracy. If the world is to become politically global it must be after a thorough debate and by consent of the majority of people concerned.

TO STOP GLOBALISM

We aim at the wrong targets. Therefore the real enemy within escapes our bullets. Let us from now on focus on the right target and aim for the centre.

1. Take back the power of money creation from the bankers.
2. Make sure arms manufacturers and suppliers are not controlled by banking interests.
3. Bring back the National religious atmosphere in schools and stop the slide of morality.
4. Leave the United Nations and form a new International Group to represent all free people.
5. Lead the world into a democratic Union of **Sovereign States.**
6. Uphold Capitalism and rebuild the main pillar**; Competition**.
7. Make sure the media represents all democratic views, and is controlled by no single minority view that follows one agenda, as it does at present.
8. Build up the self-sufficiency of nations by funding a strong agricultural policy.

At the beginning I said that I would not hold back the truth that I found while researching this history, even if it crossed forbidden territory. Well I found that a strong group (that fund the Jewish agenda and therefore control it) called the Guardians within Zionism was behind the plot for a One World Government under Communism but I have done my best to show they do not follow the Zionist cause which is for a return to their promised land. (The Torah commands that they should be led back by their Messiah, in **Peace. This is yet to pass). That is why I call them International Zionists.**

A group of very rich and powerful International Zionists **and others**, led by the Rothschilds (International Zionists believe that the world is their state) have used finance to move them back to Israel without their Messiah and certainly not in peace.

The inner group of about two thousand powerful people, including the Multi-National companies that also wish to move the world of politics to a single world government, ruled by their own funded brand of politics, Communism, I have exposed. This group, through their power of money, has taken over the political agenda of Zionism and has ignored the commands of the Torah. **They are the enemy of the Jewish race as much as the enemy of Christians and Moslems.**

This is why it is so dangerous to give a blanket censorship to all Jewish comment because behind this mirror of silence they can move forward untouched and corrupt the world with their power towards the Communist super state, that will deliver their desire for ultimate power; over **money and politics**.

I hope the ordinary Jewish people will understand what I am saying, as I believe they have as much to gain as the Christian world in stopping this group of powerful men reaching their goal**.**

For the Jewish race the prize for delivering up this small group for judgement is the freedom and heartfelt thanks of a grateful world, who will not hold them responsible for the greed of a few.

Remember only the bankers and Multi-National companies' gain from Globalisation and Europe is just one part of their plan.

If they succeed the people of the world will live in perpetual debt slavery subservient to the will of the Bankers and their Communist regime.

So if you, having read this, fear for your future, join in and help us defend all Sovereign Nations. If you are a Catholic, Moslem or any true religious believer, come and help us to stop this Hidden Agenda. If you are Jewish, and agree that a tiny minority of Jewish power barons have taken over the agenda of your religion, join us and fight. If you are a farmer, suffering from the decimation of your proud industry, join us and fight back against those who wish you harm. If you are a deep-sea fisherman and have suffered under the unfair political laws of Europe, join us and fight for your rights. If you are a Trades Unionist and have lived under the falsehood of Communism, join our fight back. If you fear for your children's future, join our cause. If you are a director or manager of a Multinational or large company, and fear the direction your company is travelling, join us and fight back.

If we are to win this battle we need you to help. We need all the help we can get for our David to beat their Goliath. People power can win. Britain is well placed to lead the come back of National Identity, and the future of true capitalism with its pillar; competition, that has delivered the free world prosperity for its people.

No other system has had such success. These bankers wish to destroy capitalism and democracy along with our chosen religion and our nation state. We, together, can stop them.

This history has set about to prove that a secret plot, assembled over two hundred years ago, calling on the secrets of mythical, pre biblical times, is in an advanced stage of taking over the world through secrecy and deceit. At every point of the history where we see the word 'direction' we find the agenda has moved towards far-left ideology, but its impact hidden, because it is attributable to so many different organisations. We have tried to show how these organisations are linked through the Illuminati to Communism, to the Masonic movement and the lodges of the Grand Orient. To International Zionism and the International bankers.

It is certain if we based our proof on a few isolated events the chance of error would be possible. But our proof is massive and links to make the events of world politics so easy to understand, and the final doubts are expelled by the proof of direction which supports our detailed bibliography which is the source of the history we present.

I do not claim to have the full history but the evidence that I have recorded is compelling and it would be wise of the world to at least debate the evidence I have laid before you. I believe that this conspiracy theory is now a fact and the world would be prudent to wake up to its truth before it is too late. Chemical war is imminent.

KNOWLEDGE IS PEOPLE POWER

BIBLIOGRAPHY

INTRODUCTION

(1) Taken from the Daily Mail Advertisement, Friday January 10th. 1997. The Referendum Party.
(2) Taken from the Daily Mail Advertisement, Friday January 10th. 1997. The Referendum Party.
(3) Taken from the Daily Mail Advertisement, Friday January 10th. 1997. The Referendum Party.

CHAPTER ONE

(Elon, Amos. 'Founder' Meyer Amschel Rothschild and His Time. Page 108
(4) Harper Collins 1996. ISBN 0 00 255706 1.
(5) Heine, H. 'Samtlighe Werke' Berlin 1887.
(6) Prince Clemens Von Metternich's Meeting with Napoleon that ended in Austria joining the coalition against Napoleon. 10th. august 1813. (Source Count Corti's book 'The Rise of the House of Rothschild' Page 143 .Victor Gollanz, 1928).
(7) The Illuminati. Refer to Chapter 2, 4 and 5.
(8) Corti, Count. 'The Rise of the House of Rothschild' Page 367. Victor Gollanz, 1928.
(9) Corti, Count. 'The Rise of the House of Rothschild' Page 367-368. Victor Gollanz, 1928.
(10) Gentz's Diary. Printed in 'The Conversational Encyclopaedia', Brockhous 1826. It was a form of paid promotion of the House of Rothschild. (Source: The Rise of the House of Rothschild').
(11) Griffin, Des. 'Fourth Reich of the Rich'. Page 97. Emissary Publications 1976.
(12) Corti, Count. 'The Rise of the House of Rothschild' is considered to be a prime source of information on the Rothschild dynasty. The history in this chapters based on its knowledge as well as other references attributed to other authors.

CHAPTER TWO

(13) Oliver, Dr. Revilo. 'Conspiracy or Degeneracy' Page 30-40.
(14) Isaiah, verses 12-14.
(15) Ezekiel 28, verses 16-18.
(16) Corinthians, 11 4 : 4.
(17) Corinthians, 11 11-14.
(18) Revelations, 12 : 9.
(19) Genesis 6, verse 5.

(20) See Weishaupt's policy page 54, chapter two.
(21) Hislop, Alexander. 'The Two Babylons' Page 52-55.
(22) See Weishaupt's policy Page 60, chapter two. The World and Europe.
(23) Druids, page 437.
(24) Hislop, Alexander. 'The Two Babylons. Page 66-67.
(25) Corinthians, 11 11-14.
(26) Luke, Chapter 4.
(27) Luke, Chapter 4, verse 8.
(28) Corinthians, 11 : 4.
(29) Jeremiah, 17 : 9 and Romans, 8 : 7.
(30) Fraser, Sir James. 'In Golden Boughs' Vol. 1, page 471-475.
(31) Hislop, Alexander. 'The Two Babylons'.
(32) Keller, Werner. 'The Bible as History' Page 368.
(33) Hurlbut, Jesse-Lyman. 'The History of the Christian Church' Page 80.
(34) Adam Smith, the father of Capitalism. 'Wealth of a Nation'.
(35) Manifold, Deirdre. 'Towards World Government' second edition. Page 3. Published by Canisius Books, Canada. 1993.
(36) Robison, Professor John. 'Proofs of a Conspiracy' (copy) Americanist Classics. Western Islands. Originally published 1798. (A book to read if you want to understand the Illuminati).
(37) Barruel, Abbe. 'Memoirs Illustrating the History of Jacobinism' Published in four volumes. The fourth volume covers the Illuminati.
(38) Manifold, Deirdre. 'Towards World Government' Page 3. Canisius Books 1993.
(39) Robison, Professor John. 'Proofs of a Conspiracy' Page 60. Americanist Classics.
(40) Robison, Professor John. 'Proofs of a conspiracy' Page 121. Americanist Classics.
(41) Robison, Professor John. 'Proofs of a Conspiracy' page 220-223 Americanist Classics.
(42) Robison, Professor John 'Proofs of a Conspiracy' page 233. Americanist Classics.
(43) Robison, Professor John. 'Proofs of a Conspiracy' page 236-237. Americanist Classics.
(44) Scott, Sir Walter. 'Life of Napoleon Bonaparte'.
(45) Toynbee, Arnold. Extracts from his speech to the Institution of Scientific Study of International Relations, in June 1931.
(46) Marsden, Victor. Translator of Professor Nilus' Russian script of; 'The Protocols of the Meetings of the Learned Elders of Zion' Found around 1905 and translated by Marsden 1920.
(47) Izoulet, Jean. From his 'Israelite Universëlle' paper 'La Capitale Des Religions'1931. Paris.

CHAPTER THREE

(48) Mr. Oudendyke, Dutch Minister at St. Petersburg, published in the British White Paper produced by the English War Cabinet, January 1919.

(49) Walsh, William Thomas. 'Philip II' Page 308-309. (Taken from Ref. in (52) Page XII)).
(50) Lazare, Bernard. 'L'Antisémitisme' Page 339. (Taken from ref. in (52) Taken from Ref. in (52) Page XII).).
(51) Cowan, A. 'The X-Rays in Freemasonry' Page 61. (Taken from ref. in (52) Page XIII).
(52) Dillon, Monsignor George. 'Grand Orient Freemasonry Unmasked' In the Preface. From lectures delivered in Edinburgh in October 1884. Page XII. M.H. Gill and Sons 1885. Reprint ISBN 0-89562-095-2 (Lost lectures reprinted) Page XII.
(53) Robbin, Sir Alfred. 'English Speaking Freemasonry'.
(54) Dillon, George Monsignor. 'Grand Orient Freemasonry Unmasked', chapter six. M H Gill and Sons.1885 Reprint ISBN 0-89562-095-2.
(55) Robison, Professor John. 'Proofs of a Conspiracy' Page 11-13. Reprint Americanist Classics.

CHAPTER FOUR

(56) Varange, Ulick. 'Imperium' Volume II 1948.
(57) Quotation from a Jewish Banker, by the Comte de Saint Auldire in 'Geneve Contre la Paix' Libraire Plan, Paris 1936.
(58) Quigley, Carroll. 'Tragedy and Hope' Page 51. The Macmillan Company 1966.
(59) Quigley, Carroll. 'Tragedy and Hope' Page 51-52. The Macmillan Company. 1966.
(60) Gibb-Stuart, James. 'Hidden Menace to World Peace' Page 30-31. Ossian Publishers. 1993.
(61) Sutton, Professor. 'National Suicide' The book about his evidence to a Republican Sub-Committee that was completely hidden from the public by the Media. This book should be read.

CHAPTER FIVE

(62) Hurst. 'History of Rationalism',Page 27.
(63) Lubec, Henry de. 'Atheistic Humanist'. Page 10.
(64) Arriaga, PnD, The Reverend. 'The New Mountain Church' and 'The Vacant Chair'.
(65) Isaiah, 14. 12
(66) Robison, Professor John. 'Proofs of a Conspiracy', Reprint Americanist Classic. Original book printed 1798.
(67) Robison, Professor John, 'Proofs of a Conspiracy', Page 71 Reprint Americanist Classics. 1967.
(68) Webster, Nesta. 'World Revolution - The Plot Against Civilisation'. 1921 Constable and Company.
(69) Robison, Professor John. 'Proofs of a Conspiracy', Page 64. Reprint Americanist Classics. 1967.

(70) Webster, Nesta. 'World Revolution - The plot Against Civilisation'. Page 13. 1921. Constable and Company.
(71) Webster, Nesta. 'World Revolution - The Plot Against Civilisation'. Page 18.
(72) Robison, Professor John. 'Proofs of a Conspiracy', Page 195. Original 1798.
(73) Roosevelt, Clinton. 'The Science of Government'.
(74) Queenborough, Lady. 'Occult Theocracy' Page 208-209.
(75) Dr. Bataille. 'Le Diable au XIX Siecue'. Page 346.
(76) Queenborough, Lady. 'Occult Theocracy'. Page 220-221.
(77) Queenborough, Lady. 'Occult Theocracy'. Page 581.
(78) Quigley, Carroll. 'Tragedy and Hope', Page 130. The Macmillan Company. 1966.
(79) Quigley, Carroll. 'Tragedy and Hope', Page 130. The Macmillan Company. 1966.
(80) Rakovsky. At NKVD headquarters. Interviewed by Gabriel. A convincing piece of evidence for the proof of Conspiracy. Taken from the translation by George Knupffer. In his book 'Red Symphony'. The Plain Speaker Publishing Company.

CHAPTER SIX

(81) Marcus Tullius Cicero. 105-43 BC.
(82) ."Focus on Facts" page 150, Rakovsky's interview at NKVD Headquarters 1936 page108. Also Manifold, Deirdre. "Towards World Order", page 3, Canisius Books 1993 Second edition.
(83) Report 3 "Focus on Facts" page151, op cit.
(84) On Target, Volume 22, 9th.-23rd. January 1993. Published by Bloomfield Books.
(85) Sovorov, Viktor. I.G.U. SM. "The Soviet Service of Strategic Deception", International Review, August 1985.
(86) Tether, C. Gordon. "The Banned Articles of C Gordon Tether". Privately published, 1977.
(87) Marmur, Rabbi Dow. "Beyond Survival - Reflections on the Future of Judaism".
(88) Madame Chiang Kai-Sheik. "Conversations with Mikhail Borodin". Privately published c. 1978.
(89) Schuman, Tomas D. "Love Letters To America". Almanac Panorama, Los Angeles, 1985.
(90) Goode, Stephen. "Eurocommunism". Franklin Watts, 1980.
(90a) A collection of British Embassy reports on Bolshevism in Russia, dated April 1919. Published by His Majesty's Stationary Office.

CHAPTER SEVEN

(91) Little, Dr. K. "Treason at Westminster", pp 1-4. Text submitted in October 1978, to The Royal Commission on Criminal Procedure.
(92) The Media Review.
(93) "On Target", Volume 23, 5th.-19th. February 1994. Page 12 (188).
(94) Dye, Thomas R. "Who's Running America - The Carter Years". Page 95. Prentice Hall Inc. NY. 1979.
(95) Webster, Nesta H. "Surrender of the Empire", page 122. Boswell Printing and Publishing Co. Ltd. 1931.
(96) H Du B Report. Vol. 32 letter 4th. July-August 1989.
(97) Sutton, Antony C. "National Suicide - Military Aid to the Soviet Union". Arlington House 1973.
(98) Knuppfer, George. "The Struggle for World Power - Revolution and Counter Revolution". Page 19. The Plain Speaking Publishing Company.
(99) Webster, Nesta H. "The Surrender of the Empire", Page 122. Boswell Printing and Publishing Company Ltd. 1931.
(100) Martin, Rose L. "Fabian Freeway - High Road to Socialism in the USA 1884-1966". Page 174-175 Western Islands. 1966.
(101) Toynbee's speech, November 1931 to the Royal Institute of International Affairs.
(102) The Plain Truth - A Magazine of Understanding. Nov./Dec. 1989. Article "All I Know is What I see in the News". By Norman L Schoaf.
(103) Schuman Tomas D. "Love Letters from America" Page 33.
(104) Turner Colonel B S. "Control of the Communications Media and Conditioning of Public Minds". Bloomfield Books 1992.
(105) op sit. Page 8-9.
(106) Spotlight Newspaper. 25th. December 1949.
(107) Stead, Henry Wickham. "The Hapsburg Monarchy", Constable and Co. Ltd. 1913.
(108) Reed, Douglas "Lest We Forget", Page 280 Jonathan Cape.
(109) Reed, Douglas "The Controversy of Zion", Dolphin Press Pty. Ltd. 1978. (In the preface).
(110) Finlay, Paul, "They Dare To Speak Out - People and Institutions Confront Israel's Lobby". Lawrence Hill and Company. 1985.
(111) Gabler, Neal. "An Empire of Their Own - How the Jews Created Hollywood". W H Allen. 1989.
112 McClintick, David. "Indecent Exposure - A True Story of Hollywood and Wall Street". Columbus Books 1983.
(113) Webster, Nesta. "The Surrender of a Empire". Page 122. Boswell Printing and Publishing Co. Ltd. 1931.
(114) H Du B Report, Volume 32. Letter 4 July - August 1989.

(115) Knupffer, George. "The Struggle for World Power". The Plain Speaking Publishing Co. 1971.
(116) Spotlight. June 20th. 1984. (Newspaper) Article on Rupert Murdoch.
(117) Daily Telegraph 21st. July 1987.
(118) Manners, Elizabeth. "The Vulnerable Generation". Page 72. Cassell and Company Ltd. 1971 p. 72.
(119) Cox, Barry. "Civil Liberties in Britain" pp. 76, 79, 105, Penguin Books Ltd. 1975.
(120) Davies, Christie. "Permissive Britain - Social Change in the Sixties and Seventies" Page 46- Publishing. 1975.
(121) Daily Telegraph, 13th. October 1989.
(122) Howard, Peter. Britain and the Beast" Page 82 William Hanimann Ltd. 1963.
(123) Mc Millan, James. op cit. pp 32-35.
(124) Cox, Barry. op cit. p 106.
(125) Mc Millan, James op cit. pp 71-77.
(126) Manners, Elizabeth. op cit. pp 181-184.
(127) Schuman, Tomas. "Black is Beautiful, Communism is Not" Page 31. NATA Almanac, Los Angeles 1886.
(128) Sunday Times, 4th. December 1989 and Independent, 19th. December 1989.
(129) Independent 19th. December, 1989.
(130) New Music Express. IPC Magazines.
(131) Standard, 21st. December, 1986.
(132) Daily Telegraph, 22nd. April, 1987.
(133) Sunday Times, 26th. April, 1987.
(134) Provincial Press 7th. October 1989; and Daily Telegraph 14th. October 1989.
(135) Today, 2nd. July 1986.
(136) Daily Mail 10th. April 1987.
(137) Radio Times 18th.-24th. February 1989; and TV Times 25th.-31st. March 1989.
(138) Sunday Times 26th. November 1989
(139) Guardian, 27th. August 1986; Times, 15th. September 1986; Daily Telegraph 16th. September 1986.
(140) Daily Telegraph 15th. December 1989.
(141) Woolwich Mercury 19th. May 1987.
(142) Sunday Telegraph 28th. January 1990.
(143) Sunday Times 10th. November 1990.
(144) Sunday Telegraph 19th. November 1989.
(145) Sunday Times 7th. January 1990.
(146) Smith, Antony (Editor) "The British Press Since the War". pp 32-41, David and Charles. 1974.
(147) Dye, Thomas R. op cit. pp 95-111.
(148) Habastram, David. "The Powers That Be" Chatto and Windus 1975.

(149) Sampson, Antony. "The Changing Anatomy of Britain" pp 382-417. Hodder and Stoughton. 1981.
(150) Financial Times. 22nd. June 1988.
(151) Independent 20th. May 1989.
(152) Independent 28th. August 1989; Sunday Telegraph 23rd. June 1991, "The Alien Porn Loopholes are Letting the Sleaze Merchants Mock Britain's Laws".
(153) Dye, Tomas R. op cit. "Who's Running America" Page 96.
(154) Financial Times, 19th. January 1989.
(155) Burrows, Lynette. "The Fight for the Family" page 1. Family Publications 1998.
(156) Scotsman, 22nd. March 1988, 12th. January 1990; Daily Express, 11th. January 1990.
(157) Manners, Elizabeth. "The Vulnerable Generation" pp 131-132. Cassel and Co. Ltd. 1971.
(158) Reader's Digest, March 1986. "When Television Threatens Young Minds".
(159) Independent, 20th. November 1986.
(160) Sunday Times, 3rd. May 1987; Daily Telegraph 25th. March 1989.
(161) Sunday Telegraph 3rd. March 1987.
(162) Daily Telegraph 21st. February 1988.
(163) Daily Telegraph 23rd. February, 2nd. November 1989; Sunday Times 23rd. July 1989.
(164) Times, 29th. April 1987.
(165) Daily Telegraph 19th. December, 1989.
(166) Sunday Times 18th. February 1990.
(167) Matthew, 6 - 24.
(168) Koestler, Arthur. "The 13th. Tribe" and the Book of Revelations.
(169) Reader's Digest February 1993. By Joseph Harriss. "The Gospel According to Marx".
(170) le Fever, Professor Ernest. "Amsterdam to Nairobi". 1979, and "Nairobi to Vancouver" 1987.
(171) From a lecture given by Elizabeth Segrue, "A Record of Education - A Hidden Agenda".
(172) From papers and correspondence held in the European Union Headquarters in Brussels. Taken from a speech by Sir James Goldsmith at a meeting of the Federation of Small Businesses, Newcastle-upon-Tyne, on Tuesday 27th. June 1996.
(173) On 6th. May 1970 Monnet communicated to Edward Heath the Procedure of the Common Market (Towards Federalism). From Monnet's original correspondence.
(174) November 1990 on BBC1 Television. Edward Heath interviewed by Peter Sissons.

CHAPTER EIGHT

- **(175)** Tether, C Gordon. 4th. January 1993. The Spotlight Newspaper. Cordite Fidelity Inc.
- **(176)** Jenkins, Lindsay. "God Father of the European Union. Altiero Spinnelli". Eurofacts Bookshop.
- **(177)** Sir James Goldsmith's speech to the Federation of Small Businesses, Newcastle-upon-Tyne. Thursday 27th. June 1996.
- **(178)** Nexus Magazine, August - September 1994. Seeds-- Survival or Servitude
- **(179)** Nexus Magazine, February - March 1998. Article on dangerous substances.
- **(180)** Connolly, Bernard. "The Rotten Heart of Europe". Faber and Faber, 1995.
- **(181)** See Rakovski's evidence, page 108.
- **(182)** Reed, Douglas. "The Controversy of Zion". Publishing Co. Pty. Ltd.
- **(183)** Weinstock, Nathan. "Zionism. False Messiah". Pluto
- **(184)** Yogev, Cedalia. "Diamonds and Coral - Anglo Dutch Press. 1989.
Jews and Eighteenth Century Trade". Leicester University Press, 1978.
- **(185**) Koestler, Arthur. "The Thirteenth Tribe. The Khazar Tribe and its Heritage". Random House, 1976.
- **(186)** Reed, Douglas. "The Controversy of Zion" Veritas Publishing Co. Pty. Ltd. July, 1995.
- **(187)** Montefiore, Bishop. Church Times. 24th. January.1992.
- **(188)** Schwartz, Rabbi E., "The Torah Will Never be Changed".
- **(189)** Sutton, Antony C. "The Best Enemy Money Can Buy". Liberty House Press, 1986 and "National Suicide - Military Aid to the Soviet Union". The Australian League of Rights, 1973 and "Wall Street and the Bolshevik Revolution" Veritas Publishing Co. Pty. Ltd. 1981.
- **(190)** Mc Connachie, Alistair D. Social Creditor, Volume 75 Number 3 of May - June 1996.

CHAPTER NINE

- **(191)** Lord Beaconsfield, around 1844 in his novel "Coningsby".
- **(192)** Douglas C. H. "Dictatorship by Taxation". 1936.
- **(193)** Dr. Little, K. "Treason at Westminster". Pages 1-4. Text submitted in October 1978 to the Royal Commission on Criminal Procedure.

(194) Dr Little, K. op cit Pages 6-12.
(196) Neuberg, A. "Armed Insurrection". Published in English by B.N.L.B. in 1970.
(197) Heydte, Professor Frhr. Fredrich Von Der. "Modern Irregular Warfare" translated by George Gregory. New Benjamin Franklin Press, 1986.

CHAPTER TEN

(198) Ezekiel: Chapter XXII. Verses 12 and 15.
(199) Leviticus. Verses 36-37.
(200) Deuteronomy Chapter 23. Verse 19.
(201) Ezekiel: Chapter 18 Verses 10-14.
(202) Ezekiel: Chapter 22. Verses 12-13.
(203) Search, Dr. R. E. "Lincoln Money Martyred. Omni Publications 1965.
(204) Op. Cit. Dr. R. E. Search. Page 32.
(205) Appleton Cyclopedia. Page 296. 1861
(205a) Search, Dr. R.E. "Lincoln Money Martyred". Omni Publications. Page 44-45.
(206) New York Tribune. Lincoln's letter of thanks to Colonel Taylor. December the 6th. 1891.
(207) Search, Dr. R. E. "Lincoln Money Martyred". Reprint Jan 1965, Omni Publications. Page 46.
(208) Howe, C. K. "Who Rules America" London Times.
(209) Op. Cit. Dr. R. E. Search.
(210) Op. Cit. Dr. R. E. Search. Page 51.
(211) Abraham Lincoln's address to the nation November 19th. 1863,Gettysburg.
(212) Op. Cit Dr R. E. Search. page 64.
(213) "The Fatal Challenge of President John F. Kennedy" The Final Call, Volume 15 number 6. 17th. January 1996.
(214) Wells, H. G. "Experiment in Autobiography" Macmillan Co. New York,1934 pp 658-9.
(215) Helfferich, Karl. "Der Weltkrieg: "Vorgeschichte des Weltkrieges".Ullstein and Co. Berlin 1919 pp 120-165.
(216) Paish, Sir George, Letters to the Chancellor, Lloyd George, dated Saturday August 1st. 1914. Public records Office T170 14.
(217) Engdahl, F. William. "A Century of War. Anglo American Oil
(218) Politics and a New World Order". Dr. Böttiger, Verlags-GmbH. 1993 English Edition Chapter 4 pp 45-59.
(218) Lawrence, T. E. "Seven Pillars of Wisdom" London, Care. 1935 page 24.

(218a) Rose. N.A. "The Gentile Zionists: A Study in Anglo – Zionist Diplomacy.1929-1939. London. Frank Cass 1973.
(219) Op. Cit. Engdahl, F. William. Page 54.
(220) Quigley, Professor Carroll. "The Anglo American Establishment from Rhodes To Cliveden". New York 1981. Books in Focus Inc. Page 5.
(221) Op. Cit. Engdahl, F. William. Page 65.
(222) Quigley, Carroll "Tragedy and Hope. A History of the World in our Time" .Collier-Macmillan Ltd. London 1966.
(223) Op. Cit. Engdahl. F. William. Page 96-7.
(224) Painter David S. "Oil and the Marshall Plan" Business History Review no.58. 1984. Harvard University.
(225) The Economist. "ENI Minus Mattie" November 1962 Page 449.
(226) Op. Cit. Engdahl, F. William. Page 134.
(227) Op. Cit. Engdahl, F. William Page 147.
(228) Op. Cit. Engdahl, F. William. Page 149.
(229) Gibb-Stuart, James. "Hidden Menace to World Peace". Ossian Publishers. June 1993 pages 49-65.
(230) Op. Cit. Quigley, Professor Carroll. (Tragedy and Hope) Page 324.
(231) Op. Cit. Engdahl, F. William. pages 150-156.
(232) Quigley, Carroll. "Tragedy and Hope" The Macmillan Co. New York. 1966.Page 324.
(233) Quigley, op. cit. Page 326.
(234) Quigley, op. cit. Page 122.
(235) Quigley, op. cit. Page 955.
(236) Quigley, op. cit. Page 130.
(237) Clarke, Kenneth. "Ruskin Today" Dinehart and Winston, New York 1964. Pages 267-268.
(238) Quigley, op. cit. Page 132.
(239) Quigley, op. cit. Page 950.
(240) Quigley, op. cit. Page 951.
(241) Quigley, op. cit. Pages 938-939.
(242) Quigley, op. cit. Page 953.
(243) Quigley, op. cit. Page 953.
(244) Quigley, op. cit. Page 954.
(245) Quigley, op. cit. Page 954.

(246) Sutton, Anthony C. "Western Technology and Soviet Economic Development 1917-1930. Hoover Institute, Stanford University. 1968.
(247) Wormser, René. A. "Foundations - Their Power and Influence". The Devin Adair Company, New York. 1958.
(248) Wormser. op. cit. pages 301-305.
(249) Quigley, op. cit. Pages 945-946.
(250) Quigley, op. cit. page 946.
(251) Quigley, op. cit. Pages 946-947.
(252) Quigley, op. cit. Pages 946-947.
(253) Quigley, op. cit. Page 947.
(254) Quigley, op. cit. Pages 947-948.
(255) Reece Committee, summary of findings.
(256) Quigley, op. cit. Page 938.
(257) Quigley, op. cit. Page 948.
(258) Skousen W. Cleon. "The Naked Capitalist" Private Publication. Salt Lake City. 1970. pages 66-67.
(259) Victor. and Toledano, Ralph de. "Seeds of Treason" Funk Wagner And Co. New York 1950. Page 69.
(260) "Seeds of Treason" Lasky and Toledano, op. cit. Pages 78-79.
(261) Lasky and Toledano, op. cit. Page 83.
(262) Lasky and Toledano, op. cit. Pages 108-111.
(263) Lasky and Toledano, op. cit. Page 112.
(264) Lasky and Toledano, op. cit. Page 115.
(265) Blum II, Page 3.
(266) In Henry Morgenthau Jr's Diary. Vol. 769, Page 3. September 5th. 6th. 1944.
(267) Deane, John R. "The Strange Alliance" Viking. 1947.
(268) Farr, Finis. "FDR" Arlington House, New York. 1972. Page 40.
(269) Farr, op. cit. Page 78.
(270) Farr, op. cit. Page 113.
(271) Bullitt, William C. "Life" August 30th. 1948.
(272) Churchill, Winston. "The Hinge of Fate" Page 201.
(273) Deane, General John. "The Strange Alliance" Viking. 1947. Page 295.
(274) Fuller, Major General J. F.C. "The Second World War" Eyre and Spottiswoode. London 1948. Pages 258-259.
(275) The New Republic. September 6th. 1943.
(276) Wedemeyer, General Albert C. "The Wedemeyer Reports" Holt 1958. Pages 370-376.
(277) Statement to the press, International News Service. February 26th. 1957.
(278) Churchill, "Closing the Ring" Houghton Mifflin, 1951.
(279) Stimson, Henry L. and Bundy, McGeorge. "In Active Service in War and Peace" Harper 1947.
(280) Churchill, Winston, "Triumph and Tragedy" Haughton and Miffin. 1953. Page 456.

CHAPTER ELEVEN

(281) Sovorov, Viktor. G.U.S.M. - "The Soviet Service of Strategic Deception". An International Defence Review, 1985.
(282) Schuman, Tomas D. "Love Letters to America Panorama, Los Angeles, 1985
(283) Quigley, Carroll. "Tragedy and Hope". The Macmillan Company 1966.
(284) Booker, Christopher. Daily Mail 1st. April 1999.
(285) Brooks, Richard. Sunday Times 4th. of April 1999.
(286) Baigent, Michael. Leigh, Richard. Lincoln, Henry. "Holy Blood and Holy Grail". Jonathan Cape Ltd. Book Club Associates Edition 1982. Page 162.
(287) Webster, Nesta H. "World Revolution - The Plot Against Civilisation". Constable and Co. 1921.
(288) Barruel, Abbe. "Memoirs Illustrating the History Of Jacobinism" 1798.
(289) Queenborough, Lady. "Occult Theocracy". The Christian Book Club of America. Reprint 1933 Edition.
(290) Pollard. "The Secret Societies of Ireland".
(291) Webster, Nesta H. "The Surrender of the Empire". Boswell Printing and Publishing Co. Ltd. 1931.
(292) Murray, John. "Memoirs of the Secret Societies of the South of Italy, Particularly the Carbonari" 1821.
(293) Dillon, Martin. "The Shankill Butchers". Hutchinson 1989.
(294) Phillips, Alison. "The Revolution In Ireland 1906-1923. Longmans, Green and Co 1923.
(295) Pike, Henry. "History of Communism in South Africa". Christian Mission International of South Africa 1985.
(296) Shimoni, Gideon. "Jews and Zionism: The South African Experience. 1910-1967". Oxford University Press 1980.
(297) Daily Telegraph 20th. April 1990.
(298) Hunter, Andrew. "Twilight and Terror - Sinn Fein - IRA; The South African Dimension". Report on IRA-ANC collaboration.
(299) Executive Intelligence Report. 14th. May. 1993.
(300) Hobson, J.A. "The War in South Africa - Its Cause and Effect". James Nesbet and Co. Ltd. 1990.
(300A) Cartwright, A.P. "The Corner House - The Early History of Johannesburg" Purnell and Sons SA Ltd. 1965.
(301) Schwarzschild, Leopold. "The Red Prussian - The Life and Legend of Karl Marx". Charles Scriber's Sons 1947.
(302) "A Collection of Reports on Bolshevism in Russia". H.M. Stationary Office April 1919
(303) Marmur, Rabbi Dow. "Beyond Survival - Reflections on the Future of Judaism". Darton Longman and Todd. 1982.
(304) Pike, Henry R. "A History of Communism in South Africa". Christian Mission International of South Africa 1985.

(305) Saron, Gustin and Holtz, Louis. "The Jews in South Africa – History". Geoffrey Cumberledge. 1955.
(306) Shimoni, Gideon. "Jews and Zionism: The South African Experience. 1910-1967".
(307) Clausewitz, General Carl Von. "On War". Translated by Colonel J Graham. Began, Paul, Trench, Turner and Co. Ltd. 1908.
(308) "On Target". Volume 25. 5th.-19th. August 1995.
(309) Pike, Henry R.A. "A History of Communism in South Africa". Christian Mission International of South Africa. 1985.
(310) SACP; Emerging from the Shadows?". The International
(311) Freedom Foundation. 1990.Bulletin - Committee to Restore the Constitution. April 1993 Features; United States in South Africa - What's Going on at the Embassy".
(312) Waldmer, Patti. The Financial Times. 29th. April 1993.
(313) Hobson, J.A. "The War in South Africa - Its Causes and Effects". James Nesbet and Co. Ltd. 1900.
(314) Benson, Ivor. "The Truth out of Africa". Veritas Publishing Co. (Pty) Ltd.
1995 3rd. Edition with a new chapter, "South Africa and the Zionist Factor".

CHAPTER TWELVE.

(315) Douglas, C.H. "Dictatorship by Taxation. 1936.
(316) Government Debt and Credit Creation. Research report no. 9 . 1981, Economic Research Council.
(317) The Institute of Economic Democracy, 1981. History of Commonwealth Banking.
(318) Butler, Eric D. "The International Jew - The Truth About The Protocols of Zion". 1947.
(319) Tankerville, Lord. "Poverty amidst Plenty".
(320) Australia League of Rights. Intelligence Survey May 1998.
(321) Financial Review, Weekend Edition. May 30th.-31st. 1998.
(322) Financial Review, April 14th. 1998.
(323) The Weekend American. April 1998.
(324) "On Target" 6th. and 20th. June 1998.
(325) Wilton, Robert. "Russia's Agony". E.P. Dutton and Company. New York. 1919.
(326) Finlay, Paul. "They Dare to Speak Out - People and Institutions Confront Israel's Lobby". Lawrence Hill and Company 1985.

CHAPTER THIRTEEN.

(327) **The United Nations was planned to replace the League of Nations and introduced to the world as a 'Last chance' when the planners knew it would succeed.**

(328) Ruggs, Dr. Harold. "The Great Technology" Page 32.
(328a) Lee, Robert W. "The United Nations Conspiracy" Appendix C Page 243.
(329) 'Life' Magazine. July 16th. 1945.
(330) 'Political Affairs' The official theoretical journal of the Communist Party, USA. April 16th. 1945. Stevenson, Adlai. Speech quoted in Guardian of Peace' State Department Publication 7225, September 1961. Page 36
(331) Clark, General Mark. "From the Danube to the Yalu" Harper and Brothers. 1954. Page 11.
(332) McArthur, General Douglas. "Reminiscences" McGraw Hill, 1964. Page 365.
(333) United States Code, Title 22, Foreign Relations and Intercourse. Chapter seven. Sec. 287, page 5639. 1970.
(334) Utt, James B. "Communism's Trap for our Youth" Speech delivered to the house of representatives.
(335) Utt's landmark speech delivered on the 4th. September 1962.
(336) II Corinthians 4:4.
(337) Griffin, Des. "The Fourth Reich of the Rich" Emissary Publications. Page 145-160. 1976. USA.
(338) Quigley, Carroll. "Tragedy and Hope". Page 324.

CHAPTER FOURTEEN.

(339) **Federal Reserve System of 1913 and Graduated Income Tax System of 1916 were both major policy statements in The Communist Party Manifesto.**
(340) **House, Colonel. "Philip Dru" – Administrator" Intimate papers of Colonel House. Edited by Charles Seymour. Page 152-157, and page 45.**
(341) "The Invisible Government" Page 7.
(342) Quigley, Carroll. "Tragedy and Hope" Page 952.
(343) "Basic Aims of US Foreign Policy" 1959 Study No. 7. Review of the News, September 19th. 1973.
(344) Rarick, John. Congressman. House of Representatives, April 28th 1972.
(345) Ward, Rear Admiral Chester, and Schlafly, Phyllis. "Kissinger on the Couch" Page 148
(346) Op cit. Page 148.

(347) Chicago Tribune, December 9th. 1950.
(348) Griffin, Des. "Fourth Reich of the Rich" Page 130-140
(349) Op cit. Page 135.
(350) Op cit. Page136.
(351) Op cit. Page139.
(352) Aydelotte, Dr. Frank. "The Rhodes Trust 1903-1953. Published 1956.
(353) Wormser, René. A. "Foundations" page 202.
(354) Reece Committee Report. Page 171.
(355) Op cit. Page 71
(356) Op cit. Page 169.
(357) Op cit. Page 174.
(358) Reece Committee Hearing one, Page 901 Report page 264.
(359) Reece Committee Report. Page 178.
(360) Barnes, Professor Harry Elmer. "The Historical Blackout and the Perpetual war for Perpetual Peace".
(361) Mc Carran, Committee Report. Page 84.
(362) Reece Committee Report. Page 28.
(363) Wormser, René. "Foundations" Page 212-213.
(364) Reece Committee Report. Page 168.
(365) Op Cit. Page 178.
(366) Barnes, Professor Harry Elmer. "Historical Blackout and Perpetual War for Perpetual Peace".
(367) Wormser, René. "Foundations".
(368) Gardner, Richard N. "Stirling Dollar Diplomacy" Revised Edition. Page 287. 1969.
(369) Op cit. Page 259.
(370) Government White Papers Pul File 35. November 30th. 1945.
(371) Churchill, Winston. Speech Fulton Missouri. March 1946. (Iron Curtain Speech).
(372) Dexter White, Harry. May 1948.
(373) Rees, David. "Harry Dexter White" Chapter 24 page 395.
(374) Cicero, Marcus Tullius. 105-43 BC.
(375) Rees, David. "Harry Dexter White".
(376) Harry Dexter White's letter of resignation. March 1947.(377) US Senate Committee of Finance, International Trade Organisation Hearing. 80th. Congress first session, US Government printing office. 1947 pp 619 ff.
(378) White Papers, Concord Files Hearings. Pages 1239-40.
(379) Rees, David. "Harry Dexter White" Pages 406-408.
(380) Brownall, Attorney General Herbert. Address to executive's Club, Chicago.
(381) Roosevelt, Clinton. "The Science of Government Founded on Natural Law" Published by Dean and Trevent, New York, 1841.
(382) House, Colonel. "Philip Dru – Administrator" Intimate papers of Colonel House. Edited by Charles Seymour. Page 45.

(383) Quigley, Carroll. "Tragedy and Hope" Page 952.
(384) Esty, Daniel. CFR Journal, 'Foreign Affairs' Nov 1995.
(385) Information from the Social Creditor, Volume 74 No. 6, Nov-Dec 1995.
(386) Taken from a group set up to fight the MAI agreement found on Web site http:www.greenecon.org/MAI/index.html
(387) Goldsmith, Sir James. Washington Times. December 6th. 1993.

CHAPTER FIFTEEN

General details are mainly from Spotlight or the Global Manipulators.

(388) Garrison, Colonel Ely. "Roosevelt, Wilson, and the Federal Reserve Law".
(389) Griffin, Des. "The Fourth Reich of the Rich". Emissary Publications. 1976. Page 124.
(390) Kissinger, Dr. Henry. Forum at a Bilderberg meeting. Printed in Spotlight, August 1991.
(391) Griffin, Des. Op cit. Page 124.
(392) Toynbee, Arnold. Speech to the fourth annual Conference of the Institutions for the Scientific Study of International Relations, Copenhagen, June 8th. – 10th. 1931.
(393) Heath, Edward. From Focus on Facts, Volume One, Report Five.
(394) Turner, Colonel B. "On Target"
(395) Stuart Gibbs, James. "The Hidden Menace to World Peace" Ossian Publications. Page 86.
(396) Eringer, Robert. "The Global Manipulators" Page 34.
(397) Passages from Protocol Twelve. "The Protocols of the Elders of Zion".
(398) Swinton, John. Former Chief of Staff, "New York Times". In reply to a toast at the New York Press Club, 1953.
(399) Disraeli, Benjamin. "Coningsby" Page 233.
(400) Quigley, Carroll. "Tragedy and Hope". Page 324.
(401) Tucker, James P. Jr. Article, "Thatcher Targeted by Elite". Spotlight, 29th. May 1989.
(402) Eringer, Robert. Op cit. Page 38.
(403) Eringer, Robert. Op cit. Page 38-39.
(404) List of attendees at the first Bilderberg Conference. May 1954.
(405) Members of the Steering Committee, Bilderberg Group, 1980 and National Members. Taken from "Global Manipulators" Page 46-49.
(406) Draft agenda for the Bilderberg Conference, June 6th.-9th.1991 at Baden Baden plus the provisional list of invited guests. Taken from 'Spotlight', September 1991.

CHAPTER SIXTEEN.

- **(407)** Eringer, Robert, "The Global Manipulators" Pentacle Books 1980. Page 57-58.
- **(408)** Eringer, Robert. Op cit. Page 78.
- **(409)** Trilateral Commission members at November 20th. 1979. Taken from "The Global Manipulators". Page 83-95.